BRITAIN & JAPAN
BIOGRAPHICAL PORTRAITS
VOLUME IV

BRITAIN & JAPAN

Biographical Portraits

VOLUME IV

Edited by

HUGH CORTAZZI

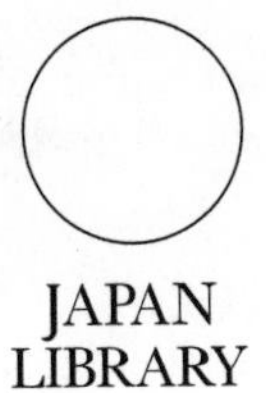

JAPAN
LIBRARY

JAPAN SOCIETY PAPERBACK EDITION Not for resale

BRITAIN & JAPAN: BIOGRAPHICAL PORTRAITS
Volume IV
Edited by Hugh Cortazzi

First published 2002 by
JAPAN LIBRARY
Japan Library is part of Taylor & Francis Ltd
11 New Fetter Lane, London, EC4P 4EE

ISBN 1-903350-14-X [Case]

British Library Cataloguing in Publication Data
A CIP entry for this book is available from the British Library

Set in Bembo 11 on 11½ point
Typesetting by Mark Heslington, Scarborough, North Yorkshire
Printed and bound in Great Britain by Bookcraft, Midsomer Norton, Avon

Table of Contents

Introduction

HUGH CORTAZZI
Compiler & Editor

THIS IS THE SIXTH VOLUME published for the Japan Society devoted to the lives of people who have contributed in various ways to the development of Anglo-Japanese relations. The first volume which marked the Japan Society's centenary and the Japan Festival in the United Kingdom in 1991 was published that year under the title 'Britain and Japan, 1859–1991: Themes and Personalities' which was edited by Gordon Daniels and me. There then followed three volumes of 'Biographical Portraits'. The first two volumes were edited by Ian Nish and the third by Jim Hoare. In 2001 'Japan Experiences: Fifty Years, One Hundred Views: Post-War Japan through British Eyes, 1945–2000', which I compiled and edited was published as part of the Japan 2001 celebrations.

At first there was some scepticism in the Society about whether there were still enough important personalities in Anglo-Japanese relations to justify another volume. Would we have 'to scrape the barrel' to do so and would we have to include pieces about personalities of marginal interest? I was confident from the outset that this would not be the case and that even after this volume there would still be many gaps to fill. I am sure that this remains true.

We have still not given adequate attention to British artists who worked in Japan and to Japanese artists who worked here. Dr William Anderson, our first Chairman and one of the main sources of Japanese art in the British Museum, has not yet been the subject of biographical portrait. There are British poets and writers who worked in Japan and should be covered. More British scholars of Japan and journalists who worked there deserve to be the subjects of biographical portraits.

Our volumes have been dominated by pieces about British people who lived and worked in Japan and insufficient attention has been paid to Japanese who lived and worked here. This has not been our intention but has arisen from the fact that for many of the Japanese who lived and worked in Britain their British experience was not central to their lives. We have also had difficulties in finding writers willing and able to do the necessary research about Japanese personalities and submit papers in English.

We should have liked to have seen a better balance between British and Japanese writers, but because compilation and editing have been done here this proved difficult to achieve.

We are often asked why some of the more significant contributors to Anglo-Japanese understanding are not represented in our volumes. This is often because they have already been the subject of at least one monograph and we did not want to include pieces, which simply replicated what had been said elsewhere and were not based on original research. We have often made exceptions to this rule and it can be argued that more exceptions should be made in the future. I am appending to this introduction a list of some of the monographs about Anglo-Japanese personalities, which have to my knowledge been published. This list, I am sure, is not exhaustive and I would welcome details of other relevant monographs. I have also attached a list of the personalities covered in previous volumes in the hope that this may help students and historians to trace relevant material.

We have so far been generally reluctant to include portraits of people who left their own memoirs of their life in Japan. Again there have been exceptions and some of these could well be the subject of biographical portraits when we come to put together further volume(s).

A significant part of the book is devoted to studies of the work of diplomats especially British heads of mission in Japan not covered in previous volumes. This is not because as an ex-diplomat I have any illusions about the extent of their importance as individuals. It reflects, rather, the fact that in the first hundred years after 1858, when diplomatic relations were established between our two countries, Britain was a significant factor in Japan's international relations and British diplomats at least up to 1941 had fairly wide access to Japanese politicians at the highest level and when it suited Japanese interests their advice was sometimes sought.

Since the end of the war the situation has changed. For Japan Britain remains an important country for reasons of language and history, but also because Britain is a permanent member of the UN Security Council and of the G8 with particularly close relations with the USA. It is also a key member of the Atlantic alliance and of the European Union. But Britain cannot now be as important to Japan as the USA or for that matter Japan's neighbours in Asia. Political relations between the two countries still matter but economic and cultural relations have become more important.

In the nineteenth century, as the portraits of Sir Francis Plunkett and Hugh Fraser show, a major element of the work of the mission was renegotiation of the 'unequal treaties'. The new treaties did not come into force until 1899 in the last year of Sir Ernest Satow's time as Minister in Tokyo. As the piece by Ian Ruxton based on Satow's diaries shows he had unprecedented access to top Japanese politicians not only because he had known almost all of them in the 1860s before the Meiji Restoration but because of his outstanding knowledge of Japanese and Japanese culture. The inclusion of this piece is an exception to our general rule. He was the subject of an essay by Peter Kornicki in the 1991 volume and has been the subject of a number of monographs, but Ruxton's portrait gives an interesting picture of a scholar diplomat and fills a gap in the coverage of British heads of Mission in Japan. This volume also includes portraits of other pre-war British Ambassdors not previously covered in our volumes namely Sir William Conyngham Greene, Ambassador to Japan during the First World War, by Peter Lowe, Sir John Tilley by Harumi Goto-Shibata, Sir Francis Lindley by Ian Nish and Sir Robert Clive by Anony Best. Of these the most interesting personality was Lindley.

Japanese heads of mission have not been neglected although they have been less fully covered, but for this volume Ian Nish has contributed a portrait of Kato Takaaki. One of the early Japanese Ministers in London Mori Arinori who later became Japanese Minister for Education and was assassinated is the subject of a portrait by Andrew Cobbing.

We have not hitherto paid sufficient attention to the business side of our relations. We have begun to rectify this omission in the current volume by including in this volume a portrait by Jim Hoare of William Keswick, the first representative of Jardine Matheson in Japan, whose offices were established at *Eiichiban* (England No. 1) in Yokohama in 1859, another portrait by Peter Davies of Frederick Cornes, who was the founder of the merchant house Cornes and Company, and also a portrait by Charlotte Bleasdale of John Samuel Swire and the early days of Swires in Japan. These three portraits cover some of the most important British businessmen in early Meiji Japan, but there are other interesting business figures who should be the subjects of studies in future volumes. In addition, Sonia Ashmore has provided a portrait of Lasenby Liberty who established the London firm of Liberty and Co Ltd. From the post-war era I have included a portrait of Peter Hewett, the eccentric and successful head of Cornes and Company in Japan, by Merrick Baker-Bates who worked for him.

Another major area, which has been covered in previous volumes, is that of British experts and others who worked in Meiji Japan. In this volume there are pieces about the engineers W. K. Burton by

Olive Checkland and H. S. Palmer by Jiro Higuchi. There is also a portrait of W. E. Ayrton, who taught physics, by Ian Ruxton and a portrait of Henry Faulds, doctor and missionary, by Ian Nish.

This volume includes portraits of the early photographers F. W. Sutton by Sebastian Dobson and H. G. Ponting by Terry Bennett. W.K.Burton mentioned in the previous paragraph was also an important photographer.

Judo is represented by portraits of Koizumi Gunji by Richard Bowen, and Trevor Leggett, who was also a Buddhist and broadcaster, by Anthony Dunne and Richard Bowen.

Journalists have not been neglected. This volume includes two interesting portraits by Peter O'Connor. One covers the editors of the *Japan Chronicle*, the other deals with the strange life of O'Conroy or Conroy, author of *The Menace of Japan* who claimed to be an expert on Japan. Freda Utley, idealist and one time enthusiastic Communist, is the subject of a fascinating portrait by Douglas Farnie.

Scholars and writers are also covered in this volume. The portrait by Akiko Ohta of the Japanese Confucian scholar Nakamura Masanao who translated Samuel Smiles' *Self-Help* into Japanese is an interesting commentary on an often-overlooked element in early relations between Japan and Britain. Two of the many British poets who came to Japan were Sir Edwin Arnold, whose year in Japan is described by Carmen Blacker, and William Empson, whose experiences in Japan are described graphically by John Haffenden. Richard Smith and Imura Motomichi have given us an account of the life of Harold Palmer, the pioneer teacher of English language in Japan in the inter-war years. The outstanding scholar of the Dutch and Portuguese in Japan, Charles Boxer, who died in 2000, is the subject of an evocative portrait by James Cummins. Nobuko Albery has written a sympathetic account of the strange character of her former husband the scholar and translator Ivan Morris.

The biographical portrait of Lord Sempill, an aviator Japanophile, by Antony Best describes a friend of Japan whose loyalty to Britain is open to question.

One essay, which is rather different and deals with a particular theme namely that of inter-racial marriages in the early days after the reopening of Japan, is 'Three Meiji Japanese married to British women' by Noboru Koyama. Another essay by Amanda Herries on 'Early Plant Collectors in Japan', covers a subject, which has been particularly topical in 2001/2 in view of the Japan Society's exhibition 'A Garden Bequest'.

This is thus both a varied and eclectic selection of personalities and contains much of interest to all involved in one way or another with Anglo-Japanese relations.

JAPANESE NAMES

Japanese names are shown in the Japanese order (surname followed by given name) except for those of Japanese contributors whose names appear in the English order (given name before surname).

ACKNOWLEDGEMENTS

I should like to thank all the contributors to this volume for their excellent biographical portraits and their patience with me as editor. I am particularly grateful to Dr Carmen Blacker, FBA, and Professor Ian Nish, CBE, and Paul Norbury for all their invaluable help and advice. My thanks go also to Anne Kaneko and Patrick Knill for their help in checking proofs.

I also wish to thank:

1. Professor Ivan Hall for permission to reproduce the portrait of Mori Arinori which forms the frontispiece for his two-volume biography of Mori Arinori, Harvard, 1973.
2. Westminster City Library for permission to reproduce the photograph of Lazenby Liberty in their collection.
3. Cambridge University Library for permission to reproduce the portrait of Nakamura Masanao (Keiu) from their stock of Japanese books.
4. The Royal Aeronautical Society Library for the photograph of the portrait of Lord Sempill, which is on display at the Society's headquarters at Hamilton Place, London W1.

The Joint Chairmen, Council and Members of the Japan Society wish to thank the UK-Japan History Research Project Promotion Fund and the Anglo-Japanese History Project for their generous support.

British Personalities and Japan

about whom monographs have been written

ADAMS, William. Various studies including William Corr, *Adams the Pilot:The Life and Times of Captain William Adams 1564–1620*, Japan Library 1995

BINYON, Lawrence. *Lawrence Binyon: poet, scholar of East and West*, by John Hatcher, Oxford and New York, 1995

BIRD, Isabella. *Isabella Bird and a Woman's Right* by Olive Checkland, Scottish Cultural Press 1996; *A Curious Life for a Lady:The Story of Isabella Bird*' by Pat Barr, Secker and Warburg 1970

BLUNDEN, Edmund. *Edmund Blunden and Japan* by Sumie Okada, Macmillan 1988

BRUNTON, Richard Henry. *Building Japan, 1868–1876*, edited Hugh Cortazzi, Japan Library 1991

CHAMBERLAIN, Basil Hall. *Portrait of a Japanologist* by Yuzo Ota, Japan Library 1998.

DIOSY, Arthur. *A biography of Arthur Diosy, founder of the Japan Society: home to Japan*, by John Adlard, New York and Lampeter, 1990

DRESSER, Christopher. *Christopher Dresser* by Widar Halen, Phaidon, 1990

GLOVER, Thomas Blake. *Scottish Samurai* by Alexander McKay, Canongate Press, 1993

HEARN, Lafcadio; Various studies

KIPLING, Rudyard. *Kipling's Japan*, edited by Hugh Cortazzi and George Webb, The Athlone Press, 1988

LEACH, Bernard. Various studies

MILNE, John. *Father of Modern Seismology* by L. K. Herbert-Gustar and P. A. Nott, Paul Norbury Publications, 1986

MITFORD, A. B. (Lord Redesdale). *Mitford's Japan* edited by Hugh Cortazzi, The Athone Press, 1985 (New edition in paperback, Japan Library, 2002)

MURDOCH, James. 'James Murdoch (1856–1921), Historian, Teacher and Much Else Besides' by D. C. S. Sissons. *Transactions of the Asiatic Society*, fourth series, volume 2, Tokyo 1987

PARKES, Sir Harry. *Sir Harry Parkes, British Representative in Japan 1865–83* by Gordon Daniels, Japan Library, 1996, *The Life of Sir Harry Parkes* by F.V. Dickins and Lane Poole, Macmillan, 1894

RIDDELL, Hannah. *An English Woman in Japan* by Julia Boyd, Tuttle, Tokyo, 1996

SAMUEL, Marcus, *Marcus Samuel, First Lord Bearsted, Founder of Shell Transport and Trading Co.*, by Robert Henriques, London, 1960

SATOW, Sir Ernest. Various studies including *The Diaries and Letters of Sir Ernest Satow* (1843–1929), by Ian Ruxton, Lampeter, 1998

STORRY, Richard. *The Story of Richard Storry and Japan* by Dorothie Storry, Paul Norbury, 1986

WALEY, Arthur. *Madly Singing in the Mountains. An Appreciation and Anthology of Arthur Waley* edited by Ivan Morris, Allen and Unwin, 1970

WILLIS, Dr William. *Dr Willis in Japan, British Medical Pioneer 1862–1877* by Hugh Cortazzi, The Athlone Press, 1995

Japanese Personalities:

FUKUZAWA Yukichi. *The Japanese Enlightenment: a study of the writings of Fukuzawa Yukichi* by Carmen Blacker, Cambridge, 1964; *Yukichi Fukuzawa 1835–1901: the spirit of enterprise in modern Japan*, by New York, 2001

MORI Arinori by Ivan Parker Hall, Harvard University Press, 1973; *The Political Thought of Mori Arinori* by Alistair Swale, Japan Library, 2000

TAKETSURU Masataka. *Japanese Whisky, Scotch Blend*, by Olive Checkland, Edinburgh 1998

List of Biographical Portraits

Themes and Personalities, 1991, Biographical Portraits Vol. I, 1994, Biographical Portraits Vol. II, 1997, Biographical Portraits Vol. III, 1999

GASCOIGNE, Sir Alvary by Peter Lowe
JAPAN-BRITISH EXHIBITION of 1910, Japanese organisers by Ayako Hotta-Lister
JAPANESE ENGINEERS in Britain before 1914 by Olive Checkland
MACDONALD, Sir Claude and Lady by Ian Nish
MAEJIMA Hisoka, founder of Japan's Postal System by Janet Hunter
MARKINO Yoshio by Carmen Blacker
MATSUDAIRA Tsuneo by Ian Nish
MATSUKATA Nakai and Takahashi, Adoption of the Gold Standard by Norio Tamaki
MINAKATA Kumagusu by Carmen Blacker
MINGEI MOVEMENT and Bernard Leach by Hugh Cortazzi
MUNRO, Gordon by Jane Wilkinson
OCCUPIED JAPAN through eyes of British journalists and authors by Roger Buckley
PARKES, Sir Harry by Hugh Cortazzi
TOGO Heihachiro by Kiyoshi Ikeda

BIOGRAPHICAL PORTRAITS, VOL II [1997]

ALCOCK, Sir Rutherford by Hugh Cortazzi
ANGLO-JAPANESE COMMERCIAL TREATY by Robin Gray and Sosuke Hanaoka
BATCHELOR, John by Hugh Cortazzi
BRITAIN'S JAPAN CONSULAR SERVICE by Jim Hoare
CHOLMONDELEY, Lionel Berners by Hamish Ion
CROWN PRINCE HIROHITO in Britain by Ian Nish
GUBBINS, J.H. by Ian Nish
HEARN, Lafcadio by Paul Murray
HUMPHREYS, Christmas by Carmen Blacker
INOUE Masaru by Yumiyo Yamamoto
JAPAN'S POST-WAR NOVELISTS (Impact in Britain) by Sydney Giffard
JAPANESE BUSINESSMEN IN THE UK by Sadao Oba
MOREL, Edward by Yoshihiko Morita
MUTSU FAMILY by Ian Mutsu
OLIPHANT, Laurence by Carmen Blacker
PONSONBY-FANE, Richard by Dorothy Britton
REDMAN, Sir Vere by Hugh Cortazzi
RIDDELL, Hannah by Julia Boyd
ROBERTSON-SCOTT J. W. by Mari Nakami
ROYAL VISITS to Japan in the Meiji Period by Hugh Cortazzi
SHAND, Alexander Allan by Olive Checkland and Norio Tamaki
SHIGEMITSU Mamoru by Antony Best
YOSHIDA Shigeru and Madame Yoshida by Ian Nish

BIOGRAPHICAL PORTRAITS, VOL III [1999]

Alphabetical List of Contributors to this Volume

ALBERY, Nobuko (Lady), writer and novelist, widow of the late Sir Donald Albery; formerly married to Dr Ivan Morris.

ASHMORE, Sonia, historian and author of thesis on Lasenby Liberty and Liberty and Co Ltd.

BAKER-BATES, Merrick, (CMG), former diplomat and businessman.

BENNETT, Terry, CEO, PIFC Benefit Consultants, expert on the history of photography in Japan and Korea.

BEST, Antony (Dr), Lecturer in International History at London School of Economics, author of books and articles relating to Japan.

BLEASDALE, Charlotte, Archivist to John Swire and Sons, Ltd.

BLACKER, Carmen (Dr, FBA), Lecturer in Japanese at Cambridge University 1958–91, author of *The Japanese Enlightenment, The Catalpa Bow* and other works relating to Japanese religion.

BOWEN, Richard, Judo expert and writer.

COBBING, Andrew, Professor of Japanese History at Kyushu University, author (among other studies) of *The Japanese Discovery of Victorian Britain*, 1998. Has translated Volume 3 of Kume Kunitake's *Beiokairanjikki*, 2002.

CORTAZZI, Hugh (Sir, GCMG), former British Ambassador to Japan, author and editor of books and articles relating to Japan (c.f. *Collected Writings*, 2000).

CUMMINS, James, Emeritus Professor of Spanish, London University. His last book was *Christianity and Missions 1450–1800*, 1997.

CHECKLAND, Olive, formerly of the University of Glasgow, writer specialising in Japanese history.

DAVIES, Peter (Professor), International Commission for Maritime History, The School of History, University of Liverpool.

DOBSON, Sebastian, expert on the history of photography in Japan, writer.

DUNNE, Anthony. Practised Yoga and Vedanta under Trevor Pryce Leggett.

FARNIE, Douglas (Professor), University of Manchester, edited *Region and Strategy,* a comparative history of Lancashire and the Kansai. He was helped in the study of Freda Utley by Minoru Sawai and Jon Utley.

HAFFENDEN, John, Professor of English Literature, University of Sheffield, Fellow of the Royal Society of Literature, author of *The Life of John Berryman,* 1982, and *Novelists in Interview,* 1985; has edited the writing of William Empson and is working on a biography of him.

GOTO-SHIBATA, Harumi, Associate Professor of International History, Chiba University, author of *Japan and Britain in Shanghai, 1925–31*, 1995.

HERRIES, Amanda, lecturer and writer.

HIGUCHI, Jiro, author of *The Biography of Major-General Henry Spencer Palmer R.E. F.R.A.S. (1838–1893),* 2002.

HOARE, James (Dr), diplomat, scholar and writer: recent publications include *Embassies in the East,* 1999.

IMURA, Motomichi, Visiting Professor at Takushoku University, President of the Historical Society of English teaching in Japan, author of *Harold E.Palmer and teaching English in Japan,* 1997.

KOYAMA, Noboru, Librarian for the Japanese Collection in the Cambridge University Library, historian.

LOWE, Peter (Dr), Reader in History, Department of History, University of Manchester, scholar and author of books and articles relating to Japan.

NISH, Ian (Professor, CBE,) Emeritus Professor of International History, London School of Economics, author and editor of numerous books relating to Japanese History, UK Coordinator of the Anglo-Japanese History Project.

O'CONNOR, Peter, currently an Associate Professor at Musashino Women's University, Tokyo. Recently edited *Informal Diplomacy and the Modern Idea of Japan*, Japan Forum 13(1) 2001. Now completing a London University PhD on the interwar history of the English-language press of East Asia.

OHTA, Akiko, Professor of Modern History, Keio University.

RUXTON, Ian, Associate Professor, Department of Human Sciences, Kyushu Institute of Technology, author of a study of Sir Ernest Satow.

SMITH, Richard, Lecturer in ELT/Applied Linguistics, University of Warwick, co-author of *Japanese: Language and People*, BBC, 1991 and author of *The Writings of Harold Palmer: An Overview.*

PART 1

Diplomats

1

Mori Arinori, 1847–89: from Diplomat to Statesman

ANDREW COBBING

Mori Arinori

IN JANUARY 1880, Mori Arinori arrived in London as the third resident minister from Japan to be appointed to the Court of St James. Still only 32 years of age, he brought with him a reputation as an outspoken champion of radical social reform. Enlisted by the new government after the Meiji Restoration, he had quickly gained notoriety in 1869 for his infamous proposal to remove the samurai's traditional right to bear his swords. Then, in his time as Japan's first minister to the United States from 1870 to 1873, he had advocated religious freedom and even suggested adopting English as the official language. On his return from Washington he had gone on to found the Meirokusha, Japan's first modern intellectual society, which spread progressive ideas through the distribution of its *Meiroku Journal*. This was the man whom the indefatigable Victorian traveller Isabella Bird described as an 'advanced liberal' when she met him on a visit to Tokyo in 1878.[1]

Once likened to a 'lone pine atop a winter mountain', the young Mori frequently cut an isolated figure in the world of Meiji politics.[2]

Four years of diplomatic service in London, however, were to effect a profound change in his outlook and bring him closer to the mainstream of government affairs. He returned in 1884 as a statesman in the making, and went on to impose such a centralized and elitist structure on Japan's education system that he was even suspected of forsaking his radical past. Ironically, perhaps, the catalyst in Mori's apparent transition from liberal to conservative was none other than Herbert Spencer, the celebrated Victorian pioneer of social science. It was under his guidance that Mori would consciously set about diagnosing the prevailing maladies in the body politic of Japan and devise his own prescriptions to revitalize the Meiji State.

On their arrival early in 1880, Mori, his wife and their two young sons moved into the Japanese legation building at No. 9 Kensington Gardens in Notting Hill. Clara Whitney, an American friend of the family passing through, observed: 'We found them luxuriously situated and very well pleased with London.' Equipped with an 'elegant barouch [*sic*]', Mori, it seems, felt quite at home, as he escorted his guests to city sights from the Tower of London to St Paul's. Some weeks later, Clara recorded how, on one occasion at dinner, 'Mr Mori regaled us with tales of his boyhood and what a savage he was when he first came to London some fourteen years ago.'[3]

Mori's appointment as minister to Britain thus marked something of a nostalgic return. Born in 1847 in Satsuma, Japan's southernmost domain, he received a traditional Confucian education in his early years under the strict supervision of his parents – he told Clara over dinner they were 'real ancient Samurai'.[4] He was sixteen years old when the Royal Navy bombarded his home-town of Kagoshima in 1863, an experience that prompted Satsuma to try and learn from Britain rather than challenge the military supremacy of the Treaty Powers. Two years later, he was one of the nineteen young Satsuma officers who were sent abroad to study as a result, smuggled out of the country in defiance of the Tokugawa regime's ban on overseas travel. He spent two years at University College, London, including trips to Russia and France. Increasingly short of funds, however, he and his five remaining companions were persuaded by their mentor, Laurence Oliphant, to cross the Atlantic for a further year abroad at a Utopian Christian colony in New York State. There, in the company of the eccentric Thomas Lake Harris' 'Brotherhood of the New Life', he pursued his studies on life in the West to the extent that, when he returned to Japan in 1868, he brought with him not just polished English skills but also a passionate belief in the powers of rationalism and an almost Western-style persona that set him apart from other young leaders in the new Meiji government.

Twelve years later, back in London, the Mori family spent the first few months of their stay in England entertaining guests, attending diplomatic functions, and travelling abroad on short holidays to Holland and Switzerland. By now they were accustomed to the social side of diplomatic life, as Isabella Bird had noted when remarking that 'his wife dresses tastefully in English style, and receives his guests along with himself'.[5] Perhaps the most singular development in these early months was on 1 June, with the removal of the Japanese Legation to a new location at No. 9 Cavendish Square. Costing more than double the rent of their former residence, Ernest Satow thought it 'a fine house' when he called on Mori for lunch some time later. He found 'his wife as bashful as ever', and commented that the boys were now speaking English 'quite naturally', having 'entirely forgotten their Japanese'.[6]

MORI AS MEIJI DIPLOMAT

Mori's new surroundings were in keeping with his keen awareness of outward appearances. In practice, his everyday duties consisted largely of correspondence relating to the Imperial Navy, from purchasing and refitting cruisers to training Japanese cadets and preparing visits to dockyards. As one attaché at the legation later recalled, the diplomatic staff also spent much of their time polishing their social skills and refining their knowledge of current affairs so as 'to show what a fine impression the Japanese could make on foreign soil'.[7] This was all part of the Foreign Ministry's new initiative to try and raise Japan's profile in the eyes of the Treaty Powers. Ultimately, the objective was to win support for a fundamental revision of the 'unequal' Ansei commercial treaties of 1858, which the Meiji government had inherited from the Tokugawa regime. Now the strategy was to attain recognition for Japan as a 'civilized' state by conforming to Western standards in institutional development and the trimmings of diplomatic protocol. As an imposing house at a central location in London, No. 9 Cavendish Square was eminently suited to the task.

Japanese hopes of revising these treaties had initially foundered in 1872 during the Iwakura Mission's visit to Washington, when Mori himself was there as minister. The issue had then pursued him in successive diplomatic posts, as minister to China from 1875 to 1877 and subsequently as assistant to the Foreign Minister, Terashima Munenori. There were some encouraging signs, particularly when Yoshida Kiyonari obtained a promise of support from the Americans in 1877. This was conditional on the blessing of the other Treaty Powers, however, and came to nothing when Britain insisted that it endangered free trade, prompting the resignation of both Terashima and Mori the following year.

When Mori was next dispatched to London by Terashima's successor, Inoue Kaoru, his assigned mission was to solicit British approval for a Tokyo conference on treaty revision. Convinced that justice was on his side, he arrived full of confidence and impatient for success, but unprepared for the blithe indifference of the Foreign Office. As Hall has pointed out, 'Britain, with the greatest vested interest in her treaty rights, was least responsive to Japanese hopes for revision'.[8] Now in the grip of a major economic slump, the British were guarding their overseas interests with jealous care. Moreover, in the mind of the ageing Foreign Secretary, Lord Granville, Japan's affairs paled in significance in comparison with more pressing matters like the Afghan War, French expansion in Africa and the Khedive's appeal for British protection in Egypt. Mori's overtures also met with suspicion from Sir Harry Parkes, his counterpart in Japan, who was now back in Britain on leave. In recent years, in fact, Parkes had frequently been at loggerheads with Mori in Tokyo over the growing menace of cholera, for he saw his efforts to impose quarantine controls in the treaty ports as an underhand attempt to reassert Japanese jurisdiction and undermine the commercial treaties.[9]

The response of the Foreign Office was to seize the initiative by sending circulars to other Treaty Powers behind Mori's back calling for a conference to be held in London instead.[10] Mori reacted by confronting Granville with Japan's demands for some fundamental changes to the treaties. In April 1881, he called on him at his Walmer Castle home with Parkes also in attendance, only to be told that Japan should concentrate on nothing more than partial amendments.[11] Granville then rejected Japan's agenda altogether and proposed a summit in Tokyo to address the limited issue of tariff reform alone. Convinced that the European Powers were orchestrating a campaign to dictate their own terms to Japan, a furious Mori complained to Itō Hirobumi in October that Britain, now in league with Bismarck, was simply trying to protect her reputation and commercial power. His efforts were to no avail, however, as the following month Inoue accepted the Europeans' plan and a Tokyo summit was opened in January 1882. The talks lasted for several months with little tangible result, in spite of Inoue's attempts to impress his guests with lavish Western-style receptions. It was to be another decade before the British, prompted by fears of Russian expansion in the East, showed genuine receptivity to the Meiji government's crusade against the unequal treaties.

Mori felt that Japan had simply caved in to European pressure, but with the centre stage of negotiations moving to Tokyo there was little he could do. Later, when the summit was over he would feel vindicated enough to remind Britain of Japan's claims to be treated on equal terms with the other Western powers. The Foreign Office, however, either ignored his letters or delayed for weeks or months before sending any reply. When he finally did manage to meet Granville in person, he found it impossible to conceal his frustration. Granville, under fire, considered his tone 'dictatorial and presumptuous', and on more than one occasion, Inoue Kaoru in Tokyo was called upon to try and soothe the British by reminding them that Mori was still 'a very young man,' or that his language was 'unauthorized'.[12]

Mori, in truth, was not a natural diplomat. He owed his posts in Washington and London rather to his undoubted intellect, his command of English and his clan affiliation. After all, the Foreign Ministry in these years was filled with Satsuma compatriots such as Terashima, Yoshida and Sameshima Naonobu, all of them veterans of the domain's expedition to Britain in 1865. Now in 1882, with negotiations out of his hands, he found relief from his ordeals with the Foreign Office in the more relaxing atmosphere of the Athenaeum Club in Pall Mall. His status as minister carried with it the privilege of honorary membership, which not only enabled him to indulge his passion for billiards, his only known hobby, but gave him the opportunity to meet some of the most prominent Victorian intellectuals of the day.[13] As a somewhat scathing article observed the following year, 'It cannot be said that Mr Mori has achieved signal success as a diplomatist,' but it did concede that 'his reputation as a philosophical disputant is quite formidable,' even if this was 'scarcely quite what Japan expects of her Minister in London'.[14]

ATHENAEUM DAYS WITH SPENCER

Soon the Athenaeum was 'the pivot of Mori's social life'.[15] This allowed him to renew his acquaintance with another member, Herbert Spencer, who spent much of his time there whenever he was in London. Mori had first met him during a brief trip to Britain in 1873, having read his works extensively in his years as minister in Washington. This in itself was not unusual, for Spencer was something of a cult figure among progressive thinkers in Japan, where some of his works were already available in translation. Spencer had set about applying Darwinian theory to the world of human relations in order to chart organic models of social and political evolution. By distinguishing between the Knowable (Science) and the Unknowable (Religion), this offered Japanese readers a refreshingly accessible approach to Western civilization, uncomplicated by the mysteries of the Christian tradition.[16] Moreover, his emphasis on minimal government interference was welcomed by many in the growing campaign for liberal rights in Japan who found their interests effectively marginalized by the authoritarian approach of the Meiji government.

Mori's visits to the Athenaeum were also of more than passing interest to Spencer, as he frequently cited the case of Japan in support of his own theories and was now seeking a reliable source of information for his new project, Part V (Political Institutions) of his major work, 'Principles of Sociology'.[17] Usually highly selective in his choice of acquaintances, he actively cultivated Mori's company, once hosting a dinner party held at the club in his honour. Mori returned the compliment by introducing him to a number of his own contacts including Ernest Satow, Itō Hirobumi and Itagaki Taisuke, founder of the Jiyūtō (Liberal Party), Japan's first genuine political party.[18]

The intellectual climate of the Athenaeum served to reinforce Mori's general optimism for the future. At the time, prominent thinkers like Samuel Smiles and Spencer, originally doctors and engineers by training rather than men of letters, were expounding 'an enlightenment of steam locomotives and gas-lit streets'.[19] Now at the height of the age of Jules Verne, they were confident that nothing was beyond the capacity of man and machine, a message that appealed to the radical side of Mori's nature and his belief in human progress. Impressed by the utility of electric power, for example, he displayed 'a typical mid-Victorian faith in the unlimited peaceful potentialities of scientific discovery'.[20]

In the field of political ideas, however, the Athenaeum experience served to temper Mori's radical spirit. By Spencer's own admission, in fact, the counsel he gave him was considerably more cautious than the views he espoused in his written works. As his diary record of the very first meeting with Mori back in 1873 reveals, 'he came to ask my opinion about the reorganization of Japanese institutions. I gave him conservative advice - urging that they would eventually have to return to a form not much in advance of what they had and that they ought not to attempt to diverge widely from it.'[21] In future years he would recall his talks with Mori in London in a similar vein: 'I gave him very conservative advice, contending that it was impossible that the Japanese hitherto accustomed to despotic rule, should all at once become capable of constitutional government.'[22]

Spencer's guarded response to Mori was not an isolated case but just one example of a marked tendency by Western liberals to shy away from their beliefs when dispensing advice to prominent Meiji politicians. It seems they feared that their own theories might lead to chaos should they be misconstrued and applied out of context in Japan. Victorian paternalism may also have featured in their thoughts as they tried to help nurture political development in the fledgling Meiji state. What men such as Spencer perhaps did not foresee was that their cautious advice might contribute to an authoritarian reaction instead by 'inducing political conservatism' in men like Mori.[23]

Spencer's influence, however, certainly helped to bring Mori's thinking closer in line with some of the more pragmatic minds within the Meiji government. Significantly, for example, his ideas won the sympathy of Itō Hirobumi, now the ascendant figure in Japanese politics. In 1881, Itō had emerged triumphant after a government purge featuring an open confrontation on the question of a modern constitution for Japan.[24] Now in 1882, he had arrived in Europe to study under legal experts in Vienna and Berlin with a view to realizing the government's resulting pledge to deliver a new constitution within ten years. Mori promptly requested an interview and, after some delay, they finally met in Paris. There, over the course of three days, he explained his growing conviction that a centrally controlled system of education would be a key element in any new constitutional structure. The talks proved to be a turning point, for Itô was so impressed by Mori's argument that he wrote to him shortly afterwards announcing his intention to make him the first Minister of Education in the new Prussian-style cabinet he was planning to create following his own return to Japan.[25]

A PRESCRIPTION FOR MEIJI JAPAN

Enthused by Itō's vote of confidence, Mori returned to London determined to draft his own proposals for educational reform. These took the form of two papers, '*Shintai no Nōryoku*' [Physical Capacity] and '*Gakusei Hengen*' [Educational Administrative Reform]. Spencer's influence was evident here in Mori's growing tendency to use the human body as a metaphor for Japanese society as a whole. Later, in a clear reference to Spencer's guidance, he even revealed how he had been 'taught' about Darwinian concepts such as 'natural selection' and 'survival of the fittest'.[26] He now showed a deep concern for historical continuity, evolutionary development and balance. Spencer's advice enabled him to plot his vision of progress within a gradualistic framework that reconciled his own radical disposition with his growing awareness of the need for pragmatism. Moreover, by approaching Japan as a complex social organism, he also felt empowered to diagnose ailments and identify potential remedies.

When he arrived in Britain in 1880, Mori had still been advocating a radically decentralized system of education. Now he saw educational administration as critical to the general health of the national polity (*kokutai*), and supported a more active role for the state. Japan's current weaknesses, he thought, were symptomatic of more than two hundred years of Tokugawa rule. In his mind, centuries of Confucian culture had exercised a morally debilitating effect, and he claimed that the Japanese people now lacked any sense of 'internally regulating principles'.[27] The Tokugawa social environment, he felt, was also responsible for what he saw as the relative frailty of his own generation, for he insisted that 'there are few, even in fact amongst the warrior class, who have managed to avoid falling into an inferior physical condition.'[28]

Mori thus held out little hope for older people raised under these conditions, so the prescriptions he devised concentrated on educational programmes aimed at raising the moral fibre and physical vitality of the younger generation. He drew encouragement from his belief in the people's innate spiritual strength, notwithstanding the impact of the Tokugawa years. This fortitude, he suggested, might be related to the historical continuity fostered by an imperial line unbroken since ancient times. Drawing on his own experience of living abroad, he observed: 'Go all over the world, take any Japanese you like, no matter how Americanized or Europeanized he may be, and you will find in him the same stout heart which beats in the breast of every native of Japan.'[29] He was also confident in the people's capacity for progress in the modern industrial world since, as he pointed out: 'I don't know how it is, whether from the genius of our nation, or from whatever other cause, the Japanese have ever been prompt to appropriate whatever is best in foreign nations.'[30]

The intensive course of physical training that Mori also recommended was conceived in 'a quasi-moral sense', for he thought this would be beneficial for 'cultivating the character of the people.'[31] His own fixation with physical vitality was nothing new. In his letters to his brother from Britain nearly twenty years before, he had described how his own regime of daily exercises was helping him to survive the rigours of student life in London.[32] His year of devotional labour in America, too, had reinforced his belief in physical training, but what began as a personal interest had now developed into a blueprint for Japan as a whole. By the end of his stay in Britain, it had become something of an obsession.

During his last few months in London, Mori went on to work in consultation with Spencer on developing his own proposal for a new constitution. Spencer recalled: 'My advice to Mr Mori was that the proposed new institutions should be as much as possible grafted upon the existing institutions, so as to prevent breaking the continuity.'[33] The resulting paper, 'On a Representative System of Government', reflected this influence, and even included Spencerian terms such as the 'engrafting' of representative government on the national polity of Japan.[34] Mori was again at pains to strike a balance in order to guard against any abuses of power, but the representation he outlined was in fact extremely limited. Arguing that a system of popular representation was essentially unsuited to Japan, he suggested limiting any franchise rights to patriarchal family heads, with only consultative powers for the first few generations at least.

Mori also expressed a deep mistrust of factional politics, insisting that 'popular representation' did not necessarily reflect the 'popular will'. Like Spencer, he was somewhat disenchanted with the infighting at Westminster, where individuals like Parnell and Churchill could practically hold Parliament to ransom as they struggled for personal advantage with their 'spoiling politics'.[35] Moreover, the early development of political parties in Japan in the wake of the 1881 purge hardly gave him cause for encouragement. Mori, in fact, confessed that he had little faith in parliaments, for he doubted 'whether parliamentarism can be successfully grafted on Japanese habits of thought'. In his mind, the real barrier was that 'it is hardly in the natural line of our historical development'.[36] While he considered a parliamentary system unavoidable in Britain, he added that 'I doubt whether we shall find it equally inevitable in Japan'.[37]

MORI AS MEIJI STATESMAN

Mori left London for the last time on 26 February 1884, and returned to Tokyo where he took up a new post in the Ministry of Education. As planned, he was then appointed minister when Itō Hirobumi formed Japan's first modern cabinet the following year. This gave him the chance to put into practice some of the theories he had formulated in Britain. His thoughts on a new constitution may have made little impact, but the sweeping reforms he introduced in the field of education during his brief time in charge were to have a profound effect on Japanese society for decades afterwards.

Mori applied his educational theories in two phases, the first reminiscent of his dialogue with Itô and the second more indicative of the influence of Spencer. In 1886, during his first year as minister, he established the New Educational Ordinance, which reasserted central control over Japan's colleges and schools by stipulating objectives and structural frameworks from university to primary school level. At the top, Tokyo University was renamed the Imperial University and came under the direct control of the Ministry of Education, guaranteeing civil service posts for an élite rank of graduates from the faculties of Letters and Law. It was the realization of an idea he had pondered years before in Britain, when he had favoured a strict examination system for entry to the civil service.

The second phase targeted cultural integration through a series of reforms aimed at standardizing the school curriculum and choice of texts. These introduced the moral and physical training that Mori considered necessary to strengthen the character of the people. Ever the patriot, his notion of moral education was based on the ideal of national service. He stressed, for example, that the people should be 'taught to the very marrow of their bones the fervent spirit of loyalty and patriotism'.[38] In 1888, the Ministry of Education published the *Rinrisho* [New Ethical Handbook], incorporating many of the ideas to be found in Spencer's *The Data of Ethics*, which had appeared in Japanese translation four years before. It was entirely secular in content, for Mori harboured no agenda to impose Western religion and, as Isabella Bird had noted a decade earlier, he saw Shinto 'only as a useful political engine'.[39] The *Rinrisho* revealed instead his desire to nurture what he called a 'common sense morality'.[40]

Concerned as ever with physical vitality, he also introduced a military-style training programme into Japan's schools. In years to come this initiative would earn him something of a reputation as the Meiji statesman who mobilized the Japanese population into a national militia. He was certainly not militaristic in outlook, however, for he expressed some ambivalence about the suitability of such a scheme from the start, conscious that it could be prone to abuse. Nevertheless, he was convinced that this was the only way to restore the Japanese people to full health after generations of Tokugawa rule, and concluded that his national physical training programme at least deserved a trial.[41]

Mori's reforms were later described by Inoue Kowashi as 'a philosophy of education based on the national polity'.[42] In some ways they started a trend, for his strong emphasis on national service was reinforced by the unity between ruler and subjects that Inoue and others stressed when they drafted the '*Imperial Rescript on Education*' in 1890. Between them they appeared to lay the foundations for the institutionalized loyalty to the Emperor that became such a feature of Japanese colonial expansion in the early twentieth century. It is only natural, therefore, that he should have been denounced in some circles as a reactionary after World War II, and that his educational reforms should be labelled orthodox, authoritarian and even statist. Mori, however, was never a statist in the mould of some Meiji oligarchs who consolidated their authority through a static system of political control. His was a more progressive conservativism, with an open-ended Spencerian vision of social evolution.[43] Moreover, even in his last years as a Meiji statesman, he could still come across to his contemporaries as a highly Westernized radical who threatened the bastions of traditional Japanese life.

Mori never did have the chance to find out whether a parliamentary system was 'inevitable' in Japan. He was assassinated on 11

February 1889, the inaugural day of the Meiji Constitution. A victim of the tide of ultra-nationalist reaction sweeping across the country, he was shot as he made his way on foot that morning from his government residence towards the Imperial Palace. His assassin, a Shinto fanatic called Nishino Buntarō, left a suicide note justifying his action by claiming not only that Mori was a Christian but also that he was guilty of insulting the Emperor. During a visit to Ise Shrine in November 1887, he had apparently neglected to take off his Western shoes on entry, and used his walking stick to lift the curtain that veiled the inner sanctum. It was an ironic end for a man who was such an inveterate patriot himself. As he confessed to a London reporter on the day before he left Britain in 1884: 'I am Japanese by blood[:] I cannot be impartial.'[44]

One of the most outspoken politicians of the Meiji period, Mori Arinori remains an intriguing figure, conspicuous as much for his radical views as he was for his later conservative agenda. Paradoxical though it may seem, he never consciously betrayed either approach, for his aims remained broadly consistent throughout as he struggled for a balance between his liberal nature and his concern for stability. To some extent these characterized successive stages in his career, from the impetuosity of youth to the pragmatism of middle age. His encounter with Herbert Spencer in London, however, was undoubtedly a critical factor, encouraging him to believe in the possibility of a gradualist compromise incorporating both. The counsel that Mori received at the Athenaeum was, in fact, a heady concoction of conflicting signals, so it is hardly surprising that his own ideas have also defied easy categorization ever since. In this light, his career as a diplomat and statesman perhaps reflects traces of underlying tensions in the Victorian world as well as some of the essential dilemmas of political life in Meiji Japan.

2

Katō Takaaki, 1860–1926: Japanese Ambassador to London and Japanese Foreign Minister

IAN NISH

Katō Takaaki

KATŌ TAKAAKI (1860–1926) had a remarkable record as diplomat and Foreign Minister. He spent about a quarter of his career overseas and was Foreign Minister four times. He had the good fortune to be able to combine diplomatic service abroad with high office in Tokyo. Since his only overseas postings were in Britain, he occupies a special place in the diplomacy of Anglo-Japanese relations. Among Japanese he was one of the greatest admirers of the institutions of Victorian-Edwardian Britain. Both in the Japanese Embassy in London and in Japan he achieved many of the goals he set for himself. But his temperament was brusque, puritanical, straight-talking and individualistic. Perhaps for that reason he is not generally given the credit for his achievements as one of Japan's greatest diplomats.[1]

Katō was born in Owari outside the area of the clans who had engineered the Meiji Restoration in 1868 and therefore without any special connections in government. In December 1882, after graduating from Tokyo Imperial University, which had just been established, he took up his first employment with Mitsubishi. He joined the sea transportation department, the main branch of the company at the time. After postings at Kobe, Osaka and Otaru, he was sent to London in April 1883 for study abroad (*ryūgaku*). He stayed at 33 Kings Road, Finsbury Park, north London.[2] But much of his time was spent in Liverpool, which had the reputation as the hub of global shipping at the time. In order to learn the technicalities of his trade, he was assisted by James Bowes, a prominent merchant who is described in Katō's biography as a Japanophile (*'shin-Nichi'*). Returning to London, Katō studied customs procedures and the shipping and insurance market, staying at 190 Stanhope Street, NW. There he got to know Mutsu Munemitsu, later to become foreign minister, who was spending 18 months in Europe for study and was based in London for most of that period. Katō developed a great respect for Mutsu which had much effect on the direction his career would take. It was Mutsu who persuaded him on two occasions to join the Foreign Ministry. Katō left London in April 1885 and travelled around Europe on his way back to Japan. These early experiences of Britain were to influence his career deeply.[3]

At the end of his overseas stint he married the eldest daughter of Iwasaki Yatarō (of the Mitsubishi house) who had died shortly before. This gave him wealth and valuable connections. He was charged with planning the merger of his company and the state-owned shipping line. Soon, however, he chose to desert the private sector and entered the Foreign Ministry in January 1887. He became private secretary to Ōkuma Shigenobu as foreign minister and was to play an important part both as interpreter and negotiator in the talks on treaty revision. After Ōkuma 's fall from grace, he switched to the Finance Ministry. This double-barrelled experience in the bureaucracy was to prove helpful in his career, though he was later to claim that he was a non-bureaucratic politician.

His old friend and senior, Mutsu, became foreign minister in the Itō ministry from August 1892. When the Sino-Japanese war began in August 1894, Katō gladly returned to the Foreign Ministry and was appointed temporary chief of the political affairs section (*seimu kyokuchō*). He attained the rank of minister plenipotentiary and negotiated the conclusion of the Japan-Korea Defence Agreement. In October he became attached to the General Headquarters (*Daihonei*) at Hiroshima, an indication of his importance to Mutsu. With Hayashi Tadasu and Hara Takashi, he made up a strong team of young officials who supported Mutsu during the travails of wartime diplomacy.[4]

SINO-JAPANESE WAR, 1894–5

The military and naval aspects of the war swung in Japan's favour; and the Chinese were forced to sue for peace. The Sino-Japanese peace negotiations were convened at Shimonoseki on 20 March 1895. But China had already been canvassing for the support of the Powers, hoping that they would intervene or exercise some influence on her behalf. It was vital, therefore, for Japan to preempt any desire they had for intervention.

Foreign Minister Mutsu had been expecting action by the Powers since early in the war. He recognized that Japan was unpopular with Britain because she had not taken up British offers of mediation before and during the war. Mutsu assumed that this frigidity was also due to Britain's friendship with China and made it his objective to win over Britain to goodwill towards Japan. Japan found herself, as happened all too often, under-represented abroad for the task. The existing incumbent who superintended the legations in Berlin and London, Aoki Shūzō, could not cope with the two posts during wartime and had in any case antagonized Mutsu. With great urgency Katō was appointed Minister to the Court of St James on 23 November. He set off by way of Canada one month later, reaching London on 23 January 1895. For Katō to receive this responsible assignment at the young age of 35 was a sign of Mutsu's confidence in him. He was naturally overjoyed to take over Japan's top diplomatic post at a critical time for his country.

From his first meeting with the Foreign Secretary of the Liberal government, Lord Kimberley, on 4 February, Katō felt that they established a fine personal rapport but perceived that Japan had still much persuasion to do.[5] Japan passed over the draft of her peace terms to China, which were leaked by the Chinese to most of the powers including Britain. Katō reported to Tokyo his impression that Britain had no firm position and was watching the movements of Russia and France over eastern developments. When the commercial terms reached him on 6 April, Katō assured Britain that all trading nations would enjoy equal rights under them. The London government received no complaints from commercial circles about these terms and broadly accepted them.[6]

In the crisis atmosphere on 6 April Kimberley asked the Prime Minister, Lord Rosebery, whether Britain should give advice to Japan as the continental powers were proposing to do. 'If that advice is not followed, are we prepared to enforce it? … We could advise Japan not to press the cession of Liaotung etc or we might ask that the cession shall not extend beyond the actual peninsula. My mind inclines to non-interference as presenting the least objection'.[7] Rosebery replied that the Japanese terms were not unreasonable and 'we could not therefore interfere by force to reduce them ... If we are not prepared to back the representations by force, it is useless in the present state of Japanese feeling to make any.' The view that Britain could not go to war with Japan unless she directly and immediately threatened British interests was endorsed by the cabinet on 9 April.[8] From this it would appear that Britain's attitude was not as yet cut and dried and that Katō's persuasiveness was still much needed.

When the treaty of Shimonoseki was signed on 17 April, the Rosebery cabinet on 23 April confirmed its former decision not to advise the Japanese 'without knowing the ulterior measures to which it is in contemplation to have recourse [*sic*] in the almost certain event of Japan refusing to yield to the desires of the Powers.' Clearly Katō had given the British ministers the strong impression that Japan would reject any outside 'advice' and resist.[9]

Meanwhile, the Tokyo representatives of Russia, France and Germany on the same day gave Japan their friendly 'advice' to reverse the clauses of the treaty of Shimonoseki, asking in effect for Japan to return the Liaotung peninsula to China. Britain did not join this Tripartite (*Dreibund*) intervention in spite of her desire for a rapprochement with Russia. She recognized that, while Japan's political demands on China were severe, she could not apply any diplomatic pressure on Japan because she was not willing to back it up by force or threats of force. Katō was worried that Britain, in spite of her assurances, might still join as a late-comer. In the end she declined to do so.[10]

Could Katō then persuade Britain to lend her support to Japan against the coalition of European powers? Kimberley had almost daily meetings with Katō over this period. At the meeting on 27 April, which was probably the critical one, Katō asked how far Japan might count on Britain's support against the *Dreibund*. While Kimberley was in Katō's view 'very cordial', he defined British policy as being one of non-interference, his principal interest being the restoration of peace in the area. Though this was not said, the British cabinet felt that China should accept the terms and that there was no practical way in which it could influence the situation.[11] Britain did not want to depart from neutrality; but Kimberley who was regularly in touch with the three Powers did tell Katō that they too were in earnest and were not likely to be fobbed off by unacceptable compromises.

On receipt of this report, Tokyo replied to Katō in English: 'Your telegram gave us a good guide in determining our action'.[12] Japan would have to handle the problem without positive external support. That meant a climb-down which she eventually made on 5 May and was thankfully accepted by the three Powers. It resulted in an agreement to retrocede all mainland territory granted under the treaty in return for monetary compensation.

When the Rosebery ministry collapsed on 24 June, Katō had a final meeting with Kimberley at which he expressed his appreciation of the actions of the cabinet and the friendliness of the foreign secretary. But his judgment may have been over-optimistic. From the British archives it would appear that Britain did not budge during the crisis from her policy of safeguarding her national interests and observing strict neutrality. Katō received lofty and accurate advice from London but no practical offers of assistance.

If Britain was circumspect during the crisis, there can be little doubt about the importance of Katō's own role. Japan's worry was about Britain's supposed alliance with China and Katō's task was to wean her away from that. In fact, Britain soon lost any confidence she had formerly had in China. It is probably true to say that Katō had great success in improving relations from the low level they had reached in 1894. Then all Britain's initiatives for peace had been firmly repudiated by Japan and Britain was in serious contention with her over the Kowshing incident, the undertakings over Shanghai and the Korean customs. The situation improved dramatically during 1895, largely due to the energetic activities of Katō. By the time the crisis had passed, Britain's cordiality towards Japan had been restored.

FOUR YEARS IN LONDON

Katō drew comfort from the thought that a favourable turn in Anglo-Japanese relations had taken place as a result of the ambitions the continental powers had shown during the crisis over the Triple Intervention. With the coming of peace he wanted to continue his collaboration with Britain. But the ministry changed in London and Katō had to cope with Lord Salisbury as Foreign Secretary – a more distant figure than Kimberley. Indeed Katō's contacts tended to be with Joseph Chamberlain, the Colonial Secretary, and younger members of the cabinet.

When Ōkuma Shigenobu came to office as foreign minister in the Matsukata ministry in September 1896, he addressed his ministers overseas about the new age (*shin jidai*) on which Japan was embarking after her massive victory in the war and called on them for their reactions.[13]

Katō gave a lengthy response on the steps he wanted to take over relations with Britain. In particular Katō called for an increase in expenditure on the London legation and a change of location for its building. He wanted the legation raised to an embassy. He saw these as essential to project a new image of Japan as a victorious Power. After Ōkuma's visionary approach, Katō's response was down to earth. Under his leadership the quality of diplomats at the London legation improved thereafter; and the number increased. They paid much more attention to hospitality and took the Japanese Legation to a new level of popularity by offering lavish entertainment. Katō never failed to turn up for the annual dinner of the Japan Society. Peter Duus makes the point that perhaps one of the reasons for Katō's appointment to London was his ability to pay the hospitality expenses of the legation from his private fortune. Katō also attached much importance to cultivating relations with the London press. He also succeeded in moving the legation from Sussex Gardens to more prestigious Grosvenor Gardens on 27 August 1898.[14] Still the subjects which engaged most of Katō's attention were the humdrum affairs of an overseas legation with a special emphasis on the consequences of Japan's revised treaties which came into effect in 1899 when all the other Powers had agreed. There were, too, the financial dealings over the large indemnity which Japan was to receive from China.

The highlight of Katō's term of office was Queen Victoria's Diamond Jubilee in June 1897 celebrating her accession to the throne 60 years earlier. This was a most exhausting issue for him. It also offers the historian many insights into Japan's world-view at the time. It occurred when Ōkuma was serving as Foreign Minister. An invitation to attend the celebrations was sent to the Japanese court and it was decided to send a delegation headed by Prince Arisugawa (Takehito Shinno no miya), who had completed his education as a naval officer in England, being the first prince of the blood to study abroad.[15] The problem was that the Japanese leaders had the feeling that their delegation had not received proper recognition at the ceremonies ten years earlier to mark the 50th anniversary of Victoria's accession to the throne. It was important to reverse this. All the more so because Japan had in the interval defeated China in the war of 1894–5 and had claims to be regarded as a Great Power.

The prince, therefore, proposed to the throne that he should be accompanied by Itō Hirobumi who was Japan's most senior statesman and the closest adviser to the Emperor but was then out of office. The Emperor (temporarily in Kyoto) was reluctant to allow Itō to leave the country for an extended period but ultimately gave in under the combined pressure of the prince and the cabinet.

In order to understand Kato's position in London, it is necessary to quote some of the correspondence, which was being exchanged between the leaders in Tokyo at this time. This illustrates the high expectations, which the Tokyo government had from Itō's visit to London and European capitals. Foreign Minister Ōkuma wrote:

> I am very satisfied that Itō is going to Britain. We cannot escape from dissatisfaction over the way that country treats our royal

> family, which may be because of religious considerations in the national character. If she knows that Itō is coming with the delegation, she will treat it more favourably. This would, of course, be important for Prince Arisugawa and for Japan as a whole. In addition I think Itō's journey would be useful both in broadening his views and in improving his health. Moreover the fact that he is not connected to officialdom would be useful in making contact with major statesmen and allowing him to speak more freely than those who have official responsibilities. There are many points, which I cannot mention openly to diplomats and where I want to rely on Itō's help. So, when Itō goes travelling from Britain to the continent, I shall send Nabeshima Keijiro to accompany him with the telegraphic codes.
>
> Though Itō is merely one member of the delegation, he is well known around the world as the former Prime Minister of a victorious country. It is natural that he will incur expenses while he is travelling. I would ask you to give him 560,000 yen. I believe that it is necessary for Itō and me to be able to communicate with one another on diplomatic affairs without going through Japanese ministers or secretaries [*kōshi mata wa shokikan*] overseas. In this way secret exchanges which are difficult to explain to others can be passed over by you to Itō.[16]

Ōkuma's proposal was endorsed by the cabinet as the following letter from a top politician of the time shows:

> … at the cabinet the other day, Count Ōkuma said that Prince Itō's proposed journey was, of course, crucially important from the point of view of Japan's diplomacy and he relied greatly on Itō's help. Though Itō is not in any way in government service, it goes without saying that Britain will accord him considerable respect both as Japan's front-ranking statesman and as the former prime minister of a victorious country.[17]

Katō's skill as a diplomat was sorely tested by Tokyo's ambitious scheme and he insisted that the over-large delegation, which Japan was intending to send, should be slimmed down. On the other hand, he argued effectively the need for receiving more funds in order to entertain as many of Britain's élite as possible since Japan was more prosperous than she had been during the royal visit ten years earlier.

Itō left Tokyo on 7 May and reached Britain after joining up with Prince Arisugawa in Paris in time for the opening ceremonies on 21 June. We need not detail the ceremonial duties, which the prince had to endure because the correspondence quoted shows that the cabinet set most store on the activities of Itō. This placed a special burden on Katō who had to try to get introductions to Britain's major statesmen. This was a task he shared with Sir Ernest Satow who happened to be on leave from his post in Tokyo at this time and was often in contact with Katō. It was not easy to secure interviews with the elderly Prime Minister and Foreign Secretary, Lord Salisbury (1830–1903) who was never keen to fulfil his social obligations by glad-handing foreign envoys. He was happy to hide behind the excuse of his jubilee preoccupations. In the end it was arranged that the two should have a conversation and Itō claims that they discussed China at length. More detailed discussions were left to Itō's and Katō's talks with George Nathaniel Curzon, the Parliamentary Under-Secretary, whom Itō knew already. The Itō connection at this time was to prove important for Katō's later career.[18]

In the middle of Katō's spell in London there occurred the serious Far Eastern crisis of 1898 when the stability of the area was threatened by the actions of European powers. It was always Katō's bent to want to influence high policy. In days before the examination system began for entry to the Foreign Ministry, diplomats were really politicians. Katō in spite of his youth felt strong enough to urge policies on his home government. When his patron Mutsu left office, he still continued this under his successors Ōkuma and later Nishi. In particular he consistently urged the necessity of an arrangement with Britain. But in Tokyo there was an influential contrary view that a deal should rather be done with Russia over Manchuria and Korea (*Man-Kan kōkan*). In a memorandum of March 1898 Katō stepped in to criticize the view of his seniors, which he considered to be weak (*nanjaku gaikō*), and advocated a more robust policy of cooperation with Britain.[19]

Katō was aware that Britain shared the anxieties felt in Japan about the actions of Russia in the east in particular. It was in this context that he proposed to such as Joseph Chamberlain, the Colonial Secretary, the idea of an Anglo-Japanese alliance. Japanese sources tell us that Chamberlain at one of his dinner parties spoke in favour of some sort of alliance. But it has to be said that there is no mention of it in British sources or in the private papers of the nation's leaders.

From 1898 onwards Katō made several attempts to get permission to return to Japan. Japan was however raising a public loan on the London money market and wanted him to stay because of the skill he had shown in clinching the China indemnity payments. Katō, however, wanted to leave for family and health reasons. Tokyo found the London market difficult because of the deteriorating situation in South Africa and would not give permission. After a dispute with

Foreign Minister Aoki, Katō took off for home via the USA and Canada. Arriving in Tokyo in May 1899, he did not attempt to clear his name. In July after consultation with Aoki, he formally handed in his resignation from the diplomatic establishment. Being married into the Mitsubishi family, he was financially independent and was not inclined to be ordered about. He went on an extended trip to Korea and China. Aoki wanted him to go back to London. When he visited Itō Hirobumi who was acting as adviser to the Foreign Ministry, Itō asked him to go on transfer to Russia or Germany for a while but Katō refused on family grounds. His visit abroad, however, suggests that he was not distancing himself from foreign policy issues.[20]

Katō was already taking some part in journalism. Though it cannot be proved, it seems likely that he inspired the following article in the *Nichinichi* on 5 May 1900 from which the following is an extract:

> That Great Britain took the lead in the revision of the Treaties, that she held aloof from interference after the Sino-Japanese war, that she showed her good-will in the matter of payment of the indemnity and of the occupation of Weihaiwei and that her political relations with us have year by year become more intimate – these are facts which cannot be concealed ... We consider that the great increase in friendship existing between our two countries is largely due to exertions of these two gentlemen in the past [Satow and Hayashi] and that our friendship will depend more and more upon them in future.[21]

This account served as a farewell message both for Sir Ernest Satow as he left the Tokyo legation at the end of April and for Hayashi Tadasu who was about to take up his post as minister in London.

SPELLS AS FOREIGN MINISTER

Katō was appointed Foreign Minister by Itō Hirobumi in October 1900 in the aftermath of the Boxer rebellion. His former associate in the crisis of 1895, Lord Kimberley, wrote to congratulate him and received the following reply:

'I feel grateful for your kind expression and also for your assurance that you have not forgotten our pleasant relations while I was in London, which indeed live vividly in my remembrance. I beg to condole with you on the death of your beloved Queen whose loss is, I assure you, sincerely regretted by my countrymen.'[22]

There are puzzles about this appointment. There was no doubt that Katō was experienced and fully competent. He was the first Foreign Minister who had been to university. Itō seems to have preserved good relations with Katō during his resting-period and had discussed beforehand the possibility of giving him a cabinet seat, if Itō returned to power. But Katō had resigned from the foreign ministry and his appointment has to be seen as a political one. He was known to have different views from the new prime minister on a number of issues such as dealing with Russia. It is strange, given Itō's own attitudes, that such a hard-liner on Russia as Katō should have been appointed. Indeed, it was rumoured that Itō might have preferred to appoint Katō's contemporary, Hara Takashi, who was probably less strong-minded.[23]

No sooner had Katō come to office than an opportunity came to advance causes which he had cherished while he was attached to the Court of St James. In October 1900 an agreement was signed between Britain and Germany for an application of the open door principle to all Chinese territory 'as far as they can exercise influence' and Katō sought to convert it into a three-sided Anglo-German-Japanese treaty by announcing Japan's adherence to it. Alas, the treaty was so vaguely worded that there were basic misunderstandings between the signatories. While Britain and Katō considered it applied to Manchuria, Germany was not willing to turn it into a challenge to Russia there. Almost inevitably Katō became highly suspicious of and disillusioned with Germany. Katō's hawkish policy towards Russia was in tune with the increasingly vociferous domestic opinion. In the aftermath of the Boxer movement where Russia took advantage of her position in Manchuria, Katō looked vigilantly at everything Russia did. He protested at the terms Russia imposed on China and Manchuria and resisted Russian proposals for the neutralization of Korea.[24] When Eckardstein at the German Embassy in London floated the idea of a more elaborate agreement in March, it is scarcely likely that Katō or his colleagues could have taken it seriously.

After the collapse of the Itō cabinet in May, Katō's vision of an exclusive agreement with Britain was carried forward by the Katsura cabinet and came to fruition in the Anglo-Japanese Alliance of 1902. Katō became a reluctant member of the Diet (*daigishi*). Thanks to help from Mitsubishi, he was able to become the owner of the *Nichinichi Shimbun*, and his hands-on involvement with it made him someone who had to be wooed by the political parties.

His second stint as foreign minister came in the Saionji cabinet. But it only lasted for two months as Katō offered his resignation in March 1906. It was a case of *tatemae* and *honne*. In the *tatemae*, one of the reasons for his resignation was his objection to the government's railway nationalization plan, which was valid enough. But the *honne*, the real reason, was almost certainly the unstated one: his failure – and that of his ministry – to implement the policy of the Open Door in Manchuria to which he felt the Japanese were committed. This was primarily caused by his two *betes noirs* – the elder statesmen and the army. But he also failed to convince the majority of the cabinet to his views. Katō was preaching in Tokyo the views on the Open Door held in Washington and London.[25]

While he was out of line with his cabinet colleagues, Katō was in fact attacking the *genro*, the elders in the political world, for their unwillingness to exercise any control over the military who were occupying Manchuria. It was one of the instances where he stood up to protest against *genro* and military interference in foreign policy-making and uphold the Foreign Ministry's independence and autonomy.[26]

AMBASSADOR TO LONDON (1908–13)

Another surprise in Katō's career comes with his appointment to London in 1908. This was in accordance with the recommendation of the retiring ambassador there, Komura Jutarō, who had become foreign minister. He thought that there had been so much ill feeling between London and Tokyo over Manchuria that Japan needed to have there someone who could revive relations with Britain. He recognized that Katō was the person best suited for the London post and recommended him to Prime Minister Katsura as his successor. Komura himself who had had the reputation of shunning social occasions recognized Katō's social aptitudes.[27]

Katō held the post from February 1909 to January 1913, presiding now over a much larger staff than in 1895. He was ultimately responsible for many historic developments: the revision of Japan's commercial tariffs; Britain's acceptance of Japan's annexation of Korea; conclusion of loans in the London money market; and the Great Japan Exhibition of 1910. But the highpoint was the continuation of the Anglo-Japanese Alliance. Katō who regarded himself as one of its authors believed deeply that the alliance, which had been revised in 1905, needed to be resuscitated *(fukkatsu)* after some of the disagreements of the intervening years. The idea of revising the alliance four years before it was legally necessary was in fact being considered quite independently in inner circles both in Britain and Japan. It is interesting that the revision was being sought by the Japanese (largely because of the Korean clause) as much as by the British. Eventually, the renewal of the alliance took place in July 1911. Katō was acknowledged by being made a Baron *(danshaku)* for his role in negotiating the third treaty.[28]

After his exertions, Katō took leave in Tokyo from September 1911. During the course of this he met Katsura whose thinking over parliamentary institutions and political parties differed widely from his own. The two got on unexpectedly well together. After Katō's return to London, Katsura was invited to form his third ministry on 21 December but he could no longer choose Komura who had hitherto been his partner as foreign minister as he had died in the previous month. To everyone's surprise Katō was offered the post. Katō accepted, having reconciled himself with someone who had hitherto been regarded as his political adversary. The British Ambassador remarked that he had 'for reasons not clearly discernible thrown in his lot with the new party and accepted the portfolio of Foreign Minister'. Katō left the London embassy, which had moved to Grosvenor Square in September 1912, early in January.[29]

When Katō took up his new post, Britain rather preened herself on being close to the seat of power in Tokyo. Dr Peter Lowe in his study of this period has emphasized the special empathy, which existed between Katō and Sir Edward Grey, the Foreign Secretary in the Liberal administration (1906–16). In almost their last encounter Katō mentioned that, when the Japanese lease of 25 years on the Liaotung peninsula expired in 1923, no Japanese government would be strong enough to give back the territory to China: 'after the great and bloody war which Japan had fought with Russia, she could not cede Port Arthur and the leased territory'.[30] It was a telling warning about the views of Katō and Japanese generally; and Grey did not appear to be too antagonistic in his response.

Katō's tenure at the Foreign Ministry was again short-lived, not on this occasion because of any intemperate resignation but because of the downfall of the ministry. Katsura resigned in February and died in October. His successor asked Katō to stay on as foreign minister but he declined. Instead Katō cautiously entered the Rikken Dōshikai, the political party, which Katsura had been building up and left behind leaderless. Eventually Katō became its first president when the Dōshikai held its inaugural meeting in December. This was a remarkable transition. Doubtless he considered that he had reached the top of his profession while he was in Britain for such was the standing of the London embassy at the time. He now saw the opportunity presented by a new career in party politics at the age of 53.[31]

It was in this new capacity as a party leader that he was admitted to Ōkuma's cabinet as Foreign Minister during the first two years of the world war – his fourth and longest period in the office. The course, which Japan steered in becoming a belligerent in the First World War, was greatly influenced by him. He seems to have got his way in cabinet to take Japan into the war against Germany. He was, he thought, acting consistently with the spirit of the alliance but did not claim that Japan was carrying out the letter of the treaty. There were many contrary voices, which claimed that the start of the

European war would present an opportunity to leave the alliance or at least to diversify by associating with Russia and France. But Katō declined to consult the *genro* or public opinion. The same applies to Japan's wartime policies towards China launched by the so-called Twenty-one Demands, which were the responsibility of the Foreign Ministry. Whether Katō personally bore the major share of blame for them or whether he was merely the tool of the military is still a matter of dispute among historians.[32] Whatever the feeling about his policies, Katō's term at the Foreign Ministry left it in a stronger position than ever before. He had established the autonomy of the cabinet and ministry and challenged interference by the *genro* in state affairs.

★ ★ ★

Katō never returned to Britain after February 1913. One may therefore ask what influence his three sojourns there had on his later career as a party politician, as party president and ultimately as Prime Minister between 1924 and his death in office two years later. His London years established his reputation for intellect and leadership. He was universally regarded as an Anglophile statesman thereafter. He saw himself as the author of the Anglo-Japanese Alliance and was its most consistent advocate. Even though he took Japan into the Treaty of London with France and Russia in 1915, he still insisted on the primacy of Japan's links with Britain. In 1921 when the Anglo-Japanese Alliance was about to lapse, Katō wrote that the two countries had 'up till now acted together like relatives; this should continue. It is vital that we should not end up as utter strangers'. In any case, the German influences, which had existed in Japanese politics and society since Meiji times, also lapsed after Germany's defeat in the First World War.[33]

Katō's dedication to party politics in the latter part of his career may also have come from Britain. Of course Meiji-Taisho political parties differed widely from those of Britain; but he was still persuaded of the cut and thrust of debate and the electoral process. Thus, in January 1914 he spoke in favour of the concept of 'His Majesty's Opposition' – a concept of adversarial politics at odds with bureaucratic politics as were then widely favoured in Japan. Many of his acts as Prime Minister such as the universal franchise act (*fusenhō*), which expanded the franchise to include almost all adult males may reflect his respect for Britain's way of doing things which he had seen there before 1914.

Yet his 'British connection' should not be exaggerated. Just as he was extending the franchise in 1924, he was also responsible for clamping down on demonstrations and left-wing political parties and for repressive police legislation *(jian ijihō)*. As Katō became increasingly embroiled in domestic party politics, his ties with Britain became attenuated. He was, after all, a most independent, individualistic Japanese and an opportunistic statesman.

3

Sir Francis Plunkett, 1835–1907: British Minister at Tokyo, 1884–87

HUGH CORTAZZI

Sir Francis Plunkett

IN THE HISTORY of Anglo-Japanese relations in the latter part of the nineteenth century Francis Plunkett has been overshadowed by the image of his forceful and abrasive predecessor Sir Harry Parkes. But Plunkett, who went on from Japan to more senior posts in Europe and who retired with a string of high honours, played a key role in the efforts, which were made while he was in Japan, to achieve agreement on revision of the 'unequal treaties' between the Western Powers and Japan. These efforts proved abortive but he was not responsible for the failure and his contribution to Anglo-Japanese relations deserves to be recorded.

Francis Richard Plunkett was the sixth son of the Earl of Fingall (an Irish peerage) and consequently had the courtesy title of 'honourable'. He was born on 3 February 1835 at Corbalton Hall in County Meath. He was educated at St Mary's Roman Catholic College, Oscott. He was appointed attaché at Munich in January 1855 when he was not yet twenty. From Munich he was transferred to Naples, then to The Hague and Madrid. In July 1859 he was appointed as a paid attaché at St Petersburg. In 1863 he was appointed Second Secretary at Copenhagen. After service at Vienna, Berlin, and Florence he was nominated in 1873 as Secretary of Legation in Tokyo under Sir Harry Parkes. He left Tokyo in 1876 and served as Diplomatic Secretary in St Petersburg, Constantinople and Paris before being appointed Minister at Tokyo in succession to Sir Harry Parkes on the latter's transfer to Peking. He was made a KCMG in 1886 while at Tokyo. (The notification of this award in a telegram from Lord Salisbury was timed to arrive on his birthday!) After Tokyo he served as head of mission to Sweden and Belgium where he was made a GCMG. In 1900 he was appointed Ambassador at Vienna and made a Privy Councillor. While he was in Vienna he was awarded a GCB and a GCVO. He retired in 1905. He died in Paris in 1907 and was buried at Boulogne. In 1870 he married May Tevis by whom he had two daughters.[1]

The Times of 2 March 1907, reporting the news of his death, recorded that in Vienna Plunkett had been liked in society and by his diplomatic colleagues. 'The Emperor constantly showed him marks of esteem, and gave him and Lady Plunkett upon their departure unusually flattering tokens of regard.' His 'kind and courteous bearing made him popular, while his keen interest in Austro-Hungarian affairs and solicitude for the welfare of the Dual Monarchy gained for him a place in the category of those diplomatists whom the Austrians cease to regard altogether as foreigners'.

On his first appointment to Tokyo as Secretary to the Legation under Sir Harry Parkes he came with his wife, two daughters and a governess. He was expected to live in the house built in the legation compound for the Legation Secretary. This was a single-storey house with a drawing room, dining room and three bedrooms (one quite small), a kitchen and various servants quarters, with a large open yard to the rear. Water came from a well in the garden. Plunkett refused to accept this house unless it was adapted to include an additional bedroom, a wine-cellar, storeroom and quarters for European servants. His wishes were apparently complied with.[2]

Plunkett seems to have been a competent diplomat and there is nothing to suggest in the Public Records that he was other than a satisfactory subordinate to his demanding boss. However, unlike A.B.Mitford who was also a diplomat and not a consular officer and had a similarly aristocratic background, there is no indication that he acquired any competence in the Japanese language. When in August 1875 he was sent on a mission to Korea and Tsushima he had to take with him a member of the Japan Consular Service, Vice-Consul Longford, to act as his interpreter.

Parkes had sent Plunkett to investigate the situation at Port Hamilton, an island harbour off the coast of Korea. As Gordon Daniels records,[3] Plunkett discovered 'that the thirty year-old description of Port Hamilton's sparse population was completely inaccurate for there were over three thousand Koreans living there'.[4] On their arrival at Port Hamilton the party seem to have been greeted rather like beings from outer space and had to undergo a 'ludicrous and unpleasant ordeal' during which the natives 'put their hands in our pockets, examined our clothes, tried on our hats, ran their hands up our sleeves and trousers'. They were served various fish dishes and expected to consume a 'horrid drink' of what seemed like sour saké [probably '*doburoku*']. In Tsushima Plunkett had seen no signs of Russians, nor had he heard news of an advance of Russian troops or ships from Vladivostock. His expenses for the journey, as reported to the Foreign Office, came to 355.41 [Mexican] dollars.

Plunkett, who was not yet fifty, was appointed as Minister Plenipotentiary at Tokyo in 1883, but did not arrive until 15 March 1884. He and his family had travelled via Hong Kong on the P and O ship *Kashgar* which called first at Nagasaki where he was given a warm welcome. On arrival in Tokyo he paid a courtesy call on Count Inouye, the Foreign Minister. He was received in audience by the Emperor on 21 March when he presented his credentials. The letter from Queen Victoria was addressed to His Imperial and Royal Majesty, The Mikado of Japan. The audience seems to have followed the usual form. Subsequently he made courtesy calls on all Cabinet Ministers.

Plunkett seems[5] to have been an active diplomat. He travelled in Japan occasionally, but not extensively. One of his first trips was to Aomori, Hakodate and Sapporo in the late summer of 1884. He noted that in all the places in which he stopped there were Japanese Post Offices from which he was able to send telegrams in English or Japanese. He was treated with due honour and did not meet with any dangers.

Because of the continuance of extraterritoriality he had to supervise the consular courts. Among the routine matters which were dealt with by the Legation in these years were such issues as shipwrecks of which there were a number, changes in lightships and buoys, precautions against cholera and problems over applications for passports by British subjects wishing to travel outside the settlements, Japanese regulations on the sale of gunpowder etc. He was also responsible for concluding the perpetual lease on the Legation's premises (the present British Embassy).

The shipwreck in 1886 of the *Normanton* in which 23 Japanese passengers died caused much ill feeling in Japan as the crew managed to escape in the ship's boats and did not do all they could to save the passengers. Captain Drake, the Master, was eventually tried in the Consular Court in Kobe and being found guilty of manslaughter was sentenced to three months imprisonment.

Plunkett and his wife seem to have been hospitable. Plunkett would have liked to have had a ballroom built for the Legation residence but this was not approved.[6] Nevertheless, Lady Plunkett as she became was reported in the *Japan Weekly Mail* at one time as giving two receptions within a month. The Queen's birthday was celebrated (e.g. in 1886) with a grand dinner attended by Imperial princes and princesses and by cabinet ministers. The Queen's golden jubilee in 1887 was the occasion for major festivities in Yokohama. The jubilee committee in Yokohama decided to collect money for the establishment of a school in Yokohama to be called the Victoria school. Reporting on the festivities the *Japan Weekly Mail* for 25 July 1887 declared: 'The twenty-first was a day to be remembered with satisfaction by the British residents of Yokohama and Tokyo. If the celebration was preceded by some essentially British grumbling, it was carried out with a thoroughness not less essentially British.' A morning service at Christ Church in Yokohama was attended by the Minister and Lady Plunkett. In the afternoon the weather being surprisingly good for late June in Japan there were sports, including tugs-of-war and 'assaults of arms' on the cricket ground. Miss Plunkett presented the prizes. The British Consulate and other buildings were adorned with flags. 'All the British residents of Yokohama threw their houses open for the entertainment of their Japanese, American, and European friends from Tokyo'. 'Beef and bread were at a premium, and as for the less substantial accessories of feasting, they were practically unprocurable.' In the evening there were theatricals and dancing. All the ships of the British naval squadron in port were lit up and 'all around the port streamed the great beam of electric light from the *Leander*'. A supper for five hundred people began shortly after midnight in a huge tent that had been erected in the Naval depot. Plunkett, who sat at a table especially reserved for distinguished guests and the Corps Diplomatique, proposed the Queen's health in suitably pompous terms.

The Plunketts were present at the famous fancy dress ball given by Count Itō in April 1887. Miss Plunkett (presumably the elder daughter) is reported by the *Japan Weekly Mail* to have 'appeared in the gaily coloured dress of a Russian Peasant Girl and one of the attachés as a Russian peasant, in black velvet and red silk sleeves. The *Mail* did not state what costumes were worn by the British Minister and his wife, but reported that there was 'a fine clerical figure of the later days of George II'. 'King John, in his royal crown and robes, moved about familiarly'. 'A portly Henry VIII was there'. Was Plunkett King John or King Henry VIII?

Plunkett seems to have had the usual interests of the British aristocracy. He and other members of the Legation applied for and were granted shooting licences. At one point the Legation were told that their request for the Imperial Fukiage Gardens to be kept open during daylights hours every day for skating had been accepted. The Plunketts attended the Yokohama race meetings and the Minister seems to have been instrumental in getting the Emperor to attend and to bring people down from Tokyo for the meetings. In 1886 Plunkett resigned after two years service as President of the Nippon Race Club, which was regarded as 'a thoroughly British institution' but he continued to belong to the Permanent Committee of the club.

Plunkett was also involved with a more serious institution, the Tokyo English Law School. The annual dinner in January 1887 was a very grand affair attended by Japanese judges, the Governor of Tokyo and the President of Tokyo Imperial University. After a ten-course dinner Plunkett proposed the health of the Emperor. All the Japanese who followed spoke in English.

A more important part of Plunkett's work was to keep in touch with the Japanese authorities over developments in the Far East, in particular over Korea where the Japanese were coming into conflict with the Chinese. This led to exchanges with Sir Harry Parkes in Peking. In a letter to Aston dated 17 January 1885[7] Parkes wrote:

> Plunkett has telegraphed me several times that the Cabinet anxiously desire to maintain peace, but that the party of action are crying out for war. But war for what and on what grounds? Plunkett also telegraphed yesterday that Japan was prepared to embark 50,000 men in thirty days. I replied that I doubted her ability to do anything of the kind, and that she had better be warned not to rashly engage in war with China, that France was fast making China a military nation.

No doubt this was sound advice from one of Parkes's experience.

The most important theme during Plunkett's stay was, as had been made clear in his instructions on leaving London, revision of the 'unequal treaties' of 1858. His efforts perhaps inevitably brought him into conflict with the resident British business community. He also clashed with them over his strictures on their attitudes towards doing business in Japan. For their part they criticised him severely for not doing enough to support British trade against German competition whereas in fact Plunkett took every opportunity to urge the Japanese not to show favouritism towards Germany.

TREATY REVISION

The voluminous files in the PRO about Treaty Revision during Plunkett's term of office in Japan show that Plunkett was willing to interpret his instructions flexibly and make appropriate concessions if these would secure a settlement, which would be acceptable in London. But Japanese opinion hardened more quickly than he or the Japanese officials with whom he was negotiating anticipated and the task of maintaining a united front among the representatives of the Western Powers was an impossible one.

Almost as soon as he had arrived Plunkett received representations from the British merchants in Yokohama and from British missionaries about Treaty revision. The merchants basically wanted to preserve their privileges especially in relation to consular jurisdiction, but also sought the opening of the whole country. The missionaries were more sympathetic to the Japanese point of view.

Plunkett was not inclined to take his line from the British merchants and displayed his willingness to be flexible from the beginning. On 10 April 1884 he reported to the Foreign Office that he had made alterations in the memoranda, which he had given to the Minister of Foreign Affairs, 'so as to bring them nearer to the spirit' of his instructions. 'I have softened considerably the stress laid in the original memorandum on the period of probation' during which Japanese would be expected to prove that their laws and administration of justice were acceptable. He rightly thought that this would be a sticking point for the Japanese and that concessions on this point would have to be made. In discussions with the Japanese Foreign Minister Count Inouye Plunkett said that he would take responsibility for waiving altogether the demand for a period of probation 'provided Japan would practically give me in another way the security to which I felt British subjects had a right'. This led to lengthy, arduous but unproductive discussions with Inouye and Yoshida, the Vice-Minister.

On 14 May 1884 Plunkett reported that: 'Neither Japanese nor foreigners care about Treaty Revision. What is wanted is a decent, practical "modus vivendi". Most people, and personally I entirely share this view, seem agreed that the time has come for admitting the first small end of the wedge, and the British merchant himself will, I am sure, be grateful to whoever has the courage to make the small beginning of gradual and prudent demolition, which will prevent the sudden collapse of the whole fabric of consular jurisdiction, which is what foreigners are so much afraid of.' Plunkett was still understandably cautious in view of opinion in both London and the settlements, but he saw that change had to be made fairly soon.

He was also conscious of the increase in trade, which could accrue if the whole of Japan was opened. On 22 July 1884 he reported that 'I have no hesitation in saying that the general interest of Great Britain is to create those fresh outlets for trade, and to help as far as she can, in the early opening of Japan to foreigners'. He noted that 'the home manufacturer and the General English Merchant have most to hope for from the opening of as many outlets for trade as possible. The shipping interest is most anxious for the opening of accessible ports.' But Japan had 'more real reason than anyone to desire the complete opening of the country'. In support of his thesis that concessions should be made he drew attention to 'the progress which Japan is daily making in Western civilization' and said that this was 'changing not only the relations between Japan and the Western Powers, but also is affecting the relations of these Powers amongst themselves as regards Japan'. The interests of the Powers were no longer identical and this caused a problem, as solidarity was needed in the negotiations.

Among the difficulties, which he faced was not only that of reaching agreement with the representatives of the other Western Powers but also the delays in receiving instructions. He reported on 22 June 1884, 'things are moving so rapidly in Japan that there is great disadvantage in constant references home, for by the time the answers are received from all the various governments, which appears to take from nine months to a year, the state of things here has altered and the instructions, when they arrive, are no longer applicable'. He stressed that 'the idea of a mere tariff treaty [which had been mooted] pleases no one'. He noted that 'Great Britain was the only Power which has made entirely adequate provision for the discharge of duties imposed on them'.[8] He was 'strongly of the opinion that it is prudent to make some concessions now, or at least at a very early date, in order to prevent serious complications in a not very distant future'.

Discussions continued throughout 1885. On 30 January 1886 Plunkett reported that he had spoken to Count Inouye and to Aoki Shūzō, the then Vice Minister, and pressed them to agree to a commercial treaty to last for 12 years and a jurisdictional convention which might be revised at the end of five years. He suggested that if Japan continued to make as much progress during this time the Foreign Powers would be prepared to make further jurisdictional concessions. Not surprisingly, the Japanese rejected this suggestion pointing out that they had no guarantee that the Powers would agree to changes in five years time.

On 21 March 1886 Plunkett warned that 'the importance of our Foreign Settlements is bound to decline'. He noted signs of decay in Yokohama and the foreign settlement at Tsukiji in Tokyo and pointed out that the 'Japanese seem to prefer, when possible, dealing direct with manufacturers in Europe'. They wanted to be free of foreign middlemen and avoid the commissions they had to pay when dealing through foreign merchants in the settlements. The Japanese saw the foreigners resident in the settlements 'as the main obstacle to the realization of their hopes for the recognition of the autonomy of Japan.'

Plunkett was appointed as the senior British delegate to the Treaty Revision Conference between Japan and the Western Powers held in Tokyo from mid-1886 to mid-1887. This was launched with the presentation of a joint Anglo-German note, prepared by Plunkett and his German colleague Baron von Holleben, which was based on the Japanese proposals of 1882 and provided for mixed courts including foreign judges. The Japanese seem to have thought this initiative a helpful one. They told the two Ministers that in recognition of their efforts to reach a settlement the Emperor wished to confer on each of them the Grand Cordon of the Rising Sun. Von Holleben accepted, but Plunkett, aware of the British rules about acceptance of foreign decorations, had to decline. However, the two Ministers were received in audience by the Emperor on 16 July 1886. Plunkett reported that the Emperor, after asking him to be seated, read out in Japanese a highly complimentary speech. The Emperor then told Plunkett that he wished to confer the Order of the Chrysanthemum on the Prince of Wales and proposed to send Prince Komatsu to England for this purpose.

The Treaty Revision negotiations dragged on for months with many disagreements, often over minor points, among the Western delegates. The first and second German delegates were frequently in open disagreement with one another. On 10 November 1876 the French delegate refused to admit that English should be the sole official language of the future courts. Eventually, a compromise suggested by the Russian delegate, whereby the official language of the courts was to be Japanese with English as the only foreign judicial language, seems to have been accepted. But all these time-consuming negotiations came to nothing as when the agreement was reported to the Japanese cabinet it was turned down. Opinion in Japan was no longer prepared to accept the derogation to foreign powers of their jurisdiction within Japan.

The British merchant community who feared that Plunkett had given too much away were critical, but *The Times* correspondent (possibly H.S. Palmer) in an article which was dated 12 August and which appeared on 17 September 1887[9] noted that Plunkett was 'known to have been conspicuous throughout for the display of a liberal and helpful spirit'. Praise was also lavished on the 'brilliant and indefatigable' Count Inouye who led for the Japanese.

PLUNKETT AND THE BRITISH MERCHANTS

In a despatch of 25 May 1885 to Earl Granville, then Secretary of State for Foreign Affairs, which was published in *The Japan Daily Herald* on 20 September 1886, Plunkett wrote:

> I cannot help feeling that the days of 'foreign settlements' and 'enforced tariffs' are rapidly passing away, and that the small profits on which trade must now be carried on will make it every day more and more difficult for the English merchant to compete on the spot with the native, whom education and the telegraph are every day placing more on a par with him. If, therefore, our home manufacturers hope to force the sale of our goods on these Eastern nations, they will have to look to native agents to do it, or they will find themselves beaten out of the field by the Germans and other foreigners who work at lower rates than we do.

On 26 July 1886 in a despatch from Nikko, where Plunkett was escaping the summer heat, the Minister enclosed a memorandum by Vice-Consul Longford on the import trade from Britain to Japan. Plunkett drew attention to Longford's comments on the necessity for British merchants [to cultivate]:

> … friendly and intimate relations with their Japanese customers. At present too many of them take little trouble to enquire what are the requirements of the local buyers, but methodically deal year after year, through the same channels, in almost the same articles.

When Japan was opened further the British merchants

> … must awaken to the fact that Englishmen are not alone in the field, and that if they are not up and stirring, the new opportunities will be utilised by more active competitors from the Continent or from America.

These comments not surprisingly infuriated the merchants who protested vigorously. In a letter to Plunkett they rejected his comments as 'unjust'. They asserted that 'a Merchant is likely to consult his own interests better by being on the spot to attend to the Japanese merchants, who receive orders from all parts of the country, than by seeking business from the small country dealers themselves'. They also rejected his view that the English merchants were losing their supremacy as premature. The bulk of the import trade remained in their hands as in addition to imports from Britain they were responsible for a large proportion of the imports from other countries. Plunkett curtly acknowledged the merchants letter.

In May 1886 the British merchants found some encouragement in the instructions which Lord Rosebery, the new Secretary of State for Foreign Affairs, had issued to British missions in the Far East to support British commercial interests. There was in fact nothing new in such instructions and the controversy, which it aroused, was artificial. Plunkett took the view that the instructions did not require him to back one individual merchant but to support British trade interests generally. He believed justifiably that the Legation should remain neutral between British merchants.

The merchants separately accused Plunkett of not doing enough to stand up for their interests, which were being undermined by Germans who had the backing of the German Legation.

ANGLO-GERMAN RIVALRY IN JAPAN

In fact, Plunkett did all he could to counter what he saw as a mistaken Japanese penchant for things German. On 1 March 1886 he reported that he had taken the opportunity of 'a friendly conversation with Count Itō to speak at length of his marked preference for Germany and the harm that so mistaken a policy must necessarily entail on Japan.' 'I thought it wise to attack his Excellency thus abruptly, because Baron von Holleben, the new German Minister, has already passed Hong Kong. Itō was kind enough to say that I had given proofs of goodwill towards Japan during the two years of my residence here quite sufficient to ensure a friendly hearing, but he on his part must claim a similar freedom of rejoinder.' Plunkett said he knew von Holleben well and welcomed his arrival. The late German Minister Herr Doenhoff 'had steadily worked against British interests here'. Plunkett pointed out the danger for Japan of trying to play off Germany against England in the treaty revision negotiations. He complained in particular about pressure on the railway department to buy German products.

Itō said that there were two causes for the Japanese attitude. The first was 'the continuance for years after it ceased to be appropriate of the policy followed by Sir Harry Parkes ... Was it human nature that while being, as they considered harshly and unfairly treated by the British Minister, they should not to a certain extent, yield to the continued blandishments of the German Minister, who was steadily inviting them to come to him for support and consolation as the British Minister repelled them by his criticisms and advice.' Itō admitted that 'in this respect the policy of Her Majesty's Government had entirely changed for the last two years, but the seed previously sown had necessarily thrown out roots and they could not be eradicated at once'. The second cause was that 'after much careful thought and examination, it had been decided to form the new constitution and codes of Japan on the model of the constitution of Prussia and of the German codes'. 'The constitution of England was abandoned as a model because it was a growth of centuries, which could not be summarily transplanted to an Eastern soil, and it had no corporate shape in which it could be studied, or altered so as to be more suitable to the totally different state of things in Japan.' Plunkett pressed Itō to encourage the study of English arguing that English was the language of the East.[10]

Plunkett spoke to Itō again on the same subject a year later (his despatch of 8 March 1887) in forceful terms: 'I reminded Count Ito that nobody was more friendly than I to an independent Japan but that I should very strongly object to assist any further a Japan the wires of which were pulled at Berlin.' Von Holleben, the German Minister, who had heard of Plunkett's complaints protested to him. Von Holleben was particularly annoyed that the Japanese demanded that Germans whom they employed should speak English.

Plunkett, who had heard the complaints about German activities from British merchants, had also been approached by Inouye Masaru, head of the railway department, who had been a student in Britain in the early 1860s and who was bitter both about the pressure put on him by the Germans to buy German equipment and about Aoki Shūzō who as Vice-Minister for Foreign Affairs was likely to develop strongly pro-German policies. Plunkett seems to have taken a strong dislike to Aoki whom he regarded as pro-German and anti-British.

DEPARTURE

Despite Plunkett's quarrels with the British merchants they were seen off by many Yokohama residents as well as by many high officials and colleagues when they embarked on the Canadian Pacific *Parthia* in early August 1877 on his transfer to Stockholm. The *Japan Weekly Mail* commented that this 'was a demonstration worthy of the high esteem that the departing Minister has won in his official capacity and of the sincere regard entertained for Sir Francis and Lady Plunkett by all who have had the good fortune to make their acquaintance'. Perhaps the paper was just being polite but the paper also took issue with the *Hochi Shimbun* which suggested that Sir Francis having become particularly popular among the Japanese 'by the liberality of his politics and the kindly courtesy of his ways, lost favour with his own nationals and was consequently obliged to leave Japan'. There was no truth in this suggestion. The government in London were most unlikely to take cognisance of the grumbles of British merchants in Yokohama and he was going on to another senior post. Lady Plunkett was not in good health and a change of climate was thought desirable for her. In any case he was due for home leave.

PLUNKETT AND SATOW

Ernest Satow who left Japan at the end of 1882 took his new post as Consul General in Bangkok in early 1884. He visited Japan on leave in October and November 1884 and again to convalesce from June to August 1886. During this latter visit he and Plunkett visited in early August the Ashio copper mines together presumably from Nikko. The mining company did their best to make their distinguished visitors welcome. Tables, chairs and cooks were brought from the Seiyoken restaurant in Tokyo and the hill sides were illuminated with covered lanterns. A feature of the entertainment was 'a peculiar dance performed by the miners; a dance which is said to have been novel even to Mr Satow. Sir Francis went all over the works, inspecting even the shafts which were farthest underground.'[11]

Satow was on very friendly terms with the Plunketts. On 21 March 1884 in a letter to his friend W.G. Aston he wrote: 'I am very sorry not to be in at the Revision of the Treaties. And I like the Plunketts so much that it is a real grief to me not to be in Tokio during their reign.' In 1883 Satow had written a long memorandum to Plunkett about the need to abolish extraterritoriality,[12] which may well have influenced the latter's thinking in the negotiations. In 1895 he noted in his diary after taking up his appointment as Minister in Tokyo that Count Ōkuma had said to him: 'Since Sir Harry [Parkes] left H.M.G. had not sent any man of weight here. Neither [Sir F.R.] Plunkett, [Mr Hugh] Fraser nor [Hon P.H.Le Poer] Trench [the three British Ministers before Satow] understood Eastern problems. Very friendly but nothing more.'[13] Satow had hoped to be appointed to Tokyo in succession to Plunkett and might have gone there as early as 1885 but Plunkett who had been offered the post of Minister in Peking in succession to Parkes declined to move to China.[14] Satow's expertise and knowledge of the language could have been invaluable in the Treaty Revision negotiations which were concluded in 1894 before Satow was appointed to Tokyo. The Foreign Office was unwilling to grant equal status to members of the Diplomatic and Consular Service, which Satow had joined. And they had not yet come to recognize the importance of having in Tokyo a head of mission with a good knowledge of Japanese. Satow was in fact the only head of mission with an effective command of the Japanese language until the appointment of Sir Esler Dening in 1951. Plunkett and his successor Hugh Fraser had to rely greatly for advice from the Japanese Secretary of the Legation, J.H.Gubbins.[15]

ASSESSMENT

Bearing in mind Plunkett's ignorance of the language and culture of Japan the records show that he was a competent and generally agreeable head of mission. His judgements seem to have been fair and reasonable. He had served under Parkes, but does not appear to have used the same kind of hectoring style.[16] In negotiations he tried to be flexible and in his comments on the changes taking place in Japan he was generally sympathetic to Japanese aspirations. Plunkett may have been an old-fashioned aristocrat but his gentlemanly style no doubt pleased the Japanese with whom he came in contact.

4

Hugh Fraser, 1837–1894: British Minister at Tokyo, 1889–94

HUGH CORTAZZI

Hugh Fraser

HUGH FRASER headed the British Legation in Tokyo as 'Minister Plenipotentiary and Envoy Extraordinary' in the final stages of the negotiations, which led up to the signature on 16 July 1894, of the revised treaty between Great Britain and Japan. This replaced the so-called 'unequal treaty' signed by Lord Elgin in 1858 and led to the abolition of extraterritoriality in Japan. This was one of the most significant developments in Western relations with Japan in the nineteenth century and was one in which Britain took the leading role. His period of service in Japan was thus a crucial one concerning relations between the two countries. Hugh Fraser is much less well known than his wife Mary Crawford Fraser whose book *A Diplomatist's Wife in Japan: Letters from Home to Home*[1] was deservedly popular with its sensitive depiction of the Japanese scene.

FAMILY

Hugh Fraser came from the Balnain (Inverness) branch of the Fraser clan. His father, John Fraser, who seems in his youth to have been fond of duelling and something of a daredevil, had been an officer in the Light Dragoons in India. On selling his commission he had been appointed, through the good offices of his cousin Lord Glenelg, then Secretary of State for the Colonies, as Secretary to the Lord High Commissioner for the Ionian Islands which included Corfu. In this capacity he was appointed one of the first Knights of the order of St Michael and St George, an order founded expressly for services in the Ionian islands (later extended to cover overseas services generally).

CAREER

Hugh Fraser who was born on 22 February 1837 was sent to Eton at the age of eleven in January 1849 and remained at the school until December 1854.[2] He spent some of his holidays with his parents in the Ionian Islands where he met General Charles Gordon (the charismatic figure who became known because of his part in crushing the Taiping rebellion as 'Chinese Gordon' and who was killed in Khartoum in 1885) and fell under the spell of his personality. Almost immediately after leaving Eton Hugh Fraser was appointed as an unpaid attaché at The Hague in January 1855 (before his eighteenth birthday), but was sent to Dresden in the following month. Here, apparently for a wager, he swam down the Elbe from Dresden to Pirna. He moved to Copenhagen in November 1857 and passed an examination in August 1859 to become a paid attaché. He was appointed to the British Legation in Central America in September 1862.

Mary Fraser records[3] that Hugh whose headquarters were in Guatemala was on his own with 'a native clerk'. 'His only means of travel was a mule'. 'He used to tell me how he would journey from capital to capital through the forest, in uniform, cocked-hat and all, this latter for the benefit of any stray bandits that might have been driven there for shelter. They would not touch a foreign representative in a cocked-hat and gold lace, though they might have made a mistake and cut his throat in mufti. England [i.e. Great Britain] was a word to conjure with in those times.' When he visited Honduras and sent in his card as British Chargé d'Affaires to the President, 'that dignity looked it over and then burst out, "Who the devil are are you? I never heard of any such person!" He never had and it took Hugh some time to explain himself.' Hugh Fraser wondered whether he had been forgotten by London who did not answer his requests for directions. 'He began to brood over his troubles, even going so far as to cuff the native clerk at times.' In the end he 'locked up the

Legation, put the key under the door, and sailed away for England.' When he reported to the Foreign Office 'Authority [i.e. the official responsible for personnel] was infinitely amused. "Good Lord, my dear boy!" it said. "We expected you home ages ago – we had no idea that you would last it out as long as that."'

Hugh Fraser later served in Stockholm, Peking and Rome. In 1874 he met and married Mary Crawford[4] in Italy. After a brief engagement of six weeks they set out for Peking where Hugh Fraser had been appointed Secretary of the Legation and served for over two years as Chargé d'Affaires in the absence on leave of Wade, then British Minister to China. He was transferred to Vienna in 1879 and then in 1882 to Rome. In 1885 he was appointed Minister at Santiago, Chile, where his prime task was to be the settlement of claims resulting from the war between Chile, Peru and Bolivia. He had to serve on a three-man committee with Brazilian and Chilean colleagues. The Brazilian infuriated him and eventually Fraser determined to bring the proceedings to an end by imposing a compromise. His appointment to Tokyo was announced in April 1888 and he was glad to get away from Chile, but the Frasers did not arrive in Tokyo until 1 May 1889.

CHARACTER AND QUALITIES

Mary Fraser seems to have been devoted to Hugh Fraser, but her brief comments on his character[5] suggest that he was not an easy or sensitive husband. His apparently dour Scottish character was in total contrast to Mary Fraser's Mediterranean and sensitive temperament.

There can be no doubt that Hugh Fraser was a brave man and cool when threatened. As a young man he might indeed have seemed foolhardy. Mary Fraser commenting on the anti-foreign bullyboys (*sōshi*) who threatened foreigners in Tokyo at this time said that Hugh Fraser refused to 'take the slightest notice of the agitation, and walks all over the town, quite alone, rather to my terror'.[6] On another occasion Gubbins, the Japanese Secretary to the Legation and Hugh Fraser's right-hand man, told her of an incident when 'quite close to our own gates they had suddenly been surrounded by a band of *sōshi*, armed with their favourite sword sticks. An attempt had been made to distract the Chief's attention by hustling him behind, and at the moment when he was intended to turn his head a sword was drawn to strike him in front. But he refused to look behind him, and kept his eyes fixed on the face of the man in front, who lowered his sword at once. H[ugh] laughed a little, and went on and finished his walk.'[7]

In addition to courage he had an austere sense of duty. This led Mary to say: 'I do not think Hugh would have been happy if he had been popular. He would have thought himself to have failed, in some respect, of duty.' He was never popular with the British community in Yokohama with whom indeed his contacts seem to have been very limited if not minimal.

His strong sense of duty ensured that he devoted his main energies to his work, which he appears to have tackled with both thoroughness and conscientiousness. Mary recorded that in Japan 'Poor Hugh is terribly busy, for all the hard work comes as a rule at the hottest time' and he often had to 'gasp over cipher telegrams'.

In his judgements of individual cases he appears to have been firm and unswayed by sentiment.

He was never accused of pomposity and although he did what was necessary in terms of protocol he did not allow it to dominate his attitude. Mary had to be presented to Queen Victoria before they went to Vienna, but Hugh refused to attend a levée although he did have a coat of arms registered.

Hugh Fraser seems to have had a jealous streak. At any rate Mary said that she had found it prudent to give up acting 'after three or four years of marriage. Violent love-scenes on the stage with good-looking men are not conducive to harmony at home.'

Mary was a devout Catholic. Hugh seems to have retained some anti-Catholic prejudices. 'Once Hugh got on to that subject, there was no arguing or pleading with him. His views were deeply rooted in the heavy soil of the "Early Walnut and Antimacassar" [presumably early Victorian] period, and, the soul of sweetness and reasonableness in every other relation of life, let that topic creep into any discussion and he was another person in an instant.'

He could be very inconsiderate in other ways. Mary suffered badly from rheumatism. Yet in Santiago when Mary urged him to go the police about a missing servant he insisted that they should walk half way across town and refused to call a cab.

Hugh Fraser could also be witty or, some might say, sarcastic. Mary records that for a reception at the Palace in Tokyo in 1894 she had 'found a brocade all over strawberries and in spite of Hugh's quotation, "Ce n'est pas la mode de s'asseoir sur son blazon" wore it bravely.'[8]

Mary Fraser described Hugh as having 'a philosophic temperament'. 'He never wasted time and effort in complaint when complaint was useless. Later in life he appeared not to notice ordinary discomforts and inconveniences at all … I remember once in Japan, when I had been away from the Legation for a couple of days, I asked the English butler what he had given him for dinner the evening before. "We gave His Excellency a very good dinner, madam." He replied assuringly; "a real old-fashioned English dinner – boiled bacon and cabbage, madam." And Hugh had never said a word!' Yet he had insisted on their appointment to Santiago in taking an English cook with them as he did not believe that native servants were reliable. 'He refused to be poisoned by the native messes, as he called them.' The Chilean habit of consuming large steaks at every meal did not appeal to either Hugh or Mary Fraser.

Mary does not comment on his attitude to money perhaps because this was not a suitable subject for a gentleman, but she does refer from time to time to the expense of running their establishments overseas and it is possible that Hugh Fraser, as a traditional Scot, was careful over money matters, but they cannot have been without private means. In the nineteenth century a British diplomat had to have a private income and Hugh had been an unpaid attaché for some four years. His mother and sister lived in apparent comfort in Bath even if to Mary there was an 'awful melancholy and dullness in all their surroundings'. As Minister in Tokyo he had an annual salary of £4,000, which was fair if not generous by the standards of the time.

Mary described her 'dear Hugh' as 'a splendid traveller' who entertained her on their difficult first journey to Peking with 'many queer accounts of his former sojourn in China'. The Frasers had two sons (Hugh and John). Mary was a devoted mother worrying greatly when her younger son was wounded in the stomach during the Boer war. There is nothing to suggest that he was not an adequate father, but travelling with children was clearly a trial. At one point she wrote: 'Hugh's nerves were always rather over-strung and just now in crying need of rest.'

In commenting on his rather complex character Mary wrote: 'Hugh was very patient, and his Highland ancestry had given him a sense of humour, that sword of the afflicted, grim and keen, against whose edge the storm burst in vain.' 'Hugh was rather a queer person in some ways. When he might be expected, and reasonably, to lose his temper, he would be quite likely to laugh, or to display a gentleness so utterly impersonal and yet so understanding, so sympathetic and so selfless that one looked up to him with a certain awe, as not being entirely of this world. At others, a trifle, unnoticed by anyone else, would stir that Scottish nature to its depths and for days he would brood over it, never speaking. One was left to conjecture what it might have been but one never, never found out – except by accident.' When the manager of an English store in Santiago wanted to marry the maid whom Mary had brought out to Chile at their expense Hugh treated the man concerned to an explosion of temper. Mary had to try to smooth him down. 'It was a long business, for Hugh had entangled himself in the depths of that Highland temper of his, where I could not follow him'.

Mary Fraser does not tell us much about her husband's hobbies and cultural interests. At one point she noted in China that he was knowledgeable about 'keramics' and at another that while in Central America he wrote a monograph arguing that the builders of the stone monuments at Copan in Guatemala 'were Mongolians who crossed over the straits from the north and wandered down'. It was in Central America that he got 'his guitar, which afterwards proved to be one of the great comforts of his life, a friend that never failed to soothe his soul when it descended into the pit of Celtic depression. And the marvellous airs! I cannot remember them … but I know that no music that I have ever heard was sweeter than that which he would whistle sometimes of an evening, strumming on the guitar.'

It is not clear how good a linguist he was. It is improbable that in those days he received much practical teaching in modern languages at Eton, but he presumably had to do some study of European languages, especially French, before he was granted a paid attaché appointment. His value to the Legations in Vienna and Rome would have been very limited if he had an inadequate knowledge of German and Italian. Mary writing of their stay in Chile said that he knew Spanish, 'perfectly', but was most reluctant to use it. During two postings to China where he worked for that great Chinese linguist Sir Thomas Wade and was a friend of Robert Hart, the head of the Chinese customs he must surely have learnt some Chinese, but it seems unlikely that he became at all fluent. In Japan he seemed to rely greatly on his Japanese Secretary, J.H.Gubbins and other members of the Japan Consular Service. All in all Hugh Fraser seems to have been rather taciturn even in English unless deeply roused.

IN JAPAN

The Japan Weekly Mail for the period when Hugh Fraser was Minister in Japan contains remarkably few references to him and his activities. It reported that the Frasers arrived in Yokohama from Hong Kong on 1 May 1889 by SS *Verona* and had an audience at the palace in Tokyo on 17 May. It noted that he was elected as a member of the Asiatic Society, but it does not seem from reports of the Transactions of the Society in *The Japan Weekly Mail* that he was an active member of the Society. In November 1890 the Frasers are reported to have attended the St Andrews Society Ball. They left Japan via the United States on leave at the end of June 1893. They returned to Yokohama on 24 February 1894 on SS *Ancona*. But the *Mail* had nothing of substance to say about Hugh Fraser until his death (see below).

TREATY REVISION

The most important theme for *The Japan Weekly Mail* in the Fraser's time was the subject of Treaty Revision.[9] This subject also predominates the papers covering the Tokyo Legation in the years 1889–1894 which have been preserved in the Public Record Office. It is clear from these papers and from Mary Fraser's account of her life in Japan that treaty revision was the dominant issue for Hugh Fraser during his service in Japan.

The substance of the Treaty Revision negotiations and the numerous communications between Hugh Fraser and the various Japanese Foreign Ministers during his time in Tokyo and with the Foreign Office in London cannot be covered in a brief portrait of him.[10] But there is one important question for which an answer should be given in any account of Hugh Fraser in Japan. Did his actions and comments have any significant influence on the outcome? It is not easy to give a definitive answer to this question, but it is clear from the papers in the PRO that Hugh Fraser, no doubt taking account of the advice of J.H.Gubbins, his right-hand man and Japanese expert, took a realistic view of what could be achieved for British interests. He firmly rejected the emotional and reactionary views of the British community in Yokohama and urged on London a common sense approach.

At a meeting of Yokohama residents on 9 September 1890, as reported in *The Japan Weekly Mail*, three resolutions were passed which were critical of moves to revise the treaties. The most important of these declared that the time had not yet arrived 'when questions in regard to rights, whether of property or person, … can be safely subjected to the jurisdiction of Japanese tribunals …'. The resolution also said that it was not possible to estimate 'the period within which the unconditional relinquishment of extraterritorial jurisdiction in Japan can be safely promised'. A leading advocate of the resolutions was a resident named J.A. Fraser (not apparently any relation of the Minister).

Over a year before these resolutions were passed Hugh Fraser in his despatch[11] of 16 August 1889 had recorded to the Secretary of State in London a view from which he did not swerve: 'I do not think that there is any probability that Her Majesty's Government will be able to obtain additional guarantees [presumably about the administration of justice] on the part of Japan in relation to jurisdiction.' He noted 'the serious agitation' in Japan 'on the subject of the concessions they have already made'. Such agitation 'might take a more acute and dangerous form at any moment,' and 'such agitation in this country is apt to lead immediately to political assassination.' He thought that 'amongst the causes of our present weakness must be reckoned, I fear, a fault: that of requiring too much'. Bearing in mind that the Americans and the Germans had accepted Japanese terms, 'Alone, or with but weak support from the Powers I do not think Her Majesty's Government can obtain additional guarantees of Justice.' These were strong words, which would not make him popular with British residents.

On 25 June 1891 after he had called on Viscount Enomoto, then the Japanese Foreign Minister, he commented to London on the difficulties, which the Japanese Government faced over Treaty revision that it was difficult to know what was 'the dominant fear' of the Japanese Ministers – 'opposition at home or complications abroad'. He surmised that what the Japanese really wanted was 'the faculty of repudiating the Treaties altogether, on a plea that the revision clause had been rendered inoperative by faults on the part of the Treaty Powers. I do not think that any such faculty can be claimed in the actual circumstances … It is impossible now to assert that England stands in the way of Treaty revision.' Fraser commented that 'The foreign relations of the Empire are hardly satisfactory at this moment. The Japanese do not seem to have a friend anywhere, unless it is Russia, and their sympathy with Russia rests absolutely on fear, that is to say, principally on momentary panic.'

Separately Fraser rejected an approach by Mr Piggott (presumably Sir Francis Taylor Piggott (1852–1925)).[12] He told the Foreign Office that Piggott 'can have no knowledge at all of the recent history of the questions he writes on …', but demonstrated that he was critical of Japanese justice by declaring: 'Mr Piggott is wrong in his good opinion of Japanese jurists.'

OTHER ACTIVITIES IN JAPAN

In Hugh Fraser's time the other work of the Legation did not seem to include commercial work, which has become the primary task of so many of the British missions abroad today. Hugh Fraser's only involvement seems to have been to forward the returns of trade prepared by British consular posts in Japan.

Hugh Fraser had to cope with the unofficial visit in April 1890 of Their Royal Highnesses The Duke and Duchess of Connaught. I have given an account of this visit in my essay entitled 'Royal Visits to Japan in the Meiji Period'.[13] The Connaughts were clearly out to have a good time and cannot have been easy visitors. They did not endear themselves to the British Community in Yokohama by refusing the ball, which the community offered.

Hugh Fraser was not directly involved with the visit to Japan in 1891 of the Czarevitch who was attacked and injured on his way from Ōtsu to Kyoto, but the affair caused a major scare at the time.

Not least because British subjects in Japan were subject to the yet-to-be-revised treaties under British consular jurisdiction he was inevitably involved in consular issues. These included the tragic murder in Tsukiji in April 1890 of the Reverend T.A. Large, a British missionary. The incident, which was described at length in *The Japan Weekly Mail* dated 12 April 1890, appears to have been perpetrated by burglars and not to have had any anti-Christian motive. The *Mail* commented that 'The absolute immunity yet enjoyed by foreigners in Japan from all personal violence during the past twenty years, invests this sad event with peculiar interest.' After the violence and insecurity, which had prevailed in the years up to and immediately following the Meiji Restoration in 1868, the lives of foreigners in Japan had been relatively peaceful, but in view of the threats of violence against Hugh Fraser and others from *sōshi* at this time such a comment seems inappropriate.

The Times of 12 April 1890 drew attention to an incident, which did not enhance the British reputation for even handed justice. In July 1889 a Spanish subject fled to Japan from Manila to escape arrest. Arrested by the Spanish consular authorities he 'was thrown into the British gaol in Yokohama where he lay until March 1 1890, without any form of trial'. When the Spanish authorities came to remove their prisoner from his cell to a steamer bound for Manila, 'they found the prison guarded by a strong posse of Japanese constables, who declined to let the man be taken from Japanese territory'. *The Times*, however, reported another case, which demonstrated Hugh Fraser's sense of justice. Campos, a Portuguese domiciled in Hong Kong escaped to Japan and was arrested by the British consular authorities in Kobe who held him for return to Hong Kong. This led to a protest by the Japanese Ministry of Foreign affairs to the British Legation. 'Mr Fraser took a singularly courageous and conscientious course. Disregarding the precedents set by his predecessors and the procedure prescribed by the Order in Council, he caused Campos to be liberated and then procured his arrest and extradition by the Japanese Government. This act, performed entirely, on the Minister's own responsibility, produced a most happy effect, and went far to teach the Japanese that they can always count on justice from Great Britain if only they succeed in getting her to listen to them.'

Hugh Fraser's contacts with Japanese Ministers were primarily connected with Treaty revision, although he no doubt drew on them for his political reporting. The reports kept in the PRO do not, however, suggest that Hugh Fraser had achieved any deep insights into the Japanese political scene. In his despatch of 30 October 1889[14] he wrote: 'It is feared that a real cabinet, one representing clear views and identical policy, can hardly be established without a serious conflict and the employment of material force; a measure to which no known leader would willingly have recourse.' In his despatch of 14 November 1889[15] he noted the continuance of the Satcho oligarchy commenting that 'The Satsuma men form a solid party and understand one another, but there is endless discussion, intrigue, and self-seeking in the Choshiu camp, and very little cohesion in the whole administration.'

Just before he went on home leave in June 1893 he commented on the confusion of thought in Japan, which was 'at all times remarkable for extremes of sentiment and violence of temper'.

Hugh Fraser relied greatly on J. H. Gubbins for whom he obtained the appointment of Japanese Secretary to the Legation, but it seems likely that Fraser's austere personality and uncertain temper may have made relations with his diplomatic secretaries difficult. There is a hint in one report in *The Japan Weekly Mail*, dated 27 December 1890, that there may have been problems with the Honourable W. G. Napier, his diplomatic first secretary. The *Mail* reported that M. W. G. de Bunsen another diplomat without any expertise in Japanese, had been appointed to succeed Napier whose departure was described as 'somewhat sudden', his term of service not having expired.

DEATH AND FUNERAL

Hugh Fraser who had only returned to Tokyo from home leave in March 1894 became ill early in May. He complained of pains in the stomach and was seen by Dr Baelz, the German Doctor who was the main medical practitioner for the foreign community at the time. According to the report by Dr Baelz, sent to the Foreign Office after Hugh Fraser's death by R. S. Paget who took over as Chargé on the death of his chief, a stoppage of the bowels was suspected. Castor oil and enemas having failed Dr Baelz called in a Japanese surgeon and they opened the small intestine, but the operation did not lead to a removal of the stoppage and a second operation was thought to be needed if the patient's condition allowed. Hugh Fraser however weakened and died on 4 June 1894. Dr Baelz commented that he was surprised by the absence of fever despite the existence of peritonitis. He did not think that there had been a malignant growth in the bowel. Hugh Fraser's illness must have been extremely painful at a time when abdominal surgery had advanced so little. Perhaps with modern surgery he would have survived.

Hugh Fraser's funeral took place on 6 June 1894. According to *The Japan Weekly Mail* of 9 June 'the body lay in state' throughout the afternoon, and 'was visited by a great concourse of mourning friends, among whom were the Japanese Ministers of the Crown and the

Foreign Representatives. The floral tributes sent were numerous and beautiful.' The ceremony was apparently arranged by Josiah Conder, the British architect.[16] The coffin was carried out of the Legation at 3.00 and reached St Andrew's Church at 4.00. 'The steep approach and the narrow road presented serious difficulties for the great crowd of carriages that followed the hearse.' The tiny Church was packed. The full choral service was performed by Bishop Bickersteth. The interment took place immediately afterwards at Aoyama cemetery where a brick vault had been built during the previous night. 'Mrs Fraser was present from first to last, bearing with indomitable courage the terrible grief of this last parting.'

The Japan Weekly Mail in its obituary described him in these words:

> Mr Fraser was one of those rare men, who with abilities of the highest order and perfectly balanced judgement, live lives of perpetual self-effacement and find their highest reward in a conscientious sense of duty faithfully discharged. His abnormally retiring disposition narrowed the circle of his appreciators and impaired the public's estimate of his capacity … If he lacked the power to dazzle, he possessed in the fullest degree that of inspiring confidence … No British Representative ever acquired larger influence in this country or wielded his influence more conscientiously. The Japanese learned very quickly that Mr Fraser could be thoroughly relied on never to lend his support to any cause tainted by the least injustice … Fate did not will that he should finally solve the complex problem of Treaty Revision, but that he materially facilitated a solution by the clearness of his insight and the dignified firmness of his methods, there can be no manner of doubt …

Japanese newspapers seem to have echoed these sentiments. The *Nichi Nichi Shimbun* published the following statement:

> The singularly just and impartial views taken by him on all occasions were erroneously supposed by these narrow-minded persons to be unwarrantably friendly to Japan … unswervingly true to the maintenance of the rights of his country, and in the discharge of his duties he was always heedless of what outsiders might say about him … In private life, he was kind, modest, and reserved, winning the respect and love of everybody, both Japanese and foreign, that came into close contact with him. A man of firm resolution he was never moved from the path of duty by the clamours of his nationals in the settlements …

Hugh Fraser, who was 57 at the time of his death, was the only British head of mission to Japan to die while still in post. He was also the only one not honoured with a knighthood or an appointment to the Order of St Michael and St George. Surely as a conscientious and upright official, even if he lacked sparkle and flair, he would have been so honoured if he had survived.

5

Sir Ernest Satow (1843–1929) in Tokyo, 1895–1900

IAN RUXTON

Sir Ernest Satow

SIR ERNEST SATOW (1843–1929) is generally regarded as the best-qualified official and the most outstanding scholar of Japanese to have been appointed head of the British Mission in Japan. He would have liked to be the first British Ambassador to Japan but was transferred in 1900 to Peking, then regarded as a more important post than Tokyo, in succession to Sir Claude MacDonald who needed a transfer following the Boxer rebellion. In the event, Sir Claude became the first British Ambassador to Japan when the legations were raised to the status of embassies following the conclusion of the Anglo-Japanese Alliance in 1902. The mission in Peking remained a legation throughout Satow's service there. Sadly, therefore, he never became an 'ambassador', although he became a Privy Councillor and was awarded the GCMG. The status of ambassador was more important at that time than it is these days when every mission is called an 'embassy' – however unimportant the country involved. Brilliant but seemingly aloof, the best way to arrive at an understanding of Satow is through his voluminous personal diaries and other papers kept in the Public Record Office. This brief essay introduces the man and his chief concerns during the above period, based mainly on his diaries.[1]

Satow arrived back in London at the end of May 1895 following his brief posting as Minister in Morocco where he had been since September 1893. He was almost 52. He had received a telegram from the Foreign Secretary Lord Kimberley (1826–1902) on 2 May offering him the legation at Tokyo, and another confirming the appointment on 17 May.[2] This was the post for which Satow was the ideal candidate, having spent almost twenty years in Japan (September 1862 – December 1882 with only two home leaves) successively as student interpreter, interpreter and Japanese Secretary to the legation.

Since leaving Japan in 1882 he had been British Consul-General in Bangkok where, early in 1885, he had been promoted from the Consular to the Diplomatic Service and made Minister to Siam.[3] But he did not care for the climate or official corruption there.[4] Bouts of malarial fever rendered him ineffective, so that from June 1887 to October 1888 when he was offered his next post in Uruguay, he was on sick leave in England.[5] Uruguay was 'an earthly paradise in which he found nothing to do'.[6] Early in June 1893 he was transferred to Morocco where his task was to promote gradual internal reform through tact and patience. His success there led to his receiving the KCMG.

NEW JAPAN: THE BACKGROUND

The Anglo-Japanese Treaty of Commerce and Navigation had been signed in London on 16 July 1894, providing for the abolition of extra-territoriality with regard to British subjects with effect from 17 July 1899, and the immediate introduction of an *ad valorem* tariff. This revision of the first of the 'unequal treaties' was an important turning point, both in Japanese history and in Britain's attitude towards Japan.[7] The First Sino-Japanese War had been won by Japan, leading to the Treaty of Shimonoseki, signed on 17 April 1895, but it had to be drastically modified after pressure in the form of 'friendly advice' from Russia, France and Germany (the so-called Triple Intervention). Japan was thereby forced to give up the newly ceded territory of the Liaotung peninsula in the southern tip of Manchuria, which included Port Arthur and Talienwan, in exchange for an increased indemnity from China.[8]

SATOW IN ENGLAND (MAY-JUNE 1895)

The Permanent Under-Secretary, Sir Thomas Sanderson, briefed Satow at the Foreign Office. They discussed the compensation that Japan would receive for withdrawing from Liaotung; the apparent rejection of Japanese reforms in Korea; and the Japanese annexation of Formosa, where the Chinese seemed to be supplying arms secretly to the anti-Japanese guerrillas, the 'semi-savage Hakkas'.[9] Sanderson told Satow that he should leave as soon as possible for Japan. The Chargé d'Affaires, Gerald A. Lowther, was doing well enough, but without Japanese language skills he was dependent on the legation interpreters, John H. Gubbins (who was then Japanese Secretary, and thus chief interpreter) and the Second Secretary, Ralph S. Paget.

Satow also had meetings with Lord Kimberley who described Japan as 'our natural ally, as against Russia'[10] and stated that he regarded China as both 'unreliable and useless'. Britain should remain friendly to her, but not rely on her as a counterweight to Russia. Kimberley also remarked that he thought the English newspapers at Yokohama did a lot of harm to Anglo-Japanese relations. Japanese vanity should be humoured, and their goodwill cultivated. In an oblique reference to Sir Harry Parkes, British Minister in Japan, 1865–83, he added: 'It was no longer possible to treat them as semi-civilized and to bully them; they must be treated on a footing of equality …'

Following the change of government from Liberal to a Conservative-Unionist coalition in June 1895, Lord Salisbury took over as both Prime Minister and Foreign Secretary. He was more sceptical about Japan's capability and reliability than Kimberley had been. When Satow wrote to him from Tokyo asking for instructions on 15 August, Salisbury in his reply of 3 October doubted whether the Japanese were capable of preventing Russia from obtaining an ice-free port on her eastern seaboard, which she could easily take by marching overland from Siberia. Satow was told instead to concentrate on the promotion of trade in the face of German commercial rivalry.[11]

Before his departure from England for Japan Satow was summoned to dinner at Windsor Castle on 25 June 1895 where Queen Victoria invested him with the accolade of a Knight Commander of the Order of St Michael and St George (KCMG), but apparently little was said. A more significant meeting took place on 11 August 1897 at Osborne House on the Isle of Wight during Satow's leave from Japan to attend the Queen's diamond jubilee. After dinner they privately discussed Siam and Japan:

> Then she said the Japanese prince [Arisugawa, in England for the Jubilee] was nice but not handsome, and I said Japanese thought him good looking. Japanese women she thought were not so either. I said that travellers coming to Japan were shocked to find the men so ugly.
>
> She asked if Japan were not a very difficult post. I replied that fortunately the three Powers [Russia, Germany, France] had made it very easy, and that being able to talk Japanese was a great help. She was much surprised at this, and asked if it were not a very difficult language. I said it was because one could not learn it by living in a Japanese family as one would do in Europe.

ARRIVAL IN TOKYO

Satow left Liverpool on 29 June 1895, arriving in Japan on 28 July via New York and Vancouver. The business community and the legation staff greeted him at Yokohama. The next day he called on Saionji Kinmochi, the acting Foreign Minister. On 1 August he met Itō Hirobumi of Chōshū, his old friend of Bakumatsu days, now Prime Minister. Satow congratulated him on Japan's beating China and discovered the conditions on which Japan would give up Liaotung. They also discussed Korea, Formosa and treaty revision.

On 9 August at 10.00 am Satow had an audience with the Emperor and Empress, at which his credentials were presented. He was fetched in an Imperial horse-drawn carriage 20 minutes before. In the reception room Satow following the prescribed protocol, bowed three times and read his speech in English. The Emperor replied in Japanese, later translated thus: 'We are exceedingly gratified to think that a greater cordiality in the friendly relations existing between our respective countries will be facilitated by the fact of your many years' residence in Our country and by your thorough knowledge of our national affairs.' Then Satow saw the Empress, who expressed pleasure at seeing him after so many years, echoed the Emperor's words on Anglo-Japanese friendship being enhanced and referred to Satow's being a 'great scholar in Japanese things'. Satow replied humbly before taking his leave.

MAIN POLITICAL ISSUES

The main problem with China from American, British and Japanese viewpoints was how to prevent her partition among the land-grabbing European powers and preserve the 'Open Door' to free trade. Satow wrote to Sir Nicholas O'Connor, then Minister in Peking, on

3 September 1895 that he supposed Salisbury's views would be the same as Kimberley's 'that China has shown she can never be of any use to us as an ally'[12] and agreed in a conversation with Admiral Buller later that month 'that China is hopeless in the matter of reform'. Her government system was 'thoroughly rotten'.[13]

When Satow saw Itō on 26 September he was told that Japan had tried desperately to come to an agreement with China over a sound system of government for Korea, but she had refused to cooperate, leading to the Sino-Japanese War. Satow himself told Count Inoue Kaoru of Chōshū (1836–1915), the former Foreign Minister (1879–87) and Minister to Korea (October 1894–September 1895) on 4 October that he thought Japan was a much better country than China to lead Korea's modernization. On the same day Foreign Minister Count Ōkuma Shigenobu denied that Japan had tried to pick a quarrel with China; the Japanese had been anxious about the Chinese navy with its powerful ships and foreign officers, but the Chinese army was poorly trained and led. Itō had told Satow that beating China had been easy.[14]

In 1899 two Chinese commissioners visited Japan. On 27 July Satow mentioned them in a private letter to Salisbury, commenting that they were unlikely to achieve anything significant:

> Japan does not wish to be tied to a corpse, nor to undertake the defence of China against Russia. Her chief care is for the maintenance of her position in Corea, and nothing but a Russian attempt to swallow up the Peninsula will in my opinion turn her aside from her present policy of lying low till her armaments are completed in 1903.[15]

After the commissioners left Satow reported again to Salisbury on 5 October that the Foreign Minister Aoki Shūzō[16] had talked to him 'in a very aggrieved tone' about their behaviour:

> By the way in which they went on they had made it impossible to have any serious negotiations with them. He added of course there had been no question of an alliance [between Japan and China], but only of a friendly understanding, which was frustrated by their conduct here.[17]

KOREA

Korea had for centuries been a vassal of China within the Confucian hierarchy, and attempts by Japan to displace the latter were in general much resented in Korea and China. Korean hatred of the Japanese could also be traced back to the invasions by Toyotomi Hideyoshi in

1592 and 1597, and more recently to the unequal Treaty of Kanghwa forced on Korea by Japan in 1876.

When Satow saw Itō for the first time on 1 August he was asked if Britain had any interest in Korea. Discounting commercial considerations, Satow stated that like Japan, Britain wished to prevent Russian annexation. Satow asked Itō if Russia was planning to extend the trans-Siberian railway down to a port in Korea. Itō replied that they aimed at 'something much greater'. He read a memo from the Russian Minister stating that Russia expected Japan 'to conform her acts to her declarations as to the independence of Corea'. Itō and Satow agreed that neutralization of Korea guaranteed by several Powers would be better than independence, which would allow Russia to deal directly with Korea and 'obtain her aims more easily'.

On 25 August Satow reported to Salisbury that Viscount Miura Goro had been appointed Japanese Minister in Korea. Satow believed he was a moderate in favour of gradual reform, but events soon proved him wrong. On 26 September Satow reported that Miura had refused a request by the Korean government for Japanese troops to subdue an armed rebellion. It was Satow's view that Korea was 'quite incapable of reform from within'. Itō himself believed that Korea could not survive as an independent state, but Japan could not prevent Russian annexation at this stage, because her navy, though increasing in size, was still too weak.

On 8 October 1895 a *coup d'état* occurred in Seoul. It was engineered by Miura Goro, and the Korean Queen Min Bi was assassinated: as Satow discovered on 14 October, she had been beheaded. On the following day Satow observed in a letter to his friend F.V. Dickins that Korea would be 'another Morocco, a rotten fruit which no one may touch, and which will be carefully propped up lest it should fall into some one's hands of whom the others would be jealous to the point of fighting'.

On 13 February 1896 Satow received a visit from a Korean fugitive from Seoul, where the King had taken refuge in the Russian Legation. He appealed strongly for British help for Korea, but Satow was unable to assist. In May he wrote to Salisbury that the Japanese viewed Korea as 'their Alsace-Lorraine'. On 4 June he told Kokugaku scholar Viscount Fukuba Bisei[18] that Inoue Kaoru had been 'in too great a hurry' in trying to reform Korea along European lines.

On 18 February 1897 the new Foreign Minister Ōkuma Shigenobu suggested to Satow that Britain might establish a legation in Korea, but Satow replied: 'It would probably excite umbrage in the minds of the Russians if we suddenly without any apparent reason converted our consulate general into a legation.'[19]

While on leave in England, Satow discussed Korea with Salisbury on 6 October. When Salisbury said the Russians wanted a port in Northeast Asia, Satow replied that a Korean port would be of no use, but that Port Lazareff (Wonsan on the east coast of Korea) in Russian hands would 'cause great popular commotion' in Japan.

Again on 2 March 1898 Satow received a well known Korean exile, Pak Yong Hyo, who asked if Britain would take a more active role in Korea. Satow said that Britain 'had no direct interests there. Only Russia and Japan had. But the latter neither spoke nor acted. Coreans must be patient for a few years.'

On 30 March 1899 Satow spoke with Aoki Shūzō, then Foreign Minister, who said:

> If Russia has Corea Japan cannot sleep in peace. Unfortunately the interests of England there are not sufficient to make it worth her while to support Japanese policy. But if Russia gets command of the peninsula she will have a great and damaging position as regards commercial nations. I observed that Japan would not be ready [for war] till 1903. He replied that she might be obliged to act before.[20]

Satow and Aoki talked again on 12 October about Russian moves on Masanpho as a coaling station and naval base for policing the Straits of Tsushima, which had been frustrated by Japanese land purchases.

Satow saw Itō for the last time on 2 May 1900 before returning to England. When Satow observed that all seemed quiet in the Far East, Itō replied that no one could tell how long it would last. Satow replied:

> As to war, I said no one could suppose it was to the advantage of Japan to fight Russia. Yet many people talked about it. Japan and Russia as to Corea like England and France as to Siam, a pretty woman with two suitors; no need however to come to blows. One thing however seemed clear, Russia regarded Japan as the only obstacle to her designs in the Far East.[21]

FORMOSA

Kimberley told Satow on 31 May 1895 that the government 'saw no reason for interfering about Formosa, though of course would rather they [Japan] had not taken it'. It was therefore not a political issue, but rather a commercial one for Satow, who had to preside over new consulates on the island as the Japan consular service was extended. In particular, he had to negotiate with the Japanese government over the camphor trade. Anglo-Chinese regulations of 1867 allowed foreigners to enter Formosa, buy and export camphor, but they were forbidden to manufacture it. In spite of this five or six British and German firms were, in fact, allowed to do so. When the Japanese took over in October 1895 they tried to enforce the regulations: several Chinese acting for the foreign firms were imprisoned. After protests by Satow and the German minister Gutschmid, the camphor trade was conceded to foreign firms until the new treaties came into effect in 1899.

Opium was another matter. On 13 September 1895 Satow and Saionji discussed it. Saionji asked if it would be safe to take a permissive line, to which Satow replied that the British Opium Commission had said it was less harmful than alcohol, and that opium was frequently smoked outdoors by Chinese labourers.

ISSUES IN JAPAN

With a new treaty only just negotiated and not yet in force, there were bound to be many issues which arose. The Yokohama branch of the China Association were against it as an 'undue sacrifice' of British (i.e. their) interests, as they told Satow in a memorandum.[22] They saw no benefit in further opening the country, unlike home-based British firms looking for new markets.

Leases caused problems, especially in Kobe. The Japanese tried to put a time limit on perpetual leases and effectively prevent foreign ownership of land altogether. Satow discussed the issue with Foreign Minister Nishi Tokujiro on 3 March 1898. Nishi thought there would be no objection. Satow replied that 'under the new Treaties foreigners would have the same rights as the law gave to Japanese and hence no need for fixing a limit. As to Kōbe I would wait till he got his information, but hoped he would eventually see that the Governor ought not to have fixed a limit on his own account when the agreement between the Japanese government and foreign ministers left everything to be arranged between the owner and the lessee.' He added that only Itō and he understood the situation in Kobe, as they had been present when the settlement was established.

Prison conditions and the access of Consuls to arrested foreigners were discussed on numerous occasions, as were certificates of origin for imported goods, taxes on land, and press laws. But the most sensational case was that of Mrs Carew, accused of poisoning her husband with arsenic in October 1896. This was tried in the British consular court at Yokohama, under the old extraterritorial system. Satow found a way of avoiding having Edith Carew hanged and accordingly her sentence was commuted to life imprisonment.[23]

SATOW'S PERSONAL LIFE IN TOKYO

Satow would have been pleased to return to Tokyo, not only for professional but also personal reasons. It would give him the opportunity to spend time with his Japanese 'wife', Takeda Kane, whom he could not marry as a diplomat, and their two sons, Eitarō and Hisayoshi (also referred to as Hisakichi, and sometimes in the diaries as 'Cha-chan', an affectionate term used only in the Kantō region). Eitarō had been born in 1880, and Hisayoshi in 1883. They were therefore fifteen and twelve years old respectively when Satow returned in 1895. Lightly coded references to Satow's Japanese family are interspersed throughout his diaries, using other languages such as Latin, Italian and Spanish. For example on 26 March 1898 Satow wrote: 'Dined at Totsuka [Shinjuku ward, near the present JR Takatanobaba station] with tutti e tre.' The three here were Takeda Kane, Eitarō and Hisayoshi. Another frequent entry is "Dined at Gembei [Totsuka] con los muchachos."[24] Yet there are usually few details given. An exception is 30 December 1895:

> Started at 10 with the boys for Shidzuura near Numadzu, a brilliant day, on foot and to the top of the pass by 11.20 reaching Karuizawa at 12.15. Started again at 1.5 and walked to Hirai where we rested half an hour, and off again on foot at 2.55. Here Saburō [Satow's manservant] and Hisakichi took *kuruma*, while we continued on foot thro' Daiba and Yamashita, crossing a low pass just behind the village of Tōgo, and getting into the main road at Yamakiwa arr. at the Hōyōkan in Shidzuura at 5.15, standing betw. Saigō's villa and the Kai-hin-In a hospital. This is a new and elegant house. I gave a chadai [tip, *pourboire*] of 5 yen and we were well treated in consequence. There is a fine grove of pine-trees on the sandy shore, and the position is a beautiful one. Temperature much warmer than Atami.

There were also old friends, foreign as well as Japanese, with whom to renew acquaintance. Professor Basil Hall Chamberlain, in Japan since 1873, was still there. And among diplomatic colleagues Satow would have been pleased to find Albert d'Anethan, the Belgian minister, who had first been in Japan 1873–75 and his English wife E. Mary Haggard, sister of the novelist Sir Henry Rider Haggard, author of *King Solomon's Mines*, and of the diplomat Sir William Haggard. Other 'old Japan hands' included J. H. Gubbins who had taken over from Satow as English Secretary to the treaty revision conference in 1883. Henry W. Denison, an American, had acted for the Japanese foreign office as a legal adviser for many years, and the Englishman William H. Stone had advised on telegraphy since 1872.

Satow decided that he liked Lake Chuzenji near Nikkō better than Hakone as a retreat from Tokyo, especially in the hot summer months.[25] To F.V. Dickins on 21 August 1895 he wrote:

> Yesterday I came here, to a small house on the bank of the lake which I have taken till the end of September. I forget whether you know the place. It is very small and quiet. The only other foreigners who have houses here are Gutschmid, the Lowthers, the Kirkwoods and a German savant name unknown.

And on 17 September he wrote in his diary that he 'rowed Gutschmid's boat in 12 min. over to Tozawa, where my house is to be built.' The villa which he had built is still used today by the British Ambassador. On 30 May 1896 Satow went with architect Josiah Conder to the building site and decided where the boathouse would be. Later, he ordered a sculling boat for 70 dollars from A. Teck, probably to replace a leaky boat.[26]

Freiherr von Gutschmid did not remain long as German minister, being the author of several gaffes. The first was when he sent a telegram to Itō congratulating him on the Treaty of Shimonoseki, and then two days later joined in the protest about Liaotung.[27] The second was when he wrote a 'foolish note' to Saionji[28] and on 30 December 1896 he allegedly struck a student[29] with his whip. He was replaced by Graf von Leyden.

Asaina Kansui was employed as Satow's spy from 2 December 1895, in the days before MI6. He was from a 'hatamoto' family, and his father had been Governor of Nagasaki. Asaina was also Governor from 1864–66 though he did not serve there. In March 1867 he was appointed Commissioner for Foreign Affairs, and in January 1868 Commissioner for Financial Affairs. Thereafter his career is unknown. Asaina appears in the official despatches as 'a confidential source' and gave Satow such materials as the shorthand notes of the financial committee of the Lower House. Sometimes Satow asked for specific information: on 12 March 1898 he 'told him to try and find out whether the Russians have informed his government of their desire to lease Port Arthur and Talienwan'. Asaina was paid regularly, usually in dollars or yen, but it is not clear how useful he was to Satow, and on 19 February 1896 Satow thought Asaina was trying to 'pump' him.[30]

On 11 December 1895 Satow was made President of The Asiatic Society of Japan, of which he had been a founder member in 1872, and to which he had frequently read papers in the 1870s. At one point on 30 November 1897 he discussed with Chamberlain a proposal for winding it up because there were too many 'twaddly papers'; fortunately, it continues to this day. Satow lectured to the ASJ on 'The Jesuit Mission Press in Japan' on 29 March 1899[31] and on 21 June at the Legation on 'The Cultivation of Bamboos in Japan.'[32]

Satow retained a scholarly interest in other languages, including Greek and Latin. He read Virgil with Mrs Kirkwood, wife of the legal adviser to the Japanese government William M. Kirkwood (1850–1926).[33] He discussed Jesuit scholarship with a Catholic priest, Père Evrard. He frequently attended concerts and amateur dramatics, and was a keen member of a glee club, for which he persuaded Mrs Blakiston (widow of Captain Blakiston[34]) to continue to play. He played whist regularly and was chairman of the Nippon Race Club in Yokohama, receiving the Meiji Emperor at the races on 29 October 1896. Other social engagements included dinners of Japanese Cambridge graduates on 24 January 1896 and 12 May 1898, and another of British and Japanese barristers at the Metropole Hotel, Tsukiji on 4 February 1899 to celebrate the founding of the Anglo-Japanese Inns of Court Association on that day.

FAREWELL TO JAPAN

On 29 March 1900 a telegram from Lord Salisbury indicated that he wanted to send Satow to Peking, and that MacDonald would 'not improbably take your place'. Satow replied that he was '[g]reatly pleased at this mark of Your Lordship's confidence' and accepted the transfer gladly, being better paid (£5000 rather than £4,000 pa) as well as being more prestigious.[35] Several high-ranking Japanese regretted his departure, including Itō and Imperial Household Minister Tanaka Mitsuaki, to whom Satow said on 3 May that he 'was only the faithful representative of the friendly feeling of England, and whether I came back or not would make no difference'. His final audience with the Emperor and Empress was on 24 April and he sailed from Yokohama on 4 May.[36]

6

Sir William Conyngham Greene, 1854–1934: British Ambassador to Japan, 1912–19

PETER LOWE

Sir William Conyngham Greene

WILLIAM CONYNGHAM GREENE came from an Anglo-Irish background. Born on 29 October 1854, he was the elder son of R. J. Greene and the Hon. Louisa, daughter of the third Baron Plunkett and grandson of Richard Wilson Greene. He was educated at Harrow and Pembroke College, Oxford, where he was an open classical scholar in 1873. He gained first class moderations in 1874, a B.A. in 1877 and M.A. in 1880. Greene entered the Foreign Office with a Clerkship on 9 October 1877 when Disraeli was prime minister. He passed an examination in public law in March 1880 and served in Athens, Stuttgart and Darmstadt, The Hague, Brussels and Tehran. In 1884 Greene married Lady Lily Frances Stopford, daughter of the fifth Earl of Courtown; they had two sons and a daughter. The two principal diplomatic appointments held by Greene were in South Africa and Japan. In both cases he assumed post at times of accelerating tension and turbulence. Before turning to his service in Tokyo, it is necessary to consider briefly his experience in Pretoria.

After three years serving in Tehran (where he gained an allowance for knowledge of Persian), Greene was appointed Her Majesty's Agent in Pretoria, under the Colonial Office, with the personal rank as a Chargé d'Affaires in the Diplomatic Service. He assumed post on 25 August 1896. Greene arrived at a period of deep mutual suspicion between the British government, headed by the third Marquess of Salisbury, and the government of the South African Republic, headed by Paul Kruger. Boer hostility to the British was based on anxiety over the erratic extension of British imperialism and was driven by a tenacious resolve to defend Boer culture from British domination. The discovery of gold rendered the situation more combative because of the influx of Uitlanders keen to make money fast. Greene was faced with challenges that would have taxed the skills of the most hardened diplomat: he had to deal with the vacillating approaches of the government in London, an ambitious and ruthless British High Commissioner in Capetown (Sir Alfred Milner) and the obduracy of Kruger and his senior colleagues.[1] Greene succeeded Sir Jacobus de Wet as Agent in Pretoria. When he arrived the High Commissioner was Sir Hercules Robinson but the latter was soon replaced by Sir Alfred Milner.

The acrimony between Britain and the South African Republic need not have led to war. Younger members of Kruger's administration, notably the brilliant J. C. Smuts, were more conciliatory in approach: the passage of time, had caution prevailed, would have permitted a change in leadership in the South African Republic which could have led to the attainment of warmer relations with Britain.[2] This would have entailed the pursuance of moderate policies in London and Capetown. The heavy defeat of Lord Rosebery's Liberal government in the general election of 1895 led to the formation of a Unionist government, bringing together the Conservatives, headed by Lord Salisbury, and the Liberal Unionists of whom the most outstanding was Joseph Chamberlain. The most combustible element, however, came in consequence of the fateful appointment of Sir Alfred Milner as High Commissioner. Milner was deeply committed to the expansion of British control in South Africa and was reluctant to compromise. Chamberlain also favoured the growth of British power but he was, in part, constrained by the cabinet, notably by the Chancellor of the Exchequer, Sir Michael Hicks Beach. The latter eventually discerned the fundamental error in appointing Milner: he had 'outChamberlained Chamberlain' through his aggressive policy towards the South African Republic.[3]

Conyngham Greene arrived to achieve a diplomatic solution if possible. Left to his own devices, he might well have done so. On the eve of the outbreak of war in 1899, Greene engaged in important discussions with Kruger's State Attorney, J. C. Smuts. These occurred in July and August 1899: Greene encouraged Smuts to accept that the British government would respond positively to compromise proposals devised by Smuts. Milner disliked Greene's reaction to Smuts' initiative and criticized Greene for having gone 'much too far' in conciliation.[4] Both Greene and Smuts were handicapped by the prejudices of their superiors: Milner wanted to place the South African Republic under British control and Kruger wanted to rally the Boers against the British. F. W. Reitz, State Secretary in Pretoria, who was fond of *Treasure Island* by R. L. Stevenson, cynically remarked that Kruger's government was preparing to hand 'the black spot to Long John Conyngham Greene'.[5] And so Greene's endeavours to reach a diplomatic solution failed because of the intransigence of others. He departed from Pretoria on 11 October 1899 and was granted a temporary pension. He was knighted in 1900 and was appointed as Envoy Extraordinary to the Swiss Confederation. Subsequently he served in Bucharest and Copenhagen before receiving appointment as Ambassador Extraordinary and Plenipotentiary at Tokyo and Consul-General for the Empire of Japan on 1 December 1912. He was sworn a Privy Councillor in the same month. Greene served in Tokyo until April 1919..

Greene arrived in Japan during a time of fundamental transition in Anglo-Japanese relations. It differed from his experience in South Africa in that an alliance existed between Britain and Japan and there was no likelihood of armed conflict arising between the allies in the near future. But there were certain similarities with his service in Pretoria. The Anglo-Japanese Alliance was concluded in 1902; it was then revised and extended in 1905 and 1911.[6] The Alliance was important for both signatories and neither thought seriously of ending the agreement. However, storm clouds were beginning to gather. The interests of the two countries were gradually diverging. Britain wished to defend its global interests as best it could and had no interest in extending the empire before the outbreak of the First World War in 1914. Japan was a developing, expanding power and this factor was bound to produce friction. The catalyst was the Chinese revolution of 1911–12 which brought about the end of the ancient empire and the proclamation of a republic of China. Japanese civilian leaders and generals feared that instability in China could jeopardize Japanese interests. Some army officers and financiers began to increase support for the southern republicans, led by Dr Sun Yat-sen. Sen had lived in temporary exile in Japan in the first decade of the twentieth century and had cooperated with the nationalist adventurers (the *shishi*) of the Kokūryukai (the 'River Amur Society' or 'Black Dragon Society').[7] The British foreign secretary, Sir Edward Grey, wished to discourage Japanese ambition in China while recognizing that some degree of Japanese expansion, as in Korea and Manchuria, was unavoidable. Clashing British and Japanese interests in China led to some of the most challenging problems faced by Greene during his six years as ambassador.

How well placed was Conyngham Greene for the demands of his new appointment? He was fifty-eight years of age in 1912 and had served in a wide variety of posts. He had been tested profoundly in Pretoria and, as we have seen, the situation there was beyond his ability - or the ability of any career diplomat - to surmount. Greene possessed a calm personality and he could bring a fresh perspective to bear on Anglo-Japanese relations, not encumbered by previous bias of having served in Eastern Asia. On the other hand, he lacked detailed knowledge of Japan and was compelled to learn fast. While conscientious and competent, he was not a man of deep perception or originality. He succeeded Sir Claude MacDonald, a soldier turned diplomat, who possessed much experience through having served in Peking and Tokyo.[8] It would have been preferable for Greene to have started in Tokyo in a placid period during which he could have established his bearings before concentrating on the more contentious issues. But the same could be said of his arrival in South Africa in 1896.

Greene was soon faced with the demands of the deteriorating situation in China and the associated criticisms of Japan advanced by the British Chargé d'Affaires in Peking, Beilby Alston. The latter had temporarily replaced Sir John Jordan who was on leave in Britain. A rebellion broke out in China in April 1913: the supporters of Sun Yat-sen took up arms against the autocratic president, Yuan Shih-k'ai. They were given financial support and arms by Japanese sympathizers including some army officers; Yuan proved successful in crushing the rebellion. A fierce debate resulted between critics and defenders of Japan within the Foreign Office in London. Suspicion of Japanese motives was growing and some officials entertained doubts as to the viability of the alliance in the longer term. Alston expressed his criticisms vehemently and Greene was compelled to respond. He sent a despatch to Sir Edward Grey on 12 September 1913 in which he pointed out that Alston could not prove that the Japanese government was undermining the alliance: 'I have endeavoured to make it clear that while there is little doubt that individual Japanese were active in the recent events in China, there is no evidence that the Imperial Government were a party to them.'[9] Greene argued that

Japan would consolidate its position in Manchuria and would not withdraw from Manchuria in order to expand in central and southern China. He held that the alliance remained a cornerstone in Japanese foreign policy. His South African experience led Greene to remark that Lord Salisbury's government had failed, during the 1890s, to prevent arms reaching South Africa and the Japanese authorities were in a similar predicament over China.[10] Greene was correct in stating that the Japanese government had no intention of ending the alliance in 1913 but Alston was right to emphasize the emerging political and economic differences between Britain and Japan as a consequence of developments in China.

Britain had taken the lead in establishing occidental imperialism in China during the nineteenth century. British firms dominated much of the trade in the treaty ports. Grey and the Foreign Office were adamant in defending British investments; they were determined to ensure that British influence in the Yangtze valley was maintained. Curiously, Britain's relations with Japan, France and Russia encountered increasing strain because of diverging interests in China between 1911 and 1914. Britain had an alliance with Japan and ententes with France and Russia, dating from 1904 and 1907. Yet Britain's partners in these agreements wished to foster their own economic ambitions at Britain's expense in China. Railway concessions were particularly valuable for combined political, economic and strategic reasons. Foreign avarice in China was aptly compared by *The Economist* newspaper to an episode in a famous Edwardian farce - 'It reminds us of a scene in *Charley's Aunt*'.[11] Greene believed that the most sensible approach would be for Britain and Japan to observe the continuance of each other's spheres of interest in the Yangtze valley and Manchuria respectively.[12] The Gaimusho contemplated developing the Anglo-Japanese Alliance into an economic, in addition to the existing political-strategic, vehicle. Greene was not in favour of such a development, writing privately to the Foreign Office: 'If the Alliance is good enough as it stands, why enlarge its scope? However that may be, it seems to be beyond doubt that the Japanese are disliked and distrusted in our sphere in China and that our co-operation with them would not be likely to be popular with our own commercial community.'[13] The permanent under-secretary in the Foreign Office, Sir Arthur Nicolson, and Sir Edward Grey concurred that Britain should not enter into a closer economic relationship with Japan.[14]

In March 1914 Greene delivered a note to the Gaimusho reiterating Grey's determination to preserve the British sphere of interest in the Yangtze region: 'I have the honour to remind, your Excellency, that the Japanese interests referred to cannot compare in magnitude or extent with the immense British interests which have been so long established in the Yangtze region and which are increasing every day; and I am to state that the policy of His Majesty's Government aims simply at safeguarding these British interests by maintaining control over the lines of communication …'[15] A change in administration occurred in Tokyo in March 1914 when the government headed by Admiral Yamamoto Gombei fell in consequence of serious bribery allegations involving the navy. The new government was led by Count Ōkuma Shigenobu, long an advocate of a more democratic system in Japan. The foreign minister was Baron Katō Takaaki who had served successfully as ambassador in London. Katō strongly supported the Anglo-Japanese Alliance but also favoured a more aggressive approach in advancing Japanese economic activity in China. Katō's marital links with Mitsubishi might well have stimulated his forward policy. Katō indicated, in June 1914, that Japanese interests in the Yangtze region would be advanced. In addition, he spoke privately to Greene to complain of the negative British policy.[16] Greene was broadly sympathetic to Japan but he entirely agreed with Grey's approach over China: 'I am glad we are all agreed about Japanese interference in the Yangtze Valley. Anxious as I am to help the Japanese, I cannot help feeling that while they will never let us into their spheres, they are trying to steal a march into ours, and this is not cricket between Allies'.[17]

Therefore, in the summer of 1914 Anglo-Japanese friction was growing and Greene was confronted with the problem of standing firm over British interests in China while not allowing this to rock the alliance too severely. At this point the grave crisis in Europe, resulting from the events in Sarajevo on 28 June 1914, led to swift descent into war in July-August 1914. Britain's relationship with Japan was important from several angles of approach. In fulfilment of the assumptions underlying British naval policy since 1907, the assistance of the Japanese navy was required in Far Eastern and Pacific waters. However, this in itself caused profound suspicion in the United States, Australia and New Zealand. They had regarded Japan with anxiety since Japan's defeat of Russia in the war of 1904–5. It was essential to maintain cohesion within the British Empire and Britain's relationship with the United States would be of crucial significance in the midst of a huge war. This contributes to explaining the way in which Sir Edward Grey dealt with issues concerning Japan's entry into the First World War. Grey was a skilful and perceptive foreign secretary but he erred in handling relations with Japan in August 1914. In his attempt to allay concern in the United States, Australia and New Zealand, Grey offended Japan by making obvious the lack of trust in future Japanese conduct. Grey's doubts possessed some validity but the maladroit way in which Japan was treated in August 1914 pushed the Ōkuma government towards a more assertive policy. Greene had to find the most appropriate diplomatic means, in 1914–15, of preventing a pronounced deterioration in Anglo-Japanese relations.

Katō Takaaki was the key personality in determining the response in Tokyo to the outbreak of war in Europe. Katō believed that Japan must participate and declare war on Germany. During the hectic activity in London following the British decision to go to war against Germany, Sir Edward Grey requested Japanese assistance on 6 August. Katō wished to act at once under the terms of the Anglo-Japanese Alliance. Japanese involvement would facilitate expansion in China. Grey feared that a Japanese formal declaration of war would alarm the United States, Australia and New Zealand. Accordingly, he endeavoured to dissuade Japan from formal entry and he tried to set limitations to Japanese actions. The Admiralty deemed Japanese naval assistance to be necessary in order to protect trade routes from a German squadron headed by von Spee and from German raiders. Greene was engaged in delicate exchanges with the Gaimusho. Katō emphasized that the Okuma government had decided to declare war on Germany, although he assured Greene that 'Japan's action will be strictly limited to measures which are absolutely indispensable … British Government may rest assured that Japanese Government, in deciding her present attitude, had not been prompted by any desire for territorial aggrandisement or by any motives of prompting her selfish ends'.[18] Greene realized how necessary it was to establish a basis for Anglo-Japanese co-operation, the alternative being unilateral action by Japan. He implied some criticism of vacillation in London:

> It is, in my opinion, absolutely necessary that the intentions of His Majesty's Government should be made known as soon as possible … What we have to decide is whether it would be more advantageous for us to allow Japan to act alone, after having asked her aid, or to give in to her now, and by so doing so put her under an obligation which we can bring up when, after operations are ended, the process of cleaning up in China is begun.[19]

Grey was preoccupied in defining geographical restrictions to Japanese action. Operations should 'not extend beyond Asiatic waters westward of the China Seas or to any foreign territory except territory in German occupation on the continent in Eastern Asia'.[20] Katō informed Greene that his government could not accept the geographical constraints proposed by Grey. On 15 August Japan sent an ultimatum to Germany demanding withdrawal of German armed ships from Japanese and Chinese waters plus the surrender of the leased territory of Kiaochow in Shantung province of China, within one month. If Germany did not comply, by noon on 23 August, Japan would be in a state of war with Germany.[21] Therefore, on 23 August 1914, Japan entered formally into the First World War. Greene dealt with various diplomatic exchanges, involving Anglo-Japanese military operations against the German fortress at Tsingtao, and Japanese, Australian and New Zealand action against German-occupied islands in the Pacific. Considerable friction occurred, since the Japanese armed forces were determined to assert primacy and to make the most of this splendid opportunity to advance Japanese expansion in East Asia and the Pacific. The fortress of Tsingtao was duly captured in November 1914. By the end of 1914 the German-held islands north and south of the Equator had been captured, the Japanese occupying the more northerly islands and Australian and New Zealand forces assumed control of those below the Equator. The United States viewed matters with much concern but President Woodrow Wilson's Democratic administration had no shortage of problems to contend with in the Atlantic as well as in the Pacific.

The next stage saw Japan acting unilaterally, as Greene had feared in August. Predictably this comprised a resolute Japanese attempt to strengthen Japan's role in China. Within Japan different official and unofficial circles formulated specific and broad aims for political, economic and strategic exploitation of China. The Gaimusho wished to extend the leases of the territorial concessions inherited from Tsarist Russia in 1905. Financial interests (the *zaibatsu*) joined with the Gaimusho in wanting to develop Japanese activity in the Yangtze valley at the expense of Britain and France. The army was particularly interested in Manchuria. Unofficial groups included the nationalist societies, notably the Kokuryūkai, which advocated Pan-Asianism with Japan liberating Asian brethren from occidental domination: this would be assisted through persuading (or, more accurately, coercing) the Chinese government into appointing Japanese advisers, so as to consolidate Japanese influence. Thus the notorious 'Twenty-one Demands' materialized in December 1914 and this marked the start of another serious crisis for Greene to handle.

Katō met Greene on 24 January 1915 and gave him a summary of the demands but omitted the fifth group, as conveyed to President Yuan Shih-k'ai. Katō observed that the demands 'were not as far-reaching as some parties in Japan desired, but he was putting them forward with the hope that they would result in the establishment of good relations between Japan and China. They were made in pursuance of a scheme which had been elaborated long ago by him'.[22] The Foreign Office soon learned from a Russian source that

Japan had put forward more extreme demands than those communicated to Greene. In an interview with a correspondent of *The Times* newspaper, on 10 February 1915, Katō admitted that he had forwarded 'wishes' in addition to 'demands': these included a preference for obtaining railway concessions in the Yangtze valley.[23] Greene visited Kato upon hearing the news from the correspondent (Kato had asked that it not be published) and the foreign minister replied truculently that Japan was prepared to act independently in advancing its interest, just as Britain had done in the past.[24] Kato modified his stance subsequently when faced with a robust response from Grey and a recommendation from the Japanese Embassy in London that he should adopt a more conciliatory approach.[25]Greene did all he could to achieve a more positive response from the Gaimusho. The Minister in Peking, Sir John Jordan, was critical of the 'British admirers' of Japan who had not revealed sufficient tenacity in protecting British interests.[26] Beilby Alston expressed blunt criticism of Greene in a personal letter to Jordan. He commented sardonically on:

> … the faith which the Tokio [*sic*] Embassy appear to have placed in the Japanese all through that period in spite of all we did at Peking to enlighten them. The idea that they were not continuing to play straight never seems to have been shaken until the full text of the demands must have given Greene a rude awakening. They, the Japs., seem able to hypnotize our people over there - Greene wrote some time ago that he did not know what he would do if Kato was turned out of office …[27]

It was true that Greene had placed particular faith in Kato, bearing in mind the latter's close identification with the creation and maintenance of the Anglo-Japanese Alliance. But Britain could not afford a full-scale dispute with Japan in time of war, which could result in Japan deciding to change sides and support Germany. This was ultimately the answer to the criticisms expressed by Jordan and Alston. The Chinese president showed much skill in delaying concessions to Japan for as long as he could. Yuan's aim was to encourage foreign representations to Tokyo and to stimulate dissent within Japanese ruling circles over Kato's diplomacy. This proved a successful strategy up to a point. Britain, France, Russia and the United States protested at the scope of Japanese designs and at the want of frankness in Kato's conduct. Kato had already alienated the *genro* (elder statesmen) by refusing to consult them, as his predecessors had done. Kato's inability to compel Yuan Shih-k'ai to accept the Twenty-one Demands precipitated a domestic crisis from which Katō emerged the loser. The *genro* insisted on a full review of policy, the outcome being agreement between the Ōkuma government and the *genro* that an ultimatum would be sent, to Yuan, based on groups one to four of the demands while group five, which was of a generalized character, was withdrawn. China was in no position to fight Japan and Yuan had no choice other than to sign treaties in which he conceded an extension of Japanese rights in Manchuria and the Yangtze valley. It was an empty victory for Katō: his diplomatic reputation was undermined by the acrid international and domestic controversy and he resigned as foreign minister later in August 1915.

Greene experienced disillusionment with Japan, as he revealed in a letter to Sir Horace Rumbold:

> It has all been a very bitter experience for me after the close and personal relations in which I had been with these people during the critical stages of the war and up till the fall of Tsingtao. I need not tell you how disappointed I was, and so were my Allied Colleagues, when this was sprung upon us all, when our hands were full elsewhere. It is very typical of Japan, but it leaves an unpleasant impression behind.[28]

In a subsequent letter to Sir Walter Langley, Greene described the Japanese as 'opportunists to the backbone'. He added, accurately, that 'The fortunes of war had placed the ball at Baron Kato's feet and he kicked it, that was all'.[29] Diplomatic pressure from the Western powers led by Britain and the United States, combined with the acrimonious domestic crisis in Tokyo, brought the Twenty-one Demands crisis to an end in May 1915. It was a major watershed in the evolution of the Anglo-Japanese Alliance. The Foreign Office, and Conyngham Greene personally, were pushed towards the conclusion that the long-term continuation of the alliance was not desirable.

Anglo-Japanese relations were still strained later in 1915 and into 1916. Towards the end of 1916 changes in administrations occurred in London and Tokyo. The coalition government led by H. H. Asquith was replaced by another coalition headed by David Lloyd George. In Japan Ōkuma Shigenobu was succeeded by Field Marshal Terauchi Masatake, a protégé of Prince Yamagata Aritomo. Thus Japan reverted to a bureaucratic government of the older type. At first sight this might have suggested that Britain would encounter more difficulty but the Terauchi government presided over an improvement in relations. The new foreign minister, Baron Motono Ichirō, had served previously as ambassador to Russia and he wished to rectify the damage caused by the adventurous China policy of his predecessor.[30] Motono advocated a cautious policy of advancing Japanese interests in China more gradually and of establishing cordiality in relations with the Occidental powers. Greene observed that 'we can hardly hope for a more friendly Government than the present'.[31] Urged on by Yamagata, Terauchi worked to achieve closer cooperation with political parties represented in the Diet. This was in part accomplished with the establishment of the Advisory Council on Foreign Relations which included representatives from the cabinet, privy council and political parties.[32]

The exigencies of war in the form of the dire pressure faced by the Royal Navy led the Lloyd George government to request Japanese naval assistance in the Mediterranean and south Atlantic. Greene forwarded the proposal to the Japanese government in January 1917. Motono made clear that Japan would require assurances relating to Shantung and the Pacific islands occupied by Japan earlier in the war. Greene held that Japan was merely asking for formal confirmation of the status quo and there was no point in arguing over this. As a sign of good faith Japan swiftly agreed to provide the naval help requested by Britain.[33] In return Britain acknowledged Japanese claims regarding Shantung and the Pacific islands north of the Equator. Britain requested reciprocal acknowledgement of the occupation, by forces from the British Empire, of islands south of the Equator: this was forthcoming.

In April 1917 the United States entered into the First World War. Relations between the United States and Japan had encountered growing friction for the previous decade and the arrival of the United States as an ally compelled a reassessment of Anglo-Japanese relations. Greene produced an important analysis in a communication to Langley, sent in August 1917. Greene referred to the discrete sources of tension in relations, citing Japanese arrogance and opportunism; the long-term trend of Japanese expansion; the support for Indian dissidents expressed by some Japanese; economic aims advanced by Japanese companies with official endorsement; alleged Japanese aspirations regarding the Netherlands East Indies (Indonesia); Japanese ambitions in China; and racial strife, illustrated in problems concerning Japanese residence in the British dominions. Suspicion between the United States and Japan was deep and was unlikely to be reversed in the foreseeable future. Greene suggested that the Anglo-Japanese Alliance should be continued for the time being but that, in the longer term, the alliance might be merged 'in a triangular arrangement between Great Britain, the United States and Japan'.[34] Greene added that 'I cannot help thinking that the present hollow friendship cannot be continued and must in due course be resolved into some relation at once less intimate and more genuine; and that we might well try to bring in America on our side to redress the balance in the Far East'.[35] The Foreign Office was sympathetic but could discern only too clearly the difficulty of surmounting American isolationism which was likely to reappear after the First

World War. However, the exchange between Greene and the Foreign Office pointed interestingly to the post-war debates in which Greene participated prior to the deliberations in the Washington Conference.

The Bolshevik Revolution in Russia in November 1917 led to renewed tension in Anglo-Japanese relations. Japanese leaders were alarmed at the instability in Siberia and the dangers this could pose for Japanese interests in East Asia. In addition, reports from Japanese representatives in Europe conveyed doubt as to the outcome of the war.[36] Some in the Japanese army believed that Germany would triumph and the Terauchi government revealed a less enthusiastic approach to cooperating closely with Britain in the latter part of 1917 and early in 1918. After lengthy debate on the merits of intervening in Siberia, ruling circles in Tokyo approved the dispatch of a military expedition in August 1918. Large-scale bribery was used in China to strengthen the warlord, Tuan Chi-jui. Domestic discontent in Japan over the price of rice caused serious riots which brought about the fall of the Terauchi administration in November 1918.[37] Speculation in Japan that German forces might break through decisively in March 1918 and lead to allied surrender evaporated in October 1918 as internal disaffection in Austria-Hungary and Germany contributed to the termination of the conflict. Greene reiterated opinions he had expressed in 1917 - 'the proposed League of Nations will ... create a new situation in regard to the whole question of Alliances and enable Britain to merge the Anglo-Japanese Alliance - which I venture to think has lived its day and done its great work - in such a League'.[38] Greene thought that the alliance should be given 'a decent burial without hurting Japanese susceptibilities'.[39] It might be possible to achieve the former but it would be extremely difficult to fulfil the latter.

* * *

Conyngham Greene departed from Tokyo in April 1919. He retired with a pension in September 1919. Greene was succeeded eventually by Sir Charles Eliot who assumed post in April 1920.[40] Greene was invited to serve as a member of a small sub-committee established in order to assess the future of the alliance. His fellow members were Sir John Jordan, Sir William Tyrrell and Sir Victor Wellesley. They reported in January 1921 that 'A careful consideration of all the arguments both for and against the renewal of the Alliance has resulted in the unanimous conclusion that it should be dropped and that in its stead should, if possible, be substituted a Tripartite *Entente* between the United States, Japan and Great Britain, consisting in a declaration of general principles which can be subscribed to by all parties without the risk of embarrassing commitments'.[41] If the United States proved reluctant to participate, the committee envisaged a new agreement with Japan so framed as to facilitate American adhesion at a future date. The ambassador in Washington, Sir Auckland Geddes, recommended that the alliance should be continued, in a modified form, because of anticipated difficulties in inducing the new Republican administration of Warren G. Harding to cooperate. The new ambassador in Tokyo, Sir Charles Eliot, recommended extending the alliance.[42] The Foreign Secretary, Lord Curzon, was dismissive of the committee's report. The Prime Minister, David Lloyd George, was quite sympathetic towards Japan. When the imperial conference met, in June-July 1921, he urged the extension of the alliance: he felt that while Japan looked after its own interests, Japan did not act more selfishly than any other power. Indeed, Lloyd George quoted part of Sir Edward Grey's address to the imperial conference in May 1911 in which Grey urged continuance of the alliance. Therefore, Greene's contribution to the debate did not influence the prime minister and the foreign secretary in the direction he desired. The Harding administration took the initiative in summoning a major conference in Washington in October 1921 and this led to the replacement of the alliance by a four-power agreement comprising the United States, Britain, France and Japan. Thus the United States helped to implement the kind of solution envisaged by Greene in 1917. The alliance ended finally in August 1923.

* * *

Conyngham Greene's diplomatic career was dominated by two major appointments in the course of which he contributed to deliberations of profound significance - in South Africa in the 1890s and in Japan between 1913 and 1919. Greene was a hardworking but rather colourless individual. He lacked the flamboyance of Sir Claude MacDonald or the erudition of Sir Charles Eliot. Greene was steady and realistic: he possessed the patient and conciliatory qualities required in a successful diplomat. He discerned the perils inherent in South Africa and worked to achieve a compromise. His efforts were thwarted by Paul Kruger and Sir Alfred Milner. In Japan Greene appreciated the value of the Anglo-Japanese Alliance at a time when Britain was encountering intensifying problems in Europe, culminating in the outbreak of war in July-August 1914. Greene lacked previous Far Eastern experience and when he arrived in Tokyo he was not fully aware of the diverse pressures that were pushing Japan in an expansionist direction. Thus he had to grapple with the arguments concerning the respective British and Japanese spheres of political and economic interest in China. Greene endeavoured to promote compromise but Grey and Katō were each resolute in defending their approaches. War in Europe temporarily averted further friction over the Yangtze valley and instead led to differences of opinion surrounding the circumstances of Japanese entry into the First World War. Grey's usual adroitness was missing in his clumsy attempts to define limits to Japanese activity in August 1914 and Greene had to point out to Grey that Japan must not be alienated. The Twenty-one Demands presented Greene with a formidable challenge: he understood that British disapproval of Japanese policy had to be conveyed but argument had to be contained amidst the greater demands of war. At the same time Greene's opinion of Japan changed fundamentally in 1915 and he regarded Japanese policy far more critically than before. This explains his advocacy of a new agreement to replace the alliance: Britain would move closer to the United States while obviating alienation of Japan. This was more difficult to accomplish than Greene appeared to believe. The significance of Conyngham Greene's service as ambassador is that it marked a decisive change in the climate of Anglo-Japanese relations, away, it might be said, from a certain warmth (if cooling gradually) to a bracing, chilling wind. The interests of the allies were diverging, as British decline became more obvious and as Japan's emergence as a major regional power became more striking. Greene was a loyal and competent facilitator of policy but he was not a commanding personality. Greene died on 30 June 1934, four months short of his eightieth birthday.

7

Sir John Tilley, 1869–1951: British Ambassador to Japan, 1926–31

HARUMI GOTŌ-SHIBATA

Sir John Tilley

SIR JOHN TILLEY was the British Ambassador to Japan from 1926 to 1931. His autobiography, *London to Tokyo,* was published in 1942, soon after the war broke out between Britain and Japan. His name does not appear in the *Dictionary of National Biography* and it seems that he has been largely forgotten. In contrast the achievements of Sir Miles Lampson (1880–1964) as British Ambassador to China from the end of 1926 to 1933 are still widely acknowledged. Lampson's association with East Asia dated back to 1906 when he went to Japan as secretary to the Mission of Prince Arthur of Connaught to invest the Meiji Emperor with the Order of the Garter. Tilley on the other hand had had limited contact with the region until he was appointed as Ambassador to Japan. Tilley was not a scholar-diplomat such as his predecessor Sir Charles Eliot (1862–1931) or Sir George Sansom (1883–1965), who was the commercial counsellor under Tilley.

Tilley was born on 21 January 1869. Educated at Eton and King's College, Cambridge, he entered the Foreign Office in March 1893. He was first assigned to the Eastern Department, where Sir William Conyngham Greene, who was to be Eliot's predecessor as ambassador to Japan, was also working. Tilley's next assignment was to the Far Eastern Department at the time of the first Sino-Japanese war and Tilley described the experience as his 'first, though distant, acquaintance with Japan as a world power'.[1] In his late thirties, he worked in Constantinople for several years as a first secretary. As the Foreign Office and the Diplomatic Service were still in theory separate, he had to effect a temporary exchange with a member of the Diplomatic Service. The two services were amalgamated in 1916 by the work of a committee appointed to consider reforms. Tilley participated in the committee as the Chief Clerk of the Foreign Office.[2] Apart from his experience in Constantinople, he worked mainly in London, but towards the end of 1920 he was asked to go to Brazil as the ambassador. Tilley described this as a 'thunderbolt', although 'of a pleasant nature'.[3] He remained in Brazil until 1925 when he learnt that he was to be appointed to Tokyo. Tilley, who was 56, does not seem to have been consulted before the Foreign Office sought Japanese *agreement* to his appointment. In June and July 1925 before he had been informed of the Foreign Office's decision, he was surprised to find friends congratulating him on his appointment to Tokyo.[4] Tilley accepted the appointment and sailed for Japan on 7 January 1926.

TILLEY IN JAPAN, 1926–31

The five years Tilley spent in Japan can be divided into two periods. The first was from the time he first arrived in Japan until he was granted home leave in January 1928: the second started in October of the same year when he resumed his job. In the first half, Tilley did not enjoy his life in Japan at all. It seems that he took an instant dislike to the country, although this feeling might be exaggerated in *London to Tokyo,* which was published in 1942 after the outbreak of war. The first reason why Tilley felt his life so difficult was that when he arrived only two years had passed since the Great Kantō Earthquake and Tokyo was still in the early stages of rebuilding. 'The old Embassy house, … everything in fact, had been destroyed in [September] 1923.'[5] The new embassy building was completed in 1932, but Tilley had no chance of living there. The physical discomfort in a 'bungalow' infested with rats was almost unbearable.[6]

Secondly, the Taisho Emperor died in December 1926, and national mourning continued for a full year. The emperor had been weak since childhood, and he was a 'lunatic'[7] when Tilley arrived in Japan. His eldest son was acting as Regent, whom Tilley initially did not rate highly.[8]

Thirdly, although Britain needed Japanese cooperation during this particular period, Tilley failed to secure it.[9]

Since the Anglo-Japanese Alliance was abrogated at the Washington Conference of 1921–22, the 'decline of British popularity' and the 'downward trend' persisted. According to F. S. G. Piggott, the military attaché under Eliot, 'outward relations with Japanese of all classes seemed as good as ever', but 'the very fact that we were always on the look-out for opportunities to maintain good relations meant that their maintenance was to some extent artificial; fundamentally they were not the same as in old days, when no special efforts were required'. As Eliot made 'unremitting efforts' to stop the fading of British popularity, Piggott thought Eliot's departure together with the death of Katō Takaaki (1860–1926) was a heavy blow to Anglo-Japanese relations.[10] This seems to imply that Piggott did not think highly of Tilley as ambassador. He later wrote that he was pleased when a change of ambassadors took place in 1931.

> … I had known Sir Francis [Lindley] slightly twenty-five years before when he was a junior secretary, and I now had the pleasure – a pleasure shared by several others at the War Office – of reading his pungent dispatches from Tokyo; a spade was invariably called a spade, much to our satisfaction.[11]

In the meantime Britain was facing serious problems in China. The Chinese were rapidly becoming aware of their inferior status in international society and began to make efforts to recover their rights. As Britain was the country, which from the middle of the nineteenth century had the largest interests in China, she was the first to be singled out as the target of attack. British trade in south China had been paralyzed because of a boycott against Hong Kong. Britain tried to cope with the situation in cooperation with other powers and wanted in particular Japanese assistance.

The Japanese Foreign Minister then was Shidehara Kijūrō, who had been a career diplomat. His diplomacy has been praised in Japan, and he wrote in his autobiography published in 1951 that he rated British diplomacy highly and tried to adopt the same general guidelines.[12] However, in the mid-1920s, the British government were displeased with Shidehara's policies towards China, because he did not seem to be willing to cooperate with Britain. He had the reputation of being 'anti-English' and instead, in favour of conciliating China and the United States.[13] Shidehara was unpopular among the British, because the interests of Britain and Japan often conflicted. The two governments, for instance, differed over whether tariff autonomy should be granted to China or not. Before the Peking Tariff Conference opened in October 1925, Britain believed that agreement had been reached to grant tariff autonomy step by step in return for effective guarantees for the gradual abolition of *likin*, a kind of internal customs. Nevertheless, when the conference met, the governments of Japan and the United States decided to grant to the government in Peking tariff autonomy in full and at an early date. In addition, Shidehara tried to secure low customs duties for Japan. As a result the conference was prolonged without the prospect of any early settlement. Another example was Japan's lack of military cooperation when Britain dispatched an expeditionary force to 'defend' the Shanghai International Settlement from the advancing Kuomintang in 1927. Shidehara considered that military intervention in China was counter-productive. Tilley's role as ambassador was to protect British interests; so he was displeased with Shidehara whom many British thought was only interested in enhancing Japan's economic interests.[14]

When the change of government took place in Japan in April 1927, however, Tilley learned 'with horror' that the new Prime Minister cum Foreign Minister, Tanaka Giichi, spoke neither English nor French, and intended always to have an interpreter at his side. Tilley disliked using interpreters and knew several European languages as well as a little Turkish, but had given up 'the attempt to learn any Japanese beyond a few ordinary expressions'. Tilley and all his colleagues greatly lamented the departure of Shidehara, 'who had a perfect command of English and an equally perfect command of his temper, and who was, moreover, very reliable in what he said'. Shidehara was a man similar to themselves. His retirement led Tilley to wonder whether he had done the former justice. Tilley wrote a farewell letter to Shidehara regretting his resignation as Foreign Minister; Shidehara wrote a charming letter back.[15]

Ex-army general Tanaka, however, was much more interested in closer communication and cooperation between the two countries than Shidehara. The change he brought to Japan's China policy was welcomed by Britain, and Tilley found him 'pleasant to deal with', although he did not rate highly Tanaka's talent as a politician. In December 1927, Tilley came to think that Tanaka had 'very little to say':[16]

> … The Prime Minister at first gave me the impression of being a man of some determination who knew his own mind. Unfortunately, although these qualities do in a way belong to him, they are not backed by much power of thought. Consequently he dashes off without very well knowing where he's going. This has several times become evident in his dealings with China: …[17]

The Tanaka government sent expeditionary forces to China in 1927 and 1928. The Sino-Japanese military clash at Jinan in May 1928 led to a serious deterioration in relations between the two countries. As Japan became the sole target of the Chinese boycott, she started to seek cooperation with Britain. Uchida Yasuya, former Foreign Minister, was sent to Europe in the summer 1928 partly to promote such cooperation. In the meantime, China started to show goodwill to Britain and the trade situation improved for the latter. Britain no longer needed Japan's support. On the contrary, close relations with Japan might have destroyed the favourable position which Britain secured in China.

Tilley was on home leave while the relations among the three countries thus changed drastically. When he came back to Japan in October 1928, his job turned out to be much easier and life more enjoyable. The Japanese started to make tremendous efforts to entertain Tilley and improve the prospect of Anglo-Japanese cooperation. Although the efforts were fruitless at the international level, Tilley himself at least was much happier.

ENTHRONEMENT OF THE SHOWA EMPEROR

The latter half of Tilley's ambassadorship started with celebrations. On 28 September 1928, Prince Chichibu, the second son of the late emperor, married Matsudaira Setsuko. The couple received greetings from ambassadors and ministers on 4 October. This was followed by a banquet a week after and a luncheon on 12 October. Princess Chichibu was the elder daughter of Matsudaira Tsuneo, an able diplomat and the fifth son of the former daimyo of the Aizu domain. The princess was born in Walton on Thames, Surrey, while her father was serving as a secretary at the Japanese Embassy in London. Although the Matsudairas left England when she was only eight months old, the princess was quite Westernized as she attended a high school in the United States where her father was Shidehara's successor as Japanese ambassador.[18] After the wedding, her father Matsudaira Tsuneo was due to leave for Britain where he had been appointed Japanese ambassador. Prince Chichibu had also stayed in England and studied at Magdalen College, Oxford, although after a term he had left because of the illness of his father the Taisho Emperor. Tilley liked both the Chichibus and the Matsudairas.

The Showa Emperor was enthroned in November 1928. All the foreign representatives including Tilley went to Kyoto where the ceremony was held. They were the guests of the Japanese government and expected to witness the emperor ascending the throne. They were among the immediate onlookers during one of the ceremonies.

Together with them were only the imperial family and the highest officials.[19]

Although the ceremony was 'extraordinarily picturesque'[20], Tilley was aware that it was an 'invented tradition'.[21] He compared it with another invented tradition, namely the British Coronation ceremony, but noted three points of difference. First, he noticed that the Japanese crowds were kept at a considerable distance from any route along which the Emperor was to pass and there was no cheering. Secondly, he observed the extreme remoteness of the emperor and empress even from their guests including himself. Although they shook hands with foreign representatives, they never spoke. Thirdly, he thought it strange that the emperor ascends the throne by the grace and favour of his own ancestress, although after all it was claimed that she was a goddess.[22]

Tilley could not believe that there was any popular enthusiasm for the emperors. He had already noticed that a considerable proportion of the crowds who prayed for the Taisho Emperor during his illness were organized schoolchildren and boy scouts.[23] Although the press reported that enormous crowds of people flocked into Kyoto for the enthronement, he could not believe it, because he did not see any sign of them. He felt that the feeling of awe to the throne was maintained with difficulty and imperial ceremonies were rather a triumph of organization than anything else. While there was no spontaneous cheering along the route when the emperor passed, Tilley was impressed with the tremendous shout of three banzais conducted by Prime Minister Tanaka in front of a palace during the ceremony:[24]

> ... to the European mind the general idea suggested by the treatment of the Emperor ... is rather that of a Being who must be propitiated than a Father of his country who must be surrounded with affection. To the Japanese mind this outward display of veneration of the Emperor may have seemed ... a natural respect for symbolized authority. At the same time it is really of quite modern invention dating only from the time of the Emperor Meiji, and is strictly inculcated by the authorities rather than spontaneous. In earlier days and for centuries many of the Emperors, although the object of some theoretical veneration, lived lives of miserable poverty and neglect and were merely made use of by the Shoguns for such purposes as the latter thought convenient. It seems to me doubtful whether this compulsory veneration of the Sovereign, in its modern developments, will conduce to the stability of the Throne better than attempts to win the genuine affection of the people; indeed, given the great development of education in this country, I

> imagine that the present system may have the opposite effect to that intended.[25]

However, Tilley was not absolutely sure whether his observation was correct. The experts at the embassy told him that there was still a very strong feeling towards the emperors among the peasantry away from Tokyo.[26] He also noticed that almost 'no Japanese would say what he thought to a foreigner on such a matter, nor, indeed, would he say what he thought to anyone at all but an intimate friend, for fear of trouble with the police'.[27]

The enthronement ceremony was followed by a lot of entertainment for foreign representatives: a garden party, a performance of *Miyako-odori* [Dance of the Capital], a trip on Lake Biwa, an excursion to Nara, banquets both in Japanese and Western style. Tilley seems to have enjoyed most of them. After spending about ten days in Kyoto, the representatives returned to Tokyo on 19 November.[28]

In May 1929, a Mission led by the Duke of Gloucester, younger son of King George V, arrived in Japan to bestow the new emperor with the Order of the Garter. On arrival at Tokyo station the duke was met by a group of British schoolchildren outside the station who had been told not to cheer, 'in deference to Japanese custom'.[29] Among many events during the duke's visit to Japan was a 'mammoth' garden party at the British Embassy: 'Sir John having been determined to invite all available British to meet the Duke … British from Yokohama of every degree; Indian women in their saris – wives of merchants – a Scout Parade, Salvation Army lasses who busily tackled the middies from HMS *Suffolk* in their traditional style, whilst teachers from all over the country, including elderly persons from distant outposts, poured forth exuberant and impassioned loyalty to anyone handy.' The party was a tremendous success.[30]

Tilley's evaluation of Japan in this period rose to a certain extent. He wrote:

> The people are mainly, … peaceable and frugal in their own lives; they are neither adventurers nor warlike, nor fond of display. I should not even describe them as hardy although they may be accustomed to hardship and are certainly ready to endure hardship if necessary. There seem to me excellent reasons why they should wish their Government to refrain from dangerous or extravagant enterprises, and why, happily, we need not expect that Japan will kindle war on this side of the world if she can possibly help it.[31]

He also wrote in the annual report for the year 1929 that the Showa Emperor had 'since the enthronement, developed unexpectedly', and his bearing, manner and voice showed greatly increased self-confidence. Shidehara, who returned to office after the Tanaka cabinet fell in the autumn of 1929, was described as being ready to work with Britain. In other dispatches written at the beginning of 1930, Tilley stated that 'in the main, Japanese policy [was] wise and farseeing, and by no means always selfish'; that 'Japan's constant schemes and intrigues in China [were] exaggerated'; and that she would not be so foolish as to annex Manchuria with a population of twenty millions of another race, which was constantly growing by immigration, and thus to annoy both China and the United States.[32]

OBSERVATIONS OF JAPAN AND THE JAPANESE

As Tilley had given up the attempt to learn any Japanese beyond a few ordinary expressions, all Japanese with whom he made friends spoke good English. Apart from Prince and Princess Chichibu and Matsudaira Tsuneo, he liked and respected Tokugawa Iyesato, Makino Nobuaki (Shinken) and Chinda Sutemi.[33] All of them spent one of the happiest periods in their lives in Britain. Tilley preferred Japanese naval officers to soldiers, because the latter usually spoke no English and were 'less inclined to be friendly'.[34] On the whole, Tilley's autobiography makes one aware of the class difference in Japan in the 1920s.[35] People whom Tilley mentioned were mainly peers or the highest officials. For example, Tokugawa Iyesato, 'unusually fine example of the old territorial nobility'[36], was heir to the last shogun. On the other hand, the names of ordinary people including servants at the ambassador's residence were hardly mentioned.

Tilley seems to have had few friends in Tokyo not only among the Japanese but also among the diplomatic corps. He had known the Belgian ambassador for many years and talked with the American and German ambassadors, but he wrote that he never knew well Paul Claudel, the French Ambassador from 1921–27 and a poet.[37] This situation was very different from the social life of Lampson in Peking, who enjoyed good communication with fellow ministers. Lampson formed a friendship with Yoshizawa Kenkichi, the Japanese Minister to China, and was invited to Yoshizawa's residence several times.[38] On the other hand, Tilley described the life of diplomats as follows:

> It is quite obvious that the relations between an Ambassador and his staff must be something quite different from those between the various members of an office in London, more especially at distant posts. It must be remembered that the idea that diplomats are constantly entertained by the people of the country where they live is generally speaking, entirely fictitious. For one thing,

> apart from official entertainment, it is only in the English-speaking capitals that people habitually entertain, even each other, in their own houses, and since the War this has become more true than ever. Diplomats, therefore, depend chiefly on each other for society.[39]

In his autobiography, Tilley complained about not being invited to Japanese houses, and even when he was invited, he sometimes had to spend tiresome hours because the hosts hardly spoke English.[40]

His communication with the Foreign Secretaries back home was also insufficient. He wrote that he talked with Sir Austen Chamberlain twice and with Arthur Henderson once. 'I did not therefore feel that I had any sort of personal relation with my chiefs. I cannot recollect anything in the nature of a personal letter, and very few private letters of any sort.'[41] His attitude was completely different from that of Eliot and Lampson. Eliot believed that it was his duty to explain the situation in Japan and things Japanese to the Foreign Secretaries, and without expecting answers, continued to write private letters. Lampson worked directly under Chamberlain when the latter was enthusiastically working towards the Locarno Treaty and came to be deeply trusted by him. There were naturally a certain number of private letters exchanged between the two. Lampson was a good writer; both his dispatches and diary are long, detailed and thus useful for historians.

Tilley was fortunate to have many competent staff at the embassy including Sansom. He delegated various tasks to them. For example, when he wrote the general summary of the annual report for the year 1929, he acknowledged that the remaining sections had been written by his staff.[42] Thanks to their capable support, observations sent from Tokyo seem mostly accurate and some are valid even today: The situation of the Diet in those days for example, was described as 'pathetic'. Although manhood universal suffrage was introduced in 1925 and the first general election was held in 1928, a parliament sat only for two months per year, and the impression Tilley gained was that its members were intellectually incapable of discussing any subject of importance intelligently.[43] The education of the public by the press was also considered to be extremely poor, because its criticisms on current events were generally of the feeblest kind. The general public had no other choice but to believe what they read in the papers, because their own knowledge and intellectual powers were limited especially in relation to foreign affairs. They seemed to have taken interest only in matters of local interest.[44]

Slowness of apprehension and decision-making were also noted. Tilley considered this was partly due to a definite fear of being trapped by the Europeans, but he also mentioned other reasons – the temperament, education and the necessity to refer every point to a multiplicity of advisers. Even when the matter had been fully considered, those who should make decisions were inclined to wait further to see how things were going to turn out. No one wanted to take responsibility and turn into a scapegoat. Tilley wrote, 'political and civic courage [the Japanese] have not'.[45]

Another problem Tilley noticed was the low status of women. Women tended to be completely excluded from social gatherings and even when they were allowed to attend some, 'only those who had had a diplomatic training talked at all'. The exception was only when Tilley visited Taiwan in January 1929. A dinner was given for him by the Governor-General and guests included a large number of Japanese, both men and women. He wrote: 'The excitement was that this was the first time that ladies had been included in such a banquet. It was a very friendly gathering.'[46] However, the general situation was not improving. In March 1930, the Ministry of the Imperial Household announced that invitations to the imperial garden parties would, except in the case of diplomats, no longer be sent to unmarried daughters, because the presence of girls on such occasions was a Western custom.[47]

Tilley felt that Westernization and the spread of English culture in Japan was insufficient, but that efforts to assimilate Western civilization were on the decline. On the contrary, he noticed the inclination of reverting to Japanese tradition. In 1927, he wrote that 'hostility to Great Britain' did not arise from the abandonment of the alliance, nor from fear of the British base at Singapore, but from some deeper 'nationalist feeling, not only in favour of Japan for the Japanese, but of Asia for the Asiatics'; and it was as 'the enemy of Asia generally' that the British were looked upon.[48]

He also observed that the system of teaching English to Japanese students was very unsatisfactory, and expressed concern that the Ministry of Education might reduce the hours for the study of foreign languages.[49] In fact he took a keen interest in education and made a number of contributions in this field. It was through his efforts that the Shakespeare medal and a library of beautifully printed books were presented to the Imperial University of Tokyo. He attended oratorical exercises at various schools and universities. His interest encouraged and inspired all those engaged in teaching and learning English. The very successful visit and lecture tour by art-historian and poet Laurence Binyon of the British Museum, who gave a series of lectures, was also largely inspired by Tilley. An exhibition of English water-colours was opened under the supervision of Binyon.[50] However, Tilley later wrote of British visitors to Japan:

> Unfortunately, the Japanese with whom our visitors made friends were the cultivated class, men with wide views of human affairs, whose influence in their own country was diminishing in favour of the ultra-nationalists, who cared nothing for cooperation, intellectual or otherwise with Europeans, unless it could contribute to the aggrandizement of Japan.[51]

Perhaps Tilley was aware that the same could actually be said of himself.

During his stay in Japan, Tilley visited various parts of the country including Kyushu and Wakayama where he was entertained by former daimyos of those regions. In November 1929, he went to Korea, Mukden, Dairen and Peking. In Peking, the Tilleys spent a week with the Lampsons. Tilley also enjoyed his visits to Nikko and Chuzenji, where he revived the use of the Ambassador's summer villa, a two-storied Japanese-style house first used on a regular basis by Sir Ernest Satow when he was Minister to Tokyo in the late 1890s. He claimed to be the one who first started using a car in the region and put an end to the 'pace of the ox', which still to a large extent prevailed in the entire country.[52]

SOME CONCLUDING THOUGHTS

Tilley left Tokyo on the evening of 18 October 1930. On returning to Britain, he retired from the service. After he retired, he wrote two books, *The Foreign Office* and *London and Tokyo.*

Tilley's contribution as British Ambassador to Japan was limited. Although Anglo-Japanese relations improved slightly during his term of office, the improvement was not the result of Tilley's efforts but of the failure of Japan's China policy. Neither did he make any contribution in the same way as such scholar diplomats as Eliot and Sansom. Tilley was an old-fashioned diplomat who took great pride in the superiority of his own country. It was fortunate for him that he left Japan in autumn 1930, because within a year after his departure, Japan started to invade northeastern China. It would probably have been too difficult for a man of Tilley's mediocre diplomatic talents to deal with such a seriously deteriorating situation.

8

Sir Francis Lindley (1872–1950) and Japan

IAN NISH

Sir Francis Lindley

SIR FRANCIS OSWALD LINDLEY (1872–1950) had his exposure to Japan in three doses. He had first been posted there as second secretary between 1905 and 1908 in the heady days of the Anglo-Japanese Alliance, the Japanese victories in the Russo-Japanese War and the excruciating formalities of Britain's Garter Mission to Japan (1906). I have written of this period previously and do not propose to repeat it here.[1] The second immersion was as ambassador in Tokyo from 1931 to 1934, a comparatively short period bearing in mind that it included six months leave in the UK. The third and longest immersion was as chairman of the Council of the Japan Society of London from 1935 to 1949 at a time when political relations between the two countries collapsed and then revived.

In the second of these encounters, Lindley who had just served as ambassador in Lisbon, set off from Southampton via Canada in order to assume his appointment as ambassador in Tokyo in July 1931. He did not take up residence in the ambassador's residence, which was not ready for him after reconstruction following the Kanto earthquake of 1923, but spent most of the summer at the embassy house in the hills at Chuzenji.[2] In an assessment of the situation penned on his return to Tokyo on 2 September, he wrote that the Japanese government of the day wanted to avoid friction with the Nanking government and were vacillating over Manchuria. He predicted: 'I shall not have a great deal to do here.'[3] I quote this to illustrate how the actions of the Imperial Japanese Army which were about to take place on 18 September came to the British Embassy as a surprise. It is arguable that the army had been skilful in keeping its intentions secret and taking the Japanese government and the various embassies by surprise. Within two months of reaching Japan, Lindley was faced by a serious local crisis between China and Japan over the latter's treaty rights in northeast China, generally known as Manchuria, and this escalated into an international crisis which involved not only the Powers individually but also the League of Nations as a peace-making organization. Sir Francis, so far from being idle, suddenly became the most active of British diplomats overseas and had to try to interpret the delicate balance of forces struggling for the upper hand in Japan and forecast the outcome of the power struggle.

Lindley has been summed up in an affectionate assessment: 'He was a rather tough old character in some respects and very outspoken in his likes and dislikes.'[4] Undoubtedly, he brought to his post considerable experience as a diplomat and had had tough postings, mainly in Europe. Most notably he had been in Riga at the time of the Bolshevik takeover and was left in charge of the embassy after the withdrawal of Sir George Buchanan. This experience had given him a deep suspicion of Soviet Russia (as it later became). He saw it as expansionist and as Britain's main global problem. He then served successively as Minister to Austria (1919–20), Greece (1922–3) and Norway (1923–9) and Ambassador to Portugal (1929–31).

He had had no experience of the United States and was sceptical about its ambitions in the East. The United States had during the 1920s taken over from Britain the role of the major outside player in the Japanese economy and society. Lindley deplored the fact that cricket, 'our national game', was 'in a less satisfactory condition in Japan' and had symbolically been displaced by the loathsome baseball.[5] Though he remained on good terms with W. Cameron Forbes and Joseph C. Grew, successive American ambassadors in Tokyo, he seems to have been convinced that it was the inclination of administrations in Washington to strike poses in East Asia without any intention to see things through and to rely on Britain 'to carry the baby'.

His likes and dislikes were vocally expressed. He was not favourable to the Foreign Office as an institution and was courageous in defending his views versus the mandarins in Whitehall. He had never had a desk in the Office and so was not overawed by officials there. He thought that ministers and top officials in Whitehall were distinctly lacking in experience of East Asia and in the understanding of countries there. Sir Esler Dening would later state quite openly that the ignorance and gullibility of the Foreign Office was a standing joke.[6]

Lindley belonged to that group in the Foreign Service who were profoundly sceptical of the League of Nations, of collective security as a means of preventing war and of the use of sanctions against an aggressor. He had disliked it long before he set foot in Japan and was to distrust it more when he saw the way in which the League's councils and committees handled the Manchurian Crisis, which was developing. In private correspondence he railed against Whitehall for its unquestioning acceptance of impracticable League principles. Moreover, Lindley was critical of Sir Miles Lampson, his colleague at Peking, for encouraging China to rely on the League and building up her expectations.

MANCHURIAN COMPLICATIONS

The Manchurian Crisis matured quickly. Firstly, the Japanese Kwantung army pushed out from Mukden, the focus of Japan's rail network, occupying Chinese cities in all directions with scarcely any long-lasting opposition. Secondly, the Chinese appealed to the League of Nations in Geneva, converting a local issue into an international one in a way that greatly embarrassed the Japanese government. Just as China's Nationalist government did not really control affairs in Manchuria, Tokyo was not able to control its own military there. Moreover, Japan was not especially adept at operating within the procedures of the League. Such were the difficulties with which Lindley was confronted.

For Lindley the embarrassment increased when the League passed a resolution on 24 October calling on the armies of both Japan and China to pull back from occupied territory within a prescribed time limit. Britain as one of the leaders of the League was understood to have devised these proposals. Evacuation was unacceptable to the Japanese who were known to oppose the resolution. Moreover, there were rumours circulating around the League that Japan's action warranted the application of sanctions. Lindley's problem was that he was not privy to the attitude of the British Government on this resolution, which had been prepared and sponsored by the French. He had to assume that it had the backing of London and was promoted by the substitute British representative on the League, Lord Robert Cecil.

The Japanese, both official and the media, were also of that impression, taking a very hostile narrow view of Britain's attitude. The more extreme among them were already talking of leaving the League. Lindley was alarmed at the hostility of the Japanese press and the political power of the military party, which was determined to resist sanctions. He felt exposed to personal criticism on two grounds: firstly, that the British government was anti-Japanese because France and the United States had dressed up their criticisms of Japanese actions more tactfully; and secondly, that he personally must have been misinforming and misadvising London. This was of course unfair because he did not agree with the alleged British line, which Japan was condemning. He was to be placed in an awkward position for the rest of the crisis, satisfying neither his home government nor the government to which he was accredited.

In fact, the Foreign Office was not too far removed from Lindley's position. In reality Whitehall officials thought that there was not a remote possibility of sanctions. When the National Government was reformed in November with Sir John Simon as Foreign Secretary, Lindley was courageous enough to write of 'the naïve follies of Reading and Cecil' - the previous ministers. For the rest of the crisis he continued in his private correspondence to the court and ministers, fulminating against a government which seemed to have followed Cecil's views rather than his own.[7] Lindley was also paranoid about Henry L. Stimson's statement of 7 January 1932 declaring Japan's actions to be unacceptable to Washington but making clear that he was unwilling to do anything about it. This confirmed Lindley's prejudices against the United States.

The next problem was Shanghai, which was occupied (apart from the International Settlement) by Japanese armies in February 1932. Lindley feared that the world Powers might take offensive naval action and get into conflict with Japan on Chinese soil in a way that naval Powers could never win. He again took a serious view of the danger: 'a false step might precipitate catastrophe'. External criticism of Japan's actions would only harden opinion in favour of the army and navy; a tough international stance would play into the hands of the Japanese. Lindley reassured London that Japan had probably stumbled into a situation at Shanghai where her prestige was at stake and was not seeking territory in central China. On what grounds he made that claim is not clear. But, luckily for him, the incident was brought to a negotiated settlement in May by the skilful use of international diplomacy under the auspices of the League. Lindley was right that the Shanghai crisis was a sideshow but it was good luck for him that his projection that the Japanese would be restrained in their actions turned out to be correct.

Lindley's advice led to accusations in Britain that he was becoming pro-Japanese in his judgements. His Tokyo colleagues and acquaintances did not accept this. Nor did his old friend, the American ambassador, Joseph Grew, who had known him in pre-1914 days during postings in Cairo. Grew always spoke of 'good old Lindley' whom he regarded as robust and realistic in his judgements.[8] While on one occasion he earned a stern rebuke, the Foreign Office by and large took a tolerant view of Lindley's effusions, concluding that he was over-wrought and was affected by his anti-League bias and his anxieties about Soviet Russia.

British representatives at Tokyo and Peking appear to have been fairly confident that the aim of the Japanese General Staff at the end of their campaign in Jehol was to round off its position in Manchuria (now renamed Manchukuo) rather than to embark on an invasion of northern China. This minimalist view of Japanese ambitions suited Britain and the British Empire. If Japan confined herself to the north of the Great Wall, she was likely to present less of a threat to Britain's colonies.

Nonetheless, the West felt that Japan should be taught a lesson. Under the severe pressure of public opinion, the British cabinet decided on 27 February 1933 to discontinue the supply of munitions to Japan and also even-handedly to China. The limited arms embargo did not attract the support of any other Power and was eventually withdrawn a fortnight later on 13 March. Lindley commented that, as seen from Tokyo, the embargo policy held nothing but disadvantages for Britain; the situation he faced would be easier were it known by the public that sanctions were out of the question. Another proposal, which followed soon after, was that the Powers should withdraw their ambassadors from Tokyo. Asked to comment, Lindley wrote: 'I cannot sufficiently deplore the proposal which will do nothing but harm. Anything in form of a rebuke would be deeply resented by Japan.'[9] He was so convinced of Japan's strength that he was opposed to any international attempts to discipline her.

MANCHURIAN AFTERMATH

In the resolution finally adopted by the League in February 1933, Japan was mildly criticized but some criticisms were reserved for China. This was merely a tap on the wrist for Japan. But she did not like to be criticized internationally and retaliated by giving notice of leaving the League of Nations. Her relations, therefore, became frosty with all the powers: hostile to the League and to Britain by extension. Lindley was embarrassed. In a letter unprecedented for an ambassador to write, he regretted that he had failed to bring home to

London 'the peculiarities of the case which political prudence, common sense and above all a regard for British interests demanded ... I blame myself grievously for my failure to convince HM Government of the risks they were running by allowing matters to take their course according to the fixed and immutable principles of the League. I now find myself faced with the imminent danger, if not the actual probability, of the supreme failure of not having prevented a disastrous and avoidable conflict with the country to which I am accredited.'[10]

Once a ceasefire in the area had been established, the Foreign Office privately examined the criticism that Lindley's Embassy in Tokyo had been pro-Japanese throughout the crisis as many were saying. This seeped through to Tokyo. George Sansom, the Commercial Counsellor, defended the Tokyo embassy's views resolutely.[11] This was supported by W. R. Connor Green who had previously served in Tokyo but had returned to the Japan desk in London. He reversed the criticism, writing that, when he had been in Lindley's embassy, 'we were never given any indications as to what if any was HMG's policy ... The Embassy tried to point out exactly what was going to happen. We were right every time.' This was a bold defence even if one that the historian can scarcely accept today. Over Japan's intentions at Shanghai and Jehol the Embassy was fortunate to get it right.[12]

In mid-April 1933 Lindley who had not taken leave between Lisbon and Tokyo spent six months in Britain. He had the expected consultations with the Japanese ambassador. He drew up an important memorandum for the cabinet on the Far Eastern situation on 20 May. He also met Neville Chamberlain, the Chancellor of the Exchequer and strongest member of the cabinet, and seems to have told him that, if Japan could not settle her people in China, there would be trouble in British colonies. This idea, which was not unique to Lindley, impressed some leaders; and his views are quoted at meetings of the Committee of Imperial Defence.[13]

The impression that Lindley was on an evangelizing mission found its way to Tokyo. Lady Sansom wrote that he had been doing some mighty spade-work and she was amused at 'the picture of the delightful man [Lindley] with his understanding of Japan's sheer necessities and forceful trading habits, stumping up and down the Office'. The impression he left in Whitehall is buried in the archives. The fact that he returned to his post for a mere three months is also something of a mystery. He reached Tokyo around Christmas 1933 and presented a message of British goodwill from the Foreign Secretary to the newly appointed Foreign Minister of Japan, Hirota Koki. This was of course reciprocated. Nothing particular happened after his return. But it was with some relief that Lindley was able to report that Britain had reverted to the 'well-tried policy of making friendly relations with Japan the cornerstone of our Far Eastern policy'.[14]

A COUNTRY RETIREMENT

After a bout of illness, Lindley left Tokyo for good on 28 April 1934. He had his final audience as Ambassador with King George V on 2 June 1934. Though he had earlier entertained hopes of being offered a final post in 'a good European embassy',[15] he gladly went into retirement one week later. He felt, he wrote, liberated from the stultifying atmosphere of 'The Office': 'I can't describe my joy at being quit of the Foreign Office and all its works for good. Bureaucrats are top dog and it is impossible to get anything done.'[16]

Others thought his retirement was a waste of resources. Sir Samuel Hoare, formerly Secretary of State for India and currently Foreign Secretary, expressed his regret at Lindley's departure from public service: 'he retired from public life far too soon! He has decided to retire to Hampshire; instead of which, he could still be devoting his valuable services to the Empire.' This may be a tell-tale remark, indicating Lindley's reputation for conservatism and his undoubted dedication to the long-term interests of the British Empire.[17]

At this point, it seems appropriate to offer some assessment of Lindley's professional career in Japan. Among his strongest admirers were the Sansoms. George Sansom, who was a senior and highly regarded member of Lindley's embassy, was interviewed by Professor Allan Nevins at Palo Alto on 11 June 1957. He said that Lindley's good point as ambassador was that he 'used his experience and kept his temper'. Interviewed on this subject following the Suez crisis of 1956, Sansom drew a contemporary parallel. He said that Lindley's approach was in marked contrast to that of the protagonists of the 1956 crisis, namely Anthony Eden, John Foster Dulles and even President Dwight Eisenhower. He kept his cool and held his tongue.

Lady Sansom spelt out Lindley's virtues in even greater detail:

> … what a superb public servant he was. And particularly valuable here in these last years when it was advisable to keep a wary eye on America whose policy as a rule has been neither good nor bad but simply all over the place in partial enthusiasms. That we the British should not be left carrying the baby may not sound a noble aim, but by Jove! it was practical enough. And in such matters Sir Francis was throughout able and shrewd and courageous.[18]

Retirement was alien to Lindley's vigorous nature. He was still active at the age of 62 and mapped out a new life for himself. On the one hand, he settled in the rural paradise of the Weir House, Old Alresford, Hampshire. There he indulged his passion for fishing and became the chairman of the Test and Itchen fishing association. He was interested in country pursuits, becoming from 1943 an official verderer of the New Forest.

JAPAN SOCIETY OF LONDON

While Lindley took on some responsibility as Chairman of the Anglo-Portuguese Society, his prime task in retirement was that of Chairman of the Council of the Japan Society of London in 1935 in succession to the merchant banker, Charles Sale. He was to continue in office until 1949. Since Lindley's tenure in Tokyo was relatively short, his contribution to Anglo-Japanese relations comes equally from these Japan Society years. This was likely to be a difficult assignment because the Society had been riven apart by the Manchurian crisis. Some of its members had forced it to discuss whether it should play an increasingly positive political role in favour of Japan. While some leaders had favoured this course, others including the chairman were against it, because it ran counter to the constitution.[19]

Instead, that issue passed and problems of a different kind arose. Early in his term of office there was held a landmark conference in the history of naval disarmament, one of the important initiatives of the interwar period. The Japan Society, which had a tradition of offering hospitality to delegations visiting London, proposed to hold a dinner in honour of the Japanese delegates to the London Naval Conference. The dinner was fixed for Claridges on 20 January 1936, right in the middle of the conference. Unfortunately, the Japanese visitors under instructions from their government had a week earlier pulled out of the conference and refused to accept any international mechanisms for restricting naval building. The dilemma, which this presented for the dinner, was a challenge for Lindley's digestion. But he handled the situation with considerable aplomb. In welcoming the guests, he was in sprightly mood and said 'No reporters being present, one can say what one likes.' (This alas was a misapprehension because his remarks were quoted in the papers the next day.) Later in his speech he is reported as saying *sub specie aeternitatis* as it were:

> It did not do to take the withdrawal of the Japanese Delegation from the Naval Conference tragically. The speaker has seen too many conferences end in smoke to be in the least depressed by the partial failure of this one. At the same time, all regretted the withdrawal, and he could assure the Delegates that their further participation in the Conference would be heartily welcomed. He expected that good work would still be done.

Admiral Nagano, one of the chief delegates, said in reply that 'in the present Naval Conference our proposal for a sweeping reduction of armaments having unfortunately failed to gain the support of the other Delegations, there has been left for us no other choice than to leave the Conference'. But he assured the audience that Japan was 'not embarking upon a policy which tends to disturb the general peace and, particularly, the good relations now subsisting between our two Empires.'

From this point onwards Anglo-Japanese relations deteriorated and Lindley as Chairman of the Council may have played an important part in slowing the rate of deterioration by explaining Japan's thinking to the British people and offering advice and hospitality to Japan's diplomats. He welcomed Yoshida Shigeru who became Ambassador to London during the summer of 1936. Recalling his days as ambassador Yoshida on 30 April 1959 described Lindley as 'my very dear and very old friend' who had established the '*family tradition* of cultivating friendship and goodwill between Japan and Britain' (my italics). This last refers to Lindley's widespread family connections. He had three married daughters who are mentioned gratefully in Japanese memoirs as welcoming Japanese guests. They were equally welcoming to Shigemitsu Mamoru, the Japanese Ambassador from 1938 to 1941.[20]

CONTRIBUTIONS TO THE MEDIA

Perhaps because of his friendship with Geoffrey Dawson, the editor of the *Times* from 1923 to 1941, Lindley became a fearless controversialist in the letters columns of that paper. This was not solely on Japan. Lady Sansom, observing the scene from Tokyo, wrote that: 'Lindley was writing furious letters to the press *on the situation in general*'. (my italics) He wrote frequent letters on Spain and Portugal, but particularly on the League of Nations and the unwisdom of sanctions. He acquired a considerable reputation as a correspondent of a conservative bent. When he became a parliamentary candidate for the Combined English Universities seat in the National Liberal interest at a by-election, he was even more inclined to cultivate the media. He was nonetheless defeated in February 1937 with vote of 4,952 against the Independent Progressive (Liberal) candidate who gained 6,596.

Naturally, he was also in demand to comment on Japan, partially in criticism and partially in explanation of Japanese institutions and attitudes. His attitude was generally to explain but not to reproach. A good example comes after the notorious incident of an army mutiny on 26 February 1936 in Tokyo. He gave a talk on the BBC (British Broadcasting Corporation), trying to explain the Japanese perspective on the mutiny by the Imperial Japanese Army and its attempts to assassinate several major Japanese politicians, including an abortive attempt at killing the prime minister:

> The habit of political assassination is a grave danger to any country, and it is, I consider - and my opinion is shared by a large number of intelligent Japanese - the greatest blot on Japanese civilisation at the present time. But whilst we all condemn it, we ought also to make an effort to understand the circumstances which give rise to it, and this can only be done if we look for a moment at the history and traditions of Japan [in respect of violence.] … These young officers who have murdered [some of the best men in Japan] had become imbued with the idea that their country was being led astray by the example of such statesmen; was being led away from those ancient traditions which had made the country great, and encouraged in a way of living and to follow ideals which were incompatible with the future which these so-called patriots had mapped out for their country. That their ideas were wrong-headed and impervious to reason has little to do with the case. Fanatics are wrong-headed and impervious to reason by their very nature. They fail to see that it is possible that their judgement may be completely erroneous and that so far from doing their country a service by their violence, they are inflicting upon it a very grave injury.[21]

He was also an author. In 1928 early in his career he had written his autobiography *A Diplomat off Duty,* which showed the benefits of a diplomatic career for a good all-round sportsman. In 1935 he published a biography of his brother-in-law, Lord Lovat. He also wrote political works such as the tract '*The legacy of Spain*' which seemed to condone the activities of General Franco and Dr Salazar in Portugal:

> There is no reason to suppose that General Franco is a Fascist. As far as one can judge, he is cast in the very Spanish mould of General Primo [de Rivera]. It has long been the practice of the Bolshevists and their admirers here to appeal to the simple-minded by dubbing their enemies Fascists … That there are some Fascists in General Franco's forces is probable, though Fascism is neither an article of export nor suited to the Spanish character. But the bulk of his forces outside the regular soldiers, Moorish and Spanish, is quite obviously composed of ordinary people who are there either because their religious feelings are outraged or because their relations and friends have been

> murdered and they know that they would suffer the same fate themselves if the 'Legitimate Government' prevailed ...[22]

With the coming of war in Europe, Britain's purpose was to remain on good enough terms with Japan to prevent her becoming a belligerent. This made Lindley's responsibilities at the Japan Society more sensitive. He discussed with the Foreign Office in 1940 his position as chairman in the event of war, interestingly anticipating that such a contingency would take place earlier than it did by 18 months. He circulated a letter in May 1942 suspending the operations of the Society. Subscriptions were stopped; and its library was put into storage.

When peace was restored, Lindley was involved with the appeal to General Douglas MacArthur for clemency to be shown to Shigemitsu Mamoru, the last pre-war Japanese ambassador in London and later wartime Foreign Minister who was under sentence as a war criminal at the International Military Tribunal for the Far East (IMTFE). While he was not the main promoter of this, he associated himself with those who had known Shigemitsu well in his London years: R.A. Butler, Sir Robert Craigie, Sir Edward Crowe, Arthur H.F. Edwardes, Howell Arthur Gwynne, Lord Hankey, Major-General F.S.G. Piggott and Lord Sempill. While the appeal was not successful, Shigemitsu was duly released on parole in 1950 and resumed a political career.

On 2 March 1949 a meeting of Trustees agreed to revive the Japan Society. Lindley presided over an extraordinary general meeting of over 100 members on 28 September at the Royal Society of Arts, which confirmed this. Soon he found it necessary to retire owing to advancing age and his place as Chairman of the Council was taken by Sir Robert Craigie. His wife died in 1949 and Sir Francis died at Alresford on 17 August 1950 aged 78 and was buried in the churchyard there.

ASSESSMENT

I have already written my assessment of Lindley the diplomat, I should in conclusion speak of Lindley the man. Ambassador Ohno Katsumi, one of Japan's post-war ambassadors, said that Lindley: 'won great affection and respect from Japanese people not because he was British ambassador, but because he was Francis Lindley the man'. He was obviously a larger-than-life individualist, a robust character with an irrepressible zest for living. The impression he gave was of being a person friendly, patient and welcoming. Professionally this 'enabled him on many occasions to gain his ends without any rancour left behind, where subtler and more calculated methods would in all probability have failed'. He had a much wider perspective on the world than many others and did not take himself too seriously. He often expressed the view -presumably rather unfashionable for diplomats - 'that the only thing worse than a military defeat was a diplomatic victory'.[23]

This quality is neatly illustrated by the light-hearted poem he wrote in the form of a hymn to be sung by bureaucrats which reveals a mischievous *joie de vivre*:

Thou who seest all things below
Grant that Thy Servants may go slow
That they may study to comply
With regulations till they die.

Teach us Lord to reverence
Committees more than common sense.
Impress our minds to make no plan
But pass the baby when we can.
And when the tempter seems to give
Us feelings of initiative,
Or when alone we go too far
Chastise us with a circular.

Mid war and tumult, fire and storms
Strengthen us we pray with forms.
Thus will Thy Servants ever be
A flock of perfect sheep for Thee.

The fact that this 'hymn for use in government departments' is treasured in the Foreign Office archives demonstrates a commendable broad-mindedness.[24]

Ambassador Ohno summed up Francis Lindley by saying that he knew 'all the good and the bad about Japan and the Japanese'.[25] Japan was the summit of Lindley's career and, though it was not his only interest in retirement, it was important to him. It would be wrong to say of him that he was pro-Japanese or anti-Japanese, but he was more sympathetic to Japan than most of his generation. While those in Whitehall were striving to make the League work by giving it teeth, Lindley gave priority to realism and pragmatism. He was always looking to British interests and the interests of the British Empire. This suited his conservative bent and strongly anti-Communist disposition.

9

Sir Robert Clive, 1877–1948: British Ambassador to Japan, 1934–37

ANTHONY BEST

Sir Robert Clive

SIR ROBERT CLIVE holds a curious position in the history of Anglo-Japanese relations, for although the period in which he was ambassador to Japan has been the object of much study, the man himself remains a mystery.[1] This is particularly so when he is compared to those who preceded and followed him as ambassador to Japan, Sir Francis Lindley and Sir Robert Craigie. The reason for his relative anonymity is not difficult to explain. Unlike Lindley and Craigie, he did not spend much of his time in Tokyo arguing with the Foreign Office or with his British counterpart in China.[2] These may have been years of diplomatic fluidity but they were not ones of controversy between the British Embassy and London.

Sir Robert Clive was born in 1877 and entered the Foreign Office in 1903. He first went to Japan from 1905 to 1909 as Third Secretary at the Tokyo Embassy and then had further East Asian experience as the Counsellor at the Peking Legation from 1920 to 1923. Prior to his term as Ambassador to Japan he had served for a long period as the Minister to Tehran, where he had successfully negotiated an end to the British extraterritorial regime in Persia.

Clive arrived in Tokyo in July 1934 at a difficult time in Anglo-Japanese relations. Since the final act of the Manchurian Crisis when Britain had initiated a month-long arms embargo against both Japan and China relations between London and Tokyo had become tense. The central issue was the inability of Britain and Japan to agree about the future of China, notably because Japan was seeking to implement its own Monroe Doctrine in East Asia, which would allow it a veto over Western dealings with the Chinese. Another pressing problem was the rise of antagonism between the two countries over trade issues. A huge surge of Japanese exports into the British colonies in Asia, including India, had led to an outcry from textile producers and the protectionist lobby in Britain and accordingly quotas had been introduced to curb Japan's incursion. This in turn provided ammunition for those in Japan who sought to whip up anti-Western sentiment and a raison d'être for the desire to create an economic sphere of influence in East Asia. As if these were not enough another contentious issue was rapidly coming to the fore, the future of the naval limitation process that the United States, Britain and Japan had initiated at the Washington conference in 1921/22.

At the same time, however, there were countervailing forces in operation that sought to dampen down the burgeoning ill feeling. In London the development of the threat from Nazi Germany had led some politicians and officials, particularly the Chancellor of the Exchequer, Neville Chamberlain, and his civil servants in the Treasury, to conclude that Britain could ill-afford tensions with Japan and they were thus interested in cultivating a rapprochement. Similar thoughts were entertained in some quarters in Tokyo where there was an interest in finding common ground over China and a mechanism that would allow Japan naval equality in principle with Britain and the United States. However, not all were sanguine about the prospects of renewed friendship; most notably the Foreign Office in London felt that Britain had to proceed cautiously in its dealings with Japan lest it offend China and the United States. This then was the complex environment within which Clive had to work.

Before he could even become acclimatized the fluid nature of Anglo-Japanese relations plunged Clive into the middle of a controversy. In his first meeting with the Japanese Foreign Minister, Hirota Kōki, on 5 July 1934 the latter raised the possibility of Japan signing non-aggression pacts with Britain and the United States in order to pave the way for an agreement over naval limitation. This overture provoked much debate in London about whether Britain should use this opportunity to orchestrate a rapprochement, an episode that has been extensively analysed by historians such as Ann Trotter, Hosoya Chihiro, and Gill Bennett.[3] Clive's role in these events was largely to act as a messenger and to try under orders from the Cabinet to get Hirota to elaborate on his proposals. His efforts were in vain, and the whole affair seems to have heightened his innate caution.

His suspicion of the Japanese was further reinforced by the welcome provided by the Japanese to the mission sent by the Federation of British Industry (FBI) in September and October 1934 to investigate the potential for British trade and investment in Manchukuo. The FBI mission was unofficial and supposed to deal solely with commercial issues, but the Japanese government and media treated it as if had a political purpose much to the embarrassment of the British Embassy. The most problematic aspect of the mission was that on its arrival in Japan Clive discovered to his horror that an audience had been arranged for its members with the Emperor. Clive's initial reaction was to prevent the audience from going ahead but once it was clear that this would mortally offend the Japanese he demurred.[4] However, this episode, added to the artificially cordial atmosphere cultivated by the Japanese, aroused his distrust. At first glance it might appear that he was allowing an adherence to traditional diplomatic formality to cloud his judgement, and that he should have welcomed this outpouring of Japanese affection which was surely just what Britain needed at this juncture. However, what Clive surmised, perhaps under the prompting of his astute Commercial Counsellor, George Sansom [later Sir George], was that there was no real substance to Japan's words of friendship beyond a desire to persuade Britain to accept a subordinate position in East Asia.[5]

After this baptism of fire and with his wariness duly reinforced, Clive settled down to a more normal routine. Over the next two and a half years he became a careful observer of the political scene in Japan, although by his own admission he found Japanese thinking difficult to understand. In November 1935 he noted in exasperation to King George V's private secretary, Sir Clive Wigram:

> The inner workings of the Japanese are often beyond our comprehension and one learns with time never to judge these people by our own standards or to expect them to react as we should.[6]

In regard to British policy towards Japan Clive did his best to make sure that Britain steered a middle course neither engaging in outright appeasement nor leaning towards the construction of an anti-Japanese bloc with the United States. In January 1935 following Japan's abrogation of the Washington and London naval limitation treaties he produced a lengthy and strongly worded despatch in which he opposed the view recently propounded by Lord Lothian that Britain should draw closer to the United States. Instead he argued that Britain should seek to use its long-standing ties to Japan, such as memory of the alliance, to act as a 'moderating influence' and to see whether Hirota's vague overtures could be made into something more substantial.[7] This analysis was well received in the Foreign Office. Indeed the Permanent Under-Secretary at the Foreign Office, Sir Robert Vansittart, who resented the intrusion of amateurs such as Lothian, praised Clive's professionalism and ordered that the ambassador's views should be circulated to the Cabinet.[8]

However, it was not easy to follow such a balanced policy, as ironically the enthusiasts for rapprochement in both countries tended to make progress more rather than less difficult. The problem with the Treasury was that its enthusiasm for a deal with Japan clouded its judgement. Notably in the autumn of 1935 Chamberlain sent out the government's chief economic adviser, Sir Frederick Leith-Ross, to assist the Chinese with currency reform and attempted to link this endeavour to a political settlement of the region's political problems by proposing that Britain and Japan should offer a loan to China in exchange for Chinese recognition of Manchukuo. In September 1935 Leith-Ross arrived in Tokyo and attempted to sell this idea to the Japanese, but neither the Foreign Ministry nor the Finance Ministry were interested. In a state of disappointment he then proceeded to China where he again flew the recognition kite, only for it to be shot down by a firm Chinese rebuff. This sort of amateur diplomacy did not impress Clive and during a visit to Shanghai in November to meet the British Ambassador to China, Sir Alexander Cadogan, he informed the latter of his fury about the whole business.[9]

On the Japanese side there were also elements that strove for better Anglo-Japanese relations but here, too, the approach, as far as Clive was concerned, was fundamentally flawed. The leading Japanese figure in 1936/37 pressing for a rapprochement was the new Ambassador to Britain, Yoshida Shigeru. From the first Clive was not enthralled by the prospect of Yoshida in such a key position. In March 1936 on learning of the latter's appointment Clive noted in a letter to Wigram, now the private secretary to Edward VIII, that Yoshida was 'a very agreeable smiling little man' but that he was not of the calibre of his esteemed predecessor, Matsudaira Tsuneo.[10] Clive's fears about Yoshida's judgement were confirmed in the autumn of 1936 when he learnt that the latter was, without explicit approval from Tokyo, attempting to interest Britain in an over-arching settlement of all problems in Anglo-Japanese relations. Afraid that Britain might take Yoshida seriously Clive sent a number of warnings to the Foreign

Office, stating that the new ambassador was not so influential in Tokyo and that he had only been sent to London to save his face after the Imperial Japanese Army (IJA) had vetoed his appointment as Foreign Minister in March 1936.[11]

Clive may therefore have had some hopes that a settlement of Anglo-Japanese difficulties was possible but he was not prepared to support rushed and ill-conceived diplomacy to support such a goal. Moreover, from late 1935 to 1937 his belief in the need for caution was reinforced by a revival of Japanese bellicosity both by its rhetoric about its foreign relations generally and by its policy towards China. In particular the IJA's support for the autonomy of north China and for the smuggling of Japanese goods into this region, thus evading paying duty to the Chinese Maritime Customs, suggested that there was little point in expecting Japan to negotiate reasonably. In addition, Clive was outraged in October 1936 when a number of Royal Navy ratings visiting the port of Keelung in Formosa were arrested and then beaten by Japanese police. Clive believed that this incident was symptomatic of Japanese arrogance and its lack of respect for British interests and was therefore convinced that Britain should push hard to achieve a satisfactory settlement of this incident, which he hoped would bring the Japanese to their senses. Indeed, in this episode he took a harsher line than the Foreign Office and feared that his forthright refusal to compromise might have annoyed the latter.[12]

Clive's increasingly tough stance towards Japan had both its admirers and detractors. Among the former was the Commander-in-Chief China station, Admiral Sir Charles Little, who noted approvingly to the First Sea Lord, Admiral Sir Ernle Chatfield, in July 1936 that Clive recognized that the only language that the Japanese understood was force.[13] The Foreign Office also generally approved of Clive's actions and assessments, which were much in line with its own thinking. However those in Britain who longed for a return to Anglo-Japanese friendship saw Clive as failing to take advantage of some crucial feelers from the Japanese and therefore acting as an obstacle to their goal. In his diary entry for 3 March 1936 the Japanophile former army language officer and Reuters journalist in Japan, Malcolm Kennedy, noted that during a lunch he had with two prominent supporters of close Anglo-Japanese relations, H.A. Gwynne, the editor of the *Morning Post*, and Arthur Edwardes, the financial adviser to the Manchukuo government, Clive had been heavily criticized. All three men had lamented the fact that Clive had recently turned down an offer from the IJA to provide a 1,000 man guard of honour at the ceremony to commemorate the recent death of George V, and noted that he had also blundered over the FBI mission's audience with the Japanese Emperor in September 1934.[14]

Divisions also existed within the embassy in Tokyo. In 1935 the War Office decided that in the interests of better Anglo-Japanese relations it would appoint the stridently Japanophile Major-General F.S.G. Piggott as its military attaché. Clive was not impressed with this choice on the grounds that 'It might be embarrassing to have on my staff an officer on whose judgement I could not rely and with whom I might differ on broad questions of policy.'[15] Unfortunately, the War Office was adamant and Piggott duly took up his post in the summer of 1936. Almost immediately his views began to clash with those of Clive, for Piggott was convinced that the general mood within the IJA favoured a rapprochement with Britain. Clive was prepared to acknowledge that the IJA's mood might have recently improved but, drawing on the opinion of the vastly more experienced Sansom, he argued that this did not by any means suggest that an agreement was practicable, for any terms acceptable to Japan would necessarily offend China and the United States.[16] Clearly, Clive felt that of his Japanese experts, Sansom and Piggott, the former was by far the more reliable and after his return to London in the summer of 1937 he lobbied for Sansom to be promoted as a means of ensuring that he stayed in Tokyo.[17]

Towards the end of his tour of duty Clive again became more optimistic about the prospects for Anglo-Japanese relations. This had nothing do with the machinations of the Treasury, Yoshida or Piggott, but was rather linked to the appearance of Satō Naotake as the Japanese Foreign Minister in March 1937. Clive had a high opinion of Satō and believed that he was a genuine Anglophile who would work for real reconciliation. He felt, however, that Satō had to be allowed to bring around the IJA in his own time and that Britain could not and should not try to force the pace of events by making any ill-timed overtures.[18] Given time and latitude Clive believed that Sato could achieve a great deal; he noted to the head of the Far Eastern Department, Charles Orde, in March 1937 that 'my own view about the immediate future is that the Japanese are likely to be less aggressive and more amenable to reason than they have been in the last few years'.[19]

Clive's time as ambassador came to an end in May 1937 immediately after the coronation of George VI. On his departure Japan appeared to be clawing its way back from international isolation and seemed ready to engage in talks with Britain on a basis of equality. Such hopes were, however, soon to be dashed, for the government of which Sato was a member collapsed at the end of the month and in July 1937 fighting broke out in north China. Clive's optimism thus proved to be woefully misplaced. The Sino-Japanese War would lead to new, even more serious problems in Anglo-Japanese relations, but

Clive had now bequeathed these to his successor, Sir Robert Craigie. Clive did not, however, throw off the Japanese yoke entirely, for he soon found in November 1937 that his new posting, Brussels, was to be home to an abortive conference to end the Sino-Japanese hostilities.

Sir Robert Clive thus took the helm in Anglo-Japanese relations in a particularly difficult period. The overall impression that Clive gives is of a diplomat who was very much in tune with the thinking of the Foreign Office. He was a cautious man who wanted diplomacy handled in the traditional channels or not at all. He did not dismiss the chance that Anglo-Japanese rapprochement was possible but at the same time felt that it could not be forced or hurried. As such he appears as the quintessential careful diplomat and as a man deserving of the description given him in the *Dictionary of National Biography*, namely that he was 'a superb public servant'.[20] Whether Britain needed a more dynamic figure who was less likely to toe the Foreign Office line remains however a matter of debate.

PART 2

Businessmen

10

William Keswick, 1835–1912: Jardine's Pioneer in Japan

J. E. HOARE

William Keswick

WILLIAM KESWICK was an important figure in Jardine-Matheson's role in China and Japan, and in the London-based Matheson and Company, from the mid-nineteenth century onwards until his death in 1912, yet he has scarcely received the attention that might have been expected from this long involvement in East Asian trade. He is curiously absent from the current *Dictionary of National Biography*, though several of his Jardines' relations are so honoured. His *Who was Who* entry, based on his own account of himself, is amazingly brief, omitting both his wives, and what many would see as his major role in the China Association, for example, though noting his one-time membership of the Hong Kong Legislative Council. His role as a Conservative MP from 1899 and his appointment as JP and High Sheriff for Surrey receive as much prominence as his work in Asia. His years in Japan, where he established Jardine's presence immediately after the 1858 treaties allowed foreign residence, go wholly unnoticed.

William Keswick was born on 1 January 1835, according to his *Who was Who* entry, though most sources say 1834, in the Scottish lowlands. A nephew of William Jardine, he attended Merchiston's school in Edinburgh, and went out to China in 1855, the first of five generations of the Keswick family to be associated with Jardines. His younger brother, James Johnstone Keswick, also joined the company in China. By that stage, Jardine, Matheson, which can trace its origins back to 1782 and a bewildering collection of intermediate names, was well-established on the Chinese coast, though faced with major rivals such as Dent and Company, and was distancing itself from its early role in the more questionable aspects of the China trade.[1]

Naturally enough, Jardines was interested in the new trading possibilities opening up in East Asia in the 1850s, as the pressure increased on Japan to abandon its isolation. Before the treaties permitted formal trade with Japan, Jardines had traded in Japanese products usually through the Ryukyu Islands or Taiwan, although there was also contact with Chinese merchants established at Nagasaki. The trade, officially forbidden by the Japanese authorities, was always small, but no doubt it served to whet appetites.[2]

The earliest treaties with Japan, concluded by United States' and British naval officers in 1853 and 1854, had been little concerned with trade. Supplying ships and coaling stations were at the forefront of the sailors' minds, not the needs of merchants; the latter had to wait for later treaties, beginning with the Dutch and Russian treaties of 1857. These allowed trade at Nagasaki and the northern port of Hakodate. Using these treaties, Western merchants from the China coast began to test the Japanese market. Not surprisingly, Jardines, increasingly seen as among the principal China coast traders, was among these pioneers.

William Keswick, now just 24, first visited Nagasaki on a Jardines' ship in January 1859, returning again in March 1859. He was impressed by the Japan trade's potential, although in fact early attempts at trade were not very successful. But the quality of Japanese silk, in particular, struck Keswick as good and he was optimistic about the future possibilities. This early trade included the standard staples of the China coast trade; textiles of various sorts, special woods and medicines were bought by the Japanese, while the Westerners bought Japanese coal, dried fish, seaweed, shark skins and rice.[3] Later, in summer 1859, Keswick visited Hakodate, the northernmost of the ports open to trade, which he found sadly lacking in both amenities and trade potential.[4] It was already obvious that neither Nagasaki nor Hakodate had the hinterlands that would allow them to develop into major trading settlements. They were indeed destined to remain commercial backwaters for the rest of the nineteenth century.

The real beginning of the Japan trade had to await the United States and British treaties of 1858. The American treaty came first, negotiated by Townsend Harris, and signed on 4 July 1858. It provided for foreign trade and residence at Kanagawa, near to the capital, Edo, as well as at Nagasaki and Hakodate. The British treaty, the Treaty of Edo, was negotiated by the Earl of Elgin and signed on 26 August 1858. It drew on Harris's treaty but also reflected British experience in China, from where Elgin had come after lengthy negotiations to settle the second Anglo-China war, also known as the 'Arrow War'. Scarcely had the treaty been signed, indeed, when Elgin returned to China, where the Chinese refusal to accept the 'Arrow War' settlement led to two more years of fighting.[5]

The 1858 treaties came into force on 4 July 1859. By that date, a number of ships were already awaiting entry to the newly-opened port at Kanagawa, bringing with them some twenty merchants. Among the ships was the Jardines' vessel, *Nora*, with William Keswick on board. Keswick had with him a cargo of cotton goods, sugar, candy and elastic bands, together with $40,000 Mexican, during this period the standard currency on the China coast. The merchants who arrived at the Kanagawa port found that there was nothing prepared for their arrival and that its anchorage was a poor one.

Instead, the Japanese had erected a number of houses and jetties, across the bay at a small village called Yokohama. These arrangements were designed to attract the foreign merchants away from Kanagawa. Yokohama had a good deep-water anchorage, which appealed to the foreigners, but it had other advantages that appealed to the Japanese authorities. Kanagawa sat on the Tokaido, the great road connecting Edo with Kyoto, where the Japanese Emperor lived in seclusion, and the Japanese had no desire to see foreigners established there. Instead, by digging ditches they had turned Yokohama into an easily controlled enclave, reminiscent of Deshima, the artificial island in Nagasaki harbour that had been home for the visiting merchants of the Netherlands East India Company from the mid-seventeenth century onwards.[6]

At the same time as the merchants arrived, so did a number of Western diplomats, joining Townsend Harris, whose lonely vigil now came to an end. The diplomats were appalled by the Japanese moves, and strongly advised the merchants against accepting what they saw as a Japanese trick. Instead, they argued that Kanagawa was the port named in the treaty, and the foreign settlement should be at that place and not at Yokohama.

Their entreaties fell on deaf ears. To the merchants, the advantages of having prepared buildings and access to the better anchorage at Yokohama outweighed the disadvantages of Japanese control. To a man – there were scarcely any women in those early days – they accepted the Japanese offer. Among the first to do so was William Keswick of Jardines. He wrote that he could understand the diplomats' position, but that for those engaged in trade, the advantages of Yokohama far outweighed those of Kanagawa. The latter might be written into the treaty, but it was the former that had the deep water, the jetties and the buildings that were needed to start trading.[7] Sir Rutherford Alcock,[8] the British representative, and his fellow ministers were not impressed by the merchants' decision, which played into the Japanese wish to isolate foreigners, but they were powerless to prevent it. The only redress left to British officials was the formal refusal to accept that Yokohama was the treaty port; until the 1880s, therefore, consular despatches were dated from Kanagawa, ignoring the fact that, like his trading fellow countrymen, the consul sat in Yokohama. The decision to occupy the Japanese-built premises at Yokohama was to be one of the many incidents that would build up mutual resentment between merchants and diplomats at Yokohama. In Alcock's case, this led to an estrangement that lasted until he left Japan for China in 1865.

That is to run ahead. In Yokohama itself there was another immediate problem in July 1859. Whatever the advantages of Yokohama over Kanagawa, they were not reflected in the early trade of the new port. The Japanese government might have established a port at Yokohama, and the foreigners might have decided to use it, but major Japanese companies such as Mitsui[9] were not at first interested. They took the decision to isolate the foreigners as a sign that expanded trade was not welcome to the Japanese government, and that it would be better not to engage with the new arrivals. Such Japanese merchants as came to Yokohama were operating on a small-scale and were underfunded. They were also restricted in every way by their own authorities, who, having been forced to accept the opening of the ports, were now doing their best to prevent the development of commerce. The result was that trade remained poor. As one historian has written, 'Seaweed and lacquer boxes' could not provide the basis for a worthwhile trade.[10]

Soon there was another dispute involving the merchants, with Jardines, and Keswick, (almost certainly) taking the lead. This, too, was an attempt to control trade, by currency exchange. Because of the difficulties over exchange that he had faced in his residence in Japan from 1857 onwards, Townsend Harris included in his 1858 treaty a provision whereby the Mexican dollar, could circulate alongside Japanese coins on a weight-for-weight basis. However, Japanese merchants would not take Mexican dollars because the Japanese authorities would not allow their use outside the treaty ports. And when the Japanese traders came to exchange Mexican dollars for Japanese currency, they found that they could only do so at a heavily discounted rate. Not surprisingly, the Japanese traders began to refuse Mexican dollars, to the chagrin of those like Keswick, who had brought with him Mexican $40,000 from China. The Japanese did allow some exchange of dollars for Japanese coins, but in such tiny quantities that the foreigners could do little more than buy daily necessities.[11] The result was that, apart from some barter, trade came to a standstill for most of July and August 1859.

Then, for reasons that remain unclear, the Japanese authorities changed their approach, and in early September, large amounts of silver coins became available for exchange. Now trade could properly begin. The foreign merchants brought in more funds from China, so that they could purchase the large quantities of silk and other products that were now being readily offered by the Japanese. There was one other item that suddenly became available, and was eagerly sought by the foreigners, namely Japanese gold coins. The rate of exchange between gold and silver hitherto fixed by the Japanese overvalued silver and undervalued gold. The foreign merchants therefore soon began a brisk trade in Japanese gold coins, and Jardines were once again at the forefront. This 'Japanese gold rush' led to many claims of unscrupulous behaviour and huge profits, and put a further distance between Rutherford Alcock and the British merchants, but the reality was that the trade lasted for a relatively short period, probably no more than six weeks, and the profits, while real, were nowhere as vast as some later writers were to claim. Jardines and Keswick were indeed in the forefront of it, but even Jardines did not make a great fortune from the gold trade.[12]

Although it would be some years before Jardines established a branch office in Japan, relying until 1870 on local agents, by the end of 1859, Keswick seems to have been convinced that a reasonable trade was possible at Yokohama. Early in 1860, therefore, he bought 'Lot Number One Yokohama' as the Jardines' offices. It was well situated on the waterfront, and he was also able to buy lots 22 and 23 behind it, which allowed room for expansion. Despite trading difficulties, despite the hostility of many Japanese, and despite the bad blood between diplomats and merchants, Jardines were in Japan to stay.[13]

Having made that decision, which was supported by the company in Shanghai, Keswick was not impressed by the nervousness of Sir Rutherford Alcock in the face of continued Japanese hostility. In particular, he did not think that the removal of the legations from Edo to Yokohama following a series of attacks on premises and personnel, which was very much Alcock's policy, was a sensible move.

Not only did it appear to be giving in to Japanese pressure, but it also brought additional dangers to the foreign community at Yokohama.[14]

Keswick's time in Japan was now coming to an end. He may have played a small part in organizing the illegal visit to Britain by a group of young Chōshū samurai in 1863, but it is clear that it was S. J. Gower who was the chief member of Jardines' staff involved in Yokohama. William Keswick's role may have been conflated with that of his younger brother James, then in Shanghai, who handled the transients at that end.[15]

By then, William Keswick had become a partner in the company and soon after the students left for Shanghai he followed them. Until 1886, he was based in Hong Kong or Shanghai, and only seems to have made one return visit to Japan. How closely he followed the Japan trade that he had pioneered is not clear. At the time of the Meiji Restoration in 1867–68, he apparently advised caution, but it is hard to imagine that he did not have some say in the decision to establish a branch of the firm in Japan in 1870 and the rebuilding of the Yokohama premises on a grander scale about the same time.[16] Later, he was no doubt kept informed of things Japanese by his younger brother, James Johnstone Keswick, known in the firm as 'James the bloody polite' from his gentle disposition. James arrived in Japan in August 1875 and took over the running of the Japan branch in January 1876. He remained in Japan until August 1880, when he returned to Shanghai.[17]

In 1874, William Keswick became 'taipan', or head of Jardine, Matheson and Company, and, in the words of his obituary in the London *Times*, the 'most prominent private European in the Far East'. He continued to serve the company in both Shanghai and Hong Kong, and was chairman of the Chambers of Commerce in both places. He also held a number of honorary consular posts, and served on the Hong Kong Legislative Council. Although he had a reputation for being a progressive businessman, in Hong Kong matters he appears to have been somewhat conservative, and he clashed frequently with Sir John Pope-Hennessy,[18] Governor of Hong Kong from 1877–82. Pope-Hennessy's view that Japan was a much-wronged country may not have appealed to one who had lived through the excitements and attacks of the early days of treaty relations. In 1886, Keswick left the China coast, never to return, settling at Eastwick Park near Leatherhead in Surrey. He remained closely involved in Jardines' affairs as a director of Matheson and Company, and in East Asian matters more generally. He was, for example, a founder member of the London Chamber of Commerce, known for its interest in East Asian trade.[19]

More important was his role in the China Association, by far and away the most important representative body for British traders to China and Japan at the end of the nineteenth century. Soon after its establishment in 1889, Keswick took over the chair of the association from Sir Alfred Dent, and it was he who shaped its early years.[20] Most of Keswick's attention during his chairmanship focused on China, but occasionally, the association turned its attention to Japan. There was, for example, a Yokohama branch of the association, which took a firm line of opposition to the revision of the treaties in Japan's favour in 1894, a line echoed by Keswick himself at the association's annual dinner in London on 26 February 1895.[21] However, the China Association seems to have been in favour of the Japanese approach to China, which led to the Sino-Japanese War of 1894–95, and was keen on the idea of special 'spheres of influence' for foreign countries in China.[22]

Although Keswick never abandoned his interest in East Asia, he had other things to occupy his attention. After his return from China, he was a Justice of the Peace. In 1898, he became High Sheriff for Surrey, and in 1899, he was selected as the Conservative and Unionist candidate for the Epsom constituency, although 'he had not up to then taken any very active part in political matters'. He represented the constituency until a few days before his death, when it passed to his son, just as his position as China coast 'taipan' had done some years earlier.[23]

Jardines of course continue in Japan, though Lot Number One, Yokohama, has long ceased to be the company's headquarters. The original site was destroyed in the 1923 earthquake. Today a stone marks the site where the foreign trade of the city really began, though it is now well back from the waterfront. The story of how Jardines ignored the diplomats and began trading at Yokohama is well known, although now few probably know Keswick's name. His association with Japan may have been relatively short, but his was one of the most important early contributions to the history of Anglo-Japanese relations.

11

Frederick Cornes, 1837–1927: Founder and Senior Partner of Cornes and Company (1873–1911)[1]

PETER N. DAVIES

Frederick Cornes

FREDERICK CORNES' GRANDFATHER was a tenant farmer at Hall-on-the-Heath, near Haslington in Cheshire. John Cornes, Frederick Cornes' father, was born in 1805. Although the family were relatively prosperous the growing silk industry at nearby Macclesfield offered him a better future and John obtained employment at Park Mill operated by Messrs. H. & T. Wardle. After learning the trade as a weaver he showed an aptitude for design on which he later concentrated. He subsequently became the firm's manager and by the time of his death in 1855 was a partner in the enterprise.

Soon after arriving in Macclesfield he married Ellen Wilshaw, the daughter of a neighbour, who was also employed in the silk industry as an operative. Their sons followed in the same line of business.

Their eldest son William was born in 1826. Having inherited his father's feeling for art William joined Wardles as a designer and spent the whole of his career at the Park Mills. When the Wardle brothers retired he took over the firm, which was then reconstituted as W. W. Cornes and Company. By the time of his death in 1885 the enterprise had been renamed Cornes and Johnson, and William was described as one of the leading silk manufacturers of the town.[2]

John Cornes' second son Frederick was born in 1837. Although educated at the local grammar school Frederick like his elder brother attended classes at the 'Useful Knowledge Society' and was awarded a prize for his drawing in 1848–49. After leaving school in 1852 he spent some time learning the basics of the silk industry. In 1857 Frederick Cornes moved to Manchester and joined the firm of Holliday Wise and Company as a silk buyer. Then after a brief period of training he travelled out to Shanghai to act as one of its representatives. His new duties brought him into contact with the buyers from many other expatriate firms and he quickly gained a reputation as a shrewd and knowledgeable agent. He soon acquired a wide understanding of the trade.

The European silk manufacturing industry was traditionally based in France and Northern Italy.[3] Although these areas originally produced much of their own raw material the expansion of output in the late eighteenth and early nineteenth centuries meant that more and more raw silk needed to be imported from Southern Italy and the Middle East. The further growth in demand then led to the development of a long-distance trade with Asia and by the 1840s China had emerged as the principal supplier. It was for this reason that Holliday Wise and Company had established a branch at Shanghai. The outbreak of the pebrine disease in the Mediterranean during the 1850s further increased the demand for Chinese silk.

This was one of the reasons, which had encouraged the firm to expand its operations and to appoint Frederick Cornes. The situation was not, however, quite as promising as it appeared for the long-running Tai'ping rebellion was beginning to damage a number of the silk-producing areas. By 1860 this conflict was starting to threaten the Shanghai region. This may well have been an important factor in Frederick's decision to reconsider his position with Holliday Wise, but the opening of a number of Japanese ports for foreign trade was another factor. After much careful consideration, he resigned from the Manchester firm and early in 1861 made his way to Yokohama, which had been made a treaty Port under the Commercial Treaties signed with Japan in 1858 and which had opened for trade in 1859. Yokohama had quickly attracted large numbers of foreign merchants and adventurers. Although the land allocated for business enterprises soon proved to be too small the area was rapidly expanded by the draining of the adjacent swamp. With the advantage of near-by deep water Yokohama was subsequently able to cope with the largest ocean-going vessels and so was able to evolve into one of Japan's most important ports.[4]

William Gregson Aspinall was one of the first group of traders to arrive in Yokohama. He was the latest in a long line of Liverpool-based merchants as the Aspinall and Gregson families had been engaged in various aspects of commerce for many generations. Both had been prominent in privateering and in the slave trade before diversifying into more general activities including insurance broking and banking. The success of these enterprises permitted some member of these families to enter into local politics and several were elected mayors of Liverpool. After various periods of on-the-job training, which may have included time with his elder brother Richard, a London tea broker, William Aspinall set up on his own account and became a partner in Aspinall, Mackenzie and Company in Shanghai. After learning of the opening of the Japanese Treaty Ports he decided to move to Yokohama. In May 1860, at the age of 38, he established himself as a 'Tea Inspector and General Commission Agent' in the newly-opened port.

William Aspinall rapidly became an important and respected member of the local foreign community. The disturbed nature of Japanese society and anti-foreign feeling in the country made Japan a dangerous place. Many expatriates took to keeping a pistol available at all times. However, in the autumn of 1860 the carrying of weapons was made illegal. Aspinall played a significant role in organizing a protest against this order and although it does not seem to have been revoked it appears to have been subsequently interpreted in a fairly relaxed manner: this was certainly the case after January 1861 when Henry Heusken, the assistant to the US Consul in Tokyo, was murdered.

In spite of difficulties of this kind the trade of Yokohama continued to expand and in its second year of operations exports valued at over £1,000,000 including more than 3,000 bales of silk and 1,250,000 pounds of tea were recorded.[5] The increasing level of activity encouraged many additional entrepreneurs and merchants including Frederick Cornes to come to Yokohama.

Cornes seems to have travelled from Shanghai to Yokohama in a sailing vessel as the first merchant steamer, the SS *Scotland* of 759 tons, did not berth at the port until March 1862.[6] It is not known whether Cornes previously knew Aspinall in Shanghai, but on his arrival in what was still a tiny community of perhaps less than one hundred expatriates it was inevitable that their paths would quickly cross. They must soon have discussed the possibility of working together as such an arrangement would be mutually beneficial. After careful consideration of the other available options Cornes decided to join his knowledge of the silk trade with Aspinall's expertise with tea. On 1 April 1861 they commenced in business together under the title of Aspinall, Cornes and Company.[7]

Under the terms of their agreement Aspinall and Cornes were to be equal partners for an initial three years. Both were to contribute their entire capital and were to receive 6% interest on whatever they invested. Their partnership agreement was to be subsequently renewed for further three-year periods in 1864, in 1867 and in 1870 but was not renewed in 1873. The enterprise was then re-established as Cornes and Company. Frederick Cornes remained the major partner in the firm until his retirement in 1911.

During the first three years of the partnership their principal function was to export raw silk and green (not fired) tea. The silk in various formats was shipped almost entirely to England and France while the tea was practically all sent to the United States. The American Civil War (1861–65) resulted in an enormous reduction in the ability of the Southern States to export cotton. As a result the demand for Japanese cotton increased and total quantities exported rose from only 4,616 piculs (15 piculs equals a short ton of 2000lbs) in 1862 to 46,697 piculs in 1863.[8] Aspinall, Cornes and Company played a significant role in this unexpected bonanza and helped to place the firm on sound financial foundations even though it only lasted a few years.

Raw silk, cocoons and (later) silkworm eggs were for many years the focus of the company's commercial activities. Thus, although William Aspinall was the older and more experienced of the two partners it was Frederick Cornes' expertise with silk which was the critical factor in their continuing success. Yokohama was at the centre of the country's silk districts and its products were brought to the port's Japanese quarter by long-established local traders. Negotiations for sales to overseas merchants were held at various inns where, until warehouses were constructed, the silk was kept until it could be shipped. As Frederick Cornes soon discovered transactions of this kind usually began early in the morning and frequently lasted for many hours before a deal could be finalized.

Aspinall, Cornes were also soon engaged in the import trade. Among the most important items were Lancashire cottons, metal products, coals and other raw materials while kerosene and a wide variety of consumer goods gradually developed into a significant trade. Both the export and import sides of the business were at first conducted largely on a commission basis, but as the firm's capital expanded through retained profits more and more transactions were undertaken on its own account. Speculative ventures were carefully avoided, but in the 1860s the silk trade was a highly volatile business and many competitors were obliged to either withdraw from the trade or became bankrupt.

The major problem, which faced the firm and all its rivals, was the length of time it took for information to pass between Japan and the West. This meant that Aspinall, Cornes were forced to buy in London or New York for a market in Yokohama, which was many months away and where prices could easily have appreciated or collapsed in the meantime. Similar difficulties were faced when purchasing in Yokohama items for export as by the time they reached Europe or North America their value might have depreciated. This problem was gradually solved by improvements in communications. When Aspinall, Cornes formed their partnership sailing ships took an average of 120 days via the Cape of Good Hope to reach London. The inauguration of a service to Shanghai, with a feeder route to Yokohama, by the Peninsular and Oriental Steam Navigation Company (P and O) subsequently reduced this to approximately two months each way. When the Suez Canal was opened in 1869 voyage times were cut by a further ten days and the evolution of an alternative route across the United States meant that messages could be received in only 40 days. However these very considerable improvements only lessened the difficulty and it was not fully solved until the international cable network reached Japan in 1872.[9]

Frederick Cornes, who rapidly became the dominant partner, clearly recognized the dangers inherent in both the export and import sides of the business. Accordingly, he attempted to design a strategy, which could broaden the economic basis of the firm. As many agencies as could be conveniently managed were acquired and from an early stage the partnership acted on behalf of many individual sailing vessels. This was soon extended to include a number of steam ships. This expertise enabled Aspinall, Cornes to obtain, for a limited period, the P and O agency, despite competition from many other expatriate firms such as Jardine, Matheson, W. R. Adamson and Dent and Company. The association with the P and O, which remained tenants of Cornes for the next forty years, enabled further appointments to be secured. These included some important British insurance companies and in 1868 Aspinall, Cornes became the first representatives of Lloyds in Japan. In addition, the firm continued to act as agents for individual vessels in both Yokohama and Kobe and later was appointed to act for the Ben Line of steamships.

A second initiative to lessen the dependency on purely trading activities was the purchase of land and property. It is not known where either of the partners lived during the early months of their business in Yokohama, but they soon secured trading premises, which could also serve as residential quarters. In September 1862 after the murder of Charles Lennox Richardson in the so-called Namamugi incident, the inquest was held at Aspinall's house.[10] By the following year the firm was reported to possess property valued at over £15,000. This amounted to 2.7% of all British-owned real estate in Yokohama.[11] In addition to houses, the company's assets included a number of 'go-downs', which had been acquired for the storage and handling of both exports and imports. These also provided office and living space on their upper floor. Additional buildings and land were later secured in other parts of the port and these were subsequently joined to form what became a company compound. By 1869 the partnership was the largest expatriate owner of land in the centre of Yokohama and also possessed substantial areas in the Bluff residential quarter, which overlooked the harbour. Many of these assets were not required for the firm's commercial activities and had been purchased to provide a rental income. They thus played a significant role in widening its financial base.

William Aspinall and Frederick Cornes worked closely together in Yokohama from the establishment of their partnership in 1861 until October 1863 when the latter returned to the UK for a twelve-month period of leave. During this time he visited many suppliers and clients and did his utmost to strengthen potential business contacts. On his return Aspinall departed for a twenty-one month stay in Britain and Cornes was left in sole control. By all accounts he then took an active part in the political life of Yokohama becoming a founder member of its Municipal Council in 1865. He also appears to have established a liaison with a Japanese lady whom he later referred to as 'Otama-san' or 'OTS'.[12] Recent research in Japan indicates that she was a member of the highly respected Yamada family and that their association was on a long-term basis.[13] The couple had a child before Cornes left Japan for a second period of leave in October 1866. He then made arrangements for an allowance to be paid to his consort via his Yokohama office and although this was continued for many years he refused to raise it[14] and in 1878 asked that no further letter should be sent on to him.[15]

The child conceived by Cornes in Yokohama was a girl whose Japanese name was Yamada Chiyo. However, she became better known as Amy Cornes and attended Soshin Girls School in Yokohama until the age of 12. She is then reported to have joined the household of Ernest Satow[16] who became British Minister in Tokyo from 1895–1900[17] but whether it was as an employee or as an adopted or foster daughter is not clear.[18] Whatever the truth of these suggestions there is no doubt that Cornes and Satow enjoyed a considerable friendship: the latter frequently staying in the Cornes' residence when visiting London.[19] In any event, four years later Amy entered Kyoritsu Girls School from where she graduated in 1887. She then returned to Soshin Girls School and served there as a teacher of English and the Bible for the ensuing 39 years.[20] Apart from visiting the United States in 1906 she continued to live in Yokohama until her death in 1960. Amy never married and never seems to have had any contact with her father.

Although Frederick Cornes' second period of leave was originally intended to last for two years he did not, in fact, return to Japan until 1871. There were a number of reasons for this change of plan.

His first motive was purely commercial. The size of Aspinall Cornes' business was now of such scale that it seemed advantageous to end the practice of leaving third parties to handle purchases and sales. As a result Cornes began to deal with an increasing number of items from the Bath Hotel in Paddington (London), where he was living, and gradually established a small group of clerks to assist him. By April 1867 he had come to the conclusion that it would be best to cater for all the firm's transactions and took rooms in 62, Cornhill in the premises of Broughall and Company who were one of the principal clients of the partnership. This remained its London Headquarters until 1876 when a move was made to 7–8, Great Winchester Street to which Broughall and Co. also moved.

This decision enabled greater control to be exercised over many of the firm's activities and it seemed wise for Frederick Cornes to stay in situ and see the new system firmly established. Once it was up and running, it proved to be very difficult for him to leave its operation to anyone else.

A second, personal, factor also encouraged him to remain in London. It seems that Cornes came home with 'intentions towards a mutual friend in Wales but was soon informed that there was no chance there …'[21] Although he subsequently developed a distinct fondness for Frances Steele Perkins, the third daughter of R.S. Perkins and Elizabeth, the older sister of William Aspinall and visited their home in Overton, Flintshire, on many occasions, this never became a serious attachment.[22]

By 1868 Cornes had taken a cottage in Hampton Wick close to the home of Richard Aspinall, William's older brother. At the end of November, 1869, he wrote to his partner in Yokohama that he had become engaged to Henrietta Alice Bull, the daughter of John Pannett Bull of 15, Hyde Park Street, London.[23] This was an excellent match for Frederick as her father was the sole partner in Bull and Wilson, cloth merchants, which possessed extensive premises in St Martin's Lane, Westminster. Although he had a total of six daughters he was well able to provide a handsome dowry and on 7 April 1870, the pair were married in style at St John's, Paddington. His marriage induced Cornes to take a long lease on 'Woodbury' a substantial house in Teddington, which remained the couple's home for the next ten years.

While Frederick Cornes was thus engaged in London William Aspinall was in charge of the firm's activities in Japan. This new arrangement worked well and from 1867 to 1869 the partnership was the largest exporter of raw silk from Yokohama with 7% of the total.[24] In spite of this progress the trade remained highly volatile and even the largest firms were not immune – Dent and Company failing in 1868. By then Aspinall and Company had over £18,000 invested in real estate, providing an income of more than £2,500 a year. This was a valuable hedge against losses elsewhere. This success in Yokohama encouraged expansion and a branch at Kobe was opened in April 1869. An indication of the status of the firm came during the visit in 1869 of HRH The Duke of Edinburgh, the son of Queen Victoria, to Yokohama. After landing from HMS *Galatea* and receiving a small deputation, Aspinall presented a loyal address, signed by over 250 British residents.[25] Aspinall was also a prominent guest at the celebrations, which marked the departure of Admiral Sir Henry Keppal from the port later that year.[26]

While the partnership was making such good progress Aspinall's personal affairs were steadily deteriorating. For reasons, which are not now clear, by 1867 he had become estranged from his wife and was also experiencing considerable financial difficulties. Both of these problems may have played a part in his decision to stay in Japan and agree that Cornes should stay in London. Aspinall's failure to send sufficient funds to pay for school fees and other family expenses first alerted Cornes that something was wrong and he became steadily more exacerbated when matters did not improve. By September 1869 Aspinall had withdrawn so much from the firm that their capital accounts had become greatly distorted. Thus, although both had started with equal amounts, by then Frederick Cornes share was £8,600 and William Aspinall only £1,600.[27] For this reason Cornes then insisted that in future each partner should only withdraw a maximum of £1,000 each year. However, he pointed out that as Aspinall would continue to receive half of the rents, which had now reached £4,000 per annum, he would still have an annual income of £3,000. As he was provided with a rent-free bungalow Cornes estimated that Aspinall could live very well on less than £600 a year in Yokohama.[28]

In spite of these problems Cornes decided to renew his agreement with Aspinall for a further three years until 1873. At the same time he insisted that William Henry Taylor be appointed as a junior partner.

He was to play an important role in the firm until his retirement in 1889. These events took place at about the same time as Cornes' marriage and it was not until the following year that he decided to return to Japan. At first he proposed to take his wife and son, Herbert Frederick, but learning of the ongoing hardships of the two-week rail crossing of the United States he finally concluded that it would be best to leave them at home. On his arrival in Yokohama in December 1871 Cornes found that the port had changed enormously over the past five years and was astonished to see how quickly the inhabitants had adopted European dress.[29] He also found that the partnership's books and accounts were in good order and as he then stayed with Aspinall in his house on the Bluff, it must be assumed that they remained on amicable terms.[30]

After a brief hand-over period Aspinall returned to the UK and Cornes followed at the end of February 1872 leaving Taylor in charge of the Japanese end of the business. Aspinall, having completed his spell of leave, was to undertake some selling of tea from the London office but poor health and family commitments prevented this from being a regular activity. Lengthy discussions about the renewal of the partnership failed in January 1873 when Aspinall refused the final terms offered by Cornes. Negotiations then hinged on the arrangements for terminating the previous enterprise, which by then was almost entirely owned by Frederick Cornes. The agreement, finalized at the eleventh hour, recognized this fact and on 1 April 1873 Cornes and Company was established to carry on the existing business.[31] In return William Aspinall was to receive £1,300 per annum from the rents of his share of the property (which was now leased by the new firm) and a further £500 a year for three years on condition that he did not begin trading on his own account in Japan.[32]

Cornes and Company was also constituted as a partnership in which Frederick Cornes retained control until his retirement in 1911. On its formation W. H. Taylor and A. G. Winstanley (1873–93) were appointed as junior partners. They were later joined or replaced by W. W. Till (1890–1900), A. G. M. Weale (1896–1910) and Archibald John Cornes (1900–49). At least one of these individuals was then always resident in Japan so that he could oversee the firm's affairs: this task was considerably lightened after the direct telegraphic link was established with Yokohama in May, 1873.[33]

Frederick Cornes controlled the enterprise from his office in Great Winchester Street in Central London for the next thirty-eight years during which Japan emerged from near feudal status to become a modern, industrial, nation and her patterns of trade with the outside world changed. At the beginning of this era exports consisted almost entirely of primary products while imports were largely of capital and consumer goods. By the end of Frederick's tenure many raw materials were being imported and Japanese textiles had not only replaced Lancashire imports but were being exported to neighbouring countries. Furthermore, Japan was now approaching self-sufficiency in many items and the functions of expatriate companies like Cornes were being increasingly undertaken by Japanese firms.

Cornes and Company, unlike many of its competitors, was remarkably successful in adapting to the changes in its trading environment. Thus it steadily reduced its direct involvement in both the export of raw silk (and later piece goods) and green tea and largely confined itself to working on a commission basis or via joint accounts. However, following the discovery of fraud by the principal silk buyer in 1902, Cornes closed their silk piece goods department; at that time its stock was still valued at over £41,000.[34] The firm also greatly extended over time the range of its imports into Japan so that while these continued to include the finer quality textiles and yarns from the U.K. it also provided cheaper yarns from Bombay. Other items supplied on either a regular or occasional basis were fine iron, kerosene, nail rods, rice and wire rope. In addition coal was imported which could be used as ballast in ships chartered by Cornes. The firm was also involved with others in the provision of large capital projects such as cotton mills. Cornes further extended their agency work so that while continuing to act for Lloyds Register of Shipping it represented many marine and fire insurance companies. Its ongoing work on behalf of many individual vessels was subsequently strengthened when in 1888 it was appointed as agents for the Ben Line at Yokohama. Taken together with its property interests the firm thus had a broad range of businesses, which helped it to survive the numerous crises, which afflicted the trade with Japan.

Although Frederick Cornes never returned to Japan after 1872 he did visit North America on several occasions. These business trips took him to the Eastern parts of the United States and Canada during 1874, 1875 and 1876. These were mainly in connection with Cornes' exports of Japanese tea, which had been originally arranged by a branch office in New York but which was increasingly dealt with by agents or on a commission basis.

Throughout this period Frederick continued to direct operations from London and to live at Teddington, where the birth of Herbert in 1871 was followed by those of Archibald in 1873, Julian in 1874, Edith in 1878 and Hugh in 1879. The growth in his family may have been an important factor in his decision to acquire Rivermead in Hampton Wick during 1880. It was there that his last child, Alice Beatrice, was born four years later.

Frederick's oldest son, Herbert, joined the firm but after acting as its London Manager during 1889 and in a similar capacity in Kobe from 1891 to 1899 he decided on a change of career. Against his father's wishes he resigned and eventually qualified as a Middle Temple barrister. Archibald, Frederick's second son, duly replaced his brother and succeeded his father, serving as a partner from 1900 to 1949. Frederick's third son, Julian, acted as a Judge in Bengal from 1897 to 1919 but then entered the family firm and worked as a partner from 1919 to 1949. Neither the fourth son, Hugh, nor Frederick's two daughters played any part in Cornes and Company.

Frederick Cornes' major concerns during his working life were always his business and his family. He also enjoyed an interest in sport and was apparently one of the principal founders of the Kobe Regatta and Athletic Club during his time in Japan. The Kobe Golf Club was not founded until 1902, but he played golf on his return to London although time constraints appear to have restricted his rounds to odd occasions and holidays.[35] Riding was another activity, which Frederick enjoyed in Japan, and he subsequently kept a horse at a farm in Hertfordshire. However, he later complained that he had few opportunities to ride. He also enjoyed fishing and made many trips to both Ireland and Wales to fish. His wife does not seem to have shared these interests, but they both appreciated walking in the countryside and family holidays were frequently spent in the mountainous parts of Europe.

Following his retirement in 1911 Frederick Cornes remained for a number of years involved in the affairs of Cornes and Company. It took some time for his outstanding accounts and loans to be settled, but even when he had no direct financial involvement, he continued to keep a watchful eye on the firm's prosperity under the guidance of his sons. He died on 7 September 1927 just before his ninetieth birthday. His wife, Henrietta Alice Cornes, died on 24 May 1928 at the age of 81. Both were buried at Teddington Cemetery near his former home in Hampton Wick.

On his death Frederick Cornes' estate was valued at £338,314. This very substantial amount shows both the profitability of his business enterprises and his shrewdness in maintaining his capital over such a long period of retirement. Frederick Cornes, who began with little except a sound education and a sharp intellect, became a highly successful entrepreneur and played an important role in the development of Japanese trade.

Frederick's second son, Archibald John Cornes, who had become a partner in 1900, ran the business until the outbreak of the Second World War. The firm then lay dormant, but was reactivated before being sold to Wheelock, Marden and Company at its book value of £20,000 in 1949. Wheelock, Marden and Co were in turn acquired by the Hong Kong and Kowloon Wharf Company in 1985 and the chairman of this vast enterprise, Sir Y. K. Pao, later arranged for what is now the Cornes Group to hold all of his Japanese interests. In 2001 the group continues to operate as a large scale, interanational trading company.[36]

12

John Samuel Swire (1825–98) and Japan, 1867–98

CHARLOTTE BLEASDALE

John Samuel Swire

JOHN SAMUEL SWIRE (1825–98) arrived in Yokohama in April 1867, just before the Meiji Restoration of 1868 and just four months after establishing his first Far Eastern 'house' at Shanghai, under the style of Butterfield & Swire. Although he initially 'took an unfavourable view of the place as a business centre'[1] he was confident that he could improve upon the efforts of his Yokohama agent, the American firm of Augustine Heard & Co., and on 1 August a new branch office opened for business.

Butterfield & Swire's principal imports into Japan were woollens, worsteds and Manchester cotton piece goods, later amplified to include potentially lucrative exports of tea and silk. In the general downturn of the 1870s, however, these trades failed to live up to expectation, and John Swire came close to closing down in Yokohama. He persisted in the knowledge that the Blue Funnel Line – the great Liverpool shipping line for which the company was managing agent in China – must eventually extend its services to Japan.

Blue Funnel began to call at Yokohama in 1881, but did not establish a regular service to Japan until 1888. In the meantime, the house developed slowly, gradually moving away from trading to concentrate on a variety of commission businesses and on shipping. By the 1880s, John Swire was able to say with confidence that 'in China and Japan we – with Jardines – stand head and shoulders above all competitors'.[2] Two events in particular assisted this turning of the tide. One was the establishment by Swire in 1872 of the China Navigation Company; the other was the formation in Hong Kong in 1881of the Taikoo Sugar Refinery – Butterfield & Swire becoming agent in Japan for both of these enterprises.

In 1887, twenty years after the opening of the Yokohama house, Butterfield & Swire established a branch office at Kobe. The firm also retained agents at Nagasaki (mainly for coal), and at Tainan, in Japanese Formosa, but John Swire steadfastly rejected suggestions from his partners that he should open at additional ports. By keeping the bounds of his enterprise within these well-defined parameters, 'The Senior' (partner) was able to exert an iron grip on his business interests in Japan – even though he was to return to that country only four more times after 1867, during extended tours to the East in 1873, 1878, 1883 and 1891.

John Swire is, however, best remembered as 'the Father of Shipping Conferences,'[3] and arguably his most important contribution to Japan's overseas trade was the inception and development of the Far Eastern Freight Conference – providing a blueprint for the organisation of liner shipping both during his lifetime, and in the century following his death.

'THE SENIOR'

John Samuel Swire was born in Liverpool on Christmas Eve 1825. His father, also John Swire (1793–1847), established a general trading house under his own name in 1816, and gradually built a modestly successful business, based around a core trade in New Orleans cotton. On his death, his two sons John Samuel and William Hudson (1830–84) took over the management of the family firm. Plagued by ill-health for much of his life, William eventually retired from business in 1876; John Swire was thus destined to be the driving force behind the firm's early development.

In the 1840s, the young John Swire travelled widely in America in search of new opportunities: at one stage reputedly holding the postal franchise for the State of Arkansas, and pushing 'further alone amongst the Indians than any other man not a trapper'.[4] In 1846, he became engaged to a Miss Lizzie Gordon, but she died before the marriage could take place. It was to be the first in a series of personal tragedies.[5]

In 1854, he sailed for Australia, where he tried his hand at sheep farming, fossicked for gold at Ballarat, and became a founding member of the Melbourne Hunt Club. More importantly, in 1855, he established a branch of his business: Swire Bros. in Melbourne becoming the focus for a growing trade in goods ranging from fencing wire, sardines, cement and Guinness,[6] to tallow, wheat and wool.[7] In 1859, he returned to Liverpool, where William, left in charge, had been finding business 'very uphill work';[8] soon afterwards, the Melbourne firm was placed in the hands of agents.

In November 1859, John Swire married Helen ('Nell') Fairrie. The daughter of a Liverpool businessman, he had known her since her schooldays.[9] But tragedy continued to stalk John Swire, and his wife died soon after the birth of their only son, John ('Jack') Swire (1861–1933), and after only thirty months of marriage. A widower at 37, John Swire immersed himself in his business.

Perhaps it was the need to forget this personal loss that spurred John Swire to seek wholly new areas of enterprise in China and Japan, after the outbreak of the American Civil War began to disrupt the trade in raw cotton. Initially, he consigned piece goods to Augustine Heard and to Preston, Bruell & Co. (in Shanghai), but frustrated by the lacklustre performance of these agents, he was soon determined to run these businesses himself.

John Swire arrived in Shanghai towards the end of 1866, establishing Butterfield & Swire in partnership with Richard Shackleton Butterfield, a Yorkshire worsted manufacturer, who was one of his principal export clients. Within eighteen months the partnership had been dissolved: 'He was grasping and he bothered me,'[10] Swire later wrote. At Butterfield's request, the dissolution was not gazetted,[11] and the name of the company remained unchanged into the 1970s[12] – although the firm was soon more widely known by its Chinese *hong* name of *Taikoo,* meaning 'Great and Ancient'.

One of John Swire's first achievements in Shanghai in December 1866 was the acquisition of the China agency for the Ocean Steam Ship Company (later, better known as the Blue Funnel Line), having obtained – against considerable odds – a return cargo for the vessel *Achilles*, in which 'B&S' had shipped its first consignment of 'shirtings' from Liverpool.[13] Swire was a shareholder in Ocean, formed by the brothers Alfred and Philip Holt a year earlier in 1865. Prior to this date, the China trade had been dominated by fast tea clippers, but the Messrs. Holt – to quote an article that later appeared in the *Japan Herald* – were 'practical ship-constructors and mechanics, [who] planned a vessel that would combine four qualities: first, to carry a large cargo; second, use a compact compound engine possessing sufficient steam power at the cost of a small consumption of coal; third, carry coal enough for a voyage of 6,000 or 7,000 miles; fourth, [have the] ability to make a voyage under canvas if necessary. The vessels, therefore, were able to do what no other packets had done before.'[14]

The fact that the Holts chose Butterfield & Swire, rather than one of the established China hongs, is an indication of John Swire's standing within shipping circles of the time. At the age of 40, he had already established a reputation as a man of acumen and integrity. Imbued with a strong work ethic by his Yorkshire-born father, he was decisive and determined, with an innate ability to grasp the bigger picture. Although considered too bold[15] by some, his unwillingness to speculate was a major reason for The Senior's periodic disagreements with his partners in later years. Many times he missed opportunities, rather than 'cut out' companies that he believed to have prior claim. 'I never knew a man with a stronger sense of justice in business' said Philip Holt of Swire.[16]

THE YOKOHAMA HOUSE

In December 1866, John Swire's Shanghai staff included William Lang, J. H. Scott,[17] R. N. Newby, and a Portuguese junior clerk called de Sa.[18] Scott, a member of the Clyde shipbuilding family,[19] had arrived in Shanghai with an introduction from Alfred Holt. He was taken on as bookkeeper and soon became a valued colleague, partner and personal friend – ultimately taking over as Senior Partner[20] on John Swire's death. Newby, a Butterfield's man, and a specialist in Yorkshire woollen goods, accompanied Swire to Japan as his first Yokohama manager.

John Swire later maintained that he was '... burdened by an engagement with Newby, who, unbeknown to us, had got a written guarantee from RSB [Butterfield] that he should *always be in charge* at the port where he resided. He was totally unfit for Shanghai or Hong Kong, and we opened in Yokohama as a place where he would have but little opportunity of doing an injury to the firm.'[21]

Given this inauspicious beginning, it is perhaps hardly surprising that the branch failed to prosper under Newby's guidance. Early in 1869, the firm was 'mercifully relieved of his presence'[22] by his resignation, and Scott was hastily despatched to Yokohama. He could not long be spared, however, because plans were now in train to establish a new branch in Hong Kong. By the end of the year, Scott – who clearly showed outstanding promise, since he was only 24 years old at the time – had returned to take charge in Shanghai.

During this 'crisis of management' the fate of the Yokohama

branch hung in the balance – Newby's failure to sell goods having resulted in a large surplus stock.[23] 'Then, and oft time subsequently, we wanted to close the house, but Lang was always averse to the course, stating that better times *must* be at hand, to which we as often replied, that meantime we *might* be ruined.'[24] Swire was reluctant to admit defeat, however: 'The very fact of the trade being so wretchedly bad, makes us disinclined to abandon it.'[25] While prospects for piece goods[26] did not look bright, he urged that exports of commodities such as tea and silk were more promising, and he undertook to engage a 'thoroughly experienced silk inspector',[27] Thomas Merry, formerly with Reiss & Co in Shanghai. This time, malaria – a perennial hazard at Yokohama – took its toll: Merry was invalided home in the spring of 1872 and died during the voyage. His successor, J. R. Turner, also died suddenly a few months after taking up the post. At last, in May 1873, James Dodds arrived in Yokohama to begin a thirty-two-year reign.

The journalist Harold Williams, a former employee of B&S in Yokohama, described the foreign trading houses on the Bund in the last quarter of the nineteenth century as follows: 'Each was set in its own compound. The Chinese and Japanese clerks dressed in their native costumes and the foreign staff wore bowler hats or headgear of an earlier era. Generally, the only mechanical equipment in the office consisted of a massive press used for press-copying hand-written letters and invoices into copy books[28]... Around the hongs there hung an aroma of cutch and spices, the smell of tea firing, or of silk cocoons, and sometimes the mustiness of age hung about them also ...'[29] This, then, was the scene at No. 7 Kaigan-dori,[30] presided over by Dodds.

At 35 years of age, Dodds' salary of £750 per annum 'all found' made him a wealthy man by Yokohama standards. From 1878, he received 25% of the branch's profits, with a guaranteed minimum of £1,000, enabling him to invest in stock in the new Japan Brewery Company – the forerunner of Kirin Beer[31] – and also to contemplate matrimony. In 1879, on his first home leave, he married a young widow,[32] Mrs Wilcox: 'a wonderfully energetic woman,'[33] who was fond of getting up amateur theatricals; they soon produced a brood of children.

Dodds grew sleek and prosperous: 'There is nothing the matter with Dodds except too good living. If he had to earn his living one day a week by pulling a jinricksha and feeding on the earnings, he would be all right.'[34]

He cultivated a set of patriarchal whiskers, and an epistolatory style that clearly tried the patience of his Senior: 'I had a characteristic and facetious chit from Mr Swire by last mail commenting on the voluminousness of my inter-port correspondence and recommending the use of postcards!'[35]

Coincidental with Dodds' arrival in Yokohama in 1873, was the establishment of Swire Bros. in New York, whose principal *raison d'être* was the marketing of Japanese green tea: 'New York was necessary to Yokohama – Yokohama to New York, and the two houses had to stand or fall together.'[36]

Unfortunately, the trade did not fulfil Swire's ambitions. Part of the problem was that soon after opening in New York there was a tremendous slump in trade, resulting in the bankruptcy of a number of houses and a serious financial panic in 1875. 'You have no idea what a crash we have had,' wrote John Swire from London: 'our interest in silk and tea to this country is still heavy and N.Y. cannot sell. I cabled to suspend all operations for the time being …'[37] For a while, John Swire clung to hopes of an upturn, in 1882 appointing H.J. Baggallay as *cha'zee*[38] to Dodds; a year later, with no sign of a market rally, he admitted defeat and the New York branch closed.

The Japanese tea trade to other markets (principally to Australia and the UK) staggered on for a few more years. By 1886, however, Jack Swire, writing home to his father during a visit to Japan, commented: 'Our tea business does not seem to be very great anywhere,' and that poor Mr Baggallay 'seems to think that he is rather wasting his time in Yokohama.'[39] In the same year, the firm's firing premises were given up and John Swire decreed that he refused to 'burden himself with such property' at the soon-to-be-opened Kobe branch: 'better make up our minds that we are <u>out</u> of this branch of trade'.[40]

Despite overall losses totalling £44,000 between 1875 and 1880,[41] Yokohama did not 'fall' with the loss of New York, because Butterfield & Swire's Japan interests had meanwhile developed in a number of new directions. In the early 1870s, John Swire obtained the fire insurance agencies in Japan for several UK insurance companies, including Royal Exchange Assurance, and the London & Lancashire Assurance Company, to whom he wrote in 1875: 'If you would like our house to take the management … our folks could do as well for you as any others … if we accept it – you shan't have cause to complain.'[42] These moves reflected a shift in Swire's attitude to his Far East businesses. Although he had remained confident during the 1870s slump that 'no House is in a safer position than we are,'[43] one of the effects of the downturn was to give him a greater appreciation of the relative security of agency (i.e. commission) businesses, as opposed to trading. While early in 1875 he was still maintaining that: 'I am not keen after agencies',[44] later in the same year, he was to say 'I want to get a snugger compass and increase our steam and commission business'[45] – an approach that was to set the trend for Butterfield & Swire's development over the next few decades.

The agencies undertaken by Dodds at Yokohama were varied: in addition to insurance, they included at one stage the seaweed business of Hokkaido Baitom Gumi, and for bottled mineral water produced by the Apollinaris Company.[46] More exotically, the branch also depended on commissions from an appointment – obtained through Baring Bros. in London – as paying agent for the Russian Imperial Government. This function must have been quite remunerative, as the Yokohama house continued to cash credits in favour of the Russian Far Eastern Fleet, (of which a goodly portion wintered at Nagasaki[47]), up to 1896. In 1891, Barings were asked to secure similar appointments for B&S in Hong Kong, China and elsewhere in Japan – however, their efforts were unsuccessful.

Also unsuccessful were Swire's strenuous attempts during the 1870s, 80s and 90s, to obtain the Japan agency for one of the Trans-Pacific shipping lines – tendering at various times for the agency for the Pacific Mail Steamship Company, the White Star Line,[48] and the Canadian Pacific Railway. John Swire cherished ambitions for his own shipping interests in what he considered to be a greatly under exploited trade and clearly 'the possibility of our controlling the Pacific route'[49] sustained his decision to nurse the Yokohama branch through its early difficulties.

Outside Japan, the 1870s and early 1880s saw a number of important developments for the firm. In 1872, John Swire formed the China Navigation Company – initially to operate on the Yangtze River, as a feeder service for Blue Funnel's ocean-going liners. Two years later, Swire bought a pair of steamers 'off the stocks' from Scotts' Shipbuilding and sailed them out to China, where he began to make great inroads into the coastal trade. With Butterfield & Swire as managing agent, the fleet grew rapidly: 'CNCo' coasters under charter called periodically at Japanese ports with cargoes of 'bean-cake', (a fertilizer produced from soya bean husks)[50], or when en route to Vladivostock carrying Chinese tea. They also bunkered at Nagasaki. By 1883, China Navigation was operating vessels from Hong Kong to east coast Australia, and by the mid-1880s, this line had extended northwards to Yokohama and Kobe.

Southbound, the major cargo was Japanese rice. The principal northbound cargo from Hong Kong was sugar, carried on behalf of the Taikoo Sugar Refining Company. The establishment of the refinery by John Swire in 1881 was something of an act of war against the rival firm of Jardine Matheson, who were already operating such a plant in the colony.[51] Drawing its supply of raw sugar from Java, the Philippines, and later, Queensland, the new refinery was in production by 1884. By 1886, Taikoo Sugar had become the mainstay of the Yokohama branch: 'Mr Dodds has delivered 24,000 more bags of sugar this half year than the last, both here [Yokohama] and in Kobe[52] we have sold more sugar than Jardines have.'[53]

By 1888, Taikoo Sugar was selling 37% of its output in Japan, as against 23% in China (other markets being India and Australia), and by 1894, Taikoo was supplying 46% of Yokohama and Kobe's demand.[54] This date marked a high point for Taikoo Sugar in Japan. Thereafter, sales declined due to the effects of the Sino-Japanese War of 1894–5, and of competition from local producers and from Jardine's China Sugar Refinery. In 1898, a further blow was dealt by the introduction of import tariffs designed to protect Japan's domestic industry. Perhaps it is fortunate that The Senior did not live to see Dodd's fall from grace in 1900, when his (Chinese) comprador[55] contrived to steal a large quantity of sugar from the firm's godown, resulting in a spectacular loss of ¥50,000.[56] Sales of Taikoo Sugar in Japan came to end with the retirement of James Dodds at the age of 67 in 1905; by this date however, the company had begun to develop a more successful market on the Chinese Mainland.

The Refinery was John Swire's 'last child'.[57] Soon after opening at Kobe in 1887, he considered the feasibility of a rice-cleaning mill there to complement CNCo's trade to Australia,[58] but his interest in this proposal eventually waned. In general, he rebuffed the recurrent suggestions of his Eastern managers that the firm should further diversify, his attitude summed up by the following diktats: 'If you *must* invent schemes, please place the prospectuses under lock and key and don't send them home. *But we would prefer that you devote your time to actual business.*'[59] And: 'We are all determined that there shall not be any speculation, but that the transactions of B&S shall be conducted on the basis of a purely commission business.'[60]

THE FAR EASTERN FREIGHT CONFERENCE

The company's most important Principal (though by no means consistently generating rewards commensurate with this status[61]) was Alfred Holt & Co. John Swire had a fierce loyalty to Ocean – perhaps because Holts had given him his first 'break' in the East. Although he did not always see eye to eye with the Holt brothers on matters of shipping policy, he staunchly defended their interests and often put them before those of CNCo. It was John Swire's ambitions on behalf of Ocean that led him to become the architect and first Chairman of the Far Eastern Freight Conference in 1879.

By this date, there was a serious overcapacity of vessels involved in the China and Japan trades, exacerbated by a seasonal fluctuation in demand[62] and an imbalance between outward and homeward cargoes: 'For half of each year, irrespective of rates of freight, the existing lines cannot secure anything like full cargoes to and from China and Japan. Imports and exports do not suffice for it.'[63]

This situation had led to bitter rate wars between the various steamship companies operating in the trade. To compound matters, the livelihood of the warring 'liners' was threatened by incursions by 'tramp' operators, who further undercut freight rates.

John Swire had fought and brokered peace terms in similar rate wars with CNCo's competitors on the coastal and inland waterways of China and had plenty of cause to discredit 'the wholesome rule that supply and demand will regulate themselves'[64] and to form instead a favourable opinion of various combinations of 'pooling' and 'joint purse' agreement as a means of ensuring that all received an equitable slice of the pie. His experience showed such arrangements did not extinguish competition, but kept it within sensible limits.[65] They were a force to keep freight rates at workable levels year-round, by allowing steamer companies to benefit mutually from higher freight rates during peak periods and to share the disadvantages of supplying tonnage during off-peak periods at lower rates.

Needless to say, there was considerable opposition to what one newspaper described as 'the ill-advised attempt by the great steam-owning firms to combine and crush out all opposition to their freight trade between England and Japan'.[66] The FEFC came under attack from steamer companies who were excluded from Conference arrangements[67], and from the merchants that shipped their goods in Conference vessels;[68] it also suffered from the internecine squabbling of its own members – and in particular, from the very organization that it had been designed to benefit: the Ocean Steam Ship Company.[69]

The FEFC suffered a number of setbacks in the first decade of its existence, including partial and near collapses in 1880 and 1887, but thanks to 'Mr Swire's discrimination, judgement and fair dealing,'[70] its critics – including Ocean – were gradually won over. By the mid-1890s, Conference principles had been extended into the regional trades, and membership expanded to include the newly-established mercantile marines of China and Japan – providing a pattern for the modern shipping consortia arrangements that exist to this day. By John Swire's death in 1898, it was 'generally admitted to be one of the strongest and best conducted of the trade organizations'.[71]

'IN THE FOREFRONT AMONG BRITISH STEAMSHIP COMPANIES IN JAPAN'[72]

By 1880, Blue Funnel vessels were carrying around two-fifths of the Yorkshire and Manchester goods shipped in Conference vessels bound for Japanese ports.[73] In August of the same year Ocean's *Agamemnon* docked in Yokohama,[74] as the 'pioneer' of a proposed new extension to Japan – probably as part of a private agreement to share outward cargoes forged between Blue Funnel and Glen Line.[75] John Swire pressed the B&S claim as manager: 'Altho' the agency was not worth much, we did not want others to get the thin edge of the wedge into that business.'[76]

Presumably, however, Holts did not find trade worth their while, for the line petered out and it was not until 1888 that Philip Holt again wrote to John Swire: 'We must tackle the Japan trade; it is interwoven with that of China and we cannot let others have a monopoly.'[77] Thereafter, the *ao-entotsu-no Battanfaru* – the 'blue funnelled ships of Butterfield' – began to be a familiar sight in Japanese waters.

In anticipation of this event, H.J. Baggallay was sent to Kobe to open a new branch office on 13 May 1887 – his contract assuring him 40% of the net profit generated by the new branch, with a guaranteed minimum of £700 per annum. Since his decade of tenure coincided with the height of Butterfield & Swire's fortunes in prewar Japan, he probably had little cause to regret this arrangement.[78] Popular, and considered a 'good businessman,'[79] photographs[80] of Baggallay show a serious and somewhat anaemic-looking man – evidence, perhaps, of the recurrent malaria that eventually forced his retirement in 1898. He established an office at No. 103 Edo-machi,[81] where his main businesses were Taikoo Sugar, and 'drumming' for cargo for Blue Funnel – for whom he built a niche business shipping Japanese 'curios' for the Bond Street market.[82]

In 1888, the same year that Ocean extended its service to Japan, the former government coalmines at Miike in southern Kyushu, were taken over by Japan's leading *sōgō shōsha*[83], the Mitsui Bussan Kaisha. Butterfield & Swire found Miike 'dust' economical for bunkering, especially when mixed with higher grades of coal, and both Blue Funnel and CNCo ships began to bunker at Miike – their custom serving to promote the use of Miike coal by other foreign lines.[84] Coal from Japan was also carried to China ports to be stockpiled for CNCo use. Miike coal apparently did not suit the boilers of some domestic lines,[85] and when a number of rival coalmines went bankrupt, following massive overproduction in the 1890s,[86] B&S became especially valued customers, cementing a lasting relationship with Mitsui[87].

The association with Ocean also led to B&S being asked during the mid-1880s to advise on ship construction and officer training[88] for the newly established Nippon Yusen Kaisha (NYK).[89] In 1894, NYK's parent company, Mitsubishi, approached B&S to manage their shipping interests (i.e. bring them under the British flag) during the ongoing hostilities between Japan and China.[90] While keen to further the relationship with Mitsubishi, John Swire was not about to be drawn into an arrangement that might damage the company's reputation in either country.[91] He declined the invitation and took a similar stance when B&S in Shanghai received a request to join forces with Jardines in such an arrangement for the China Merchants Steam Navigation Company: 'We are satisfied that our refusal to take charge of the Japanese or Chinese fleets was politic in every way. Don't let us be parties to any equivocal transactions.'[92]

Benefiting from operational and shipbuilding subsidies, after the Japanese Government declared the route between Japan and Australia to be one of national importance, NYK became a formidable rival. Eager to avoid a battle he knew CNCo could not win, John Swire counselled: 'We hear the NYK contemplate running Japan/Hong Kong/Australia – better suggest they buy us out. We would take £150,000 for the four ships,[93] which cost us £184,000 laid down – we engaging not to run. Better for them to buy than to fight.'[94]

His Eastern managers were reluctant to give up a relatively new and 'prestige' line, and CNCo soldiered on despite disappointments.[95] John Swire continued to woo the Japanese line, however, and in 1896 invited them to join with CNCo and the other main protagonist in this trade, Eastern & Australian Steam Ship Co.,[96] in an agreement to maintain freight rates – a move that foreshadowed Swire's induction of NYK into full Conference membership soon afterwards.

The Japanese Government's protectionist stance towards trade and its rapidly developing industries, as well as the rise in nationalism associated with the Sino-Japanese War, certainly coloured The Senior's view of the long-term viability of B&S in Japan. 'Our chief interest is in China, not Japan, where the future for foreigners is very doubtful,'[97] he cautioned, rebuffing a suggestion for a new branch at Moji in 1894. Clearly, he also came to regard his Japan managers as 'specialists' who could not easily be interchanged with managers at other ports, admonishing Dodds, who believed he had been passed over for promotion in 1889: 'For "Head" either at Hong Kong or Shanghai you have not the requisite experience … besides you, like myself, are too old to transplant.'[98]

Swire's repeated mantra was that it was vital to choose good men and to know them personally and continuity of management helped him to maintain a degree of personal control in Japan that is surprising, given the nature of communications that existed in his day. Although the telegraph service extended to Japan in 1872, cables were discouraged because of the cost involved. However, inter-port mail was religiously copied home to The Senior in London, affording him exhaustive access to the routine minutiae, and daily he sat down to write to his managers in longhand,[99] his communications by turns didactic, bantering or sardonic.

The acerbic wit apparent from John Swire's correspondence masked a kinder nature. He was devoted to his son, and to judge from surviving letters, theirs was a warm and easy relationship of a kind that belies the Victorian stereotype. Whilst he could be personally parsimonious, he could also be magnificent in his generosity to his friends,[100] and his 'rigorously fair, but absolutely uncompromising manner'[101] inspired great loyalty amongst his staff: 'My one merit is that managers or partners in the House will accept my decisions with perfect confidence … every dispute is left for my award, and with it, they have heretofore been satisfied,'[102] he wrote to his future wife in 1881.

After twenty years of widowhood, and to the great delight of his family, John Swire married Miss Mary Warren, the daughter of a Liverpool ship-owner, and 26 years his junior. They had one son, (George) Warren Swire (1883–1949). Mary accompanied her husband during his final trips to Japan in 1883 and 1891, but she was not present in August 1891, when Baggallay's 'seaside house,' in which Swire was weekending, was destroyed in a typhoon. Fortunately, the party had decided to brave the storm and walk the seven miles back to the Foreign Settlement[103].

13

Lasenby Liberty (1843–1917) and Japan

SONIA ASHMORE

Lasenby Liberty

LIBERTY'S, JAPONISME, AND THE TRADE IN JAPANESE GOODS

AFTER THE OPENING of Japan to the West, and with the reduction of tariffs, Japanese artefacts became sought after by artists and architects, particularly in Britain, France and the United States. In 1874, the London Furniture Gazette announced that 'Fashion has declared for Japanese Art'.[1] In 1888, the Woman's World reported that 'There is hardly a drawing-room in the kingdom in which the influences of Japanese art are not felt … most of the Japanese wares that are sold in England are exceedingly cheap, and there is consequently some danger that they may be vulgarized'; nonetheless, it recommended a visit to 'some great warehouse', where, 'a little taste and a five pound note will work miracles in the most sombre and puritanical of houses'.[2]

Liberty & Co. of Regent Street were influential in the dissemination of Japanese and other oriental artefacts in Britain. The shop became the principal retail source of the Japanese 'look' in London, whether in the form of silks and embroideries, a paper fan, an antique kimono, a print, a folding screen, antique or modern Japanese porcelain, or 'Tokio Tooth Powder'.

Arthur Lasenby Liberty, who became known as 'Lasenby', developed his business against the background of both the Arts and Crafts movement and its concern about the pernicious effects of industrialization, and of growing interest in Oriental countries and their regenerative possibilities for the fine and decorative arts of the West. There was a high level of interest in the Islamic arts of Spain, North Africa, the Middle East and Moghul India in parallel to the 'discovery' of Japan as a source of inspiration and novelty. Liberty's was instrumental in both.

Lasenby Liberty achieved a dominant position in both the West End luxury trades and the emerging department stores; with this success came personal wealth, influence and social standing, including membership of influential organizations, the positions of J. P. and High Sheriff of Buckinghamshire, and a knighthood. Liberty's progress from the modest milieu of the small provincial draper (his father had a drapery business in Chesham, Buckinghamshire) was directly linked to both the old East India trades and to the newer commerce with Japan.

Although dealers and collectors had bought Japanese artefacts before the opening of the Japanese ports in the 1850s, the International Exhibition of 1862 was effectively the first occasion when specifically Japanese goods were shown to the wider London public. After 1862, Japan took full advantage of the trade opportunities offered by the international exhibitions, participating in all but two of those held between 1862 and 1910. Rutherford Alcock's[3] selection for the Exhibition 'included non-art objects', ranging from sixty-seven kinds of Japan paper to traditional Japanese medicines.[4] Lasenby Liberty later commented that at this exhibition:

> The art of Japan was first fully revealed to the Western world and we should not forget that the revelations of Japanese art assisted in no mean degree the renaissance of our own minor constructive arts, and that its beneficial influence can readily be traced in our pictorial, ceramic and decorative arts, and in improvements in our textile fabrics.[5]

At the close of the exhibition, Farmer and Rogers bought many of the artefacts for their new 'Oriental Warehouse'. Their 'Great Shawl and Cloak Emporium' at 171,173, 175 Regent Street, succeeded J. & J. Holmes, dealers in shawls and 'Oriental Curiosities', mostly from India. In 1862, Lasenby Liberty joined the business, and found his metier:

> It was the only shop in London that then dealt in things from the East. The products of Japan were then an absolute novelty, and they attracted the attention of the artistic world … By the time I was twenty-one I was manager of the shop.[6]

By the time Liberty was in trade on his own account in the mid-1870s, there were a number of import houses in London from which he could supply his shop. By 1900, the London trade directory listed nineteen 'Oriental Warehouses' (sometimes meaning large shops, sometimes wholesalers), eleven 'Japanese Fancy Goods Importers', five 'Japanese 'Fine Arts' dealers (both English and Japanese), and five importers of 'Japanese Leather Papers', besides East India Merchants and Agents.

In May 1875, Arthur Lasenby Liberty, then thirty-two years of age, opened a small shop at 218a Regent Street. He had three assistants including a sixteen-year-old girl, Hannah Browning and a Japanese boy, Hara Kitsui (or possibly Kerosaki), the first of several Japanese employees.[7] Fifty years later, the third assistant, William Judd, by then seventy-eight years old, opened the first of two new Liberty shops on Regent Street, with a staff of 'a thousand or more'.[8] These two linked buildings are still familiar London landmarks today.

At first the shop sold 'coloured silks from the East [India, China and Japan] nothing else'[9] By 1881, when Liberty's first catalogue was published, the stock imported from Japan had expanded to include ceramics, bronze and enamel work, scrolls, carved wood panels, lacquer ware, which 'bids fair to entirely supercede the papier maché manufactures of the world,' and necklaces of aventurine, 'sparkling with gold'. An 1882 catalogue included Japanese robes and embroideries including a coat embroidered with '*Kaku-re-minu*, supposed to be of angelic origin and to render the wearer invisible.' By 1884, Liberty's could supply a whole room decorated in Arabian, Chinese or Japanese style; the latter included folding screens, lacquer and enamel cabinets, trays, paper lanterns, embossed 'leather' wallpaper, 'fine grass matting', and bronze and porcelain jars. Liberty's Japanese furniture, clearly manufactured for the export market, was made of 'pressed lacquer' or 'hand-carved' in the form of 'Whatnots',[10] inlaid brackets from Nagoya, and cabinets inlaid with ivory and mother of pearl. In the 1890s, after Lasenby Liberty's visit to Japan, the company began importing Japanese silver, 'a quite recent production of the resourceful and artistic craftsmen of Japan … a development of the bygone art of the Armoursmiths and Silversmiths of Old Japan … changed or modified, in order to meet the requirements of altered conditions.' The silver took the form of teasets, matchboxes, salt cellars, porridge bowls and spoons, suggested as being suitable for Christening gifts.

LIBERTY IN JAPAN

Lasenby Liberty's notions of the 'East' were not formed entirely at second-hand. Given the demands of running a business with which he maintained such a close personal identity, he managed to travel extensively. The Libertys visited Europe, North Africa – Tunisia, Algiers, and Tangier, Constantinople, Egypt, Ceylon and Japan, returning via San Francisco, and other unrecorded locations.

In December 1888, Lasenby Liberty, by then the owner of a thriving business on Regent Street, embarked on a 'world tour' with Alfred East, Charles Holme and his wife Emma. In February 1889 they arrived in Nagasaki from Hong Kong on the P and O ship *Verona*, and stayed in Japan until June of that year. For Liberty, the tour, which also took in Egypt and Ceylon, combined tourism with business, which was built upon goods imported from the 'East', principally India, China and Japan.

Liberty's friend Charles Holme (1848–1923) had a background in the silk and wool trades, but 'retired' to found the influential art magazine, the *Studio* in 1893. In the 1870s Holme had also started trading with Turkestan, India and China and subsequently went into partnership with Christopher Dresser,[11] opening oriental 'warehouses' in Japan at Kobe, and London (1878/79), supplying Liberty's and other retailers. The opening of their London warehouse on Farringdon Road was attended by Sir Rutherford and Lady Alcock.

Liberty had also become a friend of the artist Alfred East R.A (1849–1913). In 1888, East was commissioned by the Fine Art Society to go on a painting tour of Japan This enabled him to travel with his richer friends, Lasenby and Emma Liberty and Holme, and it is thanks to his diaries that we have a written record of the Libertys' visit to Japan.[12]

Guide-books of the period confirm that the Libertys' journeys were typical of those made by numerous contemporary traders, artists, writers and tourists, and indicate a well-organized network of hotels, banks, guides and traders, ready to cater for their needs and lure the money from their purses. Shops which were listed in contemporary guide-books and which might have been patronized by Liberty included in Nagasaki, for instance, in addition to 'curio' merchants, dealers specializing in silk, porcelain, tortoise-shell, *cloisonné* and ivory, embroideries, fans, screens and toys.[13] Murray's *Handbook* commented that 'Japan is now almost denuded of old curios. Some have found their way into the museums of the country, while priceless collections have crossed the sea to Europe and America.' Liberty frequently complained on his travels that there was nothing left to buy, and grumbled about prices, but nonetheless he appears to have done business constantly.

Besides Alfred East's *Diary*, two other documents give us an idea of Lasenby Liberty's first-hand ideas of Japan: an album of photographs, and Liberty's lecture to the Society of Arts in 1890, *The Industrial Arts and Manufactures of Japan'*.[14]

The volume of fifty photographs, *Japan: A Pictorial Record by Mrs Lasenby Liberty* (1910)[15] has captions by her husband. The photographs themselves, 'selected from over a thousand' taken by Emma Liberty, are well-composed representations of the 'traditional' and picturesque Japan that might have appealed to any Victorian, or indeed later, tourist: shrines, monasteries, scenery, street scenes, itinerant traders and musicians. Liberty's text is purely descriptive, apart from a few passing comments such as the caption to a photograph of a street near Yasaka Pagoda, Kyoto: 'The gas lamp marks the bald usurping influence of the Western World'. About the 'Courtyard of an Inn' at Sakamoto, near Lake Biwa, Liberty wrote: 'The youths leaning over the barred gateway are taking full advantage of the opportunity to gaze, probably for the first time, at a European lady.' He noted a general inquisitiveness about Europeans, and the strict rules for monitoring passports at inns. The photographs reveal the Libertys' itinerary through Japan, which included Nagasaki, Nagoya, Kyoto, Nara, including Horyuji, Karasaki, Sakamoto, Ikao (Mt Itanna), Dogashima, (Izu-hanto peninsula), Jigokudani (the boiling sulphur valley at Hakone), Mt Fuji, Nikko and Tokyo.

Alfred East's *Diary* gives more insight into the Libertys' activities in Japan, although East himself generally travelled alone, since his mission was to paint, and stayed on for several months after his companions left. East noted that his friends spent a good deal of time examining and buying 'curios'. At a shop in Nagasaki, their port of arrival,[16] East recorded that 'Sato, the owner of the shop, was delighted to see some Europeans as they were generally his best customers. My friends ordered a considerable number of curios to be sent to the boat'.[17] In Osaka, he sketched while the others went in search of artefacts. 'After an hour or two I found them up to their eyes in curios at the principal shop and as a result of this strange infatuation we scarcely caught our train back.'[18]

East also gave one of the only physical descriptions of Liberty, returning from an inland trip with 'Mrs Liberty … in a *kago* on the shoulders of four coolies … Holme and I had just sat down when we heard English voices and saw through the open *shoji* a short stoutish man with a bronzed and merry face. He was wearing a shirt and trousers. On turning round I discovered that it was our friend Liberty.'[19]

East, Holme and the Libertys traveled from Kobe to Osaka in an 'English railway carriage' accompanied by Mr Sale of Mawe and

Company of Yokohama, the company which had taken over Holme's business in London and Japan, originally established with Christopher Dresser. Dresser and Holme's Kobe branch, run by Dresser's sons, had been listed at 81 (*Hachi-ju-ichi-ban*) in the *Japan Directory for the Year 1880*.[20]

In Kyoto, they stayed at Yaami's Hotel, patronized by Christopher Dresser and Rudyard Kipling[21] on other occasions. In Tokyo, the travelers were entertained at the British Legation near the Imperial Palace, by the Secretary of the Legation, the Master of Napier, who arranged for Liberty and East to be invited to the Emperor's Garden party, for which they had to borrow frock coats and hats. Napier apparently took a dislike to Holme, however, for pretending not to be in trade. 'Liberty scored with Napier by saying that he was in trade'.[22] They were also entertained at the house of Viscount Sano Tsunetami (1822–1902) an influential government Minister.

East's Diary described 'Liberty's farewell lunch' in Tokyo, in June. The scale of the occasion suggests that Liberty was well regarded in Japan, at least in his capacity as a trader: It was held at Ueno Park, which besides temples and tombs of the shoguns, contained the Ueno Museum and a restaurant. East noted:

> There I met Count Okuma, the Foreign Minister, the Lord Chamberlain, the Honourable the Master of Napier, Sale and about eight other European and Japanese gentlemen who had entertained Liberty or done business with him during his stay in Japan. It was an elegant tiffin.[23]

East was appalled by the furnishings however. 'The crimson satin chairs for the Europeans came from France and the rugs from us. What a conjunction! What a horror! I wonder if they felt as uncomfortable as I did.'[24] Liberty's response, though unrecorded, was no doubt similar.

LIBERTY ON 'JAPANESE ART INDUSTRIES'

After the luncheon Liberty gave his lecture, with the aid of an interpreter, Mr N. Ariga. According to the *Japan Weekly Mail*,[25] the event was held in 'the buildings of the *Bijitsu Kiokai*, at Sakuragaoka, Uyeno'. The subject was 'Japanese Art Industries'; he later gave a version of this talk to the Society of Arts on his return to England. 'He managed to explain very well our point of view', East commented in his Diary, mentioning also that 'Captain Brinkley and Professor Fenollosa were there together with an appreciative audience of kneeling listeners sitting on scarlet rugs over the mats'.[26] They had already met Fenollosa at the Emperor's Garden Party the previous day. Liberty thus met two key individuals connected with the appreciation and collection of the traditional arts of Japan.[27]

Lasenby Liberty's paper on 'The Industrial Arts and Manufactures of Japan', for which he was awarded a Silver Medal from the Society of Arts in 1900, now reads as a mixture of insight and opportunism. Liberty singled out for admiration the kind of objects he promoted through his shop, whether or not they were genuinely 'Japanese', while also regretting the Westernizing influence. On the other hand, he made a sincere attempt to understand the cultural determinants of Japanese 'industrial art', and looked at 'character', religion, and factors such as the influence of earthquakes on the design of buildings. He argued that what he called 'the vitality of the race-genius', had enabled the Japanese to absorb a variety of cultural forces and to adapt them to their own needs and abilities. In his paper, Liberty referred to Buddhism, Confucianism, and Catholicism – to the failure of which he ascribed the origin of Japanese isolationism, and 'more recently the example of the industrial West'. He expressed ambivalence about 'Western' influences, suggesting that the opening of Japan to the West:

> … was followed by a rapid absorption of western scientific and mechanical ideas and influences. Perhaps no period could have been more unfortunate for Japanese art, as it coincided with the Western climax of art retrogression, and the Japanese being an emotional people, for a while failed to discriminate between material and art advantages.

While Liberty acknowledged that market forces had caused some deterioration in quality, in lacquer work, for example, and in the 'designs and colourings of silk', he also argued that the Japanese craftsman would benefit by adapting to Western markets. He particularly admired the resourcefulness of Japanese metalworkers in adapting their skills from traditional, military applications to domestic ones, noting 'Nielo' inlaid metalwork, 'the variety and beauty of Japanese iron nail heads', and the hammered copper finish of traditional water kettles – 'happily adopted' by Tiffany's of New York.

On the subject of new developments, Liberty gave the example of antimony, 'Quite a recent invention … promising to be very successful, and again, suggestive of the ability of the Japanese to adapt their industrial arts to Western requirements.' Antimony pieces were promoted in Liberty's catalogues from 1890. Lead was moulded into the required shape and coated with harder antimony;[28] the material could also be coloured. This was a means of producing overtly European goods, such as photograph frames, match boxes, button hooks, cuff-links, sugar sifters and salt cellars 'at trifling cost' yet retaining an element of the 'sharp quaintness and originality' of more traditional Japanese craft work.[29] according to Liberty's Catalogue (c.1890). Liberty also mentioned jewellery in his lecture, as an example of the 'ready versatility of the Japanese craftsmen' although, apart from hairpins, jewellery making was not a notable Japanese tradition. Another example of adaptation mentioned by Liberty was 'the embossing of paper leather', developed specifically for the export trade, and a long-running best-seller in Liberty's shop.

Turning to the subject of textiles, Liberty found a mixture of good and bad. Deterioration in 'both designs and colouring' he ascribed to Western influence; 'The Japanese colour printer and fabric designer has become utterly paralyzed; and deranged by contact with European influence.' On the other hand, its effect had also been 'to reduce the substance of these silks, which was indeed thicker and heavier than seemed necessary or desirable'. Presumably, he meant that these were not suited to Western tastes and therefore difficult to sell, notwithstanding the requirements of the Japanese winter climate or court traditions for which the 'abnormally thick, rigid and stiff' textiles may have evolved. Liberty admired the 'supple silken fabrics … ordinarily worn by the women and children'. Liberty noted that the adoption of industrialized silk production combined with cheap labour and low shipping costs would enable Japan to provide serious competition for European manufacturers. Japanese silk made on power looms lacked 'the meretricious surface lustre, and the substance produced by artificial weighting in Lyons silks at the same cost'. Liberty found the 'purity of material and prospective durability' of the Japanese silks, 'far more satisfactory'. Regarding embroidery, he regretted that 'recent influences have separated this beautiful craft into two divergent schools'; in one, 'the evil "sweating system"' results in 'vulgarism and deterioration', in the other 'progress and a higher standard is the motto'.

While Liberty found some of the Japanese Government's efforts to develop and promote 'art industries' admirable, he also regretted that 'Japan had erred precisely as Great Britain had erred', and had 'too hurriedly absorbed the scientific materialism of the West'. The pernicious effects of industrialization were a fundamental reason for the appeal of hand-made, Oriental goods in the West.

Liberty's lecture was greatly admired when given to the Society of Arts on his return to England. Caspar Purdon-Clarke, who had been unable to attend, subsequently wrote 'The whole paper was so rich in suggestive matter that I should be led into writing a book in attempting to illustrate its influence on my mind.'[30] The Chairman, Sir George Birdwood (1834–1917), Special Assistant in the Revenue and Statistical Department at the India Office in London, speculated that Japan's isolation might account for the closeness to nature of Japanese art. In his summary, Birdwood stressed the 'impassable gulf' between Japanese and Western art, emphasizing its 'diabolical cleverness', and also revealing some of his own prejudices:

> It was a complete mystery to him how the Japanese could have attained to such artistic perfection. The aborigines of the country were the Ainos, and mixed up with them were Papuans, Malayans and Chinese, all people outside the pale of historical humanity, and always looked upon as the most degraded types of the human race. It was very remarkable, therefore, that they should possess so perfect an art.[31]

The day after the lecture in Tokyo, Liberty's party traveled to Yokohama, where the Libertys and Holme embarked on the British steamer *Oceanic*, bound for San Francisco.[32] East, who was staying on to continue with his painting, recorded that:

> I felt I confess miserable about it and the dinner Holme gave me at the Grand Hotel[33] little helped me to forget. It was a pleasant enough evening but the morning was to separate us after many months of companionship in travel in which we had shared so many pleasures together.

LIBERTY AND THE LONDON JAPAN SOCIETY

Like other contemporary visitors to Japan, Liberty developed his contacts with the country and interest in things Japanese through the Japan Society of London (as the society was then called), of which Liberty, East and Holme became active founder-members, sitting on its Council. Liberty was also on the Publications Committee of the Society until 1912, Holme became Secretary, and later Chairman. In Japan, Liberty and Charles Holme were also elected (as Life Members) to the Asiatic Society of Japan,[34] according to a report in the *Japan Weekly Mail*, 29 June 1889.[35]

Founded in 1892, the Japan Society's aim was 'the encouragement of the Study of the Japanese Language, Literature, History and Folklore, of Japanese Art, Science and Industries, of the Social Life and Economic Condition of the Japanese People, past and present, and of all Japanese matters'.[36] Among its members were Gleeson White, editor of Holme's *Studio*, and Marcus Huish, the English editor of Siegfried Bing's *Japon Artistique*. Siegfried Bing (1838–1905), a pioneering dealer in Japanese art in Paris, publisher of *Le Japon Artistisque,* and leading promoter of *Art Nouveau*, was an early (corresponding) member of London's Japan Society, responsible for introducing Liberty and East among other members, at its inception.[37] In March, 1898, Holme read out Bing's paper on '*The Thirty-Six Views of the Fuji-Yama*'. Liberty was in the Chair; commenting diplomatically that:

> He was sure that the members must be impressed with the enthusiastic and poetic manner in which M. Bing had expressed himself. Personally he thought the paper would have had additional interest if the author had also dealt with the technical side of the subject.[38]

Liberty's link with Bing is significant. Their professional careers and promotion of Japanese art and artefacts in the West were in many ways comparable. Although Liberty's aesthetic ideas were less formalized, and more eclectic than Bing's, both men developed new approaches to design, inspired by oriental models, and promoted a domestic design aesthetic which, in the Japanese manner, did not separate the fine and applied arts. Liberty's bought goods from Bing from 1876; although the nature of the purchases is not recorded, Bing dealt almost exclusively in Japanese artefacts at the time.

Further links between French and English *Japonisme* were made through international exhibitions. Liberty and others were invited by Hayashi Tadamasa[39] to choose ceramic objects for the Japanese pavilion at the 1900 Paris Exposition. In 1891, Liberty was invited to contribute an article to Bing's journal *Artistic Japan*, an example of the rapid and influential expansion of art publishing at the end of the nineteenth century.[40] '*The Industrial Arts and Manufactures of Japan*', was an illustrated version of Liberty's lecture in Tokyo to the Society of Arts. Although Bing's journal had only thirty-six issues (1888–91), and was criticized by some scholars as being an opportunistic venture - a means of promoting his business, it was widely read and appeared in three languages. Lasenby Liberty was appearing in print in a high quality, scholarly and internationally influential journal, surely a sign that Liberty was taken reasonably seriously in the world of *Japonisme*.

LIBERTY AND THE MIKADO

In the context of popular *Japonisme,* Liberty & Co. was associated with the D'Oyly Carte Opera Company, and particular with its production of Gilbert and Sullivan's Mikado (1885). This was a huge success and ran for 672 performances, followed by several revivals. 'Authentic' Japanese detail was achieved with the assistance of Lord Redesdale,[41] and the Japanese craftspeople appearing at Humphrey's Hall, Knightsbridge in 1885 in an exhibition, which included two hundred Japanese men, women and children. About six years earlier,

Liberty's had also held a 'Japanese Village' exhibition. 'A Japanese house was erected in the large hall, and this was advertised by men dressed in Japanese costumes, carrying sandwich boards'.[42]

The *Cabinet Maker* referred to W. S. Gilbert 'availing himself of the native talent … brought over in order to thoroughly Japan the Savoy Company. Thus the Anglo-Japanese in *The Mikado* are "to the manner born" … These Japanese makers are useful living examples of that much-praised race of artist-workmen whose disappearance has been so much deplored by writers of the Ruskin school'.[43] Liberty's supplied 'The Ladies' dresses' together with a certain 'Madame Léon'; Gilbert may also have used Japanese prints from Liberty's as source material. Liberty's employee Jessie Flood recalled a show for the press in Liberty's shop in 1882, at which she modeled a 'beautiful white and gold embroidered kimono, which was sold to Jessie Bond, the actress, to play in the Mikado.'[44]

The Japanese authorities attempted to have the play stopped on the grounds that it poked fun at the Emperor. As Gilbert's biographers Dark and Grey observed: 'Though the scene is Old Japan, and though the characters have Japanese names and imitate Japanese manners, the satire and the fun are English in their objective.' Gilbert, surprised, and probably alarmed at the potential loss of earnings, thought it 'a poor compliment to the Japs to suppose they would be offended by it'.[45]

LIBERTY, LIBERTY'S AND JAPAN

The relationship of Lasenby Liberty and his business with Japan was influential and complex. It expressed the aspirations and contradictions of the age. Japan was offered to English consumers as an 'authentic' experience of a pre-industrial culture, embodied in traditional, hand-made artefacts. At the same time, Liberty's wished to supply Japanese goods to a Western mass-market; this required the invention of new forms for production by crafts people whose traditional patronage base was disappearing. Lasenby Liberty himself spent five months enthusiastically investigating Japan at first hand and establishing contacts with dealers and manufacturers. As his lecture on 'Japanese Art Industries' indicates, Lasenby Liberty was as aware as any of his contemporaries of the degenerative effect of Western demand on Oriental artefacts and the societies that produced them. Through its commercial activities, the company was inevitably implicated in this process.

Liberty & Co.'s imaginative introduction of Oriental elements, both Japanese or Islamic, into both dress and home furnishings, became the precursor of a more general move towards lighter, more flexible and less cluttered domestic interiors than those opulent and overstuffed styles generally favoured in the late Victorian and Edwardian periods, an age for which Veblen[46] coined the phrase 'conspicuous consumption'. As the Cabinet Maker recognized, 'A Japanese house is full of emptiness ... for the Japanese have learnt the art of doing without'.[47] Paradoxically, Liberty's, that great emporium of Oriental treasures on Regent Street, may have contributed to that essentially modernist sentiment.

14

Peter Hewett, 1920–82

MERRICK BAKER-BATES

Peter Hewett

FOR THIRTY-FIVE YEARS in post-war Japan Peter William Hewett, known to his colleagues at Cornes and Company as PWH, projected his enigmatic personality on the Anglo-Japanese business scene. As Chairman from the mid-1950s of the long-established trading house that he ran with an iron, sometimes capricious, hand, Hewett made a major contribution to the growth of Anglo-Japanese trade. The holder of a Military Cross, and with an MBE attesting also to his distinguished war record against the Japanese, he spent his most productive years amongst them, helping to rebuild and consolidate the Anglo-Japanese relationship through commerce. In this he was very successful. At a time when the Japanese market was heavily protected, Hewett showed that barriers could be surmounted profitably and, by that example, he encouraged many British, and other European and American exporters, to develop their Japanese connections. These achievements and his chairmanship of the British Chamber of Commerce were recognized by his appointment as a CBE in 1965. By virtue of his long residence in Japan, he remained a leading, if towards the end of his life increasingly detached, personality in the foreign community at large and among the Japanese who moved in those circles. Yet he was not gregarious, he rarely spoke in public and he jealously guarded his private life. Even now, some twenty years after his death, as he would have wanted, much about the real Peter Hewett remains a mystery.

By his own account Hewett's early life was undistinguished. His father, who at one time had been in the British army, sent him to Haileybury, a breeding ground for colonial Civil Servants and officers in the armed forces, many destined to serve in India. At the age of seventeen he announced that he wanted to be a journalist, which prompted his father to respond that he had nothing more to learn at an expensive public school. He then introduced young Peter to the editor of *Sporting Life*, the only newspaper that the father professed to read. Hewett stuck to sports reporting for only six months (longer than most new entrants, he later claimed) and with a fair sized nest-egg of £250 from his racing bets, he moved to a provincial newspaper in Dorset as a junior reporter covering local news from church bazaars to murder trials. The horse-racing nest-egg soon disappeared on cars and beer and after a year or so he tired of his impecunious life in provincial lodgings.

By the summer of 1939 Hewett had moved to London to seek work on a national newspaper. He was about to join the *Daily Mail*, having landed a job on the newspaper's Features Page, when war broke out, newsprint was rationed and the job offer was withdrawn. The armed forces beckoned. However, the Royal Naval Reserve for which he was on the waiting list could give him no firm date to join. Moreover, having developed poor eyesight, it was impossible for him to become a naval deck officer. By chance he discovered, however, that the Brigade of Guards would take volunteers and somewhat to his surprise, after a perfunctory examination, he was able to join the First of Foot.

Next day, when he appeared with shaven head, uniform and boots several sizes too big, his Company Commander noted on his report 'appearance against him', sending him nonetheless for basic training. Later, Lance Corporal Hewett, unpaid, since he was described as a 'potential officer', was briefly stationed at Windsor Castle ready to defend the Royal Family to the last should the Germans invade.

After that it was the Royal Military College at Sandhurst for officer training. But on passing out at a respectable level Hewett did not return to the Grenadier Guards. An officer in that regiment needed a considerable private income of some £600 a year to augment his pay, support which his father was unable or unwilling to provide. Since his family and his school, had connections in India he decided to seek an appointment in the Indian Army.

In 1941 Hewett joined the 4/14 Regiment in the Punjab. He moved first to the North West Frontier where he hoped to join the Waziristan Scouts, but found himself instead in Burma confronting the Japanese. After that it was a good war during which he seems to have acquired a scar on his left cheek which, when combined with his neatly trimmed beard gave him a somewhat piratical look. Cornes men later dubbed him *ohige-san,* 'Mr Beard'. He came to admire Japanese fighting spirit and that of the Gurkhas amongst whom he moved. In later life he would often refer to his war experience as the time when his interest in Japan was first kindled.

Demobbed with his MC and an MBE (Military) Major Peter Hewett decided to seek a job in the Far East. The commercial prospects in devastated Japan did not look good; so he briefly joined a textile firm in the UK. By 1948, however, he had started to look again at Japan. He made contact with Stanley Dodwell, Chairman of Dodwell and Co. He wrote:

> It has been suggested by Mr Marlowe of the London Chamber of Commerce that I should write to you. Ever since I returned in 1946 from the Far East, where I spent five years with the Indian Army in India, Burma, Siam and Malaya, I have been determined to make my career in Japan. My duties in the Army in the last year brought me into close contact with Japanese and I learned something of their language and customs … It now seems that the commercial position has improved there and as I want to join a firm whilst I am still of an age to make a worthwhile career in it, I am approaching you.

Dodwell commended the application to John Ewing in his Tokyo office, describing Hewett's army testimonials as 'most satisfactory' and suggesting that his name be put on the list in case there was another vacancy.

For whatever reason, Dodwell and Co. did not offer him a job. How Hewett eventually found Cornes and Company remains obscure. One must assume, however, that he had an introduction to the swashbuckling entrepreneur and old China hand, George Marden, Chairman of Wheelock Marden and Co, in Hong Kong, who had acquired Cornes and Company from the family in 1947 for its book value of £20,000.

There is no need here to review the history of the company in Japan as this is traced in the biographical portrait by Peter Davies of its founder Frederick Cornes, which is included in this volume.

When Hewett arrived in Tokyo in 1948 the trading climate was not as propitious as he had believed. Japan was still occupied and commercial life was only slowly recovering after wartime destruction. He found Cornes operating out of a Nissen hut and struggling. By 1955, however, the company had acquired a number of prestige agencies including de Havilland aircraft, Yardley, Rowntree and Robertson's Jams. But it was not making money and George Marden was threatening to close it down. One difficulty lay in the expatriate staff, mostly a group of old China hands who in the words of one former Cornes executive 'expected to live and operate as they had in pre-war Shanghai with Japanese instead of Chinese coolies'. Moreover, the company's main competitors, Dodwell and Jardine Matheson, could use their Hong Kong experience and connections, whereas Wheelock Marden had little to do with import export business.

This was Hewett's opportunity. He promised Marden that he would turn the company around within two years if he were appointed Chairman and Chief Operating Officer and joined the Board of Wheelock Marden in Hong Kong. Marden agreed. Some expatriate staff left and Hewett began the task of rebuilding the company in his image and making his own fortune in the process. He did this by a combination of luck, entrepreneurial flair and personal relationships. He projected the company to principals abroad as 'Japan Merchants', experienced people who operated only in Japan, specialising in two main areas – insurance and trading, mostly in high technology products. Insurance became the most important aspect of the company's business with Cornes acting as agents and brokers. Ship surveys and claims settlement were handled in Yokohama, Nagoya and Kobe with the underwriting and broking done in Tokyo and Osaka.

On the trading side, Hewett acquired electronic interests in both marine and industrial equipment. Cornes also had important aviation and defence agencies and a large agricultural machinery business launched in the mid-1960s. Sometimes a successful agency or division would be hived off to form a separate company in which Cornes would retain a shareholding. Hewett created half a dozen such affiliated companies, whose activities ranged from the manufacture of electronic components and the distribution of business machinery, to selling children's books and making pork pies and pizzas.

Business Machinery was one of his most successful ventures. Cornes began importing Gestetner's stencil duplicators in the early 1960s which, in a PR coup, were supplied to the Olympic Village during the Tokyo Games of 1964. As the business grew Hewett formed a joint venture company with Gestetner, staffed by seconded Cornes men, creating what many foreign companies wished to emulate but few achieved, a countrywide distribution and service system for his product.

All the while Hewett ran Cornes with a small group of colleagues virtually as a private fief, following very few of the rules of modern management and frequently, by some accounts, off the seat of his entrepreneurial pants. Being his own man, he did not feel the need to consult the Wheelock Marden in Hong Kong in anything more than a nominal way. He made his mind up quickly, sometimes wrongly, about people although he prided himself on an ability to read character. Wartime experience had led him to regard the Ghurkas as a breeding ground for managerial skills; so on more than one occasion he employed Ghurka officers with results that were not always happy. The inner workings of the company were shrouded in secrecy. For example, a 22-year-old management trainee, deputed to sell Robertson's jams, recalls how he had little idea of the landed cost of the product and no knowledge of his budget and, therefore, of profit or loss. Whilst thus trying to sell in the dark, he was surprised to be told by the Chairman that one day he would head the company. Hewett gave that particular nod to several people over the years.

He also managed to create a strong personal relationship with some of the Japanese staff who held him in respect, not to say awe, and not least because he so evidently cared about their welfare, creating for them a company spirit. Yet, despite his thirty-five years of residence in the country, Hewett never got near to mastering the Japanese language, although he understood more of it than he liked to admit. In that he was typical of many expatriates of the time. At the office he liked to cultivate a rather gruff, remote, exterior. If something displeased him, he would roar '*urusai*!!' (bloody nuisance!) and then subside with a slightly sheepish grin and a pull on his ever present cigarette.

In his more outspoken moods, Hewett claimed to despise the human race. He liked to be provocative, as when at a British Embassy dinner he denigrated the expensively refurbished panelling in the dining-room as 'cheap Filipino plywood'. But he only did it to annoy because he knew it teased, and one felt that his provocative comments were a cover for shyness and a sense of insecurity. He did not want to be regarded as rude or overbearing. In reality, he was a kind and considerate man – particularly towards animals, being a keen supporter of the Japan Animal Welfare Society. He showed generosity to many people. Steak and kidney pies, beef stew and apple pies, prepared by Hideko Endo his cook, would be delivered by Rolls-Royce to ease some domestic crisis. His talks to new entrants to the company were famous for their easy humour and frankness, and are still recalled with affection and respect.

He was also a man for the underdog, the non-conformist, the less privileged in a society that lays emphasis on rank and conformity.

Typically, he once gave a job to someone because his father was in prison; but he was then deeply hurt when that employee turned to thieving himself and had to be dismissed. There was never a hint of marriage. He ostentatiously preferred male company, though he also had some firm female friends devoted to him. Inevitably, however, questions were asked about his sexual proclivities, questions never answered with any certainty.

Cars, preferably big and expensive, were his passion from childhood. But selling them in Japan was at the best of times an uphill slog. Cornes acquired the Rover agency, later moving up market to Rolls-Royce and Ferrari for which Hewett designed a splendid service garage in Yokohama. He regarded those agencies as the crown jewels of his trading business, never a very profitable part but one that projected Cornes to the outside world as a company of quality.

By the early 1980s, Hewett was beginning to think of retirement. He had made his fortune and had devised elaborate plans to ensure that the taxman did not lay hands on it. He spent more time at his seaside villa at Arai, some 60 miles south of Tokyo where he regularly entertained. On a summer's Saturday morning Kosegawa, the butler, would drive the navy blue Rolls-Royce Corniche convertible to the seaside, with Hewett beside him and Hideko's supplies for the weekend in baskets in the back. The last couple of hundred yards or so to the house had to be covered via a steep, narrow pathway precipitously perched between paddy fields. Here the butler would alight and Hewett would drive at speed up the hill, believing that only he knew how to navigate the hazards on route in a Rolls-Royce.

The house at Arai was his indulgence. A white wooden bungalow on top of a cliff, it was tastefully and luxuriously furnished with antiques and decorated with English wallpapers. The roof was of slate, also imported expensively from England. Hewett would pad around the house barefoot enjoying the magnificent views over the sea, smoking incessantly, consuming glasses of John Begg whisky and reading the British weekend papers. One of his eccentricities was to subscribe to the airmail edition of *The Times* at some considerable expense, but never to read it. Hundreds of unopened copies remained neatly stacked in a large alcove behind his desk at the office.

At Arai, whilst he would recommend a stroll, he never seemed to indulge in exercise himself. On one occasion he proposed an expedition to the beach with a picnic for some guests and their children. When the party arrived there, only a few minutes walk away, they were dismayed to find it covered in refuse and the sea full of flotsam and jetsam. Gingerly, a space was cleared on the sand and they waded out to swim beyond the floating refuse. It was decided not to describe the embarrassing state of the beach to their attentive host. So when

Hewett asked how they had enjoyed themselves he received a suitably bland reply. He then confessed, with a twinkle in his eye, that he had not been on the beach for fifteen years and that when he had swum there last he had caught an ear infection from the polluted water.

As he grew older, his bachelor habits and routine became more pronounced. He always wore a navy blue knitted tie, and usually a blue shirt. Being highly sensitive to human odour – there had been a problem with a colleague's socks – he doused himself (some claimed he showered in it) with Estee Lauder Eau de Cologne. Invariably, he arrived at the office in mid-morning. This was a ruse, he claimed, to persuade any inspectors who might be snooping in the building that he was indeed, as he had declared on his tax return, a part-time Chairman.

Lunch in the office followed an unvaried pattern. Mrs Kaga, widow of a British Embassy chauffeur, clad in a kimono, would appear with a large dry martini and two dainty sandwiches, always of the same white bread with the crusts removed and always containing cheese. Hewett would carefully remove the top layer of bread, consume what remained of the sandwich and then order a second martini. That was lunch. At 4 o'clock Mrs Kaga would appear again with a large pot of tea and at 6.30 pm she would bid him good night, leaving a bottle of John Begg whisky, ice and a glass on his desk. He then consumed a first generous tot before ordering up his Rolls-Royce Silver Shadow from the garage.

At the house in Kamiyama-cho, Kosegawa, in jacket and cummer-bund, would be waiting at the top of the front steps with a glass of John Begg and water. That was the pattern for the evening: whisky, reminiscences and clouds of tobacco smoke. Around 8.30pm dinner would be announced then delayed whilst he ordered another Scotch and water, and puffed at another Winston cigarette. The meal was modest in quantity, designed to trim the figure. A consommé might be followed by cold cuts, home grown radishes and a little salad, the meal being finished off with fruit. Then back in the sitting-room he would return to reminiscences and the John Begg. Despite the large quantities of alcohol and the fifty or so cigarettes that he consumed daily, to all appearances Hewett had an iron constitution unaffected by these indulgences.

By the early 1980s, with business booming in Japan, Hewett talked openly of retirement and planned to divide his time between his London home, in Edwardes Square, the houses in Tokyo and Arai and a farm near Obihiro in Hokkaido. He became ever more preoccupied with elaborate, legal, schemes to keep his assets beyond the reach of punitive death duties. If that meant becoming virtually a non-person for taxation purposes, so much the better. He had acquired the

Hokkaido farm from Cornes in the late 1960s. It was run by his Japanese protégé, Tateki Sasaki and Hewett hoped one day to live there at least part of the year with him and his family.

In the summer of 1982 Hewett took his annual home leave in Britain, accompanied by Kosegawa and the cook Hideko. The day before departure he had a drinks party at the office, talked about the new management structure recently put in place and mused about eventual retirement. In Britain he made his usual round of visits to his sister at Cork in Ireland and friends in England. In early September news of his sudden collapse during lunch at his house in Edwardes Square came as a shock. For some weeks, after a lengthy operation, he lingered unconscious in a London clinic. It seemed that, at best, early retirement would be forced upon him. But it was not to be. He died on 15 October 1982. The funeral took place at the Golders Green crematorium. Hewett being an atheist, there was no religious over-tone, no ceremony. Nothing was said. Shirley Bassey, Julio Iglesias and others of his favourite recordings were played. According to one version, the coffin disappeared to the strains of Shirley Bassey's hit *Hey, big spender!* – a touch one cannot help but think that Hewett would have enjoyed. In Tokyo a traditional, full-blown, Japanese company memorial service followed. Hewett himself would probably have preferred more muted obsequies. But the company that he had joined in a Nissen hut was now expected to blow its trumpet even in mourning. As he wished, his ashes were laid to rest on a hillside over-looking his beloved Spring Farm in Hokkaido and near to the family that he had adopted.

Within two years the company that he had built was a very different animal. Wheelock Marden, and with it Cornes, had become part of the commercial empire of the Hong Kong shipping and prop-erty magnate, Sir Y. K. Pao. The Rolls-Royces were still blessed annually by the Shinto priests, but of Hewett's idiosyncratic, often eccentric, management style little else remained. He saw himself in the Frederick Cornes tradition, a Victorian entrepreneur in Japan, taking risks, sailing near the commercial wind. That was not the style of the Hong Kong Chinese management. His legacy lies in the flour-ishing company that he revived and in the strong impression that his personality, with all its contradictions, made on those around him. One can see him now lurking on the fringes of a cocktail party, with his erect military bearing, in one hand a Winston cigarette and in the other a glass of scotch, as he surveys the scene with an enigmatic smile and a detached, somewhat cynical, eye.

ACKNOWLEDGEMENTS

The author gratefully acknowledges contributions from many sources, in particular from Mrs Satsuko Uchiyama, Mrs Colette Tsugi, Mr L. A. Radbourne OBE, Mr Jonathan Rice, Mr T. Takahara OBE, Mr Tadami Tsusumu, Mr Stephen Jones, Mr Masahiro Ogihara, Mr F. M. Wilson and others who knew Peter Hewitt and provided reminiscences. Without their kind cooperation this biographical portrait could not have been written.

PART 3

Engineers & Teachers in Meiji Japan

15

Professor W. E. Ayrton, 1847–1908: the 'Never-resting, Keen-eyed chief'

IAN RUXTON

Professor W.E. Ayrton

> When I arrived in Japan in 1875, I found a marvellous laboratory, such as the world has not seen elsewhere. At Glasgow, at Cambridge and Berlin, there were three great personalities; the laboratories of [Lord] Kelvin, and of [James Clerk] Maxwell, and of [Hermann von] Helmholtz, however, were not to be mentioned in comparison with [that of] Ayrton. Fine buildings, splendid apparatus, well-chosen, a never-resting-keen-eyed chief of great originality: these are what I found in Japan.
>
> J. Perry, untitled obituary ['Death of Professor Ayrton'], *Journal of the Institution of Electrical Engineers*, 1909, Vol. 42, 3–6 on pp. 3–4; and also in *Central*, Vol. 7, (1910), p. 708.[1]

As the above frequently quoted (but apparently somewhat misleading) observation[2] by his great research associate and Ulsterman colleague John Perry (1850–1920)[3] suggests, William Edward Ayrton was a British physicist and electrical engineer of considerable verve and distinction. He was the first Professor of Electrical Engineering in Japan – and thus in the world[4] – at the ICE (The Imperial College of Engineering, from 1886 the Faculty of Engineering of the Tokyo Imperial University), and thereafter the first in Britain.

Born the son of a London-based lawyer, Ayrton studied at University College (part of London University) after his eminent Japan *senpai* (Sir) Ernest Satow, and was also taught in Glasgow by the above-mentioned Lord Kelvin of Largs (1824–1907, called Sir William Thomson 1866–92) who 'virtually single-handedly engineered the cables, galvanometers, and other electrical components for the first successful telegraph cable beneath the Atlantic Ocean in 1866.'[5] After working for the Indian Telegraph Co. Ayrton was in Japan from 1873 to 1879 at the ICE (the *Kōgakuryō* founded in August 1873, from 1877 known as the *Kōbu Daigakkō*) lecturing on Physics and Electrical Engineering (especially telegraphy).[6]

On 25 March 1878 the first carbon arc lamps in Japan were lit at the ICE under Ayrton's direction to celebrate the opening of the Tokyo Central Telegraph Station, and thereafter 25 March became 'Electricity (Commemoration) Day' in Japan, a clear measure of the very high regard in which his name was and is held up to the present day.[7] This paper focuses on Ayrton's Japan experience as a crucial formative stage in his development as a major pioneer in the study of, and teaching about, Electricity.

EARLY LIFE AND EDUCATION

In the 1901–11 Supplement to the *Dictionary of National Biography*[8] W. E. Ayrton was deemed to merit a substantial entry (pp. 72–75) by one 'P. J. H.' (Philip James Hartog, a family friend). He was born in London on 14 September 1847, the son of an able barrister Edward Nugent Ayrton, and had other eminent relatives.[9] 'Ayrton's father, a distinguished linguist ... tried, without much success, to enforce on his son the practice of speaking different languages (including Hebrew) on each day of the week.'[10]

Ayrton proceeded from University College School (1859–64)[11] to University College (founded 1826) in 1864, where in July of 1865 and the following year he won the Andrews mathematical scholarship. In 1867 he passed the first BA exam of the University of London with a second-class in mathematics and also passed the entrance exam for the Indian telegraph service. He was first sent to Glasgow to study electricity under Thomson, of which Hartog says he gave 'a vivid account' in *The Times* of 8 January 1908.

In 1868, after practical work at the Telegraph Construction and

Maintenance Company, Ayrton went to Bombay where, from 1 September, he was appointed assistant-superintendent (fourth grade). He received rapid promotion as a result of work with the Electrical Superintendent on 'developing a speedy method for locating the prevalent faults in the overland telegraph lines.'[12] This made it unnecessary to go to the trouble of laying costly submarine cables around the coast of India. On 21 December 1871, in London, Ayrton married a cousin, a practice apparently not uncommon in the Victorian era with its large families. She was Matilda Chaplin (1846–83), and was destined to teach midwifery to Japanese women.[13] On a second leave from India in 1872 Ayrton was elected a member of the Society of Telegraph Engineers (the STE, from 1888 the Institution of Electrical Engineers) and assisted Thomson in testing a new transatlantic cable.

Ayrton, whose notepaper (according to Perry) was fittingly embossed with his motto 'Energy', was appointed to a five-year contract as Professor of Physics and Telegraphy at the ICE through the patronage of Thomson and W. J. M. Rankine, both of Glasgow University. He arrived in Japan with his wife in September 1873, a rising star in a new academic field, aged just 26. But the Scottish principal of the ICE Henry Dyer (1848–1918), who had arrived in June 1873 after appointment the previous year, was almost a year younger. The pioneering new college, suggested by Rankine to Itō Hirobumi during the Iwakura Mission's visit to Scotland in October 1872,[14] and the creation of Dyer and then Vice Minister of Public Works Yamao Yōzō (a member, with Itō, of the Chōshū Five who had himself worked and studied in Glasgow, 1866–68) would clearly lack for nothing in terms of youthful dynamism and energy!

AYRTON IN JAPAN

The ground breaking and key research, which Ayrton did in Japan, was mainly conducted with John Perry, who at the age of 25 took up the Chair of Mechanical Engineering at the ICE in 1875. Together they published many papers in British and Japanese journals between 1877 and 1880.[15] Topics were wide-ranging and included earthquakes (i.e. seismology, in which John Milne,[16] professor of mining and geology at the ICE from March 1876, was to specialise from 1880 onwards and ultimately make his name), and Japanese 'magic mirrors'.[17]

The main focus of Ayrton and Perry's research was, however, the exciting and still relatively unknown properties of the new energy source, electricity. They wrote on: 'telegraph tests, the ratio of electrostatic and electromagnetic units, electrolytic polarization, atmospheric electricity, the resistance of galvanometers and the electric arc, the viscosity of dielectrics, and the theory of voltaic action in the electric cell [i.e. battery]'.[18] To a layman some of these words may be obscure, but that the research was cutting-edge in the Victorian age seems obvious.

The leading Japanese academic researcher on Ayrton is Dr Yūzō Takahashi of the Faculty of Engineering at Tokyo University of Agriculture and Technology. His seminal 1991 article '*Ayrton to sono shūhen*' (Ayrton and his circumstances) provides much useful and detailed material. He explains that the Telegraphy course at the ICE was the first independent course of electrical engineering in the world, and that Ayrton and this course were crucially important for the institutionalization (*seidoka*) of electrical engineering education worldwide. In other words, the ICE itself was one vast (and hugely successful) experiment!

What did Ayrton think of Japan and its seemingly sudden passion for Western technology? Perhaps the clearest answer is the one he gave shortly after his return to England, near the end of his lengthy inaugural lecture at the new City Guilds Institute (funded by the City of London), of which he was the first professor, on 1 November 1879. In the address, entitled 'The Improvements Science can effect in our Trades and in the condition of our workmen', he spoke in glowing terms of his admiration for the country:

> And yet another nation, small and apart from the world, a people like the Swiss, dwelling in a mountainous country, and like them too dearly loving their pine-clad hills – *the Japanese – have set us an example that our ambition should lead us to emulate.* [My italics, not in original text.] Much have we heard of Japanese art, much have we seen of Japanese lacquer, Japanese fans, but only a few of us are acquainted with the Japanese modern technical education.

Ayrton went on to describe the Meiji Restoration, and the drive to catch up with the West which had created the new ICE:

> Ten years ago a feudal country, tyranised [*sic*] over by barons with power of life and death in their hands, distracted by the conflict between the rightful sovereign and their hereditary military usurper, that nation whom we regarded as barbarous, that nation of whose manners we were comparatively ignorant, whose very modes of thought are so different from our own that we can hardly be said to understand them now, that people had but three years emerged from a state of almost slavery, when up grew, in its very midst, *a technical college, with its staff of carefully-chosen English professors, with its laboratories, its class-rooms, museums, libraries, and workshops, costing Japan, a poor country be it remembered, at least twelve thousand pounds a year to support, and many many thousands to build.* [My italics]

The Japanese egalitarian and meritocratic pursuit of academic excellence clearly appealed to Ayrton as 'an example to emulate' in his new post, for he continued and concluded:

> And to enter and study at this college, neither cash, nor position, nor any qualification is necessary but ability and desire to study; so that working at the lathe, or conning over their books in the class-room, or experimenting in the laboratory, may now be seen, side by side, the young noble and the young artisan.[19]

AYRTON AND PERRY'S JAPANESE STUDENTS

In imitation of Thomson's practice, of which Ayrton later wrote enthusiastically,[20] Ayrton and Perry made use of their Japanese students as 'research assistants' in their laboratories. This turned the whole educational process into a highly positive and mutually beneficial exchange: the bright and knowledge-hungry young students, fiercely patriotic and determined to acquire engineering knowledge for Japan, learned the practical skills of experimentation by doing, and the canny professors used the results of these experiments in their research papers. The trust which Ayrton, unlike other European colleagues, was ready to place in his students as independent researchers paid handsome dividends.

This convenient two-way symbiotic mechanism (which, incidentally, continues to flourish in little-modified form in many Japanese technological universities and faculties to this day[21]) was specifically and properly acknowledged by Ayrton and Perry. For example, in a paper on the gravitational acceleration for Tokyo, published three years later in England, they wrote:

> We have to thank several of our late [i.e. former] students, and especially Messrs. Honda, Kikkawa, A. Kasai, J. Nakabara, and H. Nobechi for assistance rendered … And it may be here mentioned that this investigation, like the many others we have been enabled to carry out during the last few years, has resulted from the plan we have followed of teaching the laboratory students not … to repeat well-known experiments, but to endeavour … to advance, in some small degree at any rate, the bounds of existing knowledge.[22]

The authors went on to claim, no doubt with some justification, that this approach of spurning the received wisdom of the few text books available and harnessing the curiosity of the young created 'an enthusiasm in experimental work otherwise unreproducible'.

Ayrton had clear ideas about good and bad teaching. In his 1908

Times tribute to Thomson, who died on 17 December 1907 ('Kelvin in the Sixties'), he wrote with scorn of 'the stereotyped teacher … the talking text-book, who instructs his students what it will pay them to read, payment being made in examination marks …' and with contrasting reverence of great teachers such as Thomson, 'the inspired teacher, he who soars above scientific fashion, whose doxy becomes scientific orthodoxy, who produces thinkers, not mere successful examinees'. Judged by these standards, Ayrton was indeed a worthy successor to his distinguished Scottish mentor, whom he recognized as the inspiration of his professional life.[23]

While at the ICE Ayrton taught about twenty students,[24] but supervised only one through his thesis to graduation. Like Ayrton before him, Shida Rinzaburo (1856–92) was in 1879 ordered to study at Glasgow (by the Japanese government) where as the first of several Japanese pupils of Thomson[25] he became an outstanding student. On his return to Japan in 1883 Shida became the first Japanese to teach in the telegraphy department at his alma mater, and in the same year he founded the Institute of Electrical Engineers of Japan. Three others who graduated in 1881, Fujioka Ichisuke (1857–1918), Nakano Hatsune and Asano Osuke, stayed on to become Shida's research and teaching assistants, in the pattern established by Ayrton and Perry which persists today.[26]

In their subsequent careers Nakano was a professor at the ICE, while in 1886 Fujioka became chief engineer at Tokyo Electric Lighting, Japan's first electricity supply company (established 1883) and made significant contributions in electric-powered rail transport and incandescent light production.

Dr Asano was the first director of the government-funded Electric Experimental Station (the *Denki Shiken-jo*, founded 1891), which led research on the wireless telegraph. He 'played a leading role as a technical adviser and senior researcher on telegraphy, telephone communication and electricity supply, as well as improving government administration in these fields'.[27]

In 1924 Asano wrote a brief memorial tribute to Ayrton in which he mentioned that he routinely worked through public holidays and weekends, and even researched on the morning of his final day in Japan before catching the boat at 3 pm with barely time to spare, telegraphing the results back to London from Suez on the way home! On arrival in London Ayrton went directly to the Royal Society to give a lecture. Such was the passion of the man for his lifework.[28]

Ayrton also taught students sent by the government from the Telegraph Operators' Training School; many of these later made their mark in Japanese electrical engineering.

AYRTON IN ENGLAND

This portrait focuses on Ayrton in Japan and I cannot comment here in detail on Ayrton's illustrious career after Japan, which has been described elsewhere. He played a leading role in England in electrical engineering and technical education, becoming a Fellow of the Royal Society in 1881 and winning a Royal Medal, awarded by the Royal Society in 1901, in recognition of his achievements in physics and engineering. His time in Japan had certainly laid the foundations for his subsequent success and fame.

In 1882 Perry rejoined Ayrton at Finsbury Technical College where 'the reunited pair translated their unique Japanese experience of laboratory-based technical education into a rather more frugal English form'.[29] The renewed partnership lasted till 1889–90. After Matilda died of tuberculosis in July 1883, William (known as 'Will') Ayrton married Sarah 'Hertha' Marks – a Cambridge-educated mathematician – on 6 May 1885. They shared research interests, and in 1899 Ayrton, a public champion of womens' rights, helped Hertha to become the first woman to read a paper at the Institution of Electrical Engineers (IEE), now based in Savoy Place, central London, of which Ayrton himself was briefly President (1892–93). Continuing the Ayrton family's political traditions, their daughter Barbara Gould (née Ayrton) became a Labour MP in 1945.

CONCLUSION

William Edward Ayrton was a most industrious, dedicated and brilliant academic, who led and taught his Japanese students by his example rather than kindness. (The phrase 'live wire' seems peculiarly apt to describe him!) Bearded and handsome, he was enormously influential at the ICE despite his relatively short period of employment there, and effectively used it as a stepping-stone to international recognition, which he had certainly achieved by 1890 when *The Electrical World* commented:

> The name of Professor Ayrton is a familiar one in every corner of the world where electrical apparatus is used today, for by his long connection with the development of practical electricity and his valuable additions to the theoretical part of the science, he is singularly well known to practical men.[30]

Ayrton's Japanese employers clearly respected his obvious abilities as a researcher and teacher, even if they did not particularly appreciate his unrestrained frankness. When his contract expired in 1878 it was not renewed, it has been suggested, because of his insistence that foreign supervision was necessary for the operation of the national telegraph system, and his 'tactlessly neo-colonialist conduct towards the officials of the Japanese telegraph service'.[31] This resembled his previous treatment of subordinates in India (1868–72), and perhaps also echoed the treatment of some of his students at the ICE.

In short, and in clear contrast to the diplomatic Dr Dyer and other colleagues, the electrifying Professor Ayrton was probably perceived as rather rude and arrogant, trading too heavily on his god-like (and self-assumed) reputation for omniscience. Yet Ayrton himself was probably not inclined to stay in Japan longer than the five years needed to make his name: although he admired Japan and was for a while treasurer of the Asiatic Society of Japan in Tokyo,[32] his self-investment in the country was not enough to make him desire permanent residence, and he followed Matilda and their daughter Edith home.

Nevertheless, the work Ayrton did in Japan was to serve both him and his students, to say nothing of the Japanese nation, in remarkably good stead in their respective future careers: it is the 'phenomenally energetic' and 'often fearlessly critical'[33] W. E. Ayrton who deserves the credit for first sowing the seed that subsequently blossomed in the field of Japanese electrical engineering, which in its modern corporate form (Sony, Toshiba, Sanyo et al.) has been envied and admired around the world.

PRINCIPAL SOURCES

- Graeme J. N. Gooday and Morris F. Low, 'Technology Transfer and Cultural Exchange: Western Scientists and Engineers Encounter Late Tokugawa and Meiji Japan' in *Osiris*, (a research journal devoted to the history of science) 1998, Vol. 13, pp. 99–128.
- Graeme J. N. Gooday, 'Teaching Telegraphy and Electrotechnics in the Physics Laboratory: William Ayrton and the Creation of an Academic Space for Electrical Engineering in Britain 1873–1884', *History of Technology*, 1991, Vol. 13, pp. 73–111 (esp. pp. 85–90 re Japan).
- Yūzō Takahashi, '*Ayrton to sono shūhen*', *Gijutsu to Bunmei*, 1991, Vol. 7, No. 1, pp. 1–32
- Yūzō Takahashi, 'William Edward Ayrton at the Imperial College of Engineering in Tokyo: The First Professor of Electrical Engineering in the World,' *IEEE Transactions on Education*, 1990, Vol. 33, pp. 198–205.

I am most grateful to Dr Gyōichi Nogami, Professor of Electrical Engineering at the Kyushu Institute of Technology (KIT, or *Kyūshū Kōgyō Daigaku*), for first suggesting W. E. Ayrton as a subject for a portrait in

February 2001, and providing many materials in Japanese about him. Thanks are also due to Dr Graeme Gooday of the Division of History and Philosophy of Science, University of Leeds, Leeds LS2 9JT for much help with articles and advice, and to Ms Kazue Akagawa, librarian of KIT.

16

W.K. Burton, 1856–99: 'Engineer Extraordinaire'

OLIVE CHECKLAND

W. K. Burton

WHICH SCOTTISH ENGINEER planned water supply systems for most of the major cities in Meiji Japan? Which Scottish engineer was responsible for the design of Ryōunkaku – the first skyscraper in Japan? Which Scottish engineer was, with John Milne, the founder of the first Photographic Society in Japan? The answer is William Kinninmond Burton[1] (1856–99) who, despite his hard work, has received none of the public recognition which fell to other British engineers who worked for the Japanese in the late nineteenth century.

Burton was an old-style engineer, trained, on the job, in the traditional manner, with none of the prestige of the young graduates, products of the new courses in engineering which had been imposed by the government on universities in England and in Scotland. By their attendance at University College, London, and, especially, at the University of Glasgow,[2] the Japanese gave much needed support to the idea of Engineering as an appropriate subject for university education. Japan benefited greatly by having a small cadre of graduate engineers who were of initial importance in late Meiji Japan.

When Henry Dyer[3] (1848–1918) was appointed principal of the Imperial College of Engineering in Tokyo in 1872 he was Henry Dyer, CE (Certificate of Engineering), MA, BSc,[4] degrees awarded by the University of Glasgow, after years of training. When William Kinninmond Burton was appointed to the Faculty of Engineering of the University ofTokyo in 1888, he had no recognizable qualifications. He relied on the training he had received as an apprentice engineer and on the support of his mentors and colleagues. It is not known who introduced Burton to the Japanese government, but it is possible that Burton's work as resident engineer of the London Sanitary Protection Association proved to be a strong recommendation.

William Kinninmond Burton was born in Edinburgh in 1856. He came of good family. His father was John Hill Burton (1809–81), his mother Katherine Innes. Cosmo Innes,[5] Burton's maternal grandfather, was a figure of some note in Edinburgh's cultural and legal circles. His father, J. H. Burton MA,[6] Aberdeen, was of a respectable but impoverished family in Aberdeen.

W. K. Burton was educated at the Edinburgh Collegiate School.[7] In 1873 he was apprenticed for five years to Messrs Brown Brothers, Hydraulic and Mechanical Engineers, of Rosebank Ironworks, Edinburgh.[8] During the last two years of his apprenticeship he served as chief draughtsman. In 1879 at the age of 23 years he moved to London where he started work with his maternal uncle, called, like his grandfather, Cosmo Innes. At that time the London Sanitary Protection Association had Cosmo Innes as its secretary. W. K. Burton became resident engineer of the London Sanitary Protection Association.

On the strength of his experience in engineering projects, both in Edinburgh and in London, W. K. Burton was appointed by the Japanese government in 1887. He was to work at the Faculty of Engineering of the University of Tokyo as 'Professor of Sanitary Engineering and Lecturer on Rivers, Docks and Harbours'.

On 5 May 1891 Burton became an Associate Member of the Institution of Civil Engineers, in London. The citation requesting his membership, dated 11 December 1890,[9] was brief, almost perfunctory, mentioning his apprenticeship in Edinburgh and his service in Japan for the Japanese government. The recommendation was proposed by Charles Scott Meik,[10] and signed by nine other engineers.

The supporters were:

F. H. Trevithick	W. Silver Hall	K. Fujikura
Francis Elgar	G. Eedes Eachus	W. L. Williams
P. Walter Meik	E. B. Ellice-Clark	C. A. W. Pownall

Several of the engineers who backed Burton's application were working in Japan,[11] especially on Japanese railways. Their work was known to James Forrest, then Secretary of the Institution of Civil Engineers, in London. Meik, the proposer, certainly worked in Japan. Reports of C. S. Meik, including plans for harbour building in Hokkaido, are held in the archives in Sapporo, Hokkaido, Japan.

Francis Henry Trevithick (1850–1931) had arrived in Japan in 1877. He worked as deputy locomotive superintendent in Kobe and in Shimbashi, Tokyo. F. H. Trevithick wrote up 'Japan's Railway System' for the Japan Society of London in 1909. F. H. Trevithick was one of the influential Trevithick family, from Cornwall, long engaged with steam engines.

Charles Asheton Whately Pownall was the Principal Engineer for Japanese Government railways in 1891. He, like John Milne and W. K. Burton, was much involved in assessing the impact of the severe earthquake in 1891 on the recently built railways, and in particular, in Pownall's case, in examining the effect of earthquakes on the bridges built over rivers to carry the railways. Francis Elgar (1845–1909), a distinguished naval architect, had served in Japan, briefly, between 1880–81. He was later director of HM Dockyards in Britain.

The only Japanese supporting Burton's application was Fujikura Kentatsu (1851–1923). He had been elected Associate Member of the Institution on 6 December 1887. Fujikura's citation is as follows:

> He was selected by the Government of Japan as one of the Engineering Pupils to be sent to Great Britain, for the purpose of studying for the profession, and was placed by his Government under the care of Messrs. D. and T. Stevenson, MM. Inst. C.E., Edinburgh, for training. During his pupilage with the Messrs. Stevenson he attended the Engineering, Chemical, and Mathematical Classes of Edinburgh University, from 1872 to 1874. In 1875, he was recalled by his Government, and placed in charge of their Lighthouse Establishment, at Yokohama. In this capacity he has erected lighthouses and lighthouse apparatus at Soyasaki, Hakodate, Rokkosaki, and Kurasaki. He is now in the service of the Japanese Government as Chief Commissioner of Lighthouses, which post he has held since 1885.[12]

Proposed by Alan Brebner.

D. A. Stevenson	R. C. Reid	James Leslie
Charles A. Stevenson	John Cooper	Alan Brebner, Jun.
Alexander Leslie		

There are several reasons for giving Fujikura's citation in full. In the first place he was a Japanese candidate who relied on the support of the Edinburgh engineers from the lighthouse building company David and Thomas Stevenson for whom he had worked. But secondly, in recommending him to the Institution of Civil Engineers his sponsors referred to the University classes which he had attended in Edinburgh. These were considered as an asset. But the rise of the University educated engineer would be at the expense of the Institution of Civil Engineers, whose easy casual self-regulating arrangements were being challenged by those newly qualified with University degrees in Engineering.

For the purpose of this brief study an attempt will be made to survey Burton's work as Sanitary Engineer, as pure water engineer, as designer of the Ryounkaku, as photographer and as a family man in Japan.

SANITARY ENGINEER

At the age of 31 W. K. Burton was appointed Professor of Sanitary Engineering[13] on 5 May 1887 at the Imperial University of Tokyo. Burton was a capable, honourable engineer but he had not, as far as is known, attended lectures, and had no experience of teaching. The Japanese took him on trust. In addition, on 1 January 1888 he became adviser to the sanitary department of the Home Ministry. His career in Japan for the Japanese government was to be a busy one. Burton's appointment specifically as a sanitary engineer reflected the Japanese government's recognition of the perils of disease which were an increasing threat to people in the burgeoning Japanese cities. As Tokyo, already in the 1880s a large city of one and a half million people, grew, so the hazards of disease became greater.

It should be remembered that the dual problems of providing pure water and disposing of sewage had not been easy to solve even in industrialized and affluent Britain. For a long time it was widely believed that bacterial disease was spread by 'a miasma'. The idea that water supply could be polluted, by being contaminated by sewage, was resisted, especially by those who profited from the status quo.[14]

The position in London was a scandal. The river Thames was, as late as the 1850s called 'The Great Stink'. Prince Albert had died, possibly of a fever, in December 1861. Queen Victoria mourned and withdrew from public life. Only in 1865 was a solution found. Joseph Bazalgette[15] designed the Crossness engines, named Victoria, Albert, Albert Edward and Alexandra beyond Woolwich, on the south bank of the Thames. These great pumping engines would bring together the sewage from London and pump it into the river at high tide. This would mean that it would be swept out to sea by the receding tide. Until recently the steamship Gardez-loo sailed regularly from

Edinburgh down the Firth of Forth, skirted the Isle of May, to discharge its cargo of sewage into the North Sea. Even in modern times it has remained acceptable practice to allow the high tide to disperse the sewage.

As Burton was to find in the 1880s, the position in Japan was very different. According to E. S. Morse 'the secret of sewage disposal has been effectively solved by the Japanese for centuries, so that nothing goes to waste'. Accordingly arrangements in Japan, even in Tokyo with its huge population, ensured that the *benjo*, 'place for business', or toilet, had an opening in the outer house wall. This enabled the *benjo* collector to remove the sewage regularly. As Morse explained, 'this material is carried off daily to the farms outside, the vessels in which it is conveyed being long cylindrical buckets borne by men and horses'. It was even said in Hiroshima that 'in renting the poorer tenement houses, if three persons occupied a room together, the sewage paid the rent of one, and if five occupied the same room no rent was charged'. The fact was that the Japanese farmer depended on the use of this 'night soil for the enrichment of his land'.[16] It was in this sense a very efficient system.

As the rural economy of Japan depended on the availability of manure from the 'night soil' it was difficult to see how other methods of disposal could ever have been considered. Indeed, Morse took a certain mischievous delight in explaining that in Japan 'there are no deep vaults with long accumulations contaminating the ground, or underground pipes conducting sewage to shallow bays and inlets, there to fester and vitiate the air and spread sickness and death'.

In this sense Burton's appointment to teach 'sanitary' engineering and later to be adviser for the Sanitary Department of the Home Ministry was a misnomer. The 'night soil' culture was too important for agricultural Japan; there could be no thought of changing it. Effectively W. K. Burton was to search out ways of providing a pure water supply for various cities of Japan. This he did in the late 1880s and 1890s with energy and enthusiasm.

PURE WATER ENGINEER

From the early days of his arrival in Japan, Burton was committed to providing plans and drawings for the water supply of many towns and cities in Japan.

W. K. Burton's reports on the Water Systems of Japan and Taiwan[17]

Year	Name of City	Contributions
JAPAN		
July 1887 (Meiji 20)	Hakodate, Aomori,	Inspection of sanitary conditions and proposal of water supply systems for Akita, Sendai
	Numata (Gunma)	Inspection of sanitary conditions and advice on improvement of its water supply system
1888 (Meiji 21)	Tokyo	1st report on the design of its water supply system
	Nagasaki	Examination to improve its water supply system
1889 (Meiji 22)	Tokyo	2nd (revised) report on the design of its water supply system. (This served as the basic design to improve Tokyo's water supply system)
	Fukuoka	Design of its water supply and drainage system
1890 (Meiji 23)	Osaka	Design of its water supply system (1895: supervised its construction works)
	Okayama	Design of its water supply system
1891 (Meiji 24)	Yokohama	Expansion programme of its water supply system
	Shimonoseki	Design of its water supply system
1892 (Meiji 25)	Kobe	Examination of its water supply system and design proposal submitted (1893)
	Moji	Examination of construction works of its water supply
	Omuta	Examination and design of its drainage system
1893 (Meiji 26)	Kofu	Examination of its construction plan of water supply
	Nagoya	Examination and design of its water supply construction plan
1894 (Meiji 27)	Niigata	Inspection of its sanitary conditions
	Hiroshima	Design of its water supply system
1898 (Meiji 31)	Takamatsu	Inspection of its sanitary conditions

Burton is also believed to have examined the water supply systems of Fukui, Matsuyama and Yanagawa. According to family legend, Burton visited all the places listed in Japan. These visits, it is believed, were 'much appreciated' by the local authorities. It is also possible that Burton supervised, or overlooked, water supply plans for various towns which had been prepared by new young Japanese graduates. If Burton did visit all the towns listed, he would have travelled by steamship. These journeys would have been long and arduous. It is possible, and indeed likely, that Burton was acting as senior consultant to various young Japanese water engineers.

IN TAIWAN

Once Japan had taken over Taiwan, the island of Formosa, which was one of the prizes from the Sino-Japanese War of 1895–96, Burton was quickly on the island advising on water supply.

W K. Burton's Involvement in Taiwan's Water Systems

1896	Tan-shui	Design of its water supply system
	Chi-lung	Design of its water supply system
	Tai-chung	Design of its water supply system
1899	Tai-pei	Design of its water supply system

He is known to have made design works of water supply systems for Tai-nan and two other cities, but the details are unknown.

Burton can only be described as an astonishingly energetic man. As will be seen from the list of reports on sanitation and water supply he was amazingly productive.

In 1894 in London, Crosby Lockwood and Son published W.K. Burton's *The Water Supply of Towns and the Construction of Waterworks, a practical treatise for the use of engineers and students of engineering.*[18] This book is a clear practical account of how to set up waterworks. There can be no doubt that the material used here had developed from Burton's work in Japan. While the book is a general study some examples are given specifically of problems encountered in Japan. One of the major concerns of the book is the supply of 'palatable' water.

In his book Burton discussed eight categories of palatable water.

These were:

Wholesome	1. Spring Water 2. Deep well water 3. Upland surface water	Very palatable
Suspicious	4. Stored rain water 5. Surface water from cultivated land 6. River water to which sewage gains access	Moderately palatable
Dangerous	7. Shallow well water 8. Water from paddy fields	Palatable

Source: W. K. Burton, *The Water Supply of Towns*, p. 14.

It is worth noting that Category 8 'water from paddy fields' had been added to this list by Burton himself. Clearly, if only three of the eight water categories listed could be regarded as 'wholesome', and five other commonly used sources of water were 'suspicious' or 'dangerous' the Japanese had problems ahead.

In this sense Burton's task was an impossible one. Edward Morse noted:

> It must be admitted that their water supply is very seriously affected by this sewage being washed into rivers and wells from the rice fields where it is deposited, and the scourge of cholera, which almost yearly spreads its desolating shadow over many of their southern towns, is due to the almost certain cultivation of the land by irrigation methods; and the consequent distribution of sewage through these surface avenues renders it impossible to protect the water supply from contamination.[19]

Burton thought he had found a way forward by establishing various 'impounding reservoirs'. As he explained '... The best site for a reservoir is one where a valley widens out into a flat bottom bounded by steep sides, the sides coming close together, forming a contraction just below this flat bed'.

The case of Nagasaki was cited:

> The following are particulars about the works: It was proposed to provide for a population of 60,000; the quantity of water proposed per head per day was twenty gallons. It was assumed that the consumption would be uniform during the whole year, the rains occurring in Japan, and particularly in Kiushu, during the hot weather, the cold weather being, for the most part, very dry. Of course, such an assumption can in no case be absolutely correct, but experience since the waterworks were opened has shown that, with an ample allowance for average consumption, it was a safe one. The catchment area was 865 acres.[20]

It should be noted that W. K. Burton, in the case of Nagasaki, was acting as senior adviser to 'Mr C. Yoshimura' who had designed the water-works at Nagasaki. It seems likely that W. K. Burton was adviser to most of the water-work projects, the basic design of which may have been done by Japanese water engineers.

There is no doubt that W. K. Burton made a considerable contribution to modern water engineering in Meiji Japan. It is a curious reflection that Burton arriving in Japan in 1887 had an advantage, working in a country with no modern systems. Burton and his Japanese colleagues in Japan were also working on the problems of filtering water through sand.

As a result of Burton's interest in water purification an article was published. This was W. K. Burton's, 'Regulating the Rate of Filtration through Sand'.[21] In this Burton refers to the work of Mr. B. Nojiri, Chief engineer to the Osaka Waterworks, 'who was occupied with elaborate experiments on the effects of varying the speed of filtration at the time of his death in 1892'. Earlier, in 1888, Burton himself had been designing a waterworks for Tokyo; he also had spent much time 'regulating with precision the flow of water through the filters'.

THE RYŌUNKAKU

Burton was commissioned sometime in the late 1880s, not long after his arrival in Japan, to design an extraordinary tall 'Twelve Storeys' which opened to the public in 1890. It was some 220 feet high, was octagonal in shape, made of brick and boasted the first elevator ever installed in a Japanese building. In 1890 this 'confection'[22] was the tallest building in Tokyo. It is not known how Burton came to be involved with this project, but his willingness suggests a man pleased to be working with the Japanese.

'Twelve Storeys' was an extraordinary, successful, Japanese-inspired, commercial enterprise, designed to attract workingmen and their families to visit Asakusa, in Tokyo. On the top floor, for example, it was possible to search out other Tokyo landmarks by peering through the telescope provided for the purpose. Other attractions were to be found on various floors of this astonishing place. The Ryōunkaku was near the famous temple of Kwannon, where public ground was 'the quaintest and liveliest place in Tokyo. Here are raree-shows, penny gaffs, performing monkeys, infant prodigies, cheap photographers, street artists, jugglers, wrestlers, …'.[23]

Kubota Mantarō (1889–1963) the novelist and playwright who lived in Shitamachi, the 'low' part of Tokyo, all his life, wrote affectionately of 'Twelve Storeys';

> In days of old, a queer object known as Twelve Storeys reared itself over Asakusa. From wherever you looked, there it was, that huge clumsy pile of red bricks. From the roof of every house, from the laundry platform, from the narrowest second-floor window, there it was, waiting for you. From anywhere in the vastness of Tokyo – the embankment across the river at Aukojima, the observation rise at Ueno, the long flight of stone steps up Atago Hill, there it was, waiting for you.[24]

The 'Twelve Storeys', which had survived the earthquake of 1894, was damaged in the Great Kanto earthquake of September 1923. Sadly, the top four storeys fell off. The novelist Kawabata Yasunari described the final hours of the Ryōunkaku in 1923, writing: 'It seems to have been a rather festive occasion. More properly the Cloud Scraper, the 'Twelve Storeys' was a pleasure and retailing centre, a somewhat ungainly brick tower ... Army demolition squads completed the destruction.'[25]

Indeed there was more:

> There was an explosion and a cascade of bricks. The wall on one side had not fallen. It was like a thin sword. Another explosion and the sword fell. The crowds on the school roof cheered, and then how we all did laugh. As the sword collapsed a black mass of people raced up the mountain of rubble.[26]

PHOTOGRAPHER

In 1887, the year in which Burton left Britain for Japan, the seventh edition of W. K. Burton's *Modern Photography* was published in London. This book was No. 7 in a series of Photographic Handy Books, which sold well and was in print for many years. In 1892 Marion and Co. of London, published Burton's *Practical Guide to Photography* which also remained in print for many years. Clearly, Burton was an expert in the new art of photography. Once settled in Japan Burton lost no time in making contact with the world of Japanese photographers.[27]

The Photographic Society of Japan (Nihon Shashin Kyōkai) was founded in Tokyo in 1889, partly due to the enthusiasm of W.K. Burton and John Milne. As has been noted, 'It was an immediate success, attracting an impressive cross-section of photographers, working in Japan and it continues to function to this day'.[28] There is an account of a meeting of the Society on Saturday, 22 March 1890 held in the Public Hall, Yokohama. New members of the Society were admitted and John Milne gave a lantern slide lecture on earthquakes.[29]

Between 1890 and 1894 Burton publicised two Japanese photographers in British photographic journals. He wrote important articles on Ogawa Kuzumasa[30] (1860–1929) and Kashima Seibei[31] (1866–1924). The 'series' consisted only of these two Japanese photographers. It is not known why Burton's articles on Japanese photographers came to an end.

As a small boy, Ogawa was said to have remembered 'being on the battle-field with his father and being wounded during the civil war of 1868–69 which ushered in the new Meiji regime. What is certain is that Ogawa was a young man of resource. He, like many others, was determined to learn English and become a photographer. Somehow, in July 1882, as a 22-year-old, he hired himself as a sailor on the American vessel *Swatara*. In course of time he was discharged in the United States, where, in Boston, he was able to study 'portraiture, carbon printing, and collotype'. He also lived in Philadelphia before returning to Japan in 1884. By good fortune Ogawa had met Viscount Okube Nagamoto (1855–1925) in the United States. Okube provided the finance for Ogawa to set up a photographic studio in Tokyo. Over the years Burton was much involved with Ogawa and recorded his indebtedness in the preface to one of Burton's own books on photography:

> I must on the whole, declare my indebtedness to Mr. K. Ogawa of this city than to anyone else. It has been my pleasure, and has certainly been to my profit, to be associated with him in much experimental work in connection with various photographic processes, mechanical among others. Mr. Ogawa has put in operation the greater number of the photo-mechanical processes described at the end of this book on more than an experimental scale, and he has made me free to publish all results whether of our joint work or of his own.
>
> (signed) W. K. Burton, Imperial University, Tokyo.[32]

In his discussion of Kashima Seibei, Burton wrote that Mr Kajima was 'not only the most enthusiastic amateur photographer in Japan, but also the most enthusiastic amateur that it has been my privilege to meet anywhere'.

Burton also explained the career of Kashima Seibei, a wealthy young saké-maker whose hobby was photography. There is no doubt that Mr Kashima's enthusiasm and energy did much to transform the expectations of the photographic industry in Japan. Mr Kashima ordered materials from England, including a camera like that of W. K. Burton but he did more, trying to manufacture similar cameras in Japan. As in other industries, those in Japan, quickly tried to copy the photographic items which were imported.

W. K. Burton also gave details of the help given by Kashima Seibei to the Photographic Society of Japan. The enthusiasm of the Japanese for photography was engaging, and resulted in small workshops turning out photographic supplies, at much cheaper cost than similar items when imported. Fortunately for the Japanese photographer, as this was a new industry, there were no Japanese traditionalists to oppose progress.

W. K. Burton was a friend of John Milne,[33] Professor of Mining and Metallurgy, and as a result W. K. Burton became involved with photographing earthquakes. Their most famous work together was that for the Neo Valley earthquake of 1891 when a most devastating event occurred in the Nagoya area of Japan. On 28 October 1891, at 6.30 am (as John Milne reported from his base in Tokyo) he was awakened by the 'creaking of the house and the pictures swinging and flapping on the walls'.

Milne and Burton were requested to proceed at once to the centre of the earthquake area. Remarkably, they succeeded in being in the

Neo Valley within two days and they studied and photographed with enthusiasm. Their book *The Great Earthquake of Japan, 1891* is very rare but if available will give a good impression of the disaster. It 'consists of thirty pages of excellent illustrations whose printing plates were prepared by F. Ogawa, together with a further forty pages of concise explanatory text'.[34]

Burton and Milne also produced a more general book, also very rare, entitled *The Volcanoes of Japan*.

FAMILY MAN

William K. Burton arrived in Japan in May 1887. He seemed to settle into Japanese society with remarkable ease. He learnt to speak Japanese and by 1892 he had a daughter, Tamako, by his young wife Orakawa Matsu. On 19 May 1894 he married the mother of his child at a ceremony at the British Consulate in Tokyo. Consul Joseph H. Longford officiated; Burton's own signature was 'illegible'. Angus MacDonald signed on behalf of Burton's wife.[35]

There were many 'marriages' of British men to Japanese women in Japan at this time. Few went to the lengths of presenting themselves and their partners to the British consul for a formal marriage ceremony. Burton must therefore be ranked among a minority of those who regularized their relationship with Japanese women. John Milne, for example, a close friend of Burton's, also had a Japanese wife, Tone. They may have had a marriage ceremony in 1881 in Tokyo, at the Rananza-ku church[36] but the civil ceremony, which married them officially, for the British authorities, was not undertaken until 12 June 1895, on the eve of the Milne's departure for England.

Burton's apparent assimilation into Japanese society was remarkable in its day. Although the professional work done by men like Burton was invaluable, there was some resentment in Japan, especially about insensitive, ignorant foreigners. Burton like T. B. Glover and Frank Brinkley, who both married and settled permanently in Japan, seem to have had the gift and to have lived and worked happily in Japan, despite the cultural differences.

W. K. Burton died on 14 August 1899 in the University Hospital, Tokyo. He was 43 years of age. He is said to have died of a fever. His extraordinary commitment to the provision of pure water for Japan and Taiwan, must have kept him constantly at work. One can only wonder at the dedication of this man to his adopted country. During his residence in Japan, a period of some twelve years, he crammed a lifetime of work experience.

AFTERWORD

There is a sequel, or rather a prequel, to this story of William Kinninmond Burton. In the summer of 1862 Fukuzawa Yukichi was in London, as one of a party of Japanese visiting the West. Fukuzawa frequented the bookshop of W. & R. Chambers, publishers of Edinburgh, at 47 Paternoster Row, by St Paul's Cathedral. Fukuzawa became friendly with the Chambers brothers who showed him some of the sights of London. Fukuzawa purchased a number of books including Chambers' *Political Economy* for use in schools and for private instruction. As Fukuzawa readily acknowledged he had based some of his work on *Economics in Conditions in the West* on Chambers' *Political Economy*. The author of Chambers' *Political Economy* … was none other than John Hill Burton, William Kinninmond Burton's father.[37]

The contribution of the Edinburgh Burtons to modern Japan was considerable. The economic and philosophic ideas of John Hill Burton were translated into easily understood Japanese by Fukuzawa Yukichi. But the practical ideas of the pure water engineer W. K. Burton kept the Japanese people alive.

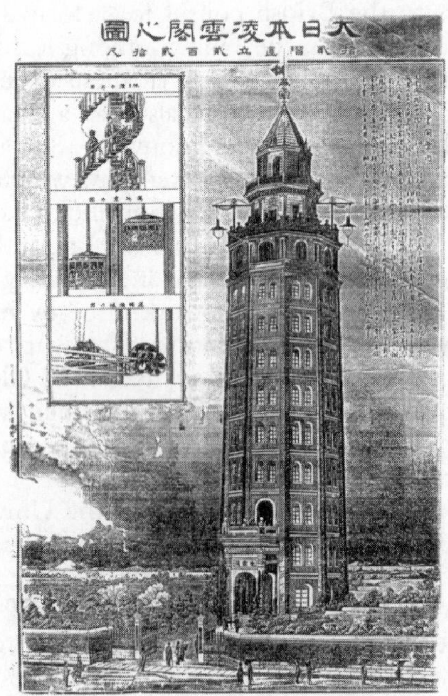

Burton's Ryōunkaku ('Twelve Storeys')

17

Henry Faulds, 1843–1930

IAN NISH

Dr Henry Faulds

HENRY FAULDS is one of those Scotsmen more famous abroad than in his own country. He stayed in Japan as a missionary doctor for twelve years at a critical time for that nation's development. This is what the standard Japanese account of his life says:

> Faulds is ... known to the world today for his skill as the man who laid the foundations for fingerprinting methods which are now widely used. But beyond his fingerprint studies, we should not forget him as the man who preached harmonization between Evolution and Religion or as the man who promoted public medical care and the education of the blind.[1]

Faulds was born in Beith, Ayrshire on 1 June 1843. He studied a full range of arts subjects at Glasgow University (1864–7) and then took a four-year course and qualified in 1871 as a Licentiate of the Faculty of Physicians and Surgeons (LFPS) at Anderson's College, Glasgow (now University of Strathclyde). Influenced as a Sunday School teacher by the Rev. Norman McLeod at the Barony, he became a missionary and served briefly (1872–3) at the Church of Scotland mission at Darjeeling. But his service there was 'terminated by discord', as it is euphemistically described. He then turned to the United Presbyterian (UP) Church, his father being an elder at Erskine, Glasgow. It was possible in the climate of the times for that church to raise in Scotland the sum of £8,949 for missions in Japan; and this was enough to send out two bachelor missionaries (at £300 p.a.) and the Faulds (at £350 pa). Faulds thus became the first Scottish medical missionary to Japan.

In his student days, Faulds had been affected by two movements: the Darwinian revolution in scientific thinking stemming from the publication of *The Origin of Species* in 1859; and the Evangelical revivalism associated with the names of Moody and Sankey. Moody's first and most effective Scottish campaign had begun in 1873 and was targeted at the student body, especially medical students, and Faulds may, therefore, have been affected as a graduate.

Faulds married shortly after his return from India and set off with his newly-wed wife into the unknown late in 1873, travelling by way of Singapore and Hong Kong. Lest we weep tears for the tragedy of the Victorian housewife being dragged off without a honeymoon on a two-months' sea journey through the tropics to an unknown destination, it should be stated that she had a brother already resident in Japan, R. Stewart of the Imperial Japanese Survey.[2] The Faulds reached Yokohama in March 1874 and took the train to Shimbashi, then the terminus for Tokyo of the first Japanese railway which had only been officially opened in October 1872. He was grateful for this modern convenience but complained about the 'odious and depressing stink of coarse and ill-flavoured tobacco which filled the compartment'.[3]

One can say that the Faulds were entering 'the unknown' because there had just been a quasi-revolution in Japan – the Meiji restoration of 1868 – the exact consequences of which were still not entirely clear. On the one hand, the new government was progressive in seeking knowledge from all over the world. In particular, it had sent the Iwakura Mission to the United States and Europe (including Scotland) between 1871 and 1873. While the commissioners were largely inspecting and reporting on the industries they saw, they were also looking for talent and had an agent in Edinburgh recruiting people who had experience of the new technology, more numerous in Glasgow than in Edinburgh.

On the other hand, the new government was not so progressive over its attitude to freedom of religion and Christianity. Officially there was a ban which was not withdrawn until 1873. The Japanese were under continuing strong pressure from all the foreign diplomats to relax their policy further but gave way only slowly. Faulds as a missionary was taking on a risky assignment. Yet he and his Church backers must have thought that a more open-minded, progressive climate which would be conducive to missionary endeavour would prevail shortly. In practice missionaries were from the time of his arrival not prevented from preaching the gospel and Christianity was not officially proscribed, though there were restrictions.[4]

Faulds had to settle at No 18 Tsukiji. Tsukiji was a district of Tokyo which lay between Tokyo bay on the east and Tokyo castle to the west. The rationale behind the government's insistence on having a foreign concession was separation: protecting the foreigner from the native and the native from the foreigner by keeping them apart. Tsukiji was in effect an isolated foreign enclave during times which were still quite violent.[5] Only foreigners employed by government were allowed to reside elsewhere in the city of Tokyo; commercial nabobs preferred to live in treaty ports like that at Yokohama. Others had to tolerate life in Tsukiji if they wanted to live in the nation's capital.

Tsukiji was, Faulds wrote, an old marshy spot which had been reclaimed from the sea and was the site of Tokyo's fish market which had moved there from Hitotsubashi. Tokyo was near and yet so far. Tsukiji was separated from Tokyo city by canals and initially gates. 'I was now', wrote Faulds, 'almost like the Dutch in Deshima, cooped up in a dreary concession – a few acres of flat, reedy forced ground, giving no chance of enjoying a rustic walk without first crossing monotonous miles of uninviting streets.' Tokyo was not as attractive to him as the free mountain life in Darjeeling he had just left. He asked the question:

> Is this quiet, sleepy-looking county-town on a large scale Yedo 'the largest city in the world' of our infallible school geographies? Certainly its 700,000 or so of inhabitants contrive to keep themselves wonderfully well out of observation … I have never been in any city – always excepting, of course, dear little St Andrews – whose citizens made so little noise.[6]

Despite its drawbacks, this was where Faulds was to be based for twelve years.

MEDICAL WORK AND EVANGELISM

Faulds records that he was able through a Japanese Christian to rent the buildings of the extinct Cosmopolitan Restaurant, 'a rather pretentious edifice seated on the bank of a romantic artificial lake'.[7] This enabled him to set up a dispensary and surgery from which he both practised medicine and undertook missionary work. In 1875 he built and superintended a UP mission hospital in the Tsukiji foreign concession which was the precursor of St Lukes Hospital today. This was the first mission hospital in Japan and served large numbers of out-patients (1400 per annum). Faulds was among the foreign doctors who introduced Lister's antiseptic methods and the treatment of fevers by an exclusive milk diet.

The hospital was eventually recognized by the government. It was invaluable at a time of cholera epidemics when Faulds was invested with government authority. Despite being offered temptation to join government service, Faulds resisted and developed a small medical school in 1876, which gave him important fee income when church resources were reduced. It is said – but I have not been able to confirm this – that he was also approached to become physician to members of the Japanese court and refused.

Among his medical interests he was specially concerned with the poor and the blind. Thus, in 1875 he helped, with a number of Japanese associates, to found the Rakuzenkai, Japan's first society for the blind, which led to the founding five years later of the Kummoin (訓盲), a solidly-built school for the blind in Tsukiji. It attracted few students until the Ministry of Education took it over shortly thereafter. While the later developments did not accord with Faulds's ideas, he continued his pioneer work by offering training and a reading-room at the Tsukiji hospital. He also helped produce a Braille type bible in Japanese.[8]

Faulds came to be associated with the mission school 'Hebonjuku' (i.e. Hepburn school). The scholarly Presbyterian missionary and medical doctor, Dr James Curtis Hepburn (1815–1911), one of the earliest foreigners to study the Japanese language, had set up this school at Yokohama primarily for teaching English. In this endeavour he was joined by Dutch Reform churchmen, Congregationalists, Baptists, Methodists Old and New. But Tokyo as the centre of government with its large population was a temptation to those seeking to educate the next generation. In 1880 Hepburn's school was transferred to Akashi-chō in Tsukiji close to where Faulds was staying and became Tsukiji College [*daigaku*] which in later days became Meiji Gakuin. As though he had nothing else to do to fill his time, Faulds became special lecturer in English.

Like most missionaries around the world Faulds was anxious to establish a printing press. He worked with James Summers, a foreign teacher who went to Japan hopeful of publishing the *Phoenix*, a bilingual oriental journal which he had originally published in London. The venture was not a success; but Faulds writes of distributing a good number of books (presumably Bibles) to villagers as he went on his rounds.[9] Faulds undertook another of his publishing enterprises, namely the editing of a journal covering matters of medical interest. This displeased the United Presbyterian Home Board which thought it inconsistent with his primary task and pressed him to give it up. One member of that Board, William Gray Dixon (1854–1928),[10] formerly a professor of English Literature in Imperial College, Tokyo, and a member of the Union Church there, stood up for Faulds on the grounds that he was specially fitted for such work as 'a man of science and general culture'. Faulds survived the rebuke but the journal did not prosper and he was forced to give up this journalistic work. Later, in 1881, when a number of Presbyterian missionaries, mainly from Canada, came together to produce *Chrysanthemum*, described as 'a monthly magazine for Japan and the Far East', Faulds was again on the editorial staff. Ernest Satow and Basil Hall Chamberlain were to be found among the early contributors. But it also ceased publication prematurely two years later.[11]

Faulds extended his interests well beyond medicine to those of amateur scientist and experimenter. He became a member of the remarkable Asiatic Society of Japan, founded in 1872, and presented two papers to its meetings in 1878. In other words, he was accepted into expatriate intellectual circles in Tokyo and held discussions with those who had come to help Japan set up the University of Tokyo and other colleges. His scientific papers, though slight, were duly published in the Society's journal.

It was a sign of Faulds' abundant energy and self-confidence that his experiments led him towards the science of fingerprinting. The story goes that in 1879 while examining prehistoric pottery uncovered by E. S. Morse at Omori in Tokyo, he discovered that the prints of the potters' hands could be discerned on it. When he turned to more recent pottery, it became clear to him that finger ridges differed between individuals. His experiments led him to compare prints also from different races. He reached the conclusion that 'the lines of the ulno-palmar margin of a particular Japanese are of the parallel sort in both hands and are quite symmetrical, thus differing from the Englishman's considerably'.[12] From these experiments he argued that it would greatly improve police methods if the distinctive furrows of a person's fingers were used for personal identification. But Faulds also claimed that fingerprinting would aid the general public by preventing false arrest being made by the police. This was particularly relevant to Japan where the custom was not to sign documents but to authenticate them by a person's han, a sort of personal seal with a red imprint, while poorer people who did not possess a han had to authorize documents by their thumb-print. He published his findings modestly in a letter to the editor of *Nature* in September 1880 entitled 'On the skin-furrows of the hand'. But in the following issue of the journal Sir George Herschel of the Bengal branch of the Indian Civil Service put forward findings of a similar kind, saying that he had been using them in the course of his legal work for as much as two decades. Faulds put his ideas to the Japanese police who were generally sympathetic and ultimately adopted them. He made similar approaches to the police in Britain but they preferred to give credit for the discovery to Herschel. This was a life-long disappointment to Faulds.

ATTITUDES TO JAPANESE

In October 1882 Faulds left Japan on furlough. In Scotland he entered into dialogue with the United Presbyterian Church about the continuation of the mission which had won few converts and managed to convince publishers to finance the publication of his major work, *Nine years in Nipon: Sketches of Japanese Life and Manners*. This appeared in 1884 from Alexander Gardner of Paisley and 12 Paternoster Row, London, and had, I suspect, been written during the long journey home. It was dedicated to his father. It was eloquently written and informative. In the preface he explains that he was forced to omit the part related to the religious and moral systems of Japan and proposed to devote another book to these subjects. This did not materialize. The book must have had some success because it was separately published in the United States and went into a second edition in 1887. It is a minor classic among travel books on Japan in the early Meiji period.[13]

Judging from this work, what appealed to Faulds about the Japanese was their enthusiasm for education and their desire to acquire knowledge, especially Western knowledge. Even before the government lifted its ban on Christianity in 1873, scores of young Japanese came to learn English at makeshift mission schools and often became Christians.[14] But it attracted older people as well. Faulds observed:

> During my whole residence in Japan, I was meeting daily with large numbers from the lower strata of people, but I can only recall one or two clear instances of Japanese people having been unable to write and read. The fact struck me very much even in the first year of my sojourn that people have all had at least a fair elementary education.[15]

Towards the many-sided aspects of Japanese religions, Faulds displayed a remarkably sympathetic attitude. Unlike so many missionary writings, his were not swiping wildly at heathens and pagans and infidels. The explanation was that early on he came to respect and love Japan, Japanese literature and scenery. He seems to have taken an intermediate position towards Japan's major religions. He describes Buddhism as 'that humane religion' but also regrets that it was in decay and part of 'the degraded Buddhism of the Far East'. It will be remembered that Faulds had encountered Buddhism in Darjeeling earlier in his career. He now felt that Buddhism in Japan had forgotten 'its old, clear, cold message' which he had encountered in India.[16]

Henry Faulds had, therefore, a special approach to evangelism: he believed in debate and dialogue. By its very nature his approach was confrontational; and Japan's religions are not by their nature normally confrontational. On one of his up-country expeditions, Faulds records that he 'expressed great joy in anticipation of a little friendly conversation before the company [with the local Shinto priest] on the subject of the merits of our respective religions. But the *Kannushi* [priest] avoided it'.[17]

There remained in any case restrictions on evangelism, both legal and practical. It was difficult for missionaries to hold public meetings which could only be 'arranged with some caution on account of certain regulations'. It was, Faulds wrote, 'as yet very difficult to organize evangelistic work in the interior not on account of any bigoted intolerance of our teaching, but simply from the fact that passports are needed for foreigners and the only objects for which they were given were "scientific research" and "health". I have never gone out except on "bona fide" errands of the one class or the other.'[18] As against that, the enthusiasm of Japanese citizens for education – and Western education – offered opportunities for missionary teaching in the cities; and mission schools, colleges and universities of every denomination were being opened all over the country to which he had access.[19]

This optimistic picture was not exactly how the mission boards judged the case – the stern fathers of the church were looking less at activities than at statistics of conversion. During his furlough Faulds came up against their scepticism about the continuation of his mission. He at first tabled his resignation but eventually withdrew it when it was agreed that he could return for another term. We do not know the arguments that Faulds deployed but we can judge his attitude from the final words of his book:

> Christianity through translated Scriptures, its pure literature, its vernacular and higher schools, its stimulating lectures and sermons, and its medical missions has done much directly – it has done very much more indirectly – to leaven public opinion with lofty and manly sentiment.[20]

A word should be said about another of Faulds' ventures which brought him into the public eye: his defence of the Christian position against evolutionary theories. Tolerant as he was of most things Japanese, he was not so for the ideas of evolution derived from the writings of Charles Darwin in the *Origin of Species* (1859) which he saw as the critical debate of the age. He believed that the Japanese were aware that educated Westerners were deeply divided over the controversy between scientific agnosticism and Christianity. While he was in Tokyo, Edward Sylvester Morse, the professor of zoology at the newly founded university, frequently addressed public meetings expounding Darwinian thinking and attracted many Japanese students. Faulds who had evidently been schooled during his university days in arguments over Darwinism was one of the few in Tokyo who was confident enough to attack Morse and spent much time campaigning and publishing against his doctrines. In particular, he established in Tsukiji cottage hospital a Thursday Club which met weekly for the free and open discussion of current issues, and the question of Science and Christianity was the major topic. His approach was that evolution was quite compatible with Christian faith; and he preached a doctrine of harmonization. His lectures were translated and published as a book in Japanese but not in English.[21]

Faulds returned to Japan after a long leave covering two springs. He was appointed by the government as Honorary Surgeon-Superintendent of the Tsukiji Hospital. He was evidently highly regarded in Japan. But, as the Meiji government expanded the number of up-to-date state hospitals, his poorly funded missionary hospital fared badly. It is likely that he would ultimately have been forced to give up his various activities. In any case, the health of his wife who appears to have followed him out deteriorated rapidly; and he eventually left Japan for good in November 1885 at the age of only 42. He was generously treated by the church and returned to St Thomas's Hospital in London for further training. He may have felt that his medical knowledge needed updating. Some of his former Japanese colleagues visited him there and reported that he was still much preoccupied with fingerprinting, this time with British furrows.[22]

For the first five years Faulds resided in the London area, initially staying at 197 Isledon Road, Finsbury Park and acting as surgeon to the Self-Help Society. He later lived and presumably practised at 40 Victoria Road, Stroud Green, North London. He next moved to Staffordshire where he acted as assistant to Dr W.J. Dawes at Longton and settled as medical practitioner at Fenton in the Potteries, serving as police-surgeon for eight years. By 1904 he had moved to Hanley, where he seems to have practised for two decades.[23]

Throughout this period Faulds was a man with a grievance, determined to take up his pen in defence of his claim to be the originator of a novel form of identification by fingerprinting. Although he had presented his arguments to Scotland Yard many times, it was not favourably regarded by the Yard or the Home Office. Nonetheless, Faulds published his *Guide to Finger-Print Identification* through Wood, Mitchell of Hanley in 1905 which became a standard work in Europe and around the world. When the matter of Faulds' recognition was raised in parliament in 1910, a written answer was given implying that he had made a false claim. From then on he issued no less than five major publications in defence of his honour.[24] One of the rival claimants for the 'discovery', Sir George Herschel, before he died, published a statement in 1917 giving full credit to Faulds' discovery alongside his own. Faulds established an international reputation in Japan, the United States and globally and obtained membership of all relevant professional bodies. But he was fighting the British establishment over fingerprints unsuccessfully till his dying day. While content with his profession of medicine, he was increasingly obsessed with his failure to obtain government recognition in Britain.

After selling his practice, Faulds retired in 1924 with increasing deafness and ill health to Wolstanton, Stoke-on-Trent, where his daughters stayed. That was where he died on 19 March 1930 at the great age of 86, his wife having predeceased him by some two years. There were a tribute in the Osaka *Asahi* newspaper and obituaries in the *Glasgow Herald* and *The Times*. The last of these (which still pretended in those days to be a journal of record) stated:

> Faulds who was an authority on the finger print system of detecting criminals died at Wolstanton, Staffs, yesterday at the age of 86. He was an honorary member of the International Association for Identification … He had held medical appointments in India and Japan. While in Japan he was responsible for the introduction into that country of milk treatment for typhoid fever and of antiseptic surgery.[25]

CONTINUING JAPANESE LINKS

But the sad ending of this symphony leads on to a happier coda. Lucky the man who has supporters who will take up his cause after his death! Faulds was fortunate in having a man like Sheriff George Wilton Wilton (1862–1964), BL (Edin.), QC, Sheriff-substitute in Lanarkshire, to pursue his cause. For a quarter century from 1938 to 1963, Wilton, a lively centenarian, argued pugnaciously with the Home Office and successive prime ministers in order to defend the reputation and claims of Faulds and secure adequate compensation for his elderly daughters. He published his correspondence in a multitude of little books – possibly at his own expense. He was convinced that Faulds did not get the credit for his discovery from the British government which was his due and that others did for similar discoveries and obtained titles and monetary rewards for them. But, without looking at the Home Office archives, it is hard to deduce why that Office was prejudiced against Faulds. Eventually, after many negative responses, Winston Churchill gave a reply in the House of Commons in 1952, stating that Faulds' contribution was fully recognized; and a pension was given to his daughters.

Wilton who did not consider the compensation enough received unexpected support from the Japanese in continuing his campaign. Where Britain was stingy, the Japanese Home Ministry establishment was appreciative. The Japanese police had early on approved of the Faulds system and adopted it officially as early as April 1911. In a letter to Wilton in 1961, Dr Furuhata Tanemoto, Director of the Scientific Research Institute of Japan, explained their continuing loyalty to Faulds: '1 April 1961 falls on the day when the [Japanese] Police began to practice the fingerprint system fifty years ago, so on this day we are planning to commemorate Henry Faulds' contributions … I am to lecture on fingerprinting and Henry Faulds.'[26]

Yasoshima Shinnosuke, professor of legal medicine, Sapporo Medical College, Hokkaido University, further reported: 'A stone monument, pointing out the residence of Henry Faulds has been unveiled by the roadside of Tsukiji, Tokyo on 28 October 1961. The unveiling ceremony was held on the memorial day of the publication of his paper "On the skin-furrows of the hand" in *Nature*, 28 October 1880.'[27] The legend on the back of the memorial stone which the Police Bureau (*Keisatsuchō*) placed at 18 Akashi-chō, Tsukiji where Faulds had once lived reads as follows: 'Dr Henry Faulds (1843–1930), Pioneer in fingerprint identification lived here from 1874 to 1886'.[28]

In a subsequent letter of 20 May 1962, Dr Furuhata wrote that he was 'glad to know that the erection of our monument in Tsukiji to the memory of Dr Faulds greatly troubled the [British] Government Departments and forced the leading officials to declare their justification for all the senseless opposition to which the application for financial aid to the aged daughters of Dr Faulds was subjected.'[29] The last of Wilton's books published in 1963 carried the secondary title 'Victory Won'. So Sheriff Wilton at least was satisfied that Faulds' claims had been fully vindicated.[30]

As with so many foreign pioneers in Meiji Japan, Faulds had a disjunction in his career. The contributions which he made to Japan in medical science, hospitals, education for the blind, were overtaken by superior services initiated by the Japanese government in the 1880s. His funding by the church was not sufficient to allow his hospital to keep up with the resources of the newly-established state hospitals. Even if his wife had not fallen sick, he might have had to leave Japan. Like most foreigners of his generation, he was never to return to that country. Yet there were continuing links. From the Japanese side, there was, as we have seen, admiration by the Japanese police for the pioneering work which Faulds had done. Long after his death – and unsolicited – they chose to commemorate his life by erecting a memorial stone in his honour. From the side of Faulds also, Japan lingered in his memory. Even as he was struggling to re-establish his medical career in the Potteries in the late 1890s, he took time out to publish from Longton in Staffordshire a journal, *East Asia*, a quarterly on lore and literature for the general reader. Though it was short-lived and only three numbers appeared, it was a symbol of Faulds' abiding affection for Japan.[31]

18

Henry Spencer Palmer, 1838–93

JIRŌ HIGUCHI

Henry Spencer Palmer

MAJOR GENERAL Henry Spencer Palmer died in Tokyo on 10 February 1893 at the age of 54.[1] Palmer, who was well known not only as a soldier but also as a scientist, became ill and died while he was engaged in the construction of Yokohama harbour. He was buried in Aoyama cemetery in Tokyo where a tomb stone[2] was erected by his friends in Tokyo.

Palmer, who was the youngest son of Colonel John Freke Palmer, a member of the East India Company's service, was born at Bangalore in the Madras Presidency on 30 April 1838. He was educated at private schools and by private tutors before being admitted in January 1856 to the Royal Military Academy at Woolwich through a public competition in which, although he was the youngest candidate, he achieved the seventh place among forty successful candidates. On 20 December 1856 he was commissioned as a Lieutenant in the Royal Corps of Engineers. In October 1858 he was appointed to the expedition to British Columbia. Palmer was actively engaged with the expedition in making surveys and carrying out explorations. One of these expeditions was a reconnaissance survey of the Cariboo gold region in 1862, which was 'accomplished under great difficulties. In that year he and his party were only saved by his coolness and address, and his knowledge of the Indian character, from massacre by the Bella Coola Indians at North Bentinck arm'.[3] The reports and maps, which he prepared during his service in Canada were published from time to time in parliamentary and colonial papers. Palmer was also involved in superintending the construction of roads, bridges and other public works in Canada. While in Canada Palmer married on 7 October 1863 Mary Jane Pearson, daughter of Archdeacon Wright, by whom, according to the *Dictionary of National Biography*, he had a large family.

On his return to England he joined the Ordnance Survey, working in the south of England. In 1867 he was appointed an assistant commissioner in the parliamentary boundaries commission. Between October 1868 and May 1869 he took part in the survey of the peninsula of Sinai. In 1873 he was promoted to the rank of Major and after some practical preparation at the Royal Observatory in Greenwich he was appointed chief astronomer on the expedition sent to New Zealand to observe the transit of Venus in 1874. While in New Zealand he advised the governor on provincial surveys throughout the then colony. He also helped the French authorities to determine the longitude of the Campbell Island.

Palmer returned to England in June 1875 and in November that year went to Barbados as resident engineer and aide-de-camp to the Governor John Pope-Hennessy[4] remaining there until March 1878 when he was transferred to Hong Kong where he was appointed engineer of the admiralty works and continued as aide-de-camp to Sir John Pope-Hennessy who had been appointed as Governor of Hong Kong. While in Hong Kong he designed a physical observatory for astronomical, magnetical, meteorological and tidal observations and determined exactly the position of the Hong Kong observatory at Mount Elgin, Kowloon.

PALMER AND JAPAN

Following a visit to Japan by Sir John Pope-Hennessy in 1879 Palmer was ordered to go to Japan where he arrived on 1 October. Palmer used his annual leave entitlement to pay another visit to Japan where he stayed from the end of July to September 1880. This led him to write a memorandum dated 6 October 1880 entitled 'On the importance of placing the departments of surveying and astronomy in Japan on a sound scientific footing.' This was submitted to Inouye Kaoru, then Japanese Foreign Minister, in October 1881 when Palmer accompanied Queen Victoria's two grandsons Prince Albert Victor and Prince George (later King George V) to Japan on HMS *Bacchante*.[5]

In this memorandum Palmer commented as follows on surveying in Japan:

> There is indeed no public undertaking to which the maxim that what is worth doing at all is worth doing well applies more truly than to a National Survey. Especially is this the case as regards triangulation. No pains, therefore, should be spared to execute it thoroughly once for all. It will then amply repay its cost. In the case of Japan, the importance of a good and precise survey has special weight. The tax upon land is the chief source of imperial revenue, forming on the average at least two-thirds of its whole amount.

On astronomy he noted:

> Eastward from India, until the Atlantic seaboard of the United States, the only public observatories in existence are those at Melbourne and Sydney in Australia and at Batavia of Java; that is to say, the vast region which extends from pole to pole, and over more than 190 degrees of longitude, with these exceptions, destitute of fixed observatories. It is plain, therefore, that Japan has before her a fine opportunity for helping to supply this deficiency and for earning appreciation and grateful acknowledgements from Governments and scientific men in all parts of the world.
>
> In astronomy, as with survey, a modest beginning with caution and moderation is urged. But the sooner a beginning is made, on sound principle, and the sooner a small staff of Japanese gentlemen of scientific tastes are brought together and interested and instructed in the work, the easier and cheaper will it be hereafter to expand that beginning into an institution which shall do credit to the Government of Japan.

An article by Palmer dated 27 July 1882 entitled 'Recent Japanese Progress' appeared in the British *Quarterly Review.* In this article Palmer drew on the material which he had collected during his 1879 and 1880 visits and drew attention to the reforms which had been made in the army, navy, education, the press, postal services, railways, telegraphs, prison system, police, hospitals, public engineering works, lighthouses, mint and mining industry. He attached detailed statistical data.

This article was noted in an article dated 27 July 1882 in the British scientific weekly *Nature*. It commented that the article 'was by far the most valuable that has been published on this subject for many years past' and after summarizing its contents it declared: 'It is gratifying to notice that a careful and impartial observer like Colonel Palmer is able to conclude his article with confidence in the future of the country to which he has devoted so much study.'

Palmer also commented sympathetically in his article on the controversial topic of treaty revision. Negotiations for revision of the 'unequal treaties' had taken place in Tokyo during 1881 and 1882, but had foundered in large part as a result of the uncompromising line taken by the British who were in the lead and who were strongly influenced by the abrasive British Minister Sir Harry Parkes. Palmer wrote:

> In Japan the question of treaty revision is one of burning interest to the Government and the educated classes, who have long smarted under tariff restrictions and under extraterritorial stipulations which denied them any jurisdiction whatever over foreigners. It certainly is but natural that an intelligent and progressive race should view as unfair and oppressive treaties according to which they have no power to regulate their own customs dues for purposes either of protection or of revenues; and that they should grudge clauses which deprive them of rights of government over the very foreigners whom they are called upon to protect, and for whose safety they are held responsible. The Japanese Government, accordingly, feel that the time has come at which they may fairly claim to be relieved from the humiliation of conditions applicable only to barbarous or semi-barbarous races.
>
> Much objection will doubtless be made to the proposed revision by foreigners resident in the country, but it will be hard for European Governments to refuse to a nation like Japan that which they have granted to such countries as Tripoli, Tunis and Morocco.

Palmer was recalled to London in 1882 and on 1 October that year he was promoted to the rank of Lieutenant Colonel. On his way home he visited Japan arriving in Yokohama on 19 December 1882 and stayed with Sir Harry Parkes at the British Legation in Tokyo. At Parkes' suggestion Inouye Kaoru, the Japanese Foreign Minister, arranged for Oki, the Governor of Kanagawa Prefecture, to call at the Legation with a Japanese engineer to meet Palmer. This led to Palmer being employed by the Japanese Government for three months to advise on the project for the new Yokohama waterworks. Palmer checked the designs and estimates prepared by Mita, the Japanese engineer responsible for the project. On 11 April 1883 and 31 May 1883 he submitted to the Governor of Kanagawa two alternative schemes for the supply of water to Yokohama. One was for water from the Tama river, the other from the Sagami river.

Inouye to whose attention Palmer's article in the British *Quarterly Review* must have been drawn considered Palmer to be a good and influential friend of Japan. He believed that Palmer could not only assist in the development of Japanese infrastructure but could help to interpret Japanese development to other countries. Palmer for his part intensified his studies of Japan and came to regard Japan as the country where he could find fulfilment.

On reaching England in July 1883 Palmer was appointed to command the Royal Engineers in the Manchester district. He retained this post until 28 February 1885. While in Manchester he contributed articles to leading British newspapers. These included an article in *The Daily News* on 22 March 1884 on 'Our commercial relations with Japan', in *The Manchester Guardian* on 7 March on 'Japan and the Treaty Powers' and in *The Times* on 9 June on 'The Capitulations in Japan'. In his article of 9 June Palmer was again sharply critical of the extraterritorial privileges in the unequal treaties and urged that they should be amended. In an editorial in the same issue *The Times* commented: 'A correspondent raises a question which is pretty sure at no distant date to force its way to the front...what our correspondent clearly shows – what ought not henceforth to be forgotten – is that it rests with England in the main to say what will be the character of the relation to the outer world of a great Empire inhabited by 37,000,000 of human beings gifted with rare industry and aptitude and moving steadily along the high road of civilization'.

This editorial prompted Inouye Kaoru to write privately to Palmer in Manchester on 13 September 1884. Inouye welcomed Palmer's untiring efforts to explain to the English public through his articles the wrongs, grievances and aspirations of Japan. In particular Inouye was impressed by Palmer's article in *The Times* and the accompanying editorial. These had been translated for the Emperor.

Inouye went on to say that the Yokohama waterworks project, which Palmer had designed, would soon be approved by the Japanese Government and Palmer would be invited to superintend the work. He asked Palmer to arrange with some leading British newspapers for him to be appointed their special correspondent in Japan. Inouye added that the Hon Francis Plunkett,[6] who had been appointed British Minister at Tokyo in succession to Sir Harry Parkes, was very popular in Japan for his conciliatory attitude and friendly sympathy towards Japan.

In the autumn of 1884, the Japanese Government decided to build the works needed to supply Yokohama with water from the Sagami river and confirmed their invitation to Palmer to superintend the work.

On 19 February 1885 Kawase, the Japanese Minister in London, sent a telegram to Inouye in which he said: 'When I contacted Palmer in accordance with your instructions to check on the feasibility of his being appointed special correspondent in Japan of leading British newspapers such as *The Times* he told me that he had been able to arrange with Mr Buckle of *The Times* to be appointed as the paper's Tokyo correspondent. This has been confirmed to me in a letter addressed to me by Mr Buckle.'

Palmer sailed from Liverpool at the end of February 1885 and reached Yokohama on 11 April. He was promoted full Colonel on 1 July 1885. On 1 October 1887 he retired on a pension with the honorary rank of Major General.

CONSTRUCTION OF THE YOKOHAMA WATERWORKS

As soon as the necessary materials had reached Japan from England full-scale construction began. The work was completed on 17 October 1887. The work took only two-and-a-half years as a result of the hard work put into the project by the Japanese engineers and workmen who quickly mastered the new techniques, which their advisers taught them. J. H. T. Turner, who assisted Palmer in the work, commented: 'Praise is due to the entire body of the junior engineering staff engaged in the works for the zeal and intelligence they displayed in work that was new to them in almost every respect.'[7]

For the important part, which he had played in the construction works, the Japanese Emperor on 2 November 1887 conferred on Palmer the Order of the Rising Sun (third class). The obituary of Palmer in *The Japan Weekly Mail* of 18 February 1893 declared: 'The excellence of the design and the thoroughly efficient manner in which it was carried out are attested by the fact that though the conditions of the work were exceptionally difficult, no defect of any kind has developed in the course of five years' operations.'

On 30 April 1987 a bronze bust of Palmer was unveiled at Nogeyama Public Garden in Yokohama, near the old water reservoir at Nogeyama, to commemorate the centenary of the completion of Yokohama's first modern waterworks designed and superintended by Palmer.

OTHER WATERWORKS

Japanese cities including Yokohama had been badly hit by epidemics of cholera and this had highlighted the need for supplies of clean drinking water. The Governor of Osaka requested the Minister of Home Affairs to send Palmer to Osaka to design and construct modern waterworks for the city. Once the construction of the Yokohama waterworks was progressing satisfactorily Palmer drew up designs and estimates for waterworks not only for Osaka but also for Hakodate, Tokyo and Kobe.[8] He also completed the design and superintended the construction in 1887 of a filtration plant for the government managed Oji Paper Mills in Tokyo.[9]

In 1891 Palmer designed and completed a large irrigation siphon at Misaka village near Akashi in Hyogo prefecture.[10] The siphon irrigation system has remained in use up to the present day.

In 1889 Palmer was appointed engineer to the Yokohama Dock Company and designed an extensive system of graving docks and repairing basins.[11] Even while he was involved in the waterworks project Palmer had begun to take an interest in schemes for Yokohama harbour and had produced on 25 January 1887 a 'Report and Estimate of a Project for constructing a Commercial Harbour at Yokohama'. This report was submitted on 17 June 1887 by the promoters of the Yokohama Harbour and Dock Company through the Governor of Kanagawa to the Ministry of Home Affairs. It was, however, turned down on 7 December 1887 by the Public Works Bureau of the Ministry, which was at that time controlled by Dutch engineers.

In April 1888 Count Ōkuma, then Japanese Foreign Minister submitted to Itō Hirobumi, then Prime Minister, a petition for the reconstruction of Yokohama harbour utilizing 1,300,000 yen, which had been refunded from the United States. On 5 September 1889 a Dutch engineer named D'rijke in the Public Works bureau produced a plan for harbour works in Yokohama. On the following day Palmer presented a revised and enlarged design for harbour works in Yokohama based on his original 1887 plans. Rivalry between British and Dutch engineers had become intense.

In the end Palmer's plan, which had Ōkuma's backing, rather than D'rijke's plan, which was backed by Yamagata Aritomo, then Minister for Home Affairs, was approved by the Japanese cabinet under Prime Minister Kuroda, in the absence in Europe of Yamagata. Ōkuma, who like Inouye before him was determined to accomplish revision of the treaties, appreciated the support for treaty revision given by Palmer and wanted to help Palmer in his work in Yokohama. Palmer, however, was now subjected to a barrage of abuse from the two Dutch engineers and Japanese engineers in the Bureau of Public Works in the Ministry of Home Affairs who instigated slanderous and critical articles in the Japanese press against Palmer.

Under Palmer's superintendence construction of the harbour works began. Unfortunately, some of the cement used to make concrete blocks was substandard and not of the quality specified by

Palmer. This was the result of some shady dealing by manufacturers and businessmen affiliated with certain Japanese politicians. Some concrete blocks cracked after being lowered onto the seabed and construction of the harbour had to be temporarily suspended. The issue threatened to become serious as those involved tried to conceal the true facts in order to protect themselves against possible legal action. In the midst of the resulting confusion Palmer died suddenly on 10 February 1893. This was a tragic end for someone who had striven so hard to help in the modernization of Japan and to introduce modern Western technology to the country to which he had devoted so much of his life and energy.

PALMER AND *THE TIMES*

Despite his preoccupation with his engineering duties Palmer found the time to furnish regular reports to *The Times* on the political, social and economic situation in Japan as well as on the problem of treaty revision. In all Palmer submitted seventeen letters devoted to the treaty negotiations and the political background to the talks. Palmer also did his best to explain to British readers the nature of modern Japan and its manners and customs. He introduced readers to aspects of Japanese traditional arts and entertainments and noted the frictions which inevitably resulted from the collision between the old and the new and between Japanese and foreign ways. About one third of his reports dealt with the records of surveys of the geological and geographical features of Japan, especially of volcanoes, earthquakes and hot springs, which had stimulated his interest as a scientist. But he was not oblivious to the charms of the Japanese landscape. Twenty-six of his more general pieces were selected by Palmer and his friend Captain F. Brinkley for publication in *The Japan Mail* under the heading 'Letters from the Land of the Rising Sun'. (A detailed list of all Palmer's articles/letters is attached).

Palmer developed a deep affection for Japan. In one letter[12] he wrote:

> Japan, indeed, has the enviable reputation of inspiring love at first sight in the heart of every comer. Nor is this a mere passing sentiment. It grows steadily as acquaintance ripens. There is something about the country and its people that never fails to win lasting and even affectionate regard.' In another private letter[13] he wrote: 'I much prefer the East to the West'. The kindness and courtesy of his Japanese friends had turned him into an enthusiastic Japanophile. He felt that all races and nations were equal before God. In one article[14] he declared: 'If there is one

> doctrine, which we Westerns have hammered into the minds of Orientals, more forcibly than any other, it is the doctrine of their inferiority. The idea of most Europeans, from noblemen to tailors, is that an Oriental, though possibly one of God's creatures, hails from some substratum far down on the human scale, and is to be treated accordingly.

Palmer did his best to understand and interpret the processes and conflicts involved in the Westernisation of Japan symbolized by the Rokumeikan, designed by the British architect Josiah Conder, which was used by the new Japanese élite for balls and other Western entertainments. Palmer, while he admitted that the kimono was the most becoming garb for Japanese women, understood the campaign to introduce Western costume. He thought it important that intercourse should be promoted between Japanese and foreigners.

Palmer's support for treaty revision was remarkable. He was a subject of Queen Victoria and served for much of his life in the British army as a member of the Royal Engineer Corps. He had worked for many years in British colonies including the then largely self-governing dominions of Canada and New Zealand and later in the colonial territories of the Windward Islands and Hong Kong. His experience in the colonies had made him sensitive to Japanese aspirations. He also saw that British industrial prowess was increasingly threatened by quickly industrializing countries such as Germany and the United States. He realized that Japan had great potential and constantly urged that Britain should do nothing to alienate the Japanese and should take the initiative in developing friendly relations with Japan in the face of imminent Russian expansion into Asia. Sadly, he did not live to see the conclusion in 1902 of the first Anglo-Japanese Alliance.

Palmer's advocacy of revision of the treaties and positive steps to promote Anglo-Japanese friendship inevitably antagonized a large number of his fellow-countrymen in Yokohama, but he had undoubtedly brought great benefits to the people of Yokohama ensuring they had an ample supply of pure water.

In the treaty negotiations Ōkuma basically maintained the concessions, which Inouye had made to the Western Powers about the employment of foreign judges and which were regarded understandably by public opinion in Japan as humiliating. Palmer explained and supported Ōkuma's efforts in his letter from Tokyo to *The Times* on 11 March 1889. This was taken up in an editorial, which appeared in the paper on 19 April 1889. This editorial was picked up and translated into Japanese by the anti-Ōkuma newspaper *Nippon* and aroused a strong popular reaction against Ōkuma. Ōkuma, however, ignored the furore and continued the negotiations. This action provoked an extremist to attack him in his carriage. As a result of this attack he lost a leg[15] and his scheme was abandoned. The anti-Ōkuma campaign appears to have been started as a result of Palmer's report. The campaign made it clear to the Japanese Government that negotiations could not be pursued if they involved similar humiliating concessions to the Western powers.

Palmer's position as an advocate of treaty revision had become extremely difficult. Many of his fellow countrymen excoriated him for his advocacy of concessions to Japan and he had unwittingly been the instrument, which had led to the breakdown in the negotiations and had resulted in serious injury to Ōkuma, who had supported him in his endeavours in Yokohama.

The *Dictionary of National Biography* described Palmer's letters to *The Times* as 'graphic' and 'written in a genial and sympathetic spirit which did much to familiarize Englishmen with the remarkable people among whom he dwelt.' 'He possessed a keen sense of humour and power of anecdote.' Palmer demonstrated some of the best qualities of the Englishman abroad in Victorian times. His contribution to Yokohama and the development of Japan deserve to be remembered by British and Japanese alike.

Palmer as the Tokyo Special Correspondent of *The Times*

PARTICULARS OF FORTY-NINE LETTERS PALMER SENT FROM JAPAN:

		From Japan	In *The Times*	The title of the letter
C-	1)	1885– 5– X	1885– 7–28	The treaty between China and Japan
A-	2)	6–19	8–19	England's Policy in Japan
C–	3)	10– 2	12– 4	A New Phase of Japanese Progress
C–	4)	12–28	1886– 2– 3	Cabinet Change in Japan
A–	5)	1886– 1–22	3– 6	The Treaty Problem in Japan
A–	6)	2– X	4–30	An Extradition Case in Japan
C–	7)	4–12	6–16	Japan's Reformed Polity
A–	8)	7–21	8–28	Treaty Revision in Japan
B–	9)	8–20	10–20	Life at a Japanese Spa
B–	10)	30	27	Asamayama; a Japanese Volcano
B–	11)	9– 2	11–16	Kusatsu; a Japanese Sanitarium
C–	12)	11–23	1887– 1– 7	Earthquake Researches in Japan
B–	13)	1887– 2– 5	5– 7	The Miyako Odori; a Japanese Ballet
B–	14)	3– 1	——	The Story of an Earthquake
A–	15)	4– 5	14	England, Germany and Japan
B–	16)	14	21	Social Problems in Japan
A–	17)	8–12	9–17	A New Phase of Japanese Treaty Revision
A–	18)	9–29	12– 2	Changes in the Japanese Cabinet
A–	19)	10– X	27	Japanese Politics

A–	20)	1888– 2– 9	1888– 4– 5	Japanese Political Progress
A–	21)	3– 9	23	Japanese Material Progress
B–	22)	4–24	6– 2	A Japanese Story from Real Life
C–	23)	5–11	23	Japan's New Privy Council
B–	24)	7–28	9–11	The Recent Volcanic Explosion in Japan
B–	25)	10–12	11–24	The Bandai-san Eruption
B–	26)	11– 6	12–27	The Shrines of Ise, in Japan
B–	27)	1889– 2–12	3–22	The Birthday of a Constitution
B–	28)	16	4– 3	
A–	29)	3–11	19	The Treaty Drama in Japan
B–	30)	5– 8	6–22	Japanese Polo
A–	31)	6–19	8– 5	England's Position in Japan
B–	32)	7–17	21	Cormorant Fishing in Japan
B–	33)	10–21	11–28	The Attempted Assasination of Japanese Foerign Minister
B–	34)	22	12– 5	The Shinto Festival of Ise, in Japan
A–	35)	28	27	Affairs in Japan
A–	36)	1890– 1–11	3– 1	The Reconstruction of the Japanese Cabinet
B–	37)	9–21	11–22	Japanese Ways
B–	38)	11–30	1891– 1– 6	The Birthday of Japan's First Parliament
B–	39)	1891– 2–26	3–30	The Death & Burial of a great Japanese noble
B–	40)	4–29	7–11	Parliamentary Procedure in Japan
B–	41)	5–15	6–13	The Attack on the Czarevitch from Japan
B–	42)	16	9– 1	Parliamentary Reporting in Japan
B–	43)	27	——	The Departure of the Czarevitch from Japan

	From Japan	In *The Times*	The title of the letter
B– 44)	10– 3	1892– 4–19	The Flower Art of the Japanese
B– 45)	11– 7	1891–12– 8	The Great Earthquake in Japan
B– 46)	1892– 2– 2	——	The Great Japan Earthquake
A– 47)	7–15	1892– 8–26	An Incident of Extraterritoriality in Japan
A– 48)	9–24	11–22	Political Development in Japan
A– 49)	10– 1	23	Political Situations in Japan

A – THE PARTICULARS OF SEVENTEEN LETTERS ON TREATY REVISION

		From Japan	In *The Times*	The title of the letter
1)	(A– 2)	1885– 6–19	1885– 8–19	England's Policy in Japan
2)	(A– 5)	1886– 1–22	1886– 3– 6	The Treaty Problem in Japan
3)	(A– 6)	2– X	4–30	An Extradition Case in Japan
4)	(A– 8)	7–21	8–28	Treaty Revision in Japan
5)	(A– 15)	1887– 4– 5	1887– 5–14	England, Germany and Japan
6)	(A– 17)	8–12	9–17	A New Phase of Japanese Treaty Revision
7)	(A– 18)	9–29	12– 2	Changes in the Japanese Cabinet
8)	(A– 19)	10– X	27	Japanese Politics
9)	(A– 20)	1888– 2– 9	1888– 4– 5	Japanese Political Progress
10)	(A– 21)	3– 9	23	Japanese Material Progress
11)	(A– 29)	11	1889– 4–19	The Treaty Drama in Japan
12)	(A– 31)	6–19	8– 5	England's Position in Japan
13)	(A– 35)	10–28	12–27	Affairs in Japan
14)	(A– 36)	1890– 1–11	1890– 3– 1	The Reconstruction of the Japanese Cabinet
15)	(A– 47)	1892– 7–15	1892– 8–26	The Incident of Extraterritoriality in Japan

16)	(A– 48)	9– 24	11– 22	The Political Development in Japan
17)	(A– 49)	10– 1	23	The Political Situations in Japan

B – THE PARTICULARS OF THE TWENTY-SIX LETTERS ON 'THE LETTERS FROM THE LAND OF THE RISING SUN'

1)	(B– 9)	1886– 8– 20	1886–10– 10	Life at a Japanese Spa
2)	(B– 10)	30	27	Asamayama, a Japanese Volcano
3)	(B– 11)	9– 2	11– 16	Kusatsu; a Japanese Sanitarium
4)	(B– 13)	1887– 2– 5	5– 7	The Miyako Odori, A Japanese Ballet
5)	(B– 14)	3– 1	— —	The Story of an Earthquake
6)	(B– 16)	4– 14	21	Social Problems in Japan
7)	(B– 22)	1888– 4– 24	6– 2	A Japanese Story from Real Life
8)	(B– 24)	7– 28	9– 11	The Recent Volcanic Explosion in Japan
9)	(B– 25)	10– 12	11– 24	The Bandai-san Eruption
10)	(B– 26)	11– 6	12– 27	The Shrines of Ise in Japan
11)	(B– 27)	1889– 2– 12	3– 22	The Birthday of a Constitution
12)	(B– 28)	16	4– 3	
13)	(B– 30)	5– 8	6– 22	Japanese Polo
14)	(B– 32)	7– 17	8– 21	Cormorant Fishing in Japan
15)	(B– 33)	10– 21	11– 28	The Attempted Assassination of the Japanese Foreign Minister
16)	(B– 34)	22	12– 5	The Shinto Festival of Ise, in Japan
17)	(B– 37)	1890– 9– 21	11– 22	Japanese Ways
18)	(B– 38)	11– 30	1891– 1– 6	The Birthday of Japan's First Parliament
19)	(B– 39)	1891– 2– 26	3– 30	The Death & Burial of a Great Japanese Noble
20)	(B– 40)	4– 29	7– 11	Parliamentary Procedure in Japan
21)	(B– 41)	5– 15	6– 13	The Attack on the Czarevitch from Japan

22)	(B– 42)	16	9– 1	Parliamentary Reporting in Japan
23)	(B– 43)	27	——	The Departure of Czarevitch from Japan
24)	(B– 44)	10– 3	1892– 4– 19	The Flower Art of the Japanese
25)	(B– 45)	11– 7	1891–12– 8	The Great Earthquake in Japan
26)	(B– 46)	1892– 2– 2	——	The Great Japan Earthquake

C – THE PARTICULARS OF SIX LETTERS ON MISCELLANEOUS SUBJECTS

1)	(C– 1)	1885– 5– X	1885– 7– 28	The Treaty between China and Japan
2)	(C– 3)	10– 2	12– 4	A New Phase of Japanese Progress
3)	(C– 4)	12– 28	1886– 2– 3	Cabinet Change in Japan
4)	(C– 7)	1886– 4– 12	6– 16	Japan's Reformed Polity
5)	(C– 12)	11– 23	1887– 1– 7	Earthquake Researches in Japan
6)	(C– 23)	1888– 5– 11	1888– 6– 23	Japan's New Privy Council

PART 4

Scholars & Writers

19

Nakamura Masanao (Keiu), 1832–91: translator into Japanese of Samuel Smiles' *Self Help*

AKIKO OHTA

Nakamura Masanao

Samuel Smiles

IN *THE WESTERN WORLD AND JAPAN*, published in 1950, George Sansom wrote that Samuel Smiles' *Self-Help* '... was enthusiastically welcomed by a public that was anxious to get on in the world. If the enterprising Westerners needed the kind of advice that was offered by Smiles, it was natural that the bewildered Japanese should look for similar guidance.' The Japanese translator was Nakamura Masanao (Keiu) who was an influential scholar and educationist in the Meiji era. Sadly, in comparison with Fukuzawa Yukichi, who like Nakamura was a member of the famous group of intellectuals in the Meirokusha,[1] he is generally only remembered today for his translation of *Self-Help*.

One of the reasons why Nakamura Masao tends to be overlooked was that Dōjinsha, which he founded in Tokyo in 1873, had to be closed down after his death.[2] It was regarded in the early years of

Meiji as one of the three major private schools, the other two being Keio Gijuku, founded by Fukuzawa, and Kōgyokusha, founded by Kondo Makoto.

Another reason may be that most of Nakamura's works, apart from lengthy translations, consisted of relatively short articles and monographs. This was in marked contrast to Fukuzawa who wrote prolifically.[3] Nevertheless, the cultural significance of translated works in Meiji Japan was considerable and they cannot be seen simply as cultural imports. Nakamura, who started as a Confucian scholar but who came to be deeply influenced by Victorian Britain, contributed greatly to the impact of Western culture on Japan and his role deserves reappraisal.

EARLY YEARS AS A CONFUCIAN SCHOLAR

Nakamura Masanao (Keiu) was born in 1832 to a lower ranking samurai family in the Azabu district of Edo (now Tokyo). Nakamura's father, Buhei, came from a farming family in the Izu peninsula, sufficiently wealthy to be entitled to a surname, Tsukada, and to bear swords. He later inherited the household of Nakamura Shigemasa, a low-ranking officer of the Tokugawa Bakufu, officially by adoption, but in reality by purchasing his title.[4] The purchase of the titles of low-ranking samurai, particularly by well-off farmers or merchants seems to have been fairly common in the Edo (Tokugawa) period. The life of his ambitious father, eager to climb the social ladder through hard work, no doubt had a considerable influence on his only son,[5] who went on to translate works by Samuel Smiles in which the lives of many self-made men were depicted.

Nakamura was a child prodigy. At the age of seventeen he entered the Shōheikō, one of the best Confucian academies run by the Bakufu. By the age of twenty-four he had already started teaching in Bakufu academies. At the age of thirty-one (in 1862) he was selected as one of the Confucian scholars to teach the Shogun. This was an unprecedented rate of promotion.

By the early 1860s Nakamura had thus established his status as an eminent Confucian scholar before he took up Western studies, although he had shown an interest in Dutch and Western studies even before he entered the Shōheikō academy.[6] In contrast, Fukuzawa Yukichi had from the beginning started his scholarly career in Western studies. In the 1850s and 1860s, when Japan was going through a turbulent period, it was hardly surprising that many Japanese youths wanted to learn about the West. However, this did not mean that they were all attracted to the West or became pro-Western in their outlook.

Nakamura, while continuing his study of the West, retained his position as a Confucian scholar within the Tokugawa establishment. He is sometime criticized for eclecticism in his understanding of Confucianism,[7] but it would be a mistake to assume that this tendency must have stemmed from a pro-Western way of thinking. What differentiated him from the more conservative Confucianists at that time was that he was searching seriously for a spirit or frame of mind (he often used the word *Shin* 心), which would be able to cope with the rapid changes taking place in Japanese society. His vision as a Confucian scholar was not limited to purely scholastic issues; he was also concerned with the real world. He repeatedly stressed that educating people to respect and observe moral virtues was essential to the stability and prosperity of Japan.[8] The problem was, of course, how to define 'virtue', 'spirit' or 'the frame of mind'. It can be assumed that Nakamura approached Western and Confucian studies together in his search for such new models. Judging from what he wrote in his letter to the Tokugawa Bakufu, seeking permission to study abroad, his desire to go overseas seems to have stemmed from this quest.[9] He volunteered to join the Bakufu students being sent to London in 1866. The members included Hayashi Tadasu, later Japanese Ambassador and Minister of Foreign Affairs, Toyama Masakazu and Kikuchi Dairoku, both of whom later became Presidents of Tokyo University.

NAKAMURA'S ENCOUNTER WITH VICTORIAN BRITAIN: 1866–68

Nakamura Masanao, then thirty-five, and Kawaji Tarō, twenty-three, were chosen as official supervisors of the fourteen Bakufu students who were sent to Britain.[10] Eleven of them were able to enter University College School in late 1867,[11] but Nakamura and Kawaji were considered too old to enrol in the school and had to rely mainly on private tuition. Already in his mid-thirties Nakamura's progress in the English language was relatively slow compared with that of younger students. While Kawaji studied naval technology, Nakamura studied the humanities, and in the evening both translated Japanese history books into English to improve their language skills.[12]

The memoirs of other Bakufu students and the Parkes Papers in the Jardine Matheson Archives reveal the difficulties, which the students had to face in London.[13] They spent a little more than a year there, but unfortunately quite a substantial part of their time and energy had to be spent in trying to resolve a bitter quarrel with William Lloyd who was in charge of them. Despite their desire to register at higher institutions in order to acquire advanced knowledge, Lloyd insisted that they lacked sufficient language ability and experience in the Western educational system to enrol immediately. The students found the preparatory tuition too basic and humiliatingly elementary. Lloyd also ignored the repeated requests of the students to be divided into separate lodgings like the Satsuma students, in order to improve their English. This, together with Lloyd's lavish lifestyle (although he was a naval chaplain) even made the Japanese suspicious that Lloyd was embezzling their funds.[14] Lloyd appealed in writing to Parkes and won the sympathy of Sir Edmund Hammond, the Permanent Under-Secretary at the Foreign Office. Hammond at first thought that the Bakufu students were 'insubordinate' and 'an unruly lot', unlike the Satsuma students who were also studying in London. He even wrote: 'I hope they are gone, never to return'.[15] It was only when he came to learn of Lloyd's unnecessary purchase of a house that Hammond began to have second thoughts about him.[16] Even so, he still seems to have thought of the Bakufu students as 'unruly orientals' who were 'almost impossible to keep under control'.[17]

Many of the Japanese students who travelled abroad during the 1860s were fortunate in their relations with their sponsors who had helped them to come to Britain. There was, of course, an element of self-interest in the motives of the sponsors. Merchants such as Hugh Matheson and Thomas Glover prudently maintained friendly relations with the students whom they had helped, believing that this would help them to play influential roles in the commercial development of Meiji Japan. Laurence Oliphant who tried to distance the Japanese students from their merchant sponsors, took advantage of their financial insecurity to entice them to join his chosen religious sect in America.[18] Even so, Lloyd's behaviour in exploiting his Japanese students for his own personal advantage was particularly flagrant.[19] It was unfortunate that the academic life of the Bakufu students, which was cut short by the downfall of the Tokugawa regime, was badly affected by their problems with Lloyd.

Nakamura must have had a particularly difficult time. As the eldest of the students and their supervisor he had to mediate between the two sides. However, in his autobiography he hardly referred to his hardships in London. He simply recounted how hard he had studied, how much he had been impressed by the vigour of Victorian society and how excited he was to see the thriving city.[20] The downfall of the Bakufu brought an abrupt end to their stay abroad, and in April 1868 they left London for Paris, reaching Japan in June that year. An English friend gave Nakamura a copy of *Self Help* by Samuel Smiles as a parting gift. He read the book from cover to cover during the long sea voyage home.[21]

LIFE IN EXILE IN SHIZUOKA (1868–72) - CHRISTIANITY AND TRANSLATIONS

Having been a retainer of the Bakufu Nakamura's life after his return home was not at first an easy one. In September 1868, he followed Tokugawa Iyesato, who had been exiled to Shizuoka, and started teaching in the Shizuoka Gakumonjo, a newly-established academy for former retainers of the Bakufu. He remained in Shizuoka until 1872. During these difficult years he managed to develop the ideas, which became the core of his moral philosophy, through his studies of Christianity and through translating works by Samuel Smiles and John Stewart Mill.

Nakamura's study of Christianity eventually led to his being baptized in 1874.[22] It is not clear whether his stay in Britain led him towards Christian beliefs. To a certain extent, he may have seen Christianity as the religion of a prosperous and enlightened society. However, Christianity was still proscribed in Japan in 1871[23] when he came to know E. W. Clark, a Methodist missionary from the United States. It may be more appropriate to assume that Nakamura became a Christian as part of his quest for a 'spirit' or a moral philosophy (*Shin*), which would meet the needs of the dramatically changing society in Japan.

As many Japanese scholars have pointed out Nakamura's *Keiten Aijin Setsu* (1868) and *Seishitsu Shōmon* (1869) may reveal that he was trying to interpret the idea of God in Christianity as analogous to that of *Ten* (heaven) in fundamental Confucianism.[24] In *Seishitsu shomon* he wrote that 'although there are several names such as *Ten, Jotei, Kami* (the monotheistic almighty God), the Creator, what they signify is the same'. In *Keiten Aijin Setsu* he declared that *Ten* or *Jōtei* should be regarded as a transcendental existence beyond the scope of the human intellect, and that respect for *Ten* should be the fundamental element of virtuous conduct or behaviour. It almost seems that Nakamura conceived God as a supernatural entity embracing both Christian and Confucian beliefs. This would partly explain why Nakamura did not seem fully to understand at this stage some of the basic beliefs of Christianity such as original sin and salvation.[25] However, through his study of Christianity, Nakamura managed to form an idea of what were the elements, which deserved respect, and of the basic criteria for virtuous people in the new Meiji era. He was looking for a form of ethics applicable in daily life. Therefore, Nakamura's approach to Christianity was not so much of a break from Confucianism as it seemed, but rather a continuation of his search for moral values.

Nakamura's interpretation of God and his moral philosophy were reflected in his translations. During his time in Shizuoka, he published two translations, which brought him to the forefront of the intellectual movement in Japan, but this time as a scholar of Western studies. His translation of Samuel Smiles' *Self-Help* (1859) was published in 1871 under the title *Saigoku Risshihen*. His translation of J.S.Mill's *On Liberty* (1859) appeared in 1872 under the title *Jiyū no Kotowari*. Nakamura seems to have worked simultaneously on the two translations. In his preface to *Saigoku Risshihen* he stressed that the strength of the West came from the people's firm belief in the 'Way of God' (*Tendō* 天). He noted that both Napoleon and Smiles had declared that the strength of a nation depended on the moral virtues of its people.[26] As he later wrote in his autobiography, what he found most impressive in Victorian society was that the people piously believed in the True God and that they observed moral virtues, worked hard and helped the aged without relatives, the sick and the handicapped.[27] Victorian society, as we all now know, was certainly not as morally pure as Nakamura observed, nor was its social policy particularly kind to those in need. Whether he ignored or simply did not recognize its seamy side is not clear. Nevertheless, in spite of such shortcomings, or maybe because of such embellishments of Victorian society, *Saigoku Risshihen,* together with Fukuzawa Yukichi's *Seiyō Jijō* (1866–70), became best-sellers of the early Meiji era.

Self Help was not only one of the best-selling work in Britain, but was translated into various languages throughout the world.[28] *Saigoku Risshihen* sold phenomenally well in Japan, and inspired many young Japanese. One often comes across passages in autobiographies or memoirs of Meiji Japanese saying that *Saigoku Risshihen* stimulated them to work hard and to succeed.[29] Although Smiles wrote *Self Help* in order to instruct the lower middle and working classes on how to improve themselves through self-help, Nakamura's translation was read and highly appreciated by a slightly different group of readers. Despite the references to the lives of workers and artisans in *Self Help,* Nakamura's Japanese version was mainly read by those eager, and sufficiently educated, to learn about Western society. Nakamura's message to his readers was that they should believe in the True God and observe moral virtues according to God's will. This was interpreted as instructions on how to endure the hardships of the tumultuous days of early Meiji and on how to succeed as businessmen, industrialists and intellectuals.[30] The chapters referring to social mobility in Victorian society were read with enthusiasm. The spirit of Victorian philanthropy and voluntary work, including its limitations, was not fully conveyed by Nakamura to Japanese readers.[31]

Nakamura's translation of J. S. Mill's *On Liberty* was also given a twist. Although Mill wrote that a liberal society supported by voluntary associations and 'the political education of a free people' by habituating them to act from public or semi-public motives' formed the important basis of a free constitution, Nakamura gave a different meaning to such key ideas. He even added a few passages, which did not appear in the original text, and wrote that it was the unity of the people and freedom of religion which were important in a liberal constitution.[32]

In his article *Taiseijin no Jōshō ni Gisu* which he wrote anonymously and which appeared first in English in *The Japan Weekly Mail* of 18 May 1872, and later in Japanese in *Shimbun Zasshi* in August of 1872, Nakamura praised the West for the great importance attached to religion in teaching moral values to the nation. He even went so far as to criticize the religious intolerance of Japan.[33] The fact that both this article and *Jiyu no Kotowari* appeared in the same year may suggest that Nakamura was hoping to convey his political message about freedom of religion through his translation of Mill's work. Whereas Mill stressed the significance of the identity of the individual in the original text, Nakamura tended to put more emphasis on the importance of moral virtue and endeavour to carry out God's Will. All these points were somewhat different from what Mill had intended to express in his political philosophy, but they were consistent with what Nakamura had been writing and advocating in his previous works and translations.

NAKAMURA'S LATER CAREER

Nakamura's later career, after he was summoned back to Tokyo in June 1872, covered a wide intellectual range. He became one of the leading figures in the *Meiroku-sha*, the centre of the so-called enlightenment movement in Meiji Japan, founded in 1873. Apart from writing for the *Meiroku Zasshi* he continued to work on translations. Nakamura's contribution to various aspects of Japanese education was also considerable.

Relatively well-known translations by Nakamura included Gillet's *The Federal Government*, published in 1871, and translated as *Kyōwa Seiji* in 1873, and Smiles' *Character*, published in 1871 and translated as *Seiyō Hinkō-ron* in 1878–80, as well as Smiles' *Thrift*, published in 1875 and translated as *Seiyō Setsuyo-ron* in 1886. Although they did not sell so phenomenally well as *Self Help* or *On Liberty*, they were widely read by Japanese intellectuals and had a considerable influence on them.

It is probable that Nakamura chose to translate *Character* because

Smiles devoted quite a few chapters to the roles of men and women, and wrote on the significance of marriage and the domestic environment. Nakamura had been involved with women's education since his return to Tokyo, and he was one of the pioneers to open the doors of higher educational institutions to women. In the autumn of 1874 he started to admit women to Dōjisha, which he had founded in 1873. The Dōjinsha girls' school eventually started from 1879.[34] The curriculum of the school, in contrast with other institutions of female education at that time, included as textbooks for study in lecture classes Mill's *On Representative Government* and *The Subjection of Women*. This was due to Nakamura's belief that it was important for Japan to enlighten women by teaching them about politics, history and women's role in society.[35] At the strong request of the Meiji government, Nakamura also presided as headmaster of Tokyo Women's Teachers College (*Tokyo Joshi Shihan Gakkō*) from 1875–1880. Although he preferred teaching in private institutions where there was more freedom, he managed to open the first kindergarten in Japan in the grounds of the Tokyo Women's Teachers College in 1876.

The translation of *Thrift* was published much later when Nakamura was fifty-five. By that time he had become Professor of Chinese Classics at Tokyo University.[36] It is not clear why Nakamura decided to translate *Thrift*, but it is probable that he saw it as a sequel to *Character* and *Self Help*.[37] Unlike *Seiyo Hinkō-ron, Seiyō Setsuyo-ron* was much shorter than the original text and conveyed a slightly different message from what Smiles had intended.[38] For instance, all the passages or chapters where Smiles wrote extensively on the role of the Friendly Society, the Co-operative Corn-mill Society in Rochdale, Savings Banks, and Postal Savings, were cut out in *Seiyō Setsuyo-ron*. In a passage where Smiles wrote that all that was great in man came from labour, Nakamura put more emphasis on the significance of knowledge.[39] As in the case of *Self Help*, Smiles wrote *Thrift* to enlighten the lower middle and working classes by giving detailed information on how to save from their earnings. It was intended as a practical handbook on how to save and live wisely. Such considerations must have seemed unnecessary for Nakamura, who translated this work for Japanese readers who were hardworking and eager to succeed. Thus, only moralistic general messages such as that one should not live beyond one's means, and excessive drinking is bad for the health, were left in the translated version. Such sentences as 'The men who economize by means of labour become the owners of capital' were underlined with emphasis marks in the translation.[40] Considering the type of readers for whom Nakamura was writing, the bias he gave to the Japanese translation was understandable.

Nevertheless, *Seiyo Setsuyo-ron* would have been more interesting, if Nakamura had translated the details of the savings systems in the West.

Was Nakamura's interest in Victorian society confined to ethics and political philosophy? To some extent his understanding of the British economic system was limited as compared with that of Fukuzawa or of Kume Kunitake, a member of the Iwakura Mission, which visited Britain in 1872, and compiler of the account of the Mission, which was produced under the title of *Bei-Ō Kairan Jikki* in 1878.[41] However, the impact of his experiences in Britain and his reading is reflected in his activities in education. Noteworthy are his endeavours to create educational opportunities for 'minorities' in Japanese society at that time. As already mentioned above, Nakamura devoted himself to the enlightenment and education of women. He also helped to establish a school for handicapped children. In 1875, with the help of Henry Faulds,[42] a Scottish physician and missionary, Nakamura founded a charitable organization called the *Rakuzen-kai,* for the education of blind children.[43] Although many Japanese who travelled to Britain in the 1860s and 1870s had noted the significance of schools for handicapped children in their records,[44] Nakamura was one of the first Japanese, who despite many difficulties and prejudices,[45] actually established an institution for them in Japan.

Nakamura seems to have had a frail constitution and tried as much as possible to keep regular hours.[46] He fell ill at home on 2 June 1891 and died five days later on 7 June at the age of sixty. He was survived by his wife whom he had married in 1859. As Yoshino Sakuzō has commented, while Fukuzawa showed the world of wisdom to the young people of Meiji Japan, Nakamura showed them the world of virtue.[47] Although Nakamura's stay in Britain was relatively short, his experiences there continued to influence him throughout the rest of his life.

ACKNOWLEDGEMENTS

I should like to express my sincere gratitude to Matheson and Company and the Manuscript Room of the Cambridge University Library for enabling me to consult the Jardine Matheson Archives.

20

Sir Edwin Arnold, 1832–1904: A Year in Japan, 1889–90

CARMEN BLACKER

Sir Edwin Arnold

WE HAVE HAD a delightful surprise, wrote Mrs Mary Fraser in December 1889 from the British Embassy in Tokyo. A visit from Edwin Arnold and his daughter! The poet was in Japan for the first time, and had so much fallen in love with Tokyo that he had taken a house for six months. There he insisted, much to his daughter's horror, on 'sleeping on the mats Japanese fashion'.[1]

In 1889 there was no need for Mary Fraser to explain to her correspondent who Edwin Arnold was. For it was he, no less, who only ten years before had published the long narrative poem on the life of the Buddha *The Light of Asia*, which had been such an astonishing 'Buddhist best-seller.' Edwin Arnold had other claims to fame; he was a poet, a scholar, a notable linguist and in his time editor of a famous newspaper. He had gone to India in 1857 and in only four years mastered Sanskrit, Pali, Hindi and Marathi, and been Principal of the Government College in Poona during the difficult times of the Mutiny. He had later acquired Persian and Turkish. He had served on the staff of the *Daily Telegraph* for twenty-eight years, rising eventually to be its editor-in-chief. He had written and translated many books in both prose and verse, including the *Bhagavad Gita*, the Persian *Gulistan*, and the ninety-nine names of Allah. But it was the *Light of Asia* which had made his name a household word, and which had sold in such amazing thousands in both England and America.[2]

Here, in blank verse of what has been described as 'Oriental luxuriance, in which colour and music were blended in the Tennysonian manner with heightened effects', Arnold had told the story of the Indian prince, on whom had been lavished every luxury and worldly joy conceivable in the sixth century BC. But he had chosen instead to renounce his inheritance, his palace, his beautiful wife and son, and to devote himself as a recluse to the momentous spiritual task of discovering the reason and remedy for human suffering. The poem ended with a triumphant account of his attainment, under the Bo Tree at Bodh Gaya, of complete and perfect enlightenment and the blessed state of Nirvana.

So vividly had Arnold told the story that Western readers had been deeply impressed and inspired, and bought so many copies that by 1912 no less than forty editions had appeared in England alone. So vividly indeed that 'the animosities of many pulpits' were aroused, and with a fury amazing to the modern reader, reverend clergymen and professors had denounced the poem as a devilish attack on Christianity, for misleading shallow thinkers into believing that the Buddha was as great a man as Christ.[3]

But here, in 1889, was the famous Edwin Arnold in Japan. Never before had he been further east than India. His motive for visiting this far country, Mrs Fraser continued, was an entirely chance encounter with 'that enchanting book Chamberlain's *Colloquial Japanese*'. After reading only a few sentences he decided that he must at all costs visit the land where linguistic courtesy was so prized and practised.

Indeed, for the entire length of the voyage across the Pacific, he had scarcely budged from a 'sheltered corner near the funnel', immersed in the wonderful book. Only at stated intervals would he emerge, to take charge of a small baby so that its weary mother could get a few minutes' rest. And even then he would walk up and down the deck with the baby on one arm and the open book in the other hand, learning more Japanese phrases.[4]

Such good use had he made of the *Handbook*, indeed, that he could speak to the children of the Frasers' servants in their own special language, much to their delight. (The *Handbook* does indeed contain a section on 'Baby Language etc', with examples of such special words – *tete* for hands, *wan-wan* for dogs, *baya* for granny, and the reminder that such words can also be used in addressing pet animals.)

What was more, it was largely due to the sweet and gentle presence of Sir Edwin Arnold that Mrs Fraser's Christmas children's party was such a success. No less than fifty-eight Japanese children from the Embassy compound, dressed in 'a blaze of scarlet, green, geranium, pink and orange', were all given presents from a giant Christmas tree, so splendid that one little boy of two fell flat on his back with amazement and lay there silent until rescued. With this crowd of excited children, Sir Edwin was 'a wonder of kind-heartedness', beaming at them all, and in the end beaming also at Bishop Bickersteth, an 'intensely Anglican, severe look ascetic', with whom he had already, though basking in Buddhist calm, enjoyed theological arguments at the Frasers' table.[5]

Nor was Mrs Fraser the only compatriot to sing his praises in Tokyo. Douglas Sladen, author of *Queer Things About Japan,* and the founder of *Who's Who*, recalled his native house in Azabu; so native indeed that 'you always had to take off your boots when you went to see him'. It lay outside Treaty limits, but he got permission to live there under the legal fiction that he was tutor to the daughters of his rich landlord. It came complete with *shōji*, floor cushions, finger stoves (*hibachi*) and no furniture.

It was here, during his year in Japan, that he wrote his lesser-known long narrative poem *The Light of the World*. This told the life of Christ in six books, from the Nativity at Bethlehem, the Three Kings, who had journeyed through the deserts of Bactria and past the Tigris and Ararat, bearing a chalice of Indian gold inscribed with the Buddha's Four Noble truths and the Swastika, to the great Consummation on the Cross. This book, alas, was to prove a signal failure, and in no way redeemed him in the eyes of the clergymen who had condemned his life of the Buddha.

But Douglas Sladen was delighted when it was read to him, batch by batch as it was composed, and observed that his handwriting was as beautiful as that of Lanfranc. He observed too that much of Sir Edwin's time was taken up with receiving 'Buddhist abbots and sages who by extraordinary abstinences and striking concentrations of mind and will, had acquired supernatural powers …'. He always fancied that Sir Edwin would produce a magnum opus on 'those Eastern superhumans', but no such book ever saw the light.[6]

Soon after his arrival he was invited to give two notable lectures. The first, to a meeting of the Tokyo Club, took place in the famous *Rokumeikan* in late November 1889. It was fully reported in *the Japan Weekly Mail* of 30 November, and later printed in the *Daily Telegraph*. Here he confirmed all that Mrs Fraser had said about Chamberlain's wonderful *Handbook*. His sudden interest in Japan, he told his audience, was roused not by a guidebook, but by a grammar!

Chamberlain's possessed all the fascination of a romance, not to speak of its perfect lucidity of style and method. He was instantly beguiled by Chamberlain's *Handbook of Colloquial Japanese* account of Japanese verbs without any imperative mood, interjections without abuse or anger, strong expressions free from all bitterness or blasphemy, and of Japanese syntax constructed according to the 'refined and gentle principle of exalting another and depreciating oneself'.

But such preparation was in no way adequate to convey the entrancing truth of Japan itself.' Japan astonishes, absorbs, delights, fascinates and wholly contents me', he declared. Never before had he visited a land where he so much envied the inhabitants and the residents. And though so recently arrived, he was able to enthuse about Buddhist kindliness and consolations, which would surely soon be reconciled with the lofty ethics of Christianity and the discoveries of science.

The *Japan Weekly Mail* even quoted in its report the quatrains of *The Light of Asia*, which Arnold had included to show that Buddhism was by no means out of step with modern science. The speech, the newspaper further reported, was 'repeatedly interrupted by bursts of applause, and Sir Edwin resumed his seat amid a storm of cheers'.[7]

The second lecture, in early December, was delivered to the Japanese Educational Society under the title of 'The Range of Modern Knowledge'. This, too, was fully reported by the *Japan Weekly Mail* of 21 December, and later printed in the *Telegraph*. It was delivered to an audience, which included Viscount Enomoto, then Minister of Education, an American Admiral, Japanese professors, Buddhist priests of various sects and some five hundred students. Notably too Mr B. H. Chamberlain himself, who gave a 'graceful and felicitous translation' into Japanese of the address. No mean feat considering that it covered more than eight pages of small print, and ranged over astronomy, geology and earthquakes, modern chemistry and oxidised glycerine, literature, some verses from *The Light of Asia* about Buddhism and science, and English as the future world language.[8]

The Japan Weekly Mail allotted more than two of its large pages to its report of the lecture, commenting that it was afterwards 'admirably rendered into Japanese by Mr Basil Hall Chamberlain, whose wonderful command of the exceedingly difficult language of the country was well exemplified by his graceful translation'.

The same newspaper further reported an interview given by Sir Edwin to the 'well-read Christian scholar' Mr Goro Takahashi. Mr Takahashi was delighted by Sir Edwin's reading of lines from *The Light of Asia* in such 'enthusiastic and solemn tones that we verily imagine ourselves in the presence of one who is revealing the very soul of the Great Benefactor of the World'. *The Light of Asia*, which had rightly been extravagantly praised, was at present being translated into Japanese by 'some Buddhists of Kyoto'. His name might well therefore, soon be 'adored as their sacred singer by millions of Buddhists in Oriental countries'.

Arnold's most enduring literary work on Japan, however, must be his book *Japonica*, published in 1891.[9] It is a compendium of articles written in Japan and sent to *Scribners Magazine*, and testifies to the ecstatic happiness he had enjoyed during his year's visit to Japan. He is lyrical about the blind shampooers still to be seen in the streets of Tokyo, piping three lugubrious notes as they feel their way along. He is delighted by the rickshaw men, whose speed and courtesy are notable even when loaded by birdcages and vegetables; by the thirty-eight kinds of Japanese dream and their signification, by Japanese swords and their miracles and legends, by the amazing carving on the gates of Nikko and by the brilliant throng to be seen daily in the Ginza - flower sellers, bird-dealers, tea houses, hawkers of fish and persimmons and kites. Lyrical, too, is his evocation of the Japanese bath-house, and the perfect modesty which goes with frank unashamed exposure of the body.

But his most lyrical praise goes to Japanese women -*musmees* as he too often calls them - their unselfish kindness, charm, gentleness, readiness at all times to sacrifice themselves for others. His only shadow of criticism of Japan is in fact for the casual manner in which Japanese men take these virtues for granted. In the great future, which undoubtedly awaits Japan, men will have to make themselves better aware of the goodness of their gods in bestowing such women on the country. He even composed a long poem to '*The Musmee*', with her brown velvet eyes and small faultless feet. These verses perhaps justify the remark of his brief biographer T. S. when he says that 'at times he allows his glowing imagery to vitiate his taste'.[10]

Sir Edwin also wrote a play in four acts entitled *Adzuma, or the Japanese Wife*, which was published in 1893. Its cast ranges from Morito Musha Endō a Japanese nobleman, Hōjō Tokimune a samurai, Wataru Watanabe another Japanese nobleman, and Adzuma his wife – to soldiers, attendants, priests, robbers etc. Whether it has ever been performed is doubtful, for alas for the modern reader it is marred by a good deal of 'tushery.' We may not perhaps find the very words 'Aroint thee, witch!', but there are plenty of other phrases such as 'Deign augustly, Sir', and ' I beseech your lofty pardon', 'Sir Samurai' and 'I make unexcused intrusion'.[11]

Chamberlain, alas, disliked it. He complained in a letter to Lafcadio Hearn that it used so many Japanese words, often mistakenly, that the English public would need a glossary to understand it. And anyway why call tea *cha* and chopsticks *hashi?* It is as irritating as those books on India, which say, 'I give a *hukhm* to cut their *tallabs*.' He also complained of Edwin Arnold's 'invertebrate maunderings.'[12]

But he might have remembered, when seeing the text peppered with words such as *naruhodo, dōmo* and *aoyaoya,* that in his *Handbook*, from which Sir Edwin had learned so much, he had allotted a special section to *naruhodo*. A very useful word', he remarked, it's meaning depending on the tone of voice in which it is uttered. In a tone of great surprise it corresponds to 'You don't say so!' 'Well, I never!' But in an assenting tone it means 'Oh indeed' or 'I see'. He advises its use too when someone is telling a long story and pauses for breath.[13]

The word *dōmo* he had engagingly described as 'very often a mere expletive, used to gain time and to cover paucity of ideas'.

Perhaps this is the moment for a brief comment in sympathy with the inspiration, which Sir Edwin derived from Chamberlain's *Handbook*. It has long been out of print and was never reissued during the war, as was his *Simplified Japanese Grammar,* which deals only with the literary style. It is nevertheless as fascinating, lucid and witty as Sir Edwin discovered. Seldom will chapters be found so elegantly expressed on 'The Verb' or 'The Postposition' or 'The Numeral'. Open the book at the chapter on 'Honorifics', for example, and you will find that though there may be no words exactly corresponding to our 'Sir' or 'Madam', 'the student who has perused this chapter with care will be able to judge how amply their absence is made good by the use of verbal and other honorifics'.

And, 'it is rather common, in slipshod talk addressed to inferiors, to omit the honorific imperative'. As in *cha wo irete,* for example, 'the sentence may appear to end in a gerund, but the ellipsis must always be mentally supplied'.

There is also a chapter on 'Special Phraseology' where, under the heading of Bad Language one may read that 'Japanese is honourably distinguished from most languages of the world by being totally devoid of oaths'. All you say to a difficult horse is *kore!,* lit., This. None of the expletives which disfigure English and French exist.

And under Court Language, the special words used by members of the Imperial Court, he writes: 'Although ordinary mortals can have no use for this exalted phraseology, a few specimens will doubtless not fail to interest the student.' And he gives a short list which includes the word *ase* for blood, *ogushi* for hair, and *okabe* for *tofu*.[14]

And we can be sure that it is not the Yokohama Dialect[15] that he gives us when he asks us to translate, 'I venture to hope that you will take some opportunity of letting me see it'. And, 'Excuse me for having trespassed on your valuable time'. And, 'None of your impudence!'.

No wonder that Sir Edwin, on reading such sentences, lost no time in booking his passage on the next steamer to Japan. Who would not wish to see with his own eyes how such a language, so different from the Sanskrit, Pali and Persian with which he was familiar, was reflected in the culture of Japan?

Yokoyama Toshio[16] has shown us that many Western readers and travellers in the nineteenth century cherished a longing to discover a hidden Paradise, a pocket of prelapsarian happiness and grace and natural virtue which had escaped the Fall of Man. That Japan should seem to conform with such a vision, cut off and isolated from the world as it had been for nearly 250 years, is not astonishing. The Jesuits had said so three hundred years before, and what were Isabella Bird's observations by comparison of the disease, fetid filth and flies in the north? Many had been the 'globetrotters' during the Meiji period who had carried the message home of a far-off elfland, unfallen, uncorrupted and innocent, and Professor Yokoyama's book shows how deftly the editors of magazines pruned their correspondents' descriptions of Japan so as to conform with this expectation.

By 1890, however, this bright image was beginning to be sullied by railways, factories and ill-fitting foreign clothes. Birmingham was beginning to irrupt into Arcadia. And Sir Edwin was no inexperienced globetrotter. He had spent years in India, mastered at least four Indian languages, had been Principal of the Deccan College, Poona at the early age of 24, and had conducted it so admirably during the critical times of the Mutiny as to earn the commendation of the Indian Government. He had been chief editor of the *Daily Telegraph* for more than a decade, and had written a best-selling poem on the life of the Buddha which had appreciably inclined the British reading public towards Buddhism. 'The dewdrop slips into the shining sea' had become as familiar to English literacy as was Tennyson's *Maud*.

Yet he, too, during his year in Japan had clearly fallen under the same spell. Japan in 1890 was as near to Paradise as any place on this earth. It was 'wonderful, delightful, unique and mysterious'. He had found there a high, unique, specialized civilization admirably suited to restore a mind weary with the heat and haste of Western daily existence.

He had explored Kamakura and Enoshima and Kyoto and Shiba in Tokyo. He had been invited to an Imperial Garden Party and met the Meiji Emperor. And he had climbed Fuji in August, where at the summit wrapped in coats he wrote a letter in poetry to 'a Japanese lady with whose friendship I am honoured'. Could she have been the lady who later became his third wife, Tama Kurokawa?[17]

His leave-taking at the end of his visit was heartrending. His landlord Mr Aso and his wife and daughter all composed farewell *uta*, expressing gratitude for the brotherly friendship so rare in one from across the seas. Many friends came to see him off, and to catch a last glimpse of him before he sailed away. What could he do to repay such a debt except to swear a lifelong goodwill to such remarkable people?[18]

On returning to England after this notable visit, Sir Edwin Arnold joined the Japan Society, and was one of the speakers at the annual dinner at the Hotel Metropole in 1894. The Japanese were the Greeks of Asia, he declared, and predicted that a splendid future lay before the Empire of the Rising Sun. So lavish was his praise, indeed, that *Punch* was provoked to produce a cartoon of 'Sir Edwin Mikarnoldo', fan in hand, clad in kimono and *eboshi*, greeting the rising sun to samisen accompaniment. 'A Real Good Jap', he was dubbed.[19]

FANCY PORTRAIT.

Two years later, he fully expected to succeed Tennyson as Poet Laureate. But when the Queen in 1896 appointed Alfred Austin he sent a generous telegram:

'Accept my heartiest congratulations with which no grudge mingles although I myself expected the appointment.'

To which Alfred Austin commented that he would rather be the man who in such circumstances could send such a telegram, than be incapable of sending it yet have written the greatest poetry.[20] The appointment of Alfred Austin invited much derision from people to whom he had boasted of never putting pen to paper without the guidance of 'It'. Such people might well have thought the Queen better advised to choose Edwin Arnold.[21]

21

Harold E. Palmer, 1877–1949

RICHARD C. SMITH & IMURA MOTOMICHI

Harold E. Palmer

IN MARCH 1922, Harold E. Palmer arrived in Japan to take up a post as *Eigokyōju komon* ('Adviser on English Teaching Methods', or, as Palmer preferred to describe his role, 'Linguistic Adviser') to the Ministry of Education (*Mombushō*). The initial arrangement was that he should stay for three years, but he remained committed to his task for fourteen. During this time, he was 'the most outstanding figure on Japan's foreign teacher scene',[1] and the Institute for Research in English Teaching (IRET), which he established in 1923 and directed until his retirement in 1936, carried out work which was to have a strong influence on approaches to teaching English as a foreign language (TEFL, or 'ELT') throughout the world. Before World War II there were no comparable centres of research outside Japan. As his friend Vere Redman was later to say:

> Palmer came to Japan as Linguistic Adviser to the *Mombusho*; when he left in 1936, he had become, through the work of the

> Institute and his work with and through it, Linguistic Adviser to the whole English-teaching world.[2]

The work of IRET only began to pay off on a large scale after the Second World War, and this occurred outside rather than within Japan. A. S. Hornby's *Advanced Learner's Dictionary* (which has sold more copies for Oxford University Press in its successive editions than any work other than the Bible) was originally conceived and developed as an innovative IRET project. Indeed, it was largely due to Hornby (Palmer's successor at IRET) that Palmer's ideas influenced the new British ELT enterprise so strongly after World War II. In 1946 Hornby, who had just been appointed 'Linguistic Adviser' to the British Council, founded the journal *English Language Teaching* (now *ELTJ*). In this he was directly inspired by his experience of editing IRET's *Bulletin* between 1936 and 1941. The essentially pragmatic ethos of British ELT in the immediate post-war years reflected Palmer's problem-oriented, non-dogmatic but principled approach. As another leading figure in the field of ELT, Reginald Close, who was the first head of the British Council in Japan after the war, remarked: 'most of what [Palmer] achieved was done in Japan. He was a creative pioneer who blazed a trail which Hornby and his disciples followed with great advantage to all of us who are concerned with English language teaching.'[3]

THE INVITATION TO JAPAN

As a teacher at University College London (UCL) and the recently established School of Oriental Studies (now SOAS). Palmer had, by the time he was invited to Japan, already gained a reputation as the leading authority of his day on methods of language teaching. He probably first discussed the possibility of visiting Japan with Kinoshita Masao, a colleague of his at both UCL and the School of Oriental Studies (Kinoshita was one of the first teachers of Japanese there). They had previously collaborated on a Japanese Beginner's Vocabulary, and one of Palmer's first publications on language learning and teaching theory (in 1916) had provided examples in Japanese, giving evidence of his longstanding interest in Japanese language and culture (according to his daughter he had been fascinated by Japan since childhood).[4] More importantly, perhaps, there were many Japanese students of Spoken English in the UCL Department of Phonetics (where Palmer was mainly based); among them were visiting academics, and he was both aware of the favorable reception his recent writings had already gained in Japan and excited by the apparent prospects for reform of English teaching in that context.

Palmer seems to have been thinking of taking a year's leave of absence to visit Japan in order to teach English or engage in a lecture tour when, in autumn 1921, Kinoshita introduced him to Sawayanagi Masataro (1865–1927), a former Vice Minister of Education and president of Kyoto Imperial University, who was visiting London in the course of a wider tour of inspection of European schools and universities.[5]

Sawayanagi retained close contacts and some influence with the *Mombushō*, and he proposed that a special advisory position be created for Palmer for a period of three years to undertake research into the development of reformed methods for the teaching of English in Japanese 'middle' (i.e. secondary) schools. Sawayanagi was the leading educational figure of his age: he combined progressive leanings as a founder of the so-called 'Taishō New Movement in Education' with considerable prestige due both to his previous career and to his current status as President of the Imperial Society for Education (*Teikoku kyōikukai*), a nationwide organization of teachers.

The invitation to Palmer was reminiscent of the early Meiji Era practice of importing Western experts (*oyatoi-gaikokujin*) to assist in the modernization of Japan. This approach had not previously been adopted for methods of language teaching since high standards of English had been attained in the Meiji Era as many subjects were then taught in English, particularly at university level. Students read English textbooks in most of their classes, learning '*in* English and *through* English, but never *about* English'.[6] However, with the revival of nationalism, Japanese interest in practical foreign language learning declined. English became a compulsory *subject* on the curriculum, and teaching became increasingly geared towards the needs of examinations. Foreign teachers were largely replaced by Japanese teachers who were not always proficient in spoken English. In consequence, 'studying from Japanese textbooks and having infrequent contact with native speakers of English, [students] had reached the stage of learning *about* English in *Japanese*'.[7]

There was a worrying decline in standards of English proficiency as the method known as *yakudoku* ('translation-reading', or 'grammar-translation') became dominant towards the end of the nineteenth century. In response, Japanese scholars began to be sent abroad to report on the teaching methods in use there. Around the turn of the century two well-known academics, Kanda Naibu (1857–1923) and Okakura Yoshisaburo (1868–1936), were sent on separate official tours of inspection to Europe, in particular Germany. Kanda, who had attended university in the USA, was already a firm believer in the 'natural method', or 'teaching by conversation' promoted there by Lambert Sauveur (1826–1907), and he continued to advocate this on his return. On the other hand, Okakura, who spent the years 1902–5 in Europe, found that the German reformers offered an orally-based model which sufficiently emphasized the *educational*, as well as the utilitarian value of English teaching in schools.[8] Kanda's and Okakura's textbooks were widely used and Okakura, in particular, met with some success in diffusing his ideas as head of the English department at the principal teacher-training institution for secondary schools, the Tokyo Higher Normal School. Nevertheless, as the Taisho Era (1912–26) ended, English teaching in schools had not changed much, and standards of oral English in particular had been little improved. At the same time, the defeat of Germany in World War I had brought a collapse in esteem for German educational models, and a general shift in attention to Britain.

This was the background to the offer of an advisory role to Palmer in autumn 1921. Sawayanagi quickly contacted a wealthy businessman and philanthropist, Matsukata Kojiro, who was visiting London at the time, and Matsukata readily agreed to provide financial backing for the venture. The prospect not only of an exotic location, considerable responsibility and commensurate pay but also of the independence promised to him and the opportunity to engage in research with definite reformist potential seem to have been the deciding factors in persuading Palmer to make the relatively long-term commitment requested of him. In February 1922, he left the University of London permanently.

UPBRINGING

When he left for Japan Palmer was already in his mid-forties, and his career until then had been academically unconventional. He had never himself attended university and was completely self-taught in the fields in which he was beginning to forge his reputation.

Born in 1877 in London, he had been educated initially at local elementary schools and at home – Harold's father Edward having begun his working life as a schoolteacher.[9] In 1883 the family moved to Hythe in Kent, where Edward opened a small school of his own, then a fancy goods and stationery shop, later giving up the school to concentrate on a local weekly newspaper called the *Hythe Reporter*, which he founded in 1890. For the next two years Harold attended a small private school very near his home.

At the age of fifteen he was sent to Boulogne on a six-month exchange visit to study French, but he did not yet show any of his father's interest in language learning; instead, most of his time was spent in the Art Gallery sketching and painting. He had hopes of working in a museum in London, but on returning from France he was prevailed upon to help out in the family business.

JOURNALISM AND TEACHING

Harold gained his first writing experience as a journalist for the *Hythe Reporter*, and in February 1899 he became editor of the paper, a duty he fulfilled for almost three years. However, towards the end of 1901 he resigned.[10] His daughter explained: 'Although Father found life to be full of interest and excitement, he felt that he must break away from work that was leading nowhere. So, in his mid-twenties, feeling cramped and frustrated, he had the urge to go abroad.'[11]

In February 1902 he arrived in Verviers, close to the Dutch and German borders in the French-speaking part of Belgium, and became an English teacher at a small school run along Berlitz lines.[12] The Berlitz method was a revelation to him, but, with an entrepreneurial vigour reminiscent of his father, he soon left to establish his own school. Here he began to experiment with teaching methods: 'He would devise, adopt, modify or reject one plan after another as the result of further research and experience in connexion with many languages - living and artificial.'[13] By this time he 'had become fascinated by languages, all languages, his own and other people's, fascinated by the way they worked. He was naturally eager to teach what he had learned and to learn as he taught.'[14] Esperanto was just one of several languages he studied, taught and wrote learning materials for during his time in Belgium. He read widely and became an enthusiast for phonetics and the ideas of the International Phonetic Association (IPA), which he joined in 1907. His daughter recalled him using a notebook to transcribe the speech he heard around him very much in the fashion of Henry Higgins in *My Fair Lady*.[15] Indeed, she herself first learned to read through phonetic script.

Many of the themes which were to characterize Palmer's later work had their roots in his Verviers experience, including his attachment to oral teaching procedures, his commitment to research, his deliberate avoidance of dogmatism, and his use of phonetics and vocabulary limitation to lessen the language learning load. At the same time, he developed a passionate attachment to internationalism and multilingualism at a time of mounting international tension. His sociability, talent for both writing and publicity, organizational skills and 'creative versatility' all found expression in his work in building up his school in Verviers, the *Institut Palmer*, and in producing materials associated with his own 'Palmer Method'.

WORK AT THE UNIVERSITY OF LONDON

Palmer's contributions to the IPA's journal brought his ideas to a wider audience, and, in particular, attracted the attention of Daniel Jones, who had recently founded the first department of phonetics in a British university, at University College London.[16] Palmer's contacts with Jones proved useful when the outbreak of World War I forced him to return to England with his wife and daughter. In 1915 Jones offered him part-time employment at UCL, initially to give a course of three public lectures, and subsequently to take over Spoken English classes for international students and start up a year-long course on 'Methods of Language Teaching' (the first of its kind at a British university). These launched Palmer's brief but productive academic career and enabled him to distil the experience he had gained in Belgium in a series of pioneering publications which established the study of language teaching as a serious academic pursuit.In Belgium, Palmer had developed an awareness that what language teachers most required was not a 'perfect method' but a principled or 'scientific' basis for the selection of methods. He explored this insight further in his first major work, *The Scientific Study and Teaching of Languages* (London: Harrap, 1917).

At UCL, Palmer also became involved in the research work of the Department of Phonetics, and made several original contributions, notably in relation to English intonation.[17] However, his interests extended beyond phonetics, and were firmly rooted in the needs of teachers and learners. His Spoken English courses enabled him to refine his 'Palmer Method' into what he began to term the 'Oral Method' (as expounded in *The Oral Method of Teaching Languages*, Cambridge: Heffer, 1921), but overall he had arrived at a position of principled eclecticism, arguing that teachers should be open to 'multiple lines of approach' and not be dogmatically attached to any one single method.

At the same time, Palmer became increasingly interested in how languages are *learned*, partly on the basis of ideas he developed for lectures on 'methods of language study' at the School of Oriental Studies. In another pioneering work, *The Principles of Language Study* (London: Harrap, 1921), he complemented the largely linguistic, though practical approach of *The Scientific Study*, with insights into the psychology of language learning.

Despite his growing renown as a language-teaching theorist, Palmer's academic status and financial circumstances remained insecure until 1920, when he was finally awarded a full-time assistantship at UCL. In the 1921–2 academic session he was promoted to a full-time lectureship. His initial high hopes of pioneering a reform of modern language teaching in British schools were not being entirely fulfilled, and this may have partly motivated the shift of emphasis in his work towards offering insights for learners as well as teachers into the general *study* of languages.

WORK IN JAPAN, THE FIRST PHASE

Palmer remained committed to Japan for much longer than was envisaged in the initial three-year invitation; indeed, his 'sincerity' in pursuing the task which had been assigned to him is one of the main reasons for the respect he continues to enjoy among many Japanese teachers of English today.

He was accorded considerable status, and, in the initial stages at least, a salary commensurate with his 'foreign expert' position. He was given the time and resources necessary to pursue his own practice-oriented research in a context where he could clearly 'make a difference'. The difficulties of achieving reform, and the misunderstandings and opposition with which he had to cope also kept Palmer in Japan: he did not give up easily.

Palmer was active, indeed prolific throughout his fourteen years in Japan.[18] Just one year after his arrival in March 1922 he set in motion the formation of an Institute for Research in English Teaching (IRET), the first such establishment anywhere in the world. The Institute soon began to publish a *Bulletin* under Palmer's editorship, and numerous publications were issued for both foreign and Japanese teachers with the support of the publisher Kaitakusha, which had undertaken to issue all of the Institute's publications without regard to profit. Initially, Palmer's ideas appealed mostly to foreign teachers already in Japan, who began to join the Institute in large numbers. However, after the 1923 Kanto earthquake, which resulted in the destruction of all the Institute's records, his attention began to be more firmly focused on the need to interest Japanese middle school teachers in reform.

Palmer initially seems to have believed - over-optimistically as it turned out - that, by encouraging reform-minded Japanese teachers to join the Institute, he could help bring about structural reform in the educational system, in addition to encouraging the teaching of English through oral means. The IRET conference of 1925 proposed a radical four-point programme for such reform involving reduced class sizes, increased freedom for teachers in textbook selection, improved in-service teacher education and more effective involvement of native speakers as teachers. There were also calls for university entrance examinations to be reformed to feature 'plain English' (as opposed to over-literary words and expressions) and for oral/aural testing to be introduced in counterweight to translation tasks. Although these proposals may in retrospect seem unrealistic, they coincided with the period of 'Taishō democracy' in the early to mid-1920s, when the government appeared to be willing to act upon reformist ideas. However, the proposals were not taken up. Instead, the political climate became increasingly unfavourable as Taishō democracy gave way in the late 1920s and 1930s to the ultra-nationalism which led ultimately to the Pacific War. During the latter period there were increasingly strident calls for the abolition of English as a subject on the secondary school curriculum, accompanied by a progressive reduction in the number of hours allotted to English.

After 1925, Palmer devoted his efforts to working within the system, and avoided involvement in political debates on the status of English as a subject. It is not correct, as several writers[19] have assumed, that Palmer expected to introduce his Oral Method into Japan without adaptation. Although his ideas were grounded throughout in an unswerving belief in the 'primacy of speech', he was guided also by a context-sensitive philosophy of 'principled eclecticism'. This philosophy was developed in an important 1924 document, the *Memorandum on Problems of English Teaching* (Tokyo: IRET), which offered a general statement of pedagogical principles, at the same time suggesting how reforms could be made in the Japanese context. He then devoted considerable effort to developing experimental materials for different lines of approach, and to gathering feedback from Japanese members of the Institute.

On this basis, and as Palmer learned more about Japanese priorities, a reader-centred oral approach emerged as most favoured, and Palmer's energies were increasingly directed towards the provision of readers amenable to oral work, materials for extensive reading and supplementary teacher's guides. In *The Reformed Teaching of English in the Middle-grade Schools* (Tokyo: IRET, 1927) Palmer clearly recognized the importance in the Japanese context of enhancing writing and reading abilities, maintaining nevertheless that 'direct' oral procedures rather than translation were the best means for pursuing these goals. Having established the need for a 'reader system', by 1927 (when Sawayanagi died) Palmer had produced a set of *Standard English Readers* (Tokyo: IRET, 1926-7), with accompanying resource books to aid teachers with oral work.

Throughout this initial period, Palmer had to cope with far more resistance than he had probably expected when initially invited to Japan. He seems to have realized early on that any 'advice' he gave would be unlikely to be implemented directly by the *Mombusho*, and this realization may have partly motivated the establishment of the semi-official Institute to support, provide a focus for and diffuse his research and reform efforts. From early on, most of his considerable energies were channelled through IRET rather than via the Ministry's more labyrinthine channels. Although the Institute was housed in the *Mombushō* right up until the Pacific War, and this gave its activities some prestige in the eyes of Japanese teachers, Ministry officials seem to have preferred to leave Palmer largely to his own devices, offering little further support to his reform efforts. Palmer was also surprised by the factionalism he encountered among reform-minded Japanese teachers and teacher trainers. His proudest boast after ten years was that the Institute had succeeded in replacing previous factionalism with a focused reform movement. However, his failure in the early stages to recognize sufficiently the contributions of Okakura Yoshisaburō, previously the doyen of English-language education reform in Japan and effectively sidelined by Palmer's arrival, meant that a significant faction of Japanese teachers associated with Okakura never fully supported his efforts.

This lack of support was partly related to a failure by Palmer to acknowledge the significance in the Japanese context of the educational and cultural value of English studies. Throughout, his assumption was that a practical mastery of English - whether in its spoken or its written form - was the main educational goal, and he underestimated the strength of sentiments such as the following:

> For the Japanese … the advantages of studying foreign languages are of a higher and more intangible nature than are its so-called 'practical' benefits. In some ways the most valuable advantage lies in its 'unpractical' aspect, namely, in its hidden and unutilitarian effect on the mind.[20]

Being through and through a rationalist, and resolutely utilitarian in his own approach, Palmer had no truck with this kind of statement, nor – despite his well-developed aesthetic sensibilities in the visual sphere – did he have much interest in literary appreciation, as emphasized by many Japanese scholars of English down to the present day. His own entertaining, indeed somewhat flamboyant, style did little to endear him to some of the more conventionally 'scholarly' members of his audiences; nor did he seem to fit the image of an English 'gentleman' (as represented to best effect in the foreign teacher community by A. W. Medley at the Tokyo School of Foreign Languages). Among progressive-minded Japanese teachers, and among foreign teachers generally, his theoretical but down-to-earth approach and evident commitment to practical improvements did begin to win him converts. However, there were always significant sections of the Japanese English education establishment who found reasons to look down on and side-step his efforts.

WORK IN JAPAN, THE SECOND PHASE

According to Palmer's daughter, the first phase of his work in Japan had been one of 'pioneering and experiment':

> He was getting to know Japan and the Japanese set-up as applied to the teaching of English, and it takes fully seven years to do just that. He was breaking new ground in his professional sphere. He was an iconoclast, a revolutionary and an innovator. He was always 'fighting' this, that or the other.[21]

In the second phase he 'fought' much less. He was just as much engaged in analysis and experimentation, but his statements became less combative and more authoritative: 'this authoritative accent was increasingly accepted and respected by the Japanese. He became an established institution and as such enjoyed considerable prestige and this not only in academic circles.'[22]

One honour had been conferred on Palmer early on - that of tutoring Prince Chichibu in English prior to his departure to study at the University of Oxford in 1926. In later years he began to give regular broadcasts entitled 'Current Topics' for JOAK (the predecessor of NHK), and thus became, literally, a 'household name' in Japan. He was also a keen participant in activities of the expatriate British community in Tokyo: the Asiatic Society of Japan, the Association of Foreign Teachers, the Tokyo Amateur Dramatic Society, and so on. He found time also for his many hobbies and interests including geology, map-making, typography and printing, and motoring. Accounts of his personality all emphasize his seemingly boundless energy, curiosity and versatility. One obituary was entitled 'Harold E. Palmer, phonetician, entertainer, philosopher, scholar, teacher, traveller, author, friend'.[23]

The second phase of Palmer's stay in Japan (between around 1929 and 1936) was taken up largely with intensive research into vocabulary, motivated, at least initially, by the need to determine appropriate linguistic contents for the various levels of the secondary school English curriculum. Enlisting the aid of A. S. Hornby (1898-1978), who had come to Japan in 1924 to teach at a university in Kyūshū, and who had subsequently become an active member of the Institute, Palmer embarked on an ambitious classification of vocabulary (including collocations). This research programme was to bear fruit not only in revised versions of the *Standard English Readers* and graded supplementary readers published for Japanese secondary schools but also in the *Interim Report on Vocabulary Selection for the Teaching of English as a Foreign Language* (London: King, 1936) compiled with colleagues overseas.

In parallel, Japanese teachers showed more and more willingness in the 1930s to experiment with, adapt and appropriate the Institute's 'reformed methods', increasingly contributing articles to the IRET *Bulletin* and engaging in innovative demonstration lessons at the annual Institute Conventions. This contrasted with the first phase, when foreign teachers had been the most prominent IRET supporters.

The work of the Institute had become well-known throughout the world, and Palmer undertook trips abroad of increasing length, partly to further publicise this work but also (he hoped) to acquire funding, since Matsukata's financial support had dried up as a result of bankruptcy in the depression years and the Institute was being run by this stage on a shoe-string.

As the international situation deteriorated and as IRET work became better known on a world stage Palmer and his wife began to consider leaving Japan. Prior to their departure in 1936, Palmer was awarded a D.Litt by Tokyo Imperial University for three of his major publications.

'RETIREMENT' YEARS

On returning to England, Palmer bought a house (named 'Cooper's Wood') in Felbridge, Sussex.[24] Here he set to work to construct a Japanese-style garden, combined with a model railway which would represent the 'syntax plan of the English language'. Together he termed these a 'syntax-scape'.

In February 1937 materials for the construction of a Japanese-style room were shipped to England as a token of appreciation from Japanese teachers of English, and in November Palmer sent photographs back to show that he had installed it in the sunroom at Cooper's Wood. After his death, this room was donated to the British Museum. Palmer took to wearing Japanese-style dress when at home and he used the Japanese room as his study, spreading out his papers on the tatami floor. He also engaged in Japanese-style archery in his garden, and developed his skills in the art of *bonkei*.

On 17 March 1938 Palmer was invited to address the Luncheon Club of the Japan Society, London, on 'The English language in Japan'. In this talk he expressed some frustration that his ideas had not been taken up more enthusiastically by the *Mombushō* and the majority of Japanese teachers. At the same time, he presented an optimistic view of IRET achievements.

Palmer was still working on a freelance basis as a consultant and writer, mostly for Longmans, Green. Several of his best-known publications of the period show the clear imprint of previous work carried out under IRET auspices, for example *The New Method Grammar* and *A Grammar of English Words* (both London: Longmans, Green, 1938) as well as his later *International English Course* (London: Evans, 1943–6). Although he seems to have hoped to establish an equivalent to IRET in the UK, his proposals fell on deaf ears.[25]

During the World War II Palmer served as an air-raid warden. A letter to his daughter dated 23 January 1940 reveals that he had been offered a senior lectureship in Japanese at SOAS, which he had declined, expressing a lack of confidence in his Japanese abilities.[26] Although during his time in Japan he had displayed a keen interest in Japanese, he had not mastered the written language. He had, however, made an important contribution to the contemporary debate on the romanization of Japanese, with his *The Principles of Romanization* (Tokyo: Maruzen, 1930), and his influence on the wartime and post-war history of teaching Japanese as a foreign language was to be profound, due to the work of his former assistant and publisher Naganuma Naoe (1894–1973).[27]

Following the Japanese attack on Pearl Harbor, both Hornby and Redman were interned. Owing to the strong opposition to any teaching of the enemy's language, the IRET Board of Administration in February 1942 changed the name of the *Bulletin* to *Gogaku kyōiku* (Language Education), and in March the IRET itself metamorphosed into *Gogaku kyōiku kenkyūjo* (literally, the 'Institute for Research in Language Education'). The Institute survived the war and retains the same Japanese name - often shortened to '*Goken*' - to this day.[28] On 20 April 1942 Kaitakusha succeeded, against all the odds, in publishing the *Idiomatic and Syntactic English Dictionary*, which had been instigated by Palmer and compiled by A. S. Hornby with two IRET colleagues, E. V. Gatenby and H. Wakefield. This was later (in 1948) to be photographically reprinted by Oxford University Press and reissued as *A Learner's Dictionary of Current English*.[29] In 1942, Redman and Hornby were permitted to return to the UK.

In July 1942 Palmer's only son, Tristram, was killed in action over Holland. Palmer never really recovered from the shock and from then on his health deteriorated. He did manage to undertake a lecture tour in South America in 1944, but he was forced by ill health to return prematurely to England. On 16 November 1949 he collapsed suddenly and died of acute heart failure 'surrounded by his beloved books'.[30]

PALMER'S LEGACY

Despite the undoubted achievements of IRET, overall assessments of Palmer's work in reforming Japanese English education have tended to be rather negative.[31] To some extent these assessments have been based on false premises about his mission - he had not, after all, been invited to reform teaching in Japan single-handedly but to engage in research and 'ultimately' suggest methods which teachers might find appropriate.

Nevertheless, Palmer himself seems to have had high initial hopes of leading a full-scale 'Reform Movement'. Despite his optimistic assessment in his speech to the Japan Society, London, in 1938, political events, and the increasing perception that English was the 'enemy's language', ultimately conspired to undermine his efforts. Indeed, *yakudoku* has continued to dominate foreign language teaching in Japanese schools in the post-war era, despite all attempts to reform it.

However, Institute ideas *were* appropriated by a number of Japanese teachers, who adapted them to their own contexts in the 1930s. More importantly, Palmer succeeded in firmly implanting the idea among Japanese teachers and teacher trainers that language teaching needs to be based on sound, scientific principles, not simply the dictates of tradition. He was not the first to introduce Western methods into Japan, but as a consequence of his own personal commitment and success in arguing for rational procedures, a tradition of conceptualising language teaching in terms of 'method' was established, and this has continued to guide progressive Japanese teachers of English, whatever their specific methodological persuasion. In the immediate post-war years the latest ideas on language teaching from the USA appeared more attractive, but Japanese supporters of Palmer's ideas had a major role in writing the first post-war *Mombushō* courses of study for secondary schools, proposed in 1947 and 1951.[32] Following a visit to Japan in 1956, Hornby wrote to Palmer's daughter: 'American influences are strong now (Fries, of the University of Michigan, is the new star)', but he found also that 'Palmer's work is remembered and appreciated'.[33]

The Institute experienced something of a revival as American efforts to reform English teaching foundered towards the end of the 1960s.[34] IRLT continues to be one of the most important associations for secondary school English teachers and university teacher trainers in Japan, and is active in promoting research work, editing publications and organizing teacher training seminars and an annual Convention, still very much under the influence of Palmer's ideas. Recently, members of the Institute have edited *The Selected Writings of Harold E. Palmer* (ten volumes, Tokyo: Hon-no-Tomosha, 1995) and in August 1999 IRLT organized a special programme of events to commemorate the fiftieth anniversary of his death (Palmer's great-granddaughter, Victoria Angela, was the special guest of honour).

Whereas Palmer's memory is very much kept alive in Japan (although his ideas may be seen to have had a lasting impact only on the more 'methodologically aware' members of the English teaching profession), his work is largely ignored in the UK, where it ended up having a much more pervasive influence.

Although the emergence of ELT as an independent, professional enterprise has occurred in Britain largely in the post-war era, it was, more than anyone else, Harold Palmer who, 'with his detailed and theory-based models of syllabus and course design and his principled but practical approach to classroom methodology … laid the essential groundwork on which the profession could build a strong and flexible structure'.[35] Until recently the greater part of the work he published in Japan has remained unavailable outside that country, and the full scale of his achievement there unrecognized in ELT circles. However, with the recent foundation of a British Institute of English Language Teaching (BIELT), it seems possible that his pioneering work will finally gain the recognition in Britain, which it has always enjoyed in Japan.

22

William Empson, Poet and Writer, 1906–84: Japan, 1931–34

JOHN HAFFENDEN

William Empson

WILLIAM EMPSON has been widely acclaimed as 'the finest literary critic the English-speaking world has had in our century'. Before the appearance in 1930 of *Seven Types of Ambiguity*, no critic had ever written with such persuasive detail of the effects of language, such searching and imaginative analysis. Not only did Empson achieve the main feat of inventing modern literary criticism in English, he went on to produce a series of ground-breaking works including *Some Versions of Pastoral* (1935), *The Structure of Complex Words* (1951), *Milton's God* (1961), and the posthumous *Argufying: Essays on Literature and Culture* (1987).

During the late 1930s he joined the staff of Peking National University and spent two years taking refuge in southwest China from the Japanese invasion; throughout the Second World War he worked as Chinese Editor for the BBC (where George Orwell was among his closest colleagues), and in 1947 he returned to China for five years, witnessing the climax of the civil war, the siege of Peking, the communist takeover, and the beginnings of thought reform. From 1953 till 1971 he held the Chair of English Literature at Sheffield University; and in 1979 he was knighted for services to English literature. But his career almost failed to get off the ground at Cambridge University in 1929, when contraceptives were discovered in his possession and he was summarily removed from a promised fellowship. After many months of hand-to-mouth existence as a freelance writer, he leapt at the offer of an appointment in Tokyo.

★ ★ ★

On his first night in Tokyo, Empson caused a farcical incident, which might have marred relations with his hosts. After booking into the Station Hotel, not far from the Imperial Palace, he set off in search of food, drink and tobacco. When he returned, it was so late that the hotel was already locked up for the night. He was far from sober and tried to force an entrance through a ground-floor window – which led only to the redbrick station next to the hotel. 'Two guards on duty in the staff room of Tokyo Station were astonished to be woken by two long legs appearing at the window,' it was reported. 'They thought at once that a burglar had been trying to enter the building. So they seized the legs of the unknown intruder, pulling his body down. It happened to land in a bucket of water always kept ready for such emergencies as fire or earthquakes.' The situation was eventually sorted out when the hotel register confirmed the visitor's name.

Unhappily, Empson's drunken blundering featured as an item of comic gossip in the *Asahi* the next day (1 September 1931), under the headline: 'Once caught, it was not a burglar but a university professor!'[1] Wrong-footed from the start, Empson was never strong on good or appropriate behaviour, and no one had adequately briefed him on the protocol of professional conduct in Tokyo.

His three-year contract as a professor of English language and literature at the University of Literature and Science – Tokyo Bunrika Daigaku, a newly-established government institution for teacher-training – beginning on 29 August 1931, would close with a more serious affair.

It was an inauspicious moment for a young teacher (not quite 25) to teach English literature to the youth of Japan. The Japanese attack on Manchuria began on 18 September. Empson wrote to his mother, facetiously to reassure those at home: 'There seems to be no doubt the Japanese don't want to *live* in Manchuria, which is cold and full of Chinese.'

Like every foreigner with little understanding of Japanese culture and sensibilities, he found it hard to come to terms with the country, especially in conditions of increasing regimentation. Peter Quennell held the same contract post in 1930–31 and recorded: 'every lecturer at a government school or university thinks of himself primarily as an official, and to succeed, must have the official point of view. Politically and socially, he must be irreproachable …'[2] Quennell was only too relieved to go home after a year. But then he capitalized on his wretched tour of duty by publishing in 1932 an elegant and remorselessly candid account, *A Superficial Journey Through Tokyo and Peking* – which Empson thought 'a good book … though he oughtn't to have done it'.

'I had pictured the Japanese as a sharp-witted, uncannily acute race …,' wrote Quennell. 'At first acquaintance, the very opposite proved true; hesitating, tongue-tied and always nervous, they suggested a people of adolescents, alternately assertive and depreciatory …'[3]

In one of his first letters to his mentor I. A. Richards, Empson broadly agreed: 'It is quite true that the Japanese are uncomfortable bogus people who don't really enjoy anything in sight.' He wavered between boisterous satire, second-thoughts, and shame for his self-pity:

> … the Christian converts who look at you with great liquid crucified eyes like spaniels with indigestion (a most embarrassing thing in a lecture room) seem anyway to have some emotional life: the others seem curiously toothy and bloodless, they hang on like lice to that state of life to which it has pleased the Emperor to call them. There is one teacher at the Bunrika who seems to enjoy what he reads: I think they are a good race, it is the immediate history of it that makes them so frightful … If one could get them to be less antlike that wouldn't matter: but it is hard to believe they would ever really enjoy any literature, anyway.
>
> But really … with a large salary and a good cook and only eight hours work a week a young man ought to be able to keep a stiff upper lip …

The sheer noise of Tokyo was a feature of the city he would never get used to. He rented a Japanese-style house, number 23 Fujimichō ('a pretty little house, very secluded, where I am rolling about on the correct mats'), at 5-chōme, Kōjimachi, not far from the British Embassy and the Yasukuni Shrine. The rent was met by the university. To keep a cook-housekeeper was the custom, and a necessity for Empson, who was unable to grasp enough of the language to go shopping. 'I got rather a horror of the infantilism of the language when I was trying to pick some up.' But the noise was 'the one thing at present that I can't get over,' he bewailed. In fact, he rented an additional workplace, first a room in an apartment house, later one 'beastly' hotel room after another. Without question, his first year in Tokyo caused him a lot of distress, including a 'fit of neurotic fear' (as he called it). Five years later, he recalled: 'there was a period in Japan when I had two houses and three rooms in different hotels, and spent my time going from one to another searching for a moment when I could escape fear without my hands shaking too much to handle my chopsticks.'

After a year, his ears and nerves thrumming, he moved to 519 Shirokane Sankochō, a fine and 'absurdly expensive' two-storey European-style house in Admiral Takarabe's compound in Takanawa. It suited him better than his earlier billets. Fukuhara Rintarō,[4] his closest colleague at the Bunrika, remembered 'a pond quietly surrounded by numerous plum-trees and flower-gardens'.[5] The ground floor consisted of two rooms: a sitting-room, 'decorated with a bronze statue, book-cases and gramophone etc.', and a spartan bedroom. Upstairs, it 'looked rather like a chaos with bookcases, type-writer, bed, desk, bathing-tub, etc.' Empson was in his unkempt element. Yet he still saw no hope of getting away from the ubiquitous noise:

> I think the main thing that gets on people's nerves is the noise: the men selling bean cake in the street use a little flat whistle that makes you stop whatever you are doing and howl at the moon, it is a more Buddhist sound than one would have thought possible. I have just moved into a European house hoping to escape from it, and am very cross – indeed rather hopeless – at finding it as bad as ever. But I am now fairly out of earshot of Japanese babies and my cook, and the screech of the sliding screens of a Japanese house, which were holding up all mental life before.

He could be well-disposed, if rueful: 'Everybody finds something to grumble about in Japan,' he wrote, 'which is a pity in a way because the Japanese hate not to be loved.' Yet he noted 'an infantile air of charm which easily becomes loathsome.'

His new lodging was some miles from the university. Empson got hold of a motorbike, which served him well for two years. His class would burst into applause when they heard his engine eructating into the university yard. 'Sometimes one of his favourite students was seen on the bike with the poet,' one such disciple has recalled, 'and how we admired the poet-hero on the bike and how we envied the student who had the glory to accompany the poet on the bike!'

Although Empson had been advised not to fraternize with the students, he eagerly spent time with them out of school. He had arrived with little more than the warm suit he stood up to lecture in

– according to one witness, his suitcase contained no more than a lemon and a pair of shoes – and sweated profusely. When the students invited him to go for a swim in Shiba Park after his first class, he readily agreed. But he had no trunks. They helped to tie up his loins in the length of red cloth that is the traditional Japanese costume. Empson could do little more than dog-paddle. His pupils swam round him in circles. Not to be put down, he showed off his leg muscles, asserting that Westerners had much firmer muscles than the soft-fleshed Japanese. When Horii Kiyoshi, the best swimmer, got on to the diving board to demonstrate his skill, Empson shoved him in. He even managed to knock Horii's glasses into the water. 'What a stupid thing I've done!' he exclaimed. The incident shows not just that Empson was afflicted with a fit of racial rivalry, he must also have felt jealous of these lithe youths who were of the same generation as himself. But although he was immature and competitive, he made every effort to get on better terms with his curiously opaque pupils – to treat them as chums, often going with them to a coffee house, or to the cinema. Despite his owlish looks, he was athletic, and would play tennis with anyone who felt game.

* * *

Most of Empson's teaching took place at Bunrika Daigaku, a modern place appended to the Higher Normal School in the Koishikawa district, but he was also down for a weekly class at the more prestigious Tokyo Imperial University (Teidai). His favourite teaching was Elizabethan drama and seventeenth-century poetry. He also taught an historical survey of English literature, including selected novelists like Woolf and Lawrence, and some modern poetry. John Morris, who went to Japan in 1938, discovered that 'T. S. Eliot is inextricably associated in the Japanese mind with my predecessor, William Empson, by whom they were introduced to the former's work.' In an introduction to a Japanese edition of Eliot's *Selected Essays* (1933), Empson emphasized how far Buddhism had anticipated the moral teachings of Christianity. He wanted to make Eliot's thoughts on the Christian tradition accessible to the Japanese and to show that the high ideals of Christianity were already in place in Buddhism.

However, he soon realized that the Japanese could not follow the spoken word. Even a student like Ogawa Kazuo – who attended Empson's classes for more than two years, and who would turn out to be a distinguished critic – found it 'incredibly difficult' to follow a lecture in English. The problem was compounded by Empson's airily rapid delivery. He compensated by writing the salient parts of his lectures on the blackboard, cleaning the surface as soon as he had covered it, over and over again, till his head and shoulders were blanketed with chalk-dust. Satirical disdain for his students is brusquely expressed to the editor and critic John Hayward:

> As for teaching, I quite like talking to myself in public. The thing is to look at the blackboard or anyway not at the assembled frogs. They can read what you write on the board though they can't understand what you say. If you write steadily on the board and keep up a spoken patter, *never* waiting for signs of intelligence or making jokes, the hour gets through all right.

Actually, former students recall, Empson was 'very earnest in his teaching' as well as 'kind to the students'. But ultra-nationalism was pumping through the student body. The students feared politically suspect ideas. Early on, Empson had to relay this sorry tale: 'I was reading *Mrs Dalloway* [by Virginia Woolf] with some class and asked them at the end to write an essay about "how far is she ironical?", they came and said they didn't want to write about that because it might be connected with politics. They seem so much spied upon …' He did not blame the students for being the victims of a repressive state machine. The teachers, though, had a duty to find ways of outwitting an apparatus that set limits on educational freedom. In his Inaugural Lecture at Sheffield University in 1953, he was to stress this lesson: 'Of course, in such a case, it is very much not the business of a teacher to egg the students on to get into trouble, but on the other hand he must insist on showing the real climate of opinion which surrounded and nourished the literary writings he is set to teach.'[6]

Several members of his class at the Bunrika were drafted during the the fighting in Shanghai early in 1932. Empson was astonished to find how the warfare skewed their minds. Teaching the poetry of A. E. Housman, he discovered they read it as a direct political message. Lines such as 'I wish one could know them … The lads that will die in their glory and never be old', were construed as a kind of gospel. 'We were reading Housman in one class, which I thought would suit them (suicide is the national sport, of course),' he reported home with black humour, 'but it was embarrassing to read a series of dull essays saying that Housman must be a good poet because he really did make them want to kill themselves, especially to go and die in Shanghai … I wonder if it would have made the old gentleman feel ashamed of himself?' Although he could make a joke of it, he felt genuinely shocked by his students. As a piece he was to write for the BBC late in 1941 shows:

> When the Japanese say that they want racial equality for everyone – and that is one of their propaganda lines – they are quite consciously talking humbug. I must have read Shakespeare's

> *Othello* with Japanese students at least three times, and every time some honestly friendly and puzzled student would say to me, or write down, 'Why should you or I take any interest in a story about a negro?' They were quite sure that I would feel the same as they did; they weren't boasting, it was just the natural question, they felt, from one ruling race to another. Why should the English or the Japanese have to waste their time over the troubles of Othello?

His sojourn in Japan taught him, he said on the BBC, to feel 'very sorry' for his pupils and colleagues. 'It was already obvious then that they were caught up in this hideous machine and had no way out, hardly even for a breathing space.' His disgust with the military mind-control is evident in an early letter dating from about March 1932:

> The Japanese flag (a poached egg, or clot of blood on a bandage, which gives the insanely simple and self-centered effect of an amoeba when drugged) is very much in evidence: the theatre (as excellent as they say) has the deaths of heroes at Shanghai on display … The efforts of patriotism have made the whole country crawl with babies, dirty and noisy in themselves and sure to cause famine in the next generation. This is a squalid way to look at a country, though.

Whatever his distaste for ultra-nationalism, he went on teaching with enthusiasm, without taking cynical short-cuts. As the students were to recall, he was strict and even severe with their efforts. 'What do *you* think?' he urged them; and when they seemed to have nothing to say for themselves, 'You *must* have an opinion.' He spared no one his direct criticism. Probably the most useful service he gave was to write detailed comments on their essays.

Many students benefited. All the same, there is little doubt that the educational process was a struggle on both sides; for every student who rose to Empson's methods there were several who never grasped how to examine a work of literature for themselves: they parroted the professor or some critical text. One student had the harrowing experience of being unable to understand a single question Empson asked during the oral examination of his dissertation on 'The tragic side in Joseph Conrad's work'. Empson passed him anyway.

A fair idea of their level of attainment, and of his fondly patronising attitude towards their efforts, may be gathered from this letter to Hayward:

> … a young man came in and explained with great dignity and politeness that he was sorry he had been unable to attend my examination, as he was drunk last night and had only just woken

> up ... Two young men sat down and wrote their essays [on D. H. Lawrence and sex] one on each side of the tea-table, in a war of Japanese speech with the gramophone playing. They are really rather sweet once you accept them as hopelessly silly.

Elsewhere, he reiterated with despondency: 'the Japanese are always Jap-to-European, and always afraid of losing dignity'.

* * *

Out of school, Empson liked travelling. He soaked himself in local culture, especially the theatre and Buddhist art. And he liked it equally well to lie naked in the summer sun, though always with a book on the go. He liked sightseeing and sunbathing all the better if he could do them in the company of a young male friend. He both fancied and felt irritated by what he regarded as the infantilism of Japanese youth, its puppyish look and demeanor. One young man he met by chance was three years his senior, Nakano Yoshio (a teacher), a pupil of Edmund Blunden, who later became a critic and journalist, and a professor of English Literature. They made a date to see a *noh* drama. When Nakano went to collect Empson at his home he found him naked, sunbathing in the porch-way. As Nakano would tenderly recall after fifty years, Empson was utterly unconcerned about his appearance. 'We sat drinking a cup of tea for thirty minutes or so, with his sweet little uncircumcized treasure in full view, staring me in the face.' Then they shuffled off together to see the *noh* play *Kakutagawa*, which Empson watched with absorption.

He went to the theatre once more with Nakano Yoshio, and at other times with other young men. He went with Sayama Eitaro to see a performance of *Nikudan sanyushi* ('Three heroes working as human bullets') – 'a Kabuki play which is sensational in style and propagandistic in content, endorsing Japanese militarism in Manchuria'.[7] Empson records his first impressions in a letter to the writer Sylvia Townsend Warner: 'Funny to see Noh plays after reading Mr Waley [*The No Plays of Japan* (1921)]: they're not Celtic and hopeless as you might think because the dances are terrific South Sea Island affairs, all crowing and prating and stamping like buck rabbits.' Empson became an enthusiast for Japanese theatre, its music and movement – not least because it provoked positive reflections on the differences in cultural disposition between East and West. He was captivated by the supra-personal beauty of the *noh*.

The sweltering hardships of travelling in the Far East he took in the spirit of junketing. A letter of March 1933 wonders: 'Always rather embarrassing to wonder what one gets out of travel to make up for its privations; except that it requires so much imagination to stay at home.' His most ambitious excursions took him in search of the faces of the Buddha. His learned amateur interest amounted to an obsession. 'The Buddhas are the only accessible art I find myself able to care about.' Within Japan he scoured the ancient city of Nara, where he found that the early Buddhas were 'really worth coming here to see. The later ones I can't like, though they are good sculpture (drapery and so on): the face rapidly becomes a slug-like affair with a pool of butter round the mouth. But the early ones feel as if everything was ready for an immense intellectual achievement which suddenly died.' As for Kyoto, the late examples of the artistic expression first imported from Korea had been so comfortably assimilated as to be 'a sort of whimsical family joke'. He took lessons in drawing from Marjorie Nishiwaki, an English artist married to a Japanese, so he could make skilful portraits of the Buddhas in their umpteen locations.

The ethics of Buddhism struck him as much more humane than those of Christianity; more generous in allowing the disciple to improve in moral worth through successive incarnations. However, it was the meaning of the myriad faces of the Buddha that he sought throughout the Far East. To the casual Western tourist, the inscrutable and even bland face of the Buddha is replicated throughout the Eastern world. Empson's assiduous eye discerned variations from country to country, and from one phase to another within each country. He also noted that the Buddha's expression embodied a fundamental ambiguity – 'a complete repose with an active power to help the worshipper ... The normal way of getting the effect in the great periods is a reliable and simple one; the two incompatible things are largely separated onto the two sides of the face'. Throughout the 1930s he was to work on his pet project, a monograph called *The Faces of the Buddha*, which was unfortunately lost after the war.

Just as the Buddha image spans nations, so, Empson felt, it is a pernicious fallacy for any nation to assert itself as a fixed race. 'The beautiful girl of the Utamaro woodcut has a long narrow face with a curled nose, a fine Jewish type, and she only really occurs among the Japanese aristocracy; and that element might come from Arab traders in the South Seas. In fact it's a very complete mixture of race.'

In October 1933, the start of his final year, he wrote to Sylvia Townsend Warner: 'the rice fields have settled down as rather crisp-looking stubble. It is only then that the country isn't irritatingly like Japanese prints.' He had an eye for the anomalous: 'it is most strange to ski past cottages with the snow piling up onto the rice-straw matting, whole walls open to the wind, and children lying teasing each other under quilts.' Empson also comments on suicide, 'one of the national sports': 'There was a particularly sporting man who while throwing himself into the Oshima crater ... shouted out to all the trippers "Come on – let's all do it". The crater would in fact hold most of the nation. But the police take a graver view and put up little black-and-white notices – "Your country needs you." "Think again."'

* * *

Empson's social contacts were limited. He knew certain individuals such as Vere Redman, as well as George Sansom (commercial counsellor at the British Embassy)[8] and his wife Katharine, both of whom he liked a great deal. But most of his other encounters were strictly occasional. He enjoyed the odd expatriate bar-hopping spree: 'The Fleet is in, and I was taken drinking with some Able-Bodies: considered a charity to take them to the right beer-halls,' he confessed to John Hayward. 'One knew how blue-eyed and idealist and cultured they were, but it is stirring to an exile.'

At the other extreme, he was once asked to the Japan-British Society, only to find himself conversing with Prince Chichibu, the brother of the Emperor (Hirohito, later known by his reign name of Shōwa), who had studied briefly at Magdalen College, Oxford. 'It is like suddenly finding yourself on a lighted stage without knowing your lines. I shall always think better of myself because I thought at once of a tolerable thing to say to this friendly character. I said, "Why don't you start a pack of hounds here in Japan?" and these were the only words I needed to say. Chichibu immediately said there was a fortune waiting for the first man who would start a pack of hounds in Japan, but the master would have to work in with the very peculiar fox-superstitions of the peasants.' Chichibu rattled on so enthusiastically that Empson was convinced 'royalty wants to be addressed in an unfrightened manner, so long as the manner is not impudent or politically wrong'.

Strange to say but somehow easy to believe, he took the prince's words quite seriously, and even suggested in a letter to his sister Molly that she and her husband might consider emigrating to Japan to start a pack of hounds there.

Whenever the weather was fine enough he would pass time at the Jingu swimming pool, hoping to make acquaintances with whom he need have no formal dealings. One such friend was Satō Nobuo, a medical student, who noticed that the foreigner always brought to the pool a towel, a watch, and a different book for each visit, one day a volume on Buddhism, the next a new novel. Empson spent most of his time reading on the concrete apron. He took Satō home for a drink, directing a taxi in poor Japanese. His clothes were clean but scruffy, Satō noted; his hair was 'like a sparrow's nest', his house messy. Thereafter they often met up at the pool. Since Empson's swimming was just as bad as Satō's English, Sato tried to teach him to swim properly, but to no avail. Empson kept up an air of not caring a jot about his lack of aquatic accomplishment.

One day they went hiking together, striking across the Miura Peninsula to the ancient city of Kamakura. As they walked, they talked. Sato knew nothing about English literature, so they chatted about botany, zoology, organic chemistry, and medicine. Satō was amazed by Empson's familiarity with carbon atoms, theories of probability, the structure of benzol and phenol, and even the relationship between vitamin D and ultra-violet light. When they got lost, Empson took out his penknife, stuck it in the ground, and lay down flat with his ear to it: he was listening to see if anyone was coming, he said. They set off walking again at his furious pace. Reaching Kamakura in two hours, they went to a café and enjoyed a meal of eel and rice and watermelon. But when a young couple with a baby came in, Empson said he hated babies as much as snakes, so he and Satō left.

They went swimming in Sagami Bay, and wrestled on Yuigahama Beach. Empson buried his watch in the sand before they started swimming, and could not find it afterwards. 'Never mind, it was a cheap one.' (At times he seems to have wanted to be loved for being so childish, so practically hopeless.) They left the beach – just as they were, naked and barefoot – and called at the house of Empson's art teacher. Fortunately, she was not at home. 'What I liked most about him,' said Satō, 'was his childlike naïveté, his forthrightness, his unwillingness to compromise on his opinions, and the way he would read a book at every possible spare moment.'

When he got back home to England, he told Satō Nobuo, he would give up being a teacher.

Empson's affections were not to be confined to the young men he picked up at swimming pools. Early in 1933 he was writing to I. A. Richards as if Japanese women were an unknown quantity: they were alien creatures who could never hold more than a theoretical interest for a Western male like himself.

But things changed profoundly within a few months. During the summer of 1933, he began an affair with a young Japanese woman whose given name was Haru. Her family home was in Yokohama, and she was working as a nursemaid for the German ambassador in Tokyo. A pretty woman of slight build, she wore her hair in permanent waves: the latest fashion. She is mentioned only a few times in Empson's surviving papers, the first in a letter of 8 October 1933: 'My young woman was expecting to have to sell herself to a German businessman to support her parents, but a brother-in-law has rallied and we are all right. I made no offers but bought her some clothes.' The relationship meant more to Empson – and to Haru – than just an easy or exploitative sexual encounter. It inspired a poem, 'Aubade'. Thirty years later, in an interview, he glossed the poem to reveal honourable and well-intentioned hopes. 'When I was in Japan ... it was usual for the old hand in the English colony to warn the young man: don't you go and marry a Japanese because we're going to be at war with Japan within ten years; you'll have awful trouble if you marry a Japanese, and this is what the poem is about.' Here are some verses from the first half of the poem:[9]

'Hours before dawn we were woken by the quake.
My house was on a cliff. The thing could take
Bookloads off shelves, break bottles in a row.
Then the long pause and then the bigger shake.
It seemed the best thing to be up and go.
…
Then I said The Garden? Laughing she said No.
Taxi for her and for me healthy rest.
It seemed the best thing to be up and go.

The language problem but you have to try.
Some solid ground for lying could she show?
The heart of standing is you cannot fly.
None of these deaths were her point at all.
The thing was that being woken he would bawl
And finding her not in earshot he would know.
I tried saying Half an Hour to pay this call.
It seemed the best thing to be up and go.'

While internal evidence, and the genre, might suggest that 'he' in the last stanza quoted could be the woman's husband or father, S. F. Bolt has revealed: 'This person … was a small boy in the charge of the nursemaid who was the poet's companion – as Empson explained when I wrote something which assumed a husband was involved.'[10] As soon as the earth moves for the sleeping lovers, the woman's first imperative is not merely to seek safety by getting out of Empson's villa as fast as possible but to rush home by taxi. Although the affair was not adulterous, it might still be a scandal for her to be sleeping out with her lover.

The key to the poem is its oscillation between the resonant refrains, 'It seemed the best thing to be up and go' gestures to the expatriate's pragmatism. 'The heart of standing is you cannot fly' touches on love, the possibility of marriage, making a stand. The poem closes by acceding to positive realism. The new commitment has to be surrendered to the long inalianable obligation.

'It seemed the best thing to be up and go.
Up was the heartening and the strong reply.
The heart of standing is we cannot fly.'

Those last lines, Empson said, 'chiefly meant that you can't get away from this world war if it's going to happen'. Their keynote is 'passive endurance. We have to put up with it, we can't avoid this situation of history.'

The next recorded reference to Haru occurs in January 1935, some months after they had separated. Empson says (in a letter to Katharine Sansom) that he gave the doleful Haru some financial assistance before he left Japan. 'I had a Christmas card from Haru in Tokyo in which she said she was keeping the money, very little, I gave her when I left and would send it back when I was seriously hard up, which she was sure I would be. She writes very cheerfully now. I wish there was some hopeful step that she could take.' The phrasing suggests that he must have put a good deal of emotional distance between himself and her.

The relationship did not end there. Haru visited England in the summer of 1935, working as a nursemaid for the future poet and academic David Wevill, who was to recall many years later:

> In autumn 1954 I had just started at Cambridge, coming from Canada. I wrote my parents a letter naming some of the poets I was reading, including Empson. My father, who knew nothing of writers or literature I think, wrote back asking if this was the William Empson he had confronted in our rented house in Croydon (I think) while we were on a visit to England [from Yokohama in 1935] … My parents had brought the young woman across as a baby-*amah* for me, and by law my father was responsible for her safe return to Japan, as a Japanese national. Empson knocked on the door asking to see her, telling what story I don't know, but I believe Empson tried several times to see her, by various means. I seem to recall my father might have appealed to the police to restrain Empson.[11]

This suggests Wevill's father believed Empson was harassing the woman, or was at least over-importunate. But Empson did have a number of encounters with Haru. They even went out of town together – perhaps in a state of mounting awkwardness, regret or recrimination – and took a trip to Devon. In October he told Sansom: 'Haru leaves England today, quite cheerful after wangling a last meeting yesterday.' His next bulletin, in November, conveys an unmistakable tone of relief: 'Very cheerful letters from Haru in Canada, who has met friends there... I do claim for Haru that she seems to have become a social figure as soon as let loose.'

As first published (in *Life and Letters Today*, Winter 1937), 'Aubade' included eight lines, halfway through the poem, which suggest that the end of the affair was protracted and hurtful:

> 'This is unjust to her without a prose book.
> A lyric from a fact is bound to cook.
> It was more grinding; it was much more slow,
> But still the point's not how much time it took,
> It seemed the best thing to be up and go.
>
> I do not know what forces made it die.
> With what black life it may yet work below.
> The heart of standing is you cannot fly.'

The unhappy truth is that she probably did try to keep their love alive too long after its natural term, for Empson's last word on the relationship was written to Ronald Bottrall in July 1940. He had been to China and returned home again since last seeing 'poor Haru', as he now called her: 'I found a grindingly sad letter from her when I got back to England, and then lost the address; but maybe after all that was the best thing to do.'

★★★

Empson was too much the Englishman ever to seek assimilation. Within a few months he set himself resolutely against his host nation's policies; and he took potentially perilous risks in making his position plain. Notably, he had penned a journal and 'privately circulated [it] to Europeans who have lived in Japan and continue to be interested in her problems.' The journal no longer exists, but Jacob Bronowski's account of it in *Granta* (10 May 1933) goes far enough to show that Empson, whom he over-eggs as 'a scrupulous searcher and a profound judge', had been preparing in secret a document that the Japanese authorities would have regarded as seditious. Bronowski's decision to publish its contents, however briefly and even in paraphrase, might have put Empson in jeopardy. Bronowski reported: 'He makes it clear that the Japanese students now play in Japan precisely the part of the Nazi students in Germany. Their lust is only for dominance and power, for ruling first the Pacific and then the world. With no culture of their own, they resent the cultures both of China and of the West.' One might suspect Bronowski of over-interpretation when he insists that Empson tagged *all* of his students as chauvinists and megalomaniacs, Japanese counterparts of the Nazi youth.

Bronowski's epitome is contradicted by another piece of writing that Empson happily kept to himself. Pencilled into a skimpy notebook, it is a draft of a letter home which he probably forgot. It includes an observation that – had it fallen into the wrong hands – would have laid him open to possible criminal prosecution. 'The Communists I know in Japan (every bright young man is a Communist),' he wrote, 'tell me there isn't going to be a revolution …'

The Japan Communist Party was an illegal organization. All Communists and fellow-travellers were being remorselessly hunted down. The Japan Communist Party was virtually eradicated by 1935, as a result of mass *tenkō* (conversion). Those casual words could have cost him dear.

Years later, he recalled: 'I found that all my students held liberal or leftish views … and on the other hand were very afraid of letting them be known…'

Empson was no Communist, but he was acquainted with some academics who were. He knew a 32-year-old New Zealander, William Maxwell Bickerton, who had been teaching in Tokyo since 1924. Max Bickerton had a reputation as a translator into English of Japanese proletarian novels such as *The Cannery Boat,* by Kobayashi Takiji. On 13 March 1934, he was taken into police custody – where he was ill-treated or allegedly beaten – and charged with promoting Communist interests. At a preliminary examination held in the Tokyo District Court on 30 April, evidence was given that on four separate occasions since September 1933 he had made financial contributions to the Japan Communist Party; he was charged under the Amendment made by Imperial Ordinance in 1928 to the Law relating to the Preservation of Peace and Order, and remanded for public trial. Mr Bickerton was 'well aware,' it was officially written, 'that the Japanese Communist Party was a secret organization which aimed, as the Japan branch of the Comintern, at the transformation, by revolutionary means, of the national constitution of this country …'[12] But the British Consul in Tokyo managed to get him released on bail.

Empson became involved, working to smuggle Bickerton out of the country. According to Ronald Bottrall, he took away Bickerton's clothes and provided him with an entirely different outfit, complete with dark glasses and a false moustache. Then he booked a passage for Bickerton, obviously in an assumed name, on a foreign freighter. As the pair approached the gangway, a member of the Secret Police appeared – only to present Bickerton with all of his old clothes cleaned and pressed. That final detail might not be so farcical if the Tokyo authorities simply preferred to turn a blind eye rather than risk an international incident. In any event, Bickerton certainly jumped bail and left Japan on the *Empress of India* on 8 June, bound for Victoria and Vancouver. There is no suggestion that Empson alone arranged for Bickerton to get out of the country by subterfuge. In fact, we cannot even know if he was placed under suspicion for aiding and abetting the escape, or questioned about it. But there is evidence to indicate that he certainly knew they had an eye on him by then.

Empson seemed to be looking for trouble, as if he needed a periodic crisis to relieve himself of nervous strain. Had he not been employed on a fixed-term contract, it is likely that he would have been sacked anyway. He got drunk in a bar and took a taxi home, and then he made a pass at the taxi-driver. He told Bottrall with absurd implausibility that 'Japanese men and women look so alike that I made a mistake'. But it was a compromising mistake. The taxi-driver seems to have reported the incident to the police, who in turn advised the Rector of the Bunrika that it would be better if Empson left Japan. (Peter F. Alexander, reporting an interview with Professor Kajiki Ryuichi, has confirmed that Empson 'got into serious trouble with the authorities because of his homosexual activity, and the Japanese police were involved'.) Perhaps he was more amused than deeply abashed by the incident – he was not reluctant to admit elsewhere to 'a diffused homosexual feeling'.

Empson introduced this scandal into some rough but beguiling verses written the next year, 1935. Though seemingly about a woman whose rare beauty he has lost, the piquant and wittily self-deprecating epithalamion 'Letter VI: A Marriage' is in fact addressed to his friend Desmond Lee, for whom he had yearned in his final year as an undergraduate. Driven to seek out this paragon in other forms, Empson reaches the third stanza:

'Envisioning however the same beauty in taxiboys
And failing to recognise in one case
What with drink and the infantilism of the Japanese type
The fact that it had not yet attained puberty
I was most rightly (because of another case
Where the jealousy of the driver seemed the chief factor)
- Not indeed technically, named only in vernacular newspapers,
And who knows who knows –
Deported from that virtuous and aesthetic country
Life being as strange as this traditional theme.'

On 22 June a farewell party was thrown in his honour at the Nanushinotaki Restaurant. Empson wore his customary crumpled white linen suit. A large number of students assembled to see him off on the *Kashima maru*, which slipped away at three o'clock in the stifling afternoon of 8 July. The steamer began to move, when quite unexpectedly Empson took off his panama hat and threw it down amidst the group of friends and students. As he cast off his hat, Empson fumbled and dropped his newspaper into the sea. He had no plans, only a vague hope that he could make his way in literary London.

* * *

One final mystery. There is one other document, now lodged in the Public Record Office in London, which must be taken into account. If its substance is not an outright lie, it implies a background of blackmail or bribery. On 4 December 1939, the British Embassy in Tokyo conveyed to the Far Eastern Department of the Foreign Office some gossip gleaned by Vere Redman from Major Kadamatsu of the Japanese Army General Staff. The burden of the letter was that the Japanese regretted their generosity towards British interests; and their complaints included this odd little item:

> Continuing on the subject of publicity Major Kadamatsu mentioned the name of Mr. Empson, a former resident in Tokyo and subsequently professor in Peking University when it was at Yunnan. (He also visited Chungking.) Major Kadamatsu said that his department had employed him as a sort of publicity man at large with unlimited supplies of money – in the words of the Major, 'We kept him luxuriously for a year.'
>
> The intention had been that he should influence foreign opinion in favour of the New Order. According to Major Kadamatsu, however, Mr. Empson's publicity activities were all too often detrimental to the prestige of the Japanese army. With all his brilliant intellectual gifts, he is a most erratic personality and quite unfitted to act in the capacity to which the military authorities appointed him. If Major Kadamatsu's account was true, the Japanese Army were guilty of a fantastic error of judgement.[13]

Empson would not have undertaken of his own free will to spread favorable propaganda for the 'New Order' in Japan, which he held in contempt. If it is true that he accepted an 'unlimited' sum of money from the Japanese military, we have first to consider whether he did so under duress. Perhaps they threatened him with physical abuse in consequence of his involvement in the Bickerton affair. They may have held out the prospect of a prison term as punishment for his homosexual importuning. In short, perhaps he agreed to do a deal, albeit disingenuously. But it is doubtful that he would have done anything at all if bullied. He was immensely stoical, and could tolerate a high level of pain.

Another possibility is that he somehow won their confidence and tricked them into awarding him a hefty remuneration for a hollow undertaking. In that event, Empson, delighting in roguishness, would have loved every minute of it, knowing that the whole charade was to be undertaken at the expense of Japan. It would have gone far to relieve his boredom. Whatever the case, as the British Embassy said, they had badly mistaken their man.

But the whole affair sounds like a piece of disinformation. If they had a hold over him, why would they pay him an 'unlimited' sum of money? – especially when he had small prospect of influencing anybody on his departure from Japan (though they could not perhaps know that).

If the allegation is true, he was both wise and witty. He acted deviously and got away with it (and a handsome profit). And he went on telling the truth as he saw it. There is no evidence, documentary or anecdotal, to suggest that he ever made propaganda for Japan.

23

Charles Boxer (1904–2000) and Japan

JAMES CUMMINS

Charles Boxer

'I THINK OF JAPAN every day, and I dream of Japan most nights.' Charles Boxer's remark, made in 1991, was obviously extravagant, but there are reasons for believing that the idea of Japan was deeply significant to him and was embedded in his mind and imagination from early childhood.

As a small boy he would have heard family talk of the exploits of his great uncle, Commander Charles Boxer RN who, as Captain of the *Racehorse*, took part in the retributive bombing of Kagoshima (Kyushu) in August 1863, under the command of Admiral Augustus Kuper.[1] That punitive attack followed the murder of an Englishman, Charles Richardson, at Namamugi on the Tokaido near Yokohama. Boxer's *Racehorse* bore the brunt of the action when she was grounded for several hours. In an enthusiastic letter to his brother, the Commander described how he sank one of the European vessels recently bought by the Japanese: '… the Flagship went in firing beautifully, and before they could fire, a shell sent them flying and dismounted their gun.'[2]

Besides such letters, the family had souvenirs of Japan, *netsuke* and samurai figurines, with which the child Charles Boxer played, eschewing the lead soldiers, the usual toys of small boys of the period.[3] When he learned to read he delighted in *Harmsworth's History of the World,* which, he said, first awakened his life-long interest in history. There, however, he found a different version of the Kagoshima story. *Harmsworth* was surprisingly sympathetic to the Japanese, denouncing the 'provocative and foolhardy conduct of Richardson, who looked upon the "natives" with contempt, and whose behaviour cost him his life, and led to the first act of war by Britain against Japan, and left the prosperous town of Kagoshima in ashes'.[4]

Harmsworth deplored the bullying manner and arrogance of '... some Occidentals, some with shady pasts and overbearing conduct, who began to swarm into Treaty Ports such as Yokohama'. It would certainly be in character for the later, mature Boxer to feel that Harmsworth was in the right, and to reject his great uncle's bellicosity.[5] The *History* also contained numerous reproductions of old Japanese prints of the sort that Boxer came to admire and to collect in later life. The descriptions of the samurai, 'the knights of old Japan', would make a ready appeal to any boy, and the description of one Japanese hero as 'The Bayard of Old Japan' clearly impressed Boxer, because thirty years later he himself used it of another 'pattern of devoted loyalty'.[6] Another obvious stimulus to the youthful Boxer's interest came in May 1921 when the then Crown Prince (Hirohito) visited Sandhurst where Boxer did his cadet training.

After Wellington and Sandhurst, Boxer followed his father into the Lincolnshire regiment as a professional soldier. The peacetime army left him with ample leisure to begin the study of Portuguese and Dutch so that he could read the records left by the pioneer Europeans in Japan.[7] He made frequent visits to Holland to work in the archives and was befriended there by the family of the historian J. M. C. Warnsinck, who set aside a room in their home as his own private study. In 1925 he began similar research visits to Portugal where he made contact with historians and intellectuals who shared his interests. He was soon reading voraciously in primary and secondary sources, becoming, incidentally, a skilled palaeographer. By 1925 he was also reading in the India Office Library. The following year he became a corresponding member of the Japan Society, and in 1927 lectured before the Society on 'A Portuguese Embassy to Japan, 1644–47'.[8] Eventually, he started to study Japanese in the School of Oriental Studies of London University, but he was dissatisfied because, though the teacher was good, there were only two classes a week, which failed to satisfy his keenness.

These were roundabout approaches to Japan, but in the 1920s any notion of going there must have seemed a hopeless aspiration. However, Boxer's enthusiasm had brought him to the attention of influential Japanophiles, and he was lucky in his time, because in the 1920s there were only two Japanese specialists in the Codebreaking Bureau, and Whitehall recognised the need for personnel to fill the gap.[9] Thanks to the influence of Major General F. S. G. Piggott, Boxer was one of those selected, and in 1930 was posted to Japan on secondment as a Language Officer. He thus entered the 'most peculiar branch of the small world of English Orientalists: that group of Japanophiles which consisted of British Army officers with experience of Japan and who flourished in the Military Intelligence Department'.[10] After a year's preliminary studies in Tokyo and at the school for NCOs at Hamamatsu, he was attached to the 38th Infantry Regiment at Nara.[11] He soon made himself at home in his new surroundings, throwing himself into regimental life, refusing the concessions granted to foreigners in the matter of diet and so on. He was determined to share the texture of the ordinary Japanese soldier's life. Always an enthusiastic drinker, he was made welcome in the mess and at parties. He had never been a sportsman, but he joined the regimental kendo team and became an accomplished fencer. He believed he was probably the first English devotee of 'The Way of the Sword', since most others preferred judo. In short, his attitude differed notably from that of many language officer colleagues.

Malcolm Kennedy, author of the *Military Side of Japanese Life* (London: Constable, 1924) and a noted Japanophile, saw him as a model soldier on secondment.[12] On 3 December 1932 Kennedy noted in his diary:

> Boxer, in Tokyo for a day or two, looked in to see me. He seems to be thoroughly enjoying his attachment to the NCOs School at Hamamatsu and he speaks highly of both the officers and NCOs there. It is good to hear a Language Officer speaking like this, as there has been far too much of a tendency on the part of Language Officers to inveigh against their periods of attachment … Where so many Language Officers go wrong is that they seem to consider their job is merely to watch on occasionally [*sic*]. No wonder they find their attachment boring and complain of the cold attitude of the Japanese officers toward them. To obtain the friendship and respect of Japanese officers you have to show them you are prepared to put up with the same hardships – otherwise it is hopeless.[13]

Yet the appointment was no sinecure. For three years the Language Officer's life consisted of six to eight hours' work daily in the study of the language, with special reference to military vocabulary, army jargon (essential for codebreaking) and the study of the military system. At the end of the second year there was an examination.

During those years Boxer, besides travelling throughout Japan, also visited Singapore, Taiwan, Indonesia, the Philippines, and some of the Pacific Islands. These journeys enabled him to serve his professional concerns and to indulge his personal interests. And he often had the advantage of the company of General Jean-Charles Pabst, the Dutch Minister in Tokyo. Pabst, a fervent *Namban* scholar, and a fluent Japanese speaker, had then been in East Asia for nearly two decades and consequently had much advice and wisdom to share with the novice Boxer. The two men had become firm friends almost as soon as Boxer reached Japan in 1930. In 1931 he also became acquainted with Nakayama Shozen, the *Shimbashira*[14] of the Tenri religion. He consequently made many visits to Tenri City where Patriarch Nakayama had built up a collection of rare books that made Tenri Library internationally known. For a scholar and bibliophile such as Boxer those visits to the Yorozuyo Collection of Christian mission literature (one of the finest to be found anywhere) were a source of wonder and envy. Boxer's letters show that at this same time he was himself building up his own collection of manuscripts and rare books.

At the end of his tour of duty in 1933 Boxer was posted to the Far East Department of the Foreign Office in London where he worked for the next three years with a specialized intelligence group under Major General Gordon Grimsdale.[15] Boxer, like Grimsdale, was alarmed to find that his superiors seemed to ignore the situation in the East and thought only of the possibility of war in Europe. This was a common complaint from many language officers who repeatedly warned that the Japanese would be a formidable enemy in any war. Grimsdale, who had spent 18 years as an Intelligence officer in Asia, later complained that since Intelligence work was the 'Cinderella of the services', their warnings were ignored or were criticised by Whitehall for pro-Japanese bias and alarmist:[16]

> I believe that this was the main reason why our high command had so seriously underestimated the Japanese. It was not lack of written material from Intelligence staff in the Far East that caused this underestimation. The Far East Intelligence Bureau was continually trying to bring home the fact that the Japanese was a good soldier, with first-class equipment, and was thoroughly trained. The tradition that the British soldier is worth two or three of any other army dies very hard.[17]

In 1936 Boxer was posted to Headquarters China Command (Hong Kong) and attached to the Far Eastern Combined Intelligence Bureau (FECB). He remained posted there until the invasion of the colony. In April 1937 he was in Manila for a two-day conference with an American Intelligence Officer who warned of Japanese agents on board a ship chartered for the Eucharistic Congress in Manila and, on a more serious level, to discuss the reading of Japanese codes.[18] In April-May 1938 he motored through south China and a photograph shows him interrogating Japanese prisoners in Sian. There were academic moments too on that trip, and he reported to Pabst in Tokyo that he had bought a rubbing of the Nestorian Stone, a Christian relic from the eighth century. In 1939 he again visited Japan, this time on honeymoon.[19] In October 1940 he interviewed Chiang Kai-Shek in Chungking to seek closer liaison with Chinese Military Intelligence so as to facilitate speedier and more reliable reports of any Japanese threat to Hong Kong.[20]

In March 1939, Grimsdale was appointed to head the Hong Kong Bureau. In his unpublished memoirs he describes his time there:

> On arrival I met an old friend, Major Charles Boxer. He had already worked for me in the War Office, and it was on my recommendation that he had been appointed as the junior military representative in FECB a year before. Charles is a remarkable character. He had passed a Japanese language course when a young officer. He understood the Japanese mentality very well and was always popular with them. From the time when he was a youth he had been interested in the Far East and had made a deep study of the early history of the European contacts with Japan.... He was also a very capable intelligence staff officer, with a quick and accurate mind and a fluent pen. I could not have wanted a better or more congenial assistant. Charles had always been popular with the Japanese, especially with the young soldiers with whom he went out on 'parties', and with the scholars who knew he was an expert on their history.

Grimsdale came to depend on Boxer, especially after the Japanese moved south from Canton, thus cutting off the New Territories and the Hong Kong colony. They closed the frontier, allowing no road or rail traffic thereby preventing normal supplies getting in from China. In trying to maintain friendly contact with them, Grimsdale and Boxer sometimes had a delicate and dangerous task: 'Neither of us could help feeling the drama of the moment or fail to realize the possibility of an 'incident', which might bring about the one thing we all wanted to avoid, namely war with Japan.'[21]

Boxer and Grimsdale continued visiting the Japanese Commander in Canton, picking up useful information:

> In order to find out as much as possible about Japanese activities in the area, Charles Boxer and I paid an official visit in May to the Japanese Army Commander in Canton. He was somewhat difficult to talk to under normal conditions, but became excessively talkative and friendly when, as frequently happened, he had taken too much to drink. He sent us out in his own car for a drive in the country round Canton. Contrary to my expectations we were more or less free to go where we wished. In the course of the drive we were able to get a good idea of the disposition of his troops and of the progress of the construction of several aerodromes. When on our return to Hong Kong we put in our report, giving as much detailed information as we had been able to acquire, we felt it was slightly comic to realize how much more accurate information we had got in a few hours at Japanese expense, than others had been able to get after weeks of work at British expense![22]

They both enjoyed such adventures, which in Grimsdale's account sometimes have a *Boy's Own Paper* air about them.

But in 1939, as war seemed inevitable, Grimsdale was ordered to Singapore: '... it was a hectic time, not made any easier by the fact that I was ordered to leave Charles Boxer behind as my representative'.[23] Boxer then became Chief of Army Intelligence in Hong Kong. He continued visiting the Japanese on the border and in Grimsdale's place he took with him Geoffrey Studholme-Wilson, the Hong Kong Chief of Police. Agreeable as they were, these were duty-journeys since they had to get all the information they could. To that end they naturally took with them enough whisky to induce amiable sessions together and Boxer had friendly kendo bouts with the officers, who lent him the necessary equipment.

On the morning of 8 December 1941, Boxer was the first person in the colony to learn that war with Japan had started, since he was on radio watch when the signal for hostilities was transmitted from Tokyo. Events then moved rapidly. On both 15 and 16 December Boxer received the Japanese envoys who demanded immediate surrender. From this point developments are confused since no two persons seem to agree on precise dates or details.[24] Boxer, however, was one of the early casualties, shot by a sniper on 20 December.[25] For some hours he lay delirious and loosing blood; but after dark he was dragged to safety and woke to find himself lying on a hospital mortuary slab. His days as an active soldier were over.

Boxer harboured no resentment against his captors. He had lived among them and understood them, as he understood humanity in general. Face slapping was a commonplace he had witnessed daily in his Japanese army service; bowing low was not humiliating to him: it was custom. This baffled many of his fellow prisoners who saw only a readiness to 'kowtow'. Moreover, in the early days he was fairly treated. His captors, who could converse with him, knew he had behaved well, and had done his soldier's duty: he had not surrendered; he had been shot in battle. On the other hand, many fellow prisoners resented Boxer's situation and there were frequent and ready misunderstandings. One instance is typical. It was noticed that Boxer received physiotherapy for his wounded arm, and the worst interpretation was quickly put upon this apparent favouritism.[26] The explanation, however, is different, though strange. The therapy was due to the intervention of a Canadian officer, Lieut. Colonel Jack Price. A fellow prisoner, Brian Baxter, describes what happened:

> I can confirm the story about Charles Boxer who I remember well. I know the story quite well, and it is as follows. The Crown Prince of Japan was sent around the world on a tour of education in 1921, and when he came to Canada, Jack Price looked after him. The Japanese were very pleased and showed their gratitude by bestowing on him the Order of the Chrysanthemum.
>
> One day in the POW camp in Hong Kong, the prisoners were inspected by a member of the Japanese royal family. Before the inspection Colonel Price intimated to the British General that he had this Japanese order, and that if the General thought it were of any use he could mention it. Accordingly, as the visitor was passing by Colonel Price, the British General told the visitor that the Japanese Government had awarded Colonel Price this high Japanese order. The visitor was very impressed and wanted to do something for him in return. The visitor offered to give him a house outside the camp where he could live. Colonel Price refused this offer, but if the visitor insisted, he suggested, Major Boxer's wounded arm could be given treatment. That was what happened, and I remember watching him being guided once a week (and then later once a month or so) to and from the hospital which was outside the camp.[27]

But misunderstandings were inevitable. Among those suspected of being too close to the Japanese was the Colonial Secretary, F. C. Gimson, who had obeyed an order to teach General Maejima to play bridge.[28] Similarly, Dr Percy Selwyn-Clarke ('the Albert Schweitzer of Hong Kong') was suspected of collaboration by the very people he was trying to help, because he kept on friendly relations with the Japanese so as to get medicines for his hospital.[29]

Later, when the Gendarmerie (the *Kempeitai*) took over, prison life became much harsher for everyone. Boxer, who had refused to sign a promise not to try to escape, was regarded with suspicion and mistrust. And the discovery of a wireless receiver in the camp led to torture and executions. Boxer was involved in the secret, and together with others, was condemned to penal servitude for life. He was moved from the POW camp to a common jail in Canton where, with the others, he was kept in solitary confinement until the end of the war. Conditions there were grim enough for him to recall, 'At times, I even prayed.'[30]

None of this changed his estimation of the Japanese. He, with Selwyn-Clarke, remembered occasional acts of kindness from individual guards, and after the war they presented a gold watch to one particular guard as a token of their gratitude.[31]

Boxer's first love, Japan, remained so until the end. In 1991, aged 88, he went back for the last time. Fittingly, it was in Tenri that he gave his last-ever public lecture, and visited the library known since his youth. Taken to visit the hall where sixty years earlier he had practised kendo with his colleagues from the 38th infantry regiment, he made no comment, since that was not his way. He had always recoiled from even the fringes of emotion and firmly controlled feelings that might be overwhelming.

⋆ ⋆ ⋆

In 1946 on his way home to England, Boxer was ordered to attend a New York military hospital for treatment to his war wound. While there he received the startling offer of the chair of Portuguese studies in London University. Once retired from the army on the grounds of disability, he accepted the proposal and so began a second career.

By the time he was taken prisoner in 1941, Boxer had published 81 works, most of them directly concerned with Japan. The remainder dealt with the history of those involved with feudal Japan: the Portuguese, the Dutch, and the Jesuits. At the end of his career Boxer had some 340 publications to his name.[32] It is difficult to select from such a bibliography but there are certain works of special interest to students of Japanese culture. Amongst them are two surveys of the maritime history of the first two European countries to make contact with Japan: The *Portuguese Seaborne Empire* (London: Hutchinson, 1965) and *The Dutch Seaborne Empire* (London: Hutchinson, 1969). More closely focused is*: The Great Ship from Amacon* (Lisbon: Centro de Estudos Historicos Ultramarinos, 1959), which deals with the silk trade between Macao and Japan. In part 1 (*The Annals, 1555–1640*) Boxer shows how the Portuguese monopoly of trade with Japan was broken when the Dutch came on the scene, and he goes on to discuss their subsequent rivalry. Part 2 consists of illustrative texts taken from contemporary documents. Boxer saw *The Great Ship* as complementing his *Fidalgos in the Far East* (The Hague: Nijhoff, 1948) and his *Christian Century in Japan* (California and Cambridge University Presses, 1951). The three works were intended to cover 'the political, religious, cultural and mercantile aspects of the early contacts between Farthest East and Farthest West', while *Jan Compagnie in Japan, 1600–1817* (The Hague; Nijhoff, 1936; 1950; 1968) was an *'Essay on the cultural, artistic and scientific influence exercised by the Hollanders in Japan from the seventeenth to the nineteenth centuries.'*

Amidst the hectic adjustments of the post-war years, he researched and wrote his *Christian Century in Japan.*[33] A work of formidable scholarship, many considered it his best; he himself said it was the book he had most enjoyed writing. Dedicated to an old Japanese friend, Okamoto Yoshitomo, it is his most personal work, because he allowed himself and his experiences to intrude into the text in a way unusual for him ('I too once lived in Nara and can appreciate Father Vilela's account', p. 67).[34]

It is a dense work and its opening chapter makes difficult reading for novices with its clutter of strange names and concepts. There are infelicities of style, occasional clumsiness and signs that stylistically this was still apprentice work. It tells the story of the attempt to convert Japan to Catholicism, from the arrival of Saint Francis Xavier in Kagoshima in August 1549 to the closing of Japan a century later.[35] It was partly to mark the four hundredth anniversary of Xavier's landing that he wrote the book.[36] By any standard, it is an extraordinary story in which the reader finds all the highs and lows of human conduct. In his 'Preface' Boxer wrote that 'the story of Japan's Christian century has proved a perennial fascination for students of the relations between East and West. And although the subject had been frequently treated in the past, I can claim to have contributed a good deal of new material. I have been able to use original Jesuit secret and confidential reports from the Marsden manuscripts in the British Museum and the Ajuda library at Lisbon.' In addition, though the old Japan mission was predominantly a Portuguese one, earlier historians had ignored Lusitanian sources and Boxer hoped he had rectified that omission. He also tried to avoid a Eurocentric approach to his subject: 'A residence of three years in Japan (1930–1933) and a somewhat longer captivity in Japanese hands a decade later, has enabled me to see something of "the other side of the hill".' The personal note is again apparent when he discusses the missionaries' experience of Japanese jails (p. 347) and the tortures they suffered, especially the water torture which is mentioned twice, perhaps because it was, he once admitted in conversation, the torture he himself had most feared during his imprisonment: 'This form of torture was a favourite one in the *kempeitai* jails in 1941–1945, but it is not an invention of theirs as many people erroneously imagine. It was widely used the world over' (p. 495). Here, as always, Boxer is concerned to be fair: 'it is well to remind the reader that virtually everything in this catalogue of horrors could have been paralleled in contemporary Europe. But the way in which Japanese jails functioned in the seventeenth century has left its mark down to the present day, as inmates of Japanese jails in 1941–1945 can testify' (pp. 347, 351). Relating the death of one missionary (p. 519) from malnutrition, Boxer comments wryly that that would be no prolonged feat in a Japanese prison (p. 391). So *The Christian Century* is a book that for Boxer links the past and present. A major study of the period, it earned him the nickname of 'The Father of Nagasakiology'.[37]

While in prison Boxer was introduced to the writings of the Stoic emperor, Marcus Aurelius. Dr Selwyn-Clarke describes how it happened: 'one great advantage was that I was with Major Charles Boxer.... He and I discussed poetry and I got another *Meditations of Marcus Aurelius* which proved a favourite with Charles.'[38] He was immediately converted to the stark philosophy of stoicism that appealed to the melancholy, pessimistic streak deep in his nature. It was the nearest he could get to religious feelings and later it helped him through the two years of solitary confinement. Fittingly, then, he ends *The Christian Century* with a quotation from the *Meditations* in his favourite translation by Marc Casaubon (1635): 'What is wickedness? It is that which many times and often thou hast already seen and known in the world. Generally, above and below, thou shalt find but the same things. The very same things whereof ancient stories, middle age stories and fresh stories are full. There is nothing that is new. All things that are, are both usual and of little continuance.' Boxer closed the book with the words: 'the sickening cruelties and incredible heroism, which marked the course of this story, have been re-enacted on a vaster scale in our own day and generation. If only for this reason, the history of the Christian Century may perhaps be regarded as a "tract for the times", and one from which the reader can draw his own moral.'

In short, *The Christian Century in Japan* is a work at once philosophical, picturesque, even passionate, and unique in the body of Boxer's multifarious writings in that it alone admits those personal feelings usually suppressed by him.[39]

24

Ivan Morris, 1925–77

NOBUKO ALBERY

Ivan Morris

I AM DOUBTFUL whether the mere fact that I was married to Ivan Morris for six years gives me enough knowledge to write adequately about someone who was as complex, tortured and secretive as he was. He gave me two invaluable pieces of advice about writing: 'Tell all, and bore all,' and 'When in doubt, cut it.' He applied these precepts rigorously in his own life.

During our married life Ivan told me next to nothing about the American side of his family background, nor did I have any idea how he supplemented his income from teaching to live in the style which none of his colleagues at the university seemed able to equal. I never dared ask, for example how he could afford our annual cross-Atlantic first-class voyages on the SS *France* or the *QE2*. Such questions would have prompted him to scoff in his usual way: 'Don't be so Osaka-Jewish.' (Osaka people are well known for greeting one another with 'Making money?' rather than 'How are you?')

It was only from reading Ivan's obituary in a morning paper five years after our divorce and many years later from Ved Mehta's article about the legendary *New Yorker* magazine editor, William Shawn, that

I learnt about Ivan's grandfather, who had built up a huge fortune in Chicago's meat-packaging industry and, like Mr Shawn's father, the meat-knife maker, had emigrated from Russia. During my married years I had quite naïvely considered my husband and his parents anti-semitic.

The portrait which I am able to draw of Ivan, therefore, is inevitably a mosaic of quick-brush, intuitive and disjointed impressions about someone whom I cannot think about without muttering to myself '*kawaiso na* (poor, tragic) Ivan'.

WHY *KAWAISO*?

Ivan was born in 1925 in a rented house in Hampstead, London, where his American father and Swedish mother had installed themselves only a few weeks before his birth, for the sole purpose of giving their child British nationality, so convinced were they that the next revolution, as prophesied by Marx and Engel would be in England. This was the first of many selfish and cruel whims to which his parents subjected their only son. His father, Ira, met Ivan's mother, Edita, during his last summer holiday from Harvard at his father's ambassadorial residence in Stockholm. 'In those days an American who was rich enough could buy an ambassadorship to an off-centre country like Sweden' was about all Ivan told me about his grandfather. Edita, on the other hand, often spoke about the ball at the American Embassy, which she had had to attend in her sister's old shoes and a borrowed dress, as the von Toll family, of which she was a member, had sunk into a genteel poverty, despite the eternal glory of their ancestor, the Swedish general of German origin, who had fought on the side of the Emperor Alexander against Napoleon and who was mentioned in Tolstoy's *War and Peace*.

The spoilt, lazy, but good-natured son of the American Ambassador fell in love with the vivacious, wilful Nordic beauty; their wedding gift was a small stately home outside the tiny village of Nesles, in the department of Seine et Marne, one-and-a-half-hours east of Paris, which, although the villagers called it Chateau de Nesles, lacked two turrets to be properly classed as a chateau.

How such a carefree young couple with no need to work for their living turned themselves into rabid '*communistes en cashmere*', and became considered subversive enough to figure on Senator McCarthy's red list, I never quite understood. In any event, their life in subsequent exile in a slightly dilapidated but elegant French manor house with a number of local peasants serving as cook, chambermaid, gardener and chicken-keeper must have been both comfortable and charming.

When I asked Ivan why he had been given a Russian name, he replied laconically: 'Because Mother was reading *The Brothers Karamazov* when she was pregnant.' I have read the novel twice since and I confess that I would not have liked to name my own son after that particular character, Ivan Karamazov!

Within six years, the half-American, half-Swedish boy with British citizenship and a Dostoevskian name was to experience a trauma, which marked him for life. This is how Ivan told me: 'Mother stood up from the breakfast table, and walked out, or rather simply evaporated into thin air. For the next thirteen years she existed through postcards sent from the most exotic, far-flung places on earth and through the punctual arrival (his mother was typically Swedish in her punctuality and maniacal tidiness) of birthday and Christmas presents. Then, one morning, soon after the war, she reappeared. As if time had frozen still for thirteen years and she had stepped out of the room to fetch a shawl, she walked in, sacked every domestic in the house, except the chicken-keeper, and resumed her life as before.'

What she actually did during the war was never explained to me; but once when we were looking for something in the attic at Nesles, Ivan casually nodded at a dusty oil painting of a wounded deer in the snow, saying: 'By a famous Swedish painter, Mother's friend.'

I neither met nor heard about one single Morris from his father's side, but by way of warning me of his mother's drastically intolerant nature Ivan did tell me about his beautiful Swedish aunt. After Edita's departure and the outbreak of the war, Ira left Nesles for America and Edita's favourite sister came to live in the *chateau manqué*, which was soon occupied by German officers. Soon after her imperial return with a word neither of explanation nor of apology, Edita heard from the chicken-keeper that her sister had received favours in the form of petrol, firewood, food, cigarettes and so on from the German officers billeted under the same roof. Edita thereupon cut her sister clean out of her life.

During Edita's absence Ira, easy-going, laid-back and totally uninterested in children, did the best he could and as soon as his son was old enough despatched him to Gordonstoun,[1] where the unathletic, pale, tidy and sensitive boy with impeccable manners, instilled into him by a string of nannies and governesses, suffered greatly. On his first night at school a group of jeering bullies shoved his head down the lavatory and flushed it.

Ivan's friends will remember him standing amongst a crowd at a party, his right hand clutching at a cold pipe, his left hand holding a glass of Dry Martini, with his walking stick and a smart leather bag, squeezed tight in his left armpit. He looked odd, and he knew it, but he would not be persuaded to dispense with any of these items. His horror of mislaying or losing his accustomed paraphernalia was a phobia and so was his agony whenever he felt that the trust, friendship, service or whatever he had given was not returned as he would have expected. He kept a minutely recorded list of hospitality, both offered and returned, and felt seriously sad and hurt if the statistics showed that this or that person had not reciprocated his assiduity. His sense of justice was in fact so exacting that, after his publisher had gone back on his word over the number of copies in the first print of his book, Ivan began tape-recording all his telephone conversations and locked up the numbered and dated tapes in his safe. Such behaviour kinks must surely have been due to the utter shock and disorientation he had suffered at his mother's 'now-I-see-now-I-don't' vanishing trick and his subsequent rootless existence with little constancy.

To someone like myself, brought up in the warmth and security of my family and with my mother seldom out of sight, and from one undiluted and continuous racial, ethnic, cultural and religious root, it seems a heroic feat that Ivan managed to survive his schizoid origin and childhood as well as he had, though naturally the toll had been high.

ARTHUR WALEY

In the past few decades in France the word '*tatamizer*' as a verb or '*tatamizé*' as an adjective have become common currency. Ivan was not in the least a '*tatamizé*' Japanologist, nor even a Japanophile: he did not possess many of his colleagues' natural, open-ended affinity, affection, and enthusiasm for Japan, for the Japanese or for things Japanese. Interested but objective and detached from his scholarly subject, he would never have been tempted to 'go native' which must be the nearest translation for '*tatamizer*'. He insisted vehemently that he had not married me because I was Japanese.[2]

Very seldom, if not never, did I see Ivan reading Japanese periodicals, whereas he either subscribed to or regularly bought *The New York Times, The Times, Le Monde, The Times Literary Supplement, Encounter* and from time to time other American and European magazines. As for books, he was reading at least two different books at any given time, say one by Lytton Strachey, the other by Konrad Lorenz, and on long summer holidays he would tackle, as he did one summer, the whole of '*A la Recherche du Temps Perdu*'; but I cannot recall seeing him read any of the latest best-selling Japanese novels or biographies.

His command of the Japanese language in reading and writing and hearing, from purely technical criteria, was not as competent as many other Japanese scholars or students I have met.[3] He accepted this fact, not humbly, but rather proudly, always citing the precedent set by Arthur Waley,[4] his old admired teacher, who had never once set foot on Chinese or Japanese soil, but had translated Chinese classical texts and Heian Japanese into English of the highest quality with the flavour and nuances of the original intact, sometimes in a far clearer way than in the convoluted and obscure original.

Returning from classes of graduate students at Columbia University, he often lamented: 'I have students far more fluent in Japanese than I: but their English! They can't write in their own language.'

During my first visit to England as Mrs Morris, Ivan took me to meet Waley's widow, Alison, who greeted us at the door with a large basket, which contained a bottle of vodka, blueberries and thick cream. She hurried us back to the car, which we had just parked. 'Let's picnic on Dickens' grave, shall we?' It was a fine but cold and gusty September morning. As I squatted on a frigid gravestone and learned to sing '*Dublin's fair city, where the girls are so pretty*' from Mrs Waley, I imagined Arthur Waley as an English eccentric – just the type of person Ivan often wistfully described as his ideal: 'with adequate private means, not too much, nor too little, just enough to be independent, living in a dry thatched cottage in a leafy cul-de-sac, within an hour's drive from Oxford and London. You know the kind of picture that smells of a faint odour of over-cooked Brussels sprouts …' – and definitely not '*tatamizé*'.

'EFFORTS, EFFORTS, AND MORE EFFORTS!'

Ivan insisted that in his house the Oxford Vintage Marmalade should be served each morning in a porcelain pot. Never in its own jar. I asked, full of good sense and Japanese thrift, 'Why? It's already in a pretty jar. Wasteful, you lose some each time you transfer it from the jar to the pot.'

'It's a question of style.' Ivan replied.

'Style!'

'Yes, style,' he delivered the word so solemnly that I, still so new to the West and eager to soak up Occidental wisdom and culture, moved to the edge of my chair.

'Style requires a lot of waste and fuss and all that, and the farthest possible distance from the raw original. Naturally, when there's a famine, you can't afford it and you won't dish out the marmalade.'

I was so impressed by his comment that I have never been able to forget it.

When I arrived at Ivan's Riverside Duplex apartment in New

York, more as an upgraded house pet than a bride, his own life-style, rhythm, and rituals had long been established and smoothly running. The interior decoration struck me as a southern German Baroque church; only instead of angels and saints, here were samurai armour, screens and lacquer ware with gold inlay and paint, mostly of the gaudy Momoyama period. Several antique chess sets of equally ornate near Eastern origin filled up what little space remained unadorned. I was, therefore, quite surprised to spot a stark simple ink-and-brush calligraphy: 'Efforts, efforts, and more efforts' hanging above the writing desk in his study. The calligrapher and author was Mushakōji Saneatsu, a Taishō era novelist, little read or discussed today. At first sight this seemed an incongruous choice of a motto for someone like Ivan, a stylish bon vivant, to whom, as many believed success and good things in life came easily. This was not at all the case.

Nothing came easily to him. He had been an awkward, diffident, flat-footed slow boy and he understood quite early on that without superhuman efforts, buttressed by iron discipline, he could not succeed and might become a marginal dilettante like his father. Of all Ivan's favourite phrases, which I used to look up in the dictionary and learn by heart, the one most often repeated was 'tenacity of purpose', and this quality Ivan certainly possessed to an obsessive degree.

Take, for example, his sudden, surprising decision to start playing a Baroque recorder. During the first weeks when his playing could have turned butter rancid, I expected him to throw the instrument of torture and humiliation into the Hudson River. No, he went on and on, and during his sabbatical holiday he travelled with the music stand, notes, the recorder with all its accessories, and practised every day for two hours in every hotel room in which we stayed. Some time after I left Riverside Drive Georgia Mae Brown, Ivan's elderly black maid, who called me 'Peanut', told me that 'the doctor was playing real good'.

As a chess player, too, I don't think that Ivan was exceptionally gifted from the start, but here again like a fitness fanatic with his daily work-outs, he eked out time from his already full life in order to play as often and as regularly as he possibly could. He became a competent player and joined a small exclusive band of insomniac players in New York. Whenever his sleeping tablets did not work effectively, he rang up one of them and played on the phone in the dead of night.

Efforts, efforts and more efforts … Ivan's fluid yet taut style in writing, too, did not happen the moment he put pen or pencil to paper. I saw and heard him constantly jumping up from his chair, banging open and shutting this and that dictionary, throwing himself back onto the chair, only to dart back to the bookshelf. Mrs Brown and I were asked not to disturb him so long as his study door was shut. In fact, his fear of losing concentration was such that he had an iron rule of never opening or replying to letters except on Saturdays.

Ivan's 'efforts, efforts, and more efforts' naturally extended to me, especially when it came to my speaking English, not New York English. For this I can never be sufficiently grateful. 'Please, never say "like I said." Say "As I said", for *like* precedes a noun. Also, never "he's gotten fatter". To get is not to become.' And so on and so forth. With my congenital hearing difficulty in distinguishing R from L, he found a solution: 'When in doubt, ask me simply "Rome?" or "London?" And I'll say Rome for procrastinate, London for glint.'

I imitated his pronunciation so well that I ended up having difficulty in making myself understood by a grocer's delivery boy by saying 'to-mah-toe'. My 'for-sai-shi-ah' made Mrs Brown yell with laughter. Once at a crowded upper West-side party, I was speaking with Brendan Gill, film critic of the *New Yorker*. Halfway through our conversation he suddenly turned to Ivan and barked: 'Ivan, do something about her English. She says "*More* unique!" More Unique, hell!' The very next day Ivan brought home a new copy of Fowler's *Modern English Usage*.

DR MORRIS, D.LIT[5]

After my arrival at his Riverside Duplex apartment Ivan had engaged the tooth-pick thin and tall elderly black maid, Georgia Mae Brown, and instructed her to answer the telephone by saying: 'Dr Morris's residence.'

'People ask me, is he a 'shrink', is he a surgeon? I say what Peanut?' she asked me. I repeated to her Ivan's solemn explanation to me: 'Doctor of Literature'.

Some of Ivan's colleagues used to say to me, but not to Ivan, good-naturedly puzzled and without malice: 'I, too, have a doctorate, but I don't go about calling myself doctor.'

Mrs Brown and I couldn't understand why either, as the title of Professor seemed more than enough; but we obeyed his instruction, seeing how much the title mattered to him. Yes, Ivan did value and relish titles and credentials and worked doggedly hard to obtain distinction. On top of all his literary efforts ranging from the books of puzzles,[6] products of his sleepless nights, to his magnificent translation of Sei Shōnagon's *Pillow Book*,[7] and others,[8] as Chairman of the Department of Oriental Studies at Columbia and founder-president of the New York chapter of Amnesty International, he worked with phenomenal diligence and concentration. I believe Ivan's steel-girder self-discipline, hard work and ambition came from his life-long dread: 'If I, too, ended up being like Father!'

Ira, in Ivan's eye, represented both charmed sloth and a pointlessly hectic existence of a non-achiever. Ira had travelled the world many times and befriended many famous politicians and writers; had funded a charity in Hiroshima to help atom-bomb victims; had written a few forgotten novels in his youth; and more. But he remained a rich old American child abroad. He spoke bad French with an American accent; spent his days and nights on the telephone chatting to his cronies in Paris or its suburbs, all races and colours mixed, who liked being invited to Nesles for luncheons, plotting how to subvert the American war in Vietnam. In fact he became president of the Americans in Paris against the war in Vietnam and we, too, joined their demonstrations, Ivan muttering to himself all the while, 'Oh, how embarrassing! So embarrassing! Unmitigated torture!' and so on. After one such demonstration, the mother and son ganged up together to denounce Americans as 'Yahoos'. Their major crime was to 'over-exist and be embarrassing'. Ira chortled in good humour in agreement. Since that night the word entered the family jargon and I, who have only grateful memories of GI soldiers throwing out chewing gum, felt squeamish every time I followed them in calling Americans 'Yahoos'. I also could not help wondering why Ivan seldom told people that he had served in the American forces during the war, although he talked freely about his years at the BBC World Service (where the frequent night shifts left him a life-long and confirmed insomniac) and later at the Foreign Office.[9]

TRANSLATION COMPLEX AND FRIENDSHIP WITH YUKIO MISHIMA

I met the Mishimas in Tokyo during Ivan's sabbatical year 1969–70. I believe that Mishima had by then already determined to kill himself in a way that best suited his own life-long credo and invented personality. We often met him with several of his trusted lieutenants of his private army, the *Tatenokai* (Shield Society) at the Imperial Hotel coffee shop after their swordsmanship training. Mishima and the well-mannered young men tucked into pancakes and maple syrup. Mrs Mishima, Yoko, would join us – always bubbling with a merry laugh almost as loud and hearty as her husband's.

When Mishima point-blank asked Ivan to translate into English the Shield Society's hymn and Ivan agreed with alacrity, I was appalled. 'What would your New York Amnesty International colleagues and helpers say, Ivan? Mishima is a notorious *uyoku* (right-wing extremist).'

Ivan replied: 'He needs this nonsense. I trust him. He won't tell anyone *who* translated it.' Next, Ivan was invited to observe the Shield

Society parachuting exercise at the Japan Self-Defence Forces (SDF) airfield at Numazu. Yoko and I went to see them off at Haneda airport, from where our husbands were to be flown in an SDF aircraft. Ivan in his Burberry raincoat, with his pipe and handbag, armed with an umbrella (in lieu of his usual cane), looked comically incongruous amongst the Shield Society combatants in the Society's uniform of dark brown shirt and trousers, designed by Mishima himself. Yoko was both scathing and affectionate as she teased her husband about what she called his 'play-thing'.

During our last dinner in Tokyo, Mishima asked Ivan to translate his tetralogy, which he was about to finish: 'You, Ivan, not your younger colleagues or ex-students, OK?' Ivan laughed and gyrated his whole body so amiably, so meekly that I concluded that his answer was 'Yes'.

Only three days after the unthinkable news was broadcast all over the world about Mishima's attack on the SDF headquarters and his subsequent suicide (*seppuku*), his hand-written letter, written on the eve of his death and addressed to both of us arrived. The letter had been posted by Yoko only a few minutes before the police raided their house. In this letter and in another, addressed to Donald Keene, he repeated the request which he had made to Ivan in Tokyo, that Ivan and Donald, not others, translate his last work *The Sea of Fertility*, 'which I finished on the very day of my action. I shall never be properly understood by my own countrymen of today … And I wish to sacrifice myself for the old, beautiful tradition of Japan, which is disappearing undefended day by day.'

When Ivan and Donald decided to give the work to others to translate, I was not only disappointed, but also indignant at the behaviour of the two 'star' professors. In my very 'wet' Japanese way of thinking, even if they considered translating a hack job, inferior to their status and image, in the circumstances I felt that they ought to have fulfilled the dead man's last ardent wish. Ivan declared: 'No, I shan't do it. I told you that *As I Crossed A Bridge of Dreams*[10] would be my last translation work. From now on I shall write my own books.'

To do Ivan and Donald justice, however, they did not succumb to doing what many so-called Japanologists, who had known Mishima personally, unfortunately deigned to do: cash in on his sensational end. Some young Western journalists and academics who had enjoyed Mishima's legendary hospitality and confidence began making the rounds of publishers, equipped with letters and photographs to prove their acquaintance. Although they had probably known Mishima better and longer than most others, Donald and Ivan steadfastly refused to collaborate with the publishers who wanted from them the most lurid and scandalous details of the writer's life.

Mishima's gory death plunged Ivan into one of his worst spells of depression. This naturally affected my health, physical and mental, and I was advised by a doctor to have my hypothyroidism treated in Japan. This was to turn into a prolonged separation and then divorce. Shortly before my departure Ivan told me: 'I want to pay homage to Mishima in my own way. I have always been fascinated by the so-called '*hangan-biiki*'. Japanese do not respect, neither do they love heroes who succeed, whilst they cheer and make a cult of those who are defeated or fall midway. I want to write a historical survey of failed heroes and place Mishima at the end.'

Ivan eventually sued me for desertion, but even during our unhappy telephone conversations we often talked about what we called 'the book of heroes', which became *The Nobility of Failure*.[11]

IVAN'S *KAWAISŌ-NA* DEATH IN A VERONA HOTEL ROOM

I happened to learn of Ivan's death[12] on opening a morning paper. The cause of death was given as a heart attack. The suddenness of his death, his relative youth, with so much work left uncompleted, all these were tragic and shocking but not *kawaisō*. What makes me say '*kawaisō*' is the fact that he died alone in a hot and noisy Italian hotel room, and lay there a week pending the issue of a certificate allowing his body to be flown to Paris, presumably to his mother Edita who survived him.

Ivan, paranoiac about his insomnia, abhorred noisy places and hotels. Such places in Italy, a land where noise is joy, were high on his phobia list. I shall never forget the embarrassing experience in Siena one July when we entered and left at least eight available hotel rooms between five in the afternoon and eight in the evening, when finally, near a nervous collapse, Ivan agreed to sleep the night in the eighth, which turned out to be the noisiest of all – with a *vespa* passing under our window every second minute until dawn. The following morning, he simply turned the car round and drove back to Nesles.

Although he had tried so hard to keep every aspect of his life secret and in order, as a result of his sudden death in a foreign city he left it behind, open to inspection by every prying eye. His body was then shipped, not to New York, his home of choice; nor to London, his birth place; but to Paris, where he was never more than a passing sleepless guest at the Hotel St James et d'Albany.

When I wrote to Edita, asking if she would allow me to visit her son's grave, she replied: '...Ira, Ivan and I did not go in for religious superstitions of any kind. Hence Ira and Ivan were not "buried" anywhere. No grave exists which you or anyone can visit. Sincerely, Yours, Edita Morris.' When I read this note, I took a deep breath and murmured: 'Thank God, you left us your books!'

Editor's Note – with the advice of Dr Carmen Blacker and Professor Ian Nish:

Ivan Morris was an outstanding scholar of Japan. His work spanned both the medieval and the modern, and comprised translations of a masterly distinction as well as studies of neglected themes in literature and history.

His scholarship has been recognized by the annual prize, given in his memory over the last twenty-five years, by the British Association of Japanese Studues (BAJS). This takes the form of an essay competition open to students of Japanese who are undertaking masters' courses at British Universities.

PART 5

Photographers, Judo Masters & Journalists

25

Frederick William Sutton, 1832–83: Photograher of the Last Shogun

SEBASTIAN DOBSON

Officer's of the Royal Navy's
China Station

RECENT RESEARCH into the history of photography in Japan has done much to uncover early Western travel photographers who recorded the country in the decade before the Meiji Restoration, and their work, so long overshadowed by professional photographers such as Felice Beato, can now be appreciated as a valuable and often unique contribution to the visual record of Japan in the final years of the shogunate.

Chief Engineer Frederick William Sutton of the Royal Navy produced some important early photographs of Japanese personalities. His output during the period 1867–68 was long assumed to consist only of a pair of portraits of the last of the Tokugawa shoguns, Yoshinobu, and the lack of any other attributable work consigned him to the footnotes of photographic literature as something of a 'one-off'. Thanks to recent discoveries in private and institutional collections, a significant number of his early works have been traced and his contribution, both as an individual and as part of a wider circle of amateur photographers in the Royal Navy, can be appreciated.

EARLY CAREER

Frederick William Sutton was born on 29 August 1832, the son of a civil engineer living in Woolwich. The family apparently had no tradition of naval service, but the Royal Navy made the move from sail to steam, and a new engineering branch was added to the service in 1837. This enabled Frederick to pursue his father's profession at sea. When he joined the Royal Navy as a Third Class Assistant Engineer at the relatively advanced age of 21, Sutton entered a service still accustoming itself to the presence of relative newcomers who brought with them not only specialized technical knowledge but also the whiff of lower social rank. Some progress had been made by the Engineering Branch since its establishment in 1837, when the first engineering officers were officially ranked below carpenters, so that by the time Sutton joined their ranks in 1854, their names had just appeared alongside regular executive officers in the Navy List, and their much despised quasi-civilian uniforms had been replaced by the midnight blue of the rest of the service. Nevertheless, as an engineer, Sutton joined the navy as something of an outsider, for whereas most of his contemporaries in the Executive Branch had joined as naval cadets in their mid-teens and received their education in the service, his training had taken place in a civilian milieu (specialized training for the Engineering Branch was only made available in 1864, and a dedicated Engineering College was not established until 1880). Socially as well, Sutton was not on equal terms with the sons of gentlemen who traditionally officered the Navy, and who generally regarded engineers as 'rude mechanicals' hired simply to tend the machinery below decks. While some engineers responded by pressing for executive rank – which finally came in 1902 – most simply got on with the job and affected a snobbery of their own, 'crude in language, demons for work and not ashamed of being seen in overalls with a sweat rag round their necks, they showed little love for the young gentlemen in the gunroom'.[1]

Sutton had entered the Navy in 1854 exactly four weeks after Britain had formally declared war on Russia, and his experience of the Crimean War was in many ways symbolic of the engineer's backstage role in the Victorian Navy. Initially assigned to the troopship HMS *St. Vincent*, Sutton observed the preparations for an Anglo-French naval assault on Russia's Baltic territories, before being transferred to another troopship, HMS *Simoom*, en route for the Black Sea. From Constantinople and nearby Scutari, Sutton's ship ferried troops and supplies to the Crimea, and in May 1855, in support of the allied siege of Sebastopol, she served on the other side of the Crimean peninsular in an early commando-style raid by an Anglo-French naval squadron on Russian settlements along the coast of the Sea of Azov. When campaign medals and clasps were distributed afterwards by the British Admiralty, Sutton and most of his shipmates received no tangible acknowledgement of their war service except the Crimean campaign medal issued by the Ottoman Empire to its allies.[2] For Sutton the only discernable effect of participating in this campaign was to engender an inexplicable but almost pathological loathing of his Russian former adversaries, the strength of which, even twenty years later, would shock at least one of his contemporaries.[3]

With the return to peace-time duties in 1856, Sutton's naval career proceeded steadily, if unspectacularly. The next nine years were spent mostly in home waters on stations such as Devonport, the Humber and Sheerness with several stints of unexciting coastguard and guard duty. His assignment to HMS *Exmouth* in 1858 as an Assistant Engineer placed him under the command of Chief Engineer Robert William Drummond. Sutton developed a close friendship with his chief, as a result of which he met, and subsequently married Drummond's daughter, Georgina Margaret. In 1861, he was promoted to the rank of Engineer, and then, just over three years later, to Chief Engineer.

SURVEYING IN JAPAN

In April 1865, Sutton joined HMS *Serpent* as Chief Engineer, and an exciting new chapter began in his career. The *Serpent* had just been commissioned to join the China Station, not only as part of Britain's naval presence in the Far East, but also, as the instructions issued by the Admiralty to her captain, Commander Charles J. Bullock, read, '… you are on all occasions to avail yourself of the means placed at your disposal for increasing our knowledge of the seas and shores where you may be employed'. The means by which this survey was to be undertaken were somewhat improvised. The *Serpent* was a regular steam-powered warship which had been converted for surveying duties by the simple addition of surveying equipment, while her officers were selected not so much from candidates who had any previous experience of surveying, but rather, according to Admiralty instructions, '… from amongst those who have previously evinced some aptitude for such pursuits or who have professed their readiness and desire to acquire a proficiency in them', and Commander Bullock was commissioned to provide the necessary instruction during the four-year long voyage.[4]

Although a special scale of pay took account of the extra duties involved for all officers of HMS *Serpent*, it proved exhausting work, especially since Bullock found himself short-staffed for the first half of the voyage. In February 1867, after fifteen months of surveying the coasts of Taiwan, China and Western Japan, Bullock reported in exasperation to his chief that, despite having assigned one his sub-lieutenants to the position of ship's Master (or Navigating Lieutenant, as the position was renamed later that year), this measure '... simply leaves the duties of an important office unprovided for, or to be divided amongst others who have already (in our special case) a considerable addition to their ordinary duties... For my own part, I shall be glad to be relieved of the extra night duty it has always entailed, and which I have found to be a very burdensome tax on my energies.'[5] Bullock also requested that the ship be assigned an assistant surveyor, 'the absence of such throws upon the Commanding Officer duties of detail which are those of subordinate Officers, infringing on his time, depriving him of necessary leisure, and rendering the conduct of a survey only endurable as a duty, as well as being the cause of a considerable portion of the work constantly falling into arrears.'

Until the Admiralty finally assigned Bullock an extra officer – but no assistant surveyor – in July 1867, the officers of HMS *Serpent* continued to be hard-pressed as the survey continued along the west and north-west coast of Japan, given greater urgency by the impending opening of the port of Hyogo to foreign trade on New Year's Day 1868 and the search for another port which could be opened simultaneously. Even in the engine room, it seems, Sutton was not exempt from the multi-tasking expected from the officers of HMS *Serpent*. While the vessel was anchored off Osaka in May 1867, British negotiations with the Shogun's representatives that month determined the location of foreign settlements at Hyogo and Osaka, and, as the *North China Herald* noted later that same month, 'Captain (sic) Sutton has been surveying the harbours of Osaka and Hiogo and the foreign quarters on shore, of all of which he has made good plans.'[6]

In addition to surveying the new treaty ports, Bullock could report by mid-July that his survey of the northwest coast of Japan was complete and that 'I have [also] taken every opportunity of correcting and improving the coast line of the Japanese Chart, which forms the basis of the present Admiralty Chart.'[7] The surveying continued into the following year, with the selection of possible sites for lighthouse construction. In June 1868, after almost two years surveying the Japanese coast, the *Serpent* left Nagasaki for Hong Kong, and the final stage of her voyage, which involved a survey of the Dutch East Indies in connection with a proposed submarine telegraph link between Australia and Java.[8]

PORTRAITS AND LANDSCAPES

Surveying involved not only the improvement of Admiralty charts but also a significant measure of diplomatic interaction. In July and early August 1866, the *Serpent* was part of the naval escort, which accompanied Sir Harry Parkes on unofficial visits to the western domains of Satsuma and Uwajima. As Parkes wrote afterwards to Admiral King, the commander-in-chief of the China Station:

> … the favourable impressions which I believe we are leaving at both of these places are mainly attributable to the kind manner in which at the cost of considerable inconvenience to yourself, your officers and men, you have endeavoured to meet every wish on behalf of the Princes and their officers for exhibition of your practice and drill, and have satisfied the curiosity and admiration of the people by allowing them the freest access to the ships.[9]

The exchange of gifts was also part of the process. Admiral King gave white ensigns to both princes, but perhaps the most lasting and symbolic gift to the Satsuma daimyo was a commemorative portrait photograph he had taken in Kagoshima together with the young prince when he visited HMS *Princess Royal* on 28 July.[10] The resulting print, taken by an amateur photographer serving on King's flagship, Lieutenant Lord Walter Kerr, enjoyed a wide circulation.[11] It was subsequently issued by the Yokohama-based photographer Felice Beato in the accessible *carte-de-visite* format, and if there was a symbol that Britain and Satsuma had reconciled their differences since British warships had bombarded the domain capital less than three years before, it was this portrait of Shimazu Tadayoshi photographed sitting next to the commander-in-chief of the British naval squadron in Japan, with his senior councillor and negotiator, Komatsu Tatewaki, in attendance.

Following Parkes' recommendation that '… visits of the same friendly character … are eminently calculated to promote the abandonment by the Japanese nobility of their old exclusiveness', King continued this informal diplomacy with visits by his naval escort to the domains of Chikuzen and Chōshū in late January and early February of the following year.[12] Kerr was again commissioned to take commemorative portraits of princes and councillors of both domains on board HMS *Princess Royal*, including one of the commander-in-chief seated between the Choshu daimyo, Mori Takachika, and his son, Motonori.[13]

Sutton was also an enthusiastic amateur photographer with a camera of his own, but there is no evidence to show that he used it – or was asked to use it – before HMS *Serpent* began its survey of Osaka Bay in April 1867. It was then that Sutton received a commission, which eclipsed even that of 'Kerr: a portrait of the Shogun'.

Towards the end of April, Sir Harry Parkes made a formal visit to Osaka, where he was received in audience by Shogun Yoshinobu. After a preliminary meeting at Osaka castle on 29 April, a more formal audience was held two days later, at which the captains of the Royal Navy vessels in Osaka Bay were presented to the shogun. Sutton was also present, and was invited to take portraits of Yoshinobu. An officer in Parkes' military escort later described the sitting: .

> The Tycoon was splendidly and becomingly dressed, with perhaps the exception of the state cap, which was a most peculiar shape, made of paper, it rested on the very summit of his head, and was kept in its position by strings, which fastened under his chin. His outer robe was of rich white silk, ornamented with medallions in mauve colour, and his stockings also white silk ... After the ceremony of presentation was over, the Tycoon retired, but shortly reappeared in another dress, consisting of a black silk jacket, or hào, trousers of dark blue silk with a gold pattern running through, and a rich obé, or belt, in which a handsome short sword was thrust. In both dresses he was photographed by Mr. Sutton.[14]

Yoshinobu showed a polite interest in the proceedings, leaving his English guests unaware that this was by no means his first encounter with photography. As early as 1849, his father Tokugawa Nariaki, lord of the Mito domain, had conducted a learned correspondence with his fellow daimyo and scientific enthusiast, Shimazu Nariakira of the Satsuma clan, in which the properties of the 'reflection-printing mirror' – as the daguerreotype was elegantly rendered into Japanese by clan scholars – and the latter's own initial researches into photography were discussed. Another relative, Tokugawa Yoshikatsu, head of the Owari branch of the family (one of the three Tokugawa families from which the shogun could be selected) and coincidentally another correspondent of Shimazu Nariakira's, had begun studying photography in 1858 after being placed under administrative exile at his Edo residence. Until he was officially pardoned two years later, Yoshikatsu took advantage of his isolation to conduct research and experiments, with the assistance of clan scholars and contemporaries such as Shimazu. A series of surviving glass-plate views from the ensuing Bunkyu era (1861–64) which he took of his castle at Nagoya, the clan residence in Edo, and even Hiroshima during his command of a military expedition by the shogun's administration to the area in 1864, indicate that Yoshikatsu maintained his interest in photography after he returned to political life. Yoshinobu was most likely aware of his cousin's photographic activities, and the presence in the archives of the Tokugawa family of earlier portraits of both Yoshinobu and his younger brother Akitake, which appear to have been taken in Kyoto before the former's nomination as shogun, suggests that this sitting before Sutton's camera was not even the first occasion that Yoshinobu had been photographed. Nevertheless, this was the first occasion that the shogun had been photographed by a Westerner, and Yoshinobu gratefully accepted copies of Sutton's photographs, which still remain in the archives of the Tokugawa family.

The last shogun, Yoshinobu

Outside Osaka, Sutton's portraits would prove something of a latter-day scoop, for, through the simple process of capturing Yoshinobu's likeness on collodion-treated glass, he had removed the shogun from his lofty obscurity, and created a symbol of how the barriers between Japan and the Western world were being broken down. *The Illustrated London News* reproduced the portrait of Yoshinobu in full court dress as a woodcut engraving in its issue of 10 August, introducing the new shogun to its readers as a 'handsome and able man, in his thirty-second year'. In Yokohama, Beato re-issued both portraits as hand-coloured *cartes-de-visite*, with his studio colourists faithfully reproducing the opulent hues of the shogun's court dress and the more subdued tones of his 'usual costume', and whereas Kerr's portraits had largely been uncredited, most surviving examples of Beato's *carte-de-visite* copies bore a handwritten inscription identifying the photographer as 'F.W. Sutton CERN', (Chief Engineer Royal Navy).[15]

Sutton succeeded in taking these portraits despite losing some of his lenses and chemicals when the boat carrying them ashore was accidentally upset.[16] The results were good, but for want of a larger lens, Sutton was obliged to take his portraits in a small format. This did not deter him, however, from taking other photographs in Osaka. An album in the Musée Guimet in Paris contains no fewer than 16 views taken by Sutton of Osaka Castle and other sites visited by Parkes and his suite during their two-day visit.[17] Although these views were not reproduced in *The Illustrated London News*, or distributed by Beato as *cartes-de-visite*, Sutton, apparently aware of their commercial possibilities, sent a selection to the British topographical photographer and photographic publisher, Francis Frith, who issued several of them as part of his extremely popular series of world views. Thanks to Sutton, Osaka was opened to the Victorian armchair traveller even before it was officially opened to foreign trade.

Despite the return to surveying duties for the remainder of the year, Sutton performed one more photographic coup during HMS *Serpent's* survey of the northern coast of Japan. Arriving at Hakodate on 7 July, Sutton took advantage of a four-day stay in the town to photograph Hokkaido's aboriginal inhabitants, the Ainu.[18] Although still in the course of development as an open port, Hakodate was no photographic backwater: photographers had been visiting the town since 1854, and by the time Sutton arrived there in 1867, at least two Japanese photographers, Kizu Kokichi and Tamoto Kenzo, were operating commercial studios. Surprisingly, however, no identifiable photographic likenesses of Ainu taken before July 1867 have ever been found, and Sutton's two portraits of a group of male Ainu represent the first photographic record known to have been taken of this camera-shy people. For Beato, these two examples of earlier ethnological portraiture represented the second opportunity that Sutton had given him that year to expand his portfolio, and both portraits soon made their appearance among the 'Native Types' that featured in the albums issued by Beato's Yokohama studio.

* * *

Sutton accompanied Parkes again, this time on an official visit to Kyoto on 21 March 1868. While the British diplomatic party and its 70–strong escort were quartered in Chionin temple, Sutton busied himself taking photographs of their temporary lodgings and Japanese escort, and took advantage of the commanding view, which the temple gave over the imperial city, to take a panorama of Kyoto.[19] Sutton's stay in Kyoto was overshadowed by other events. As Parkes set out for an audience at the Imperial Palace on the afternoon of 23 March, two anti-foreign swordsmen attacked his party and ran down the line hacking wildly. One of the assailants was immediately decapitated by Goto Shojiro, while the other, a Buddhist priest called Saegusa Shigeru, was soon overpowered after being shot in the jaw and placed under arrest. If Sutton had entertained hopes of having a sitting with the Emperor Meiji during Parkes' audience, as had been the case with the shogun in Osaka, he was to be disappointed, and instead the only notable portraits which he took in Kyoto were of the injured Saegusa and his accomplice Murata Teiken, whose head had been retrieved as a trophy and placed in a bucket. Saegusa was an unpromising sitter - almost less so than Murata - but photographing him in the final hours before his execution on 27 March, Sutton succeeded in capturing something of the dejection and hostility of this would-be assassin.[20]

Following the Meiji Restoration, the imperial court showed an increased awareness of the problems, which the new medium of photography brought to their efforts to control the image of the emperor. In January 1872, the Austrian photographer Baron von Stillfried illicitly took a portrait of the Emperor Meiji in Yokosuka, going to elaborate lengths to hide on board a coaling vessel, which was being used to demonstrate to the imperial party the operation of the newly constructed dry dock. The image was quickly suppressed, and the court reluctantly acknowledged the need for an official portrait of the Emperor Meiji by arranging a sitting with the Japanese photographer Uchida Kuichi a few weeks afterwards.[21] In time, an elaborate ceremonial would grow around the imperial portrait - until after the Pacific War, it was customary when developing a photograph of the emperor to use water which had been consecrated according to Shinto purification rites and drawn from a well festooned with *shimenawa*, the folded, hand-made paper streamers normally seen at shrine gates and altars. In 1868, there may have been less self-consciousness, or indeed awareness, with regard to photographing the 'true reflection' of the imperial visage.

THE CHINA STATION PHOTOGRAPHERS

There is a tendency to imagine amateur photographers like Sutton and Kerr working in isolation, partly because they were serving on different vessels, and partly because the work so far attributed to them differs significantly in terms of location and subject matter. The only point they seem to have in common is that the most remarkable examples of their work, Kerr's portraits of Admiral King with Japanese daimyo and those which Sutton took of Shogun Yoshinobu, were reproduced, if not pirated, at the time by Beato and subsequently reproduced in Elmhirst and Jephson's 1869 publication, *Our Life in Japan*. There can be little doubt, however, that Sutton and Kerr were aware of one another's interest in photography. On the occasions that Kerr took his commemorative photographs while the *Princess Royal* was anchored in Kagoshima, Uwajima, Fukuoka and Mitajiri, Sutton's vessel, HMS *Serpent,* was also present as part of the naval escort. Although Sutton might have been unaware that Kerr was taking photographs on board Admiral King's flagship, the fact that Kerr is also known to have taken photographs inside the Satsuma palace at Kagoshima during Parkes' visit there in late July 1866 makes this less likely, especially since all members of the British envoy's naval escort enjoyed this generous Satsuma hospitality.[22] Mutual awareness, of course, does not imply collaboration, and it is all too easy to imagine the young, aristocratic lieutenant and the middle-aged, middle-class chief engineer having little in common beyond an interest in photography.

Nevertheless, there is compelling evidence that Sutton and Kerr were part of an informal circle of amateur photographers that existed among officers of the Royal Navy's China Station. Three years ago, the Royal Photographic Society acquired an album of over 100 original photographs, the majority of which were taken in Japan and China during the period 1866–69.[23] The contemporary captions, which accompanied the photographs, and several of the photographs themselves, immediately suggested a strong naval connection, and in a few instances, the names of two vessels on the China Station, HMS *Pelorus* and *Princess Royal* appeared. In one instance, a view of Hyogo was attributed in a contemporary hand to Lord Walter Kerr, while several views of Osaka either precisely matched or closely resembled photographs known to have been taken by Sutton during Parkes' visit there in May 1867. Even more intriguingly, 11 photographs, all of Japanese subjects, bore the initials 'HLP'. A search through contemporary issues of the Navy List revealed three officers with those initials, only one of whom, Lieutenant Hugo Lewis Pearson, was listed as serving in the Far East during the time these photographs were taken and his ship proved to be HMS *Pelorus*. The album contained further revelations, in particular an informally-posed photograph taken in an unspecified Japanese location of two Westerners apparently preparing glass plate negatives, with a camera, portable darkroom tent and other photographic apparatus at hand, the inscription below reading 'Photographers at "Tiffin" (Thermom[eter] in shade 98 degrees).' Comparing the figures in the photograph with a later portrait of Pearson revealed that he was one of these amateur photographers, but the identity of the other remains unclear. Interestingly, there is some resemblance between this bewhiskered figure and a caricature of Kerr published almost thirty-five years later in *Vanity Fair*, but even if this second photographer can be positively identified, the question remains of who was the unseen third photographer who took this informal group. Could it be Sutton?

The album in the Royal Photographic Society, therefore, suggested that Sutton, Pearson and Kerr worked together, or at least exchanged examples of their work. Sutton's connection with Lieutenant Pearson appears even stronger when one examines the 22 extant views of China, Java and Japan held in the Francis Frith Archive at the Victoria and Albert Museum, all of which are duplicated in the Royal Photographic Society album, and in addition to the matches with Sutton's Osaka portfolio mentioned earlier, an even greater number of Frith's Japanese views can now be attributed to Pearson.[24] Evidently, both photographers had seen the commercial advantages of syndicating their work through the most important photographic publisher of the day.

Another source of distribution, which all three photographers shared, was Felice Beato. There is some evidence to suggest that Beato assiduously cultivated officers of the Royal Navy, and especially those with an interest in photography. Some views taken by Beato inside the treaty limits near Yokohama show Westerners with the distinctive cuff rings of British naval officers on their jacket sleeves, and a number of the views in the Royal Photographic Society attributed to Lieutenant Pearson raise intriguing questions about the extent to which Beato used the work of naval photographers to augment his portfolio. We know of one instance in 1865 where Beato came to an arrangement with Henry F. Woods, Master of the gunboat HMS *Kestrel*, whereby he loaned Woods his 'portable dark-room and all the necessary gear and chemicals' for a trip to Edo, on condition that he handed over the glass plate negatives of any photographs he was able to take.[25] Although Beato was quite adept at occasionally wheedling himself and his camera onto various diplomatic and naval missions to parts of Japan otherwise inaccessible to Westerners, he was still based for most of the time in Yokohama, and he probably saw that there was an opportunity to expand his stock by supporting and exploiting the efforts of amateur photographers whose duties as Royal Navy officers took them beyond the regular treaty limits.

SUTTON'S LATER CAREER

HMS *Serpent* finally returned to England for good in August 1869, and after a well deserved eight-week leave, Sutton was transferred to service with the Naval Reserve. In July 1873, Sutton returned to Japan as a member of the British naval training mission headed by Lieutenant-Commander Archibald Douglas. Based at the Imperial Naval College at Tsukiji, in Tokyo, the mission began formal instruction in January 1874, with the cadets divided into four classes. Sutton, assisted by Engineers Thomas S. Gissing and William J. Harding, took charge of the engineering class, but found that he had perhaps the most burdensome assignment. An examination sat by the cadets quickly revealed 'their utter ignorance of the most elementary marine engineering subjects', and, following Sutton's advice, a branch school for the engineering class was opened at Yokosuka in May.[26] Sutton was based in Yokosuka and given the title of 'head of the steam department' with what was essentially a roving commission in the recently constructed Naval Arsenal. He reported regularly to Commander Douglas in Tokyo, and the official diary he submitted reveals the zeal with which he threw himself into his task:

> Make arrangements to place four students in steam hammer shops, four in the foundry, and five in the fitting, turning and erecting shops. Tomorrow at 8.30am [8 June 1874], I shall commence the practical instruction in dockyard. I am not yet able to establish a satisfactory routine, but I have written out the following instructions for the ensuing week, viz.: Hours of attendance, 81/2 daily ... Saturdays and Sundays to be holidays. 7am to 11.30am, instruction in workshop; 1pm to 5pm, instruction in class room ... I cannot establish a fixed course of instruction until I have had at least a week's experience with students on the dockyard, but I hope to be able to do so about the end of the week, and will bring it over myself to Tokyo for your inspection and approval.[27]

Sutton duly completed the training schedule for naval engineers, but possibly as a result of his exertions, he fell ill, and exactly one month after beginning his work at Yokosuka dockyard, he was granted sick leave by the Japanese authorities, and spent part of the summer recuperating in Nikko. Sutton happily settled into his new life. Visitors from the survey vessel HMS *Challenger* in April 1875 found him established in a house ('a thoroughly Japanese one, of the better sort ... formerly occupied by the head Buddhist priest of the capital') near the naval college at Shiba, and according to Sub-Lieutenant Herbert Swire 'he speaks the language, likes the country thoroughly and is a first-rate photographer, so that he never finds the time hangs heavily on his hands'.[28] In addition to his half pay from the Royal Navy, and a generous salary from the Japanese Government, Sutton had the benefit of an annual three-month holiday: '... during this vacation Sutton tramps about the country on foot with his photographic apparatus in a "jinrikisha", and living on Japanese grub and in Japanese style, and thoroughly enjoys himself'. Sadly, these photographs have never been found, but, according to Swire, Sutton's eye for unusual subject matter seems to have remained undiminished:

> In the courtyard of the temple which stands on the top of the rising ground of Shiba, are two slabs of stone bearing a very

> remarkable series of carved figures representing the development of plants and animals from the lowest organisms, and bringing them up in an unbroken chain, to man. These stones have been in their present position for many hundreds of years, and are said to have been examined with interest by Mr. Darwin when he visited Japan. Thus this grand theory of Development of Species, which captivates and convinces all who throw aside superstition and set to work, in an impartial spirit, to examine it, is, after all, not a product of the science of our own times, at least not altogether. I, for one, was much disappointed to find here the very idea, the very sap of the whole scheme, depicted in a carving several hundreds of years old. Sutton is going to take large photographs of the two stones, which, I believe, have not yet been taken, strange to say; they will be most interesting pictures to men of science.[29]

Following the renewal of his contact in July 1876, Sutton was joined by his family. Sutton's three daughters established a friendship with the young diarist Clara Whitney, and, until their return to England in May 1879, the Suttons frequently appear in her diary, which remains one of the main primary sources for scholars of the Tokyo foreign community in the first two decades of the Meiji period.

In his essay on Sutton, the photo-historian Ishiguro Keisho quotes with some disappointment an entry in Clara Whitney's diary describing a visit to Sutton's house on 1 April 1878, which left her seething with disapproval. Evidently in expansive mood, Sutton bragged at length about the security of his position at the Naval College, and how even the Navy Minister was powerless without Sutton's assistance. A typically boastful Englishman was Clara's verdict. Certainly Sutton felt confident that his services would still be required by his Japanese employers, and in January of that year had allowed a deadline set by the Admiralty for his return to British service to expire, thereby automatically placing himself on the retired list at the age of 45. One suspects, however, that the date of Clara's meeting with Sutton is more significant than the gist of the conversation she describes, and that in fact the rather earnest New England teenager was the victim of a leg-pull on Sutton's part. Less than two weeks before, Clara had been describing a tea party at Sutton's house where his constant stream of jokes had his guests helpless with laughter, including Clara herself.[30]

Through Clara's diary, a picture emerges of the Suttons enjoying a comfortable life in Tokyo, hosting regular tea parties and tennis parties at their home, and Sutton himself happily confirmed as a typical

Victorian paterfamilias with the birth of a second son in the autumn of 1878. This idyll proved short-lived. In February of the following year, Sutton suffered what appears to have been a nervous collapse, and for a time lay paralyzed in his bed, unable to recognize even his own wife.[31] In April, his contract with the Japanese Navy Ministry, which had been due to expire in July, was abruptly terminated. On 19 May 1879, after he had received an audience from the Meiji Emperor, Sutton and his family left Yokohama for England.

Sutton was not to enjoy his retirement for long. His health appears to have steadily failed, despite the family's moving from London to Weston-super-Mare after 1881. 'Cerebral Softening … Enlargement of Heart and General Dropsy with Disease of Lungs and Kidneys' was the final diagnosis, and Sutton died on 28 January 1883.

Japan left a positive impression on Sutton, so much so that his youngest daughter, born shortly after the family returned to England, was christened with the Japanese name Ume, and his final home was likewise christened 'Nihon'. Like many visitors to Japan in the nineteenth century, he had been fascinated by the country, and even returned to play a role in its modernization, but it fell to few to contribute to such an extent to the visual record of Japan on the eve of the Meiji Restoration.

26

Herbert George Ponting, 1870–1935: Photographer, Explorer, Inventor

TERRY BENNETT

Herbert George Ponting

Mount Fuji by G. Ponting

AT THE BEGINNING of the twentieth century, *The Japan Times* reviewed the work of an English photographer who had taken pictures of Mount Fuji:

> It would be scarcely an exaggeration to say that Mr. Ponting has discovered a new mountain; for no one has ever seen the great quiescent volcano depicted from so many points before, except, indeed, from the pencil of Hokusai. But then, this great painter gave representations that were half true, half fanciful, whereas the pictures before us are pure and unadulterated truth.

These remarkable photographs represent Ponting's best work in Japan, and can be found reproduced in his delightful books: *In Lotus-Land Japan* and *Fujisan*.

Ponting at his best was one of the most technically and artistically competent photographers in the history of the medium. From the advent of photography in Japan until the end of the Meiji period, he is the best British photographer to have worked in that country. Few others have equalled the quality of work produced by this energetic, restless and ultimately tragic figure.

Ponting was a perfectionist, determined to obtain the best results wherever in the world he was working. That he was not easily satisfied can be seen in his account in *In Lotus Land Japan* of how he tried to capture a particular view of Fuji. He was particularly taken by a winter's view of the mountain near Lake Motosu. He wanted to illustrate a cloudless Fuji through shoots of Kaia grass in the foreground. It was a pre-requisite that the grass be completely still, in order to avoid the inevitable blurred image. In achieving the perfect combination of a cloudless and windless moment, he had to tramp back and forth to the nearby village of Nakano-kura-toge, a distance of some fourteen miles. It required more than a dozen journeys before the now world-famous photograph of 'Fuji and the Kaia grass' could be taken to his satisfaction.

Ponting worked tirelessly to illustrate a mountain for which he had genuine and deep affection; he photographed it in all seasons, circling the base on a number of occasions in order to obtain the desired views, and taking views from the summit, which he reached twice. In *In Lotus land Japan* he declared:

> Every hour of every clear day the mountain was a different picture. There was Morning Fuji, shaking off mists of night; the Midday Fuji, with a belt of cumulus cloud floating across its waist; the Sundown Fuji, a symphony of pink and violet; and a hundred other phases, for the mountain is never twice alike.

And in experiencing sunset from the summit he wrote:

> ... When the sun sank to the level of the surging vapours, flooding their waves and hollows with ever-changing contrasts of light and shade, the scene was of indescribable beauty. Never in any part of the world have I seen such a spectacle so replete with awesome majesty as the sunset I witnessed that evening from the topmost cubic foot of Fuji.

In stark contrast, Ponting gave a graphic account of how potentially dangerous a place Fuji could be. He described his first journey to the summit accompanied by a Japanese friend and four mountain guides. Between them they had the dubious privilege of carrying Ponting's 80lbs weight of photographic equipment including a dark-tent, supply of glass plates and enough food and clothing to facilitate a stay for up to a week on the summit, if that was how long it needed in order to capture the best views.

On arrival at the summit the party was caught in a severe storm and involuntarily marooned for several days. During a brief lull, Ponting ventured alone to the highest point of Fuji, Ken-ga-mine, to witness the sunset. Just as he was about to negotiate the half-mile return journey to the rest-hut he was suddenly enveloped in swirling mists, darkness and a howling icy wind which '... moaned and whistled among the crags which loomed like ominous moving phantoms in the turbulent vapours and dying light ...' He was completely disoriented and groped his way along a perilous path, almost falling over a precipice. After shouting for some time, he was eventually rescued by one of the guides.

PONTING'S EARLY LIFE

Ponting was born in Salisbury on 21 March 1870. One of eight children, he appears to have had a reasonably happy childhood. Certainly it was comfortable, since the family lived in large houses in London, Watford, Ilkley and Southport and employed several maids and servants. Herbert had an adequate, if not exceptional education – initially at Carlisle and Preston grammar schools, and then at Wellington House College, Leyland. Leaving at 18 he attempted to follow in the footsteps of his father's successful banking career, but after four years he had had enough and set off for California with the advantage of generous financial support from his father.

Ponting had great affection for his parents, and wrote and visited them whenever he could. He stayed close to them until his mother's death in 1919 and his father's fatal illness in 1923.

His father's financial support was sufficient for Ponting to purchase a fruit farm in Auburn, California, as well as to speculate with others in local gold-mining enterprises. In June 1895 he married a local girl, Mary Elliott, who came from a successful and prominent local family, and bore him a daughter, Mildred, in January 1897.

The fruit farm was soon in financial difficulties and the gold mining ultimately proved unsuccessful. It seems that Ponting had little talent for business - having no lasting commercial success throughout his career. Late in 1898, he took his American wife and child to London where a son, Dick, was born in March 1899. Ponting who was restless returned to the United States with his family a few months later and lived in Sausalito, San Francisco.

Ponting took up photography seriously in 1900. It is not clear what induced him to do so. He became fascinated and obsessed with stereoscopic photography.[1]

A chance encounter with a visiting professional photographer changed the course of Ponting's life. The photographer was on a temporary assignment, taking photographs illustrating Ponting's local area. He sought Herbert's opinion of the best locations and the professional was impressed with the would-be photographer's intuitive understanding and 'photographic eye'. When Ponting later showed some of his own work, the professional encouraged him to enter some competitions and, crucially, to submit his work to a certain company specialising in the production of stereographic pictures. This advice was followed with spectacular results. Not only was Ponting successful in a number of competitions - including having one photograph entitled 'Mules at a Californian Round-Up' displayed as a centre-piece at the World's Fair in St Louis - he also secured the patronage of the stereographic company which started buying up a number of his negatives. They also invited him on an 'all expenses paid' trip to New York to discuss future cooperation.

Lucrative commissions to photograph throughout the world followed and Ponting spent a frenetic decade globe-trotting during which he became one of the best-known and most famous photographers in the world.

PONTING'S CREATIVE YEARS (1901–12)

Ponting received his first commission in 1901 when the American journal *Leslie's Weekly* and the Universal Photo Art Co. of Philadelphia sent him on a tour of the Far East. Unfortunately, very little is known about his movements during this time and it is difficult to determine the chronology of his subsequent assignments in Europe and North America. Ponting does not seem to have kept a diary, and other sources are sparse.[2]

Ponting said that he spent three years in Japan. This would seem to cover the period 1902–5, which included his attachment to the First Japanese Army in Manchuria, during the 1904–5 Russo-Japanese War. He photographed in Korea and Manchuria in 1902 or 1903, and was working in China, India and Russia in 1906–7. It is also known that he was taking pictures of mountain scenery in Switzerland and France in 1908. At the very height of his fame in 1909 he received the great distinction of being asked by Captain Scott to become the official photographer to the 1910–13 Expedition to the Antarctic. Ponting is more widely known for his work during this ill-fated mission to the South Pole than he is for his work in Japan or elsewhere (see below).

PONTING IN JAPAN: NAGASAKI TO HOKKAIDO

Ponting travelled all over Japan in search of the unusual or the exotic. In *In Lotus Land Japan*, he describes trips to Kyoto, Nara, Nikko,

Nagasaki, Matsushima, Kamakura, Lake Hakone, the Inland Sea and Hokkaido. Photographing everywhere he went, Ponting emerges as an intelligent and sympathetic observer of Japanese life and customs. He seems to have acquired a basic level of conversational Japanese, a more than passing interest in the country's history, and a deep appreciation of Japanese arts and handicraft. His friendship with resident experts such as Basil Hall Chamberlain and Professor Edwin Emerson would certainly have helped.

Whilst in Kyoto Ponting went out of his way to visit, and photograph expert exponents in the arts of bronze-work, silk embroidery, pottery and sword manufacture and design. He became quite knowledgeable in this latter field and wrote eruditely on the subject for *Country Life*. He established good relations with members of the Japanese aristocracy and military and political leaders. This enabled him to view the personal collections of both Baron Terauchi and Ito Hirobumi – the latter inviting Ponting to his country house at Oiso where sword racks covered the walls and hundreds of books on Japanese swords were on display.

In Hokkaido to see the Ainu, experienced traveller though he was, he was nevertheless taken aback by the sounds emitted by the volcano of Noboribetsu. Looking over the edge he declared: '… it breathed a deep sigh, and then let out a wailing shriek, as if some subterranean demon were in agony. I have seen many volcanoes … in several lands, but never any other that emitted such truly horrible sounds …'

Ponting had a more dangerous encounter with another volcano – Asama-yama (in Nagano prefecture near Karuizawa). Ignoring local advice, he and a friend were looking over the edge into the cavity below when it erupted. The pair just had time to jump backwards as a stream of debris was propelled into the air, accompanied by an ear-splitting roar. Ponting and his companion fully expected to be buried beneath the falling stones and rocks but, fortunately, the strong wind ensured that the contents of the mountain were directed some distance away.

Ponting liked Japan and the Japanese. He seemed totally intoxicated by the fairer sex - affording them a whole chapter of *In Lotus Land Japan*. Ainu women, however, did not seem to get quite the same Ponting seal of approval:.

> The lot of the Ainu woman is not a happy one … dirty, slovenly, barefoot … disfigured by tattoo-marks … a wretched drudge, to whom life holds out none of the pleasures and diversions known to women of other parts of Japan. But in common with her sex the world over, she loves jewellery...she loves to adorn her scanty attractions with rings, sometimes on her fingers, sometimes in her ears.

Nevertheless, Ponting was seldom uncharitable, and finished: 'And yet she has charms - that I had almost overlooked: she is gentle and submissive as a child, and her voice is low and musical.'

PONTING AND HIS FAMILY

Ponting was in great demand and constantly travelling. His long absences from his wife and young children, however, must have put a great strain on his marriage. In either 1905 or 1906, he returned home to Berkeley and apparently informed Mary that he felt the responsibilities of marriage were holding back his artistic career. This seemingly cold, indifferent approach to his family does appear to be inconsistent with his sentimental, and generally pleasant personality. The facts, however, are that he never saw his wife again. He refused her subsequent request for a divorce (possibly because he feared the financial consequences), and specifically excluded her from his will, stating: 'I declare that in no circumstances is my wife, whom I have not seen for upwards of thirty years, to receive any benefit from my estate.' Ponting's father did not approve of his son's behaviour to his wife and supported Mary both morally and financially.

Whilst Ponting, an excellent conversationalist, had many friends and acquaintances, he seemed to be incapable of forming long and deep relationships and rarely took anyone into his confidence. He was a loner. In 1910, just before going to the South Pole, he sent a message to his children, who were in Europe at the time, to meet him in London because he wanted to say goodbye. They came, as arranged, only to find their father absent and a note saying that he decided not to meet them because he feared he would be weakened in his resolve to go with the Expedition.

THE ANTARCTIC EXPEDITION

The photographs taken of the Antarctic by Ponting are considered to be unsurpassed by any photographer of any expedition, before or since. They certainly represent the crowning achievement of Ponting's life, and sealed his reputation for all time as one of the world's great photographers. Ironically, however, his obsession with ensuring their wider distribution and recognition was to cost him his health and financial security.

On being selected for the expedition Ponting made typically meticulous preparations to ensure that the expedition would have comprehensive photographic coverage in still and movie form. He was not too familiar with the latter medium, and turned to an expert in the field, Arthur Newman. Numerous hours of practice and experimentation were required until Ponting was satisfied with his own results.

On the 1910 voyage of the *Terra Nova* from New Zealand to the Antarctic, Ponting suffered badly from sea-sickness, but refused to allow this to interfere with his work. When a storm caused flooding on board the ship, and there was danger of its sinking, Ponting seemed far more interested in protecting and safeguarding the photographic apparatus and materials.

His obsession, if not bravery, was soon all too evident to the crew once the ship encountered ice. Ponting wanted movie coverage of the prow of the ship breaking through the ice floes. To achieve this, Ponting clung perilously to wooden planks that were extended from the starboard side of the ship, which also contained his necessary equipment. Somehow, holding his camera with one arm and turning its handle with the other, he was able to take pictures of the ship breaking through the floes by leaning out under the overhanging prow and trying not to lose his balance. The results were spectacular and represented some of the most thrilling movie film of the whole expedition.

During January 1911 it was necessary to build the expedition's hut at Cape Evans. Scott excused Ponting from the tedium of unloading supplies and work associated with the hut's construction. Although the plan was to allow Ponting freedom to devote all his energy to photography, this appears to have caused resentment amongst other members of the party who thought he was not doing his share of the hard work. This may have been one of the reasons why Ponting was not thought to have been 'one of the team'. Whether this bothered him or not is unclear, but Ponting seemed only really concerned about maximising his photographic output during the fine weather before the onset of the winter on 22 April 1911. His darkroom had to be prepared in the hut itself and Ponting would often work while his companions were asleep in order to maximise the hours of daylight.

At this time, Ponting took such ultimately famous pictures as 'The Death of an Iceberg' and 'A Grotto in an Iceberg'. He was becoming increasingly excited by the results he was getting - although sometimes obtained at great personal risk. On one occasion the ice on which he was standing was attacked by killer whales, which attempted to break it. Probably his worst experience happened when he was pulling his sledge and equipment alone across the ice in search of icebergs. Suddenly, he felt the ice beneath his feet begin to sink. Aware that the extreme weight of the sledge was the probable cause, and that he was harnessed to it, he considered slipping out of the harness to save himself at the expense of his equipment. Although the ice continued to sink as he moved forward, and the water was rising above his boots, he decided that he would not desert his equipment: he would save himself and his equipment, or they would go down together. He describes what happened next: .

> Though the ice sank under my feet, it did not break; but each step I expected to be my last. The sledge, dragging through the slush, became like lead; and as the water rose above my boots, I was unable to pull it further. Just then … I felt my feet touch firm ice … I got on to it, and managed to drag the sledge on to it too; then I collapsed … it was quite a long time before my trembling muscles ceased to quake.

Once the winter arrived Ponting was, like the rest of the party, confined to quarters - although he did manage to take some flashlight photography. Otherwise he joined in the series of talks and lectures. One of the talks and slide shows he gave was of his time in Japan, and this was received enthusiastically. Ponting seems to have got on reasonably well with the rest of the party at this time and survived the long winter months despite the occasional bouts of depression and the fact that he was temperamentally less well suited to the conditions than the others.

At the end of October 1911, Scott and the other members of the polar party set off on the fateful journey from which they would not return. Ponting went with them for a few miles to capture the departure on film, but then returned, as planned, to carry out an intense programme of photography around Cape Evans and Cape Royds. This continued until March 1912 when he left for New Zealand in the *Terra Nova*.

SUBSEQUENT CAREER

Ponting was unable to exploit his Antarctic photography commercially to any great extent. There were many reasons for this – amongst them a lack of clarity in the agreement between Ponting and Scott about use of the still photography. Ponting seems to have wasted a lot of energy in trying to raise the stature of the expedition in the eyes of the British public. He always felt frustrated that his photographic monument was not more appreciated. Ponting had never shown any real business acumen and other disappointments followed as a result of the failure of two of his photographic inventions. Towards the end of his life he also invested money in collaborating with an inventor of an inner tube which was specifically designed for car tyres and for which certain advantages were claimed e.g. that it would not burst.

Although the venture was not a success, Ponting had high hopes of this invention right up until his death.

By 1935 Ponting's health, which had been steadily deteriorating, finally gave out. He suffered a coronary thrombosis and died. Ponting's later life was full of frustration and disappointment. On his death, his net estate totalled no more than £377. Certain debts emerged and his photographs and equipment were sold to meet them.

ASSESSMENT

Ponting considered himself to be a 'camera artist' rather than 'photographer'. Although he appears to have had no formal art education, his intuitive understanding of composition and lighting helped him to produce pictures that put him in the photographers' hall of fame. More than most photographers, Ponting tried to capture the 'mood' and 'feel' of the scene. It is worth bearing this in mind when criticisms are made of some of his Japanese garden scenes and portraits of women, which have been described as contrived, unimaginative and ordinary. There is no disagreement, however, regarding the timeless quality of his Mount Fuji and Antarctic work. These are the real monuments to the life and memory of the camera artist, Herbert Ponting.

BIBLIOGRAPHY

Arnold, H. J. P: *Photographer of the World: the biography of Herbert Ponting* , Associated University Press, 1969. (A very valuable source).

Bennett, Terry: Korea: *Caught In Time*, Garnet, 1997.

Ponting, H. G.: *Fujisan*, Ogawa, Tokyo, 1905.

Ponting, H. G.: *Japanese Studies*, Ogawa, Yokohama, 1906.

Ponting, H. G.: *In Lotus-Land Japan*, Dent & Sons, 1910 (An important source).

Ponting, H. G.: *The Great White South*, 1921.

27

Koizumi Gunji, 1885–1965: Judo Master

RICHARD BOWEN

Koizumi Gunji

KOIZUMI GUNJI was a man of unfailing courtesy. His two most conspicuous traits were absolute probity and iron determination. He was an elegant man not only in appearance, but also in his behaviour.

Koizumi was born on 8 July 1885, the second son of Koizumi Shukichi, a tenant farmer, and his wife Katsu. He had an elder brother, Chiyokichi and a younger sister, Iku. The farm, which formed part of the small village of Komatsuka Oaza, was about twenty miles north of Tokyo, in Ibaraki Prefecture. He attended two schools, a primary school from the age of six to ten, followed by a higher school from ten to fifteen. The newly-qualified teacher at the latter school, Eizuka Wataro, taught single-handed all the subjects in the equally new National Curriculum, which included trigonometry, geometry, algebra, chemistry, physics, and drawing, to four distinct classes, numbering sixty pupils, in one room. While still at school Koizumi had, at his own volition, started to learn English from a neighbour who had spent some time in America.

A few years before Koizumi was born, Saigo Takamori of the Satsuma clan had perished in the dying throes of the samurai class. Koizumi was inspired by such tales of heroism and this prompted him to start kendo (fencing) at the age of twelve; he studied under the same teacher for three years. 'At the time I did not fully realize it, but I owe much to this master. The force of his personality and kendo had a strong influence in moulding my ego.'[1] Koizumi also remarked that in his father's time all the farms were clustered together in the village; this was done for mutual protection against marauding former samurai (*ronin*).

As a younger son, there were at that time only two options open to him if he wished to stay close to home. Either he had to start up his own farm or he had to marry into a family without a male heir. As neither option appealed to him, he left home in July 1900 a few days short of his fifteenth birthday, and made his way to Tokyo to seek his fortune. Once there, and after trying a couple of jobs, he enrolled in December 1900 in a government-subsidized training course for telegraphists. He qualified in October 1901. As a contractual condition he was obliged to spend a two-year stint working at the Central Post Office in Tokyo; during this period he took up Tenshin Shinyo Ryu jujutsu under the master Tago Nobushige. He wrote of his experience at the Post Office:

> I became acquainted with the ways of a bureaucracy dominated by feudalistic traditions, infested with flatteries and snobberies. Realizing the incompatibility of my nature to such an atmosphere, I turned my thoughts towards a field of life where the concept of freedom and independency would be held in higher regard.

Having no desire to spend his life as a telegraphist, he decided to study electricity with the aim of eventually starting a business. He decided that the best place to study the subject would be America. At the time he was earning about twelve or thirteen shillings a month at the Post Office, a sum, which was more than adequate for life in Tokyo at that time, but hardly sufficient to purchase a passage to America. Accordingly, he decided to work his way there in a series of 'hops'. He left Japan for Korea in November 1903 and took a job as a telegraphist at the Pusan Post Office, later in 1904, changing to the Korean Railway where he was posted to a remote railway station. There he was quickly sought after as a partner for the unattached daughters of the local Japanese families: 'I realized that I was on the border of a quicksand called "first love", a condition which is reputed to have submerged many an ambitious lad.'

During 1904, with judo-jujitsu never far from his mind, he

enrolled in a *dojo* (training hall) run by Yamada Nobukatsu. He left Pusan in January 1905 bound for Shanghai where he worked for five months as an interpreter to a firm of Japanese decorators. Continuing his policy of hopping from port to port, he arrived in Hong Kong in the summer of 1905 and then on to Singapore, arriving there in August. Here, too, he joined the local jujutsu school, the teacher being Akishima Tsunejiro. Once he had saved enough for the next 'hop', he set sail to Calcutta in February 1906 accompanied by a photographer, Hirano Toraroku. Aboard the ship was Professor Harada Tasuku, President of the Christian Doshisha College (later to be a university) in Kyoto, and Dr Motoda Sakanoshin. It seemed appropriate to Koizumi to ask such knowledgeable men about the meaning of life. Dr Motoda, with a smile, replied: 'My dear boy, a one pint vessel can't hold a gallon of water.' Years later, when he met the Doctor, in London, and reminded him of the incident, the then Bishop Motoda could not recall the episode.

Arriving in Calcutta in March 1906, he and Hirano set off to visit Buddhagaya, the site of The Buddha's enlightenment, where they spent two days being guided to places of historical interest by a Japanese priest, the Rev. Fujita Tokumei, who had lived there for two years. Fujita, a vegetarian except for milk foods, regarded money as unclean and would only touch it with a pair of chopsticks.

In Bombay, by chance on a tram, he met a Japanese carpenter, Tsuchiya Tokutaro who was member of the crew of the small British cargo ship, the SS *Romford*. Following an introduction by the carpenter he was accepted as his assistant to work his passage to England. On 4 May the *Romford* anchored off Mostyn in North Wales. He had now accomplished a major part of his journey.

He was lucky. Having arrived in Liverpool with sixpence in his pocket, he found and was employed by a run-down jujutsu correspondence school, the Kara Ashikaga 'School of Jujitsu', controlled by an Englishman. The weekly wage was thirty shillings, but ten shillings was then sufficient to cover bed and breakfast for a week at a local hotel. But the school had deteriorated beyond hope of recovery. So he moved on to London, arriving on August Bank Holiday1906.

In London, while preparing himself for the final hop to America, he worked as an instructor at the Uyenishi (Raku) school of jujutsu in Golden Square, Soho, and as a visiting instructor at the Regent Street Polytechnic and for the Royal Naval Volunteers. This was the last time that he taught judo professionally; for the rest of his life he was a strict amateur.

Koizumi arrived in New York in May 1907 and set about seeking a job where he could learn about electricity. But this took a little time. In the meanwhile he was introduced by Hagiwara Mokuojo to the American Locomotive Automobile Company and taken on as a machinist. Not knowing anything about lathes he managed to smash a gear on a lathe! However, with the help of his friend he kept this job for several months until he was taken on as an electrician's help at the Newark Public Service Railway Company. He was to remain there until April 1910 studying practical electrical engineering at work, and at an evening institute, as well as taking a correspondence course.

One day, finding a large piece of metal an inch thick in the shape of a horseshoe, which appealed to his aesthetic sense, he filed and polished it until it was perfect. Not knowing what else could be done with it, he decided to magnetize it. So before leaving work for the day he pushed it under one of the dynamos.

> When I came in the next morning there was bedlam, and they were digging my horseshoe out of the machine. I nearly caused the powerhouse to blow up. Well, as it was my fault I explained to the Superintendent, Mr Smith, what had happened. He seemed speechless for a moment and I can still recall vividly the dumbfounded expression on his face, and his fatherly words: 'You nearly cost me my job. Don't do it again.' Shortly after this I was on a gantry and a cable was being hoisted towards me. I went to touch it and suddenly realized it was live. I wondered at the time if the Superintendent was trying to secure his job by execution!

By now he was confident that he knew sufficient about the subject to branch out on his own. But he did not know where he should go. After three years in America he felt he was a misfit in such a materialistic society:

> Yet I was reluctant to return to my over-populated and prejudice-bound homeland. The features of life in Britain, which had been moulded by mature common sense and stately traditions … influenced me to retrace my way to London where the Anglo-Japanese Exhibition had just opened at the great White City.

He helped Ohno Akitaro, a Kodokan fourth dan and acquaintance from 1906, in demonstrations of jujutsu at the Exhibition, meanwhile setting up as an electrical lighting supplier in London's Vauxhall Road. It was then that he realized a business needed capital, which he didn't have. By January 1912 he decided on a change of direction, more in line with his natural inclination towards aesthetics, and he opened a lacquer ware studio in Ebury Street. Soon the business flourished and he employed a staff of a dozen artists, counting among his clients HM The Queen Mary, and Lord Kitchener. He remarked that Kitchener made frequent visits to the studio, but on the solitary occasion when Queen Mary paid a visit he was out.

Bessborough Gardens is a small patch of green in Victoria, on the approach to Vauxhall Bridge. In a small church which once stood there, Koizumi Gunji and Ida Celine Winstanley were married in April 1912, a partnership which lasted until her death thirty-five years later. There was one daughter, Hana.

Koizumi had a strong social conscience. This led him in 1919 to organize the *Zaiei Dōbō Kyōsai Kwai* (The Japanese Mutual Aid Society of Great Britain) to help with the various human problems of the thousand Japanese residents and the many Japanese transients, which were not catered for in the official duties of the Japanese diplomatic service, such as assistance for the needy and unemployed, and the provision of a communal burial ground, which still exists at Hendon Cemetery. Some years later, this Society was absorbed into a new and larger organization with Koizumi responsible for relief activities. Earlier, during the First World War, he and others formed a volunteer ambulance unit, which was to operate in and around London should the need arise. When asked about the source of the necessary equipment for the unit he replied: 'We supplied everything ourselves. You helped yourself in those days and did not wait for others to do it for you.'

Earlier, during 1917, Koizumi had had the idea of starting an institution for the study of the martial arts and their related cultural aspects. This was based on a twofold premise: firstly, to further interest in the martial arts, their underlying philosophy and Japanese culture in general, and secondly, to repay his adopted country for its hospitality towards himself and his fellow compatriots. He leased premises in Lower Grosvenor Place, Victoria, and The Budokwai, a strictly democratic society run by the members (as it still is), opened its doors on 26 January 1918. Apart from being responsible for the rent and other regular expenses, Koizumi paid the membership fee of three pounds as well as donating seventeen pounds over the next few months. From now on his activities were split between his business and The Budokwai.

A document, entitled 'Dojo Diary', written in old and difficult Japanese, records the infant organization's first wobbly steps. A translation of part of the first two entries reads:.

> 26 January 1918. Saturday. Clear skies. Felt like a spring day. About three p.m., two men from Mitsui Bussan come to visit dojo. Seems they saw article in Nichi-Ei Shinshi. As they were leaving, Arata, Uchiyama, and Iwasaki arrived. Join as provisional

> members. Koizumi, Asada, Karasawa, Unno, Matsunaga, Abe et al., arrive. 28 January 1918. Monday. Good weather. Club visited by Koizumi, Negishi, Ashida, Karasawa, Takahashi. At night Ito came, becoming a full member. In middle of practice with Koizumi, hear first air raid in a long time. Booming of guns. Bright moon.

A few months later, in August, he organized the 'Thames Exploration Party', which set off from Hampton Court Bridge and consisted of himself and four compatriots. Extracts from his account include: 'Rising Sun going upstream, threading its way through meadows and flat stretches of green fields, Arrive at bustling Maidenhead at 7.00 p.m. … Past Bourne End and Great Marlow and near Temple Lock, met Australian Prime Minister Mr Hughes with two children and someone who could have been a secretary, rowing in a boat. Went along with them as far as next lock, Henley.' They reach Oxford. 'Besides being a brilliant achievement, first time Rising Sun flag travelled deep into upper reaches of Thames.'

The first thirty-six members of The Budokwai were Japanese, and included Tani Yukio[2] and nine staff members of the Yokohama Specie Bank. The first Englishman enrolled in March 1918, followed by the first Englishwoman, Miss Cooper-White. By 1920 twenty-four other ladies had joined her, including Lady Susan Ridsdale. Some other members of note in the first few years were: Rear Admiral Tosu; the writer, Komai Gonnosuke; Lieutenant John Brinkley, son of Francis Brinkley[3] of Tokyo; Christmas Humphreys, later a High Court Judge; and Lt. Colonel Strange, CBE, Keeper of the Department of Woodwork at the Victoria and Albert Museum. It was probably at Colonel Strange's request that Koizumi assisted in revising the Museum's catalogue of Chinese and Japanese lacquer ware in 1924–25. About the same time he published a book on lacquer (*Lacquer Work: A Practical Exposition*, published by Sir Isaac Pitman and Sons, 1923).

One of the features of the Society was an annual display, the first taking place on the premises in May 1918 but later at various venues: the Aeolian Hall, the Royal Horticultural Hall, the Stadium Club, and Seymour Hall, culminating in the huge displays at the Royal Albert Hall in the fifties and sixties. A report in the press stated that Koizumi was elated at the news that the Crown Prince, HIH Hirohito, was expected to be present at the fourth annual display at the Aeolian Hall on 28 May 1921; it seems that difficulties in the security arrangements prevented his attendance. In the 1927 the Society was honoured with the presence of HIH Prince Chichibu. In the 1924 display Hayakawa Sessue, the film star, gave a demonstration of kendo, and at a later display Bernard Shaw was spotted in the audience and persuaded to sit with the Japanese Ambassador.

In 1920 Dr Kano Jigoro,[4] Founder of Kodokan Judo (the full name of judo), visited the Society. This was the first of six visits. Dr Kano, a major figure in the field of education, formulated his system in 1882, drawing on and adapting techniques from the older systems of jujutsu. He repeatedly stressed that the moral and mental benefits derived from proper judo training were of far greater importance than the physical ones. Writing of the purely physical differences between the older methods and his system, he said:

> The principal difference between jujutsu and judo is that in the former case greater importance was attached to the fighting side of the art, while in the latter its fighting side does not play so important a part as the other.

Kano, as the first Japanese member of the International Olympic Committee and Founder of the Japanese Amateur Athletic Association, was very keen on the Olympics. However, Kano had no intention of seeking the inclusion of Judo in the Games as he did not consider it as a sport (a point which the present-day large judo federations ignore in their hunt for medals at all costs). For Koizumi, too, judo was not a plaything but a principle for life. As a result there was instant rapport between Kano and Koizumi as they realized their approach to the problems of life and the purpose of jujutsu/judo coincided. This led Koizumi to enroll in the Kodokan, and Kano graded both him and Tani to second dan (Koizumi's ultimate judo grade was eighth dan). Otani Masutaro and other members also joined the Kodokan. Kano's approval of the aims of The Budokwai led him in the early 1930s to propose that the Society become the London Branch of the Kodokan. This received the unanimous support of the Committee and members. However, despite two or three years work the scheme was never realized, probably due to the international situation. But even shortly before his death in 1938, returning home after having secured the 1940 Olympic Games for Japan, Kano was still talking about the London Branch of the Kodokan.

In the early years of The Budokwai Koizumi organized a series of talks on a wide range of cultural aspects of Japan. The speakers included: Komai Gonnosuke, who gave three lectures; the Rev. W. Montegomery McGovern, a Buddhist Priest, who spoke on 'Northern Buddhism' and 'Religions of Japan'; the famous artist Yoshio Markino who lectured on 'A Philosophical Point of View of Ikebana' and 'Japan's Ideal Monarchism'; and the Quaker, Dr Nitobe Inazo, whose themes were 'The Japanese Idea of Loyalty' and 'The Japanese Woman in Her Home'. Colonel Strange gave several talks on lacquer, and there were many others who contributed, including Viscount Kano Hisaakira,[5] who was a leading figure in the Japanese community in London and later head of the London branch of the Yokohama Specie Bank.

The Budokwai went from financial crisis to financial crisis and only survived because of the monetary support of its Founder. When, by the early 1930s, the loan the Society owed to him amounted to several hundred pounds, the members acted to repay and remove further financial burdens from him. A company was formed to issue debentures; in the longer term, however, these proved insufficient.

In 1929 the very first international judo match took place in Frankfurt. This led to a series of matches, both in the UK and Germany, and more importantly a series of judo Summer Schools in Frankfurt, the teachers being Koizumi, Tani Yukio and Otani Masataro from London, Kawaishi from Paris, and Dr Rhi from Switzerland. It also led to attempts by Koizumi, undoubtably prompted by earlier discussions with Dr Kano Jigoro, to set up a European Judo Union. Although opinions vary, it seems that this met with a degree of success until conflict in Europe made such international cooperation impossible.

While he would have attended The Budokwai most evenings to teach, Koizumi, who had a great deal of initiative, did not neglect his business. As the years passed he branched out from lacquer ware and oriental *objets d'art* into flower-arranging (ikebana-style), and the importation of Japanese foodstuffs. But it was learning about the curative effects of *mogusa* (*O-kyu*, or moxa) from a visiting expert in the mid thirties, which really caught his interest and prompted him to open a clinic offering such treatment in Seymour Street, near Marble Arch, in central London. Here, if required, he augmented the traditional moxa treatment with a system of his own, Spinoculture, using judo exercises to correct postural defects. Shortly before the Second World War he travelled to New York with the intention of opening a similar clinic there.

After the start of the Second World War, with so many members in the forces, the Committee of The Budokwai decided to suspend its work for the duration. For Koizumi who was not a person to give up easily this was unacceptable. So he formed a temporary organization and set to work to remedy the dire financial situation. He was successful, and within two or three years the stop-gap organization was absorbed into the parent body and The Budokwai was reconstituted. Throughout the war judo training had continued, albeit on a limited scale. Outside displays were also mounted, and instruction was given to various groups, such as the Home Guard. Koizumi was not interned and indeed suffered no restrictions.

With the end of the war there was a tremendous interest in judo and many clubs opened. One possible reason for this was the unarmed combat training, based on judo, which many in the Forces had experienced. There was also the 'missionary' zeal of Society members spread around Britain; for instance two posted to an RAF station in Blackpool started a club which, over three or four years, attracted more than five thousand RAF enthusiasts. The most unusual club was the one started by Percy Sekine, later to be Koizumi's son-in-law, in a Prisoner of War camp in Germany. Sekine, of the RAF, had parachuted into Germany when his bomber was shot down.

Such was the number of newcomers to judo and the growth of clubs that The Budokwai rapidly took over as the centre of British judo. By 1950 it had over a hundred affiliated clubs, possibly half of the clubs in existence. While pleased with the spread of judo Koizumi was not happy with the undemocratic manner in which a single club had influence over so many smaller clubs. In July 1948 he convened a meeting in which the British Judo Association was formed; various officials were elected, including a Treasurer. But as the Treasurer had nothing to 'treasure' Koizumi, as ever, supplied a five-pound loan for the fledgling organization. In the same month he had invited delegates from Continental countries to another meeting in London, at the Imperial College Union, with the aim of starting a European organization. After two days of discussions the delegates from Holland, Italy, Austria, and Britain created the European Judo Union.

By 1951 the Union had increased to eight nations: Italy, France, Belgium, Holland, Germany, Austria, Switzerland, and Britain. Countries outside central Europe were clamouring to join the Union, and though the constitutional provisions had been stretched to accommodate them a proper long-term solution had to be found. At a meeting in a Chinese Restaurant in London's Soho the European Judo Union was dissolved and replaced by the International Judo Federation. The Minutes of that meeting, on 12 July, end with:

> Let it not be forgotten that this now worldwide organization has sprang from the foresight and long experience of one who has devoted his life to Judo – Mr Gunji Koizumi. It was he who suggested and inspired that first meeting of the European Judo Union in 1948, bringing together the judo experts (*jūdōka*) of Europe for the first time since the War, to share and to discuss their problems, and now to lead Judo to the far corners of the globe.

Especially in the late 1940s and 1950s there was very little understanding of Japan among ordinary people in Britain. Any of the few

Japanese who lived in London at that time and who had any knowledge of judo were 'lured' into a judo club and this led to many friendships between British people and Japanese. Judo and the philosophy behind it, promoted so assiduously by Koizumi, made a significant contribution to the understanding of Japan in Britain. The members of the judo clubs used Japanese customs such as bowing and adopted a considerable number of Japanese words, which have found their way into the English language.

In the late 1940s Koizumi retired from business and from then on devoted the rest of his life completely to judo, travelling the country from club to club, from course to course, teaching without payment and often without even receiving his travelling expenses. What money he had saved for his old age was sadly depleted in this manner. But his opinion was that an ideal is doomed when it becomes solely concerned with financial benefits.

In the early fifties the Society moved to larger premises, and at a ceremony on 19 September 1954, the then Japanese Ambassador, Matsumoto Shunichi, declared the new premises open. Shortly after this Koizumi visited his homeland for the first time in fifty years. He was greeted at the airport by his sister and relatives and by a delegation from the Kodokan, headed by the President, Kano Risei, son of the Founder. He was treated as an honoured guest by the Kodokan, and escorted around the great shrines and other noted places by Daigo Toshiro, twice champion of Japan. The family farm had long disappeared and his closest relations now lived in Tokyo, but many of his school friends were still around. The small river spanned by a bridge, and close to his former home, was unchanged. Koizumi recalled:

> My father had forbidden me to bathe there. no doubt out of fear for my safety. But the temptation of the water was great, especially as other boys were always splashing around in it. One day I was in the water when I spotted my father coming along the road, so I ducked under the bridge till he had passed. Finally I went to get dressed, but my clothes had gone – with my father. Leaving a small boy to walk home in the nude.

He retraced the journey from the village to his school and was surprised to find that it took less than fifteen minutes. In his memory it had taken an hour or more. After so many years in London, he found the low ceilings in Japan oppressive. And the sleeping arrangements were difficult for him: 'I had to have six or more futons like a feudal lord.' On his return to London, he remarked: 'It's good to be home and have a nice cup of tea.' When asked why he did not become British, he gave a little laugh, and pointing to his face said: 'The face is wrong.'

He was well but lightly built, about five feet six inches in height, and was handsome both in youth and old age. He always wore a black suit with a cream shirt and black bow tie, and favoured dark glasses when he was elderly. The exception to this attire occurred on Sundays when, clad in what could be called a gamekeeper garb, a Norfolk jacket with breeches buckled just below the knees, and long, heavy knee-length stockings, he would, when possible, set off for a walk in the country, 'To clear my mind'. Koizumi was imbued with the Meiji spirit of discovery or adventure.

Often, he had little adventures, for instance, on one occasion at an isolated farm he was asked where he came from: 'We have never met a Japanese before, so you had better come in and have a cup of tea with us.' This particular meeting concluded with the farmer offering him a job. He had a droll sense of humour, which often emerged unexpectedly. His laugh was catching, inviting you to join in and you usually did. One final story will give a further insight to his character. An old friend had died a few days earlier. Someone told him the old friend had been afraid of dying. Koizumi burst out vehemently: 'The coward! Nobody should be afraid of dying.' It was startling. He was actually quite angry (as I personally observed).

On Thursday, 15 April 1965, aware of increasing infirmities, not wishing to become a burden, and feeling that he had little more to contribute, he decided, as he wrote to friends: 'I am going to jump the queue.' The evening before he had been teaching at The Budokwai. His passing was mourned by thousands of judo enthusiasts in Britain and on the Continent. A few days earlier when being driven home he remarked: 'I should like to see more people thinking for themselves instead of being led like so many sheep.' Part of the obituary in *The Times* of 20 April 1965 reads:.

> A traditional Japanese view is that if a man has completed his service to the world and can do no more, he is permitted to cut himself off radically, after clearing up all his affairs. It is held that only a man of pure heart can do this. Mr Koizumi towards the end became increasingly impatient of the ability of his bodily instruments to perform the tasks set it; he had given all his reserves to his ideals.

As the personification of what judo is really about, Koizumi towers above all the exponents in Britain and Europe. On Chelsea Embankment a few yards from the statue of Sir Thomas More there is a small patch of greenery. There grows a Japanese Cherry Tree dedicated to the much-loved Koizumi Gunji who was an example of the best of Japanese manhood.

28

Trevor Pryce Leggett, 1914–2000

ANTHONY DUNNE & RICHARD BOWEN

Trevor Pryce Leggett

THE BEST WORD to describe Trevor Leggett is teacher. In that role he had the rare ability, found in only the best teachers, of seeking out and training the dormant creative talents which many people possess.

He was born on 22 August 1914 in Brondesbury, north-west London, the youngest of three boys, the others being Maurice and Terence. Their mother, Isobel Mabel, a qualified nurse, came from a relatively wealthy Scottish family, named Pryce. Speaking of her, Leggett remarked that she was canny with money but, a true Victorian, she believed in paying well for good things. Ernest Lewis, the father, coming from a farming family, which was not too well off, always had a slight suspicion of luxury items and, while not actually disapproving, would refer to them as 'de luxe' objects. The father had been a child prodigy, giving public performances on the piano at the age of seven. As a violinist, one of the best of his generation, he was the leader for several years at the Royal Opera House Covent Garden (and other venues) under Sir Thomas Beecham. In addition he was musical director at a number of theatres and also a first-class musical arranger, although he admitted to his younger son that he was no composer. In later years Leggett often regretted that he had not asked his father more about the brilliant but often capricious Beecham. There is no doubt that Leggett in his formative years was strongly influenced by his father's musical talents.

Leggett retained unusually clear memories of his early childhood. For instance, his first venture into the world of music was with a tin drum and a particularly resounding arrhythmic beat of great charm to a young lad of two years. 'My poor mother, I'm surprised she didn't strangle me.' On a visit to the seaside he toddled into the sea, surviving the first wave but was knocked over by the next. 'I was supremely happy until rescued by a soldier. Meanwhile, my nanny had hysterics.' Then there was a visit to the Isle of Wight where some relations lived. 'I recall vividly walking up a long and very steep slope. It went on and on, and my poor little legs ached and ached.' Many years later, in his seventies, while on holiday in the Isle of Wight, 'I made a beeline for that wretched slope. It was nothing, just a gentle incline. It required a real act of imagination to call it a slope.' He repeated these and other little stories about his childhood many times. The listener was expected when hearing these and other stories to find an inner meaning in what he heard.

He was educated in north London at Mill Hill School. While at school he became an accomplished pianist and supplemented his pocket money by playing the organ in a local church. His ambition was to train as a concert pianist, but his father, knowing the vagaries of earning a living in the music world, dissuaded him. Instead Leggett took a law degree at King's College, University of London, graduating in 1934. Nevertheless, his father encouraged his son's musical talent on the piano and sent him to the best teachers.

Once out of college he was employed in the Bell Punch Company where, with a law degree, his position would have been relatively good. He was adept at shorthand and a phenomenally fast touch-typist, both skills, which he had no doubt learnt while studying law. It was at about this time that he learnt to drive although he never owned a car. His ability as a ballroom dancer probably dates from the same period.

He started the practice of meditation at the age of fourteen and, a year or two later, discovered and began judo. Both meditation and judo were to have a profound and lasting impact and came to dominate his life. It is not clear why he started meditation and what form it took, but he was probably inspired by Zen Buddhism. He started judo at the age of sixteen, joining the Budokwai[1] in 1930, partly for health reasons and partly for self-defence. He wrote: 'Up to the age of fifteen, I was interested only in music. I never took any exercise, so I was constantly getting ill. The doctor told me that I must build up a better constitution and I began running every day. Then I came across judo.' Once in The Budokwai, and under the teachers Tani Yukio and Koizumi Gunji,[2] judo came to dominate his life. Soon he came to be the first on to the judo mat and the last off, every day; developing Spartan habits such as only wearing a thin shirt and jacket in the winter and scorning sweaters and overcoats. Once fully into the training, he supplemented it by running from midnight on a Saturday to the early hours of Sunday, picking up a bottle of milk for breakfast and spending most of Sunday in bed – unless, that is, the Budokwai was open in the afternoon.

He was particularly influenced by Tani, a hard taskmaster, and would relate stories about him. 'One evening I stubbed my toe', a common and painful happening for beginners, 'and was loudly complaining about the awful pain and the sheer agony.' Tani, from the edge of the mat, remarked, 'Do you want your mummy?' Leggett said that after that he never again complained about minor injuries. On another occasion he looked in at the Budokwai, but, feeling a bit off colour and deciding not to train, walked away. He met Tani who asked where he was going. Responding to the five feet three inch Tani, Leggett said, 'Well, you know, I thought I'd give the training a miss tonight. I'm a bit off colour and a rest will do me good.' 'Now, Leggett San, if a man with evil intent rushes up to you in the street with a hammer, what are you going to say? I'm sorry but I don't feel too good. Can you attack me next week?' Leggett turned on his heel and went back to the Budokwai. It was incidents of this nature, and there were a number, which made a major contribution to his steely self-control and determination.

He had an intense admiration for Tani, and wrote: 'Tani had a wonderful reputation. When I was taught by him, he was already over fifty, but was still very skilful. Over twenty years before, my father had seen this small man defeating big boxers and wrestlers, apparently by magic. He was a sort of god to us, and his words made a great impression.'

In 1936 he met the man who, for the rest of his life, he regarded as his teacher in religious and philosophical studies and meditation practices, Dr Hari Prasad Shastri.[3] Dr Shastri (1882–1956), born in Northern India, was a teacher of Adhyatma Yoga, the yoga relating to the inner self, based on the classical meditation and ethical traditions found in the *Upanishads* and the *Bhagavad Gita*. His approach to the main religions was eclectic, an approach followed, as might be expected, by Leggett. Shastri spent two years teaching in Japan before moving to China and finally to Britain in 1929, where he set up an organization in London for the study of Yoga and Vedanta philosophy.

The quality of intense concentration demonstrated by Leggett was directly connected to the training he undertook with Shastri, who also warned him against the danger of following a 'false ideology' of achievement. Leggett was to write many times on the dangers of this form of 'self-deceit', using examples from Zen, judo, kendo, and other sources. He quoted an Indian teacher who wrote, 'When you are becoming respected and honoured, that's the time to leave.'[4] More succinctly, 'Do what you are to do, and then go! Don't hang about.'[5] Continuing this theme, years later, Leggett remarked about his entry in the *Guinness Book of Records,* 'It *is* nice to have your picture in the *Guinness Book of Records,* but it is nothing, it is absolutely unreal.'[6]

All of Leggett's books of a religious or philosophical nature were dedicated to Shastri. One dedication is particularly revealing: 'To the late Dr Hari Prasad Shastri who introduced me to Zen in its original Indian form, in whom the ancient traditions were always young, these pieces are reverently dedicated by this pupil.'[7] Many people assume that Leggett's interest was solely in Zen and its manifestation in judo, particularly the *koan* of judo,[8] and it may surprise some readers to learn of his intense fascination for ancient Indian meditation practices. The above dedication should explain the connection. He wrote: 'The great religions of the world, if they are gone into, have a mystical side which is not far removed one from the other.'[9]

Furthermore, the dedication has the phrase '… in whom the ancient traditions were always young …' Leggett's feeling for true tradition was based on the view that what had been tried and tested over a long time was likely to have a correct basis, and he wrote:

> Buddhism is an ancient tradition and so it knows the sort of thing that can happen. It has a line of teachers who incorporate in themselves the experience of many centuries of practising these direct experiments on consciousness. It is an experimental thing, experiments that the scientists do not make. They never consider the observer, or haven't until the last twenty years or so. Buddhism makes experiments on the 'I' – the observer and consciousness.[10]

Leggett maintained that a man or woman who is quite ordinary could produce extraordinary effects through the process of inspiration brought about by the practice of meditation.[11]

He was convinced that telepathy existed and that one day it would be proved scientifically. On a visit to a theatre he saw a mind-reading act where the performer had his eyes covered with a slab of dough and a scarf. Members of the audience were invited to write something on a blackboard and the performer attempted to copy this. Leggett, who was sitting in the dress circle with his mother and brother, rushed down and through the stalls on to the stage where he wrote three Japanese characters (*kanji*) followed by one in running script on the board. The performer was not very successful with the top character but did quite well with the rest, remarking that it was Chinese. Earlier he had reproduced some Arabic characters, even adding a correction. Leggett concluded that it must have been a form of weak telepathy with a range of a few feet. He regarded this as a hint of the existence of telepathy, but certainly not proof. 'I was glad I rushed down to the stage.'

A combination of these two factors, meeting Dr Shastri and joining The Budokwai with its strong links with Japan and its Japanese members, led to Leggett's initial interest in Japan. By the mid 1930s he was expert in judo, and was helping out with instruction, mostly outside the Society, for instance at Oxford University Judo Club, and other organizations, as a semi-professional. Indeed, he spent a year in the mid 1930s teaching judo in Germany and Czechoslovakia, with the dual aims of seeing the Continent and improving his German.[12] In 1939, when the two teachers of the Budokwai were absent, Tani had suffered a stroke, and Koizumi Gunji was in New York, Leggett was appointed Instructor to the Society.[13]

Shortly after the appointment, he was given leave of absence for one year in order to visit Japan. With the encouragement and sponsorship of Viscount Kano Hisaakira and supported by additional backing from the International Students' Federation of Japan, arrangements were made for Leggett to make a trip to Japan to further his judo training and to foster his interest in Japan and Japanese culture. A farewell dinner for him was held at the Nihon Jin Kwai in June, 1939; the guests numbered about twenty, and included staff from the Japanese Embassy and Consulate, two NYK (Nippon Yusen Kaisha) ship captains, and of course Viscount Kano; others were from the Budokwai. Two days later, on Thursday 22 June, Leggett set sail aboard the NYK's *Hakozaki Maru*, bound for Japan.[14]

His time in Japan was spent in intensive study of judo, the Japanese language and culture, and, of course, Zen Buddhism. When he arrived at the headquarters of judo, the Kodokan, he was close to fourth *dan* standard in judo. By the time he left Japan he was a fifth *dan*, at that time the highest grade world-wide ever attained by a non-Japanese. Two life-long friends from this period were Takasaki Masami, the son-in-law of Kano Jigoro,[15] the Founder of Kodokan Judo, and Nakayama Shozen, the head of the Tenrikyo sect (known as the *Shinbashira)* both judo experts. At some stage, probably in 1940, he joined the staff of the British Embassy, where the Ambassador was Sir Robert Craigie.[16] With the outbreak of the war in the Pacific, the embassy staff were interned and guards placed around the compound.

With other Britons seeking refuge the numbers in the embassy tripled. Some eight months were to pass before the repatriation of diplomats was arranged; during this time some of the social restraints broke down. For instance, minor squabbles between husbands and wives, which were normally kept private, became public altercations. Leggett said that crowded confinement in difficult circumstances led to this type of breakdown. As the men tended to group together in the evenings and spend their time drinking, Sir Robert asked Leggett to keep a weather eye on the proceedings. He said, 'I developed a reputation as a hard drinker who never got drunk, sitting at a table and swigging, from time to time, a half tumbler filled from my own very special bottle of gin. Occasionally, I would buy a round of drinks, but never offer anyone my own special gin.' The 'gin' was, of course, water! Leggett's abstinence from alcohol was a manifestation of his ascetic character, rooted in his belief in man's ability to undergo a radical change of consciousness.[17]

The staff of the embassy were evacuated in July 1942 and arrived home in Liverpool in October 1942. After joining the Ministry of Information, Leggett was sent on a refresher course in Japanese at the School of Oriental and African Studies (SOAS). Being well in advance of the ordinary classes he had private sessions with Arthur Waley. He went on to serve in India in the Ministry's Far Eastern Bureau which later merged with the Psychological Warfare Division of the South East Asia Command there; holding the rank of major, his expertise in Japanese language and culture were invaluable.[18] It was here that he met another old member of the Budokwai, Major John Brinkley, son of the famous Francis Brinkley.[19] When circumstances allowed, Leggett would certainly have studied further the great classics of India.

Sir Leslie Glass writing about his time in India during the war included several passages about Leggett. He wrote:

> Our Japanese script was often written, or rather painted with a brush by Trevor Leggett. He was a perfectionist in all he did – judo, chess, piano or Japanese lettering. I have seen him, brush in hand, practising for hours, indeed for days, a single stroke of a single letter, over and over again. I learnt from him that judo was not just a wrestling skill but a form of mental and physical discipline … Trevor was a tall, rather gangling figure. He told me he had been outsize at school and bullied. He had taken up judo to work out the resentment which had built up inside him. Once he knew he could defeat any man he met in unarmed combat, he felt exorcized, and I found him to be the gentlest and mildest of men … In wartime Delhi he usually wore an open-necked shirt, and he walked with a slight stoop. His normal meal was a

> poached egg and a glass of milk usually taken while he was reading some volume of poetry or philosophy. He started to teach me chess, and, just to demonstrate the difference of class between us, asked me at the beginning of a game to choose which particular square I should like to be mated on. I chose the most unlikely square I could think of, and in due course my king was humiliatingly shepherded on to that very square for the *coup de grâce*.[20]

He returned to civilian life in 1946, joining the British Broadcasting Corporation (BBC) and soon became Head of the Japanese Service, a prestigious position which he enjoyed as it enabled him to retain his contacts with Japan. He retired early in 1969 at the age of fifty-five. He was given the opportunity to be promoted, but this would have entailed leaving the Japanese Section and becoming an administrator, a role, which failed to interest him.[21] It is not clear why he retired early, but it may have been due to his belief that it is necessary to change direction radically from time to time. Another possible reason was that by now he was writing and lecturing extensively and wished to devote more time to those activities. His close friend John Newman, MBE, also fluent in Japanese and also a high grade judo man, replaced him at the BBC.[22]

In 1948 at a meeting in London, convened by Koizumi Gunji and chaired by Leggett, the European Judo Union was formed. Leggett was elected to be the Union's first chairman, an office from which he soon resigned, though retaining his position on the Technical Panel. Later, in 1951, the Union became the International Judo Federation.[23] While he had done some teaching earlier, it was about 1950 at the Budokwai that his talent as a teacher became apparent. He decided to run senior training sessions and invited members to attend. The class opened with over forty people but rapidly dropped to about eighteen, all experienced. Real judo training is harsh. 'Oh, you feel sick? Right, go and be sick and hurry back.' Or, 'You'er injured? Sit by the mat and take notes.'

Following the judo tradition, each year, at the coldest time winter training sessions took place. These were in the early morning from 7.00 to 8.00 and again in the evening. To step on the ice-cold mat with bare feet and clad in a thin judo kit took considerable willpower. But what was the purpose of such austerity, as obviously the body cannot function efficiently in such conditions? Life can be unfair and one must learn to function as best as one can in adverse conditions and not simply throw up one's hands. This is part of the mental training of traditional judo; do not become demoralized by injuries or unfavourable circumstances. Leggett, a chain smoker at this time, would stop for the two weeks of 'winter training'. These, indeed all, of his sessions ended with a few minutes sitting in Zen style meditation (*zazen*). 'Think of a drop of water running down your forehead and nose and dripping onto your abdomen', or, 'Think about the day of your death.' Many years later he confessed that his style of teaching judo was Zen based, and indeed likened proper judo training to monastic Zen training. Leggett, with his life-long devotion to traditional Kodokan Judo, was appalled by what has recently become a debased form, encouraged by international organizations and governments in a glorified hunt for medals. He often spoke and wrote accordingly.

When in his seventies and during a discussion on tolerance, he remarked, 'I've always been patient, quite tolerant, indeed a virtual paragon of forbearance.' Even the finest of memories can fail! When teaching judo he was anything but patient. To have six feet three inches of scowling Leggett bearing down on you, because you had forgotten last session's lesson was an awe-inspiring experience. On a few occasions he actually grabbed people and shook them. 'Wake up, wake up!' This can suggest that he was guilty of bigotry, or narrow-mindedness, or that he was a bully. But this was not the case. The exhortation, 'Wake up!' said it all. He was putting tremendous physical and mental effort into inspiring, into galvanizing, people so that they would not waste what ability they possessed – this under the cloak of pseudo irascibility. In time, but not at first, the class came to realize and acknowledge this.

There is no doubt that Leggett himself learned a great deal from teaching these judo classes and this, allied to his work at the BBC, turned him into a skilled communicator, which was to prove of tremendous value. During the decade starting in 1950 he encouraged and assisted sixteen judo men to travel to Japan to further their training. The eventual outcome of his efforts was that two became security officers at the British Embassy in Tokyo, one of whom later became a vice-consul, another judo man became a second secretary in the commercial department of the Embassy, others became schoolteachers and university lecturers, and still others, fluent in Japanese, became freelance translators or worked for Japanese companies. Although on a much smaller scale, he also arranged for Japanese to visit Britain, some as judo instructors, or to study; and others, sometimes with a judo connection, to be employed at the BBC.

His immediate pupils were encouraged to visit museums, art galleries, and plays. By a kind of mental osmosis, most of the class took up chess, sitting for hours in a nearby cafe huddled over miniature chess sets. While he was not keen on women doing judo, he had immense respect for the leader of the ladies' section, the intellectually brilliant Dame Enid Russell-Smith.[24] He usually had several books with him, carried wrapped up Japanese fashion in a *furoshiki,* a square of cloth. Sitting over a coffee (and a chessboard) one would casually glance at one, 'Yes, that's quite interesting, by Schrodinger on his Dublin lectures, y'know. Take it for a week or two.' Two or three weeks later the book would be returned to him. 'Oh, yes, thank you. What did you think of it?' He would not press for embarrassing details, knowing very well that the unfortunate victim had probably done no more than vaguely skim through one or two parts of the book. And he would be quite satisfied with, 'Yes, it's quite fascinating' or some equally bland response. But the next time, and there was always a next time, the victim, aware of how closely he had escaped intellectual death, would more or less learn the particular book by heart. And then Leggett, now aware it would not cause embarrassment, would launch into a detailed discussion.

It was in 1960 that he produced his first book, *A First Zen Reader*,[25] which has been reprinted many times. Other works, well over thirty, followed, several on judo, others on Zen and Yoga, Chivalry, and *shogi* (Japanese chess in which he reached fifth *dan*, a professional standard). Some books were in Japanese. His greatest literary effort was a translation into English of a newly discovered Sanskrit commentary by the most renowned of Indian philosophers, Sankara (circa 700 AD).[26] This occupied him, on and off, for seventeen years. When he started Sanskrit at an advanced age, he was advised not to waste his remaining years in this manner as brain-cells die at the rate of 100,000 a day, and therefore learning a language was, 'Absolutely out!' Leggett's immediate reaction was, 'Aaargh!' But then his training came to the fore and he thought he must do his very best even with the few brain-cells he was fortunate to still possess and not be scared off. Later, he made an investigation and found that the brain had 10,000,000,000 cells, enough to last 274 years.[27]

Apart from writing books, he continued right up to his death to produce numerous articles, which were published in an assortment of magazines, mostly in English but some in Japanese. He was skilled in the use of parables, which he employed widely, both in books and articles. While many came from his own pen, others originated in Christianity, Judaism, Islam, Hinduism, and Zen. He lectured widely, at the Buddhist Society,[28] the Theosophy Society, the Albion Yoga Movement, the Imperial Defence College (from 1971 renamed The Royal College of Defence Studies), and many other bodies including Dr Shastri's organization.

His taste in reading was catholic, ranging from science fiction and fantasy to learned works on religion, philosophy, and science, to most of the classics. It was alarming in conversations with him, to suddenly find that the discussion was centring around Axel Munthe's experiences in the cholera outbreak in Italy; or why did Boudica come to be mis-spelt Boadicea, and the strange myth that she is interred under platform eight in King's Cross Station; or the greatness of Ambedkar; or Saint Augustine's comment on Saint Ambrose's silent reading, a topic which lasted for several discussions.[29] He often said that he had read few books, meaning that he could grasp the sense by scanning the pages rather than word by word. There were certain books, which he did read carefully and returned to once a year or so, for instance Bernard Shaw's *Methuselah*. Poetry was important to him, and he recalled attempts in his early days to set *The Lady of Shallot* to music. Even though he subscribed to the *New Scientist*, once a year or so he would make a sustained attempt to bring himself up to date on the latest scientific advances. .

He suffered several serious illnesses and for many years was blind in one eye. Towards the end of his life the sight in the other eye came close to total blindness. With the aid of a special computer he could work his way painstakingly through documents. His reaction to his inability to read ordinary print was typical, 'Now I can sit and think without any distractions.' His attitude to death was different from that of most people. In 1863 General 'Stonewall' Jackson, accidentally shot by his own sentries, when returning from a reconnaissance, was told by his doctor that he would not last the day. The day was 10 May, a Sunday. The General, a deeply religious man, reputedly said, 'Oh, good! I've always wanted to die on a Sunday.'[30] Leggett, when told of this, remarked, 'Splendid! Marvellous! *That's* the way to go!' Following a story from the Zen tradition, he wrote, 'I can also say that in times of real crisis I have found this phrase a big help: "If you are going to die, die quick!"'[31]

His austere habits persisted until his mid-seventies when, at the insistence of his doctor and with considerable reluctance, he took to wearing warmer clothing. This austerity extended to his living quarters. Once back in London at the end of the war, he shared a flat with his mother in Cheyne Walk, Chelsea (his father had died in 1943). Later, they moved to Kensington Square, off Kensington High Street, and it was there that his mother died in 1965. His next move was to Palace Garden's Terrace, backing on to the Russian Embassy, and here, with only himself to please, he was able to indulge his Spartan habits. This resulted in all the radiators being stripped out; this included cutting off all hot water to the kitchen and bathroom. The sole source of hot water was an electric kettle. He would shower at the judo club or Roehampton Club, where he played golf; his handicap was six (his brother Maurice's handicap was four).

Leggett had an outstanding sense of humour. He was particularly fond of the fast, clever, repartee of the Marx Brothers, and this could creep into conversations. On the subject of chess he said: 'I'm going to buy the new German Mephisto chess computer when it comes out. I've played the hitherto champion, Challenger – I only lost once, and then I didn't lose, because I pulled his plug out. Man kills Robot – that's news!'

In 1984, on 3 May, his contribution Anglo-Japanese relations was recognized when, by Command of the Emperor of Japan, the Japanese Ambassador, Hirahara Tsuyoshi, invested him with the Order of the Sacred Treasure (Third Class).

The following quotation from his writings provides a fitting conclusion to this portrait:

An Indian tradition says that training is usually like setting fire to wood that is a bit damp in places. It is difficult to get a flame at all, and it keeps going out. When it does catch hold a bit, great clouds of dense smoke arise, nearly choking the fire-raisers.

Then it begins to burn briskly, and people can benefit from the light and heat. Then it roars in triumph as the whole pile blazes.

Finally it dies down into the peace of the ashes.[32]

AUTHORS' NOTE: Much of this account derives from conversations with Leggett by the two authors over many years. The notes headed Archive Documents refer to R. Bowen's collection, which will eventually be deposited as a collection in the Library of the University of Birmingham. We thank the Trustees of the Trevor Leggett Adhyatma Yoga Trust and the administrators of his estate for allowing access to his papers.

29

The *Japan Chronicle* and its three editors, Robert Young, Morgan Young and Edwin Allington Kennard, 1891–1940

PETER O'CONNOR

Robert Young

THE *JAPAN CHRONICLE* was the best of Japan's pre-war English-language newspapers. Its news reports were the most informative and its essays and opinion pieces represented the cream of Japanese and expatriate intellectual life and scholarship. *Chronicle* writers and editors demonstrated a sure grasp of contemporary events, and two of its three editors were, in their day, among the most perceptive writers on Japan anywhere.

Robert Young founded the *Japan Chronicle* and in thirty-one years made its reputation for fierce but scrupulous engagement with the politics and society of contemporary Japan. During his fourteen years as editor, Arthur Morgan Young built strongly on this foundation, and was banned from Japan for his pains. In the last five years of the *Chronicle*, Edwin Allington Kennard edited the paper with the help of a Gaimushō (Foreign Office) subsidy and benefited from the sale of the newspaper to its semi-official rival, the *Japan Times*.

ROBERT YOUNG (1858–1922), FOUNDER, PROPRIETOR AND EDITOR 1891–1922

Robert Young's writings are easy to study in surviving issues of his newspaper but, as others have found, there is little biographical information on the man himself.[1] Robert Young was born at 15 Moreton Place, Pimlico, in the borough of Westminster, London, on 9 October 1858, to Andrew Young, a journeyman piano maker, and his wife Jessie (née Dodds). Robert was one of four children, the others being George, Andrew and Margaret. The Youngs were not wealthy, but they were steady enough to see their son into the Westminster Training School, and then a printer's apprenticeship with the publishers Spottiswoode. Robert Young took to his work and became a compositor and then Reader on the *Saturday Review*. The work was arduous, but it suited Young's passion for accuracy.

Young's parents were regular church-goers, but both Robert and his brother George became interested in Positivism (before the term atheism was coined), and began attending lectures and courses at the South Place Religious Society (renamed the Ethical Society in 1887) in Moorgate, EC. Dr Moncure Conway, the American anti-slavery campaigner and revolutionizer of religious thought, who presided over South Place from 1864–1897, became a huge inspiration to Young and his brother George, who would both name their future homes, and Robert his first son, 'Conway' in his memory. At South Place, Robert Young also came to know Charles Bradlaugh (1833–91), the first militant Atheist. A large portrait of Bradlaugh would later dominate the *Japan Chronicle* offices in Kobe.

Early in life Young became one of that awkward brigade who mean what they say and act accordingly. Through lectures and study groups at South Place, and the influence of Conway and Bradlaugh, he developed an opposition to worship that would only harden with the death of two of his children in Japan, and would be observed in a clause of his Will directing that 'no Christian religious ceremony or service be performed over my remains'.[2] Trained to respect the fact, to ferret out cant and compromise and to distrust unthinking ceremony, Young's make-up would have set him at odds with late Victorian England, let alone Japan as he found it and as it would develop.

Robert Young and his English wife, Annie (née Crockett) first came to Japan in 1888, following Young's successful interview for a post as manager of the *Hiogo News* (1868–98) of Kobe. In 1891,

Young left the *Hiogo News* to establish, at the age of thirty-three, the *Kobe Chronicle*, with a starting capital of ¥1000. There were no assistants or reporters in the first three years, and Annie Young helped her husband with proof-reading and numerous other tasks. When business picked up, Mrs Young left to concentrate on family life.

The first issue of the *Kobe Chronicle* appeared on 2 October 1891. On 3 July 1897, Young began a weekly edition. In 1898, Young bought the *Hiogo News* from the Kobe syndicate that had previously employed him, ran it as a separate paper with its own editor, B.A. Hale, and hired staff from England for both papers. Just after the sale, a fire destroyed the entire *Hiogo News* plant and most of the files. Undaunted, Young found jobs at the *Kobe Chronicle* for the *Hiogo News* staff and ran the *Hiogo News* title under the *Chronicle* masthead. On 8 January 1902, the *Kobe Weekly Chronicle* became the *Japan Chronicle Weekly*. On 5 January 1905, Young renamed the daily edition of the *Kobe Chronicle* the *Japan Chronicle* and the paper grew from four to eight pages. In 1905, the new title marked the *Chronicle*'s popularity, as the best-selling English-language newspaper in Japan, and reflected Young's wish to gain a wider constituency for his paper, which 'took the world as its province'.

Thus, within a few years of his arrival in Japan, Robert Young had established himself as a newspaperman in Japan and had become, if not a pillar of the Kobe community, an active participant. Here is Young as his sometime leader writer Lafcadio Hearn saw him in 1894: 'Young is hearty and juvenile in appearance – serious face – dark beard – used to be a proof-reader on the *Saturday Review*, for which some culture is necessary. Is a straight thorough English radical. We are in perfect sympathy on all questions.'[3]

Hearn's last point goes some way towards explaining the ambivalence of Young's position in Kobe and in Japan's expatriate community. By temperament and upbringing, as a matter of principle (or disbelief), and above all because he felt that his work required it of him, Young's outlook was invariably liberal, often radical and sometimes socialist. On labour relations, armaments and militarism, on the Russian revolutions of 1905 and 1917, on Communism, on Japan's wartime plutocracy and on her political development Young's approach was always liberal. Not only did Young advance his own leftish views, but he published a regular diet of notable foreign and Japanese commentators in the *Chronicle*: Bertrand Russell, Yoshino Sakuzo, Kagawa Toyohiko, Nitobe Inazo, Ozaki Yukio, Sakatani Yoshiro and others.

Young and his newspaper soon gained a feisty reputation in Japan, largely through a series of clashes with Captain Francis Brinkley (1841–1912) and his newspaper, the *Japan Weekly Mail*. Like its junior contemporary, the *Japan Times*, the *Mail* was a semi-official organ, promoting and defending Japan to the English-speaking world and receiving subsidies and other benefits from the Japanese government in return.[4] Brinkley's *Mail* defended 'squeeze' among government officials and the sale of young girls into prostitution by their parents. Reports of Japanese atrocities in Korea were 'iniquitous falsehoods' drummed up by 'the hostile orchestra' of the *Japan Herald*, *Japan Gazette*, and *Kobe Chronicle* ('the *Kobe Quibbler*' to *Mail* readers).[5] As a contemporary sniped, 'It is impossible to conceive Captain Brinkley in a position antagonistic to the government. The training of long years will suffice to deliver him from that unenviable predicament.'[6]

The *Chronicle* decried Brinkley's indiscriminate promotion of Japanese causes. In 1922, Young's obituary maintained that 'none of Robert Young's opinions was stronger than this, that paid advocacy is not a proper function of the Press'.[7] But Young's own record was not without blemish. In the early nineties, he accepted government funds to argue the case for ending extraterritoriality. It may have been in recognition of this campaign that in 1903 Young had an audience with the Meiji Emperor (an honour never granted to Brinkley, who was asked to wait outside the reception hall on the one occasion he came close to an audience).[8]

Having little Japanese also made Young a less mellow observer than he might have been. Frank Brinkley's excellent command of the language brought him close to Ito Hirobumi and the Meiji élite, and this intimacy helped him to appreciate the Japanese perspective. Brinkley's comfortable Meath squirearchy, Dungannon School and Trinity background and his position as a scion of the Protestant ascendancy, (his grandfather was the astronomer Bishop Brinkley whose statue stands at the entrance to the library of Trinity College, Dublin), helped set him at ease among the oligarchs.[9] Coming from more ordinary stock did not prevent Young from being on good terms with some politicians, among them Tokonami Takejiro and Hara Kei, but the Japanese in his inner circle were all radical journalists and intellectuals, and he felt little pressure to toe the official line.

Robert Young's campaign against extraterritoriality was qualified by a parallel effort to prevent the surrender of the private interests of foreign residents along with their extra-territorial privileges, most notably the 'perpetual' foreign leaseholders' exemption from the Japanese house-tax, a question eventually settled in the foreign residents' favour by the International Court at The Hague.[10]

Young's relationship with the Kobe community was never cosy, but the house tax campaign and another that Young and the British Association of Japan fought against the British Status of Aliens Act, forbidding British children of parents born abroad from taking British nationality, were both followed keenly by Japan's British community (including Frank Brinkley, whose children eventually benefited). In 1922, in the week that Young died, his friend Gershon Stewart MP forced an amendment through the Commons.

In 1910, during an extended visit to England, Young was interviewed by the *Daily News* about the High Treason Incident (*Taigyaku Jiken*) of 1910, in which several hundred socialists and anarchists were arrested in Japan and twenty-six, including Kotoku Shusui, charged with plotting to assassinate the Emperor.[11] Young described the press blackout in Japan and questioned the validity of the trial by the Court of Cassation as '... both unconstitutional and unprecedented. I understand that the Court of Cassation will try the twenty-six men and women in camera, so they are to have no public trial, and no chance of appeal, and we shall never know the facts'. In a letter to *The Times* Young described the trial as 'unjust in the extreme'.[12]

Japan engaged in some well-planned news management to prepare Western opinion for a severe decision in the High Treason trial, putting out notices through Reuters in September 1910 and giving advance notice of Chief Prosecutor Hiranuma Kiichiro's decision to the *Jiji Shimpo* and to the Tokyo correspondent of the *North China Herald*. An official press conference was held for foreign newsmen in Tokyo on 16 January 1911. Two days later, the Court of Cassation commuted twelve sentences to life imprisonment and handed the death sentence to Kotoku Shusui and eleven others.[13]

Robert Young was one among a very few informed opponents of this process and these decisions. He acted as a radical gadfly, stinging not only the Japanese judiciary but also the conscience of the Japanese press, declaring in his letter to *The Times*, 'the mouths of the accused have been shut, and any newspaper which dared give publicity to their defence would have been prosecuted under the law'. Kotoku himself had been a journalist on the once-radical *Yorozu Chōhō*, and the silence of the Japanese papers over his fate marked a watershed in Japanese press history.

The High Treason Incident was one of a number of issues of national significance on which Japan's independent English-language press ventured far sharper comment than the vernacular press. Writers like Robert Young, his successor (but not his relation) Morgan Young and Hugh Byas at the *Japan Advertiser* were not restrained by the same loyalties or hierarchies as Japanese newspapermen. As nationalist sentiment increasingly modified independent comment in Japan, the gap widened between the English-language press and the vernacular press reporting of major issues. Under Robert Young's editorship, this divergence was most obvious in the two presses' coverage of the High Treason Incident, the wars with China and Russia, the 'White

Rainbow' incident (*hakko jiken*),[14] in which the Terauchi government came down heavily on the Osaka *Asahi Shinbun* during the Rice Riots of 1918, for hinting at a celestial portent of military government or assassination of a member of the Imperial family, the allied intervention in Siberia, the Korean independence movement of 1919–20, and in 1920–22, the question of the renewal of the Anglo-Japanese Alliance. Under Morgan Young, the gap widened further, especially after 1931.

An important element in the *Chronicle*'s criticism of Japanese attitudes to expatriates and foreign powers was its perception of a lack of reciprocity between the rights enjoyed by Japanese in America, Canada and Great Britain (although these did not include extraterritoriality), and the rights of expatriates in Japan. In frequent editorials, the *Chronicle* called for greater reciprocity. In 1911, Japan was attempting to renegotiate treaties made with Britain dealing with Conventional Tariffs. Reuters, in their reports, were advancing the Japanese view that the agreements reached in 1899 were 'one-sided'. In a letter to the *Manchester Guardian*, Young wrote: 'There is, it is true, a lack of equity and reciprocity in the existing treaties with Japan, but it is not the Japanese who are entitled to complain.' To Young, the inequities were obvious: land ownership, the franchise, the exclusion of non-Japanese ships from Japan's coastal trade, and the exclusion of British residents in Japan from holding shares in companies to which the Japanese government granted subsidies despite their paying both Imperial (British) and local taxes.[15]

Young's beliefs kept him out of church, but as a lifelong Spencerian, he went out of his way 'to teach the Christians Christianity', notably the foreign missionaries protesting the harshness of Japan's administration in Korea. As Young wrote in a late letter to Bertrand Russell: 'The missionaries have always been puzzled that I should so stoutly defend the right of Christian missionaries in Korea to preach their doctrines without let or hindrance, despite the fact that I am a notorious unbeliever and a keen critic of them and their beliefs. The idea that one can defend the right of others to teach what he does not himself believe permeates very slowly into their minds.'[16]

All three of his sons served in the 1914–18 war, but Young detested militarism, in Japan as in Britain and America. The *Chronicle* was highly critical of Britain's policy in South Africa before and during the Boer War, and of international intervention in Peking in the Boxer crisis. During Japan's 1894–5 War with China, Young's network of contacts in East Asia enabled the *Chronicle* to enhance its reputation by the breadth and accuracy of its war news, and it gained a world scoop on the attack on Formosa. This report and forecasts of an overwhelming Japanese victory were taken as championing the

Japanese cause, and during the war patriotic lantern processions would pause outside the *Chronicle* offices to cheer Young and his staff. A decade later, when the *Chronicle* refused to support Japan's war with Russia, the lantern processions fell silent as they passed the *Chronicle* building.

Young's principles increasingly set him at odds with Japan's foreign policy. As one obituary put it: 'Subsequent developments – the administration and annexation of Korea, the securing of rights in Manchuria – were contrary to his political philosophy, and he viewed with dislike the whole drift of Japanese policy as inimical to the sound development of the country and the true happiness of the people'.[17] The *Chronicle*'s stand often attracted charges of being anti-Japanese. Responding in 1921 to one such article in *Chūo Kōron,* Young maintained that he criticised Japan for the good of the Japanese:

> … it is the Japanese people who have obtained advantage by the criticism of individual cases of injustice. Again, it is the Japanese people who will gain most from a decline in the power of the militarists who have exerted so much influence on the country's foreign policy for the last thirty years … It is the Japanese people who would benefit and to describe criticism along these lines as anti-Japanese evinces a strange lack of perception.[18]

Even his obituary notice admits of Young, 'Occasionally, the amount of artillery, which he employed, gave the impression that his opponent was more formidable than was really the case'.[19] Young's close friend, the Kobe businessman David James, also felt that Young went too far. 'After the First World War,' he wrote, 'I saw more and more of Robert Young. By then, he was more a destructive critic of Japan than a constructive one. I felt that his work … and influence in Japanese progressive circles was being defeated by carping criticism.'[20]

★ ★ ★

The summer of 1917 saw the first issue of the *New East*, 'a monthly review, in English and Japanese, of thought and achievement in the eastern and western worlds', edited by J. W. Robertson-Scott. With Hugh Byas as Business Manager, Frank Ashton-Gwatkin, then a language trainee at the Yokohama consulate, helping out on a voluntary basis, and Nitobe Inazo translating and advising, Robertson-Scott had assembled a gifted team.

Some in Whitehall had dared to hope that in wartime even Robert Young would pull his punches for an enterprise designed to harmonize relations between the two allies in the face of a determined enemy, but Young did the *New East* no favours. 'Our own impression after perusal of the first number is that of a compound of *Titbits* and the *Review of Reviews*, with a dash of the *Daily Mail*', he wrote in the *Chronicle*.[21] In a later review, Young trashed an article by Lord Curzon on 'The Common Ideals of Japan and Britain', with telling references to Ito's *Commentaries* to illustrate divergences between the 'two island empires'. He lost no opportunity to harry the *New East* until its collapse in 1919.[22]

Young and the *Chronicle* made few friends at the Foreign Office or at the Tokyo embassy. In December 1917, Sir Conyngham Greene, the British Ambassador, acknowledged that 'the editors of the "*Japan Chronicle*" are very capable and well-informed … their criticisms on passing events show a close acquaintance with the past history of this country and with the published writings and speeches as well as the acts, of public men not only in Japan but also, to some extent, in China'. However, as Greene saw it the *Chronicle* writers:

> … seem to suffer from an exaggerated critical faculty with regard to the actions and sayings of all their fellow men and especially those in official positions – an idiosyncrasy which, in the case of the various Japanese with whose words and deeds the 'Chronicle' is naturally called upon to deal most frequently, leads to a disposition to dwell unduly upon every fault and to overlook the arguments or excuses which might be cited in favour of the persons criticised … Such a disposition, whilst apt to obscure the otherwise brilliant gifts of these writers, might nevertheless do little harm, since the Japanese recognise only the apparent ill-will of the paper and have ceased almost entirely, to pay attention to the views expressed by it; but, unfortunately, the opinions held and voiced by the British communities not only in the chief ports of Japan but also in the small mining camps of Corea, and especially in Kobe itself, are to a very great extent inspired by this journal, which thus, on the whole, exercises a detrimental influence on the relations between Japan and the British Empire.[23]

Greene and Young were bound to see things differently. For Greene, Japan was an ally to be treated with care and respect, particularly in wartime. In Young's sense of the function of an independent press, Japan and the Japanese were subject to the same unfaltering scrutiny as the rest of the world. Pleasing impressions of Japan that harmonized the Alliance were not the proper work of the *Chronicle*.

Thus, by the early 1920s, Robert Young's *Japan Chronicle* was celebrated as an uncompromisingly truthful reporter of Japanese life to the foreign community and the world at large, and deprecated as an unforgivably anti-Japanese paper that pampered the prejudices of the expatriate community and stained the image of Japan around the world. Both views attest to the influence of the *Chronicle*. By 1922, it had become that rare thing, a local newspaper with an international readership and influence. In addition to a solid subscription list among English-speaking expatriates in Japan, Korea and China, the *Chronicle* was read in all the embassies of these countries, and by newspaper men and opinion leaders in Great Britain, Europe and the United States.

ARTHUR MORGAN YOUNG (1874–1942), EDITOR 1922–36

Robert Young died suddenly of a heart attack at his home in Kobe on the night of 7 November 1922. He was sixty-four. The Youngs had five children: Arthur Conway, Douglas George, Eric Andrew, a daughter who died in childhood, and Ethel Margaret Young. The eldest boy, Arthur, had died on service in France in 1917. Douglas, the second son, had served in the Air Force as a Captain and had become a flying instructor in Kobe after the war. The third son, Eric, had been a corporal dispatch rider on the Western Front before returning to manage the *Chronicle* presses. Ethel, the youngest child, had married Reginald Steward-Scott RNR in Portsmouth, England, in March 1921, and in May 1922, a daughter was born.[24] .

Robert Young's estate including the *Japan Chronicle* business and property, was valued for probate at £749.11s.3d. Under his Will, ownership of the *Chronicle* passed to a trust, of which Robert's youngest son Eric was the sole member.[25] Eric now became managing director of the *Japan Chronicle* and the British journalist and writer on Japan, Arthur Morgan Young, who had been assistant editor since 1911, became editor.

In the summer of 1922, the new *Mainichi Shinbun* English edition had poached some of the *Chronicle*'s Japanese linotype print workers, defections which brought the paper to its knees, as new staff had to be found and trained up from the beginning. Robert Young bought two new printing machines and engaged new operators from England, but for a month, the daily paper came out in a smaller edition, and the *Chronicle* lost readers. Now, Eric Young had to meet the payroll of large advertising and printing departments, a team of translators and a sizeable editorial department (including his new editor at ¥1000 a month), cable and supplies costs, and find his own salary. These were daunting problems to someone with no financial training or management experience and in 1926, Eric Young committed suicide by drowning.[26]

It is difficult to find anyone with a good word for Douglas Young, who now replaced Eric as managing director. Eric's elder brother was a heavy drinker and notoriously ill tempered. Tokyo Embassy officials described him as 'a half-crazy misanthrope with a grudge against the Japanese and ourselves', and as being 'always against the government'.[27] The historian of expatriate Japan, Harold Williams, who knew him personally, wrote that Douglas Young '… was not a journalist, nor was he a person of any great ability nor business experience'.[28] Even the Gaimusho described him as inexperienced (*mukeiken*), arrogant (*gōgan*) and bureaucratic (*kanryōteki*).[29] .

Eric Young had been on good terms with Morgan Young, but under the new manager, the atmosphere became hard and unforgiving. In the spring of 1930, Morgan Young found that his salary had been docked ¥65 for 'free advertisement' because he had reprinted in the *Chronicle* an interesting American review of his book *Japan in Recent Times*.[30] At the same time, the *Chronicle*'s financial situation continued to deteriorate. Desperate to cut costs, Douglas Young stopped paying the salary of a Japanese employee of the advertising department and fired two other advertising staff. In 1927, in a characteristically intemperate move, he closed down the advertising department altogether. In 1929, he stopped publishing the *Japan Chronicle Year Book*, then closed the Japan Chronicle Press and fired its staff of forty-five.

The *Chronicle*'s financial problems had not been irreversible in 1926, but by these sackings and closures, Douglas Young cut off useful revenue and made recovery entirely dependent on the fortunes of the newspaper. But the *Chronicle* was on its way out. Foreign news stopped coming in when cable bills went unpaid and the *Chronicle* began copying items from other papers and using translations of vernacular press reports as page-fillers. By the early 1930s, Morgan Young's essays and opinion pieces were almost the only fresh items in the paper, and circulation had halved to a couple of thousand copies as readers moved to the blander pastures of the *Japan Advertiser*.

Unlike Robert Young, whose writing was concentrated on the *Chronicle* and correspondence for the *Manchester Guardian*, Morgan Young wrote extensively for other publications. He also published four books: *Japan in Recent Times*: *1912–1926* (1929), *Books on the Far East* (1934), *Imperial Japan: 1926–1938*, (1938) and *The Rise of a Pagan State: Japan's Religious Background* (1939).[31] Morgan Young was very close to his predecessor, even in his religious outlook. During his time as editor, the *Chronicle*'s focus changed little: Japan's lack of reciprocity, the dangers of militarism, official attempts to control 'thought', the suppression of the socialist and labour movement, Japan's sponsorship of the opium trade in China, and the errors of emperor worship, (nicely instanced by Morgan Young as 'the folly of dying for an enlarged photograph').[32]

Conyngham Greene may have had reason to maintain that Robert Young's *Chronicle* was ignored by the Japanese, but under Morgan Young it was taken very seriously indeed. Morgan, Douglas and Eric Young were under constant police observation, (Morgan Young liked to bamboozle the gendarmes by signing himself 'Douglas Young' in hotel registers), and the *Chronicle* was often marked for close inspection (*sasatsu yo-chui shi*) by the Home Ministry (*Naimusho*). Between 1932–1937, thirty-five issues were prohibited from sale and distribution by order of the Home Ministry, eighty-three inspired official warnings, and on three occasions articles were published which led to punishment of the editor by order of the Kobe district court.[33] The Gaimusho also kept a close eye on *Chronicle* articles, translating and analysing their content as a matter of course.

On 15 September 1936, a *Chronicle* article suggesting Japan compensate the families of those Chinese killed in the recent Chengdu and Pakhoi incidents led to the official suppression of the entire edition. Under circumstances that remain unclear, Morgan Young resigned from the *Chronicle*. Although he considered the offending article 'as harmless a lucubration as was ever written', Young seems to have been under official pressure to resign, remarking that 'Mr. Amau [Eiji, then head of the *Gaimusho Jōhōbu*] flatters me by being interested in my departure'.[34] In October 1936, he sailed for England.

In May 1937, Morgan Young was appointed Tokyo correspondent for the *Manchester Guardian* but his application for a permit to return to Japan was turned down by the London embassy. Young settled down in London and in Cowley, Oxford. In August1938, he began a ten-page fortnightly newsletter, *The Far East Survey*, published from his London home.[35] *The Far East Survey* was critical of Japan's activities in China and may have been financed by the Chinese Nationalists.[36] Later in 1938, Young published *Imperial Japan* and contributed articles to *Asia* magazine, the *Contemporary Review*, *Pacific Affairs*, *The Times* and other organs.

There is no sign that anyone at the Foreign Office felt that Morgan Young's twenty-five years experience as a commentator on Japan might help the Far East Department to read and understand the country. In mid-December 1938, the ex-Japan diplomat Harold Parlett was asked by London University to chair a lecture by Morgan Young on 'Imperial Japan'. Parlett sought guidance from his old employers and was advised that '… while we do not wish to discourage you in any official sense from accepting the invitation, you yourself might find it somewhat embarrassing, in view of your past and present associations with Japan, were Mr. Young to make disparaging references to the Japanese Government and perhaps even to the Throne'. Parlett made his excuses and the talk went ahead under another chairman.[37]

In retirement, Morgan Young continued to write about Japan and China and to pester the Foreign Office about the fate of former associates captured by the Japanese. He died in Oxford on 3 January 1942, aged about 68. His wife, Louisa May, and his two children, Ernest, who had been a businessman in Japan, and Lucy, survived him.[38] Louisa Young died in November 1970.

EDWIN ALLINGTON KENNARD (1902–77), EDITOR 1936–40

Following Morgan Young's departure, Douglas Young retired to England and was replaced by a Mr S. Foley, who became Business Manager of the *Chronicle*. The British journalist, Edwin Allington Kennard had been assistant editor for nine years and he now became editor of the *Chronicle*. Kennard had been in the Royal Navy for four years, then a journalist for another four years on the *Peking & Tientsin Times* before joining the *Chronicle* in March 1927.

Working in an even more forbidding atmosphere for independent comment, Kennard soon faced the same problems as his predecessors. In August 1937, the *Chronicle* published an offensive article and in mid-October Kennard was summoned by the Kobe district court and briefly imprisoned.

In June and November 1940, fearing that, as the *Japan Advertiser* had just done, the *Chronicle* might sell out to Japanese interests, the British Embassy in Tokyo offered financial assistance to the *Chronicle*. Accepting the second offer, Foley assured the embassy that a sale was out of the question. As the British Ambassador Sir Robert Craigie later reported: 'This was, of course, at a time when arrangements for the sale had already reached an advanced stage.' On 17 December 1940, Craigie learned that the *Chronicle* was to be sold to the *Japan Times & Advertiser*, and the transaction took place on 21 December.[39] To add to Craigie's vexation, on 14 March 1941, on the eve of his departure from Japan, Mr Foley confessed to Craigie that the Gaimusho had been subsidizing the *Chronicle* since 1938. On condition the *Chronicle* temper its editorial line on Japan and keep the subsidy secret, ¥3000 a month had been distributed among Foley himself, Edwin Kennard, and the Young family.

Or rather, what was left of it. Young's widow, Annie, had left Japan in September 1923 and died in London. Arthur had died in 1917, Eric had committed suicide in 1926, and Douglas had died in the late 1930s. Ethel, the only surviving child, had divorced from Mr Steward-Scott, married a Mr Harloe, and removed to Bournemouth. As the principal beneficiary of the Young Estate, Mrs Harloe, whom

Harold Williams has described rather primly as '... an inebriate and a rather notorious person', had for three years been paid ¥1000 a month by the Gaimushō and her daughter, now aged nineteen, ¥200 a month.[40] As editor, Edwin Kennard received ¥230 a month, as Business Manager, Foley received ¥200. The remaining ¥1370 a month covered 'other expenses'.[41]

In December 1940, Foley and Kennard were paid 'substantial retiring allowances' and Ethel Harloe received the lion's share of the sum 'considerably in excess of ¥300,000' paid in foreign currency by the Gaimusho (through the *Japan Times & Advertiser*) for the *Japan Chronicle*. This price was more than fair, if we recall that in 1924, when the *Chronicle* was a going concern, Robert Young's gross estate, including the *Japan Chronicle*, was valued at £749.11s.3d.

Craigie was irritated by Foley's deception, but he seems to have felt that Edwin Kennard had concealed the subsidy out of loyalty to his *de facto* employer, Mrs. Harloe, who would have had to give her assent to his breaking the terms of her deal with the Gaimusho. Not without misgivings, Craigie recommended Kennard for a post with the Malayan Broadcasting Corporation in Singapore. The last nominally independent editor of the *Japan Chronicle* sailed from Yokohama on 24 March 1941.

Whatever his involvement in the subornment and sale of the *Chronicle*, after the fall of Singapore, Kennard's BBC radio broadcasts from Southeast Asia did much to enlighten British listeners during the Pacific War. In peacetime, Kennard returned to newspaper work – on this occasion the *Straits Times* in Singapore. He died in retirement in Groby, Leicester, on 27 June 1977, aged seventy-five.

As for the *Chronicle*, under the wing of the *Japan Times & Advertiser* its subsidy went up to ¥4000 a month and, as Craigie reported, it became 'gradually more pro-Axis until at present there is nothing to distinguish it from the *Japan Times & Advertiser*'. After the sale, the British Embassy huffily did what it had so often threatened to do when the *Chronicle* was a less emasculated organ, and cancelled its subscription. Edited and staffed by Gaimusho appointees, the *Chronicle* continued to publish a daily edition until 31 January 1942.

Robert Craigie's disappointment over the *Chronicle*'s subsidy and sale to Japanese interests was real enough, but he might have seen it coming. Even in wartime, with three of his sons serving on the Western Front, Robert Young's *Japan Chronicle* never beat the drum for Britain. In all its unsubsidized history, from 1891–1938, the *Chronicle* never put Britain's (or Japan's) national interest before what it saw as the facts of an issue. Foley and Kennard had acted in bad faith, but representing an institution that had scorned unthinking loyalty for almost half a century, it would have been difficult to accuse them of treachery.

The foreign experience in East Asia has been described as 'a network of multiple overlapping imperialisms, in the interstices of which opportunistic groups carved out new livelihoods and new roles'.[42] Robert Young, Morgan Young and Edwin Kennard lived and worked in these interstices. As much as any Parsee merchant or White Russian settler, as much as any American or Ulsterman, the editors of the *Japan Chronicle* sought their own fulfilment, from Robert Young and Morgan Young's radical, engaged Positivism to Edwin Kennard's 'substantial retiring allowance' from the sale of the *Chronicle*. What made the *Japan Chronicle* so readable was not only its critical line on Japan, but its equally forthright line on British and American affairs. It is a measure of their independence and resourcefulness that today the editors of the *Japan Chronicle* and their newspaper belong as much to the history of Japan as they do to the history of Britain.

30

Timothy or Taid or Taig Conroy or O'Conroy (1883–1935): 'The "Best Authority, East and West" on anything concerning Japan'

PETER O'CONNOR

Timothy Conroy

FOR A WHILE after the publication in July 1933 of his book, *The Menace of Japan*, Timothy Conroy was treated by the British press as an 'inside' source on Japan and her intentions in East Asia. Conroy's own high opinion of his scholarship was not widely echoed outside Fleet Street, but the explosion of Japanese military activity in China in the 1930s and Conroy's early death in November 1935 lent credibility to his writings and a retrospective purpose to his chaotic life.

Timothy Conroy was born on 20 August 1883, in Castleinch, Ballincollig, Co. Cork, to Jeremiah and Hanora Conroy.[1] According to his 1932 curriculum vitae, Conroy joined the Royal Navy in 1898, serving in South Africa, Somaliland and the Persian Gulf until 1906.[2] He then spent a year teaching English at a Berlitz school in Copenhagen. In 1909, Conroy was 'Introduced to the Russian

Imperial Court by H.M. Kammer her Kajar'. He taught English in 'Petersburg (Imperial Palace)' and lived 'in the suite of General Rauch, A.D.C. to a Grand Duke' before moving to Siberia to 'study Siberian types and peasants' life'. In 1913, Conroy returned to London to manage the Ambassadors Theatre for a year. In 1914, he passed the Civil Service Commission with Honours in Languages and became a Language Officer 'attached to R.N. Airships, Belgium'. Later that year, he helped repatriate British subjects from Germany via Switzerland. Then, in 1916, Conroy began the journey that would take him to Japan.

Conroy's curriculum vitae gives the impression of an occasional author, equally at ease in a naval mess and the 'suite' of a Grand Duke's *aide de camp*, blessed with the means to 'study conditions', 'pick up on' events and see how matters 'peg out', and when things get too much, 'to rest and take cure', but Conroy's father was a labourer who could not write his own name, and Conroy spent even the years of his greatest celebrity in extreme hardship.[3]

Timothy Conroy was born Timothy Conroy but he died Taid O'Conroy. He was Taig O'Conroy to US President Coolidge in 1924, Tim Conroy to Malcolm Kennedy in 1925, Taid Conroy at Hikone College, Shiga, from 1926–28, T. O. Conroy to *The Daily Mail* in 1932, Taid O'Conroy to his publishers Hurst & Blackett and his readers in Britain and America, Timothy O'Conroy to the British and Japanese press and Timothy or T. Conroy to the British Foreign Office. Hindsight shows that there was no conspicuous profit for Tim Conroy in managing these variations, but knowing this does not help us understand why he did it.

CONROY IN JAPAN

Timothy Conroy got to Japan by a roundabout route. By his own account, Conroy travelled east in 1916 to work with the British Economic Mission to Russia. In 1917–18, he 'opened own business' with the Trans-Siberian Railway, but was held up in the siege of Moscow 'by "Lenin" Army'. According to his British detractors in Tokyo, Conroy was a deck hand who jumped ship in Vladivostock before coming to Japan. According to the *Tokyo Asahi Shinbun*, when Japan and her Allies intervened in Siberia in 1918, Conroy was working for the Harbin post office.[4]

Conroy taught English at Keio Gijuku University from 1919–20. In 1920, he married Terao Kikuko, a resident of Morikawa-cho in Hongo-ku, Tokyo. Mrs Conroy is described as a 'café waitress' in most Foreign Office correspondence, and in the Japanese press as a waitress (*jokyū*) at the 'Oolong *Kissaten*' in Ginza, a teahouse where she was known as 'O-Kiku-san'. More bluntly, the journalist and historian Malcolm Kennedy refers to Mrs Conroy as 'an inmate of the Yoshiwara'.[5] The publisher's preface to a late edition of *The Menace of Japan* describes the Terao family as 'an aristocratic family that can trace its line back through many centuries'.[6] .

In 1920, according to his curriculum vitae, Conroy went to China and 'studied Manchurian "Open Door"', returning to Japan to teach at the Imperial Naval Staff College from 1921–22. He was injured in the Great Kanto Earthquake of September 1923, and visited America to recover, accompanied by his wife. In 1924, the Conroys visited the White House and most American dailies carried photographs of 'Professor Taig O'Conroy' and 'The most beautiful woman in Asia' on either side of US President Calvin Coolidge. According to Malcolm Kennedy, Conroy had obtained an introduction to the President by 'posing as a friend of the Prince of Wales'.

As Kennedy has it, before leaving Japan, Conroy told a wealthy collector of *netsuke* that he could get a high price for his pieces in America, and he was given part of the collection with which to test the market. However, while he was in America, Conroy got into the habit of presenting new acquaintances with *netsuke* as keepsakes. When he returned to Japan, Conroy explained to the collector that he had used his pieces to 'salt the ground' for his next visit to America, but the man demanded compensation. Conroy having no funds, the collector brought a court action against him, whereupon Conroy and his wife left Japan. However, according to Professor H. I. Bird of Waseda University, writing to the *Japan Advertiser*, when he returned to Tokyo, far from facing a court case, Conroy blackmailed the *netsuke* collector out of 'several thousand yen'.[7] According to the 1933 *Asahi* report, Conroy tried to sell artworks of dubious provenance *(ikagawashii)* while he was in America, and presented President Coolidge with a *netsuke* piece that he said had been used by the Shogun (*Shogun no shiyo shita netsuke*). Eventually, the *netsuke* were exposed as fakes and Conroy returned to Japan. The *Asahi* does not mention a court case.

Sometime in 1924–25, Conroy opened a language school in Shibakoen, in central Tokyo, but it went out of business. During this lull, Conroy's main haunt was the lobby of the Imperial Hotel. On 2 April 1925, Malcolm Kennedy, Reuters' newly appointed Tokyo correspondent, dined at the Imperial Hotel with an Indian friend who introduced him to 'a man named Conroy'. In his diary, Kennedy noted that 'Conroy … was formerly a naval officer, but chucked the Service in 1906 to go to Russia. Has a Japanese wife and was, for some yrs., instructor of English at the Japanese Naval Staff Coll.' Noting his naval experience, Kennedy asked Conroy if he was a member of the Tokyo British Legion. Conroy replied that he was not, explaining that he was so immersed in Japanese society and culture that he seldom mixed with other foreigners.[8]

In a later account, Malcolm Kennedy relates that he told an embassy acquaintance about meeting Conroy. Kennedy's friend snorted, '"Ex-naval officer! University professor! My holy aunt! He has never been in the Navy, he is no more a professor than you or I, and his real name is Tim Conroy. He made his way to Japan some years ago from Vladivostock after deserting from a freighter, in which he had been working as a deck-hand... He now likes to pose as a professor and calls himself Taig O'Conroy. It sounds more distinguished than plain Tim Conroy"'.[9]

This conversation – and even the embassy man himself – may have been a retrospective creation, for Kennedy's own diary entry for 2 April 1925 shows that Conroy introduced himself as Conroy and made no claim to be a professor. Kennedy's 1966 account, written for *Blackwood's Magazine* but never published, has Conroy introducing himself as Professor O'Conroy. However, for someone who spent the best part of his week in the Imperial Hotel lobby, Conroy's claim that he 'seldom mixed with foreigners' seems rather bold.

In April 1926, Conroy's fortunes revived when he obtained an English teaching post at Hikone College, the forerunner of Shiga University. The university history records that 'he suffered from the derogatory attitudes of other teachers because of his lack of academic background (*mugakusha*)'.[10] Conroy's contract expired in 1928, and he left Hikone. Conroy's curriculum vitae has it that he went to Europe in 1928–29 to '"pick up" on changes of conditions' and to Geneva to 'study the working of the League of Nations'.[11] The same document has Conroy spending 1930 and part of 1931 in Korea, then returning to Japan to teach for a while at the 'Second Shinko College' in Kobe.

Conroy and his wife definitely left Japan in May 1932. Conroy said in a 1933 interview that they had left after he received a threat from 'a prominent member of a notorious secret society called 'The Dragons' and that his wife had come with him as far as Marseilles, 'and then returned to let me have regular information about events in Japan'.[12] In December 1933, Kikuko Conroy told a consular official in Tokyo that she had not seen her husband since July 1932, when she had been repatriated from Marseilles by the Japanese consulate.[13] Malcolm Kennedy believed that the Conroys left Japan to avoid the *netsuke* lawsuit and that Conroy abandoned his wife in Marseilles, and the Japanese consul repatriated her.

The truth lies somewhere between Conroy's melodrama and Kennedy's hatchet job. In May 1932, the Conroys sailed from

Yokohama, entered the Mediterranean through the Suez Canal, and quite possibly disembarked in Istanbul, for the next item on Conroy's curriculum vitae was an English teaching post at the Turkish Senior Naval College. This cannot have been much more than a stop-gap, however, for within a few weeks Kikuko Conroy was kicking her heels in Marseilles and Timothy Conroy was in London, planning his entrée to the Foreign Office.

CONROY AND THE FOREIGN OFFICE

On 27 May 1932, Douglas Crawford, Foreign Editor at the *Daily Mail*, sent a letter introducing Conroy to Sir Robert Vansittart, Permanent Under-Secretary at the Foreign Office in London. Crawford cautioned, 'Conroy is a queer individual, but I make bold to say that his knowledge is profound. He has lived and taught in Japan for many years. He has a charming Japanese wife who comes from a very important family and he himself, I believe, both reads and writes Japanese.'[14] Crawford wrote of 'My old friend T. O'Conroy' but crossed through the apostrophe in 'T. O'Conroy' and added a full stop so that it reads 'T. O. Conroy'.

On the morning of 1 June, Conroy came to the Foreign Office by appointment and was interviewed not by Vansittart but by another senior official, Sir John Pratt. According to Pratt's notes, Conroy believed that recent political developments in Japan 'could only be explained by the neo Shintoism … and the peculiar race cult of the Japanese people. The military caste are the High Priests of Neo Shintoism and among them there is a turning away from Western civilisation back towards the dark beliefs of an earlier epoch'.

Conroy struck Pratt as bombastic and arrogant. 'He has spent thirteen years in Japan studying Shintoism and unfortunately his mind appears to have been affected by the process'. He suggested that the Foreign Office appoint a panel of experts to debrief him, as 'It was impossible to convey in a few hours his own "infinite knowledge" (these were his actual words!)'.[15]

One hour into their meeting, Pratt interrupted Conroy to suggest that 'perhaps he had better put what he had to say into the form of a memorandum which we could study at leisure. This, to my relief, he readily promised to do. He asked if he could be loosely attached in some capacity to the Foreign Office. I said this would be difficult but we had better see his memorandum first.'[16] This last fainthearted suggestion set off a saga that would take years to unravel.

Nine days later, when Conroy delivered his memorandum, he produced a typewritten receipt.

Foreign Office 10/6/1932,

> Received a Memorandum, requested by H.M. Foreign Office, from Mr T. Conroy, consisting of six parts, and dealing with present-day conditions in Japan (1) Psychology of Neo-Shinto. (2) Economics. (3) Political Parties. (4) Military Psychology and tendencies. (5) Priests (My note: Priests' propaganda activities) (6) Manchuria. 'Open Door.' Signed, ooooooooo, Chief of the Far East Division. 10/6/1932.[17]

Pratt signed this document, 'without scanning it too closely'.[18] Over the next six weeks, Conroy sent Pratt and Vansittart a series of letters, offering, among other things, to set up 'a little group of experts on Japanese thought' and to 'procure the presence of our deepest medical psycholico-psychiatric authority: to give the expert point of thought; re the actuality of humans being absorbed with such a devouring (mental monopoly) (mono-pensation) as are the Japanese, at this present time.'[19]

When Conroy left Japan in May, he had come with his wife as far as Marseilles, left her there and gone on to London. Conroy now told Pratt that his wife was due to sail from Marseilles for Japan on 23 June. He had given up trying to finance Kikuko's *permit de séjour* or to get her to England on the proceeds from his memorandum, but he was worried about her reception in Japan for '... she *cannot fight against the type of Shinto influence that will be brought to bear on her in J-n*'.

Throughout their exchanges, Pratt insisted that there was no hope of the Foreign Office either paying Conroy for his memorandum or offering him a job. On 13 June, Conroy asked that his memorandum be returned. On 16 June, Pratt posted the memorandum to Conroy with a letter of thanks, repeating that no funds were available to pay for it and that no employment was available. On 22 June, John Norton of the Foreign Office wrote on Vansittart's behalf to thank Conroy for his letters. On 6 July, Conroy wrote to Pratt to say that his wife was still in Marseilles, adding, 'Surely there is some kind of little nook in the F.O. into which I could fit.'.

Nothing was heard of Conroy for three months. Messrs Norton, Pratt and Vansittart certainly had bigger fish to fry. On 15 September 1932, Japan signed a treaty recognizing Manchoukuo and thereby pre-empting the Lytton Commission's Report, which was published in October. In February 1933, when the League of Nations Assembly accepted the Commission's Report, which blamed both China and Japan for the state of affairs in China and Manchuria but rejected Japan's justifications of its excursions in China and named Japan as the aggressor, Matsuoka Yosuke led the Japanese walkout from the conference hall. Japan withdrew from the League of Nations on 27 March. That spring, Matsuoka's dramatic exit and his statements framing Japan's position in terms of national victimhood and even 'crucifixion' greatly excited Anglophone publics in East Asia and on both sides of the Atlantic.

On 4 October 1932, Conroy surfaced again, at the British Consulate in Brest (France) with a request for funds to return to England. Desperate to pay for his wife's *permit de séjour*, Conroy had tried to find teaching work in Toulon but failed and had run out of funds. On 31 October, the Consul at Brest advanced Conroy F300.00 for his fare to London. Conroy surrendered his passport and the curriculum vitae that informs this paper, and, for good measure, showed the Consul a letter of thanks from Sir John Pratt K.B.E., C.M.G. 'for a memorandum on Japan which he wrote recently, in London, at the request of the Foreign Office'.[20]

Back in London in mid-November 1932, Conroy wrote to Pratt 'in dire, dire, distress of mind and pocket'. He had for sale some 'hot' lines of merchandise, namely a weatherproof coat, a 'stockingette' shirt and a "Zip" portmanteau, plus some autograph writings from George Bernard Shaw, all of which he offered to Pratt and Vansittart in return for hard cash. Finally, he protested, 'It is really a surprising [thing] to me, and to those to whom I speak of it, that H.M. Government REQUESTS work and then does not give "the labourer his hire"' then asked, 'Could some way be found to give me a "leg up"?'[21] On 20 November, Pratt set aside his duties at the League of Nations World Disarmament Conference in Geneva to deny that he had made an official request for Conroy's memorandum. 'His present claim is rather an impudent try on, but I expect the poor devil is starving.'

On 25 November, Conroy sent Vansittart a copy of the receipt for his memorandum, which Pratt had signed on 10 June. In his covering letter, Conroy wrote that he had received 'a very warm letter of thanks' from Pratt, stating that his memorandum threw '"a strong light on the background of affairs in the Far East"'. 'This is but natural,' wrote Conroy, '— as I am considered the "Best Authority, East and West" on anything concerning Japan'.[22] On 26 November, Norton complained, 'the poor fellow is beginning to make himself a nuisance by calling'.[23] On 13 December, following internal discussions, Norton wrote to Conroy returning his passport.[24] On 17 February 1933, the Foreign Office formally wrote off Conroy's repatriation costs of FF300 or three pounds, fourteen shillings and one penny at the current rate of exchange.[25]

THE MENACE OF JAPAN

In July 1933, Conroy's *The Menace of Japan* came out in London. The name on the jacket spine was 'Professor T.O'Conroy', and on the front 'T.O'Conroy, late Professor of Keio University, Tokyo'. George Bernard Shaw threw a party for the author and introduced him to literary London. 'Professor O'Conroy's' revelations enthralled reviewers at the *Morning Post* and the *Daily Telegraph*. At the *Daily Mail*, Foreign Editor Douglas Crawford ran a large spread on 'Professor O'Conroy' and his book.

Despite emphasising that 'The book is not mere sensationalism; it is a cold, logical thesis compiled by the author during his fifteen years in Nippon', the blurb for *The Menace of Japan* spoke of 'authenticated stories of the debauchery of the Buddhist priests, unutterable cruelty, sex orgies, of trafficking in human flesh, of baby brokers'. The introduction stressed the author's 'special credentials and his inside knowledge of Japan'. Not only had he taught at Keio University, 'the Oxford of Japan', but he had married into an 'aristocratic Japanese family' and become 'a 100 per cent Shintoist and Japanese'.

The Menace of Japan was not the worst Japan book of the 1930s, but it was far from the best. For all Conroy's vaunted intimacy with the Japanese language, he depended heavily on the English-language newspapers of Japan for material. Citing 'the *Japan Advertiser* (Vernacular Edition)' and 'the *Japan Chronicle* (Vernacular Edition)', Conroy may have wished to dilute the impression of his dependence on English-language sources, but neither paper had a Japanese edition.

The book dusts off some very old chestnuts, notably the story, which had been going around since the 1850s, on how the Japanese dealt with foreign discomfort at mixed bathing. 'No, today a rope is slung across the middle of the bath, and men must keep to one side and women to the other, thus honour has been satisfied!' (p. 53).

There are spectacular omissions. 'An old man, named Sakae Osugi, a retired schoolmaster, lived quietly with his wife and his nephew, a boy of ten years. He had retired, but earned a little money giving private tuition. He was happy with his wife, had he not worked hard for fifty years? Neighbours, rivals possibly for his private pupils, some petty enemy, reported to the police that the family's thoughts were not loyal to the Emperor…' (p. 42). In discussing the September 1923 murder of Japan's most newsworthy anarchist, his nephew and his common-law wife Ito Noe, Conroy seems to have been quite unaware of who he was.

More than such errors, what most upset official Japan was the claim, in the introduction to *The Menace of Japan*, that 'Eamonn de

Valera, when he was preparing to act as President of the League during its consideration of the policy of Japan in Manchuria, used parts of this book in manuscript form' (p. 11). In other words, Conroy's arguments alerting the world to the 'menace' of Japan had been put before the President of the League of Nations at the time that the League Assembly accepted the Report of the four-man Commission on Japan's behaviour in Manchuria. Nevertheless, whatever the extent of the upset caused by his book, *The Menace of Japan* was openly on sale through Thompsons of Kobe and affiliated agencies: it was never banned in Japan.

PERSECUTION AND COLLAPSE

In the autumn of 1933, interviews with 'Professor O'Conroy' began appearing in the British press, to the effect that Mrs Conroy was suffering persecution or worse, because of the help she had given her husband in researching his book. On 19 October, an interview with Conroy appeared on the front page of the *Evening Standard* of London, in which he claimed that the Japanese police and 'the notorious Dragons' were persecuting his wife and might have poisoned her. Conroy told the *Standard*:

> Some time ago my wife indicated briefly that she was afraid of being kidnapped. She could not tell me much; but I was calmed when I heard no more about it. Eighteen days ago I had a letter from her saying she had gone to bed with severe internal pains. I immediately feared poison. I have not heard from her since and I am alarmed. I cannot write to her or wire her to ask what is the matter, since to do so would, I am afraid, incite those who hate us to finish off the job. So I do not know whether she is even alive.

Conroy explained that he had managed to keep his address a secret up to now, but 'one of the secret societies has a branch either in London or Cambridge, and I fear an attack'.[26] .

Three days later, the *Tokyo Asahi Shinbun* responded with a report by its London correspondent headlined 'Eight hundred Lies published in "*The Menace of Japan*"' *(Uso happyaku o narabeta "Nihon no Kyōi" shuppan)*. According to the *Asahi*, Conroy had held a number of teaching posts, including one at Keio University, but had lost them all through 'vicious and intemperate habits'. Other foreigners in Japan looked down on Conroy (*zairyūgaijin kara hinshiku sarete itta*). He had married 'O-Kiku-san', a beautiful hostess from a Ginza teahouse, whom he used in the United States as an 'envoy of friendship', pretending that she was a lady of quality and an official bearer of cordial sentiments from the women of Japan to the women of America. Under this guise, Conroy and his wife had met President Coolidge at the White House and, as mentioned above, had presented him with *netsuke* 'used by the Shogun'. Asked by the *Asahi* to comment on the report, the Gaimusho said it had no knowledge of Conroy's book, that there had recently been a flood of this type of literature about Japan, and that sensible people in England would rate the book at its true value.[27] .

Two weeks later, the *Japan Chronicle* of Kobe thought the *Evening Standard* article 'rather like a sensational piece of advertising'.[28] On 23 November, the *Japan Advertiser* published Professor Bird's letter describing Conroy as 'a plausible and clever adventurer, but of a likeable disposition'. Bird claimed that besides bilking the *netsuke* collector (see above), Conroy had recently 'slept three or four nights in the rain in the streets' of Kobe to protest the decision of an Osaka man not to engage Conroy to take his son to England where he wished him to be educated. As the professor saw it, 'England and Japan must always work hand in hand, to effect a lasting peace and prosperity in the East'. However, there were those who sought to disrupt these harmonious objectives. 'The mercurial Conroy while in Japan had expressed violent antipathy towards England and had schemes of espousing the cause of the Sinn Feiners against that country'.[29] .

Back in London, Conroy collapsed and was taken to the London County Council Hospital in Hammersmith, west London, where a doctor diagnosed a nervous breakdown, '… accentuated by the fact that for some weeks past he has been almost destitute – starving himself so that he could send money to his wife'.[30] Aroused by their author's condition and his fearful allegations, Conroy's publishers asked the Foreign Office to find Mrs Conroy and help get her out of Japan.

In early November, Malcolm Kennedy received a cable from Reuters in London to 'cover briefly disappearance wife O'Conroy'. Calling at the Gaimusho, Kennedy was shown a pile of cuttings from London and provincial newspapers playing up the 'O'Conroy' story for all it was worth. Far from their stated ignorance, the Gaimusho had been following Conroy's statements and writings closely. On 24 November, Kennedy cabled Reuters in London, 'Whereabouts Mrs O'Conroy unknown but O'Conroy well-known impostor swindler'. To his fury, Kennedy's cable was spiked and the Conroy story continued to develop, this time in the *Sunday Despatch*.[31]

SEARCH FOR MISSING BEAUTY
AUTHOR HUSBAND'S FEARS OF JAPANESE AVENGERS
The beautiful Japanese wife of Professor Timothy O'Conroy has disappeared at Tokio. A Reuter message stated yesterday that the police have been requested to search for her.

Professor O'Conroy is at present a patient in a London hospital. For 14 years he was Professor of English at Tokio University, and while there married Kikuko Terao, famed as the most beautiful girl in Tokio. When the professor came to England recently, his wife remained in Japan.

'THIS IS THE END'

'This is the end,' said Professor O'Conroy, sinking back on his pillow, when a *Sunday Despatch* representative informed him of the disappearance.

'My wife is a victim of vengeance. She is regarded as a "traitor'"because she supplied me with information for my book, 'The Menace of Japan'.

BAND OF FANATICS

She is probably in the clutches of a secret society known as 'God's Soldiers'. The society is composed of fanatical young men of good birth who are ultra-patriotic. Recently they planned to murder the whole of the Japanese Cabinet.

'If they have got her, there is no knowing what may happen. There is no limit to their inhumanity. She could be slowly tortured to death.'

THE NOBLEST CREATURE

Tears came into his eyes. 'I loved her more than I ever thought it was possible to love a woman. She was the noblest creature I ever met … Now it is all over. If she has gone, I have nothing left to live for.'[32]

On 30 November 1933, Kikuko Conroy was summoned to police headquarters in Tokyo and questioned for over five hours about her family and ancestors and her husband. She signed a statement containing an express denial that she had suffered any molestation. Other members of her family were also questioned. Soon after, the British Consulate also tracked down Mrs Conroy. She was in good health, living with her brother and his family in Morikawa-cho, Hongo-ku, and running a tea-house in Kanda. Mrs Conroy visited the Tokyo Consul on 1 December 1933 and 'emphatically denied that she had been the victim of any form of persecution' and that she been the source of any of the material in *The Menace of Japan*, which she had not even read. Conroy had not supported her since May

1932, she had not seen him since July 1932, when she had been repatriated from Marseilles by the Japanese consulate, and she had not heard from him since August 1933.[33]

Conroy slipped from public view that winter, but early in January 1934, Sir John Pratt received a letter from a City solicitor, asking for an appointment to discuss 'a Memorandum prepared at the request of H.M. Foreign Office' by their client 'Professor O'Conroy'.[34] No doubt, Pratt and his colleagues braced themselves for a resumption of the memorandum saga, but the official paper trail ends there and the outcome of this final episode is unknown.

When Conroy told the *Sunday Despatch* in November 1933, 'I have nothing left to live for', he may, at last, have been speaking the truth. Conroy died on 6 November 1935, at Hampstead General Hospital. He was fifty-two. His death certificate records heart failure resulting from cirrhosis of the liver: we can surmise that Conroy had a severe drinking problem. The name given on his death certificate is 'Taid O'Conroy'; it was witnessed by a brother, resident in London SW4, who signed it 'L. O'Conroy'.[35] The brother's signature and the name of the deceased on the death certificate give the impression that 'Taid O'Conroy' was Conroy's real name and that Conroy was the alias, whereas the opposite was true. Of course, Conroy could have changed his name by deed poll, but why would his brother do the same?

THE MAN ON THE SPOT

Ever since the murder of Queen Min of Korea in 1895 by Miura Goro and others, the British public had thrilled to the idea of Japanese secret societies. When the Crown Prince left Japan on his 1921 world tour, the *Daily Mail* had much to say about the opposition of the *Roninkai*. When Hara Kei was assassinated the following autumn, the secret society angle was rejuvenated, especially in the *Morning Post*. In the early 1930s, the 'patriotic' assassinations of Japanese politicians and industrialists were front-page news in Britain. By 1937, the boom in Japan scares had Graham Greene's feckless elder brother Herbert telling *Daily Worker* readers 'I was a Secret Agent of Japan' (and inspiring the inventive close-ups of vacuum cleaner parts of *Our Man In Havana*).[36] Conroy's book and interviews sent delicious shivers down the spine and confirmed many people's worst fears about Japan and the Japanese. With the 'Dragons' setting up in Cambridge, nobody was safe, not even in Hammersmith.

Between the 1890s and about 1919, Western readers and critics gave explanatory writers on Japan such as Nitobe Inazo and Sydney L. Gulick an easy ride. Critical books on Japan only began to sell well in the 1920s. As sales picked up, Japanese writers on Japan and Western-based foreign writers ceded credibility to writers who were 'on the spot' and took a more critical approach. Nitobe's fall from fashion did not occur on its own, but in relation to a rise in demand for critical writings by Western authors based in Japan. By the early 1930s, as far as Western readers were concerned, it was not enough to be a scholar of Japan if you were based in the West, and being Japanese gave an author of a book on Japan no advantage at all.[37] In July 1933, *The Menace of Japan* rode a swelling wave of demand for books by Western authors with an 'inside' knowledge of Japan. By May 1938, Conroy's book had gone into seven British editions and sold 13,000 copies.

Conroy's history certainly demonstrates the porosity of the British (but not only the British) establishment. The *Asahi* called him an intellectual conman (*interi goro [gorotsuki]*), but real conmen have bigger plans than the sale of 'stockingette' shirts to Whitehall functionaries. Conroy longed for access to the privileged and powerful. Above all, he yearned for intellectual prestige, and this he gained in a bull market for 'inside' information, at a time when Japan specialists were thin on the ground. Although *The Menace of Japan* sometimes illuminates little more than the unhappy life that inspired it, reading it today does throw a wobbly light on some of the jumpier aspects of Anglo-Japanese relations in the 1930s.

31

Freda Utley, 1899–1978: Crusader for Truth, Freedom and Justice

DOUGLAS FARNIE

Freda Utley

WINIFRED (FREDA) UTLEY (1899–1978) was the second child of Willie Herbert Utley (1866–1918) and Emily Williamson (1865–1945). Her father was a socialist journalist and her maternal grandfather a freethinker, a republican and a manufacturer in Manchester. Plain-featured, short-sighted and hard of hearing, Freda was a passionate and convinced believer in the causes she espoused. Educated in a rationalist and humanist mode, she was brought up to be a conscientious atheist and to see religion as only the shield of tyranny, intolerance and cruelty. Hot for certainties in life, she became imbued with an abiding passion for freedom and justice, which proved as strong as any religious fervour. She grew into a thoroughly modern woman, emancipated from the traditions of the past but retaining a tough Puritan core. From her education in Switzerland, she acquired an international outlook. She never believed in the particular wickedness or virtue of any one people, race or nation or in the intrinsic superiority of any race or nation to another. She never became much of a feminist and was saved from becoming 'the type of unsexed, frustrated or embittered woman who provides dynamic energy to all movements for the regimentation of mankind' such as Beatrice Webb or Eleanor Roosevelt.[1] Aspiring to liberate mankind from immemorial oppression, she sought to usher in, through political activity, a new era of human freedom.

In 1923 Freda graduated from King's College, London, with first-class honours in history. She undertook research under Norman H. Baynes (1878–1961), submitted a thesis on 'The social and economic status of the Collegia from Constantine to Theodosius II' and graduated in 1925 as an MA with distinction. She pursued her research at the London School of Economics under Charles M. Lloyd (1878–1946), Foreign Editor of the *New Statesman*. There she worked for two full years on Eastern competition with the Lancashire cotton industry. She was confidently expected to become as distinguished a woman economic historian as Eileen Power (1889–1940). The general strike of 1926 proved to be 'the turning point of my early political development', leading her into the Communist camp.[2] As the vice-president of the University Labour Federation she visited Russia, 'the Land of Promise' (June-Sept. 1927). 'To me it seemed that Russia had unlocked the gates of Paradise to mankind.'[3] On her return she became a member of the Communist Party (1927–30). In 1928 she travelled through Siberia to China and Japan. In Tokyo she undertook for nine months pioneer fieldwork into economic history, studying the bases of competition by Japan and India with Lancashire. That period she always remembered with an aching nostalgia as the happiest year of her life. She sought to avoid being 'overwhelmed by Japanese courtesy and hospitality'[4] and praised 'the incredible industry, devotion to their children and natural cleanliness of the poorer Japanese.'[5]

Her pioneering articles on comparative labour-costs in Japan and Lancashire established her reputation as an authority upon the cotton industry.[6] *Lancashire and the Far East* (1931) embodied the full fruits of her research in a detailed empirical study, supported by 112 tables of statistics. The book was intended to fulfil an educational function and to instruct the employers of Lancashire in the irreversible change in conditions in the world market since 1914. Freda was primarily concerned with labour conditions and labour costs. She showed that labour costs of production in Japan were one half of those in Lancashire in spinning and less than one half thereof in weaving. She concluded that the disparity in labour costs was so enormous that no reduction in labour costs in Lancashire could ever restore its competitive capacity in the markets of the Far East. The book was limited in value by its patently propagandist purpose and by its lack of sympathy with employers. Freda condemned British employers for *never* having paid a living wage to the majority of their workers. She also concluded that mill-girls in Japan clearly hated heir way of life.[8] She intended the work to form a contribution to the study of modern imperialism and indicted British policy in India as responsible for the impoverishment of its population. She refused to modify that conclusion when urged to do so. William Beveridge, the Director of the LSE, thereupon revoked his decision to permit the publication of the work under the imprint of the School. The book was published by Allen & Unwin and was translated twice into Russian (1931, 1934) and into Japanese (1936).

Freda had made two fateful decisions. In 1928 she married a Russian citizen, Arcadi Berdichevsky. In 1930 she emigrated to the USSR where she lived for five-and-a-half years in Moscow. There she served in succession as a member of the Anglo-American section of the Comintern and as a textile expert at Promexport and at the Commissariat of Light Industry. After the publication of her monograph she became in 1932 a senior scientific worker at the Institute of World Economy and Politics of the Academy of Sciences. She studied the economic and political situation in the Far East, in order to provide theoretical foundations for policy decisions. Freda had already become suspicious of Soviet 'socialist' society after meeting its representatives in the Tokyo embassy in 1928. In Moscow she speedily became disillusioned with the Soviet regime but managed to keep control of her tongue throughout her years in 'the Hell of Communist tyranny'.[9] Then on 11 April 1936 her husband was arrested and was sentenced to five years in prison. Freda never saw Arcadi again and left the USSR ten days later 'with my political beliefs and my personal happiness alike shattered'.[10] Years were to pass before she again became free in mind and in spirit.

Japan's Feet of Clay had been written in Moscow from a Marxist perspective and was published in November 1936. Launched with a sensational title and inspired by a propagandist bias, the book was written with a profound religious fervour and was intended to shock readers into acquiescent agreement. It was based upon three years of research and access to a wide range of English-language sources as well as to the eight-volume work, *Le Japon, Histoire et Civilisation* (1907–23) by Antoine Rous de la Mazaliere (1864–1937). Freda compared Japan to Tsarist Russia as it was in 1900 and described it as 'a colossus with feet of clay' and as 'Fascism's weakest link'.[11] Her intention was to undermine the myths about Japan propagated by its admirers, to explode the idea of its invincibility and to reveal the weakness of the foundations of the Japanese State. She therefore emphasized its limited resources in coal, iron and oil, i.e. in the raw materials essential to the development of modern industry. External expansion was necessary not only to supplement native resources but also to moderate the domestic conflicts endemic within society. 'The real Japan is a seething cauldron of misery and injustice, social hatreds, revengeful passions, hysteria and chauvinism; a country of continuous conflict ... Japan is a powder magazine full of mad hatred of the West.'[12] She accepted the view of the *Koza-ha* school of historians who argued that the restoration of 1868 had been an incomplete revolution.[13] The complicity of the Western powers was condemned for supplying the warlike materials necessary to Japanese expansion. Freda urged the imposition of economic sanctions, which she thought would precipitate the collapse of Japan within a few weeks.[14]

The book was praised in London for 'its comprehensive knowledge of Japan and its passionate faith in a cause' and for presenting 'a complete picture of a very strange country' which 'can only be rightly understood through the study of anthropology'.[15] It was however severely criticized by the geographer J. E. Orchard for its exaggerated assertions and by I. Clunies-Ross of Sydney as 'unnecessarily insulting to all Japanese, except those whose political sympathies are akin to her own'.[16] The recommendation to impose sanctions was rejected in the USA as an invitation to an 'imperialist adventure', obliging the UK and the USA to cut off their nose in order to save China's face.[17] The book was undoubtedly unbalanced in so far as it failed to recognize the real sources of Japan's national strength.[18] It was roundly criticized by a Japanese economist for the abundance of its incorrect, misguided and incorrect information.[19] Banned in Japan, the book became a best-seller in England and in the USA, being twice reprinted in January and February 1937. In September 1937 Faber & Faber printed it in a second and cheaper edition, with an extra chapter of fourteen pages on the Sino-Japanese War of 1937 and with an advertisement in bold type on the dust jacket 'This book is banned in Japan'. As an exposé the book proved to be comparable to Katherine Mayo's *Mother India* (1927). The Japanese held the author to be largely responsible for the initiation of a boycott of Japanese goods in America.[20] The book was translated into five foreign languages, French, Swedish, Danish, Norwegian and above all, Chinese. Tens of thousands of copies circulated in China and earned the author golden opinions as a 'great friend of China'. Thus its commercial success more than fulfilled the hopes of Freda, saving her from destitution.

Two more books on Sino-Japanese relations followed in quick succession. *Japan Can Be Stopped* (1937, 64pp.) was written in collaboration with David Wills and was published by the *News Chronicle*. It also appeared in a French translation, sponsored by the China delegation to the League of Nations. That translation was circulated by H. H. Kung to the delegates to the Brussels Conference of the signatories of the Nine-Power Treaty of 1922 which followed the outbreak of war in 1937.[21] *Japan's Gamble in China* (1938) was described by the author as 'a short book' of 302 pages, being completed in six weeks and favoured with an introduction by Harold Laski of the LSE. Therein Freda described Japan as 'a police state, governed by a bureaucracy wedded to a plutocracy' and criticized the argument from over-population as an excuse for Japanese aggression.[22] She re-emphasized the historic significance of the conflict. 'This war is a war to make or break Japan.'[23] She had begun to believe that the next world war would break out in the East rather than in the West. She began to make a transition from the study of Japan to the study of China, which had occupied only a single chapter in her monograph of 1931. Professing her belief in the 'absolute sincerity' of the Chinese Communists, she portrayed them as agrarian reformers, a view she later repudiated. 'Today Communism in the Far East stands for agrarian revolution, not the dictatorship of the proletariat'.[24] Once more she urged the imposition of economic sanctions by the UK, the USA and the Netherlands. The book ushered in a new phase in Freda's career: it enabled her to secure an appointment as a war correspondent for the *News Chronicle* and to complete a major study of the war for publication in June 1939.

China at War (1939) was based upon a stay of three months in China (July-Sept. 1938), upon two trips to the front line and upon many conversations with national leaders. In the temporary capital of Hankow Freda became one of the forty foreign correspondents who prided themselves upon remaining the 'Hankow Last Ditchers'. Together with Agnes Smedley (1892–1950), 'Freda Clayfoot Utley' became 'the centre of a high-powered, tight-knit social circle of diplomats and journalists'.[25] Freda herself served as 'the flame, uncontrolled and forever attracting all, instinctively and unconsciously'.[26] Her time in Hankow remained as memorable as her sojourn in Japan in 1928–29. 'Never had I known, or would know again, people I liked so well, felt so akin to and from whom it was so sad to part.'[27] Freda re-iterated her negative view of the Japanese as 'an under-nourished nation of robots' and 'the greatest menace to civilisation of any nation on earth' by virtue of their 'savage, simian efficiency'.[28] Together with Agnes Smedley, she revealed the terrible condition of the wounded Chinese soldiers, criticized the medical administration of their army and campaigned for help for the Chinese Red Cross Medical Commission.

In October 1938 Freda returned from Shanghai to San Francisco but was refused landing rights in Yokohama, so becoming newsworthy all over the world. Entering by the western back-door into the new and democratic society of the USA, she discovered that 'America came close to my vision of the good society'.[29] Her first article in an American paper was published in San Francisco.[30] Thereafter, she addressed meetings sponsored by the American Committee for Non-Participation in Japanese Aggression and travelled from coast to coast, urging an end to war supplies to Japan. Returning home to England, she was accepted as an authority upon the USSR and the Far East.[31] Her books on Japan were cited by G. E. Hubbard (1885–1951) as authoritative, although they were never mentioned by G. C. Allen (1900–82).[32] *China at War* won Freda much respect for the objectivity of its reporting as well as for her courage in facing 'death in terrifying shapes at close quarters'.[33] Unfortunately, the book was received with less enthusiasm than *Japan's Feet of Clay* and was indeed utterly neglected in the West, being overshadowed by the gathering storm of World War II.

The series of four books (1936–39) dealt ostensibly with the Far East. They were also conceived in terms of a covert personal agenda and formed part of Freda's desperate campaign to secure the release of her beloved husband. First, she hoped to establish her reputation in England in order to enhance her bargaining-power.[34] Secondly, she wished to prove that she was a wholly reliable Stalinist-line Communist and that Arcadi should therefore be freed to rejoin her. Thus *Japan's Feet of Clay* adopted a Stalinist type of analysis in accordance with the Comintern thesis of 1931. *China at War* reflected the Stalinist version of the new united front between Chiang Kai-shek and the Chinese Communists.[35] Freda could also have adopted coded language and may well have meant the USSR when writing about Japan in relation to the outward conformity of the population to the State creed and to the expressions of enthusiastic loyalty made under a tyrannical government.[36] Her campaign proved 'intellectually and psychologically terribly frustrating' and a total failure. The Soviet ambassador to the USA Konstantin Umanskii, declined forcefully in 1938 even to see Freda in Washington ('That bitch! Never!').[37]

Freda had agreed with her friend Bertrand Russell in approving the Munich policy of Neville Chamberlain, who thought an agreement with Hitler was more likely to preserve the British Empire than an alliance with Stalin. She was deeply disturbed by the Russo-German pact and the outbreak of war in 1939, ushering in the prospect of the unchecked expansion of Communist influence in Eastern Europe. 'National Socialism, Red or Brown, may be the new society which we cannot escape … The democratic sun is sinking.'[39] Her former membership of the Communist Party barred her from employment either in the Foreign Office or in the Royal Institute of

International Affairs at Chatham House. She therefore emigrated at the end of 1939 to the USA. 'My decision to leave the Old World for the New was the best I ever made.'[40] In New York she published in September 1940 her most important book.

The Dream We Lost. Soviet Russia Then and Now was one of the most bitter contributions ever penned to the literature of disillusion. Freda offered her own testimony to the public as 'the only Western writer who had known Russia both from inside and from below, sharing some of the hardships and all the fears of the forcibly silenced Russian people.'[41] Written more in hatred than in sorrow, the book contained a searing indictment of life endured in a virtual hell of human suffering under 'a savage and barbarous Asiatic despotism'.[42] Freda had shared in 'a comradeship of the damned' within a 'vast prison house' which had become 'a purgatory of our own choosing'.[43] The totalitarian tyranny of 'the Knouto-Soviet State' had created 'sullen apathy' 'stupified servility' and 'a more stultifying and soul-destroying system than any previously experienced by the sons of man'.[44] The Soviet way of life was one pervaded by a 'storm of terror, hate, regimented sadism, hunger, cold and wretchedness and … nauseating cant and hypocrisy'.[45] The book was didactic in purpose, like all of Freda's works. It was inspired by the mad rush of intellectuals in the West 'toward a world which will be as horrible as Russia'[46] and was intended to teach 'the plan-mad liberals of the Western world that Russia's reputedly planned economy is a myth'.[47] In the third part of the book 84 pages were devoted to a perceptive comparison of Soviet Russia with Nazi Germany, so paving the way for many imitators. In the conclusion, Freda advocated a negotiated peace between Hitler and England, even at the price of recognizing German hegemony over the Continent.[48] The alternative was the continuation of a mutually destructive war until Europe had been made safe for Stalinism.

The book was deeply moving and highly provocative, constituting the author's most ambitious and personal testament. It failed, however, to sell widely or to break through the sound barrier established by the left-wing controllers of the mass media. It was flatly rejected by Freda's English publishers, Faber & Faber, despite her readiness to eliminate the controversial Third Part, a concession, which she had declined to make to Beveridge in 1930. The publication of *The Dream We Lost* nevertheless marked the beginning of a new phase in Freda's career as a dedicated anti-Communist. She had been educated politically through her personal experiences and had recognized that Communism was in effect a substitute religion.[49] 'Never in my life have I seen a woman in whose heart and mind every hope on earth has been slain as has hers. She used to be a leading British Communist; now [she is] a black-minded cynic. She believes in nothing at all.'[50] Eight years after its original publication the book appeared in an abridged version, omitting the Third Part, as *Lost Illusion* (1948). The revised edition was widely acclaimed in England and in New York and was translated into several languages, including Danish and Swedish in 1949. It was distributed in paperback form by the US Information Service and was reprinted in America in 1959.

Immediately upon its appearance in 1940 the book gave deep offence to the 'totalitarian liberal cohorts' of the Western intelligentsia.[51] Freda had, unforgivably in their view, become 'a premature anti-Communist' and paid a heavy price for her conversion. The Friends of the Soviet Union began to campaign for her deportation, creating a threat, which hung over her head for four years. Congressman Jerry Voorhis (1901–84) introduced in March 1941 a private bill 'for the relief of Freda Utley' from the provisions of the Alien Registration Act of 1940, a bill which was not finally passed until October 1944. In 1941 Freda had reached a mass audience of over four millions with an article in *The Reader's Digest*, pleading for a negotiated peace between England and Germany.[52] She thereby incurred the wrath of the administration as well as of the progressive literati. Thus, for some years Freda found it difficult to secure contracts from publishers. She was also refused engagements as a lecturer. She did indeed become a member of the department of politics advisory council at Princeton University (1941–47) but she never secured a full-time academic appointment, much as she would have liked to secure such a niche.[53]

She devoted herself tirelessly to alerting her adopted country to the Communist menace. Inevitably, she sympathized with the aims of the America First Movement. She deeply deplored the demand for unconditional surrender adopted in 1944, believing that such a commitment to the total defeat and disarmament of Germany would lead to a second Versailles, with even worse consequences than had followed from the first. Her article of 1944 'Why Pick on China?' secured Freda a position as economist and consultant to the Chinese Supply Commission in Washington.[54] It enabled her to migrate from New York to the federal capital. In June 1945 *The Reader's Digest* published an article entitled 'The Destiny of the World is being Decided in China'. The nominal authors were Max Eastman and J. B. Powell but the true author was Freda Utley. The publisher, De Witt Wallace (1889–1981), compensated Freda for her sacrifice of credit by appointing her as a correspondent in China. A sojourn of five months (October 1945 – February 1946) resulted in the publication of her first book on the Far East in nine years.[55] On that visit Freda became the first woman correspondent to visit Yenan since Anna Louise Strong in 1938. There she was denied an interview with Mao but agreed with the contrast drawn by Tillman Durdin between 'the frightened people and the confident commissars' of Communist China.[56] Freda warned the USA that its China policies, culminating in the ending of the supply of arms to the Nationalists in 1946, had proved utterly disastrous, benefiting only the Communists. The publication of *Last Chance in China* marked the start of a new phase in Freda's career, wherein she focused attention upon the question, who was to blame for the loss of China to the Communists? In the anguished national debate, which followed, her status was so enhanced that her work was cited as authoritative in a report of 1948 from the House Un-American Activities Committee.

De Witt Wallace then appointed Freda as a correspondent in Germany, where she arrived in August 1948 after three years of Allied occupation of the country. Her resulting book, *The High Cost of Vengeance* (1949) was the bravest work she was ever to write: it denounced Allied policy as stupid, wicked, vindictive and disastrous. Her aim was once more didactic, seeking to avoid in Germany a repetition of the policies, which had lost China and had benefited only the Communists. Freda found Germany reduced to the status of an African colony with an Asiatic standard of living and inhabited by 'a people condemned by all the world, defenceless, hungry and without rights or liberties'.[57] Their hapless condition reminded her forcefully of her own struggle for existence in Moscow (1930–36). She strongly repudiated the anti-German fixation of the so-called liberals and progressives, who 'took the lead in demanding the crucifixion of the whole German people'.[58] She condemned the Nuremberg Trials as wholly extra-legal in their basis and the Dachau trials of 1946 as founded upon the brutal torture of the defendants.[59] The policy of demilitarization, denazification, decentralization and de-industrialization was benefiting mainly the USSR. The book was subsidized by the Foundation for Foreign Affairs in Washington and proved extremely controversial, generating virtually no royalties for the author. In Germany, however, Freda earned golden opinions and received from Siegerland a bronze memorial statue in gratitude for her efforts in saving the industries of the district from destruction.[60] The German translation of 1950 became a best-seller and was published in an extended form in 1962.

Freda Utley became an American citizen in 1950 and published *The China Story* in April 1951 during the Korean War. The book formed a major contribution to the debate on US policy in the Far East. Freda condemned that policy as vacillating, pusillanimous and self-defeating,[61] being responsible for 'four hundred million lost allies.'

She blamed the State Department for delaying the crucial shipment of munitions in 1948 and attributed the delay to the dominant influence of left-wingers within the department.[62] The book was naturally commended by General MacArthur and became for three months a best-seller, being reprinted three times (May-June 1951). Freda earned full national recognition as an authority upon China. She became Director of the American-China Policy Association Inc., established in 1946, and gave evidence before the Tydings Committee against Owen Lattimore (1900–1989), as the reputed architect of US policy towards China.[63] She had already supplied Senator McCarthy with the material for his denunciation of Lattimore in his speech on 30 March 1950. She gave evidence before three more Congressional Committees on 11 October 1951, 1 April 1953 and 1 July 1954 but concluded that McCarthy's campaign had been 'brief and abortive'.[64] Her work did, however, permit the public identification of such fellow-travellers as J. K. Fairbank, J. E. Johnson and Edgar Snow (1905–72).[65]

During the year of the Suez Crisis Freda undertook a seven-months tour of Asia (June-December 1956), which brought her back to Japan in August 1956 for the first time since 1938. She had been dismayed by the outburst of anti-Arab sentiment in the New York press, which greeted Nasser's nationalization of the Suez Canal Company. Believing that the problems of the Middle East resembled those of China, she hoped that the USA would not make again the same mistakes in its policy. In *Will the Middle East Go West?* (1957), she argued that it had alienated Western-oriented Arabs by its pro-Israeli policy and might push the whole region into the Communist camp. In 1968 she completed the first volume of her autobiography, which covered the adventurous years of her life down to 1945.[66] She never, however, published the second volume, analysing the intricacies of politics in Washington and showing how Senator McCarthy had been captured by the forces of the ultra-right and thereby led to destruction.

On 22 December 1978 Freda Utley died in Washington, one full year before Soviet power reached its maximum global extent with the invasion of Afghanistan. The collapse of the USSR in 1990–91 was followed by a notable and widespread resurgence of interest in her work. *Kostspielige Rache* (1951), the translation of *The High Cost of Vengeance,* was reprinted in Germany in 1993. *The China Story* (1951) was translated into Japanese in 1993. *Japan's Feet of Clay* (1936) was also translated into Japanese in 1998 and was reprinted in the original English in 2000. *Lancashire and the Far East* had become a classic monograph of economic history and in 1996 was twice reprinted. Her surviving papers in 87 boxes were deposited in the archives of the Hoover Institution in Stanford, California, and were catalogued in 1984. No biography has so far appeared.

Possessed by a zest for in-depth research, Freda had spread her energies widely. Her contributions to the history of the USSR, Germany and Asia remain of lasting value. Six of her eight books were translated into eight languages, endowing her with a global readership. Their author never, however, secured the recognition, which she sought. Disputatious by disposition, she always remained, in Rosa Luxemburg's phrase, 'the one who thinks differently'. Thus, she became an inevitable opponent in succession of the established regimes in England, Japan, Russia and the USA. Russell Kirk aptly described her as 'thorny and indomitable … full of reproaches and resentments, possessed of acerbic wit, passionately didactic and remarkably readable'.[67] Freda lost her faith in the inevitability of progress and in the perfectibility of man through the improvement of his material conditions. To the end she remained a modern Antigone, consumed by a savage indignation against injustice. Her work was carried on by her son, Jon Basil Utley, who had been born in Moscow in 1934. He became chairman from 1998 of Americans against World Empire and created in 2001 a memorial website on the internet dedicated to 'Freda Utley.com'.

the Hoover Institution in Stanford, California, and were catalogued in [illegible] bibliography has so far appeared.

Frustrated by [illegible] for [illegible] research, Fredi had turned her energies widely. Her contributions to the history of the USSR, Germany and Asia remain [illegible] lasting value. Six of her eight books were translated into [illegible] languages, [illegible] her with a global readership. [illegible] author never [illegible] the recognition [illegible] she sought. [illegible] by [illegible] she always [illegible] [illegible] in [illegible] places. [illegible] Thus, she [illegible] opponents [illegible] of these [illegible] regimes in England, Israel, Russia [illegible] Russell Kirk and [illegible] and [illegible] of [illegible] and [illegible] professionally [illegible] and [illegible] the [illegible] of [illegible] through the improvement of [illegible] conditions. At the end she remained a [illegible]. Anyone consulted by [illegible] against injustice. Her work was carried on by her son, [illegible] who had been born in Moscow in [illegible] of Americans [illegible] and created in 2001 a memorial website on the internet dedicated to Fredi [illegible].

PART 6

An Aviator and Two Themes

32

Lord Sempill (1893–1965) and Japan, 1921–41

ANTONY BEST

Lord Sempill

THE POSITION that the aviator Colonel William Forbes-Sempill (or Lord Sempill as he would become on the death of his father in 1934) holds in Anglo-Japanese relations is a strange one that is full of ironies. As the head of the unofficial British naval aviation mission to Japan in 1921 Sempill was the last major figure of the Alliance years to collaborate extensively with the Japanese. His work, however, was to backfire, for twenty years later the seeds that he had sown turned upon Britain when the pilots of the Imperial Japanese Navy's (IJN) air service were responsible on 9 December 1941 for the sinking of HMS *Prince of Wales* and HMS *Repulse*. Moreover, Sempill, the distinguished ambassador for British aviation and friend of Japan, was by then in disgrace with the cloud of treachery hanging over his head.

William Forbes-Sempill who was born in 1893 was the eldest son of the eighteenth Baron Sempill, soldier and landowner of Craigevar Castle, Aberdeen. He was educated at Eton and then from 1910–13 served an engineering apprenticeship in the workshops of Rolls-

Royce Ltd at Derby. At the start of the Great War 'Bill' Sempill who had the courtesy title of Master of Sempill joined the Royal Flying Corps, became a member of the Royal Navy Air Service (RNAS) in 1916, and was appointed as an officer in the Royal Air Force (RAF) in 1918. He thereafter rose to the rank of Colonel and assisted in an aviation mission to the United States. His acquaintance with Japan began in 1921 due to the interest shown by the Imperial Japanese Navy (IJN) in getting a British mission to advise it on how to develop an aviation service. The first Japanese overture came in the autumn of 1920. Their initial interest was in persuading Britain to send an official mission, but the Admiralty rejected this idea, on the grounds that technological secrets should not be passed to 'possible enemy nations, including Japan'.[1] However, the Admiralty was prepared to contemplate the dispatch of a civilian-led unofficial mission. The IJN took up this proposal, which also had the tacit support of the Air Ministry, and the Japanese naval attaché in London was provided with a list of recently retired officers who might be willing to be involved in such a venture. The Air Ministry, one can safely assume, saw the commercial advantages that might accrue from Britain, rather than any other country, providing such assistance.[2]

The result of the IJN's search for advisers was that by February 1921 Forbes-Sempill had agreed to head an unofficial mission that would provide help with training in both flying and technical matters. Over the next six months a team of thirty personnel was put together including both pilots and engineers. Many of the staff had, like Sempill, previously served in the RNAS. The mission duly arrived in August and training commenced on 1 September at the newly opened IJN naval base at Lake Kasumigaura, some forty miles north-east of Tokyo.[3]

At first, progress appears to have been slow. As Forbes-Sempill would later recall in a talk to the Japan Society of London in 1925, he faced a number of problems on his arrival. One of the most serious was that he found the Japanese pilots to be unused to handling modern technology, or as he put it 'mechanical contrivances', and therefore were unable to appreciate how to deal with complicated machinery such as aircraft engines.[4] In addition, Forbes-Sempill was frustrated by the attitude of the upper echelons of the IJN who he felt had no coherent policy on how the air arm should develop and who were reluctant to take his advice about purchasing airframes from British companies.[5]

However, despite these difficulties, Forbes-Sempill worked hard to make his mission a success and found his Japanese wards to be courageous and eager to learn. The mission concentrated on assisting the IJN with developing the capacity to engage in the key elements of air warfare at sea including reconnaissance work, observation of gunnery practice, flying on and off decks, the handling of flying boats, and torpedo-dropping. The more mundane world of aircraft maintenance was also not neglected and British engineers assisted in the workshops attached to the Kasumigaura base advising on armaments and design matters. Such indeed was the level of help provided by Forbes-Sempill that in May 1922 the Admiralty reiterated its concern, stating that it was 'decidedly impolitic' that the fruits of British ingenuity should be passed to the Japanese.[6]

While in Japan Forbes-Sempill kept in close touch with the embassy and entertained visits to Kasumigaura by the two naval attachés who served in this period, Captain Marriot and Captain Colvin, and by a young consular officer, Esler Dening.[7] Marriot, who does not seem to have enjoyed his period in Japan, tended to denigrate the Japanese attempt to develop an air arm, but Colvin was far more appreciative and recognized that Forbes-Sempill had brought the IJN up to near British standards of efficiency.[8] Sir Charles Eliot, the British Ambassador, was also broadly sympathetic towards the mission, partly because he was a keen supporter of close Anglo-Japanese relations, but also due to the fact that purchases of aviation equipment from British companies steadily rose during 1922.[9]

By the autumn of 1922 the IJN was keen to change the role of its British guests and use them purely as advisers rather than having them design and control the training process. As a result, some of the British contingent were surplus to requirements and made their way back home. Perhaps, surprisingly, this included Forbes-Sempill himself. However, when one considers that the IJN now wished to take charge of training it seems logical that it should have dispensed with the mission's leader as clearly he would have been less malleable than his juniors. Forbes-Sempill left Japan in October 1922 claiming that his mission had been a success and that he had secured £1 million of orders for British aviation companies.[10] The last British advisers left in December 1923 having witnessed one of the most significant moments in Japanese naval aviation history the landing of a Japanese pilot on the IJN's first aircraft carrier, *Hosho*.[11]

On his return to Britain Sempill emerged as one of the leading aviation figures in the country. Over the next few years he engaged in a number of high-profile long-range flights, offered assistance to other foreign governments in both Europe and Latin America, and from 1927 to 1930 he was the president of the Royal Aeronautical Society. He also had business interests and in 1931 he became the vice-chairman of the London Chamber of Commerce, before rising to the post of chairman in 1934–35. In 1934 on the death of his father he became a peer and took his place in the House of Lords. In the midst of all this busy activity he did not, however, forget Japan; he was a keen member of the Japan Society of London, serving on its Council, and did his best to lobby for the maintenance of Anglo-Japanese friendship.[12]

On the face of it Forbes-Sempill was a dashing member of the aristocracy and pillar of the inter-war establishment. Politically he stood resolutely on the right. For example, his maiden speech in the House of Lords on 12 May 1936 echoed the view of the die-hards in the Conservative Party by calling on the British Government to withdraw from the League of Nations.[13] However, his conservatism went beyond a mere glib reiteration of the minor aristocracy's dislike of the modern world, for there was a more controversial, darker side to his character which led him into dangerous waters. In the 1930s he became a member of some of the pro-Nazi and anti-Semitic groups that existed at the time, such as the Anglo-German Fellowship and The Link, on which he served as a council member.[14]

Controversy also surrounds his business activities and the exact nature of his links with Japan. Late in 1925 and into 1926 the Government Code and Cipher School (GCCS) intercepted a series of telegrams from the Japanese Naval Attaché in London to his superiors in Tokyo calling for £200 to be paid to an individual referred to as 'SE'.[15] The obvious assumption was that this was Forbes-Sempill, who was known to be in financial difficulties. It appears, according to an internal history of MI5 written in 1944, that the Security Service initiated an investigation into the possibility that Forbes-Sempill had passed secret information about Fleet Air Arm aircraft to the Japanese in return for money. The result was that a case alleging a breach of the Official Secrets Act was sent to the Director of Public Prosecutions and the Attorney-General. However, the latter decided that a prosecution would not be expedient at this time, presumably as a conviction could not be assured without compromising British intelligence sources. Nevertheless, the aura of suspicion surrounding Sempill had an automatic effect, for it led the Foreign Office to tell the Greek government early in 1926 that it could not support Forbes-Sempill leading an aviation mission to Athens.[16]

After 1926 Forbes-Sempill's activities were kept under surveillance by the Security Service, and were brought to the attention of successive Secretaries of State for Air.[17] There was, of course, a neat irony here, for one of his fellow members of the Japan Society of London was none other than Sir Vernon Kell, the head of MI5, who had visited Japan in the 1900s and become strongly attached to the country.[18]

Sempill next came to the attention of the intelligence services in October 1934 when the GCCS intercepted a Japanese telegram from

London to Tokyo in which Ambassador Matsudaira Tsuneo indicated that Lord Sempill, as he had then become, was interested in visiting Japan and Manchuria. Sempill had already committed himself to a solo flight to Australia and planned from there to go north to Japan via Singapore and Indo-China. He intended to visit Japan and Manchuria in his capacity as chairman of the London Chamber of Commerce and hoped to be able to build on the momentum generated by the recent mission by the Federation of British Industry. Matsudaira was keen to have the Gaimusho approve this visit, for he was convinced that it 'would bring about a situation advantageous to ourselves', particularly as Sempill was a tireless advocate of British recognition of Manchukuo.[19] Tokyo was agreeable to Sempill's itinerary, but in the end the visit did not come about, for he had to delay his flight to Australia thus cutting short his latest aeronautical adventure.[20]

During the rest of the 1930s Sempill disappeared into the background as far as British relations with Japan were concerned and it appears that he concentrated his efforts on preserving Anglo-German relations. Indeed, his commitment to this cause was such that in the summer of 1939 he became a founder member of the Right Club, a new extreme right-wing organization founded by the Conservative MP for Peebles, Captain Archibald Ramsay.[21] However, once war broke out with Germany Sempill did not flinch from his patriotic duty, he returned to the Royal Navy with the rank of Commander and served in the Admiralty's Directorate of Air Material. At this stage he appears to have distanced himself from Ramsay, for it is noticeable that when the latter was detained under Defence Regulation 18b in May 1940, Sempill remained in his post.

However, during 1940 Sempill did become far more active in the field of Anglo-Japanese relations. By the summer of 1940 the Japanophile lobby in Britain, consisting of figures such as the former Military Attaché to Japan, Major-General F.S.G Piggott, the adviser to the Japanese Embassy, Arthur Edwardes, and the businessman George Sale, were becoming greatly disturbed by the chasm opening up between Britain and Japan. They believed that Japan was not necessarily lost to the Axis cause and that a rapprochement was possible if Britain followed a more neutral line towards the war in China. Their pet plan was for the British government to send a Cabinet minister on a formal mission to Tokyo for high-level talks with the Japanese. This would impress the latter with Britain's serious regard for Japan, particularly, so they believed, if the minister in question was accompanied by an 'expert' of the calibre and experience of Piggott.[22]

Sempill was keen to help with this project and was, of course, very valuable, for as a peer and celebrated aviator he had good contacts in the upper echelons of government. In August 1940 Sempill held a lunch at his home to which he invited Piggott, Sale, and two Labour ministers from the National Government, the First Lord of the Admiralty, A.V. Alexander, and the Minister of Labour, Ernest Bevin.[23] The talk apparently focused on Japan and afterwards Sempill produced a memorandum for Bevin on Japan's position in the world in which he stressed that Japanese expansionism was solely the result of the international restrictions on Japanese immigration and trade discrimination against its goods. In his paper Sempill angrily compared the great attention given by the media to Japanese expansion with the paucity of coverage allocated to 'Soviet aggression' and acquisition of new territory.[24] Bevin apparently kept in contact with Sempill after receiving the memorandum, meeting him in October in the company of the former Ambassador to Japan, Sir Francis Lindley, but the exact nature of their conversations is unclear.[25]

Sempill's contact with Japanese issues was not, however, limited to his role as a lobbyist for reconciliation, for he also maintained his contact with the Japanese Naval Attaché's office in London. In June 1940 the British censorship authorities came across a reference to Sempill in letters from Mitsubishi in Tokyo to its branch in London that referred to the continuation of payments to Sempill in return for information. This revelation was immediately brought to the attention of the Minister of Home Security, Lord Swinton. The result was that in September 1940 Sempill was ordered before the Board of Admiralty to explain his conduct and told that he could only maintain his commission if he made a written undertaking to have no contact with the Japanese in relation to matters connected with his employment.[26]

Even following this warning Sempill's name continued to appear in intelligence reports. In February 1941 the transcript of a telephone conversation that Sempill had with Arthur Edwardes was brought to the attention of the Permanent Under-Secretary at the Foreign Office, Sir Alexander Cadogan, who noted acerbically in his diary that Sempill deserved to be crucified.[27] In August Sempill was heard to be indiscreet when talking to his wife and early in September he was given another private warning.[28] Worse, however, was soon to follow.

On 13 September the Prime Minister, Winston Churchill, was shown an intercept of a telegram from the Japanese Embassy in London to the Gaimusho that contained a good deal of information about Lord Beaverbrook's forthcoming visit to Moscow. Churchill was alarmed and promptly asked the Foreign Secretary, Anthony Eden, to find out what contacts the Japanese Chargé d'Affaires, Kamimura Shinichi, had with British sources of information.[29] Eden duly noted that Kamimura was close to Edwardes, Piggott, Sempill and a few other either naïve or unscrupulous souls. Of these men it was clear that Sempill constituted the greatest problem for not only was he the only one still in government service, but his post meant that he handled sensitive technical information about naval aircraft. At first Swinton, to the dissatisfaction of Eden, declared that there was no point in delivering yet another admonition to Sempill, perhaps believing that the problems were in the past.[30] By early October, however, it was clear from transcripts of recent telephone conversations that Sempill was still in contact with the Japanese Naval Attaché and that therefore the government could not afford to sweep the problem under the carpet. Churchill and Eden now moved on to the offensive and, on Cadogan's advice, pressed for Sempill's removal from the Admiralty.[31] There was a short debate about whether he ought to be sacked or moved to a distant posting in which he could do little harm. In the end the decision was taken to follow the latter course and send Sempill off to the northern coast of Scotland, for there was the possibility that if dismissed he might use his status as a peer to cause trouble. Unwilling to go into internal exile Sempill decided to avoid further trouble by simply resigning his commission.[32]

Sempill's link with Japan did not, however, end with his undistinguished exit from government service. In the post-war era he briefly re-emerged as one of the signatories to the unsuccessful petition for the release of the convicted war criminal Shigemitsu Mamoru, the Japanese Ambassador to Britain from 1938–41 and intermittent Foreign Minister from 1943–45.

The *Dictionary of National Biography* describes him as 'A very Scottish, thick-set, figure of medium height – he always wore full Scottish evening dress on all suitable occasions – practical, stubborn, and convivial, Sempill was an enthusiastic propagandist and 'flying for fun'. He was a sound engineer, an excellent cook who, whenever possible, baked his own bread, and a successful amateur farmer … Sempill was excellent company and made a host of friends throughout his life.'[33]

In the context of Japan, however, Sempill emerges as a controversial figure. In the inter-war period there were many Establishment figures that lamented the passing of the alliance, believing that its abrogation had led to permanent instability in East Asia and an otherwise avoidable falling out between Britain and Japan. These men were an irritant to the Foreign Office but nothing more, for their worst crime was their naivety. Sempill was different, for here was a man who not only espoused such views but also engaged in the collection of information for the Japanese in return for money. The degree to which he betrayed his country's interests is not clear, but it was serious enough for him to be a target of MI5's interest from 1925 to 1941. The final irony, however, is that in all likelihood the greatest damage that Sempill did was not as a spy but as the head of the unofficial aviation mission of 1921–22, which was approved, if not sanctioned, by the British government.

33

Three Meiji Marriages between Japanese Men and English Women

MINAMI TEISUKE & ELIZA • OZAKI SABURO & BATHIA CATHERINE • SANNOMIYA YOSHITANE & ALETHEA YAYENO

NOBORU KOYAMA

Baroness Sannomiya

MARRIAGES BETWEEN MEN AND WOMEN of different cultures, religions and ethnic groups have often aroused hostility and prejudice. Opposition to such marriages was common in Britain and Japan in the second half of the nineteenth century and the first half of the twentieth century. Some marriages were successful; others failed. .

Especially in the early years after the opening of the Treaty Ports under the 'unequal treaties' there were more foreign men than women. This led inevitably to the development of 'liaisons' between foreign men and Japanese women, some, but not all, of whom were prostitutes. Some of these 'liaisons' led to formal marriages; others were fairly permanent arrangements such as that of Ernest Satow with his Japanese 'wife' or 'mistress' as some would have called her. The term 'common law' wife was sometimes used for the women in question.

Many young Japanese were sent by the Japanese authorities to study abroad. The vast majority of these were men and there were very few Japanese women in foreign countries with whom they could consort. They inevitably developed attractions to foreign women and in a number of cases this led to marriages between Japanese and residents in the countries where they were studying.

International marriages (in Japanese *kokusai kekkon*) faced legal obstacles in Japan. Under Decree No. 103 of 1873 Japanese wishing to marry foreigners had first to obtain permission from the Japanese government, and foreign women who married Japanese men had to give up their own nationality and become Japanese nationals. The decree also prescribed that foreign men, who were adopted as *yōshi* (sons-in-law) of Japanese through marriage to Japanese women, had to acquire Japanese nationality and abandon their own. The change of nationality demanded by the decree was its most controversial aspect.

Decree No. 103 was issued in direct response to an enquiry from a British consul in 1872 about marriage between British men and Japanese women. The new Meiji Government allowed Japanese to marry foreigners under Decree No.103 because the previous Tokugawa Shogunate had in 1867 sanctioned marriages between Japanese and foreigners in response to a similar enquiry from a British consul. The enactment of Decree No.103 was brought about as a result of enquiries from Britain. Sir Harry Parkes (1825–85), the British Minister, was strongly opposed to Decree No.103. He consulted Nicholas John Hannen (1842–1900), Assistant Judge at Yokohama. Hannen argued that British nationals, such as British women who married Japanese, should be protected under the extra-territorial treaty arrangements in Japan by maintaining their British nationality. He commented: 'Whatever effect a so-called marriage between an English woman and a Japanese may have upon the status of the woman as a British subject, it is, and must be, entirely independent of the laws of Japan.'[1]

Apart from British men who were adopted as *yōshi* the cases that caused the most concern were those of British women who married Japanese and thus lost their British nationality. In this essay I propose to focus on three British women who married Japanese men in England and who were the pioneers of intermarriage with Japanese men. Their experiences in respect of the nationality issues, residence in Japan and their relationships with their Japanese husbands were all different.

Eliza Pittman (1849–1902) married Minami Teisuke (1947–15) in London in 1872. Their marriage is regarded as the first case of an 'international marriage' in Japan. Shortly after the promulgation of Decree No. 103, they arrived in Japan from England and Minami reported their marriage to the Japanese Government in June 1873.

He claimed that he had obtained permission for his marriage from the senior members of the Iwakura Mission including Iwakura Tomomi (1825–83), Ambassador, and Terajima Munenori, the Japanese Minister to London.[2] Eliza lived in Japan with Minami Teisuke between 1873 and 1883. But at no time did she acquire Japanese nationality; nor was she registered in Minami's family registration (*koseki*).[3] They were apparently divorced in 1883.

Ozaki Saburō (then Toda Saburō) (1842–1918) and Bathia Catherine Morrison (1843–1936) were married in London in 1869, three years earlier than the marriage between Minami Teisuke and Eliza Pittman. When they married, there were no laws about marriages between Japanese and foreigners in Japan and they did not seek permission for their marriage from the Japanese Government, nor did they report it to the government. However, their marriage later became an issue and Ozaki Saburō eventually received permission for their marriage from the Japanese Government in 1880. Bathia never went to Japan, but she acquired Japanese nationality for a brief period from 1880 to 1881 when she was registered in Ozaki's *koseki*. Ozaki Saburō and Bathia signed a divorce agreement in London in 1881 and Bathia was removed from Ozaki's family registration in the same year.

Alethea Raynor (1846–1919) married Sannomiya Yoshitane (1844–1905) in London in 1874. Their marriage was the fourth case of marriage between a Japanese national and a foreign woman to be approved by the Japanese Government[4] and was the second case of marriage between a British woman and a Japanese man. Alethea lived in Japan from 1880 until her death in 1919 and became a Japanese citizen.

JAPANESE STUDENTS AND THEIR BRITISH WIVES

Ozaki Saburo, Minami Teisuke and Sannomiya Yoshitane were three of the young Japanese who were sent abroad by the Meiji government to study western methods with the aim of furthering the modernization of Japan. They all belonged to the group which had led the Restoration movement and whose slogan was 'Revere the Emperor and expel the barbarians'(*sonnō-jōi*). Minami was a cousin and younger brother-in-law of Takasugi Shinsaku (1839–67) who was one of the leading figures of the Choshu clan which had led the movement against the shogunate. Ozaki was a young retainer of Sanjo Sanetomi (1837–91), one of the important court nobles fiercely opposed to the Shogunate. Sannomiya rendered distinguished service in the major battles against the forces of the Tokugawa shogunate in 1868, supporting Prince Higashi-Fushimi (1846–1903).

Ozaki Saburo arrived in London in 1868 as an attendant to Sanjo Kin'aya, the heir to Sanjo Sanetomi who was the Chief minister in the new Meiji government. Minami and Sannomiya Yoshitane both came to London in 1871 as attendants to Prince Higashi-Fushimi. This was Minami's second visit to England. He had made a brief visit to London before the Meiji Restoration and sought an opportunity to go abroad again in the hope that foreign study would contribute to his own career in the Meiji Government.

Ozaki Saburo and Sanjo Kin'aya were taught by the same private tutor, William Mason Morrison (1819–85). Morrison had been an undergraduate at Magdalene College, Cambridge, in 1883. They boarded at Morrison's home in London. Bathia was Morrison's daughter. She had been born on 18 October 1843 at Downderry, St Mary's, Scilly Island, where her father William Morrison had been a schoolmaster. Morrison taught English, law and customs of England to Japanese as a private tutor in London after about 1868. Ozaki and Sanjo may have been Morrison's first Japanese pupils. Later, he taught prominent Japanese including Suematsu Kencho (1855–1920), Nanjo Bun'yo (1849–1927) and probably Inoue Kaoru (1835–1915).

Bathia's mother was Mary Anne Morrison (née Smith). She had an elder brother, Theodore, who worked as a tutor and civil servant. The marriage of Bathia and Ozaki Saburo and the birth of their three daughters were described by Theodore Jervis, Morrison's family friend in a letter of 14 July 1887 as follows:

> It was not long after the latter's residence [Ozaki Saburo] in Mr. Morrison's house before an attachment sprung up between Mr. Ozaki and Mr. Morrison's only daughter Bathia and they were married by licence on the 4th of March 1869 and the fruit of this marriage has been 3 daughters.[5]

According to their marriage certificate, Bathia was aged 22 and Ozaki 23, but in fact Bathia was 25 and Ozaki 27 years old. Bathia seemed to be relatively old to become a new bride in the Victorian period. Their first daughter, O'yei Evelyn Theodora Kate was born in December 1870, the second daughter, Masako Maude Mary Harriet, in January 1872 and the third daughter, Kimie Florence Bathia Alexandra, in October 1873. The first and third daughters who went to Japan and lived there had Japanese names: O'Yei or Eiko and Kimiko respectively. The second daughter never went to Japan and stayed in England. According to the census report for 1871, the Morrisons together with Ozaki Saburo and Bathia and their daughter Evelyn, lived at St Alban's Cottage, Fulham, London.

The Iwakura Mission stayed in Britain from July to November 1872. The original purpose of the Mission was the renegotiation of the unequal treaties. Ozaki Saburo was sent to the United States to convey the opinion of Japanese students in Britain to the leaders of the Mission while the Mission stayed there.

Minami Teisuke who became the Director of the American Joint National Agency, a newly established bank in London, tried to persuade members of the Iwakura Mission and Japanese students in Britain to deposit their money in his bank. Minami was very successful in acquiring Japanese customers for his bank including senior members of the Mission, such as Iwakura Tomomi and Kido Takayoshi (1833–77).

Minami had originally intended to join a military school in England. He had come to England as an attendant to Prince Higashi-Fushimi who was a military man, later General. However, after discovering that he was shortsighted, he changed his course to legal studies and in 1871 joined Lincoln's Inn. He met Charles Bowles, an American banker, probably on the voyage over the Atlantic to England from the United States. Charles Bowles and his brothers were very rapidly expanding their banking company, Bowles Brothers and Company, in the United States and Europe at the beginning of 1870s. They set up the London Branch of Bowles Brothers and Company in 1870 and the American Joint National Agency in London in 1872. The American Joint National Agency was a subsidiary of Bowles Brothers and Company. Minami Teisuke became one of the directors of the American Joint National Agency in 1872. As a result of Minami's effort, the total amount of deposits from Japanese customers reached about a quarter of those of the London Branch of the Bowles Brothers Company and the American Joint National Agency.

Eliza Pittman was born at Brixton, Surrey, on 20 May 1849.[6] Her father, Charles Pittman was a gardener. Her mother was Sarah Pittman (née French). Minami Teisuke described Eliza as the fourth daughter of Charles Pittman who lived in Dulwich, although he described her as the third daughter on another occasion. So Eliza had at least two or three sisters. Probably the Pittman family moved from Brixton to Dulwich after her birth. Her death was reported by her brother James Pittman. According to Minami, Eliza studied at Dulwich and Kensington. We do not know how Minami and Eliza became acquainted with each other, but it could be possible that they knew each other through Bowles Brothers and Company or the American Joint National Agency. Whilst Minami was a director of the American National Agency, they married on 20th September 1872 and lived at 5 Canning Place, Kensington.[7] Ozaki Saburo described Minami's life at that time as follows in his autobiography:

> As the director, Minami received £200 (¥2,000) as monthly salary and rented a grand house in London, he married an English woman and lived in luxury. When Japanese students visited him occasionally, he invited them into his drawing room, greeted them with his wife and served them wine.[8]

Ozaki mentioned Minami's marriage with Eliza in his autobiography, but never referred to his marriage with Bathia.

While the Iwakura Mission was still in Britain, on 9 November 1872 Bowles Brothers and Company and the American Joint National Agency were closed down and declared bankrupt the following month. Minami lost both his livelihood and his reputation among his fellow Japanese, many of whom lost a total of over £20,000.[9] Ozaki, who acted as representative for Japanese students in Britain and had deposited money for them in Minami's bank, negotiated with the trustees for bankruptcy as the representative of the Japanese creditors and succeeded in gaining for them a quarter of the deposits.[10]

Minami returned to Japan with Eliza in the spring of 1873 and they became the first mixed marriage couple recognized under Decree No. 103.

Alethea Raynor, daughter of William Raynor and Elizabeth Raynor (née Jefferson), was born at Hull on 3 April 1846.[11] William Raynor was a draper by occupation. Ernest Satow wrote in his diary that Mrs Sannomiya was said to be the daughter of a lodging housekeeper.[12] Her family probably moved to London at a later period and she met Sannomiya Yoshitane there. They married in Hampstead, London, on 16 April 1874.[13] Their ages were described as 'full' in the marriage certificate. In fact Alethea Raynor was 28 and Sannomiya Yoshitane was 30 years old. Their marriage also seemed to be a late one by Victorian standards. Sannomiya was still a student at that time. He reported his forthcoming marriage to the Japanese Legation in London on 10 April 1874.

Sannomiya was appointed Second Secretary at the Japanese Legation in Berlin in 1877 and lived there with Alethea for about three years. After returning to Japan with Alethea in 1880, he moved from the Ministry of Foreign Affairs to the Department of the Imperial Household and became the Grand Master of Ceremonies (*Shikibuchokan*) in 1895 after being the Vice-Grand Master for some time. He remained in this post for 10 years until his death in 1905. He was made a baron in 1896. His close relationship with Prince Komatsu,[14] formerly Prince Higashi-Fushimi, continued until the Prince's death in 1903.

In 1877, when Sannomiya and Alethea lived in Berlin, he applied by letter to the Tokyo Metropolitan Government for the entry of Alethea into his *koseki*.[15] While the Tokyo Metropolitan Government was asking the Ministry of Foreign Affairs whether his marriage with Alethea had the permission of the government, Sannomiya withdrew his application. The Ministry of Foreign Affairs confirmed that the marriage had been sanctioned by the Japanese Legation in London in 1874. It is not clear why in these circumstances he withdrew his application for the entry of Alethea into his *koseki*. Was it perhaps related to the opposition of Sir Harry Parkes, the British Minister to Japan, to Decree No.103?

THE TROUBLED MARRIAGE OF OZAKI SABURO AND BATHIA

Ozaki Saburo returned to Japan in October 1873, leaving his wife Bathia and two daughters in London. The third daughter was born around the time when Ozaki arrived in Japan where in the middle of March 1874, just after his return home, he married again, this time, a woman called Toda Yae[16] who was related to the family into which he had been adopted. In 1862, when Ozaki was 20 years old, he had become the adopted-grandson-in-law of Toda Miki, who had been a retainer of the Sanjo family. Since that time, Ozaki had been called Toda and he was known as Toda Saburo when he stayed in England. His adopted mother was called Tamai and Yae, his new wife, was her niece. In 1869, the feudal lords returned their lands and retainers to the emperor. This was one of the most important reforms following the Meiji Restoration. This reform, which was termed in Japanese '*hanseki hōkan*', affected the status of the samurai class. Although Ozaki was a retainer of Sanjo Sanetomi, he could not become a *shizoku* (samurai class), because his family had been less than three generations retainers of the Sanjo family. So, Ozaki (Toda) returned to his original family name (Ozaki) and Toda Saburo became Ozaki Saburo. Bathia was called Bathia Catherine Toda when she married Ozaki, but then her name changed to Bathia Catherine Ozaki.

In order to continue the Toda family, Ozaki's adopted mother Tamai became the head of Toda family. Because of this family background, Ozaki Saburo and Yae were eventually expected to marry. Even before Ozaki had left for England, both seemed to be unofficially engaged. When Ozaki left England for Japan, Bathia did not accompany him and he might have thought that at this time his marriage with Bathia was over. He may have kept his marriage secret. Kido Takayoshi, the Deputy Ambassador of the Iwakura Mission, did not know that Ozaki was married in London and tried to arrange a marriage for him when Ozaki returned to Japan, although in fact he had married Toda Yae in 1874.

Ozaki took a mistress, Fujiki Michi (who became the adopted daughter of Toda Tamai) in 1879.[17] Since he had no children by Yae, he probably took a mistress in order to have children. Both his wife and his mistress lived in the same house with Ozaki. Eventually, he had fourteen children by his mistress, one daughter by his wife and three daughters as a result of his marriage with Bathia. He obtained rapid promotion in the Meiji Government probably as a result of the patronage of ItoHirobumi (1841–1909).

What kind of arrangements were made for Bathia and their children when Ozaki left for Japan? Theodore Jervis in a letter of 14 July 1887 wrote:

> In 1875 [1873], Mr. Ozaki left England for Japan and at that time there was no question of his wife accompanying him, but of course he was to send money from time to time to England. This he did in a very irregular and unsatisfactory manner and it would seem that in 1880 Mr. Morrison was in communication with his friend Count Ennowaye [Inoue Kaoru], Foreign Minister in Japan, and I enclose a copy letter of the latter to him marked No. 21 from which you will see that at that time 1880, Count Ennowaye [Inoue Kaoru] thought he could arrange for a sum of £1,300 being paid by Mr. Ozaki who was still in Japan where he had been since 1875 [1873], but Mrs. Ozaki [Bathia] having written herself to Count Ennowaye asking to get her husband an appointment in England or somewhere in Europe. The offer of the £1,300 fell through and Mr. Ozaki was appointed to St. Petersburg where his wife joined him in September 1880.[18]

As this letter indicates, Ozaki Saburo was appointed as First Secretary of the Japanese Legation at St Petersburg in 1880. In order that Bathia could join him in St Petersburg, he had to obtain permission for their marriage from the Japanese Government and had to register Bathia into his family registration after he had removed Yae's name from it. Bathia was duly registered in Ozaki's *koseki* and she acquired a Japanese passport in 1880. But 'further disagreements' arose between Ozaki and Bathia in St. Petersburg and Bathia returned to London in December 1880.[19] Due to the government's reduction in the number of diplomatic and consular staff, Ozaki returned to Japan in 1881. On his way back to Japan, he stopped off in London and in July 1881 he and Bathia signed an agreement of separation or divorce according to Japanese law.[20] After his return, in September 1881, he removed Bathia's entry from his *koseki* and put back the name of his former wife Toda Yae.[21]

At the beginning of the agreement to separate, it was stated that the reason for the separation was Bathia's refusal to accompany her husband to Japan. Theodore Jervis commented as follows:

> Mrs. Ozaki certainly refused to accompany her husband to Japan because she was given to understand that he had married again out there and that by the laws of the country he could have two ladies residing with him in the house. Her English friends could hardly advise her to go.[22]

The agreement provided that in so far as Bathia could manage to support her children, she could keep them with her, but if she could not afford to keep them, she could send all or any of them to Japan. In the event, Theodora (O'Yei or Eiko) and Florence (Kimiko) were sent to Japan. In 1905 Theodora married the famous Japanese parliamentarian, liberal statesman and one time Mayor of Tokyo, Ozaki Yukio (1858–1954)[23]as his second wife. Although Ozaki Saburo and Ozaki Yukio shared the same family name, they were not related to each other. Indeed, Ozaki Saburo was at one time an enemy of Ozaki Yukio. When Saburo was the Director General of the Cabinet Legislation Bureau in 1889 he exiled Ozaki Yukio from Tokyo under the so-called 'Peace Regulations'. Florence (Kimiko) married a Swede called Henrik Ouchterlony in Japan in 1909 and moved to Sweden. The second daughter, Maude, stayed in England and married Alfred James Hewitt in 1906.

Bathia Catherine Ozaki lived to a ripe old age. She died in London on 30 December 1936 at the age of 93.[24] She was described on her death certificate as 'widow of Saburo Ozaki (Baron), Japanese Diplomat'. Four years before her death, her first daughter Yei Theodora Ozaki died at London at the age of 63 on 29 December 1932.[25] Her husband Ozaki Yukio was present at her death.

THE TURBULENT MARRIAGE OF MINAMI TEISUKE AND ELIZA

The marriage of Ozaki Saburo and Bathia did not turn out happily. Neither did that of Teisuke and Eliza Pittman. Minami himself described their married life in a letter of 20 April 1884 to Eliza's father Charles Pittman, written about one year after her return home in 1883:

> Since her arrival to Japan, I had worked very hard to make her comfortable in European style and living as much as my ability allowed me to do, which you may remember by Eliza's letters, etc. But, she has been so disobedient to me in many things benefits to her lady way and has been very cruel to me and did act bodily violences on me and even she could not keep her

> written promises and acted same as before the special promises written. The copy of this promises I enclose in this. It will show you how the matters have been passing and have resulted in divorce. You may know I am very forbearing and giving, but I could not do so any more with her. It is better for her to be free from me as she is free from Japanese laws and live and settle with native people.[26]

The 'special promise,' mentioned in the letter to Eliza's father included the following points: Eliza promised not to use abusive words and violent acts, to learn Japanese, to perform wifely duties for his friends and undertake household affairs; finally, if she were to break her promises, she could not expect to receive support and protection from him. The 'promises' seem strange to modern eyes; for example, 'I promise to be obedient to his wishes firstly, that I should study the language of the country, in such a way and for such a time each day, as he may direct'.[27] The 'special promises' were signed by Eliza and Minami Teisuke on 10 and 11 March 1882. Then, according to Minami Teisuke, she broke these promises and left Yokohama for England in April 1883. This constituted a divorce for them.

Minami Teisuke was appointed as Consul at Hong Kong in August 1883 and reported his marriage with Izawa Sen to Inoue Kaoru, the then Japanese Foreign Minister, in November 1883[28]. Inoue Kaoru, who knew about the troubles of Ozaki Saburo with Bathia, asked Minami Teisuke whether he had divorced Eliza officially or whether there had merely been a separation. In replying to Inoue, Minami claimed that their marriage did not conform to the correct procedure and that Eliza was not registered in his *koseki*. Inoue, replied that Minami's marriage with Eliza seemed to be valid, citing the documents which Minami had submitted to the Ministry of the Foreign Affairs in 1873. In response, Minami gave a detailed description of the violent acts Eliza had committed against him and his family. On several occasions he had received injuries to his face, hands and legs. In February 1882, Eliza had even attacked him with a Japanese sword. Then she escaped from his house and went to his uncle's, asking for clothes and concealed herself in the house of a civil servant for several days. Minami tried to prosecute her under Japanese law, but he did not press the charges because as a result of mediation by an English friend she had signed certain 'special promises'. But she had later broken these promises; so he had no alternative but to divorce her and let her return to England.

Minami in his short autobiography[29] said that Eliza did not follow his advice and learn Japanese. She did not associate with Japanese people; nor did she bear a child. Later, she showed signs of insanity and tried to attack him with a dangerous weapon. Since we have no account of their married life from Eliza, we do not know how far Minami's claims can be believed. It is certain, however, that their marriage in Japan was disastrous. Eliza left Yokohama for Hong Kong on a British steamer, the *Bangalore,* on 5 April 1883.[30] Inoue Kaoru, the Foreign Minister, seemed to be satisfied with Minami's explanation and approved his remarriage.

Eliza died in 1902 at Beddington where she probably lived after their divorce and where according to the 1881 and 1892 census reports her father Charles Pittman lived. She was buried in St Mary's Churchyard, Beddington, Croydon. Part of the tombstone survives. The inscription reads: 'In Memory of Eliza Teiske Minami, who departed this life, July the 9th, 1902. The marriage in 1872 of the above Eliza Teiske Minami, an Englishwoman, with Teiske Minami, a Japanese, was the first known union between subjects of the two countries.'[31] Her death was reported by her brother James Pittman, who lived in Battersea[32] and who was probably responsible for the tombstone and its inscription.

THE SUCCESSFUL MARRIAGE OF SANNOMIYA YOSHITANE AND ALATHEA YAENO

Compared to Eliza Minami and Bathia Catherine Ozaki, Alethea Yayeno Sannomiya had a relatively happy marriage with her Japanese husband, Sannomiya Yoshitane. As the wife of the Grand Master of Ceremonies (*Shikibuchōkan*) and also as an English woman, she played an important role as adviser on diplomatic and foreign matters for the Court in Japan. She was also a useful intermediary for foreign diplomats in Japan. Baroness d'Anethan wrote: 'Madame Sannomiya is an Englishwoman, with very pleasant manners, and is, I am told, a great power at the Court. Her husband is Vice-Grand Master of Ceremonies … Madame Sannomiya is very charming and clever, and I am told the Sannomiyas' house is one of the most hospitable in Tokyo.'[33] Major General F.S.G. Piggott wrote about her in his autobiography as follows:

> … the stately Baroness Sannomiya, English widow of a high official in the Imperial Household Department. Her advice on foreign dress and social customs had for many years been sought by Japanese ladies, including the Princesses and ladies of the Court when they first mingled in diplomatic society. The Baroness had regular weekly At Home days, when there were always many visitors; her unique position was an echo of English influence in an unusual field in the early days of the Meiji era.[34]

Alethea was dedicated to charities, such as the Red Cross, and to social work, partly because she had no children. She was described by Mary Crawford Fraser, wife of the British Minister Hugh Fraser, as follows: 'Madame Sannomiya is one of the ladies who have done most for the Red Cross Society here, of which the Empress is the President and the ruling spirit.'[35] A visiting English woman, Teresa Eden Richardson said of her: 'Baroness Sannomiya took me under her wing and explained some matters referring to Japanese etiquette. She is an English lady, wife of the Master of the Ceremonies at Court, and was a kind friend to me all the time that I stayed in the country.'[36] Sir Ernest Satow, British Minister in Tokyo from 1895–1900, frequently referred to her in his diaries.

Alethea Yayeno Sannomiya died at Tokyo on 17 August 1919 at the age of 73.[37] At the time of her death she was a Japanese national. Presumably, she took Japanese nationality long before her death. As there is no record of her death in British consular files it would seem that she was no longer regarded by the British authorities as a British national. Her husband, Sannomiya Yoshitane, had died earlier in 1905. A Japanese newspaper reported that her life had been lonely in later years since she had no children of her own.[38] They had adopted Shizuma, Yoshitane's nephew, as a son, but he died at the age of 24, six months after his adopted mother's death.[39]

DECREE NO. 103 AND TREATY REVISION

When Decree No.103 was issued, Sir Harry Parkes sought the views of the Earl of Granville, then British Foreign Secretary about the Decree, sending an English translation and the opinion of Nicholas Hannen, Assistant Judge at Yokohama in 1873. Granville asked the Law Officers of the Crown for a legal opinion on Decree No.103. Their report was issued in August 1873. They did not agree with Hannen's objections to Decree No.103 although they accepted Hannen's last point that the Decree would affect 'an English woman domiciled in England'.[40] In general, the Law Officers thought Decree No.103 was in accordance with the standards of other civilized countries if its application were limited to residents in Japan.

Hannen was not convinced and sent his comments to Parkes who asked the Foreign Office to study Hannen's arguments. In replying to the Foreign Office in March 1874, the Law Officers clearly stated that '… an Englishwoman marrying a Japanese in England, Japan or elsewhere (if no treaty affects the case) would become by virtue of such marriage amenable to Japanese jurisdiction when in Japan'.[41] After receiving the Law Officers' reply, Parkes finally accepted Decree

No.103, writing as follows in his letter of 24 April 1874 to the Earl of Derby, the Foreign Secretary:

> I conclude from the opinion of the Law Officers of the Crown above referred to that such a claim if made by the Japanese Government in the case of English women marrying Japanese would be assented to by Her Majesty's Government, and that an Englishwoman when married to a Japanese loses in Japan the protection of the extraterritorial clauses of the Treaty, and becomes amenable to Japanese jurisdiction.[42]

Parkes accepted that British nationals who married Japanese under Decree No.103, lost their British nationality, but this did not mean that marriage under the Japanese law was accepted as valid under British law. This situation was rectified by the case Francis Brinkley (1841–1912) who married Tanaka Yasu according to Japanese law in 1886. Brinkley brought a legal case against the Attorney-General claiming that his marriage was also valid under British law. He won his case on 8 February 1890 (Brinkley v. Attorney-General).[43]

After the case of Brinkley v. the Attorney-General, the Foreign Office considered whether or not HM consuls in Japan should report marriages solemnized according to Japanese law to the Registrar-General or not, since they had hitherto sent 'nil' returns of *lex loci* marriages.[44] However, the Earl of Kimberley, then Foreign Secretary, decided in the light of the opinion given by Hiram Shaw Wilkinson, Acting British Judge at Yokohama, and John Harriet Gubbins in June 1895 not to require the registration of *lex loci* marriages to marriages conducted according to Japanese law.

* * *

After the Anglo-Japanese Treaty of Commerce and Navigation, concluded in 1894, came into effect in 1899 as part of the revision of the unequal treaties, Britain officially recognized marriage according to Japanese law. To facilitate treaty revision the Japanese Government had enacted the Japanese Civil Code, the Nationality Act, the *Hōrei* (the law governing the application of laws), etc. and Decree No.103 finally ceased to have effect in July 1898. However, British members of the foreign community in Japan did not know of the change of law affecting marriages in Japan. The Rev. William Awdry, Bishop of South Tokyo announced at Yokohama on 9 February 1908 that certain marriages of British nationals, which had been solemnized in Japan since 16 July 1899 were valid.[45] It emerged as a result of a divorce in London, Marshall v. Marshall, that more than thirty cases of marriages performed in Anglican churches in Japan were invalid since the treaty revision, because they were neither conducted at the consulates in Japan nor according to Japanese law. Following revision of the treaties, a religious marriage ceremony alone could not guarantee the validity of marriage in Japan. In December 1912 the British Parliament passed a special act in order to remove doubts about the validity of such marriages.[46] From now onwards marriages between British and Japanese people stood on a firmer footing reflecting the new era in diplomatic relations.

34

Early Plant Collectors in Japan

AMANDA HERRIES

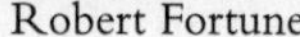

Robert Fortune

John Gould Veitch

'PLACE THE FLOWER in a situation where the side-light is cut off … when the stripes acquire the appearance of gentle streamlets of Australian gold, and the reader who has not seen it may form some feeble notion of what it is.' So the famous Dr John Lindley effused about one of the specimens newly arrived from Japan – the entrancing *Lilium auratum*. It was a spectacular success at the Horticultural Show in London in 1862: 'Fortunately some ten thousand eyes beheld it at South Kensington … and they can fill up the details'.

The sensational golden-rayed lily of Japan had recently arrived in a shipment of plants sent to London from Japan in 1861 by John Gould Veitch, one of the most famous of Victorian plant collectors. It was one of many plants introduced after his single visit to Japan, which have subsequently become so familiar in Western gardens that we never stop to question their origins.

The story of the introduction of Japanese plants to the West extends back into the late seventeenth century, with the work of a one-time physician to the Dutch East India Company (VOC), forming the first accurate descriptions. Japan was then a closed country, with the Dutch the only Western power to be allowed any contact at all. Engelbert Kaempfer, a German naturalist and surgeon, arrived at the man-made island of Dejima outside Nagasaki in September 1690. Kaempfer appreciated that the climate of Japan was broadly similar to that in Western Europe, and that therefore plants growing in Japan would be of great interest at home. Although restrictions on the Dutch meant that at that time they were kept as virtual prisoners at Dejima, Kaempfer left in 1692 with plenty of information on plants to include in his work *Amoenitatum Exoticarum* published in Latin in 1712.

Kaempfer's work was the forerunner of future 'floras' of Japan. The work and records he kept while in Japan also provided the manuscript for his two-volume *History of Japan*, published posthumously in 1727. The *History* was published first in English, after Sir Hans Sloane managed to acquire the original German text.

Kaempfer was not the only VOC officer to contribute to the discovery of the Japanese flora. Nearly one hundred years later the Swedish VOC representative, Carl Peter Thunberg, also working as a medical officer, and a passionate amateur botanist, was in Dejima in 1775. He kept a small garden in which to care for the living plants and seeds he collected, before shipping them to Holland as specimens. Like all VOC employees his travelling was severely restricted, but he accompanied the annual embassy to Edo (the modern Tokyo, usually referred to as Yedo by foreigners in those days although the Y was not pronounced), and was able to collect plants on the journey. This was no easy task, given the secrecy with which specimens had to be gathered. Thunberg was also interested in obtaining maps, an activity specifically forbidden to foreigners. Thunberg was fortunate and his *Flora Japonica* was published in 1784.

Philipp Franz von Siebold was not quite so lucky. German-born, and only 26 when he arrived, his duties as physician in Dejima began in 1823. A keen botanist, he sent two large consignments of plants back to Holland but was found to be in possession of maps, accused of treason and eventually deported from Japan in 1829. Nevertheless, his work, and publication of a two-volume *Flora Japonica* in 1826–7, exquisitely illustrated by a Japanese artist, makes him one of the most important early plant collectors in Japan. Together with Kaempfer and Thunberg he provided the background information for the great nineteenth-century plant hunters in Japan.

The Britons, John Gould Veitch and Robert Fortune, were two of the most significant of the nineteenth-century collectors in Japan, once her ports and harbours had been reopened to the West during the 1850s. Fortune is perhaps better known for his travels in China, and both men made only one visit to Japan (although Veitch interrupted his visit with a trip to the Philippines). They happened to be in Japan at roughly the same time, and although both mention the other, and were at the British Legation on the same days on one occasion, no comments were made by either about the other's achievements. They both made detailed records of their travels.

Other British collectors in Japan deserve a brief mention for the influence their activities had on gardens today. Amongst them, A.B.Mitford, closely connected with bamboos and maples, Charles Maries who discovered some well-known climbers, James Herbert Veitch (son of John Gould) and, in the twentieth century, E. H. Wilson, well known for his exploits in China, all introduced plants, which have become familiar and much-loved in the West.

Bamboos have, in recent years, become very popular in Western gardens. British gardeners first became aware of them in the nineteenth century, when many were introduced from China and Japan. Algernon Bertram Freeman Mitford, later Lord Redesdale (first Baron in the second creation of this title), served as Second Secretary to the British Legation in Tokyo from 1866 to 1870.[1] He disliked the Japanese garden: '... all spick and span – intensely artificial and a monument to wasted labour', but became passionately interested in the trees, and was one of the first in England to arouse interest in bamboo as a garden plant. Although he was an amateur collector, rather than a commercial plant-hunter, Mitford did much to further the knowledge of bamboos and of a large range of trees, including many maples.

Plant nurseries were flourishing in England by the middle of the nineteenth century, and several sent collectors worldwide to seek new specimens for their businesses. Charles Maries was one of those despatched to the Far East by the famous Veitch nurseries of London. He arrived in Yokohama in 1877 and spent the next three years travelling between Japan and China. His greater successes were in Japan, and he sent over 500 live plants back to the Veitch nurseries. Unlike many of his predecessors he was able to travel more or less freely throughout Japan, and returned with a significant haul of plants that have enhanced many Western gardens. The conifer *Abies mariesii* is named for him, and two climbers which never cease to impress, *Actinidia kolomikta* and *Schizophragma hydrangeoides*, a close relative of *Hydrangea petiolaris*, were first collected in Japan by Maries. On three visits to Japan Maries collected seeds and specimens – and not a few stories to tell, ranging from robbery to shipwreck. Maples, many varieties of *Iris Kaempferi,* primula, a number of conifers and a new lily (*Lilium auratum* var. *platyphyllum)* are amongst plants he brought back, as well as a collection of insects, which was accepted by the British Museum.

In 1891 James Herbert (Harry) Veitch embarked on a world tour, arriving first in India. Early in 1892 he was in Yokohama, and in June went from there to Korea, at that time even more isolated and forbidden country than Japan had been. In many places Veitch was the first Westerner the natives had ever seen. He left Korea less than two months later with colourful stories but little to show – it had been the wrong time of year to collect flowers or seeds. Returning to Japan he stayed until the following January. His most important contribution to the story of plant introductions was the new interest he created in flowering cherries. Although this was the result of meeting Charles Sargent (*Prunus sargentii*) while in Japan, the enthusiasm for the cherries came after his return to England.

Ernest 'Chinese' Wilson is best known for his travels and discoveries in China, where in the course of his success in making enormous collections of specimens (one shipment was of 50,000, collected in three short months), he memorably had his leg and foot badly shattered in a rock fall and was subsequently clambered over by a whole train of mules. In his description of this experience he noted that he then 'realised the size of the mule's hoof', although not one hoof landed on him as he lay in their path. Wilson travelled to Japan on only two occasions, and both were easy in comparison with his exploits in China. At the time he was working for the Arnold Arboretum in Boston, USA; he took many hundreds of photographs, and brought back several thousand specimens, including syringas, maples, lilies and thuja. He also visited azalea nurseries in the city of Kurume in Kyushu in April of 1918 and, entranced by the sight of 250 named azaleas, clipped and pruned in the Japanese manner, set about creating a collection to bring back to the West. His introductions, known as 'Wilson's Fifty', arrived in Boston in 1919, and formed the basis of the highly popular group of 'Kurume' azaleas bred worldwide today. .

Among the British collectors John Gould Veitch and Robert Fortune hold first place for their travels, collections and accounts of their time in Japan. First to arrive was Veitch, twenty-one at the time, so keen to go to the newly opened Japan that he 'eagerly sought the means of proceeding thither', and pulled every string he could to ensure his quick passage. John Gould was the great-grandson of the famous John Veitch, a Scot from Jedburgh, who acquired premises for a nursery near Exeter, in Devon, in 1808. John Gould's grandfather, James senior, took over the business, and his father, James junior, was sent to train in London aged eighteen. James junior realised that expansion of the business meant a London headquarters, and in 1853 he acquired the Royal Exotic Nursery at No. 544 King's Road, Chelsea. John Gould was fourteen at the time, and was destined, all his life, to continue the impressive Veitch dynasty.

John Gould Veitch started his voyage to Japan in April 1860, aboard the *Malabar*, armed with a large amount of equipment with which to pursue his activities on arrival in the East. As well as scientific instruments he had a number of Wardian cases – rather like miniature glass greenhouses – specifically designed to protect and nurture live plants on long journeys. The cases, invented by Dr Ward in the late 1830s, were still somewhat experimental when Veitch and Fortune decided to use them for their travels. None of the equipment was destined to arrive in Japan – the *Malabar* was shipwrecked off the coast of Ceylon near Galle and everything was lost. Veitch wasted no time in finding another ship, and arrived in Nagasaki, via Hong Kong, Canton and Shanghai, on 20 July, only three months after his departure from England.

Like most other travellers in Japan at the time, Veitch was lodged in a temple in Nagasaki. The information we have of his experiences comes from his letters home, which were passed on to the popular gardening magazine of the day, *The Gardener's Chronicle and Agricultural Gazette*. In all they published eighteen letters between 15 December 1860 and 1 February 1862.

Veitch was allowed to use the garden in the temple grounds, which gradually became the repository for his collections. His main frustration was the rule restricting him to travel only within a ten-mile radius – and the nearest nursery was fifteen miles away! On every excursion he was accompanied by an 'interpreter', who was very likely reporting his activities to a rather bemused (and often tiresome) senior official. He was swift to identify the difficulties with officialdom; his second letter home, written after fourteen days in Japan, states: '... the system of government consists so much of espionage, and every officer being a spy on the other, it is impossible to do anything with them'. On the other hand, the local people were friendly, and willing to bring him all sorts of plants. Many of them he quietly discarded, but others were kept in pots in his garden and tended until he had gathered enough for a shipment to England.

Young, and energetic, Veitch was delighted to be in Japan: 'The Japanese ... are far superior in every way to the Chinese', although to be fair his only experience of the Chinese was as he passed through their ports. He immediately started to learn some Japanese; indeed, two weeks after his arrival he wrote: 'the language I am getting hold of fast and I think that another fortnight (a month in all) will teach me as much as I require to make my way ...'! He enjoyed the interaction with the Japanese people, whom he liked. In his letters home he mentioned, in passing, that Japanese ladies were very friendly, and not at all shy. He did, however, comment that they didn't like European whiskers at all – and he clearly had some experience to go by, for as we see from his portrait, he sported a splendid set of long, black, 'weepers'. The portrait shows an attractive and gentle face, but Veitch also had enormous confidence – enough to get himself to the other end of the world, at such a young age, recover from shipwreck, settle himself comfortably in a very foreign land, and tackle a difficult local language so that he might communicate with as many people as possible.

Having arrived in July, Veitch left Nagasaki – and his plants, carefully attended by his friends at the temple – at the end of August, in the heat, and took a passage through the Inland Sea to Yokohama, where, with a letter of introduction from Hong Kong, he considered himself lucky to be invited to stay with 'Mr. Keswick, the representative of Messrs. Jardine and Co. here.'[2] He was hoping to be allowed to visit Edo but had to have the right invitation. No foreigners other than Legation officials were allowed to reside in Edo, and visitors had to have specific invitations from the senior foreign diplomat of their Legation. The British Minister and Consul General was Rutherford Alcock, and as luck would have it, Alcock arrived in Yokohama en route for an excursion to Mount Fuji two days after Veitch's steamer arrived there. The introduction was made, and Veitch was invited to join the Fuji expedition. Since he had to have an official role on the trip, he was immediately made 'Botanist to Her Britannic Majesty's Legation at Yedo'. Veitch reported that 'I at once grew six inches taller'.

Their ascent of Mount Fuji was the first that Europeans had been allowed to make to the famous, and sacred, mountain. The group took about two weeks to make the trip. The last stop, at about 8500 feet, was at a guesthouse where the eight English, their servants, and their Japanese host family all slept together in a room some 25 by 11 feet, with no windows or chimney, and, according to Veitch, liberally infested with fleas. The summit was reached with comparative ease, whereupon the party hoisted the British flag, sang 'God save the Queen', fired a twenty-one gun salute with revolvers, and toasted the health of the Queen, the Minister and, no doubt, themselves, in champagne – in the little temple on the top. The weather had not been good, with much rain, and the party was not allowed to wander off the path, (already, at this date, there was a well-trodden road up and down the mountain), but Veitch did manage to do some collecting, and he arrived at the bottom of the mountain with seeds and specimens of some twenty-five different species of conifers. It is also possible that it was on this trip that he first caught sight of the magnificent lily, the *Lilium auratum*, which he was able to collect and send home to England to become such a wonder.

Without doubt the trip to Mount Fuji was one of the highlights of

Veitch's time in Japan, but his travelling was by no means finished. Having secured the vital invitation to Edo from Alcock, Veitch set off by steamer to Hakodate, in Hokkaido, the most northerly port open to foreigners. He had only three or four days there but was well pleased to have been so far north. On his return he stayed with Alcock in Edo, where, to his chagrin, he found his movements even more restricted then they had been in Nagasaki. On every step outside the gates of the Legation he was accompanied by a large escort, all very inquisitive, and slightly hostile. Once again he was not allowed to stray from the road, and, frustratingly, he had to ride past trees and shrubs, now loaded with seed, without stopping. Once again he was befriended by locals who brought him specimens, although communication was frustrating (despite his earlier confidence about the language), and often in pictograms. He did manage to visit some of the Edo nurseries, including one trip organized by Alcock where he saw chrysanthemums, which astonished him, and which, he said, 'would not disgrace even a London exhibition'.

It was by now November, and Veitch was preparing to send the plants he had collected to England. Having lost all his Wardian cases he had much difficulty explaining to local carpenters how to construct these peculiar boxes made of glass with sealed corners, and was dubious as to the sea-worthiness of their efforts. The carpenters thought he was little short of mad to attempt to send live plants so far across the seas in such boxes. However, he had no option if he was to send his collections home. Before he left the Legation to travel to Yokohama and Nagasaki to collect plants he had left there he chanced to be under the same roof as Robert Fortune, newly arrived from England. This is one of the most tantalizing moments of the story of these two plant collectors, but Veitch's only comment was 'Mr. Fortune arrived here on the 12th inst. He is quite well'.

Robert Fortune, it must be said, made even less reference to Veitch. It has to be assumed that the two met – they may even have travelled together by steamer through the Inland Sea – certainly their specimens travelled together and were almost certainly muddled up before arrival in England. One can only imagine the opinions these two men would have had of one and other; the one young, on his first trip, full of enthusiasm and energy, the other middle-aged, by now a celebrated figure in England, an experienced collector on his fifth trip, an old China hand, travelling for his own amusement, and not the paid employee of the past.

Veitch set off soon for Yokohama, collected his plants, went on to Nagasaki, completed his business there and set off for Hong Kong. Having ensured that the plants were safely on their way to England he set sail for the Philippines on what became an extended, and very successful, trip to collect orchids. For unknown reasons his letters, at least one of which was definitely written, never reached England from the Philippines, so there is no account of his time there. He returned to Japan for another four months in August 1861 for the seed-collecting season, but his enthusiasm for the people had waned a little. He experienced an earthquake: '… one feels the uncertainty of what will happen next, and the utter inability to do anything to help oneself'. He was also irritated by the habits of his two new servants: '… unfortunately they are not in the habit of speaking the truth, and therefore little dependence can be placed on what they say. They also cheat one almost as much as a Chinaman, they get a percentage on everything you buy'. In early December, 1861, with, as he describes, views of Mount Fuji 'covered with snow, a remarkably beautiful object, particularly in an evening, with the sun setting almost immediately behind it' etched into his memory, he left Japan for home.

At the end of his travels in the Far East Veitch had sent home a remarkable collection of plants. Veitch's introductions were a stunning addition to the glories of Japanese plants then available in Britain. Just to mention a few of the many species and cultivars gives some idea of his importance: his collection of maples was one of the biggest ever received by a nursery in Britain at the time, the umbrella pine (*Sciadopitys verticillata*), which both he and Fortune found to be a magnificent tree, a Virginia Creeper called *Ampelopsis veitchii* (now *Parthenocissus tricuspidata*), the commercially very useful Japanese larch, dozens of conifers, magnolias and a number of lilies, including, of course, the sensational golden rayed *Lilium auratum*.

There was only one other opportunity for Veitch to make a journey abroad, to Australia and the South Sea Islands, from 1864–66, bringing further important plants to British collections. Sadly, he contracted tuberculosis and died at the age of thirty-one in 1870, a tragic loss, not only to his wife and young family, but also to the plant-collecting world. His place in both the family dynasty and the history of plant collectors was, nevertheless, firmly established.

Robert Fortune arrived in Nagasaki on 12 October 1860, three months after Veitch. This was his fifth (and last) trip abroad, all of them to the East. Born in Berwickshire, Scotland, in 1813, he started life as an apprentice gardener nearby, but by 1840 was working at the Botanic Garden in Edinburgh. He got on well with his superior there, William McNabb, well known as a demanding taskmaster, and McNabb recommended him for the post of Superintendent of the Hothouse Department at the Horticultural Society's garden at Chiswick. He took up the post in 1842, but within months he had been selected to spend a year in China on behalf of the Society on a plant collection expedition.

The story of Fortune's relationship with the Horticultural Society is well documented. His instructions for the expedition survive, and have been reprinted in the Journal of the Society. He was to be given a salary of £100 per year – not very generous, considering that a previous collector had received the same amount some seventy years earlier. He was required to collect seeds and plants, obtain information on Chinese gardening and cultivation, keep detailed daily journals and write home at every opportunity – and all letters must be sent in duplicate 'by separate opportunities'. 'If Chapoo [sic], the place of resort of the Japanese, should be accessible on your arrival, this would be worth an immediate visit.'

The need for good conditions for his plants was urged upon him: 'You will take care to impress upon the minds of the Captains the indispensable necessity of the glazed boxes being kept in the light, on the poop if possible, or on deck, or failing that, in the Main or Mizen-top.' The document is a marvellous example of precisely what was required of a plant collector in the nineteenth century. At the same time there was an argument about the methods with which Fortune might protect himself. The Society offered him a life preserver (a lead weighted cosh), and it took Fortune some time to persuade them that he really needed something more substantial. Eventually, with some reluctance, the Society allowed him to take a shotgun and a brace of pistols, but only on the understanding that he sold them before he left China and gave the money to the Society. The firearms later saved Fortune's life.

Despite a difficult start the trip was immensely successful, and many, if not all, the letters written back to the Society on this trip, survive in the Lindley library. They are the only examples of his correspondence still remaining, as most were destroyed after his death. The Society had clearly chosen the right man for the job. Fortune was very calm and resourceful in the face of adversity – and there were many, from shipwreck to murder attempts and frequent robberies. With such an excellent grounding in Eastern travel Fortune went on to make Chinese explorations his particular speciality. Although many new plants were introduced after his first trip, Fortune never again worked for the Society. His second trip to China, in 1848, was for the East India Company, at a 500 per cent pay increase, with a specific remit to obtain information about and specimens of tea plants, kept a jealously guarded secret by the Chinese. It was as a result of Fortune's work, he often disguised as a Chinese, that it first became known in the West that green and black teas came from one and the same plant.

A third trip was made once for the East India Company, from 1853–6, again in pursuit of information about tea – the Company had realised how immensely profitable this new habit would be to them. A fourth trip (1858–9) was made on behalf of the Government of the United States of America, which also wanted his expertise to develop their budding tea industry.

It must be presumed that Fortune wrote journals on all his trips, although they have now disappeared. He did, however, produce three books, which have survived, describing his various experiences in China. All were popular at the time, and still make fascinating reading. They are full of tales of adventure, described in a rather impersonal and matter-of- fact style. They must have made Fortune quite a hero on their publication over the years, and he was certainly well known as a traveller and plant-collector. In addition, Fortune had always kept his eye out during his travels for works of art, and shipped back a large amount of porcelain, lacquer and other items over the years. By the time he decided, aged forty-seven, to return to the East, to see for himself this newly accessible country of Japan, it appears that he did not need to find an employer to send him. He seems to have made an arrangement with the firms of Standish and Noble in Bagshot, and Glendinnings of Chiswick, to handle plants that he sent home. In the last book which he wrote about his Japanese journey, he described his purpose in going as 'with a view to making a collection of these (species of trees, and other vegetable productions of an ornamental and useful kind) and other objects of natural history and works of art'.

From his very first sight of Japanese shores Fortune showed his delight in this new country in the way he wrote about it. He visited the mudflat at Dejima and was struck at the great change that had come about there in six short years. It was no longer a virtual prison; the gate had been removed, the surrounding walls pulled down and the whole place looked ruinous. What a difference from the rigid guards and curfews, which von Siebold had known. von Siebold, now an old man, who had been allowed, indeed encouraged, to return to Japan in 1859, was almost the first person whom Fortune visited, in his small house outside Nagasaki, where he had already established a garden and was busy collecting once more. .

Fortune described the trees and plants which he saw as he travelled around Nagasaki. 'One feature of the people was rather striking, and an interesting one it is. Almost every house which has any pretension to respectability has a little flower garden in the rear, oftentimes, indeed, small, but neatly arranged, and adds greatly to the comfort and happiness of the family'. He described scenery, domestic scenes and flowering plants that would still be very familiar today in the countryside.

Compared with his Chinese travels Fortune's Japanese expedition was a gentle experience, although there were a few tricky moments. When sailing through the Inland Sea, (which entranced him and reminded him of Scottish lochs), on an English steamship called *England*, the Japanese pilots ran the ship aground having assured the Captain and all aboard that they knew exactly what they were doing. Fearing possible storms Fortune was extremely concerned. He was accompanying his plants, in Wardian cases made up, once again, by the puzzled local carpenters, through the Sea, by special permission, en route to Shanghai, to ship the plants to England. This was the same ship, on which Veitch's plants, and perhaps Veitch himself, were travelling, giving rise to confusion over the ownership of many of the plants once they arrived back in England. Fortune's only comment was: 'Mr. Veitch had also put his plants on board the same vessel, so that the whole of the poop was lined with glass cases crammed full of the natural productions of Japan.'

Like Veitch, Fortune was frustrated by, and slightly distrustful of, the constant attendance of '*Yakoneens*' (*yakunin*, literally official but probably police) wherever he went. 'Japan would be a pleasant place to live or travel in were it freed from those bands of two-sworded idlers which infest the capital'. He visited Edo on two occasions; the first at the invitation of Alcock, in the approved manner, where he chanced upon Veitch for the first time; and the second, when, due to the absence of Alcock, he engineered for himself an invitation from Townsend Harris, the United States Minister. He was desperate to visit the capital's nurseries in the spring, and needed an official invitation. Unfortunately, the Chargé d'Affaires at the British Legation became aware of his presence in the capital and felt a slight to his self-importance. A brusque series of letters followed, which Fortune detailed in his book.

Fortune travelled in Japan from October 1860 until the end of the year, when he saw his plants off to England safely from Shanghai. Three months later he was back in Japan and remained, travelling again around Edo, Kanagawa, Kamakura and Yokohama, for another seven months until July 1861 when he set sail for Shanghai and a brief, and rather unproductive, trip to Peking (Beijing). Throughout his book the people, their customs, the climate and the agricultural produce are described in great and, in some cases, quite charming detail: 'Saki, which is rather stronger than tea, is also consumed in considerable quantities. Report says that many of the visitors are particularly fond of composing and reciting poetry in one of the avenues near the temple, and that sundry draughts of the favourite beverage are taken to brighten the intellect and to excite the imagination'. Although some have thought Fortune's writings rather humourless, there is a strong sense of irony in many of his comments.

Mainly because of the confusion of the shipment that arrived with Veitch's main collection, Fortune is not credited with the first introduction of many of the plants, which he sent to England. But he certainly 'found' the *Primula japonica*, although it was delivered to his door in a basket. He thought the candelabra-shaped flower, a deep magenta colour, quite delightful, and described it as the 'Queen of Primroses'. He was fascinated by the umbrella pine and sent back specimens, together with the gingko (he called it *Salisburia adiantifolia*), *Cryptomeria japonica* and *Thujopsis dolobrata*. He too discovered the *Lilium auratum*, growing near Kamakura, and brought back saxifrage, deutzia, euonymous, new chrysanthemums, and perhaps his most successful introduction, the male form of the *Aucuba japonica*, formerly only known in the West in its female, non-fruiting, form. He himself was particularly pleased with this introduction, amongst the dozens of plants, which he sent back to England.

On his return to England, Fortune settled down to a comfortable retirement. His many purchases in China had been sold over the years at a number of auctions arranged by Christie's. They netted him a comfortable return. Many of his plants were also sold at auction. Two tantalising mentions were made of his family; a wife and young daughter, and 'an eldest son', to whose farm in Scotland he often travelled from his own farm in Berwickshire in his retirement years. On 16 April 1998 English Heritage decided that his life should be recognized by a Blue Plaque at No. 9, Gilston Road, Chelsea, where Robert Fortune died on 13 April 1880, after a long, fruitful, and fortunate life.

Fortune said that no country had so favourable a spring as Japan. Although certain parts of China remained closest to his heart, he delighted in his last journey, and the benefits to his homeland are many, both through his closely observed writings and the many wonderful trees, flowers and plants which he helped to introduce. These plants are still with us today, and are a fitting legacy to the small group of plant collectors who have given so much pleasure over the years.

NOTES

Chapter 1 ANDREW COBBING *Mori Arinori, 1847–89: from Diplomat to Statesman*

1. Isabella Bird, *Unbeaten Tracks in Japan,* 2 vols. (London, 1880) II, p. 202.
2. Alistair Swale, *The Political Thought of Mori Arinori* (Richmond, 2000), p. 1.
3. Diary entry for 15 April 1880, 'Clara's Diary' in Okubo Toshimichi et al (ed.), *Mori Arinori Zenshû*, vol.4 (Bunsendô, Tokyo, 1999), pp. 288–9, 304.
4. *Ibid.*, p. 304.
5. Bird, II, pp. 202–4.
6. PRO, Satow Papers, PRO-30–33–15–7, 'Diary, January 1882–March 1884,' entry for 5 April 1883.
7. Makino Nobuaki, *Kôkai Roku* (Tokyo, 1977) cited in Inuzuka Takaaki, 'Zaiei Nihon Kôshikan no Setchi Keii to sono Henkan' in *Seiji Keizai Shigaku*, no.330, December 1995, p. 16.
8. Ivan P. Hall, *Mori Arinori*, (Harvard, 1973.) p. 283.
9. On one occasion Mori had even refused Parkes' representative, Endymion Wilkinson, entry to a meeting on the cholera quarantine issue by insisting that he was uninvited.
10. Inuzuka Takaaki, *Mori Arinori* (Tokyo, 1986), p. 212.
11. *Ibid.*, p. 214.
12. Granville Papers, PRO-30–29–312, Further Correspondence, Part 5, cited in Hall, *Mori Arinori*, p. 285.
13. *Ibid.*, p. 290.
14. *Japan Weekly Mail*, 1 September 1883.
15. Hall, p. 289. Mori may have come across Oliphant again at the Athenaeum, although there is no record of such a meeting. In addition to this club, he also joined the Royal Asiatic Society in time for its first gathering, where he freely criticized a paper by Professor Friedrich Max Mueller of Oxford on a 'Sanskrit Text Discovered in Japan', a subject he knew practically nothing about. Hall, pp. 291, 293.
16. Swale, p. 13.
17. Hall, p. 289. See Spencer, *Principles of Sociology*, I, parts II and III, and II, part V.

18. Itagaki's interview with Spencer was not a success. Mori reported to Itô early in May 1883 that 'Itagaki had his interview with Spencer – the idol of his researches – three days ago. He went into it as though approaching the Emperor, but in the actual discussion master and pupil traded places, with the disciple doing all the sermonizing and putting forward his usual empty and unfounded theories. Finally the central idol lost his patience, got up in the middle of the conversation muttering 'no, no, no' [English in original] and took his leave of Itagaki, just like that.' Hall, p. 292.
19. Swale, p. 4.
20. Hall, p. 288.
21. David Duncan, *The Life and Letters of Herbert Spencer*, (London, 1908), p. 161.
22. *Ibid.*, p. 319. Letter from Spencer to Kaneko Kentarô. 21 August 1892.
23. Hall, p. 323. A decade later, for example, Spencer felt compelled to inform another Japanese contact, Kaneko Kentarô, that 'I give this advice in confidence. I wish that it should not transpire publicly, at any rate during my lifetime for I do not desire to arouse the animosity of my fellow-countrymen.' Duncan, p. 323. Letter from Spencer to Kaneko Kentarô, 26 August 1892.
24. Another major cause of this political purge was the financial scandal over the sale of the Hokkaido Development Agency's assets. See Cobbing, *The Satsuma Students in Britain* (Richmond, 2000), p. 128.
25. Swale, p. 17.
26. *Pall Mall Gazette*, 26 February 1884.
27. Swale, p. 102.
28. *Pall Mall Gazette*, 26 February 1882.
29. *Ibid.*
30. *Ibid.*
31. Swale, pp. 105–6.
32. Cobbing, *The Satsuma Students in Britain* (Folkestone, 2000), pp. 90–1.
33. Duncan, p. 319. Spencer to Kaneko Kentarô, 23 August 1892.
34. Only the first four parts of '*Representative Government' Nihon seifudaigai seitairon'*survive in English, but there is a complete Japanese version in nine parts entitled'.
35. Swale, p. 86.
36. *Pall Mall Gazette*, 26 February 1884.
37. *Ibid.*
38. Swale, p. 20.
39. Hall, p. 294.
40. Mori Arinori, Letters to Yokoyama Yasutake, No.10, *Mori Arinori Zenshû* vol.2 (Tokyo, 1972), p. 46.
41. Mori Arinori, '*Shintai no Noryoku'* in *Mori Arinori Zenshû* vol.1 (Tokyo, 1972), p. 328.
42. Olive Checkland, *Britain's Encounter with Meiji Japan 1868–1912* (London, 1989), p. 131.

43. For an assessment of Mori as a Spencerian 'progressive conservative' rather than a 'statist' in the mould of Stein, see Swale, pp. 184–7.
44. *Pall Mall Gazette*, 26 February 1884.

Chapter 2 IAN NISH *Kato Takaaki, 1862–1926: Japanese Ambassador to London and Japanese Foreign Minister*

1. Biographical accounts of Kato are to be found in Hosoya Chihiro in *Nihon gaikoshi jiten*; Ito Masanori, *Kato Takaaki*, Tokyo, 1929, 2 volumes [hereafter cited as 'Kato']; Peter Duus, *Party Rivalry and Political Change in Taisho Japan*, Harvard, 1968; Frederick Dickinson, *War and National Reinvention: Japan in the Great War, 1914–1919*, Harvard, 1999; Hara Kenichiro and Yamamoto Shiro (eds.), 'Kato' in *Hara Takashi wo meguru hito-bito*, Tokyo: NHK Books, 1981, pp. 177–98; Omura Tatsuzo, *Nihon no gaikokan 300-nin no jimmyaku*, Tokyo: Yomiuri, 1975. Obituaries in London *Times* for 23 January 1926 by C.J. Sale (Japan Society) and 2. Kato, i, 151–79.
2. Kato, i, 151–79.
3. *Mutsu Munemitsu haku*, Tokyo: Kasumigasekikai, 1967, pp. 50–1. Hagihara Nobutoshi, 'Mutsu Munemitsu in Europe, 1884–5' in Louis Perez (ed.), *Mutsu Munemitsu and Identity Formation of the Individual and the State in Modern Japan*, Lampeter: Mellen Press, 2001, pp. 77–9.
4. Kato, i, 235–8.
5. I.H. Nish (ed.), *British Documents on Foreign Affairs*, Part I, Series E, 'Asia', Maryland: University Publications of America, 1989 (General editors, K. Bourne and D.C. Watt), vol. 5, doc. 24 (hereafter cited as '*BDOFA*'). Kato, i, 241–2. For a more general treatment, see Ian Nish, 'Japanese diplomats and the Sino-Japanese War' in *The Sino-Japanese War of 1894–5 in its International Dimension,* STICERD International Studies pamphlet, LSE, IS/94/278, pp. 61–72.
6. Note by Kimberley, 14 April 1895 in British Foreign Office (Japan), FO 46/460; Giffen to Foreign Office, 17 April 1895 'Memorandum on Commercial Aspects of the Treaty between China and Japan' in *BDOFA*, vol. 5, doc. 353.
7. Kimberley to Rosebery, 6 April 1895 in Rosebery papers 10243 (which are to be found in the MSS room of the Scottish National Library, Edinburgh).
8. Rosebery to Kimberley, 9 April 1895 in Rosebery papers 10243. The *Dreibund* intervention is handled in more detail in Ian Nish, 'The Three-power Intervention of 1895' in A.R. Davis and A.D. Stefanowska (eds.), *Austrina*, Sydney: Oriental Society of Australia, 1982, pp. 204–25 and 'Britain and the Three-power intervention, 1895' in *Proceedings of the British Association of Japanese Studies,* vol. 5/I(1980), 13–26.
9. Kato, i, p. 250.
10. Kato, i, pp. 249–52.

11. Kimberley to Rosebery, 27 April; Rosebery to Kimberley, 28 April 1895 in Rosebery papers 10070.
12. Kato, i, p. 250.
13. Okuma to Kato, 12 Nov. 1896 in *Gaimusho no 100–nen*, 2 vols, Tokyo: Hara Shobo, 1969, i, 379ff.
14. Kato to Okuma, 11 Dec. 1896 in *Gaimusho no 100–nen*, i, 386ff; Duus, *Party Rivalry*, p. 55.
15. Ian Nish, 'Ito's Overseas Sojourns' in *Bulletin of the European Association of Japanese Studies*, 55(2000), 7–15.
16. Okuma's statement in Kaneko Kentaro (comp.), *Koshaku Ito Hirobumi den*, 3 vols (Tokyo, 1941), iii, 306–7.
17. Oishi Masami's statement in *Ito den*, iii, 308.
18. Kato, i, 340–8.
19. Omura, p. 35; I.H. Nish, *Anglo-Japanese Alliance, 1895–1907*, London: Athlone Press, 1964, pp. 59–60; Tsunoda Jun, *Manshu mondai to kokubo hoshin*, Tokyo: Hara Shobo, 1968, pp. 30–32.
20. Kato, i, 360–72.
21. Foreign Office (Japan), FO46/527,D. 57.
22. Kato [Surugadai, Suzuki-cho, Tokyo], to Kimberley, 3 February 1901 in Kimberley papers 10249 f. 106 [to be found in the MSS room of the Scottish National Library, Edinburgh].
23. Barbara Brooks, *Japan's Imperial Diplomacy, 1895–1938*, Hawaii: University Press, 2001, *passim*; Kato, i, 373ff; Okazaki Hisahiko, *Komura Jutaro to sono jidai*, Tokyo: PHP, 1998, pp. 133–4.
24. Hosoya in *Nihon gaikoshi jiten*.
25. *Gaimusho no 100–nen*, i, 496–500; Nish, *Anglo-Japanese Alliance*, pp. 104–11.
26. Brooks, p. 22; *Kato*, i, 582–6.
27. Ayako Hotta, *Japan-British Exhibition of 1910*, Richmond: Japan Library, 1999, pp. 43–9.
28. Peter Lowe, *Great Britain and Japan, 1911–15,* London: Macmillan, 1969, ch. 11. G.P. Gooch and H.W.V. Temperley (eds), *British Documents on the Origins of the War, 1898–1914*, viii, ch. LXIX, pp. 466–540 *passim*, covers the activities of Baron Kato during this period.
29. Kato, i, 685–97; Tsunoda, pp. 627–9; *BDOFA*, vol. 9, p. 354.
30. Nish, *Alliance in Decline, 1908–23*, London: Athlone Press, 1972, pp. 88–93*; BDOFA*, vol. 9, pp. 354–5.
31. Kato, i, 708–26.
32. Lowe, ch.7; Duus, pp. 92–6; Dickinson, pp. 91–2; Kato, ii, 1–14; 71–102.
33. Kato in Tokyo *Asahi Shimbun*, 20 July 1921, quoted in K. Bourne and D.C. Watt (eds), *Studies in International History,* London: Longmans, 1967, p. 380.

Chapter 3 SIR HUGH CORTAZZI *Sir Francis Plunkett, 1835–1907: British Minister at Tokyo, 1884–87*

PRINCIPAL SOURCES. FO files in the Public Record Office covering Plunkett's time in Japan (FO 46 and FO 262 series), Foreign Office lists, *Dictionary of National Biography*, *The Times* as quoted and the *Japan Weekly Mail* for 1886 and 1887.

1. DNB entry for Francis Plunkett by Thomas Henry Sanderson.
2. *Embassies in the East* by J.E.Hoare, Richmond: Curzon Press, 1999, page 115.
3. *Sir Harry Parkes, British Representative in Japan, 1865–83* by Gordon Daniels, Richmond: Japan Library, 1996, pages 160/1.
4. Plunkett's account of his journey in August 1875 in HMS *Frolic* has been preserved at the PRO (FO 46 193)
5. Papers preserved in the PRO are quite voluminous.
6. *Embassies in the Far East* by J. E. Hoare, Richmond: Curzon Press 1999, page 117.
7. Quoted in the *Life of Sir Harry Parkes* by F.V. Dickins and Lane Poole, Volume II, London: 1894, page 221.
8. In relation to Consular jurisdiction as set out in the 1858 Treaties.
9. See page 5 of a paper by Ian Ruxton of the Kyushu institute of Technology on 'The Ending of Extraterritoriality in Japan' for The History, Political and International Relations section of the 9th triennial conference of European Association of Japanese Studies at Lahti, Finland in August 2000. This paper also provides useful additional background on the Treaty Revision negotiations.
10. For a fuller account of this conversation see Ian Nish's paper entitled 'Japan's Modernization and Anglo-Japanese Rivalry in the 1880s' in *Bruno Lewin zu Ehren: Festschrift aus Anlass seines 65.Geburtstages* Band II Japan. Universitaetsverlag Dr.N.Brockmeyer. Bochum. 1989.
11. *Japan Weekly Mail*, Aug 7, 1886.
12. Satow Papers (PRO 30/33 1 / 2)
13. *The Diaries and Letters of Sir Ernest Mason Satow, 1843–1929, a Scholar Diplomat in East Asia*, edited by Ian Ruxton, 1998, Lampeter: Edwin Mellen Press, page 214.
14. Nigel Brailey of the University of Bristol who has made a particular study of Satow especially during his time in Bangkok is the source for this information.
15. See Ian Nish's biographical portrait of Gubbins in *Biographical Portraits*, vol. II, Richmond: Japan Library, 1997.
16. In his essay on the 'The Era of Unequal Treaties' in *The Political-Diplomatic Dimension 1600–1930*, edited by Ian Nish and Yoichi Kibata, Palgrave, 2000, Jim Hoare wrote of Francis Plunkett that he 'was a more easy-going man, less given to hectoring. But he had been Parkes's Secretary

of legation in the mid-1870s, and naturally continued something of that approach'. I have not found direct evidence to support Dr Hoare's comment.

Chapter 4 HUGH CORTAZZI *Hugh Fraser, 1837–94: British Minister at Tokyo 1889–94*

Sources include: PRO Records in FO 46 for 1889–1894, *The Japan Weekly Mail*, 1889–1894, Mary Fraser: *A Diplomatist's Wife in Japan; Letters from Home to Home* (first published in 1899 by Hutchinson and Co and republished as *A Diplomat's Wife in Japan; Sketches at the Turn of the Century* (Weatherhill, Tokyo and New York, 1982); Mary Fraser: *Reminiscences of a Diplomatist's Wife in Many Lands*, 1911; Mary Fraser: Further Reminiscences, 1912.

1. *A Diplomat's Wife in Japan: Sketches at the Turn of the Century* is the title of the edition which I made in 1982 and which was published by Weatherhill.
2. Eton College Records.
3. *Further Reminiscences*, published in 1912, includes more comments on Hugh Fraser's career and character than are contained in either of Mary Fraser's other books.
4. For background on Mary Crawford please see the introduction to my edition of *A Diplomat's wife in Japan*.
5. In her three books listed above.
6. *A Diplomat's Wife* page 89.
7. *A Diplomat's Wife* page 224.
8. *A Diplomat's Wife* page 334. Three strawberries (*fraises*) were part of the Fraser coat of arms ('azure trios fraises argent')
9. The Treaties concluded in 1858 with their provisions for extraterritorial jurisdiction over foreign residents as well as their trade provisions were increasingly resented by the Japanese who had made strenuous efforts to modernize their country. They limited Japanese sovereignty and extraterritoriality came to be seen as insulting. Various attempts had been made in the 1870s and 1880s to get agreement from the Powers to revised treaties. One proposal had been for the establishment of mixed courts but this aroused a furore of protest and the Japanese position gradually hardened. The Japanese recognized that at this stage in the nineteenth century an agreement with Britain was the key to revision of the other treaties, but they also saw that benefits might be had by trying to seek agreement first with other Powers e.g. the USA and Germany, thus putting pressure on Britain to make concessions.

The foreign communities, of which the British were by far the largest, while wanting to be able to travel freely outside the Treaty ports and resenting Japanese restrictions on their freedom to trade desired at the same time to retain their privileged position (consular rights, leases etc). They were highly critical of Japanese justice and vigorously opposed concessions often accusing those involved in the negotiations of not standing up for the 'rights' of foreigners in Japan.

Background on the Treaties and on some of the other personalities involved can be found in Ian Nish's biographical portraits of Aoki Shuzo and J. H. Gubbins in *Biographical Portraits*, Vols II and III (Japan Library for the Japan Society, 1997 and 1999). See also essays by James Hoare 'The Era of the Unequal Treaties 1858–99' and by Inouye Yuichi 'From Unequal Treaty to the Anglo-Japanese Alliance, 1867–1902' in Volume I of *The Political-Diplomatic Dimension, 1600–1930*, edited by Ian Nish and Yoichi Kibata, 2000.

10. Despatch No 97.

11. See Dr Carmen Blacker's essay 'Two Piggotts ...' in *Britain and Japan, 1859–1991, Themes and Personalities*, edited by Hugh Cortazzi and Gordon Daniels and published for the Japan Society in 1991.

12. *Biographical Portraits*, Volume II.

13. No 140.

14. No 144.

15. See biographical portrait of 'Josiah Conder (1852–1920) and Meiji Architecture' by Dallas Finn in *Britain and Japan, 1859–1991, Themes and Personalities*, edited by Hugh Cortazzi and Gordon Daniels, London 1991.

Chapter 5 IAN RUXTON *Sir Ernest Satow (1843–1929) in Tokyo, 1895–1900*

1. It will be assumed that readers know something of Satow's previous posting in Japan, having read *A Diplomat in Japan* (Seeley, Service & Co. London, 1921) about the years 1862–69. See also Peter F. Kornicki's chapter on Satow in Cortazzi and Daniels (eds), *Britain and Japan, 1859–1991* (London and New York: Routledge, 1991) and Ian C. Ruxton (ed) *The Diaries and Letters of Sir Ernest Mason Satow* (Lampeter: Edwin Mellen Press, 1998).

2. Diary, 17 May 1895. Satow's private diaries are in the Satow papers beginning at PRO 30/33 15/1–17 (1861–96), continuing in PRO30/33 16/1–12 (1896–1912) and ending at PRO 30/33 17/1–16 (1912–26 and various travel diaries 1879–1906).

3. See Brailey, N. (ed.) The Satow Siam Papers, vol. 1, The Historical Society, Bangkok, 1997.

4. In a letter to his former Japan colleague and friend W. G. Aston, provisionally appointed Consul-General in Korea, dated 27 June 1884 Satow wrote enviously: 'The work must be very interesting, and you have a teachable people to deal with.' Satow Papers, PRO 30/33/11/3

5. The long leave was the low point in Satow's diplomatic career, but he made good use of his time, visiting family and friends (A. B. Mitford, William Willis), reading in libraries (in Oxford, Rome, Madrid and Lisbon) and getting confirmed in the Anglican faith on 29 October 1888.

6. See Dr H. Temperley's entry on Satow in *Dictionary of National Biography, 1922–30* (Oxford: Oxford University Press, 1963).
7. Ian Nish, *The Anglo-Japanese Alliance* (London: The Athlone Press, 1966) p. 11. In Japan there had been growing pressure for repudiation of the old treaties, so that the process of renegotiation may have been an attempt by the Western Powers to keep Japan within the 'comity of nations' and prevent her sliding back into '*sakoku*' isolation (see N. Brailey, 'Ernest Satow and Japanese Revised Treaty Implementation', a paper delivered at STICERD on 9 July 1999).
8. For more detail, see Mutsu Munemitsu, *Kenkenroku: A Diplomatic Record of the Sino-Japanese War, 1894–1895.* (trans. Gordon M. Berger. Tokyo: University of Tokyo, 1982.) See also Beasley, W., *Japanese Imperialism 1894–1945* (Oxford: Clarendon Press, 1991); Lone, S., *Japan's First Modern War: Army and Society in the Conflict with China, 1894–95* (London: Macmillan, 1994).
9. From Lensen, G. A. (Translated and ed.) *The d'Anethan Dispatches from Japan, 1894–1910.* (Tallahassee, Florida: The Diplomatic Press, 1967) p. 53. For more excerpts from Satow's diary see also Lensen, G. A. (ed.) *Korea and Manchuria Between Russia and Japan, 1895–1904, The Observations of Sir Ernest Satow* (Tallahassee, Florida: The Diplomatic Press, 1966). Henceforth this latter work is cited as 'Lensen'.
10. It was quite common for Japan to be described as Britain's 'natural ally' by shrewd observers on both sides in the 1890s. (Nish, p. 11, quoting S. Gwynn (ed.), *The letters and friendships of Sir Cecil Spring Rice*, 2 vols, London, 1929, volume i, pp. 145–6, Rice to Ferguson, 28 May 1893: 'In England we regard [Japan] as a practical joker...The general feeling in Japan is that England is her natural ally.')
11. Satow Papers, PRO 30/33/5/2
12. Satow to O'Conor (private), 3 September 1895, Satow Papers, PRO 30/33/14/8
13. Diary, 20 September 1895, PRO 30/33/15/17.
14. Satow had expressed the same view in a letter dated 18 April to his friend F. V. Dickins before leaving Morocco, when he had likened it to cutting through a mouldy cheese. Satow to Dickins, 18 April 1895, PRO 30/33/11/6.
15. PRO 30/33 14/11
16. See 'Aoki Shūzō (1844–1914)' by I. Nish, Ch. 12, *Britain and Japan: Biographical Portraits* vol. 3 (ed. J. Hoare, Richmond: Japan Library, 1999).
17. PRO 30/33 14/11
18. Fukuba Bisei (1831–1907). After the Meiji Restoration he entered the Office of Shintō Worship (Jingikan) and worked to promote Shintō. Appointed to the Genrōin in 1881 and later served in the Kunaishō and the House of Peers. Elsewhere Satow calls him the 'dwarf Shintoist' Diary, 14 August 1895.

19. PRO 30/33 16/1
20. Diary. PRO 30/33 16/2
21. Diary. PRO 30/33 16/3
22. PRO 30/33 5/5.
23. Diary. 2 February 1897. See also *Shades of the Past* by H. S. Williams (Tokyo: Tuttle, 1984) for a journalistic piece on the Carew case which was controversial.
24. Gembei mura was where Satow rented a house for use at weekends to see his family, and research and cultivate plants and bamboos. It is also called Totsuka or Takata or just 'the suburbs' in Satow's diary. (S. Nagaoka, *A-nesto Satō Kōshi Nikki*, vol. 1, p. 165; Tokyo: Shinjinbutsu Ōraisha, 1989).
25. He frequently walked up from Arai's Hotel at Nikkō to the lake at Chuzenji, and also enjoyed the walks in the area. On 19 September 1895 he 'saw Mrs Bishop at Kanaya's.' This was the married name of Isabella Bird (1831–1904) the intrepid lady traveller.
26. Diary. 3 February 1899.
27. Diary. 1 August 1895.
28. Diary. 23 October 1896.
29. Diary. 12 January 1897.
30. Lensen, pp. 21–24.
31. Published in the Transactions of the ASJ Vol. 27, Part 2, 1899.
32. Published in the TASJ Vol. 27, Part 3, 1899.
33. William Kirkwood was appointed legal adviser to the Japanese Ministry of Justice in 1885, and when a Foreign Ministry judicial review committee headed by Inoue Kaoru was set up on 6 August 1886 he was appointed to it with G. E. Boissonade. Kirkwood offered opinions on Boissonade's proposed legal codes and translated a large part of Japanese law into English. His employment terminated on 31 July 1901 and he returned to England, having been awarded the Order of the Rising Sun, 2nd class, in recognition of his services to Japan. (source: *Rainichi Seiyōjin Jiten*, edited by Hiroshi Takeuchi, Tokyo: Nichigai Associates, Inc. 1995)
34. See 'Thomas Wright Blakiston (1832–91)' by Sir H. Cortazzi, Ch. 5, *Britain and Japan: Biographical Portraits* vol. 3 (ed. J. Hoare, Richmond: Japan Library, 1999).
35. Yet when Satow discussed the possibility that he might be transferred to Peking with H. S. Wilkinson he said 'that nothing in the world would induce me to ask for a post of such difficulty, but we agreed that if it were offered I could hardly decline'. (Diary, 25 July 1899).
36. He would have to leave his Japanese family, but had shared actively in the formative teenage years of his sons. He saw O-Kane and Hisayoshi again on his last visit to Japan in 1906, and on his way home visited Eitarō who was farming in Denver for health reasons. Hisayoshi, later Dr Takeda shared his interest in botany and studied in England from 1910–16. There is no indication that Satow ever fell out of love with O-Kane, and on 26 January

1916 he noted in his diary that Hisayoshi should return because his mother was lonely and he could no longer afford to pay him an allowance of £200 a year.

Chapter 6 PETER LOWE *Sir William Conyngham Greene, 1854–1934: British Minister to Japan, 1912–19*

1. For a lucid analysis of the situation during the 1890s, see I.R. Smith, *The Origins of the South African War* (London, 1996).
2. *Ibid.*, pp. 136–7.
3. *Ibid.*, p. 367.
4. *Ibid.*, p. 351. For further evidence of the discussions between Greene and Smuts, see Keith Hancock and J. van der Poel (eds), *Selections from the Smuts Papers* vol. I (Cambridge, 1966), pp. 201–4, 266–8, 283–305.
5. Smith, pp. 379–80.
6. See Ian Nish, *The Anglo-Japanese Alliance: the Diplomacy of Two Island Empires, 1894–1907* (London, 1966) and *Alliance in Decline: a Study in Anglo-Japanese Relations, 1908–23* (London, 1972) for an authoritative survey of the alliance from its origins to its demise. See also Peter Lowe, *Great Britain and Japan, 1911–15: a Study of British Far Eastern Policy* (London, 1969).
7. See M. B. Jansen, *The Japanese and Sun Yat-sen* (Cambridge, Mass., 1954).
8. See Ian Nish, 'Sir Claude and Lady Ethel MacDonald', in Ian Nish (ed.), *Britain and Japan: Biographical Portraits* (Folkestone, 1994), pp. 133–45.
9. Greene to Grey, 12 September 1913, FO 405/212, pp. 130–2, Public Record Office, Kew.
10. Lowe, p. 113.
11. *Ibid.*, p. 120.
12. Greene to Grey, 14 December 1913, FO 371/1621.
13. Letter from Greene to Sir Walter Langley, Assistant Under-Secretary of State, Foreign Office, Langley papers, FO 800/31.
14. Lowe, pp. 161–2.
15. Enclosure in Greene to Grey, 3 March 1914, FO 371/1941.
16. Greene to Grey, 10 and 12 June 1914, FO 371/1942.
17. Letter from Greene to Langley, 22 February 1914, Langley papers, FO 800/31.
18. Greene to Grey, 10 August 1914 (two telegrams), FO 371/2016. For a stimulating assessment of Japan's response to participation in the First World War, see F.R. Dickinson, *War and National Reinvention: Japan in the Great War, 1914–1919* (Cambridge, Mass., 1999). Dickinson provides a favourable assessment of Kato Takaaki, arguing that Kato was pursuing a policy of traditional imperialism, analogous to that reinforced by the Occidental powers in China during the nineteenth century. He portrays Kato as wishing to assess the control of foreign policy by the political parties with the exclusion of the influence of the *genro*.
19. *Ibid.*

20. Grey to Greene, 11 August 1914, FO 371/2016.
21. Lowe, p. 190.
22. Greene to Grey, 25 January 1915, FO 371/2322. See Dickinson, pp. 84–116. I am not persuaded by Dickinson's highly sympathetic portrayal of Kato Takaaki. While Kato was able, courageous and very experienced, he seriously underestimated the problems he faced in simultaneously expanding Japan's role in China, compelling Yuan Shih-k'ai to comply, inducing the western powers to acquiesce in Japanese aims, marginalizing the *genro* and controlling the army. Kato was very capable and tenacious - but he was not a Bismarck. Kato made serious mistakes in 1915 which damaged his standing as a diplomat and his ambitions as a party leader.
23. Greene to Grey, 10 February 1915, FO 371/2322.
24. *Ibid.*
25. Lowe, p. 235.
26. Letter from Jordan to Alston, 2 February 1915, Alston papers, FO 800/248.
27. Letter from Alston to Jordan, 19 March 1915, Jordan papers, FO 350/14.
28. Letter from Greene to Rumbold, 10 May 1915, cited Lowe, p. 256.
29. Letter from Greene to Langley, 9 September 1915, Alston papers, FO 800/247.
30. Nish, *Alliance in Decline*, p. 198. See also Dickinson, pp. 117–53.
31. Greene to Balfour, 18 January 1917, cited Nish, *Alliance in Decline*, p. 199.
32. *Ibid.*, p. 200.
33. *Ibid.*, p. 206.
34. Greene to Langley, 30 August 1917, cited ibid., pp. 220–1.
35. *Ibid.*
36. *Ibid.*, pp. 236–8.
37. *Ibid.*, p. 250.
38. Greene to Cecil, 2 November 1918, cited ibid., p. 262.
39. *Ibid.*
40. *Ibid.*, p. 300.
41. Cited Lowe, p. 309.
42. Nish, *Alliance in Decline*, pp. 310–12.

Chapter 7 HARUMI GOTO-SHIBATA *Sir John Tilley, 1869–1951: British Ambassador to Japan, 1926–31*

1. Sir John Tilley, *London to Tokyo* (London: Hutchinson, 1942), p.23.
2. *ibid.*, pp. 79–84. Sir John Tilley and Stephen Gaslee, *The Foreign Office* (London & New York: G.P. Putnam's Sons Ltd., 1933), p. 84.
3. *London to Tokyo*, p. 96.
4. *Ibid.*, p. 135.
5. *Ibid.*, p. 138.

6. J. E. Hoare, *Embassies in the East* (Surrey: Curzon, 1999), pp. 130–1.
7. *London to Tokyo*, p. 145. Hara Takeshi stated in his *Taishô Tennô* [Emperor Taishô](Asahi Shimbunsha, Asahi sensho, 2000) that stress made the emperor insane.
8. Public Record Office, Foreign Office papers, FO371/12524, F3611, from Tilley. No. 155, 15 Mar. 1927.
9. Please also see Harumi Goto-Shibata, 'Anglo-Japanese Co-operation in China in the 1920s' and Ian Nish, 'Echoes of Alliance' in Nish and Yoichi Kibata (eds.), *The History of Anglo-Japanese Relations*, vol. 1 (London and Basingstoke: Macmillan, 2000), pp. 224–278.
10. F.S.G. Piggott, *Broken Thread* (Aldershot: Gale & Polden Ltd., 1950), pp. 199, 204. Katô was the minister and then ambassador to Britain, served four times as the Foreign Minister, and finally became the Prime Minister from June 1924 to January 1926.
11. *Ibid.*, p. 226.
12. Shidehara Kijûrô, *Gaikô 50 nen* [50 years in diplomacy] (Yomiuri Shimbunsha, 1951), pp. 38–42, 247–250.
13. FO371/13965, F3909, from Tilley, no. 271, 2 July 1929. Piggott, *Broken Thread*, p. 184.
14. FO405/260, F1035, Chamberlain to Tilley, no. 127, 18 March 1929.
15. *London to Tokyo*, pp. 143, 162. FO371/12518, F5040, from Tilley, no. 249, 25 April 1927.
16. FO371/13164, F200, from Tilley, no. 623, 12 Dec. 1927; FO371/13965, F5593, from Tilley, no. 426, 2 Oct. 1929.
17. FO405/256, F203/7/10, Tilley to Chamberlain, 15 Dec. 1927.
18. Prince and Princess Chichibu, *Ei bei seikatsu no omoide* [Memories of our lives in England and the United States](Bunmeisha, 1947), pp. 105, 124, 166.
19. FO371/13964, F17, from Tilley, no. 490, 29 Nov. 1928.
20. *London to Tokyo*, pp. 176–8.
21. Eric Hobsbawm and Terence Ranger (eds.), *The Invention of Tradition* (Cambridge University Press, 1983). See also Takashi Fujitani, *Tennô no peijent* [Pageant of the emperor] (Nihon hôsô shuppann kyôkai, NHK books, 1994).
22. *London to Tokyo*, p. 179.
23. FO371/12523, F2068, from Tilley, no. 35, 31 Jan. 1927.
24. FO371/13964, F17, from Tilley, no. 490, 29 Nov. 1928. *London to Tokyo*, p. 180.
25. FO371/13964, T21, from Tilley, no. 499, 5 Dec. 1929.
26. FO371/12520, F4345, from Tilley, no. 177, 23 Mar. 1927.
27. FO371/13968, F1767, from Tilley, no. 100, 13 Mar. 1929.
28. *London to Tokyo*, pp. 176–8.
29. Nish, 'Echoes of Alliance', p. 270.
30. Katharine Sansom, *Sir George Sansom and Japan* (Tallahassee, Florida: The Diplomatic Press, 1972), p. 35.
31. FO371/13968, F1767, from Tilley, no. 100, 13 Mar. 1929.

32. FO371/14754, F958, from Tilley, no. 1 Confidential (1/13/30), 3 Jan. 1930; FO371/14756, F2622, from Tilley, no. 150 (1/237/30), 26 Mar. 1930
33. Both Makino and Chinda were diplomats. Makino served at the Japanese Embassy in London for about three years from 1880. He was the Foreign Minister from February 1913 to April 1914, and one of the Japanese representatives at the Paris Peace Conference held in 1919. Chinda became the ambassador to Britain in June 1916. He also represented Japan at the Paris Peace Conference.
34. *London to Tokyo*, p. 136, 146, 168, 180–2, 197.
35. See Takie Sugiyama Lebra, *Above the Clouds: Status Culture of the Modern Japanese Nobility* (University of California Press, 1993).
36. FO371/12525, F8585, from Tilley, no. 541, 13 Oct. 1927. Tokugawa Iyesato was one of Japanese representatives at the Washington Conference of 1921–22.
37. *London to Tokyo*, pp. 75, 148.
38. Nish, 'Echoes of Alliance', p. 265.
39. *Foreign Office*, p. 258.
40. *London to Tokyo*, pp. 143, 149.
41. *Ibid.*, p. 136.
42. FO371/14756, F2622, from Tilley, no. 150 (1/237/30), 26 Mar. 1930.
43. FO371/13964, F1400, from Tilley, no. 69, 20 Feb. 1929; F1757, from Tilley, no. 80, 2 Mar. 1929.
44. FO371/12522, F1322, from Tilley, no. 17, 10 Jan. 1927; FO371/13968, F1767, from Tilley, no. 100, 13 Mar. 1929; FO371/14756, F2622, from Tilley, no. 150 (1/237/30), 26 Mar. 1930.
45. *London to Tokyo*, pp. 206–7.
46. *Ibid.*, pp. 153, 187.
47. FO371/14752, F2188, from Tilley, no. 134(1/224/30), 18 March 1930.
48. *London to Tokyo*, p. 140. FO371/12524, F3611, from Tilley, no. 155, 15 Mar. 1927; F6510, from Tilley, no. 365, 28 June 1927. FO371/13246, F186, from Tilley, no. 616, 7 Dec. 1927.
49. FO371/12522, F9438, letter from Tilley to Mounsey, 5 Nov. 1927. FO371/13250, F6542, from Tilley, no. 453, 31 Oct. 1928.
50. FO371/13250, T13282, from Tilley, no. 247(R), 24 Nov. 1928; FO 371/14756, F6549, enclosure, from Snow, no. 556 (69/22/30), 22 Oct. 1930. *London to Tokyo*, pp. 175, 183, 195.
51. *London to Tokyo*, p. 197.
52. *Ibid.*, p. 140.

Chapter 8 IAN NISH *Sir Francis Lindley (1872–1950) and Japan*

1. I. H. Nish, 'Jousting with Authority: The Tokyo Embassy of Sir Francis Lindley, 1931–4' in Japan Society of London, *Proceedings,* 105 (Dec. 1986), 9–19.

2. J. E. Hoare, *Embassies in the East* (Richmond: Curzon, 1999), p. 136.
3. Lindley to Dawson, 2 Sept. 1931 in Papers of Geoffrey Dawson, Bodleian Library, Oxford, 76; *Documents on British Foreign Policy, 1919–39,* second series, VIII, no 495 [hereafter cited *as 'DBFP'].*
4. Letter to the author from Capt. Malcolm Kennedy, 15 Oct. 1977.
5. *DBFP*, ii/VIII, no 495.
6. Nish, 'Jousting with Authority', p. 10.
7. Lindley to Rumbold, 30 March 1932 in Papers of Sir Horace Rumbold, Bodleian Library, Oxford, 39.
8. Joseph C. Grew, *Turbulent Era,* 2 vols (London: Hammond & Hammond, 1953), vol. ii, p. 23.
9. Lindley to Simon, 15 March 1933 in *DBFP*, ii/XI, no 453, fn 5.
10. Lindley to Simon, 24 Feb. 1933 in *DBFP*, ii/XI, no 371.
11. *DBFP,* ii/XX, no 4.
12. *Ibid.*
13. *DBFP*, ii/XX, nos 1 and 39, p. 75. Philip Bell, *Chamberllain, Germany & Japan, 1933–4* (London, 1996).
14. K. Sansom, *Sir George Sansom and Japan* (Tallahassee: Diplomatic Press, 1972), p. 70; *DBFP*, ii/XX, nos 41 and 68.
15. C.G. Thorne, *Limits of Foreign Policy* (London: Hamish Hamilton, 1972), p. 99 quoting Royal Archives.
16. Lindley to Dawson, 26 May 1934 in Dawson papers.
17. Speech at the Japan Society's dinner on 19 June 1935.
18. K. Sansom, *Sansom and Japan*, p. 95. Transcript of the Sansom-Nevins interview in Columbia University, New York, Oral Archive.
19. H. Cortazzi, 'Japan Society' in Cortazzi and Daniels (eds.), *Britain and Japan* (London: Routledge, 1991), pp. 36–40 *passim.*
20. Yoshida's speech at the Industry Club, Tokyo, 30 April 1959.
The Yoshidas visited Scotland and stayed at his daughters' houses. See Yuki Yoshida, *Whispering Leaves in Grosvenor Square,* with Introduction by Sir Francis Lindley (Folkestone: Global Oriental, 1997), p. 27.
21. Lindley, 'Recent Events in Japan' in *The Listener*, vol. 15, 11 March 1936. Thanks to Dr Gordon Daniels for drawing my attention to this broadcast. Also K. Sansom, *Sansom and Japan*, p. 95.
22. Lindley, 'The Tragedy of Spain' (12pp) in *National Review*, Feb. 1937.
23. J. H. F. McEwen, 'Lindley' in *Dictionary of National Biography.*
24. Martin Morland to the author, 22 March 2000, quoting *The Times* (London), 11 June 1994, in turn quoting an obscure American Commonplace Book by George Gardner Herrick, a descendant of the poet. A slightly modified and amplified version of the poem is to be found in J.E. Hoare, *Embassies in the East*, footnote to p. 136. It cannot be said whether the version here given is earlier or later.
25. Speech of Ambassador Ohno at the House of Lords, London, 23 Feb. 1959.

Chapter 9 ANTHONY BEST *Sir Robert Clive, 1877–1948: British Ambassador to Japan, 1934–37*

The author acknowledges the permission of Her Majesty Queen Elizabeth II to use material from the Royal Archives at Windsor Castle'

1. See in particular A. Trotter, *Britain and East Asia, 1933–1937*, (Cambridge University Press, Cambridge, 1975).
2. See Ian Nish's essay on Lindley in this volume and my own 'Sir Robert Craigie as Ambassador to Japan, 1937–41' in I. H. Nish (ed.), *Britain and Japan: Biographical Portraits*, (Japan, Library, Folkestone, 1994).
3. C. Hosoya, C., '1934*-nen no Nichi-Ei fukashin ky_tei mondai* [The Problem of the Anglo-Japanese Non-Aggression Pact in 1934]. *Kokusai Seiji*, 1977, pp. 69–85, and G. Bennett, 'British Policy in the Far East 1933–1936: Treasury and Foreign Office', *Modern Asian Studies*, 1992, vol. 26, pp. 545–68, and Trotter, *op. cit.* pp. 97–107.
4. Trotter, *op. cit.* p. 120.
5. PRO FO262/1891 Clive (Tokyo) to Wellesley (FO) 12 October 1934.
6. Royal Archives Windsor, PS/GV/P510/68 Clive to Wigram 8 November 1935.
7. PRO FO371/19359 F1090/483/23 Clive to Simon 7 January 1935.
8. PRO FO371/19359 F1090/483/23 Vansittart (FO) minute 2 March 1935, and CAB24/254 CP80(35) 'The Far East' Simon note April 1935.
9. Cadogan papers, Churchill College Cambridge, ACAD1/3, diary 19 November 1935.
10. Royal Archives Windsor, PS/GVI/C/053/JAP/3 Clive to Wigram 26 March 1936.
11. PRO FO371/21029 F570/28/23 Clive to Eden 27 January 1937.
12. Knatchbull-Hugessen papers, Churchill College Cambridge, KNAT2/55, Clive to Knatchbull-Hugessen (Nanking) 14 April 1937.
13. Chatfield papers, National Maritime Museum, CHT4/8, Little (C-in-C China) to Chatfield (FSL) 6 July 1936.
14. Kennedy papers, Sheffield University Library, 4/31, diary 3 March 1936.
15. PRO FO371/19364 F4680/4680/23 Clive to Vansittart 25 July 1935.
16. PRO FO371/20279 F7400/89/23 Clive to Eden 6 November 1936.
17. PRO FO371/21044 F5093/5093/23 Ashton-Gwatkin (FO) minute 5 August 1937.
18. PRO FO371/21024 F2568/597/61 Clive to Eden 25 March 1937.
19. PRO FO371/21040 F2388/414/23 Clive to Orde (FE Dept) 22 March 1937.
20. Trotter, *op. cit.*, p. 35.

Chapter 10 J. E. HOARE *William Keswick, 1835–1912: Jardine's Pioneer in Japan*

1. Maggie Keswick, editor, *The Thistle and the Jade: A Celebration of 150 Years of Jardine, Matheson and Co.,* (London: Octopus Books, 1982), p.37.
2. Grace Fox, *Britain and Japan 1858–1883*, (Oxford: Clarendon Press, 1969), pp. 46–47. For background on the attempts at Ryukyu trade, see W. G. Beasley, *Great Britain and the Opening of Japan, 1834–1858*, (London: Luzac and Co., 1951), pp. 79–80.
3. Fox, *Britain and Japan*, pp. 51–53.
4. Fox, *Britain and Japan*, p. 66.
5. Beasley, *Great Britain and the Opening of Japan, pp.* 168–93; W. G. Beasley, trans. and editor, *Select Documents on Japanese Foreign Policy, 1853–1868*, (London: Oxford University Press, 1955), pp.156–94.
6. J. E. Hoare, *Japan's Treaty Ports and Foreign Settlements: The Uninvited Guests, 1858–1899*, (Sandgate, Folkestone: Japan Library, 1994), pp. 6–7. See also J. McMaster, 'British trade and traders to Japan, 1859–1869', unpublished PhD thesis, University of London, 1962.
7. Jardine Matheson Papers, Kanagawa, W. Keswick to J. Whittall, 21 July 1859; see also Hoare, Japan's *Treaty Ports*, pp.6–7.
8. Sir Rutherford Alcock was the subject of a biographical portrait by Hugh Cortazzi in the Japan Society's *Britain and Japan: Biographical Portraits*, Volume II, published by Japan Library, 1997.
9. The House of Mitsui, which was to become the largest business combine of the inter-war years, was the wealthiest merchant house during the Edo period (1600–1868). It had been founded in 1673. Mitsui and Co (Mitsui Bussan) was established in 1876.
10. John McMaster, 'The Japanese Gold Rush of 1859', *Journal of Asian Studies*, vol. xix (1959–60), p. 274.
11. McMaster, 'Japanese Gold Rush', pp. 274–75.
12. McMaster, 'Japanese Gold Rush', pp. 275–287, based mainly on the Jardine Matheson archive in the University of Cambridge Library, is the fullest analysis available of what otherwise is a story of vague claims and hearsay.
13. Keswick, *Thistle and the Jade*, pp. 157–58.
14. Fox, *Britain and Japan*, p. 84. For the background to Alcock's fears, see J. E. Hoare, *Embassies in the East: The Story of the British and their Embassies in China, Japan and Korea from 1859 to the Present*, (Richmond, Surrey: Curzon Press, 1999), pp. 95–104.
15. Grace Fox gives much of the credit for the students' arrangements to Keswick, but it seems clear that Gower played the more important role: Fox, *Britain and Japan*, p. 458; Andrew Cobbing, 'Ito Hirobumi in Britain', in J. E. Hoare, edit., *Britain and Japan: Biographical Portraits*, vol. III (Richmond, Surrey: Japan Library, 1999), pp. 18, 20.

16. Keswick, *Thistle and the Jade*, p. 162–64.
17. Keswick, *Thistle and the Jade*, pp. 40–41; *Japan Gazette*, 12 March 1877; Japan *Mail* (Summary), 3 Sept. 1880. James later married Marion, daughter of Sir Harry Parkes, Alcock's successor as British Minister to Japan.
18. Sir John Pope-Hennessy (1834–1891) was a controversial figure. The DNB describes him as being 'humane and sympathetic' but of 'impulsive temperament. His failure as a colonial governor was due to his want of tact and judgement, and his faculty of "irritating where he might conciliate."'
19. 'Mr W. Keswick', *The Times*, 11 March 1912. See also Keswick, *Thistle and the Jade, passim*, and Robert Blake, *Jardine Matheson: Traders of the Far East*, (London: Weidenfeld & Nicholson, 1999), pp. 151–53.
20. Nathan A. Pelcovitts, *Old China Hands and the Foreign Office*, (New York: King's Crown Press, 1948), pp. 158–60.
21. Foreign Office Records Japan (FO46)/459, R. S. Grundy, China Association, to the Earl of Kimberley, 12 February 1895, forwarding the 'Protest of the Yokohama Branch of the China Association against the Action of Her Majesty's Government in the matter of the Treaty lately concluded with Japan by Great Britain'; *London and China Express*, 1 March 1895.
22. Pelcovitts, *Old China Hands*, p. 183.
23. 'Mr W. Keswick', *The Times*, 11 March 1912.

Chapter 11 PETER N. DAVIES *Frederick Cornes, 1827–1927: Founder and Senior Partner of Cornes and Company (1873–1911)*

1. I am indebted to Professor Y. Suzuki for his assistance with the basic research for this paper and to Colin Cornes, great grandson of Frederick Cornes, for making his family papers available to me and for his valuable comments on the original draft. I am also grateful to the Leverhulme Trust and the Cornes Group for their generous support for this project.
2. *Macclesfield Courier*, 18 April 1885.
3. Giovanni Federico, *An Economic History of the Silk Industry*, CUP, Cambridge, 1997.
4. Hugh Cortazzi, *Victorians in Japan: In and around the Treaty Ports*, London, 1987, pp.54–92.
5. Pat Barr, *The Coming of the Barbarians*, Penguin, London, 1967, p.100.
6. Tomio Hora, *Ships entered at Yokohama*, Yokohama Local History, No. 128, Central Library, Yokohama, 1996.
7. *North-China Herald*, 18 May 186l.
8. Grace Fox, *Britain and Japan !8581883*, Clarendon Press, Oxford, 1969, p.322
9. Daniel R. Headrick, *The Invisible Weapon: Telecommunications and International Politics, 1851–1945*, O.U.P., Oxford, 1991, p.44.
10. *Japan Herald*: 15 September 1862.

11. Tamakusu, *The West in Yokohama.* Yokohama Archives of History, No. 5, March 1987, Table 4, p.27.
12. Cornes Manuscript: Cornes to Taylor, Book 7, 22 October 1869.
13. Evidence provided by Professor Yoshinori Suzuki, Kanagawa University.
14. Cornes Manuscript: Cornes to Taylor, Book 5, 28 August 1868.
15. Cornes Manuscript: Cornes to Winstanley, Book 26, 6 September 1878.
16. Ernest Satow had himself formed a liaison with a Japanese lady Takeda Kane, by whom he had two sons when he served in Japan in the 1860s/70s as a Japanese language student with the British Legation and junior official in the Legation (see separate biographical portrait of Satow as Minister in Tokyo in this volume).
17. See biographical portrait of Sir Ernest Satow as Minister in Tokyo by Ian Ruxton in this volume.
18. Correspondence with Dr. Nigel J. Brailey, University of Bristol.
19. Cornes Manuscript: Cornes to Taylor, Book 41, 10 August 1883.
20. Clare A. Converse, Letter to the Vermont Shaftsbury Association, printed in June 1902 by The Fukuin Printing Co. Ltd., of Yokohama.
21. Cornes Manuscript: Cornes to W.G. Aspinall, Book 5, 17 June 1868.
22. Cornes Manuscript: Cornes to W.G. Aspinall, Book 2, 25 April 1867.
23. Cornes Manuscript; Cornes to W.G. Aspinall, Book 7, 25 November 1869.
24. Tamakusu, *The West in Yokohama,* Yokohama Archives of History, No. 5, March 1987, Table 4, p. 27.
25. F.O. Manuscript 165: Sir Harry Parker to the Earl of Clarendon, 2 September 1868.
26. *The Japan Times Overland Mail,* 18 September 1869.
27. Cornes Manuscript: Cornes to Aspinall, Book 7, 9 September 1869.
28. Cornes Manuscript: Cornes to Aspinall, Book 7, 10 September 1869.
29. Cornes Manuscript: Cornes to Coysh, Book 11, 2 December 1871.
30. It should be noted that Frederick Cornes was not related to the Rev. Edward Cornes who, together with his wife and son, were killed when the *City of Edo* blew up in 1870 while on a voyage from Tokyo to Yokohama.
31. Cornes Manuscript: Cornes to W.G. Aspinall, Book 12, 13 March 1873.
32. William Gregson Aspinall, who by then was reconciled with his wife, continued to be beset by financial difficulties and these encouraged him to return to Yokohama. He then opened a small business and Frederick Cornes supported him with a number of small commissions. He died in 1879 at the age of 57 and was buried in the Foreigners' Cemetery on the Bluff overlooking the Port.
33. Cornes Manuscript: Cornes to Winstanley, Book 13, 2 May 1873.
34. Cornes Manuscript: Cornes to Weale, Book 94, 5 March 1902.
35. Cornes Manuscript; Cornes to Weale, Book 92, 20 June 1891.
36. See website.www.cornes.co.jp which provides a comprehensive guide to the group's history and range of activities.

Chapter 12 CHARLOTTE BLEASDALE *John Samuel Swire (1825–98) and Japan, 1867–98*

1. J. S. Swire to J. H. Scott, W. Lang and E. Mackintosh, 4 July 1881.
2. J. S. Swire to Mary Warren, 24 Aug. 1881.
3. Obituary in the *Liverpool Journal of Commerce* (6th December, 1898), cited in S. Marriner & E. Hyde, *The Senior: John Samuel Swire (1825–1898), Management in Far Eastern Shipping Trades*, (Liverpool University Press, 1967) p. 135.
4. J. S. Swire to Mary Warren, 15 Nov. 1879.
5. Including the premature deaths of his first wife (see later), and of his sister-in-law Mary in 1869, and his brother William in 1884.
6. JS&S in Liverpool bottled and exported Guinness to Australia under the brand 'Dagger Stout' from 1869 to 1894.
7. S. Marriner & E. Hyde, *The Senior* p. 52.
8. Mary Martin *diary*, 27 Oct. 1855.
9. J. S. Swire to Mary Warren 1881 (undated).
10. J. S. Swire to John Cunliffe, 26 Feb. 1877, quoted in S. Marriner & E. Hyde, *The Senior* p. 21.
11. S. Marriner & E. Hyde, *The Senior* p. 21.
12. The Swire Group today consists of Hong Kong-based Swire Pacific, a publicly listed company in which JS&S maintains a 28% shareholding, and whose main businesses are properties, aviation, beverages, industrial and trading, and marine services. In addition, JS&S has major wholly-owned interests in the UK, USA, Australia and Papua New Guinea. JS&S also has property interests in Japan, but the Group's main business with Japan is vested in its container shipping services and the services of Cathay Pacific Airways.
13. J. H. Scott, *A Short Account of the firm of John Swire & Sons* (privately printed by the Arden Press, Letchworth, 1914).
14. Article in the *Japan Herald*, reproduced in the *China Mail*, 7 Sept. 1880.
15. W. Lidderdale to S. G. Rathbone 11 Dec 1872, quoted in S. Marriner, *Rathbones of Liverpool, 1845–1873*, (Liverpool University Press, 1961), p. 48.
16. P. H. Holt to Mrs J. S. Swire 17 Jan. 1899, quoted in S. Marriner & E. Hyde, *The Senior*, p. 205.
17. Lang and Scott became partners in JS&S in 1869 and 1874 respectively. John Swire's other partners were Edwin Macintosh, (who became Hong Kong Manager in 1879) and Fredrick R. Gamwell – Swire's right-hand man in London. JS&S became a Limited Company, with Jack Swire as its first Chairman in 1914, after the death of the last of the original partners, J. H. Scott, in 1912.
18. J. H. Scott, *A Short Account of the firm of John Swire & Sons, op cit.*
19. Scotts' Shipbuilding & Engineering Co. Ltd.
20. J. H. Scott played a very significant role in the development of the firm,

both as John Swire's Eastern partner, and as Senior Partner 1898–1912. He also provided an important link between JS&S and Scotts' Shipbuilding & Engineering – one of the foremost shipbuilding companies in the UK. Scotts' were principal shipbuilders to the Ocean Steam Ship Company and to Swire's China Navigation Company. They also (with Holts) became major shareholders in a number of Swire projects, including China Navigation, the Taikoo Sugar Refinery and (after John Swire's death) the Taikoo Dockyard & Engineering Company in Hong Kong. JHS, as Senior Partner, was the instigator behind the establishment of Taikoo Dockyard, and Scotts' Shipbuilding acted as expert advisors during its construction (1900–1908) – thereafter providing technical staff for the facility.

21. J. S. Swire to J. H. Scott, W. Lang and E. Mackintosh, 4 July 1881, *op cit.*
22. *ibid.*
23. J. S. Swire to W. Lang 20 Sept 1869.
24. J. S. Swire to J. H. Scott, W. Lang and E. Mackintosh, 4 July 1881, *op. cit.*
25. J. S. Swire to W. Lang 20 Sept 1869, *op cit.*
26. This trade survived, primarily on a joint account basis with UK textile producers such as Dewhurst, until 1891.
27. J. S. Swire to W. Lang 20 Sept 1869, *op cit.*
28. By pressing the originals against sheets of thin tissue paper so as to expel ink onto them.
29. Harold S. Williams, *Tales of the Foreign Settlements in Japan*, (C. E. Tuttle Co., US) p. 212–213.
30. This office was rebuilt in 1923. The new building – although gutted by fire – was one of only two left standing in Yokohama, following the great earthquake of that year.
31. M. Torii *Yamate Yokohama* (extract).
32. J. S. Swire to Mary Warren, 1879 (undated).
33. J. Swire to Mrs J. S. Swire 11 July 1886.
34. J. S. Swire to W. Lang, 6 Feb. 1879.
35. J. Dodds to B&S HK and Shanghai, (undated) quoted in C. Drage, *Taikoo,* (Constable, London, 1970) p. 111.
36. J. S. Swire to J. H. Scott, W. Lang and E. Mackintosh, 4 July 1881, op cit.
37. J. S. Swire to J. H. Scott, 24 June 1875.
38. Tea buyer.
39. J. Swire to J. S. Swire 2 Sept. 1886.
40. J. S. Swire to E. Mackintosh, 1886 (undated).
41. S. Marriner & E. Hyde, *The Senior* p. 46.
42. J. S. Swire to D. Graham, 26 Feb. 1875.
43. J. S. Swire to J. H. Scott, 24 June 1875, *op cit.*
44. J. S. Swire to D. Graham 26 Feb. 1875, *op cit.*
45. J. S. Swire to J. H. Scott, 24 June 1875, *op cit.*
46. C. Drage, *Taikoo*, p. 110–111.
47. Harold S. Williams, *Tales of the Foreign Settlements in Japan*, p. 212.

48. By 1881, White Star were running ships trans-Pacific under charter to the Kansas Pacific Railway.
49. J. S. Swire to J. H. Scott, W. Lang and E. Mackintosh, 4 July 1881, op cit.
50. CNCo's fortunes were founded on the coastal trade in 'beancake', which was more usually carried from Newchwang in Manchuria to Swatow in southern China. Beancake remained important up until the early 1900s.
51. J. S. Swire to E. Mackintosh 23 Jul. 1879.
52. The agent for sugar sales in Kobe at this time was Fearon & Co.
53. J. Swire to J. S. Swire 19 July 1886. This was despite some teething troubles: 'I suppose Dr Korn [Manager of the refinery in Hong Kong] will attain the acme of excellence soon and that the turnouts of the different classes of sugar will be more uniform in quality than they are at present. Much is bought to arrive, and up-country buyers lose confidence if the sugar delivered is not as good as the standard they bought from. Mr Dodds tells me that he has a large quantity of a low grade sugar on hand which he cannot sell, the demand being entirely for the higher grades.' (*ibid*).
54. S. Marriner & E. Hyde, *The Senior*, p. 102–103.
55. This was common practice for the Japanese branches of companies operating on the China coast.
56. C. Drage, *Taikoo* p. 113.
57. J. S. Swire to S. Martin 17 June 1881, quoted in S. Marriner & E. Hyde, *The Senior* p. 99.
58. J. S. S. to E. Mackintosh 27 Jan 1888, quoted in S. Marriner & E. Hyde, *The Senior* p. 132.
59. J. S. Swire to J. H. Scott 1886 (undated).
60. J. S. Swire to J. H. Scott, 1888 (undated).
61. S. Marriner & E. Hyde, *The Senior* p. 205.
62. Arising from the fact that many of the commodities carried were primary products, such as tea.
63. J. S. Swire, letter to *The Times*, 1 Dec. 1882.
64. Editorial, *China Mail* 15 Dec. 1879.
65. S. Marriner & E. Hyde, *The Senior*, p. 143.
66. Editorial, *China Mail* 15 Dec. 1879, *op cit.*
67. Most notably, in 1885, from the Mogul Shipping Company, after it was refused entrance to the FEFC because its ships would not bear their fair share of non-peak sailings. Mogul brought a test case alleging that the Conference agreement amounted to a 'conspiracy ... to coerce and bribe shippers to agree to forbear from shipping cargo by [Mogul's] steamers.' The case dragged on through several appeals until dismissed from the House of Lords in 1891. A final line was drawn under the matter by the findings of the Royal Commission on Shipping Rings (1909), which exonerated most shipping cartels of the charge of engaging in unhealthy restrictive practices.
68. In 1882, a number of merchants banded together to create their own line, the China Shippers Mutual Company, based on the principle that the

shippers, being also mutual owners of the ships, would receive pro rata dividends on the profits of the trade. But having thus put themselves into a position wherein they could view the advantages of the conference system from both sides, within a very few years the Mutual Company had capitulated to the extent of entering into pooling agreements with the Conference lines; by 1885, they were officially included in Conference arrangements.

69. 'In justice to the other members of the conference, I must say that no man ever drove a more reasonable and willing team. PHH [Philip Holt] was the spare horse, and he amused himself by putting his head between his legs and smashing the manger with his heels. When he looks round, he will see that he has lost his corn' – J. S. Swire to W. Lang, J. H. Scott and E. Mackintosh, 4 April 1881, quoted in S. Marriner & E. Hyde, *The Senior* p. 145.

70. Minutes of the 34th Annual General Meeting of the Ocean Steam Ship Company, 8 Feb. 1899, quoted in S. Marriner & E. Hyde, *The Senior*, p. 184.

71. *ibid.*

72. Butterfield & Swire: Harold S. Williams, Tales of the Foreign Settlements in Japan, *op cit.*

73. S. Marriner & E. Hyde, *The Senior* p. 162.

74. Article in the Japan Herald reproduced in the *China Mail*, 7 Sept. 1880, *op cit.*

75. S. Marriner & E. Hyde, *The Senior* p. 168.

76. J. S. Swire to J. H. Scott, W. Lang and E. Mackintosh, 4 July 1881, *op cit.*

77. P. Holt to J. S. Swire, 1888 (undated).

78. C. Drage, *Taikoo* p. 104.

79. J. Swire to J. S. Swire 2 Sept. 1886.

80. The Kobe City Museum retain a remarkable collection of Baggallay's photograph albums.

81. Purchased from the Japanese Imperial Government in 1888.

82. C. Drage, *Taikoo* p. 104–107.

83. General trading company. See Sin'ichi Yonekawa and Hideki Yoshihara (eds) *Business History of General Trading Companies*, (University of Tokyo Press, 1987).

84. Cited in *The Hundred Year History of Mitsui* (Mitsui, 1976).

85. Nippon Yusen Kaisha, cited in C. Drage, *Taikoo* p. 103.

86. C. Drage, *Taikoo* p. 103–104.

87. The link between Swire and Mitsui at both a personal and business level was very strong and remains important to this day.

88. C. Drage, *Taikoo* p. 125.

89. Mitsubishi Shokai established Japan's first overseas shipping line, between Yokohama and Shanghai in 1875. In 1885, Mitsubishi's shipping interests (by now called Mitsubishi Mail Steamships Company) merged with Kyodo Unyu Kaisha (established in 1882) to form NYK.

90. The Sino-Japanese War of 1894–5.

91. J. S. Swire to B&S Shanghai, 23 July 1894, quoted in C. Drage, *Taikoo* p. 29.
92. J. S. Swire to B&S Shanghai, 1894 (undated).
93. Changsha, Taiyuan, Chingtu and Tsinan – built for this service in 1886. Chingtu and Tsinan were transferred to a Shanghai-Japan only line in 1907 and sold in 1909. CNCo continued to run Changsha and Taiyuan to Australia until 1912, when they gave up the line.
94. J. S. Swire to B&S Shanghai and HK, Jan. 1896.
95. S. Marriner & E. Hyde, *The Senior* p. 94.
96. E&A and CNCo had for some years maintained an agreement to pool cargo.
97. J. S. Swire to J. Dodds, 1894 (undated).
98. J. S. Swire to J. Dodds 1889 (undated).
99. The first typed letter appeared on his private letter file in 1892.
100. In 1867, when the collapse of the Royal Bank of Liverpool threatened to bring down the Liverpool White Star Line, JSS wrote immediately to White Star's owner, Henry Threlfall Wilson: 'Dear Wilson, I am very sorry to learn of your misfortune. I have lying at my bankers £20,000. You may make any use of it that you please. ' (Link with days of famous clippers, article in the Liverpool Post & Mercury, 31 Dec. 1923).
101. Dr Robert Bickers, Entry for John Samuel Swire in The Oxford Dictionary of National Biography.
102. J. S. Swire to Mary Warren, 24 Aug. 1881.
103. J. S. Swire to Mrs J. S. Swire 17 Aug. 1891.

Chapter 13 SONIA ASHMORE *Lasenby Liberty (1843–1917) and Japan*

1. 1874, 67.
2. *Woman's World*, I (May 1888) 94–96.
3. The exhibits were collected mainly by Rutherford Alcock (1809–1897) the first British Minister to Japan in 1859 and author of *Art and Industries of Japan* (1878) see Hugh Cortazzi's Biographical Portrait in *Biographical Portraits*, Volume II, 1997.
4. Watanabe (*High Victorian Japonisme*, 1991, 89–91). See also Alcock's *Catalogue of Works of Industry and Arts sent from Japan* (1862).
5. A. L. Liberty, *Journal of the Society of Arts* 38, June 1890.
6. 'The House of Liberty and Its Founder', interview in the *Daily Chronicle*, c.1913.
7. Koykama Tokuza, a 'fancy goods maker', and 'S. Eidia', a 'Japanese repairer' (subsequently Eida of Piccadilly?) had worked at the Japanese Exhibition at Humphrey's Hall, Knightsbridge in 1885. K. Kodama, hired at fourteen shillings a week, came from Eida 1898; Kodama also introduced G. Shibata, 'from Japan', taken on as 'Help' at ten shillings a week. A year later,

Fujita Heichachi, previously with A. Oestman & Co., of Yokohama, came to work at East India House for seventeen and sixpence a week.
8. Memoir of William Judd, *Liberty Lamp*, February 1925.
9. Judd, 1925.
10. Used here to mean a stand with shelves for small objects.
11. Christopher Dresser's *Japan, its Architecture, Art, and Art Manufactures*, London 1882 was a seminal work.
12. Cortazzi ed., *Alfred East: A British Artist in Meiji Japan* (1991)
13. Murray's *Handbook for Japan*, 1894. One of the authors was Basil Hall Chamberlain (1850–1935) who was the first Professor of Japanese and Philology at the Imperial University, Tokyo, author of *Things Japanese* (1890) and many other scholarly works about Japan.
14. Versions were published in the *Japan Weekly Mail*, XI, 23 (8 June 1899) 551–2, the *Journal of the Society of Arts* 38 (1890) 673–689 and *Artistic Japan*, VI (1891).
15. Published in a limited edition in 1910
16. One of the Curio shops in Nagasaki mentioned in Murray's 1901 guide.
17. East (1991), page 18.
18. East (1991), pages 26–27.
19. East (1991), page 83.
20. Yokohama: Offices of the *Japan Gazette*.
21. See *Kipling's Japan* edited by Hugh Cortazzi and George Webb, London 1988.
22. East (1991) page 61.
23. East (1991) page 87.
24. Dresser had noted with similar dismay, the European furnishings of the Mikado's temporary Palace in Tokyo, including 'cheap French wall paper' applied to the sliding panels, (Dresser, 1882, 52).
25. *Japan Weekly Mail*, XI, 23, 8 June 1899.
26. Ernest Fenollosa (1853–1908), an American who first went to Japan to teach philosophy in 1878, became a cultural adviser to the Ministry of Education and the Imperial Government. He established the Japanese Department at the Boston Museum of Fine Arts.
27. Frank Brinkley was an English journalist and collector, who bought the *Japan Weekly Mail* in 1881, was one of the founders of the Asiatic Society of Japan (1872) and wrote an 8-volume history of Japan and its cultures (1901–2). See biographical portrait by J. E. Hoare in *Biographical Portraits*, Vol III 1999.
28. These properties also made antimony a useful component of 'lead' type for printing.
29. *Liberty's Catalogue* c.1890
30. *Journal of the Society of Arts* 38 (1890) 673–689. Purdon Clarke was Director of the South Kensington Museum (V&A) 1896–1905, and subsequently of the Metropolitan Museum of Art, New York.

31. *Ibid.*
32. *Japan Weekly Mail*, 8 June 1889.
33. 'The Grand Hotel caters to First-Class Travel and is the best known hotel in the East … Wines and Cuisine (French Chef) the best the market affords. The Hotel Band plays each evening'. Advertisement, Murray's *Handbook to Japan* (1907). Kipling's view was more jaundiced: 'At the Grand … they don't always live up to their grandeur; unlimited electric bells, but no one in particular to answer 'em'. (Cortazzi, 1988, 129). Christopher Dresser also stayed there, and was surprised to find Crosse and Blackwell's potted meats, and Keiller's Dundee marmalade', on the table. (Dresser, 1882, 3).
34. *Japan Weekly Mail*, 29 June 1889.
35. See also Asiatic Society of Japan *Transactions* XIX 1891.
36. See Cortazzi's 'The Japan Society: A Hundred Year History', in Cortazzi & Daniels, Eds. *Britain and Japan 1859–1991: Themes and Personalities* (1991) 1–53. Also *The Japan Society: A History*. Hugh Cortazzi, edited Anne Kaneko, Japan Society 2001.
37. Japan Society *Transactions I* (1892–3) 213.
38. Japan Society *Transactions IV* (1898) 252.
39. Hayashi (1851–1906) was in Paris to organize the Japanese exhibit at the 1878 Exposition Universelle, and stayed on to become an influential dealer in Japanese art.
40. *Artistic Japan*, vi, 1891. With illustrations collected by S. Bing. *Le Japon Artistique*, published by Bing, was published for three years, 1888–91, in French, German and in English by Sampson Low, Marston & Company, London 1891.
41. Redesdale (Algernon Freeman-Mitford or A.B.Mitford) had been a diplomat in Japan. See Hugh Cortazzi, ed., *Mitford's Japan*, London 1985.
42. Memoir of George T. Ensworth, employed by Liberty's in 1878, one of a staff of twelve (*Liberty Lamp*, December 1925, 9).
43. *Cabinet Maker* V, 1885, 14, 181–3
44. *Liberty Lamp* VI, 4, 1925.
45. Dark and Grey, 1923, pages 97–101.
46. Thorstein Veblen (1857–1929) *The Theory of the Leisure Class*, 1899, chapter iv.
47. *Cabinet Maker* XII (1891) 120–131.

Chapter 15 IAN RUXTON *Professor W. E. Ayrton, 1847–1908: the 'Never-resting, Keen-eyed Chief'*

1. Quoted in Olive Checkland, 'Henry Dyer of the Imperial College of Engineering in Tokyo, and afterwards, in Glasgow' (in *Britain and Japan: Biographical Portraits*, Volume 3, Chapter 11, ed. J. E. Hoare, Japan Library for the Japan Society, 1999). Also in the same volume quoted by Neil Pedlar in 'James Alfred Ewing and his Circle of Pioneering Physicists in Meiji Tokyo'

(Chapter 8) and previously in O. Checkland, *Britain's Encounters with Meiji Japan* (Basingstoke, Macmillan, 1989) p. 85.

2. See Gooday & Low, 1998, footnote 39, p. 116: 'Some of Perry's obituaries of Ayrton … elided the early [ill-equipped] laboratory of 1873 with that opened in 1877.' (But why would Perry have done this – to boost his old friend and colleague perhaps? Or was a failing memory to blame?)

3. See Graeme Gooday's entry for Perry in the forthcoming *New Dictionary of National Biography* (henceforth *New DNB*) from which the following is extracted:

John Perry (1850–1920), F.R.S., engineer and educator, was born on 14 Feb. 1850 at Garvagh, Ulster, the second son of Samuel Perry and a Scottish-born wife. He graduated B. Eng. with first class honours from Queens College, Belfast in 1870. He first taught at Clifton College, Bristol, from January 1871 where he wrote *An Elementary Treatise on Steam* and established the first physics laboratory and the second mechanics workshop in an English school. In 1874 he was Thomson's assistant in Glasgow for one year, and was recommended to Tokyo where he commenced a three-year contract as professor in civil engineering at the ICE from 8 September 1875.

He lectured on steam power, mechanical structures and hydrodynamics to Japanese student engineers while researching with Ayrton. He returned to London in 1879, and in 1882 was appointed to the chair of Mechanical Engineering at Finsbury Technical College where he was reunited with Ayrton until 1889. From 1896 to 1913 he was Professor of Mathematics and Mechanics at the Royal College of Science and School of Mines in London (part of Imperial College from 1907). He enjoyed a vigorous social life, was member of the Athenaeum Club and 'an affably disputatious man … remembered fondly by both allies and one-time opponents.' Died Notting Hill, 4 August 1920.

4. Takahashi, 1991, p.1.

5. Robert Rosenberg, 'American physics and the origins of electrical engineering', *Physics Today*, October 1983, pp. 48–54) p. 48.

6. See Silvana de Maio, 'Engineering Education in Japan after the Iwakura Mission', Chapter 9 of *The Iwakura Mission in America & Europe* (ed. Ian Nish, Japan Library, 1998) pp. 162–9. Ayrton is described as a professor of 'natural philosphy' (p. 166). This is the older term for what we now call Physics. Strictly speaking, Ayrton was Professor of Natural Philosophy and Telegraphy (see Gooday, 1991, pp. 85–6).

7. From the website of the Illuminating Engineering Institute of Japan (IEI-J) at http: //wwwsoc.nacsis.ac.jp/ieij/englsh/history.html

See also *Britain & Japan: Biographical Portraits*, Vol. 3 p. 92. 'In Japan, at a banquet given at the Hall of the College of Engineering on the evening of 25 March 1878 to celebrate the opening of the Central Telegraphic Communication Office, three of Ayrton's students lit a large arc-light to illuminate proceedings. Unfortunately, after the dark banqueting hall was lit up

… for a few seconds, the arc broke with a hissing sound and darkness ensued again.' (J. Perry, *ibid.*).

8. Founded in 1882 by George Smith. (Oxford University Press, ed. Sidney Lee)

9. Acton Smee Ayrton (his uncle), Edmund Ayrton and William Ayrton. For more about 'the dark angel of retrenchment' A. S. Ayrton (1816–1886) MP 1857–84, see Roy M. Macleod, 'The Ayrton Incident: A commentary on the relations of science and government in England, 1870–1873', in *Science and Values: patterns of tradition and change* (ed. A. Thackray and E. Mendelsohn; Humanities Press, 1974) pp. 45–78.

10. Ernest Satow's Nonconformist father was also keen on strict home schooling, though more oriented towards religion. (See *The Family Chronicle of the English Satows* by E. Satow, privately printed, Oxford, 1925).

11. University College School was founded in Gower Street in 1828 as part of University College, London and moved to Hampstead in 1907. A public school with day pupils only, it had a particularly strong teaching record in mathematics, with many pupils going on to Cambridge. One of its most distinguished former pupils was the Cambridge mathematician Kikuchi Dairoku, later President of Tokyo University (1898–1901) and Minister of Education in Japan (1901–3). He attended the opening ceremony on the new Hampstead site in 1907. (See *Hatenkō: 'Meiji Ryūgakusei' Retsuden* by Koyama Noboru, Kodansha Sensho Metier, 1999.)

12. See Graeme Gooday's entry for Ayrton in the forthcoming *New DNB*.

13. See Takahashi (1991) pp. 29–30. See also Gooday & Low, 1998 pp.114–5: Matilda Ayrton was 'a refugee from Edinburgh University's expulsion of women medical students, forced to qualify at the Sorbonne and retrain as a midwife in London … Matilda exercised her medical skills in teaching European midwifery techniques … to Japanese women, but she also took the opportunity to study the physical anthropology of the Japanese. This work would become the basis of her MD thesis at the Sorbonne.' She also wrote a storybook, *Child Life in Japan* (London, 1879). She left Japan with the couple's daughter Edith in early 1877, one year before Ayrton. (She has a separate entry in the *DNB*.)

14. See O. Checkland, '"Working at their Profession": Japanese Engineers in Britain before 1914', Chapter 4, p.45, *Britain and Japan: Biographical Portraits*, Vol. 1, ed. Ian Nish (1994). But Yamao had already submitted a proposal to open a technical college in the name of the Public Works ministry to the *Dajōkan*, the Grand Council of State, in April 1872. (p. 127, *A-nesuto Satō no Shūhen*, by Shozo Nagaoka, published by Lieb Co. Ltd., Tokyo, 2000)

15. For a list see Takahashi (1991), p. 19. He lists seven papers by Ayrton as sole author and 14 by Ayrton jointly with Perry.

16. On Milne, (1850–1913; resident in Japan 1876–1895) see Chapter 3, pp. 136–141 of *Westerners in the Modernization of Japan* (henceforth *Westerners*) by Teijiro Muramatsu, professor emeritus of Tokyo University and sometime

director of the Meiji Mura Museum at Inuyama city near Nagoya (Originally *Nihon no Kindaika to o-Yatoi Gaikokujin*, translated by Lynne E. Riggs and Manabu Takechi, English and Japanese versions both published by Hitachi Ltd., Tokyo in 1995). The same volume contains brief portraits of Dyer and Ayrton (Chapter 5, pp. 194–206 in the English version) and some good illustrations of the ICE building and workshops, arc lamps and a generator used with arc lamps.

See also Gooday & Low, pp. 121–127. For his first three years in Japan the man later known as 'Earthquake Milne' (sometimes 'Earthquake Jonny'), who had been educated at King's College, London and trained as a mining engineer at the Royal School of Mines in the 1860s before gaining practical experience in a career path resembling Ayrton's, concentrated on teaching mining, architecture, chemistry and crystallography at the ICE. It was only after a severe earthquake struck Yokohama on 22 February 1880 that Milne with two colleagues (Thomas Gray and W. S. Chaplin) and some interested Japanese founded the Seismological Society of Japan on 16 April 1880 (disbanded 1892).

In a letter from Tangier to his friend F. V. Dickins dated 8 March 1894 Ernest Satow wrote that he agreed with Dickins that Milne was the best man to be *The Times* correspondent in Japan. 'He is independent, has plenty of brains and can write well enough' (See *The Diaries and Letters of Sir Ernest Mason Satow (1843–1929): A Scholar-Diplomat in East Asia*, ed. I. Ruxton, Edwin Mellen Press, Lampeter, Wales, 1998, p. 185). Satow was clearly unaware that Milne was soon to return to England with his Japanese wife Tone, the daughter of a Buddhist temple priest from Hakodate. (Tone returned to Japan in 1919, six years after Milne's death. She passed away in Hakodate in 1925.)

17. Japanese 'magic mirrors' revealed images embossed on their metallic rear when viewed at specific angles. Ayrton interpreted this phenomenon as resulting from Japanese metalworking techniques. See W. E. Ayrton, 'The Mirror of Japan and Its Magic Quality,' *Nature*, 1879, 19: 539–542, quoted in Gooday & Low, 1998, p. 118.

18. Gooday & Low, 1998, p. 118.

19. Inaugural lecture at Cowper-street Schools in connection with 'The City Guilds Institute' from *The Electrician*, Volume 3, November 8 and 15, 1879.

20. See the Engineering Supplement of the London *Times*, 8 January 1908. 'Among Thomson's discoveries was the fact that it was good for students to do laboratory work.'

21. The research of the lowly and modestly remunerated *joshu* (research assistants), who also have a teaching/tutorial load and the prospect of promotion to lecturer grade and above, is generally treated as the property of the whole laboratory which operates as a kind of hierarchical family, with the professor whose name the laboratory bears in a paternal role. This little-

studied structure might interest trained anthropologists as an example of group interaction. (Note: As a rule the research of all subordinates is acknowledged in some way by the professor and associate professors though of course there are occasionally unscrupulous exceptions !)

22. W. E. Ayrton and J. Perry, 'Determination of the Acceleration of Gravity for Tokio, Japan,' *Proceedings of the Physical Society of London*, 1880, 3: 265–76, on p. 276. Quoted in Gooday & Low, 1998, p. 121.

23. Ayrton in *Popular Science Monthly*, 1908, p. 268.

24. See Takahashi (1991) p. 15. All 21 theses (1879–84) were in English, presumably because Ayrton could not read Japanese. Shida's thesis was on the history of electricity and telegraphy. Fujioka wrote on galvanometers; Nakano on telegraphic communication; and Asano on the speed of signalling.

25. See Checkland, (ibid.) vol. 1, p. 53. Six Japanese students of Kelvin (Thomson) sent him a birthday greetings telegram in 1904, which is in the Kelvin papers, University Library, Cambridge, NB 168, 25 June 1904.

26. *Westerners*, pp. 205–6.

27. *Westerners*, p. 206.

28. *Meiji Bunka Hasshō Kinenshi*, 1924, pp. 40–1.

29. From Graeme Gooday's entry for Perry in the forthcoming *New DNB*.

30. 'Prof. W. E. Ayrton, F.R.S', Electrical World Portraits, no XIX, *The Electrical World: a weekly review of current progress in electricity and its practical applications*, Vol. XVI, no. 25, p. 432.

31. Gooday & Low, 1998, 13: 118–9.

32. Ayrton had three scientific papers published in the Transactions of the Asiatic Society of Japan, first series, volume 5: *The Importance of a General System of Simultaneous Observations of Atmospheric Electricity; The Specific Inductive Capacity of Gases; A Neglected Principle that may be Employed in Earthquake Measurement.*

33. Gooday, July 1997, entry for Ayrton in the forthcoming *New DNB*.

Chapter 16 OLIVE CHECKLAND *W. K. Burton, 1856–99: 'Engineer Extraordinaire'*

* This essay is a gift for Tsurumi Sachiko, W.K. Burton's great grand-daughter in Kyoto.

1. It was Max Inanaga, formerly of Glasgow, Scotland, now of Fujisawa, Japan, who first introduced me to Tsurumi Sachiko and W. K. Burton. With thanks for all his help.

2. The University of Glasgow *Senatus acedemicus*, deeply conservative, resisted the imposition of Engineering as a University subject. Certificate of Engineering (CE) was a grudging acknowledgement.

3. For Henry Dyer see http;//www.cs.strath.ac.uk/-rbh/hd/index.html.

4. The degree of Bachelor of Science, (B.Sc) was introduced in the University of Glasgow in 1872. Henry Dyer and Thomas Urquhart were the first to hold this distinction.

5. Cosmo Innes (1798–1874) antiquary and lawyer, was Professor of Constitutional Law at the University of Edinburgh from 1846. See *Who was Who*, pp. 457–8.
6. John Hill Burton (1809–1881) born Aberdeen, graduated from the University of Aberdeen, but moved to Edinburgh. Lawyer and writer see *Who was Who*, pp. 462–4.
7. With thanks to Carol Morgan, the archivist at the Institution of Civil Engineers, One Great George Street, Westminster, London.
8. *Candidates Circular*, William K. Burton, dated 11 December 1890, Institution of Civil Engineers, London.
9. *Candidates Circular,* dated 11 December 1890, Institution of Civil Engineers, London.
10. Charles Scott Meik (1853–1923); born and educated in Edinburgh; employed by T. F. Sharp, a harbour construction engineer; passed the national public surveyor examination. He went to Japan in 1887 and was employed as Harbour Engineer by the Japanese government. Meik prepared two important reports, on *Hokkaido Harbours* (November 1887) and on *Ishikari Navigation* (October 1889); the latter included a note on the transport of coal from Sorachi. Both these reports are held in Sapporo Prefecture Archive. My thanks to Akio Ishizaka. See also C. S. Meik, 'Around the Hokkaido'.
11. See O. Checkland, *Britain's Encounter with Meiji Japan, 1868–1912,* 1989.
12. Fujikura Kentatsu, *Candidates Circular* available prior to election as Associate Member of Institution of Civil Engineers, London, p.11, elected 6 December 1887.
13. With thanks to Margaret Lamb for her kind assistance.
14. O. Checkland and Margaret Lamb, *Health Care as Social History, the Glasgow Case,* Aberdeen, 1982, pp. 1–15.
15. *The Guardian*, 'Royal Flush', 31 January 2001.
16. E. S. Morse, *Japanese Homes and their Surroundings,* Dover ed., New York, 1961, pp. 232–3.
17. With thanks to Tsurumi Sachiko.
18. W. K. Burton's *The Water Supply of Towns* … remained in print for many years. The second edition, revised and extended, was published by Crosby Lockwood in 1898. After the author's death the third edition, revised by J. E. Dumbleton was published (by Crosby Lockwood) in 1928.
19. E. S. Morse, *Japanese Homes* …, p. 233.
20. W. K. Burton, *The Water Supply of Towns* …, pp. 46–7.
21. W. K. Burton, 'Regulating the Rate of Filtration through sand', *Institution of Civil Engineers, Minutes of Proceedings,* Vol. 112, 1892–93, pp. 321–5.
22. Dallas Finn, *Meiji Revisited, the sites of Victorian Japan*, New York, 1995, p. 159.
23. B. H. Chamberlain, *A Handbook for Travellers in Japan*, otherwise known as *Murray's Handbook to Japan,* 1907, p. 133.

24. E. Seidensticker, *Low City, High City, 1867–1923,* Tokyo,1983, p. 71.
25. E. Seidensticker, *Low City, High City*, 1983, p. 9–10.
26. E. Seidensticker, *Low City, High City*, 1983, p. 10.
27. See 'Professor W. K. Burton in Japan', *Photography*, 17 October 1895.
28. *The Theme and Spirit of Anglo-Japanese Relations, an Exhibition of Photographs*, 23–30 May, 1998. Introduction by S. Dobson and T. Bennett, p. 16.
29. See *Antony's Photographic Bulletin*,Vol. XXI, 1890, pp. 285–6.
30. T. Bennett, *Early Japanese Images*, Rutland, Vermont and Tokyo, 1996, Ogawa Kazumasa, pp. 52–4.
31. T. Bennett, *Early Japanese Images*, Kashima Seibei, p. 57.
32. W. K. Burton, *Practical Guide to Photography,* Marion and Co., London, 1892.
33. L. K. Herbert Gustav and P. A. Nott, *John Milne, the Father of Modern Seismology,* Tenterden, Kent, 1980.
34. L. K. Herbert Gustav and P.A. Nott, *John Milne* …, pp. 94–5.
35. Copy of Marriage Certificate.
36. L.K. Herbert Gustav and P.A. Nott, *John Milne* …, p. 114.
37. Albert M. Craig, 'John Hill Burton and Fukuzawa Yukichi', typescript, May 1983.

Chapter 17 IAN NISH *Henry Faulds, 1843–1930*

This paper is based on the writings of Sheriff-substitute George Wilton Wilton, on the related papers which he deposited in the National Library of Scotland [Acc. 20765 from f.59 to f. 173], and on Japanese sources. We acknowledge the help of the librarians at the Edinburgh Public Library and the National Library of Scotland, both at George IV Bridge, Edinburgh, the Wellcome Medical Library, London, and the Staffordshire Record Office.

G. W. Wilton's comprehensive publications on this subject are *Fingerprints: history, law and romance*,Glasgow: William Hodge, 1938; *Fingerprints: Scotland Yard and Henry Faulds*, Edinburgh: W Green, 1951; *Fingerprint facts*, Galashiels, 1953; *Fingerprints: Fifty Years of injustice*, Galashiels, 1955; *Fingerprints: Scotland Yard: Ruxton Trial Revelations*, North Berwick: Tantallon Press, 1957; *Fingerprints, Dr Henry Faulds and his daughters*, North Berwick: Society for the Freedom of the Individual, 1962; *Fingerprints: Six Years' Strife: Victory in Sight; Fingerprints: Swan Song of Old Dr Fingerprints: Victory Won*, North Berwick, Tantallon Press, 1963

1. Shigehisa Tokutaro, 'Henry Faulds' in Oyatoi gaikokujin, vol. 5, 'Kyoiku shukyo', Tokyo: Kajima kenkyujo, 1969. See also Nigel Cameron (ed.), Dictionary of Scottish Church History and Theology, 1993
2. *Henry Faulds, Nine Years in Nipon: Sketches of Japanese Life and Manners*, Paisley and London, 1885. [Hereafter cited as 'HF'] See also Hugh Cortazzi,

Victorians in Japan: In and around the Treaty Ports, London, Athlone, 1987, pp. 113–15, 324–5

3. HF, p. 39. Yumiyo Yamamoto, 'Inoue Masaru: Father of the Japanese Railways' in Ian Nish (ed.), *Britain and Japan: Biographical Portraits, vol. 2*, Richmond, Japan Library, 1997, pp. 24–9

4. Ian Nish (ed.), *The Iwakura Mission in America and Europe*, Richmond, Japan Library, 1998, ch. 2

5. Dallas Finn, *Meiji Revisited: The Sites of Victorian Japan*, New York, Weatherhill, 1995, p. 736.

6. HF, pp. 225 and 44

7. HF, p. 65

8. Shigehisa, *op. cit.*, pp. 179–83

9. HF, p. 95. James Hoare, *Japan's Treaty Ports*, Richmond, Japan Library, 1997, p. 163. Koyama Noboru, 'James Summers, 1828–91' in James Hoare (ed.), *Britain and Japan: Biographical Portraits*, vol. 3, Richmond, Japan Library, 1999, pp. 30–3.

10. W. G. Dixon was the author of *The Land of the Morning: An Account of Japan and its People*, Edinburgh 1889

11. A. Hamish Ion, *The Cross and the Rising Sun, vol. 2*, Waterloo, W. Laurier University Press, 1993, pp. 53–4; G. W. Wilton, *Fingerprints: history, law and romance*, p. 26

12. Letter to the editor, *Nature*, 28 Oct. 1880, Transactions of the Asiatic Society of Japan

13. Only the second 1887 edition is shown in the British Library catalogue.

14. D. Finn, *op. cit.*, p. 73

15. HF, p. 208

16. HF, pp. 104 and 95. See also p. 301 where he writes
'Confucius does not speak to the times we live in, as even an infidel or pagan Japanese editor feels that Christ does.'

17. HF, p. 120

18. HF, p. 100

19. HF, p. 101

20. HF, p. 301

21. HF, p. 182. On Morse, see Robert A. Rosenstone, *Mirror in the Shrine: American Encounters with Meiji Japan*, Cambridge, Harvard UP, 1988, pp. 132–3. Since many of Morse's pamphlets are in the Japan Society library, he must have had connections with London after he left Japan.

22. Shigehisa, *op. cit.*, pp. 172–3, which shows Faulds being visited by Tanaka Naomi.

23. Information extracted from Kelly's Medical Directories.

24. *Guide to Finger-print Identification*, Hanley: Wood, Mitchell, 1905; *The Hidden Hand*, Hanley: Wood, Mitchell, 1920; *A Manual of Practical Dactylography*, London: *Police Review*, 1923; *Was Sir E. R. Henry the Originator of the Finger Print System?* Hanley: Webberley, 1926

25. *The Times*, 20 March 1930. Osaka *Asahi* contains an obituary and a tribute from the Japanese Ministry of Justice (Shigehisa, pp. 173–4).
26. Furuhata to Wilton, 20 March 1961 in Wilton MSS 20765.
27. Yasoshima to Wilton, 14 Dec. 1961 in Wilton MSS 20765
28. Shigehisa, *op. cit.*, p. 179; Olive Checkland, *Britain's Encounter with Meiji Japan, 1866–1912*, London, Routledge, 1989. The legend in Tsukiji may need amendment because the Faulds reached the UK on 19 Dec. 1885. It is possible, however, that some of his contracts may have run on into 1886.
29. Furuhata to Wilton, 20 May 1962 in Wilton MSS 20765
30. Wilton, *Swansong of Old Dr Fingerprints*, pp. 16–17. Faulds' daughters were Isabella Jane Faulds and Agnes Cameron Faulds
31. Faulds' journal is not in the British Library catalogue but three issues are understood to have come out in 1897–8.

Chapter 18 JIRO HIGUCHI *Henry Spencer Palmer, 1838–93*

1. Captain Brinkley of *The Japan Weekly Mail* wrote an obituary of Palmer on 18 February 1893. Obituaries were also published in leading Japanese newspapers including the *Tokyo Nichi Nichi Shimbun, Mainichi Shimbun, Yomiuri Shimbun, Jiji Shimpo, and Nippon*. Obituaries appeared in *The Times* on 15 March 1893 as well as in *The Royal Engineer's Journal* in May 1893 and the journal of the Royal Astronomical Society (September 1894). A short biography of Palmer appeared in the *Dictionary of National Biography* in 1895
2. The inscription '*Non omnis mouriar*' (I shall not altogether die) was taken from a poem by Horace.
3. Dictionary of National Biography, contributed by Robert Hamilton Veitch, 1895.
4. John Pope-Hennessy became a KCMG on 21 April 1880.
5. For an account of this visit see *The Cruise of HMS* Bacchante *1879–1882*, two volumes, London 1886.
6. c.f. Hugh Cortazzi's biographical portrait of Sir Francis Plunkett in this volume.
7. See minutes of the proceedings of the Institute of Civil Engineers, 'Waterworks in China and Japan' page 75. Turner on the Yokohama Waterworks 25 February 1890.
8. Palmer's reports for these waterworks were dated: Osaka, 6 May 1887, Hakodate, 12 September 1887, Tokyo, January 1888, Kobe, March 1888.
9. Report in *The Japan Weekly Mail* dated 25 June 1887.
10. Report in *The Japan Weekly Mail* dated 4 July 1891.
11. Application submitted by the promoters of Yokohama Dock Company with Palmer's design for docks on 31 January 1890.
12. 'Life of a Japanese Spa' 20 August 1886 (see attached list of articles)
13. Letter to Sir George Biddell Airy (1801–1892), Astronomer Royal (1834–1881) at Greenwich dated 30 July 1880.

14. 'Article entitled 'Social Problems in Japan' dated 14 April 1887 (see attached list)
15. The attack which took place on 18 October 1889 was reported by Palmer on 21 October 1889.

Chapter 19 AKIKO OHTA *Nakamura Masanao (Keiu), 1832–91:* translator into Japanese of Samuel Smiles' *Self Help*

1. The Meirokusha was founded in 1873 and played an important intellectual role in the intellectual development of the early Meiji period. Other members included such famous figures as Mori Arinori, Kato Hiroyuki, Nishi Amane, Tsuda Mamichi and Nishimura Shigeki, who all contributed essays to the *Meiroku Zasshi* which circulated widely among Japanese intellectuals.
2. There were said to be more than three hundred students in the Dojinsha, which provided education in foreign languages and Western studies. The curriculum included English language, Western studies, Chinese classics and mathematics. A literary magazine called *Dojinsha Bungaku Zasshi* was issued from July 1876. The school seems to have run into financial difficulty around 1883 when the new conscription law was introduced. It was eventually closed after Nakamura's death in 1891. For further details see Takahashi M, *Nakamura Keiu*, Tokyo 1966.
3. For other reasons for Nakamura's relative obscurity, see Ogiwara Takashi *Nakamura Keiu Kenkyu*, Tokyo, 1990
4. Nakamura Shigemasa was posted to Kyoto every other year as one of the Bakufu guards at the Nijo Castle *(Nijojo Koban Doshin)*.
5. Takahashi Masao *Nakamura Keiu*, Tokyo, 1966, pp. 1–2.
6. Takahashi Masao in his study *Nakamura Keiu,* Tokyo, 1966, pp 18–31, describes several episodes and suggests some factors, which led Nakamura to take an interest in Western studies. In his autobiography Nakamura confessed that as it was officially forbidden to learn about the West when he entered the academy, he tried to conceal the fact that he was studying Dutch, but was often discovered and reprimanded by his teachers. See Nakamura Masanao *'Jijo Senjimon'*, Tokyo, 1987, p. 1.
7. Matsuzawa Hiroaki *Kindai Nihon no Keisei to Seiyo Keiken*, Tokyo, 1993, pp. 233–235.
8. Okubo Takeharu *Meiji Enlightenment to Nakamura Keiu(1) in Tokyo Toritsu Daigaku Hogakukai Zasshi,* vol. 39, No. 1, Tokyo, 1998, pp. 655–659.
9. Nakamura wrote that Western Studies in Japan tended to be too materialistic and that it was important for the benefit of his country to send a Confucian scholar like himself to look into the spiritual aspect of Western society. See Nakamura's *'Ryugaku Negaitatematsurisoro Zonjiyori Kakitsuke'* included in Okubo Toshiaki ed. *Meiji Keimo Shiso Shu*, Tokyo, 1967, p. 279.
10. For details of the Bakufu students who studied abroad in the 1860s see

Ishizuka Minoru *Kindai Nihon no Kaigai Ryugakushi,* Tokyo, 1992, pp 140–143. In the 1860s the popularity of Dutch studies was rapidly giving way to Western studies in general. This change was reflected in the Bakufu's choice of destinations for overseas study. The countries selected also depended on the subjects the students were to study. Reflecting the close relations developed between the Bakufu and France, France was the first choice for many students. This was followed by the Netherlands, Britain, Russia, the United States and Belgium. Students from the daimyo domains did not follow this pattertn.

11. For details see Cobbing, Andrew, *Japanese Discovery of Victorian Britain,* Richmond, 1998, pp. 105–110; Koyama Noboru, *Hatenko Meiji Ryugakusei Retsuden,* Tokyo, 1999, pp. 58–73.

12. Kawaji Taro, *Taiei Nisshi,* included in Kawaji Ryuko, *Kurofuneki,* Tokyo, 1953, pp. 198–199.

13. See Kawaji Taro, *ibid.*; Hayashi Tadasu, *Nochi wa Mukashi no Ki,* Tokyo reprint 1970.

14. Hayashi Tadasu, *ibid.* pp. 178–180.

15. Hammond frequently referred to the 'insubordinate' Bakufu students and expressed sympathy for Lloyd in his letters to Parkes. Parkes papers in the Jardine Matheson Archives (hereafter cited as JMA). JMA Parkes Papers; Parkes 1: H14–H16; H22; H25; H28; H36; H43–H47 Hammond to Parkes.

16. JMA Parkes Papers: Parkes 1: H53–H54 Hammond to Parkes.

17. JMA Parkes Papers: Parkes 1: H55 Hammond to Parkes.

18. Cobbing, Andrew, *Japanese Discovery of Victorian Britain,* Richmond, 1998, p. 110. See also Blacker Carmen, '*Laurence Oliphant and Japan 1858–88* in Nish, Ian ed., *Britain and Japan; Biographical Portraits,* Vol. II, Japan Library, 1997.

19. Hayashi in his memoir recorded that Lloyd suddenly visited the hotel in Portsmouth where he was staying in 1872 as a member of the Iwakura Mission. Lloyd referred to his efforts on behalf of the Bakufu students and asked for employment with the Japanese government. Ito Hirobumi, however, after consulting Hayashi refused this request. Hayashi Tadasu, *Nochi wa Mukashi no Ki,* Tokyo reprint 1970, p. 180.

20. Nakamura Masanao, *Jijo Senjimon,* Tokyo 1987, p. 3. Nakamura does not seem to have been impressed by Paris, which he thought was a frivolous and luxurious city. Unlike his compatriots who generally kept diaries and wrote detailed accounts of their experiences abroad in the 1860s and 1870s, Nakamura wrote remarkably little about his stay in Britain.

21. Takahashi Masao, *Nakamura Keiu,* Tokyo, 1966, pp. 72–73; Matsuzawa Hiroaki, *Kindai Nihon no Keisei to Seiyo Keiken,* Tokyo, 1993, p. 236.

22. Nakamura was baptised by George Cochran, a Canadian Methodist missionary in 1874.

23. Clark met W. E. Griffis when he entered Rutgers College in 1865 and they became close friends. After travelling round Europe, he came to Japan in 1871 on Griffis' recommendation and taught chemistry, physics and

general knowledge about the West at Shizuoka Gakumonjo (see W. E. Clark *Life and Adventure in Japan*, London 1878).

24. C.f. Okubo Toshiaki, '*Nakamura Keiu no Shoki Yōgaku Shisō to Saigokurisshhen no Yakujutsu oyobi Kankō ni tsuite*' in Okubo Toshiaki Rekishi Chosakushu, vol. 5, Tokyo, 1986; Maeda Ai, 'Nakamura Keiu' in *Bakumatsu Ishinki no Bungaku*, Tokyo, 1972; Okubo Takeharu, 'Meiji Enlightenment to Nakamura Keiu (i) in Tokyo Toritsu Daigaku Hogakukai Zasshi, Vol. 39, No 1, Tokyo, 1998.

25. Okubo Takeharu, ibid., p. 665.

26. Nakamura Masanao, *Saigoku Risshihen* (Kodansha paperback edition, 1981), p. 39. Okubo points out that Nakamura frequently used the terminology Shin in translating 'mind' 'soul' 'will' and 'principle'. Okubo Takeharu, ibid., p. 673.

27. Nakamura Masanao, *Jijo Senjimon*, Tokyo, 1987, p. 3.

28. See 'Samuel Smiles' in *The Dictionary of National Biography*; Matsuzawa Hiroaki, *Kindai Nihon no Keisei to Seiyo Keiken*, Tokyo, 1987, pp. 246–247.

29. For example, Magoshi Kyohei, founder of Dainippon Beer Company, recalled that he owed his success to Self Help, which had been lent to him by his friend Masuda Takashi, founder of Mitsui Bussan Company when they were both young. Shirasaki Hideo, Don ou Masuda Takashi, paperback edition Tokyo, 1998, vol. 1, p. 248.

30. For example, on translating Chapter VI 'Industry and the English Peerage' Nakamura added a slightly different meaning to the original text. He translated the title of the chapter (Chapter VII in the Japanese version) as 'On those who were given a peerage' and amongst the sub-titles, he even created a new one called 'Many of the existing peerage began as merchants'. This was the section where Smiles described the intermingling of classes, but Nakamura tried to give a clearer picture of upward mobility in society. Such sections stirred the spirits of Japanese merchants and businessmen, who had been officially placed at the bottom of the class hierarchy during the Tokugawa period, to work even harder.

31. Matsuzawa Hiroaki, *Kindai Nihon no Keisei to Seiyo Keiken*, Tokyo 1993, pp 239–241. Philanthropy in Victorian Scotland was different from that practised in England. How far Nakamura differentiated between Scotland and England is uncertain. For social policy and Victorian philanthropy, see Checkland, Sydney. British Public Policy 1776–1939, Cambridge, 1983; Checkland, Olive, Philanthropy in Victorian Scotland, Edinburgh, 1980.

32. Nakamura Masanao, *Jiyu no Kotowari*, Tokyo, 1872, vol. V, p. 342.

33. Nakamura Masanao, *Taiseijin no Josho ni Gisu*, in Okubo Toshiaki ed., *Meiji Keimo Shisō Shu*, Tokyo, 1967, pp. 281–283.

34. Takahashi Masao, *Nakamura Keiu*, Tokyo, 1866, pp. 155–166.

35. For Nakamura's views on women's role, see for example in *Zenryo naru haha wo tsukuru setsu* in Meiroku Zasshi, No 33, 1875, and *Hahaoya no kanka* in Jogakuzasshi, vol. 9, no. 82, 1887.

36. Nakamura was not appointed to this post because he had lost interest in Western studies. Chinese classics, which had lost popularity during the early Meiji period, were reappraised in the 1880s and Nakamura, formerly a renowned Confucian scholar, was asked to contribute to their revival.
37. Smiles, S., *Thrift*, London, 1875, Preface.
38. Whereas *Thrift* consisted of sixteen chapters (about 380 pages), Nakamura reorganised Seiyo Setsuyo-ron into a book divided into sixty-six sections, but of only 182 pages.
39. Smiles, S., *Thrift*, London, 1875, p. 6; Nakamura Masanao, *Seiyo Setsuyo-ron*, Tokyo, 1886, p. 15. Nakamura did mention the significance of labour, but he tended to put more emphasis on the importance of knowledge.
40. Smiles, S., Thrift, London, 1875, p. 10; Nakamura Masanao, *Seiyo Setsuyo-ron*, Tokyo, 1886, p. 26.
41. *Bei-O Kairan Jikki* was the official report of the Iwakura Mission to the USA and Europe (1871–3). It was compiled by Kume Kunitake (1839–1931), a Confucian scholar and historian. There were similarities in the academic background of Kume and Nakamura.
42. Henry Faulds (1843–1940) is the subject of a biographical portrait in this volume by Ian Nish.
43. This led in 1880 to the establishment of the Institute for the Blind, which soon started educating deaf-mute children as well.
44. See, for instance, *Seiyō Jijō* by Fukuzawa Yukichi, *Seiyō Bunken-roku* (1869) by Nomura Fumio, and *Bei-O Kairan Jikki* by Kume Kunitake.
45. Since Christian missionaries played an important part in the activities of the Rakuzen-kai, some Japanese interpreted it as a movement to promote Christianity in Japan under the guise of a charity.
46. Takahashi Masao, *Nakamura Keiu*, Tokyo, 1966, pp. 273–274.
47. Yoshino Sakuzo, '*Saigoku Risshihen*' in Nihon Bungaku Daijiten, Tokyo, 1925, vol. 3, p. 176.

Chapter 20 CARMEN BLACKER *Sir Edwin Arnold, 1832–1904: A Year in Japan, 1889–90*

1. Mary Crawford Fraser, *A Diplomat's Wife in Japan*, edited by Hugh Cortazzi, 1982, p. 113–4, and abridged from the 2-volume work of 1899.
2. A recent edition may be recommended, edited with an illuminating Introduction by the English bhikkhu Sangharakshita, Birmingham 1998.
3. Philip C. Almond, *The British Discovery of Buddhism*, Cambridge 1988, p. 1–3.
4. Mary Fraser, *ibid.*, p. 113.
5. *Ibid.*, p. 129.
6. Douglas Sladen, *Twenty Years of My Life*, London 1914, p. 116–7. *The Light of the World* was published in 1891.
7. The text is reprinted in *Seas and Lands*, 1891, p. 240–3.

8. Ibid., p. 244–57.
9. *Japonica,* London 1891, pp.62, 123,127.
10. T. S. or Thomas Seccombe wrote the entry for Edwin Arnold in the DNB 1912.
11. The story of *Adzuma,* 1893, is based on the legend of Endo Morito, or the future Mongaku Shonin, and Kesa Gozen.
12. *Letters from B. H. Chamberlain to Lafcadio Hearn*, compiled by Kazuo Koizumi, Tokyo 1936, p. 22 and 18.
13. *Handbook of Colloquial Japanese*, revised edition 1907, p. 238. The late Sir John Pilcher, (1912–1990), Ambassador to Japan 1967–1972 took great pleasure in using and pronouncing the word '*naruhodo*' in the various ways described by Chamberlain. For a biography of Sir John Pilcher see Sir Hugh Cortazzi's portrait in *Biographical Portraits, Volume III.*
14. *Ibid.*, p. 239–40.
15. For an account of the Yokohama dialect see Sir Hugh Cortazzi's *Victorians in Japan*, London, 1987 pages 340–5.
16. Toshio Yokoyama, *Japan in the Victorian Mind: a study of the stereotyped images of a nation 1850-1880*, London, 1987.
17. She was still living in London in 1945. Do any readers remember her?
18. Three *uta* are reproduced, with calligraphy and translation, at the end of his Preface to *Japonica*, p. ix.
19. The cartoon from *Punch* is reproduced in Sir Hugh Cortazzi's 'The Japan Society: a Hundred-Year History', in *Britain and Japan, 1859–1991, Themes and Personalities*, ed. Sir Hugh Cortazzi and Gordon Daniels, London, 1991.

The *Punch* cartoon must have been galling to Sir Edwin, who was always concerned to correct Western misconceptions about Japan derived from the superficial effusions of globetrotting *flaneurs* Mr Gilbert and Sir Arthur Sullivan also had something to answer for by reason of their lively misrepresentation of Japan in the comic opera entitled *The Mikado*. The characters and the general *mis-en-scène* were 'so ridiculous to the Japanese eye partly because of the gross disrespect offered to the growing empire and its sovereign', that the piece could never be produced in Japan. Nor was *Punch* to be exonerated, with his cartoon of a diminutive 'Jap the Giant-Killer' trampling on a colossal Chinaman'. *East and West*, 1896, p. 275.

20. *Autobiography of Alfred Austin*, 1911, Vol. 2, p. 259–60.
21. See, for example, E. F. Benson, *As We Were*, 1930, p. 192–6.

Chapter 21 RICHARD C. SMITH & IMURA MOTOMICHI *Harold E. Palmer, 1877–1949*

1. Lecture on 'Foreign Teachers in Japan', given by Sir Vere Redman to The Japan Society on 11 October 1966, in Japan Society *Bulletin*, 51 (1967), p. 9.
2. *ibid.*, p. 10

3. Cited in Tanaka Masamichi, 'Harold E. Palmer after he left Japan', *Annual Review of English Language Education in Japan* 2 (1991), p. 184.
4. Dorothée Anderson, 'Harold E. Palmer: a biographical essay', Appendix to Harold E. Palmer and H. Vere Redman, *This Language-Learning Business*, London: Oxford University Press, 1932/1969, p. 143.
5. For more on the circumstances and nature of the invitation to Japan, see Imura Motomichi, *Palmer to nihon no eigokyoiku (Harold E. Palmer and Teaching English in Japan)*, Tokyo: Taishukan, 1997, pp. 28–40.
6. H. Vere Redman, 'English teaching in Japan', *Oversea Education* 11 (1931), p. 79 (italics in original).
7. William Cullen Bryant II, 'English language teaching in Japanese schools'. *PMLA* 71/4, part 2 (1956), p. 25 (italics in original).
8. For more on Sauveur's 'natural method' and the work of the German reformers, see A. P. R. Howatt and Richard C. Smith (eds.), *Foundations of Foreign Language Teaching: Nineteenth-century Innovators*, London: Routledge, 2000, and A.P.R. Howatt and Richard C. Smith (eds.), *Modern Language Teaching: The Reform Movement*, London: Routledge, 2001, respectively. On Okakura, see Imura Motomichi and Takenaka Tatsunori, *Okakura Yoshisaburo*, Tokyo: Jiyusha, forthcoming.
9. Details of Palmer's life up to his departure for the Continent are presented more fully in Richard C. Smith, 'Harold E. Palmer's formative years (1877–1901)', *Area and Culture Studies (Tokyo gaikokugo daigaku ronshu)* 57 (1998), pp. 1–37. See also Anderson, 'Harold E. Palmer', and Richard C. Smith, *The Writings of Harold E. Palmer: An Overview*, Tokyo: Hon-no-Tomosha, 1999, Chapter 1.
10. In the *Hythe Reporter*, 21 September 1901.
11. Anderson, 'Harold E. Palmer', p. 136.
12. Full details relating to Palmer's work in Verviers are provided in Smith, *The Writings*, Chapter 2.
13. Anderson, 'Harold E. Palmer', p. 136.
14. *ibid.*
15. Anderson, 'Harold E. Palmer', p. 141.
16. See Beverley Collins and Inger M. Mees, *The Real Professor Higgins: The Life and Career of Daniel Jones*, Berlin: Mouton de Gruyter, 1998.
17. For more details of Palmer's lectures and research work at UCL and SOS, see Richard C. Smith, 'Harold E. Palmer's London lectures and related publications (1915–21)', *IRLT Bulletin* 12 (1998), pp. 55–85. Also, Smith, *The Writings*, Chapter 3.
18. For more detail on Palmer's work in Japan, see in particular Imura, *Palmer*, and Ozasa Toshiaki, *Harold E. Palmer no eigokyojuho ni kansuru kenkyu: Nihon ni okeru tenkai o chushin to shite* (A Study of Harold E. Palmer's English Teaching Methodology, with Special Emphasis on its Development in Japan), Tokyo: Dai-ichi Gakushusha, 1995. Also, Richard C. Smith 'The Palmer-Hornby

contribution to English teaching in Japan', *International Journal of Lexicography* 11/4 (1998), pp. 269–91, and Smith, *The Writings*, Chapters 4 and 5.
19. Including Norman Y. Yamamoto, 'The Oral Method: Harold E. Palmer and the reformation of the teaching of the English language in Japan', *ELT Journal* 32/2 (1978), pp. 151–8.
20. Nitobe Inazo. 'The teaching and use of foreign languages in Japan', *Sewanee Review* 31 (1923), pp. 338-9 (as cited by Lynn Earl Henrichsen, *Diffusion of Innovations in English Language Teaching: The ELEC Effort in Japan, 1956–1968*, Westport, Connecticut: Greenwood Press, pp. 121–2).
21. Anderson, 'Harold E. Palmer', p. 153.
22. Anderson, 'Harold E. Palmer', p. 154.
23. By W. Rudolf F. Stier, in *Gogaku kyoiku* 210 (1950), pp. 12–14.
24. Further details of Palmer's final years are provided in Tanaka, 'Harold E. Palmer after he left Japan'. See also Imura, *Palmer*, Chapters 17-20, and Smith, *The Writings*, Chapter 6.
25. See Tanaka, 'Harold E. Palmer after he left Japan', p. 154.
26. In the personal files of Victoria Angela.
27. Naganuma's own methodology and textbooks were clearly based on Palmer's work for English. For example, his *Hyōjun nihongo dokuhon* (Standard Japanese Readers), Tokyo, 1931, reflect the contents as well as the title of Palmer's *Standard English Readers*.
28. See IRLT (eds.) *Zaidanhōjin gogaku kyōiku kenkyūjo nanajūsshūnen kinenshi* (A History of IRLT to Commemorate the Seventieth Anniversary of its Foundation), Tokyo: IRLT, 1994.
29. See A. P. Cowie, 'A. S. Hornby, 1898-1998: a centenary tribute', *International Journal of Lexicography* 11/4 (1998), pp. 251–68.
30. Anderson, 'Harold E. Palmer', p. 181.
31. For example, Vere Redman, 'Harold E. Palmer: pioneer teacher of modern languages', *English Language Teaching* 22/1 (1967), pp. 10–16, and Yamamoto, 'The Oral Method'.
32. See Bryant, 'English language teaching'.
33. Hornby to Dorothée Anderson, 13 October 1956, in the personal files of Victoria Angela.
34. On these efforts see Henrichsen, *Diffusion of Innovations*.
35. A.P.R. Howatt, Foreword to Smith, *The Writings*, p. viii.

Chapter 22 JOHN HAFFENDEN *William Empson, Poet and Writer, 1906–84: Japan 1931–34*

1. Sumie Okada, *Western Writers in Japan* (Basingstoke, Hants.: Macmillan Press, 1999), p. 44; Kyohei Ogihara, 'About Emp-san', *Eigo-Seinen (The Rising Generation)*, 106: 10 (1 October 1960), p. 32.
2. Peter Quennell, *A Superficial Journey Through Tokyo and Peking* (1932; reprinted Oxford: Oxford University Press, 1986), p. 99.

3. Quennell, *A Superficial Journey*, p. 115.
4. See *The Japan Biographical Encyclopedia and Who's Who*, 3rd edition, 1964–1965 (Tokyo: The Rengo Press).
5. Rintaro Fukuhara, 'Mr William Empson in Japan', in *William Empson: The Man and His Work*, ed. Roma Gill (London: Routledge & Kegan Paul, 1974), p. 22.
6. Empson, 'Teaching English in the Far East and England', in *The Strengths of Shakespeare's Shrew* (Sheffield: Sheffield Academic Press, 1996), p. 216.
7. Okada, *Western Writers in Japan*, p. 45.
8. See Sir Hugh Cortazzi, 'Sir Vere Redman, 1901–1975', in *Britain and Japan Biographical Portraits*, vol. II (Japan Library, 1997), pp. 283–300; Katharine Sansom, *Sir George Sansom and Japan: a memoir* (Tallahassee, Florida: Diplomatic Press, 1972); and Gordon Daniels, 'Sir George Sansom (1883–1965): Historian and Diplomat', in *Britain and Japan 1859–1991: Themes and Personalities*, ed. Sir Hugh Cortazzi and Gordon Daniels (London & New York: Routledge, 1991), pp. 277–88.
9. *The Complete Poems of William Empson*, ed. John Haffenden (Harmondsworth, Middx.: Allen Lane The Penguin Press, 2000), p. 69.
10. S. F. Bolt, letter, *The London Review of Books*, 15: 16 (19 August 1993), p. 5.
11. David Wevill's letter is quoted in Okada, *Western Writers in Japan*, p. 48.
12. See FO 262/1878/ 151. 158081 (Public Record Office, London).
13. FO 371/ 24742 Political: Far Eastern – Japan 1940; files 953–1559; Public Record Office, London (letter from Tokyo Chancery, British Embassy, Tokyo, to Far Eastern Department, Foreign Office, 4 December 1939).

Chapter 23 JAMES CUMMINS *Charles Boxer (1904–2000) and Japan*

1. Professor Boxer was still taking notes on these events in his commonplace book as late as 1978.
2. Catalogue 1116 'Japan' (Maggs Bros., London, 1990), pp. 2–3.
3. 'My interest in Portuguese and Dutch maritime history started virtually simultaneously and continued on parallel lines. I came to both through my basic interest in Feudal Japan, 1500–1800, which I began as a child, collecting *netsuke*, etc' (undated autograph note by Boxer).
4. *Harmsworth's History of the World*, I (London: Amalgamated Press, 1907), pp. 553–62.
5. Harmsworth was not alone: 'The destruction of the town belonging to this strange people with whom we have only lately come in contact has caused a very painful sensation in this country.' (Annual Register (1863), pp. 301–302).
6. Harmsworth, I, p. 481; Boxer, 'Hosokawa Tadaoki and the Jesuits', *Transactions and Proceedings of the Japan Society of London*, XXXII (1935), p. 119.

7. Since the Jesuits were the first Christian missionaries in Japan Boxer became interested in their history, an interest that remained with him throughout his life. He saw 'a certain similarity of training' between stoics, samurai and Jesuits (Boxer, *The Christian Century in Japan 1549–1650* (Cambridge University Press, 1951), pp. 48–9).
8. See Hugh Cortazzi and Gordon Daniel, *Britain and Japan 1859–1991. Themes and Personalities* (London: Routledge, 1991), 33, 41. Boxer would have been amused by a comment in the *Foreign Office Annual Report on Japan* (1930): 'Propaganda of an indirect but not ineffectual kind is also a function of such cultural societies as the Japan Society of London' (P[ublic] R[ecord] O[ffice], FO. 371.15520, p. 33).
9. John Ferris, 'The Kennedy Diary', 1934–46', *Intelligence and National Security*, IV (1989), p. 422–5.
10. Between 1903–1937 about 130 such officers served in Japan (Ferris, p. 422). Piggott was an extreme Japanophile who was considered to have 'gone native' and in the 1930s his reports were dismissed in Whitehall as 'Piggotry' (Richard J. Aldrich, *Intelligence and the War against Japan* (Cambridge University Press, 2000), 30, 61–2).
11. In his first year in Tokyo he lectured in the Toyo Bunko on 'European Influences on Japanese Sword-fittings, 1543–1853'.
12. Boxer belonged to the Kennedy school of Japanophiles, and in conversation described him as 'an old and good friend, whose *Military Side of Japanese Life* is authoritative.' Boxer was fortunate in knowing Kennedy, for, as Ferris writes of him, 'in the 1930s few foreigners exceeded his grasp of Japanese policy, politics and personalities' (p. 423).
13. Kennedy Diaries, Sheffield University Archives, 3.26, pp. 47, 72–3, 131.
14. The *Shimbashira* (literally god column) was the hereditary head of Tenrikyo, a religion established in 1838 by Nakayama Miki after a divine revelation that she should become the shrine of god.
15. When he left the 38th Nara regiment, his fellow officers, in a gesture of appreciation, presented him with a sword that had once belonged to a seventeenth-century daimyo.
16. Grimsdale claimed that he himself had been selected for Intelligence Service because the recommending officer happened to know he read The Times (Grimsdale Papers, Imperial War Museum, London, p. 3).
17. Grimsdale Papers, p. 111.
18. PRO. WO 106.6095.
19. He also submitted 'Notes on a visit to Japan, July, 1939' to his superiors (PRO. FO. 371.23573).
20. PRO. WO 208.2049A.
21. Grimsdale Papers, pp. 14–15.
22. Grimsdale Papers, pp. 18–21.
23. Grimsdale Papers, p. 20.
24. A website listing every serviceman or woman who served in the 1941

Hong Kong garrison and an hour-by-hour history of the December 1941 fighting is in preparation; tony@hongkongwardiary.com This is expected to be the most comprehensive and accurate account published so far.

25. The wound crippled his left arm permanently. Ironically, some of the Japanese troops involved in the fall of Hong Kong belonged to Boxer's old 38th Nara infantry regiment.

26. Boxer said later that this therapy saved him from having his arm amputated.

27. Personal communication from Emeritus-Professor Brian Baxter, Department of Naval Architecture, Strathclyde University.

28. Gimson found Maejima 'a good friend to the internees by his favourable interpretation of the regulations'. But the tuition aroused hostile comment, which Gimson linked to 'the unstable mental condition of the large majority of the internees'. Nevertheless, he took the precaution of taking an officer with him 'for protection against false allegations and libellous statements' (Gimson's diary, Rhodes House, Oxford, Indian Ocean MSS. 222, fols. 75v, 92r, 164r). Gimson (Sir Franklin Gimson) became Governor of Singapore after the war.

29. See Emily Hahn's *Hong Kong Holiday* (New York: Doubleday, 1946), pp. 119–31.

30. The secret radio referred to was used to disseminate news amongst the prisoners, and Colonel H. W. Browne has described how discreetly this was done: 'Charles Boxer was a quiet man who kept very much to himself and I did not have any contact with him before, or during the war, but in Argyle Street Camp I attended his Japanese language classes. Also the information coming in from the wireless and from Chinese newspapers etc. was analysed by Charles and Lt. K. M. A. Barnett. Charles then disseminated this through a group of some six shorthand writers, of which I was one. We sat round him as if he was giving a class, in case any Japanese came into the hut. We then had to pass on the information to our own huts, by a similar method i.e. not having all the occupants of each hut crowding around, but to groups as if at class.'

31. Kawata San had shared his rations with starving POWs and risked his life to help the sick. The gesture recalls Churchill's gift of gold watches to some of his guards during his capture in the Boer war. Selwyn-Clark later refused to denounce any Japanese, but Boxer did not hesitate to name those considered by him to be guilty.

32. For the most up to date bibliography see *Portuguese Studies* (London, vol.17 (2001), pp. 247–76.

33. Typically, his medical treatment had not stopped him from researching in the New York Public Library where he 'took copious notes' (*Christian Century*, p. 483).

34. Okamoto was greatly respected by Boxer: 'I regarded myself as his disciple'.

35. The date and place of that landing had a personal resonance for the author.
36. Boxer liked his work to be reviewed and so was disappointed when the Jesuit journal *The Month* failed to notice the book. When they explained they had no one capable of doing so, Boxer submitted a sample 'review', including the criticisms of other reviewers, and he ended by saying 'the book is outrageously expensive, but does not cost as much as a bottle of whisky, and will do less harm.' He signed his 'review' with the name of his favourite comic figure, 'Dr. Strabismus'. In the end the Jesuits rose to the challenge and got Vincent Cronin to review the book for them.
37. Professor Tadashi Nakamura of Kyushu University in conversation (1991).
38. I am grateful to Dr Selwyn-Clarke's daughter for allowing me the use of the unpublished diary.
39. For Boxer's biography see Dauril Alden, *Charles R. Boxer, An Uncommon Life, Soldier, Historian, Teacher, Collector, Traveller* (Lisbon: Fundação Oriente, 2001). For the biography of Boxer's second wife, Emily Hahn, see Ken Cuthbertson, *Nobody said not to go. The Life, Loves and Adventures of Emily Hahn* (London: Faber and Faber, 1998. For her autobiography see Emily Hahn, China to Me (Philadelphia: Blakiston, 1944; London: Virago, 1986).

Chapter 24 NOBUKO ALBERY *Ivan Morris, 1925–77*

1. Gordonstoun is a Spartan 'public' boarding school in Morayshire, Scotland, founded by a German refugee Kurt Hahn (1886–1974) who had originally founded a school at Castle Salem in Germany, based on his ideas of what an English public school was supposed to be. According to *Chamber's Biographical Dictionary,* 'The school emphasized physical rather than intellectual activities...Hahn was a man of overpowering and autocratic personality, ...[who] dominated his school and imposed his obsessions with sex and aesthetics on his pupils.' Prince Philip, Duke of Edinburgh, as well as Prince Charles, Prince of Wales and his brothers Andrew and Edward all attended Gordonstoun.
2. Nobuko was Ivan's second Japanese wife. His first Japanese wife was a ballet dancer Ogawa Ayako whom he had met in London. Yaki, as she was popularly called, had been befriended by Otome Daniels, the wife of Frank Daniels, then Reader in Japanese at SOAS and later Professor of Japanese. Otome who had no children of her own was always hospitable and kind to anyone she thought lonely or friendless. Yaki was an unstable character who became obsessed with Communism and alcohol. It now seems from new information that Nobuko was, in fact, Ivan's third wife; his first is believed to have been South African, although very little appears to be known.
3. Yet he produced his *Dictionary of Selected Forms in Classical Japanese Literature,* 1966
4. Ivan Morris came to the School of Oriental and African Studies (SOAS) in London as a post-graduate student in 1948 to work on a thesis

on the style of *Genji Monogatari*. He had taken his first degree at Harvard University after serving in the United States Navy where he presumably began his study of Japanese. His supervisor at SOAS was Arthur Waley whose translation of *The Tale of Genji* had become a classic. After Waley's death Ivan Morris conceived, compiled, and edited *Madly Singing in the Mountains: An Appreciation and Anthology of Arthur Waley,* London 1970. This book to which Ivan Morris contributed his own tribute to Waley has been a valuable sourcebook for scholars interested in the life and work of Arthur Waley.

5. Was he a D.Lit (i.e. Doctor of Literature), a degree usually given emeritus, or a PhD/D.Phil (i.e. Doctor of Philosophy) which would have been the degree he received for his SOAS thesis.

6. One of his puzzle books was *The Pillow-Book Puzzles.* Another was *The Lonely Monk and Other Puzzles.*

7. *The Pillow Book of Sei Shonagon*, translated and edited by Ivan Morris was published by Oxford University Press in 1967 and dedicated to 'my friend and colleague' Professor Donald Keene. It was accompanied by a companion volume of detailed scholarly notes.

8. Among Ivan Morris's many books I have an especial admiration for *The World of The Shining Prince,* which brings to life the world depicted in' *Genji Monogatari'*. It was published by Oxford University Press in 1964 and dedicated to Arthur Waley.

9. Ivan Morris worked in the Japan section of the Research Department at the Foreign Office in the early 1950s.

10. *As I Crossed A Bridge of Dreams: Recollections of a Woman in Eleventh-Century Japan* was published by Oxford University Press in 1971 and dedicated to Sir Hugh and Lady Casson. In addition to this translation and his translation of Sei Shonagon's *Pillow Book,* Ivan produced many other translations from Japanese into English including *Fire on the Plain* by Shohei Ooka, *The Temple of the Golden Pavilion* by Yukio Mishima, *The Life of an Amorous Woman and other Writings* by Ihara Saikakau, *The Journey* by Jiro Osaragi, as well as numerous Japanese short stories. Translating from the Japanese into good English is a hugely time-consuming and difficult task. Ivan and Donald's reluctance to take on the task of translating *The Sea of Fertility* in addition to their many other scholarly projects is understandable.

11. *The Nobility of Failure: Tragic Heroes in the History of Japan was* published in 1975 by Holt Reinhart Winston, New York. It is a fascinating study of the hero figure in Japan with examples taken from a whole range of Japanese history. Ivan Morris had produced a study of *Nationalism and the Right Wing in Japan: A Study of post-war Trends* which was published by Oxford University Press in 1960 under the auspices of the Royal Institute of International Affairs. While in the Research Department of the Foreign Office he had worked on this theme. In 1963 he edited and supervised the translation of Professor Masao Murayama's *Thought and behaviour in Modern Japanese Politics*, published by the Oxford University Press in 1963. He

conceived the idea of producing an English version of this important book and himself translated two of the most significant chapters. At that time few students were aware of Maruyama and his brilliant essays in intellectual history. This book was crucial to Western understanding of Japanese ultra-nationalism and related issues. Ivan Morris also edited in 1963 *Japan, 1931–45: Militarism, Fascism, Japanism?*
12. There remains something of a mystery about Ivan's death, which is unlikely ever to be clarified. He was not known to have suffered from heart disease.

Chapter 25 SEBASTIAN DOBSON *Frederick William Sutton, 1832–83: Photographer of the last shogun*

1. Captain John Wells: *The Royal Navy. An Illustrated Social History, 1870–1982*, Stroud (Alan Sutton Publishing Ltd.), 1994, p. 56.
2. Turkish Crimean Medal Roll, ADM 171/28
3. See Clara Whitney's diary entry for 1 April 1878. Ichimata Namiko, Takano Fumi, Iwahara Akiko and Kobayashi Hiromi: *Katsu Kaishu no yome: Kurara no meiji nikki*, Tokyo (Chuokoronsha), 1996, volume 1, p. 521. The only complete published version of Whitney's diary exists in Japanese translation.
4. Frederick Evans to Admiralty, 16 April 1867, ADM1/6006.
5. Bullock to King, 12 February 1867, ADM1/6006.
6. *The North China Herald*, 23 May 1867, p. 74. See also Samuel Mossman: *New Japan, The Land of the Rising Sun. Its Annals during the past Twenty Years recording the remarkable progress of the Japanese in Western Civilisation*, London (John Murrary), 1873, p. 286.
7. Bullock to Admiral Keppel, 15 July 1867, ADM1/6006.
8. Note by Henry Richards dated 13 January 1869 in Bullock to Keppel, 2 November 1868, ADM1/6053.
9. Parkes to King, 10 August 1866, enclosed in King to Admiralty, 10 August 1866, ADM1/5996.
10. King to Admiralty, 13 August 1866, ADM1/5996.
11. See, for example, E.P. Elmhirst and R. M. Jephson: *Our Life in Japan*, London (Chapman) 1869, p. 280.
12. King to Admiralty, 21 January 1867, ADM1/6006.
13. Satow recalls that in February 1867, 'Lord Walter Kerr of the *Princess Royal* kindly gave me photographs of the four nobles and two of the leading councillors of Choshiu.' Sir Ernest Satow: *A Diplomat in Japan*, London (Seely, Service & Co.), 1921, p. 185. Two of these portraits are reproduced in Satow's book on p. 184. The originals are still pasted in Satow's diary in the Public Record Office, opposite the entry for 10 February 1867, with the exception of Kerr's portrait of Admiral King with the Choshu princes. According to a contemporary note by Satow, he removed and presented this

photograph to the Uwajima daimyo, Date Munenari, in Osaka on 16 May 1867. PRO30/33/15/2. This was probably intended as a memento of King's previous visit with Parkes to Uwajima. Curiously, although the prince had come on board HMS on 8 August 1866, he does not appear to have sat for Kerr. One possible explanation is that Kerr had already used up his photographic materials taking views of the Shimazu estate at *Princess Royal* Kagoshima less than two weeks before.

14. Elmhirst & Jephson, p. 127–28.

15. For example, photographs AP10824 and AP10825 in a contemporary *carte-de-visite* album issued by Beato's studio in the collection of the Musee Guimet. Coincidentally, a copy of Kerr's portrait of Admiral King with Shimazu and Komatsu in the same album bears no such identifying inscription.

16. John Reddie Black: *Young Japan*, volume 2, p. 42.

17. My thanks are due to Jerome Ghesquiere, Curator of Photographs at the Musee Guimet, Paris, for allowing me to examine this album.

18. One of the portraits was reproduced (back-to-front) as an engraving entitled 'Group of Einos' in Elmhirst and Jephson, p. 282, and is attributed to Sutton in the preface. Both Ainu portraits, in addition to appearing in the Musee Guimet's album of Sutton views, are contained in a Beato album held at the Royal Photographic Society under the shelfmark ALB-B1.

19. Ishiguro Keisho: '*Bakumatsu shashinshi Satton wo ou*', in *Bakumatsu-Meiji no omoshiro shashin*, Tokyo (Corona Books), 1996, pp. 23–37.

20. Ishiguro, pp. 24–25.

21. Luke Gartlan: '*Chronology of Baron Raimund von Stillfried-Ratenicz (1834–1911)*' in John Clark (Ed.): *Japanese Exchanges in Art 1850s - 1930s with Britain, Continental Europe, and the USA*, Sydney (Power Publications), 2001, p. 131–34. See also Ujioka Majumi's article '*"Maboroshi no kojun shashin" wo toku*' in *Asahi Shimbun*, 25 May 2001 (Evening Edition), pp. 20–21.

22. Two of Kerr's views of Kagoshima, entitled 'Prince Satsuma's Summer Palace at Kagoshima' and 'Gardens of the Summer Palace', are reproduced as engravings in Elmhirst and Jephson, pp. 388–89. Examples of the original prints from which these are taken have not yet come to light, despite the kind assistance of Lord Walter Kerr's descendant, Lord Lothian.

23. I am indebted to Debbie Ireland, formerly Assistant Curator at the Royal Photographic Society, and currently Manager of the Picture Library at the Automobile Association, for appreciating the importance of this gift to the society and informing me of its existence. At the time I examined it, the album had not yet been catalogued, and had only been assigned the provisional shelfmark S1081.

24. The Francis Frith Collection in the Victoria and Albert Museum is held under the pressmark E.208. Several views from the Far Eastern, and especially the Japanese, portion of the collection are missing, but their titles can be found in the original ledgers of the company still held by the Francis

Frith Collection in Treffont, near Salisbury. I am very grateful to Mr. John Buck for sending me a photocopy of the relevant ledger entries, which suggest that most of these missing photographs were also the work of Pearson and Sutton.

25. Sir Henry F. Woods: *Spunyarn. Strands from a Sailor's Life*, London (Hutchinson & Co.), 1924, p. 194.

26. Ikeda Kiyoshi: 'The Douglas Mission and British Influence on the Japanese Navy', in Sue Henny & Jean-Pierre Lehmann [Eds.]: *Themes and Theories in Modern Japanese History. Essays in memory of Richard Storry*, London (The Athlone Press), 1988, p. 180.

27. Quoted in Archibald C. Douglas: *Life of Admiral Sir Archibald Lucius Douglas, GCB, GCVO*, Totnes (Mortimer Brothers), 1938, p. 41.

28. Herbert Swire: *The Voyage of the Challenger: A Personal Narrative of the Historic Circumnavigation of the Globe in the Years 1872–1876*, London (The Golden Cockerel Press), 1938, vol.2, pp. 136–137. I would like to express my thanks to Luke Gartlan for giving me this reference.

29. *Ibid*, 138.

30. Clara Whitney diary entry for 20 March 1878.

31. Clara Whitney's diary entry for 3 February 1879, *Kurara no Meiji nikki*, p???.

Chapter 26 TERRY BENNETT *Herbert George Ponting, 1870–1935: Photographer, Explorer, Inventor*

1. This is a process where an image is captured by a camera containing two mounted lenses. The result is two photographs of the same scene taken from slightly different angles. When these photographs are mounted side by side and viewed through a stereograph a remarkable '3-D' effect is created. Although no longer popular, no fashionable late-Victorian nor Edwardian home would have been without such a device, and scenes and portraits from across the world would have amused and informed the occupants - young and old.

2. Further information might well be found in the archives of the commercial operations that sponsored his photographic assignments, and a careful study of the many contemporary publications that carried his photographic contributions should prove helpful. The impressive list included: *Leslie's Weekly*, *The Illustrated London News*, *Graphic*, *Sphere*, *Country Life*, *L' Illustration*, *Pearson's*, *Sunset*, *Cosmopolitan*, *Harper's Weekly*, *Century*, *World's Work*, *Metropolitan*, *Wide World* and *Strand*.

Chapter 27 RICHARD BOWEN *Koizumi Gunji, 1885–1965: Judo Master*

1. The quotations ascribed to Koizumi in this portrait are mainly from letters and other documents in the writer's archive, which eventually will be

deposited as a collection in the Library of the University of Birmingham. The collection includes an account of Koizumi's early days and travels in his hand; various reports from the records of The Budokwai; extracts from the *Nichi-Ei Shinshi* (maintained by the Oriental and India Office Collection of the British Library); Minutes of the British Judo Association; Minutes of the European Judo Union; and *The Budokwai Bulletin*. Other sources include *Chamber's Journal of Popular Literature, Science and Arts, Health and Strength Magazine; My Study of Judo* Foulshams 1960. In addition, I should like to thank Koizumi 's daughter, Mrs Hana Sekine and her husband, for access to family records. And finally, much information comes from the many conversations with Koizumi over the years I was fortunate to be associated with him.

2. Tani Yukio (1881-1950) arrived in Britain in 1900, having been brought over from Japan by E.W.Barton Wright as an instructor for his school in Shaftesbury Avenue. In 1901 Tani appeared on the stage at the Tivoli theatre in the Strand, demonstrating jujutsu with his compatriot Uyenishi (stage name Raku), and issuing an open challenge, backed by money to anyone, of whatever weight, who wished to try their luck. Once the word got out, and there were many press reports, every wrestler of note turned up. All were defeated either by Tani or Uyenishi. Tani at five feet three inches became the darling of the crowds. It was estimated that during the eight or nine years, which represented the peak of his music hall career, he earned a quarter of a million pounds.

3. Francis Brinkley. See Biographical Portrait by J. E. Hoare in *Biographical Portraits*, Vol III, Japan Library, 1999. There are several mentions in other accounts that his son was named Harry, but both his death certificate and Budokwai records give the son's name as John R. Brinkley.

4. Kano Jigoro (1860-1938), apart from creating Kodokan Judo, was a leading educationist. He had been a Professor at the Gakushuin, Principal of No 5 Junior High School in Kyushu, (where he had invited Lafcadio Hearn to teach at his school), Chief of the inspectorate for school textbooks at the Ministry of Education and Principal of the Teachers Training College. See '*The Father of Judo: A Biography of Jigoro Kano*' by Brian Warson, Kodansha, 2000.

5. Viscount Kano Hisaakira. See Keiko Itoh's biographical portrait in *Biographical Portraits*, Vol II.

Chapter 28 ANTHONY DUNNE AND RICHARD BOWEN *Trevor Pryce Leggett, 1914–2000*

1. The Budokwai, in South Kensington, founded by Koizumi Gunji in 1918, is the oldest martial arts society in Europe.

2. See the chapter on Koizumi Gunji, and the endnote in that chapter on Tani Yukio.

3. Dr Hari Prasad Shastri: obituary in *The Times* of Tuesday, 31 January 1956, page 11, col 2.
4. *The Old Zen Master.* T.P. Leggett; Buddhist Publishing Group, England, 2,000: page 135.
5. *Ibid*, page 136.
6. *Ibid*, page 21. *Guinness Book of Records* 1960, pages 250 and 257.
7. *Ibid*, dedication to Dr Shastri.
8. *The Dragon Mask and Other Judo Stories in the Zen Tradition:* T.P. Leggett; Ippon Books Limited, Judo koan, page 55: this is probably the best book to give a non-technical insight into judo. And also *A First Zen Reader.* compiled and translated by T.P. Leggett; Tuttle, 1960. This gives greater information on the Judo koan: pages 229– 233.
9. *The Old Zen Master.* page 14.
10. *Ibid*, page 22.
11. Correspondence: T. Dunne: August, 2001.
12. Archive Documents (maintained by R. Bowen).
13. *Ibid.*
14. *Ibid.* (Including seating plan of the dinner).
15. For Kano Jigoro see endnotes for portrait of Koizumi Gunji.
16. *Behind the Japanese Mask*: Sir Robert Craigie; Hutchinson 1945, this gives an account of the internment and repatriation. Leggett is not mentioned in the text but appears in a photograph of the Embassy internees.
17. Correspondence: T. Dunne: August, 2,001.
18. Archive Documents.
19. *Ibid.* (John Brinkley and Francis Brinkley).
20. *The Changing of Kings: Memories of Burma 1934–1949*: Sir Leslie Glass; Peter Owen Publishers, London, 1985: sections on Leggett – pages 164,166, 179.
21. *This is the BBC London* (in Japanese) by: Okura Y: formerly of the BBC for four years; The Simul Press, circa 1983.
22. John Newman, MBE Obituary in *The Times* of 5 April 1993. And *The Independent* of 21 April 1993.
23. Archive Documents.
24. Dame Enid Russell-Smith: obituaries in *The Times* of 18 July 1989: *The Daily Telegraph* of 17 July 1989, which included a separate appreciation by Enoch Powell.
25. *A First Zen Reader.* compiled and translated by T.P. Leggett; Tuttle, 1960.
26. *The Complete Commentary by Sankara on the Yoga Sutras: A Full Translation of the Newly Discovered Text*: T. P. Leggett; Kegan Paul International, 1990: 418 pages. In 1989 he was invited to present a paper at the International Seminar on Sankara in New Delhi.
27. Number of brain cells: Leggett used this in a 1984 lecture and later in various articles; his point was that it is not uncommon for certain people to

try and dissuade and describe as futile any creative effort. This is what happened here.

28. The Buddhist Society taped many of his talks and these are available for a small fee.

29. Discussions: *The Story of San Michele*, Axel Munthe, 1929, in various editions. The revolt by the Iceni and the supposedly interment of Boudica under platform eight at Kings Cross – a story which persists, see *The Daily Telegraph* of 22 February 1988; a good account of the uprising is *Boudica, The British Revolt against Rome AD 60*, Graham Webster, Batsford Ltd, 1978; in April 2001, two television programmes on the Celts give the site of Boudica's last battle as the area immediately in front of Kings Cross Station – perhaps the Queen is under the platform! Silent reading, a good source is *A History of Reading* by Alberto Manguel, Harper Collins, 1996. Ambedkar, see Life by Keer, 1954.

30. General 'Stonewall' Jackson's deathbed utterance comes from a excellent television series on the American Civil War. However, in *Stonewall Jackson* by J.O.A. Tate, Michigan University, 1957, Jackson when told by his wife that he is going to die, said in a low voice, 'Very good. Very good. It's all right.'

31. *The Old Zen Master: Inspirations for Awakening*; T.P. Leggett; Buddhist Publishing Group, Totnes: 2,000: page 123: 'If You're Going to Die, Die Quick!' As might be expected, this has an inner meaning.

32. *Ibid*, page 60. Used here as a comment on Leggett's Life.

Chapter 29 PETER O'CONNOR The Japan Chronicle *and its three editors, Robert Young, Morgan Young and Edwin Allington Kennard, 1891–1940*

1. Notably Tomiko Kakegawa, whose '*The Japan Chronicle* and its editors: reflecting Japan to the press and the people, 1891–1940' pp. 27–40 in *Informal Diplomacy and the modern idea of Japan* (ed. P. O'Connor) *Japan Forum*, 13 (1), April 2001, is the most considered study of the *Chronicle* by a Japanese historian. Ebihara Hachiro (1934) *Nihon oji shinbun zasshi shi* (History of Western-Language Newspapers in Japan), Tokyo: Taiseido and Ito Hitoshi (1956) *Nihon bundan-shi* (History of Japanese Literary Circles), Tokyo: Kodansha also deal with the *Chronicle*.

2. Family Division, High Court: Administration granted to George Young, 21 August 1924. Probate Index Effects ref.: 49.3.11.

3. Lafcadio Hearn to B. H. Chamberlain, 23 October 1894. Hearn wrote *Kobe Chronicle* leaders daily from 11 October 1894 to 14 December 1894, but retired because of problems with his sight. MS6681/1/80: Harold S. Williams Collection, National Library of Australia [hereafter HSW].

4. Brinkley received ¥10,000 a year from both the Nippon Yusen Kaisha and the Japanese Foreign Office in subventions for the *Japan Mail*.

5. *Japan Mail*: 23 December 1905.

6. *North China Herald & S.C.& C. Gazette*: 9 March 1894, p. 357.

7. *Japan Chronicle Weekly*: 16 November 1922, p. 632.
8. Young's presentation was kept under wraps (*Peking & Tientsin Times* obit. November 1922). As 'M.Y.M.' recalled, 'a few years ago when Brinkley, Sir Valentine Chirol, and G. E. Morrison paid a visit to the Meiji Emperor, Brinkley was denied access but the others were granted an audience. The Imperial Household Agency explained that 'no precedent existed for giving audience to resident journalists, either foreign or Japanese. This answer killed all criticism" ('M.Y.M.' 'Links with the old journalism' *Far East*: 13 March 1915, pp.675–676). Morrison and Chirol met the Meiji Emperor in 1909 according to Pearl, Cyril 1967, *Morrison of Peking*, (London: Angus and Robertson), pp. 194–196.
9. *Nagasaki Press*: 1 November 1912.
10. *Japan Chronicle Weekly*: 16 November 1922, p.632.
11. Robert Young edited the paper 1891–1922, with breaks in 1896, 1906, 1910, 1913–14 and 1919–20. During his 1913–14 visit, Young considered running for Parliament as a Liberal but business called him back to Kobe. 'He had a comfortable house on Sydenham Hill and was to be seen every day in the National Liberal Club. The outbreak of the World War raised business questions which required his presence in Japan, and he returned and remained here until his death' (Hugh Byas, 'Twenty Years After' in *Contemporary Japan*: June 1937, pp. 43–51).
12. *Daily News*: 9 December 1910; *North China Herald*: 30 December 1910, p. 769. 'The Alleged Plot against the Emperor of Japan', *The Times*: 6 January 1910.
13. Notehelfer, F. G. 1971, *Kotoku Shosui, Portrait of a Japanese Radical* (Cambridge U.P.), p. 197; *North China Herald*: 27 January 1911, dispatch dated 16 January 1911; *Jiji Shinpo*: 16 January 1911.
14. For a full account of the *Chronicle*'s line on the *Osaka Asahi Shinbun* incident, see Tomiko Kakegawa (2001) *op cit.*, pp. 31–35.
15. *Manchester Guardian*: 18 January 1911, *Japan Gazette*: 8 February 1911.
16. Young to Bertrand Russell, 27 October 1922, Russell Archive, Mills Memorial Library, McMaster University, Ontario, Canada: No. 710.048282.
17. *The Times*: 9 November 1922.
18. *Japan Chronicle Weekly*: 10 February 1921, p. 172.
19. *Japan Chronicle Weekly*: 16 November 1922.
20. David James letter to Harold S. Williams, 12 March 1963. HSW: MS 6681/1/80.
21. *Japan Chronicle* daily: 5 June 1917.
22. *Japan Chronicle* daily: 6 June 1917.
23. FO 371/3235 (F17504/-/23): 3 December 1917, Conyngham Greene to B. Munro Ferguson.
24. *Japan Chronicle Weekly* 18 March 1921.
25. *North China Herald*: 11 November 1922.
26. Gaimusho Gaiko Shiryokan, Tokyo: *Zaihonpo gaiji shinbun kankei zakken*

'Japan Kuronikeru' shi no hainichi kiji kankei, A 350, 12–1, March 1928 – December 1933: 12 December 1933, Hyogo Governor Takesuke to Foreign Minister Hirota Koki.
27. 'Misanthrope': FO 395/447 (P2303/2303/150), T. Snow, Tokyo, to A. Willert, 18 November 1934. 'against the government': FO 371/18162 (F392/392/23), Tokyo Chancery to Far East Department, 6 January 1934.
28. MS6681/1/80: HSW.
29. Gaimusho Gaiko Shiryokan: *Zaihonpo gaiji shinbun kankei zakken 'Japan Kuronikeru' shi no hainichi kiji kankei,* A 350, 12–1: 20 December 1928, Hyogo Governor to Foreign Minister Tanaka Giichi.
30. *Diary*, Malcolm Kennedy, 19 March 1930: Malcolm Kennedy papers, Sheffield University, UK. Kennedy's informant was Harry Griffiths, proprietor of the Kobe bookshop J. L. Thompson & Co.
31. Morgan Young is usually credited with the authorship of *The Socialist and Labour Movement in Japan* (Kobe, *Chronicle* Reprint), (1921), because his name appears in *katakana* at the back, but the true author was Ivan Kozlov, a Russian political writer who was deported from Kobe to Shanghai in July 1922 (*Japan Chronicle Weekly*, 3 August 1922: 'The Deportation of Mr. Kozlov'). Young's name probably appeared on the flyleaf because Kozlov's would have made publication more difficult.
32. Young, A. M., 1939, *The Rise of a Pagan State: Japan's Religious Background* (London, Allen & Unwin), p.139.
33. *Naimusho Keiho-kyoku (1937) Shuppan keisatsu-ho* (Publications Police Report) 110, December, quoted in Kakegawa Tomiko (2001), *op cit.*, n1.
34. A. Morgan Young to Hugh Byas: 18 September 1936, Byas Papers, Yale University Library.
35. Connaught Mansions, Victoria Street, Westminster. Subscriptions were 10/- per annum.
36. Williams, Harold and Jean, *East Meets West*, (Sydney, Halstead Press), Vol.1, p. 193.
37. FO 371/22181 (F13489/71/23): S. Gasalee to H. Parlett, 21 December 1938. Young's talk was published in 1939 in *World Outlook* (ed. Frederick Whyte), (London, Nicholson & Watson).
38. Ernest Young died in the 1970s.
39. FO 371/24728 (F5646/53/23): Craigie telegram, 17 December 1940.
40. MS6681/1/80: HSW.
41. Payments were withheld during the anti-British demonstrations in Tokyo in March-August 1939.
42. Bickers, Robert and Christian Henriot (eds) (2000) *New frontiers: Imperialism's new communities in East Asia, 1842–1953*, (Manchester, Manchester University Press), p. 2.

Chapter 30 PETER O'CONNOR *Timothy or Taid or Taig Conroy or O'Conroy, 1883–1935: 'The "Best Authority, East and West" on anything concerning Japan'*

I am most grateful to Professor Akiko Manabe of Shiga University and IASIL Japan, for kindly researching Conroy's record at Hikone College, Shiga, in 1926–28.

1. Conroy's birth certificate gives 20 August 1883 as his birth date (Cork Record Office, certificate No. RGB 088/0277). His CV gives 6 March 1883.
2. In *The Menace of Japan*, Conroy writes that he 'ran away to sea' at thirteen (p. 280).
3. Conroy's obituary also notes that he was born 'to poor parents': *The Times*, 6 November 1935. p. 16.
4. *'Uso happyyaku o narabeta "Nihon no kyōi" shuppan'*: *Tokyo Asahi Shinbun*: 21 October 1933, p. 2. Hereafter, all 'Asahi' references are to this article.
5. In 'Tim Conroy, Impostor', an undated addendum to his 1925 Diary. In other notes, Kennedy had 'heard it said that he came across her [Terao Kikuko] in the Yoshiwara (licensed quarters), fell in love with her & bought her from the proprietor'. Malcolm Kennedy Papers, Sheffield University Library.
6. O'Conroy, Taid (1938) *The Menace of Japan* (London, Hurst & Blackett, Paternoster Library series). pp. 9–10. The 1938 edition was the seventh in Britain. Hutchinson took over the title in Britain later that year. In America, the publishers were H. C. Kinsey and Grosset and Dunlap, both of New York.
7. *Japan Advertiser*, letter dated 18 December, published 23 December 1933.
8. Kennedy Diary: 2 April 1925: 53. Kennedy Papers.
9. Kennedy, Malcolm D., 1966, 'The Strange Affair of Tim Conroy', unpublished 1966 MSS, p. 3. Kennedy Papers. (Hereafter: *Strange Affair*).
10. *Ryōsui Rokujunen-shi*, (Ryōsuikai, Shiga Daigaku, 1981).
11. Conroy's British passport was issued by H.M. Consul General, Kobe on 1 June 1928.
12. *Evening Standard*, 19 October 1933 p. 1: 'Professor Fears Wife Has Been Poisoned by Japanese Avengers'.
13. FO 371/18166 [F19/19/23]: P. D. Butler Memorandum, 2 December 1933.
14. FO 371/16243 [F4624/40/23], Douglas Crawford to Sir Robert Vansittart, 27 May 1932.
15. According to Pratt's Minute, Conroy had also conveyed his views to US Secretary of War Henry L. Stimson, Sir John Simon and Mussolini.
16. FO 371/16243 [F4624/40/23]: J. Pratt Minute, 1 June 1932.
17. FO 371/16243 [F8373/40/23]: T. Conroy to R. Vansittart, 25 November 1932.

18. FO 371/16243 [F8373/40/23]: J. Pratt letter to C. J. Norton, 28 November 1932.
19. FO 371/16243 [F4777/40/23]: Letters of T. Conroy, J. Pratt and others, June-July 1932.
20. FO 369/2256 [K12981/12981/217]: A. Mignon Brest, to Secretary of State 4 October 1932; FO 369/2256 [K13454/12981/217]: A. Mignon, Brest, to Secretary of State, 16 November 1932.
21. FO 371/16243 [F8234/40/23]: Letters of T. Conroy, J. Pratt and C. J. Norton, November 1932.
22. FO 371/16243 [F8373/40/23]: T. Conroy to R. Vansittart, 25 November 1932.
23. FO 371/16243 [F8373/40/23]: C. J. Norton to J. Pratt, 28 November 1932, C. J. Norton to T. Conroy, 6 December 1932.
24. FO 371/16243 [F8638/40/23]: C. J. Norton to Conroy, 13 December 1932.
25. FO 369/2256 [K13454/12981/217]: Minute, 16 November 1932.
26. *Evening Standard*, 19 October 1933 p. 1: 'Professor Fears Wife Has Been Poisoned by Japanese Avengers'. Conroy's address at the time was c/o a friend in the Albany.
27. *Tokyo Asahi Shinbun*: 21 October 1933, p. 2.
28. *Japan Chronicle,* 11 November 1933.
29. *Japan Advertiser*, 23 November 1933.
30. Kennedy, Strange Affair, p. 5, Kennedy Papers.
31. Kennedy thought it 'little short of criminal' that Reuters had suppressed his message denouncing Conroy, because it enabled Conroy to continue to 'gull the public and to embitter relations at a time when, thanks to trade competition, the urgent need in both countries is to prevent further embitterment'. Kennedy to Rickardson-Hatt, Reuters London: 25 November and 3 December 1933 and 4 January 1934: 10.3 (5), Kennedy Papers. Unable to air his suspicions through Reuters, Kennedy (writing as "M.D.K.") published an unrestrained attack on Conroy in the *Japan Advertiser* of 17 December 1933 under the headline, "O'Conroy admits no one excels him in knowing Japan". In November 1966, Blackwood's Magazine turned down Kennedy's mss. "The Strange Affair of Tim Conroy": 10.1 (32) Kennedy Papers.
32. *Sunday Despatch*: 26 November 1933, p. 13.
33. FO 371/18166 [F19/19/23], P. D. Butler Memorandum, 2 December 1933.
34. FO 371/18188 [F967/967/23]: Arram, Fairfield & Co., to J. Pratt, 2 January 1934.
35. No. DXZ 857206, registration Hampstead sub-district, Family Records Centre, London.
36. Daily Worker: 22 December 1937.
37. For more on the rise of the 'man on the spot', see Ion, A. Hamish (1996) 'Japan Watchers: 1903–31', in John F. Howes (ed.) *Nitobe Inazo: Japan's*

Bridge Across the Pacific, San Francisco, Calif.: Westview Press, pp. 79–106, and Peter O'Connor (2000) 'The Locus of Credibility Heads East: The English Language Press and Books on Japan, c.1900–1941' Bulletin, 1, Musashino Women's University, Faculty of Contemporary Society, pp. 39–52.

Chapter 31 DOUGLAS FARNIE *Freda Utley, 1899–1978: Crusader for Truth, Freedom and Justice*

NOTES: The author of all works cited is Freda Utley, unless otherwise stated. The place of publication of all sources cited is London, unless otherwise stated.

1. *Odyssey of a Liberal. Memoirs* (Washington, D.C., 1970, henceforth cited as *'Odyssey'*), 61.
2. *ibid.*, 74.
3. *ibid.*, 84.
4. *ibid.*, 103.
5. *Japan's Feet of Clay* (1936), 176.
6. *Manchester Guardian Commercial*, 25 April 1929, 490; 2 May 1929, 517.
7. *Lancashire and the Far East* (1931), 220. *What's Wrong with the Cotton Trade? An Explanation of the Present Depression and the Communist Policy for Cotton Workers* (1930), 17.
8. *Lancashire and the Far East*, 72, 149.
9. *Odyssey*, 305.
10. *The Dream We Lost. Soviet Russia Then and Now* (New York), 1940, henceforth cited as *'Dream'*), 3.
11. *Japan's Feet of Clay*, 21, 288. *New Statesman*, 6 Feb. 1937, 195.
12. *Japan's Feet of Clay*, 17, 337.
13. Kaoru Sugihara, 'Economic Motivations behind Japanese Aggression in the late 1930s: Perspectives of Freda Utley and Nawa Toichi'. *Journal of Contemporary History*, 32: 2, April 1997, 259–80.
14. *Japan's Feet of Clay*, 36.
15. *The Economist*, 26 DEC. 1936, 638. *New Statesman*, 7 NOV. 1936, 736, Bertrand Russell.
16. *New Statesman* 6 March 1937, 365, with a reply by Freda Utley in idem, 13 March, 403.
17. *New York Times Book Review*, 18 April 1937, 3, W. H. Mallory.
18. *The Spectator*, 11 DEC. 1936, 1063.
19. *Contemporary Japan*, 6: I, June 1937, 95–101, a reference for which I remain indebted to Dr Janet Hunter of the LSE.
20. *Odyssey*, 212.
21. *New Statesman*, 25 SEPT. 1937, 433, 'How Japan Could be Stopped'.
22. *Japan's Gamble in China* (1938), 103, 114.
23. *Ibid.* 282.

24. *ibid*, 14.
25. Janice R. MacKinnon and Stephen R. MacKinnon, *Agnes Smedley. The Life and Times of an American Radical* (Berkeley, 1988), 208.
26. Stephen R. MacKinnon and Oris Friesen, *China Reporting. An Oral History of American Journalism in the 1930s and 1940s* (Berkeley, 1987), 43, citing Agnes Smedley.
27. *Odyssey*, 206, 218.
28. *China at War* (1939), 52, 189.
29. *Odyssey*, 222.
30. *San Francisco Chronicle*, 27 NOV. 1938, 'A Woman in China's War Zone'.
31. *New Statesman*, 1 July 1939, 20, a review of John Gunther, *Inside Asia* (1939); idem, 27 OCT. 1939, 586, 'Mrs Chesterton on Russia'.
32. G. E. Hubbard, *Eastern Industrialization and its Effect on the West* (Oxford, 1935, 1938), 395, 399, 400.
33. *Manchester Guardian*, 24 OCT. 1939, 3v, 'Death from the Skies'.
34. *Dream*, 265, 270, 273.
35. O. Lattimore, *China Memoirs. Chiang Kai-shek and the War against Japan*, compiled by Fujiko Isono (Tokyo, 1990), 233. Tillman Durdin, according to MacKinnon & Friesen (op.cit), 40), believed on the other hand that Freda Utley's categorical anti-Communism counterbalanced the left-wing enthusiasm of the united frontists in Hankow.
36. *Dream*, 122.
37. Lattimore, op.cit., 233.
38. *Odyssey*, 222.
39. *New Statesman*, 30 SEPT. 1939, 457, letter. *Dream*, 145.
40. *Odyssey*, 230.
41. *Ibid.*, 255.
42. *Lost Illusion* (1948), 94.
43. *Dream*, 268. *Odyssey*, 106, 137, 142.
44. *Dream*, 293. *Odyssey*, 143.
45. *Dream*, 84.
46. *Odyssey*, 278.
47. *Dream*, vii.
48. *Ibid.*, 359, 361.
49. *Ibid.*, 19, 88.
50. MacKinnon and MacKinnon, op.cit., 251 citing Agnes Smedley to Aino Taylor, 2 Dec. 1942.
51. *Odyssey*, 270, 275.
52. *Readers Digest*, 39: 235, NOV. 1941, 58–63, 'Must the World Destroy Itself?', reprinted from *Common Sense,* August 1941, 'God Save England from her Friends'.
53. *Odyssey*, 77.
54. *Reader's Digest*, 59: 249, SEPT. 1944, 345–351, 'Why Pick on China?'.
55. *Last Chance in China* (Indianapolis, 1947).

56. *Ibid., 153.*
57. *The High Cost of Vengeance* (Chicago, 1949), 2, 30, 44.
58. *Ibid.*, 9. Two works maybe mentioned as representative reflections of the wartime mind-set. *Germany the Aggressor throughout the Ages (*1940*)* was written by F. J. C. Hearnshaw (1869–1946), who had been Freda Utley's professor of history at King's College. The same theme pervaded *The Course of German History* (1942) by the radical socialist, A. J. P. Taylor (1906–91).
59. *The High Cost of Vengeance*, 167, 185–201. *American Mercury*, 76, June 1953, 112–118, 'Facing the Facts in Germany'. idem, 77, Dec. 1953, 35–39, 'The Book Burners Burned'. Idem, 79, Nov. 1954, 53–58, 'Malmedy and McCarthy'.
60. *The High Cost of Vengeance*, 127.
61. *The China Story* (Chicago, 1951), 130.
62. *Ibid.*, 27, 168.
63. *Ibid*, 185 *American Mercury*, 73, Sept. 1951, 101–118, 'The Case of Owen Lattimore'. *Idem*, 80, June 1955, 21–26, 'The Triumph of Owen Lattimore'.
64. *Odyssey*, 279.
65. Francis X. Gannon, *Biographical Dictionary of the Left* (Boston), 1969), I, 321, 380, 544–5.
66. *Odyssey of a Liberal. Memoirs* (1970).
67. *New York Times Book Review*, 75: 16, 19 April 1970, 32, in a review of *Odyssey of a Liberal.*

Chapter 32 ANTONY BEST *Lord Sempill (1893–1965) and Japan, 1921–41*

1. PRO FO371/5358 F2561/193/23 Admiralty to Foreign Office 22 October 1920.
2. The best description of the Sempill mission is J. Ferris, 'A British "Unofficial" Aviation Mission and Japanese Naval Developments, 1919-1929' *Journal of Strategic Studies*, 1982, vol.5, pp. 416-39.
3. The Master of Sempill, 'The British Aviation Mission in Japan' *Transactions and Proceedings of the Japan Society London*, 1925, Vol.XXII, p.41. (Thanks are due to Sir Hugh Cortazzi for bringing this paper to my attention.)
4. *Ibid*, p.44.
5. PRO FO371/8051 F2109/2109/23 Marriot (NA Tokyo) to Eliot (Tokyo) 9 January 1922 no. 1 and FO371/8050 F1065/1065/23 Eliot (Tokyo) to Curzon 6 February 1922 no. 69.
6. PRO FO371/8050 F1793/1065/23 Admiralty to Foreign Office 19 May 1922. See also Ferris, *op. cit.* p. 424 and Sempill, *op. cit.* pp. 43-4.
7. Later Sir Esler Dening GCMG, Ambassador to Japan, 1952-1957, then private secretary to Sir Charles Eliot.
8. On Marriot, see R. Colvin, *Memoirs of Admiral Sir Ragnar Colvin KBE CB* (Wintershill, Durley, 1992). (My thanks to John Colvin for bringing this

volume to my attention.) For Colvin's view of the mission see PRO FO371/8043 F3436/19/23 Colvin (NA Tokyo) to Eliot 12 October 1922 no.16.

9. PRO FO371/8050 F2704/1065/23 Eliot to Tyrrell (FO) 21 July 1922.
10. Ferris, *op. cit.* p. 428.
11. PRO FO371/10309 F1016/268/23 Colvin to Palareit (Tokyo) 18 February 1924 no. 3.
12. See the entries in *Who's Who* and *Dictionary of National Biography* for Forbes-Sempill.
13. *Parliamentary Debates, Fifth Series, House of Lords*, vol.100, col. 954–5, 12 May 1936.
14. R. Griffiths, Patriotism Perverted: Captain Ramsay, the Right Club and British Anti-Semitism 1939–40, (Constable, London, 1998) pp. 144–5.
15. PRO HW12/78 BJ.022075 JNA London to 'Oimatsu' Tokyo 21 December 1925 circulated 5 January 1926.
16. Ferris, *op. cit.* pp. 430–1.
17. PRO KV4/1 'The Security Service: Its Problems and Organizational Adjustments' Curry (MI5) March 1946. See also PREM3/252/5 Swinton to Churchill 24 September 1941.
18. Kell papers, IWM, memoirs p.176-7.
19. PRO HW12/184 BJ.058100 London to Tokyo 21 September circulated 4 October 1934.
20. PRO HW12/185 BJ.058558 London to Tokyo 15 November circulated 17 November 1934.
21. Griffiths, *op. cit.* pp. 144–5.
22. A. Best, "That Loyal British Subject"?: Arthur Edwardes and Anglo-Japanese Relations, 1932-1941', in J. E. Hoare (ed.,) *Britain and Japan: Biographical Portraits, Vol.III*, (Richmond: Japan Library, 1999) pp.227-39.
23. Butler papers, Trinity College Cambridge, RAB E13/1966.
24. Hankey papers, PRO, CAB63/177 Sempill memorandum undated in Sempill to Hankey 3 June 1941.
25. Piggott papers, IWM, Lindley to Piggott 20 October 1940.
26. PRO PREM3/252/5 Swinton to Churchill 24 September 1941
27. Cadogan papers, Churchill College Cambridge, ACAD1/10, diary 22 February 1941.
28. PRO PREM3/252/5 Alexander to Churchill 8 October 1941. See also R. Aldrich, *Britain and the Intelligence War Against Japan, 1941–45: The Politics of Secret Service*, (Cambridge: CUP, 2000) pp. 47-8.
29. Avon papers, Birmingham University Library, AP20/8/548 Churchill to Eden 13 September 1941.
30. PREM3/252/5 Swinton to Churchill 24 September 1941, and Eden to Churchill 26 September 1941 PM/41/121.
31. Aldrich, *op. cit*, p. 47.
32. PRO PREM3/252/5 Morton to Churchill 17 October 1941.

33. This entry by Peter Masefield was published in the DNB in 1981.

Chapter 33 NOBORU KOYAMA *Three Meiji Marriages between Japanese Men and English Women*

1. FO 97/503 7280.
2. Japan, Ministry of Foreign Affairs, Archives (JFMA), file 3.8.7.4 (*Naigai jimmin kekkon zakken*).
3. *Koseki* are household registers maintained in the city, town or village which is regarded as the place of permanent domicile of the household (*honsekichi*).
4. The four marriages, which had been previously approved, were those of Minami Teisuke and Eliza Pittman, William Henry Freame (British national) and Kitagawa Sei, Zhong Zhaonan (Chinese national) and Shingo Mio, Tan Bengtech (British national, Chinese Singaporean)
5. JFMA, file 3.8.7.4–1 (Ozaki Saburo *rikon no ken*).
6. Birth certificate (Eliza Pittman).
7. Marriage certificate (Shunpou Teske Minami and Eliza Pittman).
8. Ozaki Saburo, *Ozaki Saburo jijō ryakuden*, Vol.1, Tokyo, 1976. p. 119.
9. *Meiji zenki zaisei keizai shiryō shūsei*, Vol.10, Tokyo, 1935. pp. 351–353.
10. Ozaki Saburo, *Ozaki Saburo jijō ryakuden*, Vol.1. pp. 125–126.
11. Birth certificate (Alethea Raynor).
12. PRO 30/33.
13. Marriage certificate (Yoshitane Sannomiya and Alethea Raynor).
14. Prince Higashi-Fushimi Yoshiaki (1846–1903) took the name Akihito, Komatsu no miya in 1882.
15. JFMA, file 3.8.7.4 (*Naigai jimmin kekkon zakken*).
16. Ozaki Saburo, *Ozaki Saburo jijō ryakuden*, Vol.1. pp. 166–168.
17. Ozaki Saburo, *Ozaki Saburo nikki*, Vol.3, Tokyo, 1992. p. 461.
18. JFMA, file 3.8.7.4–1 (Ozaki Saburo *rikon no ken*).
19. JFMA, file 3.8.7.4–1 (Ozaki Saburo *rikon no ken*).
20. JFMA, file 3.8.7.4–1 (Ozaki Saburo *rikon no ken*).
21. *Meiji zenki mibunhō taizen*, Vol.2, Tokyo, 1974. p. 355.
22. JFMA, file 3.8.7.4–1 (Ozaki Saburo *rikon no ken*).
23. Ozaki Yukio in his autobiography published in an English translation by Princeton University Press in 2001 gives some account of his marriage (see especially pages 246 and 247)
24. Death Certificate (Bathia Catherine Ozaki).
25. Death Certificate (Yei Theodora Ozaki).
26. JFMA, file 3.8.7.4 (*Naigai jimmin kekkon zakken*).
27. JFMA, file 3.8.7.4 (*Naigai jimmin kekkon zakken*).
28. JFMA, file 3.8.7.4 (*Naigai jimmin kekkon zakken*).
29. Minami Teisuke, Kotokuin goryakureki, [Tokyo], 1915.
30. *Japan Weekly Mail*, 7 April 1883.

31. Parish Church of St Mary, Beddington, *Statement as to the tombstones and monuments in St Mary's Churchyard extension*, [Croydon], 1961.
32. Death certificate (Eliza Teiske Minami).
33. Eleanora Mary d'Anethan, *Fourteen years of diplomatic life in Japan*, London, 1912. p. 33 and p. 43.
34. F.S.G. Piggott, *Broken thread*, London, 1950. p. 67.
35. Mary Crawford Fraser, *A diplomatist's wife in Japan*, Vol. II, London, 1899. p. 363.
36. Teresa Eden Richardson, *Japanese hospitals during war-time*, London, 1905. p. 28.
37. *Asahi shimbun*, 29 August 1919.
38. *Shimbun shūsei Meiji hennenshi*, Vol. 13, Tokyo, 1934. p. 33.
39. *Asahi shimbun*, 29 December 1919.
40. FO 97/503 7280.
41. FO 97/503 7280.
42. FO 97/503 7280.
43. *Times law reports*, VI (1889–1890). pp. 191–192.
44. FO 881/8211 5810.
45. *Japan Weekly Mail*, 15 February 1908.
46. 2&3 Geo.5 C.15.

Chapter 34 AMANDA HERRIES *Early Plant Collectors in Japan*

BIBLIOGRAPHY

Fortune, R: *Three Years' Wanderings in the Northern Provinces of China*. John Murray, London, 1847.

Fortune, R: *A Journey to the Tea Countries of China*. John Murray, London, 1852.

Fortune, R: *A Residence among the Chinese*. John Murray, London, 1857.

Fortune, R: *Yedo and Peking*. John Murray, London, 1862.

Coats, Alice M: *The Quest for Plants*. Studio Vista, London, 1969.

Heriz-Smith, Shirley, *James Veitch & Sons of Exeter and Chelsea, 1853–70*, Garden History 17(2) pp. 135–152.

Glattstein, Judy: *Enhance your garden with Japanese Plants*. Kodansha International, 1996.

Musgrave, T, Gardner, C, Musgrave, W: *The Plant Hunters*. Ward Lock, 1998.

Nelson, E. Charles: 'So many really fine plants – An epitome of Japanese.

Plants in Western European Gardens'. *Curtis's Botanical Magazine* 16(2) pp. 52–73.

Barnes, P: 'Japan's Botanical Sunrise – Plant exploration around the Meiji Restoration'. *Curtis's Botanical Magazine* 18(2) pp. 117–131.

PERIODICALS

Journal of the Royal Horticultural Society, Volume 68 'Robert Fortune' pp. 161–9.

The Gardeners' Chronicle and Agricultural Gazette.

Gardeners' Chronicle Gardening Illustrated.

Journal of Horticulture and Cottage Gardener.

NOTES

1. See Hugh Cortazzi's *Mitford's Japan*, Athlone Press, London,1985.
2. See biographical portrait of William Keswick in this volume.

Index